Police Operations

Theory and Practice

SIXTH EDITION

Police Operations

Theory and Practice

SIXTH EDITION

Kären Matison Hess, Ph.D.
NORMANDALE COMMUNITY COLLEGE

Christine Hess Orthmann, M.S.
ORTHMANN WRITING AND RESEARCH, INC.

Sgt. Henry Lim Cho, M.A.
ROSEMOUNT (MINNESOTA) POLICE DEPARTMENT

DELMAR
CENGAGE Learning

Australia • Brazil • Japan • Korea • Mexico • Singapore • Spain • United Kingdom • United States

DELMAR
CENGAGE Learning·

Police Operations: Theory and Practice, 6th Edition

Kären Matison Hess, Christine Hess Orthmann, Henry Lim Cho

Vice President, Careers and Computing: Dave Garza

Director of Learning Solutions: Sandy Clark

Senior Acquisitions Editor: Shelley Esposito

Director, Development—Careers and Computing: Marah Bellegarde

Managing Editor: Larry Main

Senior Product Manager: Anne Orgren

Editorial Assistant: Diane Chrysler

Brand Manager: Kristin McNary

Market Development Manager: Michelle Williams

Senior Production Director: Wendy Troeger

Production Manager: Mark Bernard

Senior Content Project Manager: Jennifer Hanley

Media Editor: Debbie Bordeaux

Cover Design: Riezebos Holzbaur/ Tim Heraldo

Cover Image(s): Main image: © Jeremy Woodhouse/Blend Images/Getty Images

Insets, left to right: © Jeff Dunn/ Photolibrary/Getty Images; © *Washington Post*/Getty Images; © Henry Cho; © John Roman Images/shutterstock

For product information and technology assistance, contact us at
Cengage Learning Customer & Sales Support, 1-800-354-9706

For permission to use material from this text or product, submit all requests online at **www.cengage.com/permissions**
Further permissions questions can be e-mailed to
permissionrequest@cengage.com

Library of Congress Control Number: 2012941387

ISBN-13: 978-1-2850-5262-5

ISBN-10: 1-2850-5262-5

Delmar
5 Maxwell Drive
Clifton Park, NY 12065-2919
USA

Cengage Learning is a leading provider of customized learning solutions with office locations around the globe, including Singapore, the United Kingdom, Australia, Mexico, Brazil, and Japan. Locate your local office at: **international.cengage.com/region**

Cengage Learning products are represented in Canada by Nelson Education, Ltd.

To learn more about Delmar, visit **www.cengage.com/delmar**

Purchase any of our products at your local college store or at our preferred online store **www.cengagebrain.com**

Notice to the Reader

Publisher does not warrant or guarantee any of the products described herein or perform any independent analysis in connection with any of the product information contained herein. Publisher does not assume, and expressly disclaims, any obligation to obtain and include information other than that provided to it by the manufacturer. The reader is expressly warned to consider and adopt all safety precautions that might be indicated by the activities described herein and to avoid all potential hazards. By following the instructions contained herein, the reader willingly assumes all risks in connection with such instructions. The publisher makes no representations or warranties of any kind, including but not limited to, the warranties of fitness for particular purpose or merchantability, nor are any such representations implied with respect to the material set forth herein, and the publisher takes no responsibility with respect to such material. The publisher shall not be liable for any special, consequential, or exemplary damages resulting, in whole or part, from the readers' use of, or reliance upon, this material.

Printed in the United States of America
1 2 3 4 5 6 7 16 15 14 13 12

DEDICATION

Dedicated to the hundreds of thousands of uniformed law enforcement officers, past and present, whose accomplishments have made such a difference in the quality of life in communities throughout the United States, and to those who are about to join them.

BRIEF CONTENTS

CONTENTS

SECTION II

Getting the Job Done: Basic Police Operations

SECTION III
Specialized Police Operations

SECTION IV
The Personal Side of
Police Operations

13 THE IMPORTANCE OF PHYSICAL AND MENTAL HEALTH: GETTING THE JOB AND KEEPING FIT FOR DUTY   498

14 LIABILITY AND ETHICS: IS IT LEGAL? IS IT MORAL?   527

PURPOSE

Welcome to *Police Operations: Theory and Practice*, Sixth Edition. This text is *not* an introduction to law enforcement and the criminal justice system. It is intended to describe what police officers do and why. Therefore, it is short on theory and long on practical application, presenting the fundamentals of what policing is all about.

The basic reason modern society has police departments is summarized in the classic statement of police sociologist Egon Bittner[1]: "Something-ought-not-to-be-happening—about-which-something-ought-to-be-done-NOW!" This text goes beyond this reactive approach (which will always be an important and unavoidable part of policing), however, by also incorporating the techniques and philosophies of proactive policing illustrated in both *community policing*, in which law enforcement partners with the citizens and organizations in a community to make the community safer for all, and *intelligence-led policing*, a methodical data-driven approach to prevent, detect, and disrupt crime.

ORGANIZATION OF THE TEXT

The first section of *Police Operations* discusses the basics behind effective police operations, including the context in which services are provided and the skills required to provide these services (Chapter 1). Law enforcement officers must be thoroughly familiar with the citizens they are sworn to "serve and protect" (Chapter 2) as well as with the constitutional restraints within which they must operate (Chapter 3). They must be proficient in communication skills as well as in the numerous profession-specific skills required in law enforcement: conducting stops and frisks, making arrests, searching crime scenes and suspects, investigating crimes, and assisting victims.

Section II discusses basic police operations, including patrol (Chapter 4); traffic (Chapter 5); crime, disorder, and quality-of-life issues (Chapter 6); violence—domestic, school, and workplace (Chapter 7); emergencies (Chapter 8); and hometown and homeland security (Chapter 9). The third section presents specialized police operations such as those performed by detectives in investigating crimes (Chapter 10), juvenile officers (Chapter 11), and officers who deal with gangs and drugs (Chapter 12). The final section discusses the personal side of law enforcement—the physical and mental health aspects of getting a job as a police officer and what officers need to know about maintaining their physical and emotional well-being so they can continue in their chosen profession (Chapter 13) and what they need to know about protecting themselves from being sued and about acting legally and ethically (Chapter 14).

NEW TO THIS EDITION

The Sixth Edition has updated all statistics and references, with most of the more than 170 new references having been published after 2008. New to this edition is a boxed feature highlighting *Technology in Policing*, as well as practical, applied information regarding various aspects of police operations

---

[1]From "Florence Nightingale in Pursuit of Willie Sutton: A Theory of Police," in *The Potential for Reform of Criminal Justice,* edited by H. Jacob. Beverly Hills, CA: Sage, 1974, p. 30.

highlighted within *Perspectives from a First-Line Supervisor*. In addition, the following chapter-specific changes have been made:

Chapter 1   Police Operations in Context

▶ Added several new terms: *heterogeneity, information, intelligence*

▶ Updated statistics regarding women and minorities in law enforcement

▶ Added a brief section about intelligence-led policing (ILP)

▶ Created a new table comparing traditional, community, and intelligence-led policing

▶ New boxed feature: **Technology in Policing**; Contracting with Private Companies to Draft Policing Manuals

Chapter 2   Communication: The Foundation of Police Operations

▶ Added terms: *Beheler admonition, plain language, reasonable suspicion,* Terry *stop, waiver*

▶ Added two **Perspective of a First-Line Supervisor** boxes: Effective Communication; Written Reports

▶ Added two **Technology in Policing** boxes: Online Citizen Reporting; 4G-LTE

▶ Added two **An Officer's Perspective** boxes: The Downside of Translators; Well-Written Reports

▶ Updated population statistics

▶ Added brief content on regional databases, including the RISS Program

▶ Added a new section on Web sites and social media—how police use this technology to communicate with the public, both to get information and to give information

▶ Added content on the challenge of Alzheimer's to law enforcement

▶ Added content pertaining to communication barriers between those from different cultures

▶ Added the Normal, Illinois, Police Department's Early Notification Program (ENP) to address police response to autistic individuals and others with mental impairments

▶ Moved "dealing with the homeless" discussion to Chapter 6

▶ Added *Rhode Island v. Innis* (1980) to define interrogation

▶ Bolstered discussion of waiving rights (*Miranda*)

▶ Added *California v. Prysock* (1981), *Duckworth v. Eagan* (1989), and *Florida v. Powell* (2010)—wording of the *Miranda* warning

▶ Added new research about detecting deception

Chapter 3   Operational Skills: Performing within the Law

▶ Bolstered the discussion of the Fourth Amendment and how it governs police action

▶ Added terms: *Carroll doctrine, fruit of the poisonous tree doctrine, inevitable discovery doctrine, reasonable suspicion*

▶ Updated statistics about police–public contacts and arrests

▶ New content on use-of-force continuums and recent criticism of such models

▶ Added two **Technology in Policing** boxes: Documenting Use-of-Force with Body Cameras; Using GPS to Track Suspects—*United States v. Jones* (2012)

▶ Added two **An Officer's Perspective** boxes: *Terry* Stops and Officer Safety; Natural versus Tactical Communication

▶ Added *Arizona v. Gant* (2009)—restricting searches incident to arrest

▶ Added *United States v. Jones* (2012)—GPS tracking of a suspect's vehicle is a search under the Fourth Amendment (Technology in Policing box)

▶ Moved exclusionary rule discussion to the end; added the three main exceptions (inevitable discovery doctrine, valid independent source, and good faith—as well as the cases associated with the exceptions: *Brewer v. Williams*, 1977; *Nix v. Williams*, 1984; *Segura v. United States*, 1984)

Chapter 4   Patrol: The Backbone of Police Operations

▶ New terms: *hot spots, preventive patrol, random patrol, routine patrol, saturation patrol, split-force patrol*

▶ Added a new section briefly highlighting preventive patrol and the importance of patrol as a way to deter crime or provide more immediate detection of and intervention in crimes already occurring

▶ New data on the Philadelphia Foot Patrol Experiment

▶ New **Technology in Policing** box: In-Car Cameras

▶ Added **An Officer's Perspective** box: Responding to the Scene of a Fire

▶ Moved some of the GPS content related to surveillance to Chapter 10

Chapter 5   Traffic: Policing in a Country on the Move

▶ New data on cell phone use and which states ban handheld use and texting while driving

▶ Updated statistics on seatbelt use, speeding fatalities, drunk driving, traffic crashes, pedestrian injuries, and fatalities from vehicle crashes

▶ New brief section on rolling domestics

▶ New/updated content on vehicle pursuits, new statistics, new case (roadblocks: *Brower v. County of Inyo*, 1989)

▶ Added two **Technology in Policing** boxes: License Plate Readers; In Pursuit of Safer Pursuits

▶ Added **An Officer's Perspective** box: Citizens: Be Careful What You Wish For

▶ New content about hazardous material response, training, and enforcement

▶ New problem-oriented policing (POP) example related to traffic issues

Chapter 6   Crime, Disorder, and Quality-of-Life Issues: Responding to the Call

▶ Added term: *routine activity theory*

▶ Trimmed discussion on crime mapping to make room for new content on geospatial statistical analysis—emerging technology to predict crime

▶ Reworked section on "Responding to Calls about Crime and Disorder" to better follow most recent guidelines referenced by the National Institute of Justice (NIJ)

▶ Updated statistics on sex trafficking/prostitution and homelessness

▶ Added a section on the Occupy Movement (under civil disobedience and protestors)

▶ Added **Technology in Policing** box: Long-Range Acoustic Devices (LRADs)

▶ Added a **Perspective of a First-Line Supervisor** box: Barricaded Suicidal Individuals

▶ New content on suicide-by-cop

Chapter 7 Violence: At Home, in the Classroom, on the Job

▶ Updated statistics on domestic violence victimization (women, men, LGBTQ, teens, elders)
▶ Added **An Officer's Perspective** box: Dual Arrests
▶ Updated the school violence discussion (new stats on violence and illegal behavior)
▶ New studies on bullying
▶ Trimmed the discussion on workplace violence, as the police response (if they are even called) is often similar to domestic violence (versus active shooter response)
▶ New problem-oriented policing example

Chapter 8 Emergency Situations: When Disaster Strikes

▶ Added terms: *emergency management, incident management*
▶ Significantly reorganized
▶ Updated content from federal emergency response agencies: Department of Homeland Security (DHS) (most recent version: *Nationwide Plan Review*), Federal Emergency Management Administration (FEMA) and the National Response Framework (*Developing and Maintaining Emergency Operations Plans*), the Emergency Management Assistance Compact (EMAC), and National Incident Management System (NIMS)
▶ Added two **Technology in Policing** boxes: Incident Command and Emergency Operations Vehicles; Robotics for Bomb Squads

Chapter 9 Terrorism: From Hometown Security to Homeland Security

▶ Added terms: *agroterrorism, sovereign citizens*
▶ New opening section on "Homeland Security in Context" to point out that homeland security encompasses more than just efforts to prevent and respond to terrorism
▶ Changed reference source of *terrorism* definition from Terrorism Research Center to the FBI (C.F.R.)
▶ Added information on sovereign citizens
▶ New content on vehicle-borne improvised explosive devices (VBIEDs), aka car bombs
▶ New content on agroterrorism as a form of bioterrorism
▶ New content on cyberterrorism
▶ Added a **Technology in Policing** box: eGuardian
▶ New content on the "If You See Something, Say Something" DHS campaign
▶ Added two **An Officer's Perspective** boxes: Not Every Citizen Recognizes the Authority of Your Badge; How 9/11 Affected Hometown Security

Chapter 10 Criminal Investigation

▶ New term: *Locard's principle of exchange*
▶ New content on the FBI's Advanced Fingerprint Identification (or Information) Technology (AFIT), introduced in 2011 as part of their broader technology initiative called Next Generation Identification (NGI)
▶ New research on using DNA analysis in property crimes investigations
▶ Updated statistics on bias/hate crime
▶ Updated computer-related and cybercrime section
▶ Added **Technology in Policing** box: Surveillance (Throwbots)
▶ Added **An Officer's Perspective** box: Partnering with Pawnshops

Chapter 11   Responding to Children and Juveniles: Our Nation's Future

▶ Updated statistics throughout
▶ Added **An Officer's Perspective** box: Handling Runaways
▶ Added content on police mentoring youths

Chapter 12   Gangs and Drugs: Two National Threats

▶ Updated statistics throughout
▶ Added material on two new subtypes of gangs defined by the *2011 NGTA*: One Percenter outlaw motorcycle gangs (OMGs) and neighborhood/local
▶ Added a **Technology in Policing** box: National Gang Intelligence Center (NGIC) Online
▶ New content on responding to clandestine drug labs
▶ Updated Table 12.5 (Drugs of Abuse/Use and Effects) to include K2/Spice, Khat, bath salts
▶ New problem-oriented policing example

Chapter 13   The Importance of Physical and Mental Health: Getting the Job and Keeping Fit for Duty

▶ Added an important new section on the police officer hiring process
▶ New content on employee wellness programs (EWP)
▶ Added content on the color-coded Cooper Awareness Spectrum
▶ New **Technology in Policing** box: The Dangers of Technology

Chapter 14   Liability and Ethics: Is It Legal? Is It Moral?

▶ New terms: *exculpatory evidence, perjury*
▶ New data from a 2011 PhD thesis regarding law enforcement accreditation and the risk of being sued
▶ Added content on unethical deception and case law: *Brady v. Maryland* (1963) and "*Brady* Material," *Giglio v. United States* (1972) and *Giglio* doctrine
▶ Added two **An Officer's Perspective** boxes: Which Is Worse: Death or a Lawsuit?; Gratuities: To Accept or Not to Accept?

HOW TO USE THIS TEXT (PEDAGOGICAL AIDS)

Police Operations: Theory and Practice is more than a text. It is a learning experience requiring *your* active participation to obtain the best results. You will get the most out of the text if you first familiarize yourself with the total scope of law enforcement: Read and think about the subjects listed in the Contents. Then follow five steps for each chapter to get *triple-strength learning*.

Triple-Strength Learning

1. Read the objectives at the beginning of each chapter, stated in the form of "Do You Know" questions. This is your *first* exposure to the key concepts of the text. The following is an example of this format:
   ▶ What police operations are and what they include?

2. Review the key terms and think about their meaning in the context of law enforcement.

3. Read the chapter, underlining or taking notes if that is your preferred study style. Pay special attention to all information within the highlighted areas. This is your *second* exposure to the chapter's key concepts. The following is an example of this format:

> **Police Operations** refers to activities conducted in the field by law enforcement officers as they "serve and protect," including patrol, traffic, investigation, and general calls for service.

The key concepts of each chapter are emphasized in this manner. Also pay attention to all words in bold print. All key terms will be in bold and color print when they are first defined.

4. Read the summary carefully. This will be your *third* exposure to the key concepts. By now, you should have internalized the information.

5. To make sure you have learned the information, when you have finished reading a chapter, reread the list of objectives given at the beginning of that chapter to make certain you can answer each question. If you find yourself stumped, find the appropriate material in the chapter and review it. Often these questions will be used as essay questions during testing.

6. Review the key terms to be certain you can define each. These also are frequently used as test items.

A Note: This text is designed to give you *triple-strength* learning *if* you (1) think about the questions at the beginning of the chapter before you read, (2) read the chapter thoughtfully for in-depth answers to these questions, and then (3) read and reread the summary. Do not misinterpret triple-strength learning to mean you need only focus on three elements—the "Do You Know" items, highlighted boxes, and summaries—to master the chapter. You are also responsible for reading and understanding the material that surrounds these basics—the "meat" around the bones, so to speak. The summaries are intended as a *review*, not as shortcuts or replacements to reading the entire chapter. If you read only the summaries, or focus only on the highlighted key concepts, you are not likely to understand or recall the content. Remember, your livelihood and your life is on the line in this demanding and rewarding profession. Begin your habits of self-discipline now.

EXPLORING FURTHER

The text also provides an opportunity for you to apply what you have learned or to go into specific areas in greater depth. To further strengthen your learning experience, the text includes discussion questions, application exercises in which you create policies and procedures related to the content of each chapter, and critical thinking exercises. Professional law enforcement officers should be able to create reasonable, legal, ethical, and effective policies and procedures for the most common situations encountered in law enforcement. In addition, they should be able to approach each situation as a unique experience, perhaps requiring a more creative approach. Law enforcement officers must have good critical thinking skills. It is the intent of this text to provide a balance of both.

Finally, each chapter contains Gale Emergency Services database assignments allowing you to go into greater depth in areas of interest to you. Do as many of these assignments as your time permits.

Good reading and learning!

ANCILLARIES

To further enhance your study of law enforcement and criminal justice, several supplements are available:

Instructor Support Materials

Instructor's Resource Manual with Test Bank This manual includes detailed chapter outlines, chapter summaries, key terms reviews, class activity suggestions, and a test bank with a full answer key. ISBN: 9781285052632

Companion Web Site The instructor companion Web site includes enhanced PowerPoint® lecture slides, a computerized test bank, and an electronic version of the Instructor's Resource manual, as well as Lesson Plans and Real-World Resources. ISBN: 9781285052786

PowerLecture™ The PowerLecture™ with ExamView® to accompany this text includes enhanced PowerPoint® lecture slides, a computerized test bank, an electronic version of the Instructor's Resource Manual, Lesson Plans, Real-World Resources, and videos. ISBN 97812850527724

CourseMate Criminal Justice CourseMate is available for *Police Operations: Theory and Practice*, Sixth Edition. ISBN: 9781285052717 (Instant Access Card)/781285052700 (Printed Access Card)

The instructor version of CourseMate includes Engagement Tracker, a first-of-its-kind tool that monitors student engagement in the course. Instructors also have full access to the interactive eBook and other student CourseMate resources.

To access this CourseMate with Engagement Tracker, go to login.cengage.com, sign in with your SSO (single sign-on) login, and add this title to your bookshelf. (Note: Engagement Tracker monitors students who have purchased access to CourseMate.)

WebTutor™ Advantage Plus on Blackboard® with eBook Jumpstart your online course with customizable, rich, text-specific content—all easily and immediately accessible within your existing learning management system. Simply load a WebTutor™ cartridge into your course management system and add, edit, reorganize, or delete content—quizzes, learning objectives, flashcards, Web links, games, exercises, and more—as you see fit. Plus, use your book's test bank and your own grade book to make assessment easier than ever. Whether you want to Web-enable your class or put an entire course online, WebTutor delivers. Visit www.cengage.com/webtutor to learn more. ISBN: 9781285052748

Student Materials

CourseMate Criminal Justice CourseMate is available for *Police Operations: Theory and Practice*, Sixth Edition. This CourseMate includes:

▶ An interactive eBook, with highlighting, note-taking, and search capabilities
▶ Interactive learning tools including:
  - Quizzes
  - Flashcards
  - Videos
  - Study Guide (including numerous exercises and self-tests)
  - Case Studies
  - And more!

To learn more about this resource and access free demo CourseMate resources, go to www.cengagebrain.com, and search by this book's ISBN (9781285052632). To access CourseMate materials that you have purchased, go to login.cengagebrain.com, enter your access code, and create an account or log into your existing account.

Discipline-Wide Supplement Related to this Text

Gale's Custom Journals Database for Emergency Services and Criminal Justice *Police Operations: Theory and Practice*, Sixth Edition contains exercises referencing Gale's Custom Journals Database for Emergency Services and Criminal Justice, available for bundling with criminal justice titles. Containing customized portions of the Gale journal database (which is known for its accurate and authoritative reference content), this Custom Journals Database provides a 24/7 library reference of the latest information and research in this topic area. Learners who desire additional resources and research beyond the scope of their textbook will find this to be a useful tool.

Instructors, talk to your Cengage Learning sales representative to find out about adding the database to your adoption of this textbook. Students, talk to your instructors to find out whether you have access to this database.

Features include:

▶ Material drawn from magazines, academic journals, books, news, and multimedia
▶ Digital access allowing easy-to-use, powerful search capabilities, creating a great reference tool
▶ Current articles to help students prepare for their careers by way of industry journal information
▶ Additional tools such as citation tools, downloads, and even translation features
   ISBN: 9781435482326

Additional Resources Available

Careers in Criminal Justice Web Site The Careers in Criminal Justice Web Site offers extensive career profiling information and self-assessment testing designed to help students investigate and focus on the criminal justice career choices that are right for them. This resource-rich Web site includes more than 70 career profiles and more than 25 video interviews with links and tools to assist students in finding a professional position. It also features a career Rolodex, interest assessments, and a career planner with sample résumés, letters, interview questions, and more. View a demo at academic.cengage.com/criminaljustice/careers. ISBN: 9780495595236 (Instant Access Code)/9780495595229 (Printed Access Card)

Crime Scenes 2.0: Interactive Criminal Justice CD-ROM This simulation CD-ROM uses six scenarios of various crimes (juvenile murder, prostitution assault, arresting force/DUI, search and seizure, embezzlement/white-collar crime, and incarceration classification/parole) to illustrate all of the stages of the criminal justice system. The student is able to make choices about the outcomes of the simulation at various decision points in each scenario, thus illustrating the consequences of each choice. The scenarios use video, courtroom drawings, and numerous forms to build the evidence of each case. This CD-ROM can be used to introduce new material, as a reviewing device, to spark class discussions, or as a basis for group research projects. And students can use this exciting and game-like CD-ROM to explore on their own. ISBN: 9780534568313

Careers in Criminal Justice and Related Fields: From Internship to Promotion, Sixth Edition (J. Scott Harr and Kären M. Hess) This supplemental book helps students develop a job-search strategy through résumés, cover letters and interview techniques. It also provides students with extensive information on various criminal justice professions, including job descriptions, job salary suggestions, and contact information. ISBN: 9780495600329

ACKNOWLEDGMENTS

First, we would like to acknowledge Henry M. Wrobleski (1922–2007), the original lead author for the first two editions of this text. Henry was the coordinator of the Law Enforcement Program at Normandale Community College as well as a respected author, lecturer, consultant, and expert witness with 30 years of experience in law enforcement and security. He was also the Dean of Instruction for the Institute for Professional Development and a graduate of the FBI Academy. Other Cengage texts Wrobleski contributed to were *Introduction to Law Enforcement and Criminal Justice* and *Private Security*. He is very much missed.

We would also like to thank Waldo Asp for creating the *Exercises in Critical Thinking* found at the end of each chapter. We would like to thank the reviewers for the Sixth Edition: Marcia Bedard, Collinsville Area Vocational Center, Collinsville, IL; Patrick Dunworth, Albuquerque Technical Vocational Institute; Michelle L. Nichol, Colorado Technical University, Sioux Falls, SD; Mary E. Pyle, Tyler Junior College; and Jason B. Waller, Tyler Junior College.

Thanks are also due to the reviewers of the original manuscript and previous editions for their careful reading and constructive suggestions: James S. Albritton, Marquette University; Becky Allen, Minot State University; David Barlow, University of Wisconsin–Milwaukee; Michael B. Blankenship, Memphis State University; William D. Braddock, Boise State University; Laura Brooks, University of Maryland; Irl R. (Chris) Carmean, Houston Community College; David L. Carter, Michigan State University; Steven B. Carter, Kaplan College; Robert Ives, Rock Valley College (Illinois); David A. Kramer, Bergen Community College; Floyd W. Liley, Jr., Mansfield University; Neal W. Lippold, Waubonsee Community College; Steven Livernois, SUNY–Canton; Jeff Magers, Stephen F. Austin State University; James Malcolm, College of Lake County; Richard H. Martin, Auburn University–Montgomery; James L. Massey, Northern Illinois University; Donald McLean, Oakland Community College; Joe Morris, Northwestern State University; James E. Newman, Rio Hondo Community College–Police Academy (California); James T. Nichols, Tompkins Cortland Community College; Tom O'Connor, North Carolina Wesleyan University; Jerald L. Plant, Milwaukee Area Technical College; Carroll S. Price, Penn Valley Community College; Chester L. Quarles, University of Mississippi; James Sewell, Florida Department of Law Enforcement; Sandra M. Hall Smith, Indiana University Northwest; B. Grant Stitt, University of Nevada at Reno; Gary W. Tucker, Sinclair Community College; and Jay Zumbrun, Community College of Baltimore County. Any errors in the text are, however, the sole responsibility of the coauthors.

Finally, thanks to our photo researcher, Terri Wright; our editors at Delmar Cengage Learning, Senior Product Manager Anne Orgren and Senior Acquisitions Editor Shelley Esposito, for their outstanding advice, support, and encouragement; our copyeditor, Robin Gold; and our production editor at Buuji, Sara Dovre Wudali.

ABOUT THE AUTHORS

Kären Matison Hess, Ph.D., (1939–2010), was the author who first developed this text with Wrobleski and carried it through four very successful revisions. Dr. Hess was an instructor at Normandale Community College (Bloomington, Minnesota) who crafted a line of enduring, practical textbooks in the fields of law enforcement and criminal justice that include *Criminal Investigation* (10th edition), *Introduction to Law Enforcement and Criminal Justice* (9th edition), *Introduction to Private Security* (5th edition), *Juvenile Justice* (5th edition), *Management and Supervision in Law Enforcement* (4th edition), *Community Policing: Partnerships for Problem Solving* (5th edition), and *Careers in Criminal Justice: From Internship to Promotion* (6th edition). She was a member of the Academy of Criminal Justice Sciences (ACJS), the American Association of University Women (AAUW), the American Society for Industrial Security (ASIS), the International Association of Chiefs of Police (IACP), the International Law Enforcement Educators and Trainers Association (ILEETA), the Justice Research and Statistics Association (JRSA), the Police Executive Research Forum (PERF), and the Textbook and Academic Author's Association (TAA). In 2006, Dr. Hess was honored by the University of Minnesota College of Education and Human Development at the school's 100-year anniversary as one of 100 alumni who have made a significant contribution to education and human development. Her tireless dedication to authorship and the education of criminal justice students will forever be an inspiration to us.

Christine Hess Orthmann, M.S., has been writing and researching in various aspects of criminal justice for more than 20 years. She is a coauthor of numerous Cengage books, including *Community Policing: Partnerships for Problem Solving* (6th edition), *Corrections for the Twenty-First Century*, *Constitutional Law and the Criminal Justice System* (5th edition), *Criminal Investigation* (10th edition), *Introduction to Law Enforcement and Criminal Justice* (10th edition), *Juvenile Justice* (6th edition), and *Management and Supervision in Law Enforcement* (6th edition), as well as a major contributor to *Introduction to Private Security* (5th edition) and *Careers in Criminal Justice and Related Fields: From Internship to Promotion* (6th edition). She is a member of the Academy of Criminal Justice Sciences (ACJS), the American Society of Criminology (ASC), the Text and Academic Authors Association (TAA), and the National Criminal Justice Honor Society (Alpha Phi Sigma) and is a reserve officer with the Rosemount (Minnesota) Police Department. Orthmann has a Master of Science degree in criminal justice from the University of Cincinnati.

Henry Lim Cho holds an M.A. in Human Services with an emphasis on Criminal Justice Leadership from Concordia University–St. Paul, Minnesota. He has worked in the field of criminal justice for more than 12 years, having held positions in private security, as a community service officer, police officer, and detective. He currently holds the rank of Sergeant with the Rosemount (Minnesota) Police Department. Sgt. Cho has experience as a use-of-force instructor and a crime scene investigator. His professional memberships include the Minnesota Police and Peace Officer's Association, International Association of Identification—Minnesota Chapter, Minnesota Sex Crimes Investigator Association, High Technology Crime Investigation Association, National White Collar Crime Center, and Fraternal Order of Police. Sgt. Cho has been published in the *Minnesota Police Journal*, appeared as a profile contributor in *Introduction to Law Enforcement and Criminal Justice* (9th edition), and was a content contributor to *Introduction to Law Enforcement and Criminal Justice* (10th edition) and *Criminal Investigation* (10th edition).

Police Operations

Theory and Practice

SIXTH EDITION

The Basics behind Effective Police Operations

Police operations deal with what officers do in the field as they "serve and protect." To fulfill their responsibilities, law enforcement officers have been given great power, power entrusted to them by the people they serve and defined by the laws of the land, state, and municipality. This section presents an overview of police operations starting with the context in which those services are provided.

The society served, the laws it has enacted, the individuals entering law enforcement, and the police organization itself have undergone great changes in the past decade—today's law enforcement uses mission statements, value statements, goals, objectives, policies, procedures, and regulations to provide a basic structure within which officers normally function. Because law enforcement deals with such diverse problems, officers also must expect to use discretion while safeguarding citizens' constitutional rights (Chapter 1).

Law enforcement demands that its officers be multifaceted and well rounded. Officers must understand the complex communication process and the barriers that often exist within that process and within our diverse society. Officers also must be skilled in making field inquiries, interviewing, and interrogating, and they must know how to do so while

The Basics behind Effective Police Operations

protecting the constitutional rights of victims, suspects, and witnesses. Further, officers must record the information they have obtained in effective, reader-friendly reports, and officers must know how to use the various records available (Chapter 2). In addition, officers need several profession-specific skills. Officers must understand and become skilled at conducting stops and frisks, making arrests, conducting searches, and participating in undercover operations, all without violating anyone's constitutional rights (Chapter 3).

Police Operations in Context

© Henry Cho

DO YOU KNOW . . .

- What police operations are and what they include?
- What changes have affected police operations?
- How our society has changed?
- How our law enforcement officers have changed?
- How the police organization may change?
- What the Commission on Accreditation of Law Enforcement Agencies (CALEA) is and how it affects police operations?
- What community policing is?
- How advances in technology are affecting police operations?
- What a mission and a mission statement are?
- What the relationship between goals and objectives is?
- What police discretion is and what positive contributions it makes?
- What problems are associated with discretion?
- What balance presents a major challenge for law enforcement?

CAN YOU DEFINE?

broken windows metaphor
community policing
discretion
dog shift
goals
heterogeneity
information
intelligence
mission
mission statement
objectives
participatory leadership
police operations
policy
procedures
regulations
selective enforcement

INTRODUCTION

Just what do police officers do? What skills must they possess, and in what ways does the community rely on their services? Historically, police officers have been viewed as law *enforcement* officers, concerned with keeping the law from being broken and apprehending those who break it. This function, however, has broadened considerably, as evidenced in the label *peace officer* replacing *police officer* in many departments. Although *peace officer* is a general term that covers all licensed law enforcement officers, including state troopers, sheriff's deputies, conservation officers, and the like, it also speaks to the expanded responsibilities of police officers to act proactively to serve the community and problem solve in an effort to keep the peace as well as to handle crime and disorder as it occurs. No matter what priorities a law enforcement agency may have, certain basic police operations will be found.

police operations

Activities conducted in the field by law enforcement officers as they "serve and protect"; usually include patrol, traffic, investigation, and general calls for service.

> **Police operations** refers to activities conducted in the field by law enforcement officers as they "serve and protect," including patrol, traffic, investigation, and general calls for service.

Before looking at specific police operations and the skills required to perform them effectively and efficiently, it is important to understand the *context* in which these operations occur. Although police operations have changed little during the last hundred years, the public served and the laws enacted by that public, the officers providing the services, the police bureaucracy itself, and the community's involvement have changed and will continue to change.

This chapter begins by examining the various changes affecting police operations. This is followed by another important context affecting police operations: the department's mission and values, reflected in goals, objectives, and tasks to be accomplished. The chapter concludes with yet another area greatly influencing operations—discretion; the discussion includes ethical decision making, the negative and positive sides of discretion, and the interaction of discretion and critical-thinking skills.

A VIEW OF CONTEMPORARY AMERICAN LAW ENFORCEMENT

In 2008, *Police* magazine ran a 12-part series of articles painting a portrait of American law enforcement operations. Following are some of their conclusions (Griffith 2008, 10):

▶ There are not enough cops. Hardly anyone wants to pay for more. And nobody is quite sure how to add more men and women to the "Thin Blue Line."

▶ The demographics of who serves in law enforcement are changing in terms of race, ethnicity, gender, and even age.

▶ Training methods are rooted more in tradition and convention than in the realities of what you face on the street. Updating these methods elicits howls from some trainers.

▶ The public doesn't really hate you. Some of it doesn't love you that much either.

▶ You will likely gravitate toward a specialty such as K-9, SWAT [special weapons and tactics], or investigations at some point in your career. This trend will be even more prevalent as we move deeper into this century.

▶ Women will play a greater role in law enforcement in this century. They won't find it easy to balance career and family. Neither will their male counterparts.

▶ Patrol is still one of the most critical operations in law enforcement. It is both the "protect" and "serve" part of the job.

▶ SWAT's focus on physical strength and endurance is being challenged by politicians more interested in diversity than tactical performance.

▶ Since 9/11, you've actually done a [expletive deleted] fine job [of] improving your ability to prevent and respond to terrorist attacks. . . . Unfortunately, you still can't relax your guard.

▶ Policymakers make rules of engagement for the least common denominator of officers. This is true, even though the experience level and education level of the vast majority of American law enforcement officers far exceeds that common denominator.

▶ Regardless of where you work, no matter how affluent or remote, violent criminal gangs are going to be a big problem for you in the coming years. Gang investigators we have talked to say you can thank Hollywood and the music industry for making gang culture so attractive to kids.

▶ Using less-lethal force can be controversial. Not using less-lethal force can be even more controversial. Weapons technology will likely outpace policy and the political will of your local government.[1]

All of these observations are discussed in this text. Griffith concludes, "The truth is that the state of American law enforcement is a very fluid thing," noting that although the *Police* staff was working on addressing issues their audience wanted addressed, the world economy "went down a rabbit hole and we are all now living in Recessionland" (2008, 10). The "economic meltdown" is greatly affecting American law enforcement.

CHANGES AFFECTING POLICE OPERATIONS

Law enforcement is affected by a changing public and society, changing law enforcement officers, a changing police bureaucracy, standards set forth by the Commission on Accreditation for Law Enforcement Agencies (CALEA), a change in community involvement, a change in approach, and advances in technology.

---

[1]Source: Griffith, David. "The State of American Law Enforcement." *Police,* December 2008, p.10.

A Changing Public and Society

The U.S. population has changed significantly during the past several decades, and these trends will undoubtedly affect police operations[2]:

▶ An aging U.S. population: Experts at the Population Division of the U.S. Census Bureau project that by 2050, more than 88 million Americans will be age 65 and older, which is more than double the number of citizens in that age bracket in 2010 (40.3 million) (Vincent and Velkoff 2010; Howden and Meyer 2011). The increase is the result of the aging of the baby boomers as well as of the increased life expectancy. When our country was founded, the average life expectancy was 35. In 2011, it was 78.4 years. Law enforcement is now seeing more elderly victims of crime, who are considered "vulnerable adults." Such victimization most commonly occurs through abuse or fraud. Several factors contribute to this increased victimization rate, including a larger number of elderly citizens in the population and a greater willingness of such victims to report "private" family matters than was seen in previous generations.

▶ An increasingly racially diverse population: In 1950, the U.S. population was 87 percent White; that percentage is projected to drop to 51 percent by 2050. Population statistics projections expect immigration to propel the U.S. population from 308 million in 2010 to a total of 438 million by 2050. The racial and ethnic profile of Americans will continue to shift, with non-Hispanic Whites assuming a minority status.

▶ A growing number of single-parent households: One-parent families numbered 12 million in 2000 and 21 million in 2010; single-mother families increased from 3 million (12%) in 1970 to 15.2 million (13.1%) in 2010, and single-father families grew from 393,000 (1%) in 1970 to 5.8 million (5%) in 2010.

▶ A widening gap between the wealthy and the poor: A report from the Congressional Budget Office indicates incomes for the wealthiest Americans are rising twice as fast as those of the middle class.

> Our society is becoming older and has more minorities, more immigrants, and more single-parent households, and the gap between the rich and poor continues to expand.

These trends underscore the need for those in the criminal justice field to be culturally sensitive to the public they serve, especially those who work as directly with that public as police officers do. Many theories have addressed how our existing system of laws and law enforcement affects and is affected by our evolving society.

A Changing Law Enforcement Officer

Another major change affecting police operations is the type of officer performing them. Historically, law enforcement has attracted young White men out of the military. These men frequently had a high school education or

---

[2]Data from the 2010 U.S. Census (http://2010.census.gov) unless otherwise noted.

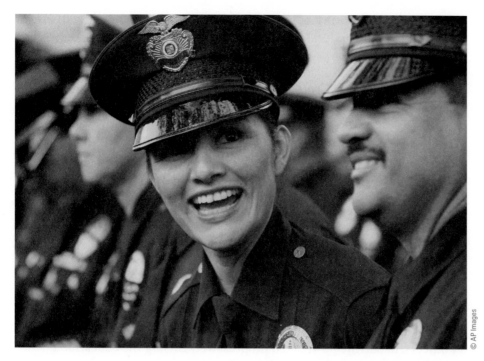

Police departments are achieving greater diversity and recruiting more women and minorities to better reflect the demographics of the populations they serve.

less and were used to following orders without questioning authority. This is no longer true. Many people entering the field have no military experience. Furthermore, the ranks of today's police departments are less exclusively White men because more women and minorities are being actively recruited and promoted, a change that has led to greater racial and gender **heterogeneity** among those in leadership positions within law enforcement organizations.

heterogeneity

Diversity.

> Today's police recruits include fewer people with military backgrounds and more women and minorities. New recruits have more formal education and police training, and they value on-job satisfaction more than they value material rewards. These recruits also are expected to perform more diverse operations and are held to a higher professional standard.

More Women and Minorities The Indianapolis Police Department made history in 1968 when it assigned the first two female officers to patrol in a capacity equal to that of their male colleagues (Harrington 2001). Since that time, women have entered the field of law enforcement in increasing numbers and played a critical role in the development of modern policing. Yet, overall, the fraction of women in law enforcement has remained small. In 2007, approximately 1 in 8 (12.5%) full-time sworn police officers at the local level was female, a considerable increase from two decades earlier when, in 1987, women composed 7.6% of sworn local officers (Reaves 2010). In general, the smaller the local police agency or sheriffs' department, the lower the percentage of female officers within its ranks (Langton 2010). Women constitute a larger proportion of sworn officers at the federal level, with roughly 20 percent of full-time, sworn federal law enforcement officers in 2007 being women (Langton 2010).

Data on the racial diversity of law enforcement officers indicates that in 2007, approximately 25 percent of local police officers were members of a racial or ethnic minority, a figure that represents a 10% increase over 2003 employment numbers of minority officers (Reaves 2010). In 2007, local police departments employed an estimated 55,267 Black or African American officers, 47,678 Hispanic or Latino officers, and 12,564 officers from other minority groups including Asians, Pacific Islanders, and American Indians. During the past two decades, the percentage of Hispanic officers has been increasing at a faster rate than that for African Americans; although the percentage of officers belonging to other minority groups has remained fairly constant since 2003, the numbers of Hispanic officers have more than tripled since 1987 (Reaves 2010).

Despite gains made during the past several decades, women and minorities continue to be underrepresented among the ranks of the police.

Better Educated In addition to recruiting more women and other minority officers, departments are also progressively raising the educational standards for officer candidates. Traditionally, emphasis was placed on potential officers' physical strength, height, weight, and such abilities as firearms skills. This focus began to change slightly during the 1920s and 1930s, when August Vollmer, considered by many as the father of professional policing, began advocating higher education for those entering law enforcement. In addition, the Wickersham Commission (1931) and the President's Commission on Law Enforcement and the Administration of Justice (1967) both recommended postsecondary education for law enforcement officers.

Research examining the effects of higher education on police officers' performance has produced varied and sometimes seemingly contradictory results. Some studies have found officers with more education perform more effectively and have a better capacity to handle the variety of tasks involved in modern policing, but other studies have concluded that higher-educated officers burn out more quickly and experience greater job dissatisfaction.

Today, college is what high school was a generation ago. An increasing number of agencies require either a college degree or some college credits. Legal barriers no longer stand in the way of police departments requiring college education. In *Davis v. Dallas* (1986), a U.S. court of appeals upheld a requirement by the City of Dallas that entry-level police recruits have completed 45 college credits with a C average.

McFall (2006, 45) cites the experience and observations of Major Stelmack of the Baltimore County Police Department: "When I started [as a police officer], they taught me how to fill out a report, do mouth-to-mouth resuscitation and drive a police car in an emergency. Now we need to be hiring people who have the temperament to deal with society. They have to be open-minded. They have to deal with people from different classes, different backgrounds, and different ethnic groups. They have to have excellent oral communication skills and be able to write. They have to come on board with some understanding of technology. They have to be able to mediate. And they have to be problem solvers." Such skills and understanding are greatly enhanced through education.

Different Generational Values Another change occurring in law enforcement throughout the country is the existence of three or four distinct generations within a single department. (*Note:* This is not to be confused with legacy hiring, which is the practice of hiring successive generations within the same family.) Today's younger police officers come from distinctly different backgrounds than did previous groups. Although different sources vary somewhat in the year they attribute to a given generation and some call a specific generation by different names, the most common breakdown of birth years is:

1922–1945	Veterans, Silents, or Traditionalists
1946–1964	Baby Boomers
1965–1980	Generation X
1981–2000	Generation Y, Millennials, Echo Boomers

Each generation has distinct attitudes, behaviors, expectations, habits, and motivations (Hammill 2005). Tables 1.1 and 1.2 compare the personal and lifestyle characteristics of the four generations and their workplace characteristics.

Slahor (2007, 66) notes, "The Generation Xers and the Millennials multitask. Their work stations and homes have music, computer screen images, and the TV news, all while they're talking on their cell phones [or texting]!" The individuals between ages 18 and 25 are often called Gamers or Generation Next; 90 percent of the latest generations use the Internet daily, and more than half send text messages daily: "With the advent of interactive technologies and online social networking as well as a growing chasm between the wired and unwired worlds, never has the gap between the generation 'in charge' and those that follow it been as wide" (Harrison 2007, 150).

Table 1.1 Personal and Lifestyle Characteristics by Generation

	Veterans (1922–1945)	Baby Boomers (1946–1964)	Generation X (1965–1980)	Generation Y (1981–2000)
Core Values	Respect for authority	Optimism	Skepticism	Realism
	Conformers	Involvement	Fun	Confidence
	Discipline		Informality	Extreme fun
				Social
Family	Traditional nuclear	Disintegrating	Latch-key kids	Merged families
Education	A dream	A birthright	A way to get there	An incredible expense
Communication Media	Rotary phones	Touch-tone phones	Cell phones	Internet
	One-on-one	Call me anytime	Call me only at work	Picture phones
	Write a memo			E-mail
Dealing with Money	Put it away	Buy now, pay later	Cautious	Earn to spend
	Pay cash		Conservative	
			Save, save, save	

Source: Greg Hammill, "Mixing and Managing Four Generations of Employees," *FDU Magazine Online* (Winter/Spring, 2005). http://www.fdu.edu/newspubs/magazine/05ws/generations.htm Retrieved January 23, 2012.

Table 1.2 Workplace Characteristics by Generation

	Veterans (1922–1945)	Baby Boomers (1946–1964)	Generation X (1965–1980)	Generation Y (1981–2000)
Work Ethic and Values	Hard work	Workaholics	Eliminate the task	What's next
	Respect authority	Work efficiently	Self-reliance	Multitasking
	Sacrifice	Crusading causes	Want structure and direction	Tenacity
	Duty before fun	Personal fulfillment	Skeptical	Entrepreneurial
	Adhere to rules	Desire quality		Tolerant
		Question authority		Goal oriented
Work Is . . .	An obligation	An exciting adventure	A difficult challenge	A means to an end
			A contract	Fulfillment
Leadership Style	Directive	Consensual	Everyone is the same	*TBD
	Command-and-control	Collegial	Challenge others	
			Ask why	
Interactive Style	Individual	Team player	Entrepreneur	Participative
		Love to have meetings		
Communications	Formal	In person	Direct	E-mail
	Memo		Immediate	Voicemail
Feedback and Rewards	No news is good news	Don't appreciate it	Sorry to interrupt, but how am I doing?	Whenever I want it, at the push of a button
	Satisfaction is a job well done	Money	Freedom is the best reward	Meaningful work
		Title recognition		
Messages That Motivate	Your experience is respected	You are valued	Do it your way	You will work with other bright, creative people
		You are needed	Forget the rules	
Work and Family Life	Ne'er the twain shall meet	No balance	Balance	Balance
		Work to live		

*As this group has not spent much time in the workforce, this characteristic has yet to be determined.
Source: Greg Hammill, "Mixing and Managing Four Generations of Employees," *FDU Magazine Online* (Winter/Spring, 2005).
http://www.fdu.edu/newspubs/magazine/05ws/generations.htm Retrieved January 23, 2012.

In addition to having different backgrounds and values from the "traditional" police recruit, police officers now are often called on to perform operations well beyond what traditionally has been provided.

A Changing Police Bureaucracy

Given the changing needs of the public, the new type of person entering law enforcement, and the growth of new services, it is logical that the bureaucracy directing police operations must also change. A basic principle held by Sir Robert Peel, often called the father of modern policing, was that the police must be organized militarily. The military model of the Metropolitan Police of London (established in 1829) was adopted in the United States and has been the model for our police departments since that time. Figure 1.1 illustrates this traditional pyramid of authority and organizational hierarchy.

This model, however, is now being questioned by many, partially because of the changes in police recruits and the transition to community policing.

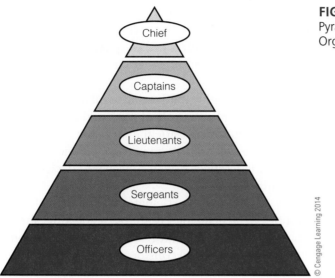

FIGURE 1.1 Traditional Pyramid of Authority and Organization Hierarchy

© Cengage Learning 2014

Some police departments are moving away from the paramilitary model and adopting a business or corporate model that flattens the organization and reduces the number of management and supervisory positions while increasing the number of officers. These officers are becoming better trained to act independently while providing more field services—that is, police operations.

It is important at this point in the discussion to recognize the differences between appearance and image (external) and philosophy and approach (internal). Some departments have attempted to shift their appearance to match the less militaristic approach, for example, by adopting a more "friendly" look in having officers wear business casual suits, but these departments have frequently encountered a plethora of negative issues involving police officer identity, safety, effectiveness, and public perception. Beyond being impractical, such attire often makes it more difficult for officers to gain compliance from "bad guys" or be taken seriously by the public. There is much to say about a "uniform" and officer presence and how our society expects a police officer to *look*. Thus, although it is entirely possible for agencies to modify the behavioral approach and response of officers to be less militaristic, the ability to alter the external image and appearance of law enforcement has met with less success. The net result has been that police still look like they always have, but they are now expected to act quite differently.

> The police bureaucracy may become less militaristic and may move toward a team approach to providing services. This includes decentralization and a shift from management to leadership.

Many people, particularly Gen-Xers, no longer depend on the authority of somebody "above" them to dictate their opinions or control their actions. They are more independent, preferring to make up their own minds and accepting responsibility for their own actions. They still, however, need the

participatory leadership

Allows officers to influence decisions affecting them and seeks to form a cohesive team.

support and guidance of a leader. Many police organizations are undergoing a change from an authoritarian management style to a leadership style that focuses on teamwork. This style, called **participatory leadership**, allows officers to influence decisions affecting them and seeks to form a cohesive team.

Participatory leadership is usually highly motivating to all members of the team. In progressive police departments, the role of rank-and-file officers is elevated significantly, with their input being critical in decision making. It is further expected that rank-and-file officers will be in close contact with the citizens they serve and, therefore, can reflect citizen concerns as decisions are made and can provide leadership.

A type of leadership closely related to the participatory style is transformational leadership, which combines the principles of shared leadership, shared vision, and the continuing improvement of the individual: "Transformational leadership uses the concepts of individualized consideration, idealized influence, inspirational motivation, and intellectual stimulation, which are referred to as the 'four I's of leadership'" (Bynum 2008, 72).

Another trend stemming from participatory leadership is customized leadership, which incorporates an understanding of generational differences. In this style, supervisors customize their leadership styles toward individual subordinates to gain optimal performance from each employee. For example, a supervisor need not offer as many supportive compliments to a baby boomer as to a millennial.

Standards Set Forth by the Commission on Accreditation of Law Enforcement Agencies (CALEA)

Many of the changes in the police bureaucracy result from a desire to comply with the standards set forth by the Commission on Accreditation of Law Enforcement Agencies. CALEA is an independent, nonprofit corporation with a professional staff governed by a 21-member commission board. Eleven members must be from law enforcement; the remaining members represent businesses, academia, the judiciary, and state/provincial and local government. Members are appointed by the four founding law enforcement organizations and serve without compensation.

> The Commission on Accreditation for Law Enforcement Agencies, Inc. (CALEA), was created in 1979 as a credentialing authority through the joint efforts of law enforcement's major executive associations:
>
> ▶ International Association of Chiefs of Police (IACP)
> ▶ National Organization of Black Law Enforcement Executives (NOBLE)
> ▶ National Sheriffs' Association (NSA)
> ▶ Police Executive Research Forum (PERF)
>
> The purpose of CALEA's Accreditation Programs is to improve the delivery of public safety services, primarily by: maintaining a body of standards, developed by public safety practitioners, covering a wide range of up-to-date public safety initiatives; establishing and administering an accreditation process; and recognizing professional excellence.

Specifically, CALEA's goals are to:

- ▶ Strengthen crime prevention and control capabilities;
- ▶ Formalize essential management procedures;
- ▶ Establish fair and nondiscriminatory personnel practices;
- ▶ Improve service delivery;
- ▶ Solidify interagency cooperation and coordination; and
- ▶ Increase community and staff confidence in the agency.

The CALEA Accreditation Process is a proven modern management model; once implemented, it presents the Chief Executive Officer (CEO), on a continuing basis, with a blueprint that promotes the efficient use of resources and improves service delivery—regardless of the size, geographic location, or functional responsibilities of the agency. ("The Commission" 2010)[3]

The Commission on Accreditation of Law Enforcement Agencies (CALEA) certifies law enforcement agencies that meet the standards set by the commission.

COUNTERPOINT

ARGUMENTS AGAINST ACCREDITATION

Although few dispute the need for law enforcement agencies and officers to hold themselves to high professional standards, some criticism has befallen the accreditation process because it can potentially impede an agency's discretion, whether in the form of overly restrictive policies, limitations on hiring practices, or some other impact on police operations. Consider, for example, the experience of one suburban police agency in Minnesota that attempted to move toward accreditation during the early 1990s.

During this process, the department realized a surge in policy requirements so great that officers were overwhelmed, which led to a disruption in proactive policing out of fear of violating one of the new, relatively unknown and unfamiliar policies. Furthermore, accreditation mandated new officer candidates hold a four-year college degree, which significantly limited the pool of qualified individuals the agency could hire. In the end, the agency chose practicality over the "gold label" of accreditation.

The CALEA *Standards for Law Enforcement Agencies*, Fifth Edition (2012) are used by agencies throughout the country and will be referred to as they relate to specific police operations.

A Change in Community Involvement: Community Policing

When Peel established the London Metropolitan Police, he set forth a number of principles, one of which foreshadowed community policing: "The police are the public and the public are the police." The Office of Community Oriented Policing Services (COPS) defines **community policing** as "a philosophy that

community policing

"Philosophy that promotes organizational strategies, which support the systematic use of partnerships and problem-solving techniques to proactively address the immediate conditions that give rise to public safety issues such as crime, social disorder, and fear of crime."

---

[3]Source: "The Commission." Gainesville, VA: The Commission on Accreditation for Law Enforcement Agencies, Inc., 2010. CALEA Online, http://www.calea.org/content/commission Retrieved January 23, 2012.

promotes organizational strategies, which support the systematic use of partnerships and problem-solving techniques, to proactively address the immediate conditions that give rise to public safety issues such as crime, social disorder, and fear of crime" (*Community Policing Defined* 2009, 3).

Community policing offers one avenue for increasing neighborhood safety: "Community policing is not a program or a series of programs. It is a philosophy, a belief that working together, the police and the community can accomplish what neither can accomplish alone. The *synergy* that results from community policing can be powerful. It is like the power of a finely tuned athletic team, with each member contributing to the total effort. Occasionally heroes may emerge, but victory depends on a team effort" (Miller, Hess, and Orthmann 2010, xix).

Community policing differs from earlier efforts such as team policing, community relations, crime prevention programs, or neighborhood watch programs. Community policing involves a rethinking of the role of the police and a restructuring of the police organization.

TRENDS IN POLICE OPERATIONS

GEO-POLICING

A recent trend in policing is called "geo-policing," which is essentially a hybrid between community policing and foot patrolling beats.

Community policing usually assigns specific officers to specific neighborhoods and actively involves them in helping the neighborhood solve its problems.

 Community policing is proactive, empowering citizens to help local law enforcement provide safer neighborhoods. It usually includes an emphasis on foot and bicycle patrol.

Community policing goes much further than traditional community relations programs or neighborhood watch programs, although it often includes these components. Community policing means that officers get to know the citizens in their assigned areas—those who are law-abiding and those who are not. It means they listen to the citizens and treat them as a business treats its customers. Community policing also capitalizes on people's natural tendency to subscribe to the Not In My Back Yard (NIMBY) philosophy. The closer to home police can get their message, the more likely they are to enlist community support.

broken windows metaphor

Broken windows in a neighborhood make a statement that no one cares enough about the quality of life in the neighborhood to bother fixing things that need repair.

A general philosophy behind community policing is explained by Wilson and Kelling (1982, 31), who suggest that crime and social disorder are "inextricably linked." They use a **broken windows metaphor** to describe the deterioration of neighborhoods. Broken windows that go unrepaired make a statement that no one cares enough about the quality of life in the neighborhood to bother fixing things that need repair. In a later article, Wilson and Kelling (1989, 49) contend, "Community-oriented policing means changing the

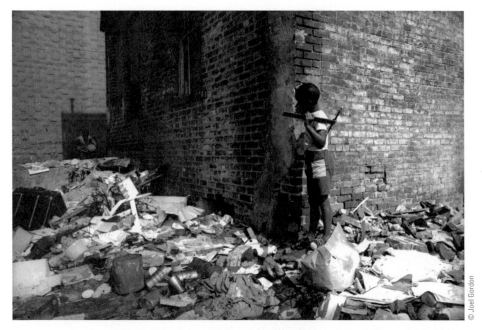

This poverty-stricken, run down, high crime, inner-city urban neighborhood illustrates the despair and disorder described in Wilson and Kelling's broken window theory.

© Joel Gordon

daily work of the police to include investigating problems as well as incidents. It means defining as a problem whatever a significant body of public opinion regards as a threat to community order. It means working with the good guys, and not just against the bad guys."

The devastated economy of 2008 and 2009 and the collapse of risky mortgages provide a present-day example of this theory in the challenge of potentially dangerous empty vacant homes: "Communities across the nation are seeing deserted houses in greater numbers than ever in neighborhoods of all socioeconomic levels. Left empty, these homes deteriorate. The grass grows out of control, windows get shattered, swimming pools turn slimy and green, walls get spray painted with graffiti. Worse yet, these vacant houses become magnets for squatters, thieves and teens looking for a place to party" (Partington 2008, 83).

The broken windows metaphor "stresses the importance of including communities in the change process, with the primary goal being the development of informal social control mechanisms within the communities in question and not merely increased enforcement of minor offenses" (Scheider 2009). The philosophy of community policing and its effect on police operations will be found throughout this text as community policing is actually implemented in the field.

A Change in Approach: The Emergence of Intelligence-Led Policing (ILP)

The terrorist attacks of September 11, 2001, in combination with the rapid evolution of technology available to law enforcement, has led to the emergence of a new era of policing—intelligence-led policing (ILP). Before the events of 9/11, *intelligence* was viewed by many in law enforcement as a clandestine operation performed by a few select entities. Separation, secrecy, and silo-ing (nonsharing) of information and intelligence were common practices. (Note the important distinction between information and intelligence: **information**

information

Raw data.

intelligence

The product of evaluation, manipulation, and analysis of information through which context, value, and validity have been added.

is raw data; **intelligence** is the product of evaluation, manipulation, and analysis of information through which context, value, and validity have been added.)

In the wake of the terrorist tragedy, many realized that these isolationist practices had contributed to missed opportunities and cues regarding the activities of those who later caused immeasurable harm to our citizens and our nation's security. Thus was born ILP, a strategic and methodical approach toward policing that involves risk assessment and risk management and uses intelligence and data as the primary resources to prevent, detect, and disrupt all manner of crime, both foreign and domestic, including terrorist activities. ILP permits early detection of crime trends, which allows police to be more proactive in preventing continued crime (Brewer 2009). ILP is separated into two categories—strategic and tactical. The strategic intelligence portion of ILP focuses on analyzing intelligence over time and contributes to broad scope, "big picture" aspects of policing such as planning and prevention. The tactical intelligence portion, in contrast, analyzes information immediately as it applies to a specific incident and more exigent concerns. Development of tactical intelligence typically leads to direct action being taken. The vital role intelligence plays in police operations will be discussed further in later chapters as it pertains to various aspects of law enforcement.

Table 1.3 compares the basic differences between traditional, community, and intelligence-led policing.

Consider next how technology has changed law enforcement.

Advances in Technology

Law enforcement has come a long way since 1931 when Dick Tracy, the hard-hitting, extremely intelligent comic strip detective, chased bad guys using his two-way wrist radio that few readers believed could actually exist. The accelerated advances in communication such as smartphones, PDAs, mobile data terminals (MDTs), video streams, and other devices, products, and applications have created "the equivalent of a technology tsunami" (Marshall 2008).

Technology has played an expanding role in the everyday operations of the frontline police officer, from the tools available in the squad car, to the equipment worn on their person, to the devices at their work stations and throughout the police department that enable them to access other law enforcement agencies and databases around the globe: "The result is a much more 'wired' officer. The technology is designed to make the officer more efficient, more effective, more knowledgeable, and better able to spend time on patrol interfacing with the community by improving reporting capabilities and eliminating the need to return to headquarters to complete and submit reports" (Roberts 2011, 72).

Advances in technology are affecting every aspect of law enforcement.

Chuck Wexler (2012, iii), executive director of the Police Executive Research Forum (PERF), stresses that technology is a crucial force-multiplier in contemporary policing:

I don't think I'm guilty of overstatement in saying that policing in the United States has undergone a fundamental transformation in just the last 30 or

Table 1.3 A Comparison of Traditional, Community, and Intelligence-Led Policing

	Traditional Policing (1840–1980)	Community Policing (1980–Present)	Intelligence-Led Policing (ILP) (2000–Present)
Era	Covers the first two eras of American policing: • Political Era (1840–1930) • Reform Era* (1930–1980) * Also referred to as the Professional Era	Emerged during the late 1970s—was slingshot into action during a time of civil unrest and widespread distrust of the government by the people. This form of policing really took hold during the 1980s and is still used.	Still in its infancy, ILP emerged as a result of the September 11, 2001, terrorist attacks on the United States. ILP continues to be developed and is the present-day era of American policing and is used in conjunction with community policing.
Policing Philosophy	*Political Era:* • Decentralization of police tactics in addressing crime • Intimate relationship with the community • Wide use of foot patrol • Police function: broad provision of social services *Reform Era:* • Centralized, efficient police organization • Professional remoteness from the community • Emphasis on preventive motorized patrol and rapid response • Focus on education and professionalization of law enforcement to execute a higher standard of enforcement of laws and justice • Police function: crime control	• Recognition that the police required a partnership with the community to prevent and control crime • Emphasis on cooperation between law enforcement and the community • Wide use of problem solving • Focus on being proactive	• Gathering, analyzing, and sharing information and intelligence among all law enforcement agencies across all levels to fight crime and terrorism • Involves the entire crime spectrum: from local crimes to crimes affecting national security • Based on a strategic managerial philosophy where criminal intelligence and data analysis are both integral to the goals, objectives, and decision making that affect crime reduction, disruption, and prevention
Police Priorities	• Addresses crime on a community level as it occurs • Security for the community from criminal activity • Used for political influence • Later, professionalization of law enforcement through higher education • Reducing corruption • Improving the quality of American policing for the community	• Engaging in a healthy and cooperative partnership with the community to effectively fight and prevent criminal activity • Being able to solve problems that re-occur, not just repeatedly addressing the same issue • Gaining mutual trust with the public	• Primary priority is national security for Americans from criminal activity, including foreign and domestic terrorism • Goal is to prevent, disrupt, or detour crime by analyzing data and developing intelligence
Policing Methodology	• Reactive patrol, addressing crime as it occurs. • Originally somewhat community-based during the political era (e.g., foot patrol), but later moved to modernization using technology to fight crime (e.g., vehicles, radios) • Enhance officer education to better fight crime	• Proactive policing and detouring criminal activity before it occurs • Working with the community to help solve community crimes • Being involved and getting to know the community	Two types of methodologies: • Tactical: short-term focused, analyzing and using information and intelligence for a specific incident • Strategic: long-term focused, analysis and use of information over time to prevent, detour, and disrupt future criminal incidents

Created by Henry L. Cho—Cho Research & Consulting, LLC. 2012
© Cengage Learning 2014

40 years. Policing today bears very little resemblance to the policing of the 1970s. . . .

Back then, police officers thought they were doing a fine job if they responded quickly to calls for service and investigated crimes thoroughly. Today's police departments have given themselves a much larger and more important mission: working with their communities to solve crime problems, and in so doing, actually preventing crimes from being committed, and reducing crime rates.

What's more, today's police have proved that they can succeed in fulfilling this bold new mission. According to the FBI's Uniform Crime Reports, violent crime rates nationwide have declined 47 percent since the early 1990s....

Technology undoubtedly played a big role in helping police to bring crime rates down.... We expect to see a new Age of Technology in policing over the next 10 to 20 years, as the technologies that we currently are testing really take hold, and new technologies that we aren't even aware of yet become available.

Furthermore, police chiefs tell us that the economic downturn that began in 2008 is making policing technology more important, to the extent that it can help officers be more effective and efficient.[4]

Although the introduction of technology has allowed law enforcement the ability to work more efficiently and effectively, it has also provided several challenges. One of the most obvious challenges involves those officers who are not as technologically savvy, often the older and more experienced generations of police officers, being placed at an operational disadvantage compared with younger, less experienced yet more technologically adept officers. The flip side to this challenge, however, occurs when younger generations become overly dependent on technology and lack the ability to respond appropriately to calls in the absence of all of their technical "tools" (e.g., not being able to run an individual's criminal history before making contact).

Technology has, indeed, become an integral part of modern police operations and will be discussed throughout the text as it applies to specific aspects of contemporary policing.

MISSION AND VALUES

This text provides a chance to engage in some thought-provoking critical thinking about important issues in police operations. To do so effectively requires an understanding of the basis for police operations. The functions undertaken by law enforcement officers should be viewed not as isolated activities, but rather as part of a master plan to accomplish the mission of the law enforcement agency. "Organizational mission statements represent the core purpose of the organization and should represent the organization's reason for existence.... The value and purpose of mission statements are that they serve as a steadfast guide for the activities of organizational members" (DeLone 2007, 219, 220).

---

[4]Source: Wexler, Chuck. "Introduction." In *How Are Innovations in Technology Transforming Policing?* Washington, DC: Police Executive Research Forum, Critical Issues in Policing Series, January 2012, pp.iii iv.

Many police departments emphasize the goals of forming partnerships with the community and serving as positive role models for young citizens.

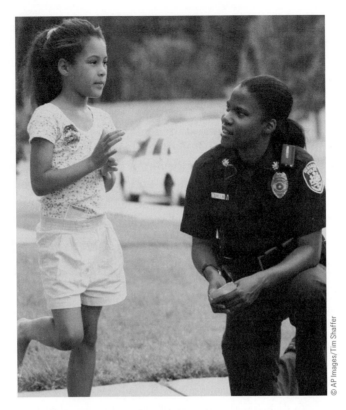

© AP Images/Tim Shaffer

An agency's **mission** is its reason for existence, its purpose. This is often embodied in a **mission statement**.

mission

An organization's reason for existence, its purpose.

mission statement

Written statement of an organization's reasons for existence or purpose.

Mission statements should be short, believable, easy to understand, easy to remember, and widely known. They should make work meaningful. Officers who see themselves as serving an important function will be more productive and more satisfied in their profession than will those who feel no sense of mission. Consider the following example:

The Charlotte-Mecklenburg Police Department will build problem-solving partnerships with our citizens to prevent the next crime and enhance the quality of life throughout our community, always treating people with fairness and respect.

Mission statements often are accompanied by the set of values on which they are based. These values must be shared by department members and the public served, or they will be meaningless. Ideally, these values also are consistent with the overall cultural values of the state and the nation. The values underlying the Charlotte-Mecklenberg Police Department mission statement are as follows:

We value:

▶ Our Employees
▶ People
▶ Partnerships
▶ Open Communications

▶ Problem Solving

▶ Integrity

▶ Courtesy

▶ The Constitution of North Carolina

▶ The Constitution of the United States[5]

Mission and value statements are important to law enforcement agencies and should be the driving force behind police operations. They are, however, only the starting point. The next steps are to develop goals and objectives that will accomplish the mission and then to decide what specific tasks must be undertaken to accomplish the goals and objectives.

GOALS, OBJECTIVES, AND TASKS

Goals may vary from one police department to another, but they usually focus on the following:

▶ To preserve the peace

▶ To protect civil rights and civil liberties

▶ To prevent crime

▶ To enforce the law

▶ To provide services

▶ To improve the quality of life in the community

▶ To participate in partnerships to solve problems related to crime and disorder

Although the words *goals* and *objectives* often are used interchangeably, most authorities agree that a *goal* is a more general term, referring to a broad, nonspecific desired outcome such as those previously listed. Goals are usually long range. Objectives, in contrast, are more specific outcomes, usually with a listing of specific tasks and a timetable attached.

goals

Broad, general intentions.

objectives

Specific activities to accomplish a goal.

Goals are broad, general intentions. **Objectives** are specific activities to accomplish goals.

The distinction between goals and objectives is clarified in the California Council on Criminal Justice's *A Guide for Criminal Justice Planning*:

Goal: A statement of broad direction, a general purpose of intent. A goal is general and timeless and is not concerned with a particular achievement within a specified time period.

Objective: A desired accomplishment that can be measured within a given time and under specifiable conditions. The attainment of the objective advances the system toward a corresponding goal.

[5]Charlotte-Mecklenburg Police Department, Charlotte, North Carolina.

Goals give purpose to what may appear to be relatively unimportant tasks. An inscription carved in 1730 in a church in Sussex, England, proclaims, "A vision without a task is but a dream, a task without a vision is drudgery, a vision and a task is the hope of the world." Consider the difference in attitude between those police officers on the **dog shift** (typically, 11:00 p.m. to 7:00 a.m.) who see the drug pusher just arrested as nothing more than an annoyance and those officers who believe they have helped make the neighborhood safer, perhaps even saving a life.

dog shift

Typically the shift from 11 p.m. to 7 a.m.

Specific objectives or individual tasks in isolation may seem to accomplish little, but in combination, they provide the direction needed to achieve the broad goals sought by the department. Common goals *are* important to team building.

How are objectives accomplished? Usually police departments establish policies that cover specific tasks that must be undertaken in basic police operations. They then create procedures to accomplish these tasks.

Policies

Goals and objectives are more easily achieved with written policies guiding the police department's activities. A **policy** is a statement of principles that guide decisions. Policies provide a course of action, help maintain organizational control, and ensure accountability within an organization. In addition, they provide a basis for fair discipline. Written policies should be generated for those areas in which directions are needed, including public and press relations, personal conduct, personnel procedures and relations, and specific law enforcement operations with emphasis on such sensitive areas as the use of force, the use of lethal weapons, search and seizure, arrests, and custody. However, officers must use common sense in differentiating between the "letter of the policy" and the "spirit of the policy," the difference being in doing things right versus doing the right thing. This is especially true when an officer must use discretion, as discussed shortly.

policy

A statement of principles that guide decisions.

Procedures

After policies are developed and put in writing, the next step is to identify procedures to carry out the policies, that is, guidelines for action or established methods. **Procedures** are step-by-step instructions for carrying out departmental policies. Written procedures promote a uniformity of action that is especially important for ongoing calls for service or when a large number of officers perform the same services. Written procedures also may reduce civil liability. Figure 1.2 illustrates a directive containing a goal, a policy, and the procedures for implementing the policy.

procedures

Step-by-step instructions for carrying out departmental policies.

Policies and Procedures Manuals

If a policies and procedures manual is to be credible, it must be easy to understand as well as concise. Manuals that are hundreds of pages long will gather dust on a shelf.

FIGURE 1.2 Sample Goal, Policy, and Procedure Directive

Mytown Police Department

Date issued: 01-01-20xx
Page 1 of 1

Procedure directive no. xx-xxxx

Effective date: 01-01-20xx
Subject: Community service officer in service operations

Goal:

To provide community service officers with uniform procedures for in-service operations. The procedures will document community service officer (CSO) activities and provide reference material for a CSO training manual. The CSO in-service operation is new. As the CSO's tasks expand, additional procedures will be added to this directive.

Policy:

Community service officers will respond to calls only when directed by the dispatcher or supervisor or by the patrol officer's request. Community service officers will notify dispatch immediately when observing any criminal or suspicious activity. Community service officers will not respond to any call, emergency or not, as an emergency vehicle.

Procedure:

I. Responding to Calls

   A. When a CSO is responding to a call at the same time as a patrol officer, the CSO will stop or slow down to allow the patrol officer to arrive on the scene first. This will prevent a CSO from entering into a situation that is or could become dangerous.

   B. When a CSO is directed to a call where a patrol officer is not assigned or that a patrol officer has requested a CSO to handle, the CSO will call for assistance in any of the following circumstances:

     1. Any situation that the CSO determines on arrival as being dangerous or that could escalate into a dangerous situation.

     2. Any situation where a criminal violation has taken place and a suspect is still on the scene, leaving the scene or likely to return to the scene.

     3. Any situation in which the CSO has not had training or experience or that the CSO feels unable or not equipped to handle.

II. Reports

   A. The CSO will turn in all reports, including daily logs, to the report basket in the squad room unless otherwise specified.

   B. A supervisor will review and approve all reports and handle accordingly.

   C. A supervisor will place the CSO's daily report in the administrative in-basket.

John J. Doe
Chief of Police

regulations

Rules put out by a lower level of government governing the actions of employees of the city, including police department personnel.

Regulations

Regulations and procedures are similar and have the same intent: to guide conduct. **Regulations** are rules put out by a lower level of government, for example, a municipality, governing the actions of employees of the

TECHNOLOGY IN POLICING

In an effort to meet certain standards and guidelines, as well as keep policies and procedures manuals effective and streamlined, many police agencies are contracting with private companies to draft their law enforcement manuals because such companies offer state-specific templates with an option to further customize, based on a police agency's individual needs. The goal of this measure is to help reduce risk and liability by staying ahead of litigation trends and using risk management analysis techniques. This is a technology innovation for public safety organizations that traditionally drafted their own policy manuals. These manuals can also be used on an online format, and many offer policy-related training and events for users and administrators. One such company is California-based Lexipol.

municipality, including police department personnel. These orders have the force of law for those people under their jurisdiction. Regulations are to a certain extent restrictive in that they force officers to adhere to certain codes of conduct. Like procedures, regulations should be in writing. Regulations help officers in decision making by eliminating discretionary action in certain areas.

A Final Note and Caution

Police chiefs and supervisors cannot establish goals, objectives, and policies in a vacuum. *All* officers, particularly those in the field, can contribute to understanding problems and can assist in developing policies and procedures. Officers in face-to-face contact with community members usually are the best informed about problems in the field and potential solutions. These officers, in turn, will better identify and understand problems through direct contact and discussion with representative community members.

Goals, policies, procedures, and regulations help make police departments efficient and effective. They are extremely important and deserve care in development and periodic evaluation. It must always be remembered, however, that not everything can be anticipated. Further, for every rule an exception usually can be found. Too many rules can be detrimental, limiting a department and its officers' flexibility. Flexibility is vital to law enforcement and includes the necessity for officers to use discretion.

DISCRETION

Discretion is the ability or power to act or decide a matter on one's own. Police use discretion because no set of policies and procedures can prescribe what to do in every circumstance. The International Association of Chiefs of Police (IACP) "Police Code of Conduct" states, "A police officer will use responsibly the discretion vested in his position and exercise it within the law. The principle of reasonableness will guide the officer's determinations, and the officer will consider all surrounding circumstances in determining whether any legal action will be taken."

Discretion *must* be allowed for several reasons. One reason is that the law *overreaches*, seldom addressing exceptions that might arise. For example, although a highway may have a posted speed limit of 55 miles per hour (mph),

discretion

The ability or power to act or decide a matter on one's own.

a driver exceeding this limit may have very good reasons for doing so. Such a driver might be a volunteer firefighter on the way to a fire, an undercover police officer tailing a car, a parent taking a seriously injured child to the hospital, or a man taking his wife who is in labor to the hospital. Technically, these people are speeding—but should they be given citations? The law overreaches in each of these instances, and discretion is the tool that allows officers to balance the letter of the law with the spirit of the law in each situation encountered.

Another reason discretion is allowed is because human behavior is too varied and complex to be accommodated by inflexible legal rules, and in some cases, the law may be better served by not being enforced. Consider the following explanations from motorists clocked at 50 mph in a 35-mph zone: "I've just come from my mother's funeral, and I'm very upset," or "I just got fired," or "I haven't ever received a speeding ticket in my life. I teach driver education at the high school."

Discretion makes enforcement of our laws *equitable*, that is, humanistic, considering the spirit rather than the letter of the law or, often, of a policy. Discretion also gives officers a sense of control over their jobs, which are, in many cases, primarily reactive.

> Discretion allows for equitable enforcement of our laws and for police officers to grow morally and professionally.

Most officers appreciate the chance to work through a citizen's problem from beginning to end. They also appreciate the acknowledgment that they have something to contribute in the form of expertise, imagination, and creativity, as well as problem-solving ability.

The ability to decide when to impose legal sanctions on those who violate the law, whether issuing traffic tickets or arresting someone, is known as **selective enforcement**. This type of discretion has only recently been recognized by police administrators and the general public as a proper aspect of officers' authority. Although such discretion is acknowledged as a necessity for effective policing, it does have some drawbacks.

selective enforcement

The ability to decide when to impose legal sanctions on those who violate the law, whether issuing traffic tickets or arresting someone.

Problems with Officer Discretion

> Problems associated with officer discretion include these:
> - Lack of accountability
> - Unpredictability
> - Inconsistency and allegations of racial profiling

Discretionary actions may also confuse citizens because they are not sure how they will be treated from one situation to the next. Discretion can be unpredictable from one officer to the next. For example, one traffic officer may allow up to 5 mph over the speed limit before stopping a motorist. Another may allow 10 mph over. The driver who gets a ticket for exceeding the limit by 5 mph when the driver who is going 10 mph over the limit does not get a ticket will see the situation as unfair.

Most importantly, discretion is often applied inconsistently. Equality under the law has always implied that people should receive similar treatment when they perform relatively the same acts. However, discretion lets officers treat different people differently. This may be seen as discrimination and, in fact, sometimes is. Some officers are harder on minorities, men, or juveniles. This may be conscious or unconscious discrimination, but it does make for inconsistent enforcement of the laws. An example of such inconsistent, biased enforcement of laws is seen in racial profiling, when an officer uses a person's race to assess the likelihood of criminal conduct or other wrongdoing. Racial profiling is discussed in depth in Chapter 5. Officer discretion, while necessary, must also be limited.

Limits on Discretion

A major challenge facing law enforcement is finding the balance between a department's clear-cut goals, policies, and procedures and its officers' discretionary actions.

Two factors must be kept in mind: (1) the primary goals of the department and (2) maintaining a balance between a need for clear policies and procedures and the accompanying need for discretion when exceptions arise. In addition, officers will be called on to use critical-thinking skills in performing police operations.

Discretion and Critical-Thinking Skills

To use discretion wisely, police officers need to develop their critical-thinking skills. Critical thinking includes a broad range of skills, such as problem solving, identifying perceptions, generating concepts from observations, applying concepts to police problems, designing systematic plans of action, and approaching social problems from several different perspectives. As a result of learning to think critically, students and future police officers will:

▶ Learn to use their diverse backgrounds and those of others to resolve social problems in a more effective, acceptable manner.

▶ Learn specific ways to move from lower-order to higher-order thinking skills.

▶ Be better prepared to enter the world of police work and further their existing or future careers.

SUMMARY

Police operations are activities conducted in the field by law enforcement officers as they "serve and protect," including patrol, traffic, investigation, and general calls for service. Law enforcement is affected by a changing public and society, changing law enforcement officers, a changing police bureaucracy, standards set forth by the Commission on Accreditation for Law Enforcement Agencies (CALEA), a change in community involvement, a change in approach, and advances in technology.

Our society is becoming older and has more minorities, more immigrants, and more single-parent households, and the gap between rich and poor continues to expand. Our law enforcement officers also have changed. Today's police recruits include fewer people with military backgrounds and more women and minorities. New recruits have more formal education and police training, and they value on-job satisfaction more than they value material rewards. These recruits also are expected to perform more diverse operations and are held to a higher professional standard.

Another change is anticipated in the police bureaucracy itself. The police bureaucracy may become less militaristic and may move toward a team approach to providing services. This includes decentralization and a shift from management to leadership. Yet another influence on law enforcement is the CALEA, which certifies law enforcement agencies that meet the standards set by the commission.

A further change is the trend toward community policing, which is proactive and empowers citizens to help local law enforcement provide safer neighborhoods. Community policing usually includes an emphasis on foot and bicycle patrol.

Advances in technology are affecting every aspect of law enforcement.

An agency's mission is its reason for existence, its purpose. This is often embodied in a mission statement. This mission is accomplished most effectively by clearly stated goals and objectives. Goals are broad, general intentions. Objectives are specific activities to accomplish goals.

Officers need to follow policies, procedures, and regulations, but they also need to use discretion. Discretion allows for equitable enforcement of our laws and for police officers to grow morally and professionally. Discretion is not without its problems, including a lack of accountability, unpredictability, and the potential for inconsistency and allegations of racial profiling. A major challenge facing law enforcement is finding the balance between a department's clear-cut goals, policies, and procedures and its officers' discretionary actions.

APPLICATION

GENERAL DIRECTIONS

When you complete each chapter, you will be asked to apply the information to develop suggested policies and procedures appropriate for your area. The Appendix at the end of the book contains a form to use for this purpose. As with any other type of administrative writing, policies and procedures should be clearly written. Consider the following guidelines:

▶ Use short, simple words, avoiding police jargon.

▶ Use short, simple sentences: 10 to 15 words.

▶ Use short paragraphs: 2 to 3 sentences.

▶ Use lists when possible.

▶ Use active verbs: Write *Clean the gun daily* rather than *The gun should be cleaned daily.*

▶ Use illustrations and diagrams for clarification.

▶ Have three or four individuals read and evaluate the policy and procedure.

▶ Most important, keep things simple. Avoid the tendency to impress rather than to express.

INSTRUCTIONS

Write a policy for writing policies, that is, outline what policies should be written for. Then write at least five procedures to be used when writing policies.

AN EXERCISE IN CRITICAL THINKING

At the end of each chapter, you will be presented with exercises in critical thinking. These exercises were written by Waldo Asp, Normandale Community College, and are based on actual decisions of state appeals courts or state supreme courts throughout the country. Read each situation carefully. Then consider the alternative responses given and select the *most logical* statement based on what you have read in the chapter.

> On September 4, State Trooper Berg was on routine patrol when he stopped a car driven by Carl Lundberg for a traffic violation. Trooper Berg arrested Lundberg for breach of the peace and placed him in the squad car's back seat. Carl's brother, Allen Lundberg, went to the scene of the arrest and, without identifying himself, got into his brother's car with the apparent intention of driving it away.
>
> Trooper Berg got out of his vehicle, approached the as-yet-unidentified individual, and asked him to get out of the car and leave. Only after Allen got out of the car did he identify himself as the suspect's brother. Trooper Berg again asked Allen to leave the scene, but Allen persisted in questioning Trooper Berg as to why he could not take the car to avoid having it towed. Trooper Berg continued to insist that Allen leave the scene.
>
> The verbal sparring continued to escalate to such a point that it drew the attention of several individuals in the parking lot of a shopping mall across the street. Various witnesses testified that Allen yelled obscenities at Trooper Berg, "leaned over and pointed to his buttocks," and gave Trooper Berg "the finger." Witnesses also testified that Trooper Berg physically turned Allen around and "gave him a shove toward the parking lot," at which point Allen "kind of turned around and came close to hitting Trooper Berg's arm." That is when Trooper Berg told Allen he was under arrest.
>
> Meanwhile, as Trooper Berg was dealing with Allen, Carl (who was in the back of the squad car) managed to cause $500 damage to the squad's interior by kicking the door.

1. Considering the way this incident unfolded, which statement best represents how Trooper Berg should have handled this event?

   a. This demonstrates that sometimes sticking to policies and procedures is not worth the trouble that is caused, for the general public will not accept impersonal execution of procedures.

   b. Officers need to understand the reasoning behind operations and be able to explain them to citizens, thereby possibly avoiding violent actions and breaches of the peace.

   c. In this case, there was insufficient evidence to support a criminal conviction for obstructing legal process.

   d. Mere words (regardless of tone, loudness, agitation, and word choice) cannot be used as a basis for a disturbing the peace charge.

   e. Only Carl Lundberg's actions should be prosecuted. Allen Lundberg should be released.

2. Officer involvement with the community would have helped Trooper Berg in what way?

   a. Witnesses might corroborate the yelled obscenities and other actions by Allen Lundberg, as well as Trooper Berg's responses.

   b. Some community members could talk the Lundbergs into cooling off and could assist Trooper Berg in physically escorting Allen away from the scene to prevent the escalation of anger.

   c. Many would enjoy the power and authority of becoming "assistant officers" with the rights of enforcing the law, as well as the status of being considered "officers and gentlemen."

   d. Fair, compassionate, and excellent police service is possible only when responsibilities are not piled on one individual.

   e. With expanded opportunities for misconduct, more eyes are needed to keep watch for undesirable activity.

DISCUSSION QUESTIONS

1. What purposes do goals serve in a police department?
2. What do you consider the most important goal for a police department?
3. What are the advantages of having written policies?
4. Are value statements necessary? How can officers best be involved in developing a department's values?
5. Who should be involved in policy development?
6. Why is discretion a necessary part of a police officer's job?
7. Have you observed police discretion in operation?

GALE EMERGENCY SERVICES DATABASE ASSIGNMENTS

▶ Use the Gale Emergency Services database (available for separate purchase) to answer the discussion questions as appropriate.

▶ Use the Gale Emergency Services database to research articles and materials on *participatory leadership and management*. Be prepared to discuss the advantages and disadvantages of participatory leadership and management with the class.

▶ Use the Gale Emergency Services database to research articles and materials on *law enforcement accreditation*. Be prepared to discuss your findings with the class.

▶ Read and outline "Law and the Parameters of Acceptable Deviance" by Mark A. Edwards.

▶ Read and outline "Community Policing: Exploring the Philosophy" by David M. Allender.

REFERENCES

Brewer, Brad. 2009. "C.R.I.M.E. Fights Crime with Intelligence-Led Policing." *Law and Order* (May): 68–74.

Bynum, Ray. 2008. "Transformational Leadership and Staff Training in the Law Enforcement Professions." *The Police Chief* (February): 72–81.

"The Commission." 2010. Gainesville, VA: The Commission on Accreditation for Law Enforcement Agencies, Inc. Accessed January 23, 2012. CALEA Online: http://www.calea.org/content/commission.

Commission on Accreditation of Law Enforcement Agencies (CALEA). 2012. *Standards for Law Enforcement Agencies.* 5th ed. Fairfax, VA: Author.

Community Policing Defined. 2009 (April 3). Washington, DC: U.S. Department of Justice, Office of Community Oriented Policing Services. Accessed January 23, 2012. http://www.cops.usdoj.gov/files/RIC/Publications/e030917193-CP-Defined.pdf.

DeLone, Gregory J. 2007. "Law Enforcement Mission Statements Post-September ll." *Police Quarterly* (June): 218–35.

Griffith, David. 2008. "The State of American Law Enforcement." *Police* (December): 10.

Hammill, Greg. 2005. "Mixing and Managing Four Generations of Employees." *FDU Magazine Online* (Winter/Spring). Accessed January 23, 2012. http://www.fdu.edu/news-pubs/magazine/05ws/generations.htm.

Harrington, Penny E. 2001. *Recruiting & Retaining Women: A Self-Assessment Guide for Law Enforcement.* Los Angeles, CA: National Center for Women & Policing. (NCJ 185235)

Harrison, Bob. 2007. "Gamers, Millennials, and Generation Next: Implications for Policing." *The Police Chief* (October): 150–60.

Howden, Lindsay M., and Julie A. Meyer. 2011 (May). *Age and Sex Composition: 2010.* Census Briefs, C2010BR-03. Washington, DC: U.S. Census Bureau.

Langton, Lynn. 2010 (June). *Women in Law Enforcement, 1987–2008.* Washington, DC: U.S. Department of Justice, Bureau of Justice Statistics. (NCJ 230521)

Marshall, Mark A. 2008. "The Cutting Edge of Law Enforcement Technology." *PoliceOne.com News* (January 2). Accessed January 23, 2012. http://www.policeone.com/pc_print.asp?vid=1645861.

McFall, Ellen. 2006. "Changing Profession Requires New Level of Education." *The Police Chief* (August): 45–47.

Miller, Linda S., Kären Matison Hess, and Christine Hess Orthmann. 2010. *Community Policing: Partnerships for Problem Solving.* 5th ed. Clifton Park, NY: Delmar.

Partington, Karie. 2008. "Abandoned Homes and 'Broken Windows.'" *Law and Order* (October): 83–85.

Reaves, Brian A. 2010 (December). *Local Police Departments, 2007.* Washington, DC: U.S. Department of Justice, Bureau of Justice Statistics. (NCJ 231174)

Roberts, David J. 2011. "Technology Is Playing an Expanding Role in Policing." *The Police Chief* (January): 72–73.

Scheider, Matthew C. 2009. "Broken Windows and Community Policing." *Community Policing Dispatch* (January). http://cops.usdoj.gov/html/dispatch/January_2009/nugget.htm.

Slahor, Stephenie. 2007. "Four Generations on the Job." *Law and Order* (December): 63–67.

Vincent, Grayson K., and Victoria A. Velkoff. 2010 (May). *The Next Four Decades—The Older Population in the United States: 2010 to 2050.* Current Population Reports, P25-1138. Washington, DC: U.S. Census Bureau.

Wexler, Chuck. 2012 (January). "Introduction." In *How Are Innovations in Technology Transforming Policing?*, iii–iv. Washington, DC: Police Executive Research Forum, Critical Issues in Policing Series.

Wilson, James Q., and George Kelling. 1982. "The Police and Neighborhood Safety: Broken Windows." *Atlantic Monthly* (March): 29–38.

Wilson, James Q., and George Kelling. 1989. "Making Neighborhoods Safe." *Atlantic Monthly* (February): 46–52.

CASE CITED

Davis v. Dallas, 777 F.2d 205 (5th Cir. 1985), cert. denied, 476 U.S. 1116 (1986)

This available CourseMate has an interactive eBook and interactive learning tools, including flash cards, quizzes, and more. To learn more about this resource and access free demo CourseMate resources, go to www.cengagebrain.com, and search for this book. To access CourseMate materials that you have purchased, go to login.cengagebrain.com.

CHAPTER 2

© Bruce Chambers/ZUMA Press/Corbis

Communication:
The Foundation of Police Operations

DO YOU KNOW . . .

- What positive outcomes effective communication can produce?
- In what directions communication might flow?
- What databases can be of value to law enforcement?
- What challenges and concerns law enforcement has encountered with communications technology?
- What some criminal justice entities believe law enforcement 10-codes should be replaced with?
- What special populations may pose especially challenging communication issues?
- When slurred speech may not be the result of intoxication?
- Which case established the right of police officers to stop and question a person?
- What rights *Miranda v. Arizona* grants to suspects?
- What would make a confession inadmissible in court?
- What purposes written police reports serve?
- Who the likely audiences of police reports are?

CAN YOU DEFINE?

absolute privilege
admission
beachheading
Beheler admonition
closed question
cognitive interview
conditional privilege
confession
felony syndrome
field inquiry
informant
interoperability
interrogation
interview
leading question
Miranda warning
open question

- What the characteristics of effective police reports are?
- What two amendments police must balance when dealing with the media?

plain language
primary victim
privileged information
rapport
reader-friendly writing
reasonable suspicion
secondary victim
statement
***Terry* stop**
totality of circumstances
waiver

INTRODUCTION

Communication is all around us. We are continually bombarded by spoken and written messages, yet most people give little thought to its importance, nor are they trained in communicating effectively. Communication at any level is an inexact art. But misunderstood communication can have grave consequences in police work. Communication skills are critical to every aspect of effective police operations.

> Effective communication can produce several positive outcomes and can be used to inform, persuade, diffuse, guide, motivate, reassure, and negotiate.

In contrast, ineffective communication can result in confusion, false expectations, wrong conclusions, negative stereotypes, frustration, anger, hostility, aggression, and even physical confrontations.

Police officers routinely communicate in every facet of their jobs, not only when they interview and interrogate individuals, but also during their interactions with the public, with coworkers in their departments, and with professionals in other fields. Officers also may testify in court and fulfill public speaking assignments, especially those for school-age children and youths.

Effective communication can be a powerful public relations tool and a means to implement community policing. A positive, service-type attitude begins with communication skills. Officers who use harsh, commanding words put people on the defensive. Many people, if pushed, will push back. Recognizing this tendency, officers must resist the temptation to engage in verbal confrontations and, instead, remain calm, using logic and reason in speaking with others. For example, compare the command "Come here!" with the request "Excuse me, but I would like to talk with you for a minute."

This chapter begins with a discussion of the lines of internal communication and technological advances in police communication. This is followed by a look at special populations that may pose especially challenging communication problems. The chapter then turns to communicating to obtain information: the field inquiry and the interview, interviewing techniques, the role of informants and anonymous tips, and the interrogation. Next, report writing is discussed, and the chapter concludes with a discussion on communicating with the media.

LINES OF COMMUNICATION WITHIN AN AGENCY

Communication within an agency may flow in different directions. It may flow vertically downward from the chief or upward from line officers. It may also flow outward or horizontally among those on the same "level" within the organization.

 Internal communication may be vertical (downward or upward) or horizontal (lateral).

PERSPECTIVE OF A FIRST-LINE SUPERVISOR
Effective Communication

It is one of our primary responsibilities to act as a gateway of communication between first-line patrol officers and administration. Administration has an expectation that we deliver their goals and mission adequately and effectively to subordinates. In the same respect, we act as a "voice" for first-line officers who want their concerns communicated to the administration. Because of this, it is imperative that mid-level supervisors are able to balance and act as liaisons between the ranks above and below them. Effective communication through this process can make the difference between a well-run agency and an agency in turmoil.

—*Sgt. Henry Lim Cho*

    In addition to the more formal lines of internal communication, informal channels also exist, called the *grapevine* or the *rumor mill*. This powerful line of communication can help or hurt an agency. The grapevine can be used positively to disseminate information quickly and as a barometer of what the workforce is thinking. However, negative information, allowed to grow unchecked, can undermine an agency's mission. Departments typically devise policies, under the area of police officer conduct, that cover the rumor mill phenomenon, yet there may be times when such rumors are allowed to persist and go unaddressed. Some of this "allowance" is attributed to the police culture because bringing an issue such as rumors to the administration may be viewed as complaining, which is not respected among law enforcement officers.

A police officer uses his cell phone to communicate with another officer on duty. Using the cell phone avoids interrupting dispatch calls.

© Henry Cho

TECHNOLOGICAL ADVANCES IN POLICE COMMUNICATION

Communication between officers in the field, officers and headquarters, and officers and local, state, and national data sources, as well as information sharing among agencies and between the police and the public, has been enhanced greatly through advancing technology. Law enforcement communications began with whistles and rattles and has advanced to handheld radios, laptop computers in patrol cars, photo cell phones, and Enhanced 9-1-1 (E9-1-1), whose geolocation feature allows law enforcement to quickly trace where a wireless call is coming from. The rapid evolution of communications technology during the past decade, however, has pushed the country's current 9-1-1 capabilities to their limit because the telephone technology simply cannot handle the increasing quantity of text, data, images, and video that are common in personal communications and critical to future transportation safety and mobility advances. The Federal Communications Commission (FCC) has recognized the critical need for an Internet Protocol (IP)–enabled Next Generation 9-1-1 (NG9-1-1) system and has placed a high priority on developing and implementing NG9-1-1 technology that can adapt rapidly to new technology, support new devices, and provide a solid foundation for public emergency communications services in a wireless mobile society.

Many wireless devices can now display and send images of a crime scene or a suspect to hundreds of officers, using only a phone and a digital camera. Furthermore, many departments have outfitted their squad cars with cameras and recording systems that are able to download to a central, fixed station server via Wi-Fi, as well as having an onboard global positioning system (GPS) that allows dispatch to monitor the real-time location of squads.

An intranet—a Web site inside a department firewall that serves the mission of the department and is not available to the public—can streamline communications and manage information cost-effectively. For example, many agencies have access to secured Web sites that police officers can use to retrieve and complete all of the necessary reports and forms associated with various calls and activities. All of these documents are shared on a secure network with other facets of the criminal justice system and can be uploaded directly to the courts and jails as soon as officers submit them.

Regional or countywide intranets are becoming increasingly popular. In addition to making operations more efficient for patrol, these Web sites also assist law enforcement and criminal justice administration. For example, in Dakota County, Minnesota, city police departments can log onto a secured Web site known as CJIIN, the Criminal Justice Information Integration Network, from which administrators can quickly tabulate statistics for various crimes, calls for service, and so on because the network compiles all of the information for them.

The trend toward community policing is bringing more officers out of the squad car to patrol on foot, bikes, motorcycles, and horses. Although this move puts officers closer to the citizens in the community, it also pulls them away from their vital link to real-time data—the vehicle-mounted laptop. Again, technology is available to assist such officers with their mobile police operations.

Smartphones, for example, have e-mail, voice telephone, and wireless Web access, making them powerful communications tools. These devices can also be loaded with specialized law enforcement programs or applications (apps) such as BIO-key PocketCop or Info-Cop, transforming the cell phone into a highly capable handheld data terminal. For example, BIO-key PocketCop lets mobile phone users query the Federal Bureau of Investigation's (FBI) National Crime Information Center (NCIC) database as well as other state and motor vehicle databases. Info-Cop also does this and lets officers download photos and look up license plates. Many similar apps are created by third-party companies and individuals.

As technology advances and smartphones become standard, the market has been flooded with the creation of different apps to help law enforcement officers do their job more efficiently and effectively. One example is an app created by Apple called "Find My Phone." A man who had reported that his phone had been stolen from his vehicle was able to activate this app using another device, which then allowed real-time GPS tracking of the stolen phone's location. When the police located the phone, they discovered that the people suspected of stealing the cell phone were also driving a vehicle that had been reported stolen; furthermore, these individuals were in possession of other stolen items as well as drugs.

Even with this capability literally in hand, police officers still rely heavily on the radio and dispatcher to retrieve critical information when dealing with incidents. Many situations either do not allow or make it unsafe for an officer to check such information by himself or herself. Departments must also be cognizant of the need to train officers in how to operate in the absence of technology, such as when equipment fails or services go down or are otherwise inaccessible. Overreliance on technology can actually impede officer effectiveness and safety in certain situations.

Enhanced Access to Databases

As law enforcement officers increasingly rely on access to information while performing their duties, emerging technology is allowing them to communicate quickly and easily with numerous databases, ensuring that officers are receiving the most current data available.

> Among the valuable databases available to police officers are the National Crime Information Center (NCIC), the Law Enforcement National Data Exchange (N-DEx), the Law Enforcement Online service (LEO), the OneDOJ Initiative, the Regional Information Sharing System (RISS) Program, the Law Enforcement Information Exchange (LInX), CrimeCog, and the Intelligence Communications Enterprise For Information Sharing and Exchange (ICEFISHX).

Many other databases exist, particularly at the regional and state levels.

The National Crime Information Center (NCIC) The FBI's NCIC is an online real-time transaction-processing database that maintains information on millions of records. Established in 1967, this database is the forerunner of newer information-sharing systems in the country. Connecting to this system, patrol officers can run local, state, and federal database checks ranging from driver's license and vehicle registration to arrest reports, stolen/recovered property, and even emergency phone numbers of business owners. The system handles nearly 4.5 million transactions daily and offers fingerprint matching capability, digital image data storage, and a mobile imaging unit to electronically capture fingerprint and camera images and incorporate them into an NCIC database query.

The National Data Exchange (N-DEx) Another initiative of the FBI is the N-DEx, an Internet-based information system aimed at linking the more than 18,000 law enforcement agencies in the nation electronically to share information beyond jurisdictional boundaries. According to the FBI ("N-DEx: Welcome to the Future" 2008), N-DEx capabilities include:

▶ Nationwide searches from a single access point
▶ Searches by modus operandi and for clothing, tattoos, associates, cars, and so forth—linking individuals, places, and things
▶ Notifications of similar investigations and suspects
▶ Identification of criminal activity hot spots and crime trends
▶ Threat-level assessments of individuals and addresses
▶ Visualization and mapping features

All of these capabilities include safeguards to protect privacy and civil rights.

The Law Enforcement Online Service (LEO) The LEO Service, launched in July 1995 by FBI staff who foresaw what the information-sharing powerhouse called "the Internet" was to become, began as a small dial-up service with just 20 members but now connects more than 100,000 members across the world. According to its Web site ("Law Enforcement Online" 2009),

Law Enforcement Online (LEO) is a state-of-the-art Internet system that is accredited and approved by the FBI for sensitive but unclassified information. LEO is used to support investigative operations, send notifications and alerts, and provide an avenue to remotely access other law enforcement and intelligence systems and resources. LEO provides all levels of the law enforcement, criminal justice, and public safety communities virtual private network access to its "anytime and anywhere" system for secure electronic communications, online training, and information sharing.

The Law Enforcement Online (LEO) network is only available to persons duly employed by a law enforcement, criminal justice, or public safety agency/department and whose position requires secure communications with other agencies via the Internet. As an information-sharing forum, all members are encouraged to contribute information in their area of interest or expertise.

LEO offers a host of features and capabilities through a Virtual Private Network (VPN) on the Internet, including:

▶ A Virtual Command Center (VCC) that allows the law enforcement community to use LEO at local and remote sites as an electronic command center to facilitate crisis management and information sharing

▶ Law Enforcement Online Special Interest Groups (LEOSIGs) that allow members who share expertise or interests to connect with each other, including sections on terrorism, street gangs, and bombs

▶ A National Alert System (NAS) directing members to the LEO site for information on emergencies (e.g., the London bombings)

▶ Access to important and useful databases, like those run by the National Center for Missing and Exploited Children

▶ E-mail services, which enable members to submit fingerprints to the FBI for processing by the Integrated Automated Fingerprint Identification System (IAFIS)

▶ Forums (bulletin boards) and Chat Rooms to allow members to post threads or have real-time discussions about topics of interest

▶ Distance learning, with several online learning modules on topics like terrorism response, forensic anthropology, and leadership

▶ A multimedia library of publications, documents, studies, research, technical bulletins, and other reports of interest to LEO users

OneDOJ Initiative The OneDOJ Initiative was developed by the U.S. Department of Justice (DOJ) for two information sharing purposes: (1) to share data among its law enforcement components and (2) to provide DOJ data access to regional systems. The OneDOJ system is a repository for data submitted and accessed by only the law enforcement components of the DOJ, namely the Bureau of Alcohol, Tobacco, Firearms and Explosives (ATF); Bureau of Prisons (BOP); Drug Enforcement Administration (DEA); FBI; and U.S. Marshals Service (USMS). Data is not contributed by external partners to the OneDOJ system ("Questions and Answers" n.d.).

Regional Information Sharing System (RISS) Program The RISS is a nationwide program consisting of six regional centers and a technology support center that is designed to link thousands of criminal justice agencies through secure communications. The RISS Secure Intranet (RISSNET) serves as the connection backbone for nearly 100 information and intelligence systems and provides information-sharing resources and investigative support to combat multijurisdictional crimes, including violent crime, gang activity, terrorism, drug activity, cybercrime, human trafficking, identity theft, and other regional priorities.

In addition to offering access to intelligence databases and connecting disparate systems, RISS provides investigative support and research; analytical support; equipment loans; confidential funds, which are monies used to purchase contraband, stolen property, and other items of an evidentiary nature or to provide for other investigative expenses related to multijurisdictional investigations; training and publications; field staff support; and technical assistance. RISS is funded through the U.S. DOJ, Office of Justice Programs (OJP), and Bureau of Justice Assistance (BJA). BJA provides funding oversight and program management for the RISS Program ("Regional Information Sharing System" n.d.).

The Law Enforcement Information Exchange (LInX) The LInX—a regional information-sharing system developed, coordinated, and largely funded by the U.S. Naval Criminal Investigative Service (NCIS)—has begun to revolutionize law enforcement in the 21st century (Dorsey and Smith 2008). This state-of-the-art collaborative information-sharing program breaks down artificial jurisdictional and technical barriers between municipal, county, state, and federal law enforcement agencies and extracts hidden data and linkages across multiple jurisdictions, bringing them together for authorized users to see. LInX is officer-friendly, making access and retrieval of data easy; enhances officer safety by providing current information to officers in the field; and improves law enforcement efficiency and effectiveness by allowing more rapid identification and processing of offenders following the reporting of a crime. LInX is currently operating in ten regions around the country, with more than 500 law enforcement agencies using LInX daily (Dorsey and Smith 2008).

CrimeCog Another Internet-based data-sharing source is CrimeCog, an information supply chain reserved exclusively for use by law enforcement and justice systems. CrimeCog provides a comprehensive software-as-a-service (SAAS) subscription-based solution called E*Justice Systems™, which collects and manages data critical to the effective operations of law enforcement and criminal justice organizations. The E*Justice System facilitates collaboration across the separate government entities that make up the nation's criminal justice community, with subscribers including local police departments, school police agencies, county sheriff departments and jails, prosecutors, courts, parole officers, state police posts, and federal agencies such as the FBI, DEA, and Immigration and Customs Enforcement (ICE).

Intelligence Communications Enterprise For Information Sharing and Exchange (ICEFISHX) The ICEFISHX is a regional internet-based intelligence sharing initiative and alert network for law enforcement agencies in

Minnesota, North Dakota, and South Dakota ("What Is ICEFISHX?" 2012). This partnership is designed to collect and disseminate information relating to terrorist operations and other criminal activities to law enforcement, government agencies, and the private sector within the tri-state area. Other regions throughout the United States have similar exchanges.

Web Sites and Social Media

Web sites and social media are becoming increasingly valuable resources for law enforcement in their efforts to gather information and enhance communication with the public. In fact, as Los Angeles County Sheriff's Captain Mike Parker states, "As technology changes, the public *expects* us to communicate with them in new ways. We now have the ability to instantly send out notifications when emergencies or other situations arise that the public should be aware of, so we are expected to do so, using the most effective technology available to us" ("Websites and Social Media" 2012, 5). In addition to sending texts and e-mails to citizens who register their contact information with the police, many agencies around the nation are tapping into popular social media such as Twitter, Facebook, MySpace, and YouTube to disseminate public safety information to the broader community. A recent Police Executive Research Forum (PERF) Survey revealed that more than 80 percent of responding agencies use social media to provide information to the public, and 70 percent use social media to receive information, including crime tips, from the public ("Websites and Social Media" 2012).

TECHNOLOGY IN POLICING

ONLINE CITIZEN REPORTING

Increasing numbers of departments are allowing citizens to file online police reports for nonviolent offenses, such as lost property, vandalism and graffiti, vehicle tampering, and harassing phone calls. In accessing the local department's Web site and the page with the crime report form, citizens are able to complete an online report with such required fields as name, address, type of incident, and loss experienced. Before the citizen can submit the report, however, a warning appears that states the penalties for filing a false report.

Online reporting of minor crimes presents several benefits to both law enforcement and citizen-victims, as Jonathan Lewin, the managing deputy director for the Chicago Police Department's Office of Emergency Management and Communications explains:

> We recently launched a Web-based case reporting program. We started with just two types

of crime—lost property and thefts under $500. This program is for crimes in which the victim is safe, there's no crime scene to protect, and the presence of a uniformed officer won't improve our chances of finding the perpetrator. Taking victims' reports online instead of in-person will reduce the number of sworn officers we take away from their street assignments. Taking a report in person can take an hour of their time on average. An advantage of online reporting for the crime victims is that they can file the report when it's convenient for them. ("Websites and Social Media" 2012, 7–8)

Source: "Websites and Social Media." In *How Are Innovations in Technology Transforming Policing?* Washington, DC: Police Executive Research Forum, Critical Issues in Policing Series, January 2012, pp. 4–12.

Concerns about Technology in Police Communication

Despite the myriad advantages and benefits technology brings to police operations, there remain several critical concerns.

> Special problems encountered with communications technology include keeping police communications secure, interference on the line and dropped calls, lack of interoperability, and lack of a common language.

Communication Security Many citizens have police scanners that allow them access to dispatcher-to-officer and officer-to-officer communications. Some criminals also use scanners, so security precautions must be taken. Listening in on cell phone transmissions is prohibited under the Electronic Communications Privacy Act of 1986, but enforcing the law is impractical. Therefore, conversations are not safe on mobile phones. As with cell phone conversations, wireless data transmissions are susceptible to interception.

Although digital technology adds a level of security greater than the analog transmissions made over police radio frequencies, it is not totally secure. Consequently, data encryption, which "scrambles" transmitted data, is considered the best way to keep outsiders from accessing inside information. As this technology becomes more accessible and affordable, more departments across the country will move toward digital radio with encryption capabilities.

Also, as increasing numbers of agencies go online, using the Internet to access and share data, keeping information secure in this medium has also become a challenge.

Interference on the Line and Dropped Calls As more people use wireless channels to communicate, the interference encountered has also increased. Interference occurs when radio channels assigned to public safety are intermingled among and adjacent to commercial channels such as cell phones.

Another problem occurs when technology to enhance communication experiences a glitch or "goes down." Earlier, communication systems were relatively uncomplicated, consisting of a microphone and a speaker, with users simply talking over them. Today's communication systems have controllers, microprocessors, and software, all of which can experience problems.

In July 2004, the FCC unanimously approved the Consensus Plan to eliminate 800-megahertz interference by realigning the current licensing of 800-megahertz systems into two distinct blocks: one for public safety and private wireless systems and one for wireless carriers such as cellular service providers.

Wireless coverage gaps (that is, dropped calls) and interruptions are other problems officers may encounter. As investigators and officers travel, they may pass in and out of wireless coverage areas; such dead zones may cause officers to lose their connections and can lead to a loss of unsaved work in progress. Unexpected automatic software updates sent directly to devices can also interrupt an officer's work and lead to time and data loss.

The mass chaos that occurred in September 2005 after Hurricane Katrina knocked out communications throughout the New Orleans area highlighted the particular vulnerability of cell towers and land lines, one response to which was that wireless carriers now have dedicated units to provide law enforcement agencies with products and services to ensure they can communicate in dead zones and even during the worst disasters: "Mobile cell towers, handsets on standby and companies' dedicated disaster response teams can help your agency stay connected" (Basich 2009, 40).

TECHNOLOGY IN POLICING

4G-LTE

As technology continues to advance in wireless communications, so does the network supporting it. Generally, most wireless communications, ranging from mobile computers to handheld radios, are run on a third-generation (3G) network with that respective technology. However, a hot topic in the wireless industry today, as networks upgrade from 3G to fourth-generation (4G) technology, is the emergence of Long Term Evolution (LTE):

> LTE is the latest standard in mobile network technology, providing an extremely high-performance radio-access technology that gives users the capabilities in a mobile setting that they get on fixed networks. LTE is a giant step forward for public safety because of its unprecedented

broadband capabilities. LTE meets the mission-critical needs of first responders in the field by providing greater data sharing in both directions. (Gavigan 2011, 32)

LightSquared's 4G-LTE network is the first of its kind in the United States and uses a combination of satellites and ground stations to "offer more immediate communication with minimal delay and faster upload and download speeds. Because the satellite component can provide reliable connectivity, first responders can maintain communications and coordinate relief efforts in the event of a disaster. There will also be connectivity in rural markets where no reliable wireless communications currently exist" (Gavigan 2011, 32).

interoperability

The ability of public safety officials to communicate with each other seamlessly in real time over their wireless communications network either by voice or through data transmissions.

Lack of Interoperability **Interoperability** refers to the ability of public safety officials to communicate with each other seamlessly in real time over their wireless communications networks, either by voice or through data transmissions. The absence of emergency response interoperability across the country has been a persistent and costly problem: "The need to provide first responders with an improved system for interoperable communications remains an urgent national priority, despite the painful lessons of 9/11 and Hurricane Katrina. Even with the attention being paid to interoperability, emergency officials around the country cannot be confident they'll be able to communicate with each other when they need to most" (Kane 2009, 52).

A successful interoperability project is the Capital Wireless Information Net (CapWIN) program, a regional coalition of public safety and transportation agencies across Maryland, Virginia, the District of Columbia, and the federal government. Headquartered at the University of Maryland's Center for Advanced Transportation Technology (CATT), CapWIN's mission is to enable and promote interoperable data communications, operational data access, and incident coordination and situational awareness across jurisdictions and disciplines, focusing on first responders in the field and the unique requirements of wireless users. CapWIN has more than 5,000 registered users from more than 80 public safety, emergency services, and transportation agencies drawn from all levels of government, including regional authorities ("Capital Wireless Information Net" 2010).

A national approach to working toward interoperability is SAFECOM, a communications program in the Office for Interoperability and Compatibility run by the Department of Homeland Security. SAFECOM provides research, development, testing and evaluation, guidance, tools, and templates on communications-related issues to emergency response agencies at all government levels ("About SAFECOM" n.d.). Its mission is to improve emergency response through more effective, efficient interoperable wireless communications. The SAFECOM Interoperability Continuum is designed to help emergency response agencies and policymakers plan and implement interoperability solutions for data and voice communications. The tool, illustrated in Figure 2.1, identifies five critical elements that must be addressed to achieve

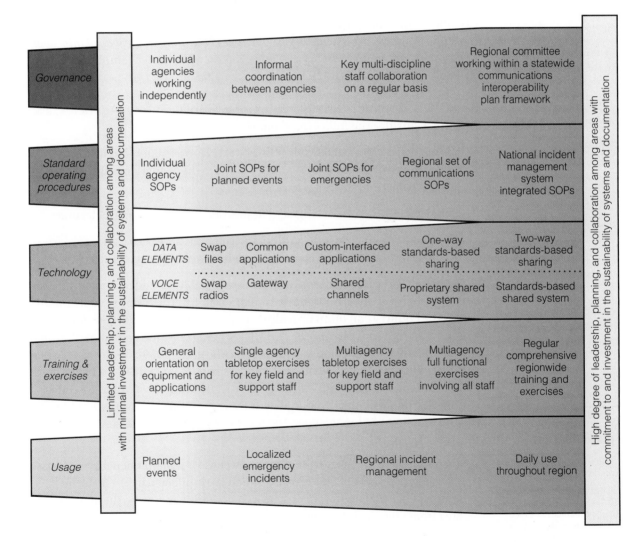

FIGURE 2.1 SAFECOM Interoperability Continuum

Source: *National Emergency Communications Plan*. Washington, DC: Department of Homeland Security, revised August 7, 2008, p. A-20. Accessed January 30, 2012. http://www.safecomprogram.gov/SiteCollectionDocuments/NationalEmergencyCommunicationsPlan_Aug08_v2.pdf.

a sophisticated and effective interoperability solution: governance, standard operating procedures (SOP), technology, training and exercises, and usage of interoperable communications. Jurisdictions across the nation are encouraged to use the SAFECOM Interoperability Continuum to track their progress in strengthening interoperable communications.

The plethora of devices and media being used by various agencies throughout the nation has created an environment in which the need for comprehensive communications interoperability has never been greater: "Creating an interoperable public safety network is a financial investment that, cities will find, pays big dividends" (Galvin 2009, 60). However, no amount of improved interoperability can overcome communication barriers that arise when officers are not speaking the same operational "language" or lingo: "Communications between and among law enforcement officers and agencies have improved significantly in the past few years, and police first responders and administrators alike have acquired and embraced numerous technological innovations. Unfortunately, however, these officers are not always speaking the same language; thus, *the largest obstacle remaining in the way of interoperability is in the human ability to communicate effectively*" [emphasis added] (O'Toole and Reyes 2008, 72).

Lack of a Common Language among Public Safety Agencies and Agents Consider the following scenario:

> You're a police officer, and a call of "10-24" crackles over your radio. It's another officer, from the next town over, and according to the coding language you use, he's just called for emergency backup.
>
> Unfortunately, in his own language, he just said he was stopping for a burger.
>
> The situation might sound absurd, but such mix-ups have been a very real part of emergency service radio communications for years. (Margetta 2009)

Although there is no national uniform standard in 10-codes, typically neighboring agencies do have a standard. Nonetheless, interoperability coordinators across the country can often provide examples of where the 10-code for taking a break was right next to another locality where the same code meant armed robbery or some other equally serious call (Margetta 2009). In any case, when considering an interagency incident, officers should be trained and have common knowledge to use plain language over radio traffic instead of 10-codes.

The National Incident Management System (NIMS), administered by the Federal Emergency Management Agency (FEMA), issued an alert on September 10, 2009, stating,

> The use of plain language in emergency response is a matter of public safety, especially the safety of first responders and those affected by the incident. It is critical that all local responders, as well as those coming into the impacted area from other jurisdictions and other states as well as the federal government, know and utilize commonly established operational structures, terminology, policies and procedures. ("NIMS and the Use of Plain Language" 2009)

Plain language is defined as "communication that can be understood by the intended audience and meets the purpose of the communicator. For the

plain language

"Communication that can be understood by the intended audience and meets the purpose of the communicator"; it is "designed to eliminate or limit the use of codes and acronyms, as appropriate, during incident response involving more than a single agency."

purpose of the NIMS, plain language is designed to eliminate or limit the use of codes and acronyms, as appropriate, during incident response involving more than a single agency" (*Plain Language—Frequently Asked Questions* 2010, 5). Alternate terms used to describe noncoded language are *common language, plain English*, and *plain talk*.

> The Department of Homeland Security recommends that first responders replace their 10-codes with plain language communications.

It is, however, critical to recognize the difference between interagency communication challenges, where the possibility of misunderstanding is high, and routine communication practices in the field among officers in the same department. In the latter case, 10-codes are still extremely common and have high pertinence to officer safety. As any first-line officer will attest, having codes when dealing with active incidents gives the officers a safety advantage. Consider the example of one officer telling his partner to "go 10-15" with a suspect. The suspect may not have any idea that the 10-code means "arrest him or her," which gives the arresting officer an edge for safety and leaves less time for suspects to think about what they might do if they had had that knowledge before being in handcuffs. Officers are well advised, however, that many 10-codes are available online to the general public.

Before looking at specific ways in which officers communicate with victims, witnesses, and suspects, consider some of the challenges officers might have in communicating with and understanding certain populations within the community.

CHALLENGES IN COMMUNICATING WITH AN INCREASINGLY DIVERSE PUBLIC

> Officers might have difficulty understanding the elderly, individuals who speak little or no English or who have different cultural backgrounds, and those with disabilities or diseases that may impair their ability to communicate.

Communicating with the Elderly

Serving and protecting the aging U.S. population is a special challenge for law enforcement. The U.S. Census Bureau predicts that by 2050, the population older than age 65 will more than double to roughly 88 million people, with this demographic constituting more than 20 percent of the population (U.S. Census Bureau 2010). Furthermore, population projections estimate that the number of people 85 and older will more than triple by 2050.

Problems in communicating with the elderly can arise from the age differences between, and corresponding generational concerns of, senior citizens and law enforcement officers. However, perhaps the greatest challenge will be for officers to recognize when they are interacting with an elderly person who has Alzheimer's disease who is either lost, shoplifting, or driving erratically. Such persons may forget where they live, where they left their cars, or even their names. Data indicate that an estimated 125,000 people with Alzheimer's disease or a similar condition wander from the safety of their homes every year and are unable to find their way back (Schaefer and McNiff 2011). In addition to missing-person calls, other incidents that may bring Alzheimer's patients or those with general dementia into contact with the police include driving and traffic difficulties (getting lost, running out of gas, causing crashes), false reports to 911, indecent exposure, shoplifting, cooking accidents, trespassing, overdoses, choking, homicide, suicide, abuse or neglect, and other types of victimization (Schaefer and McNiff 2011).

 An individual with Alzheimer's disease may have slurred, incoherent speech resembling intoxication.

If Alzheimer's disease is suspected, officers should look for an identification (ID) bracelet or other identification. Officers should identify themselves and explain what they will be doing, even if obvious. Officers should also maintain eye contact when speaking and try to keep a calm atmosphere. Physical restraints should be avoided if possible because they are almost certain to cause the person to lash out, verbally and physically.

Communicating with Non-English-Speaking Immigrants

"More than 47 million people in the United States speak a language other than English. Of those, about 19 million are classified as having limited English proficiency. Overall, nearly 2.6 million adults in the country speak no English at all. For law enforcement, the reality in the field speaks even more loudly than the statistics" (Holt 2008, 54). Law enforcement officers face daily situations where they must communicate with individuals who have limited English skills, often a dangerous situation for all involved: "Miscommunication between an officer and a victim or suspect can spark further conflict, delay needed help and escalate already tense situations" (Holt 2008, 54).

Language and cultural barriers can also severely hinder an investigation. It can be extremely difficult to conduct an effective interrogation if an officer does not speak the suspect's language, even if the communication is translated through an interpreter, because most translators typically have no law enforcement background. Many of the tactics and nonverbal communication involved in interrogation can be lost in this translation, which is frustrating to the investigator, the victim, and sometimes the suspect.

One way to enhance communication with non-English-speaking people is to recruit bilingual officers. Another approach is for English-speaking officers to learn the language most commonly used by the immigrant population in their jurisdictions. Traditional language classes are not necessarily effective because they include writing and "polite" conversation, not what police officers need. They need to master a small number of phrases with specific applications to street situations to maintain control until someone fluent in the target language arrives.

■ AN OFFICER'S PERSPECTIVE
The Downside of Translators

I once had a domestic abuse incident involving a Somali family and decided to use a language line Somali interpreter. This interpreter could barely speak English, and I later discovered he had asked the female victim why she had called the police over the incident. Apparently it is not acceptable for a woman in that culture to report an abusive husband. This had nothing to do with what I wanted translated. When using a translator who has no law enforcement background, it is important to keep in mind that, if it involves their primary culture, you may find barriers with them as well. You are dependent on them as your communication, and they have the power to place bias in the translation without either party's knowledge.

—*Sgt. Henry Lim Cho*

Another way to overcome language barriers is to compile a list of bilingual citizens in the community. This is easiest in large cities and those that have colleges and universities. Legal problems may arise, however, if confidential information is involved. When interviewing a suspect in custody, credentials count, and a court will only recognize certified translators. Often, incidents involving language barriers occur at times when it is difficult to find a certified translator, making it difficult to properly investigate or resolve an incident. The Tulsa, Oklahoma, police department has implemented the Volunteers in Police Services (VIPS) Spanish-interpreter ride-along program to draw on the valuable language skills of the increasingly Hispanic community and to build trust with this rapidly expanding segment of the city's population (Sherwood 2011). VIPS interpreters must complete an application and undergo a thorough background check as well as rigorous scenario and role-play exams before they are accepted into the program.

Another approach to the language barrier is to subscribe to the *language line*, a translation service offered by AT&T that provides direct interpretation in more than 140 languages for police and other emergency service units responding to calls. This service, however, is not without potential drawbacks, such as the lack of visual cues or body language that is often important and insightful during communication; difficulty in developing a rhythm for turn-taking during the dialogue; poor acoustics, distracting background noises, bad connections, and other technical equipment failures; and the lack of privacy that sometimes accompanies phone conversations and that may inhibit the free disclosure of certain information.

Technology is also available to help officers communicate with diverse populations, such as point talk translators, electronic devices that allow an officer to select the desired language and point to the most appropriate phrases to elicit responses from a subject. Electronic voice translators that convey basic instructions in the subject's own language are also available.

Communicating with Those from a Different Culture

Even when language is not a barrier, communication problems may result from customs and cultural differences in gestures, body language, body space expectations, and the like. For example, the Asian custom of coin rubbing to cure children of diseases leaves marks on the skin that may be misinterpreted by teachers or police officers as signs of child abuse. It is also reported that officer gender can come into play, with some individuals from non-Western cultures refusing to listen to female officers.

Another example: Unlike most Americans who know they should remain seated in their car if stopped by police, a Nigerian driver will commonly get out of the car to show respect and may ignore a request to step back because it makes no sense to him or her. Furthermore, in Nigeria, the distance for conversation is much closer, sometimes even less than 15 inches, and direct eye contact signifies deception, rudeness, or defiance. These cultural differences could easily cause communication problems and conflict between an officer and an immigrant citizen.

Immigration has been an integral part of the fabric of American society since the nation's inception. Figures from the U.S. Census Bureau indicate that of the 34.2 million persons counted in the 2005 U.S. Census survey (the most recent census year for which data analysis has been made publicly available), 12 percent were foreign born, bringing to local communities multiple cultures, languages, and "often unique perspectives on, or fears of, the police." Many new immigrants come from countries where the police are feared or distrusted rather than respected. The police in those countries keep secret files and have broad arrest powers. They may brutalize citizens, force confessions from them, or simply imprison them without any "due process." In fact, due process and civil rights may be concepts unknown to immigrants. Many immigrants also distrust public institutions, such as banks, and will keep their money and valuables at home or at their businesses, making them vulnerable to crime. Again, their fear of the police will work against them because they are unlikely to report the crimes or to assist the police in investigating these crimes.

Some jurisdictions are tapping the cultural resources of their communities to tackle trust issues as well as communication barriers by encouraging citizens from diverse ethnicities to join the ranks of their reserve units. For example, in Dearborn, Michigan, where more than 30 percent of the residents are Arab American, the police department actively promotes and supports a reserve officer program, in which 7 of the 33 volunteer reserves are from the Arab American community (Haddad 2011). In addition, 8 of the 25 youth participants in the Dearborn Police Department's Explorer program are from the Arab American community. Such efforts have proven quite effective in helping the police build inroads and relationships with members of the increasingly diverse community (Haddad 2011).

The neighboring cities of Brooklyn Park and Brooklyn Center, just outside of Minneapolis, Minnesota, have become home to what is thought to be the largest population of Liberian and Somali civil war refugees in the United States. In 2004, police officers in those communities began to recognize a pattern of escalating conflict, much of which was caused by miscommunication and inaccurate assumptions among diverse residents with various languages, family structures, social customs, and religious beliefs (Ankerfelt, Davis, and Futterer 2011). Realizing that their jurisdictions were in dire need of relationship building and better methods of communication, officers decided to take an innovative approach by assuming a leadership role that went beyond the traditional role of public safety. The Joint Community Police Partnership

(JCPP) was formed in which officers actively worked to help new immigrants assimilate into the broader community and open lines of communication between and among citizen groups and law enforcement. After several years, the approach has proven successful in fostering safe and livable communities with more effective communication and greater mutual understanding between and among local residents, new immigrants, and the police (Ankerfelt, Davis, and Futterer 2011).

Immigration is an issue for countless communities across the nation, and illegal immigration has become particularly challenging for border states. According to *The Police Chief's Guide to Immigration Issues* (2007, 7), "The distinction of 'legal' and 'illegal' immigration has existed since 1882, when Congress passed the Chinese Exclusion Act—one of the nation's first immigration laws established to keep immigrant populations out of the United States." Myriad challenges are facing law enforcement (*Police Chief's Guide* 2007, 10):

▶ One major city agency launched a new outreach initiative to work closely with its immigrant communities on the same day the local sheriff's department cross-deputized each deputy as a U.S. ICE agent to pursue and arrest illegal immigrants.

▶ Some cities have been faced with divided community opinion on "flash point" issues such as day laborer hiring sites—some calling for the police to support such locations, whereas others contend that most laborers at these sites are illegal and should be arrested.

▶ Community groups are seeking to support immigrants, but other groups are focusing on undocumented immigrants and enforcement actions.

▶ Governing body leaders are seeking to protect undocumented immigrants and other leaders are seeking to deport them.

The estimated number of illegal immigrants is growing at a rate of 100,000 to 300,000 each year. These non-English-speaking immigrants often cluster together in relatively poor neighborhoods where crime rates are high, leading nonimmigrants to equate these newly arrived individuals with crime and disorder.

The PERF report, *Police Chiefs and Sheriffs Speak Out on Local Immigration Enforcement*, states, "Increased enforcement of immigration law will have a significant chilling effect on crime reporting in immigrant communities. Fear of arrest and deportation will give illegal immigrants an even greater incentive to stay 'under the radar' and avoid drawing attention to themselves" (2008, 15).

Communicating with Individuals with Disabilities or Conditions Affecting Speech

When people think of "cultural diversity," they typically think of racial, ethnic, or even religious groups existing within mainstream America. Yet, in fact, the largest minority group in the United States, an estimated 49 million people, consists of individuals with disabilities. The DOJ estimates that about 20 percent of Americans have disabilities, a figure likely to rise as the population ages and baby boomers grow older (Kanable 2008).

To ensure that people with disabilities are treated fairly, the Americans with Disabilities Act (ADA) was enacted in 1990. The DOJ explains, "Under the

Americans with Disabilities Act, people who have disabilities are entitled to the same services law enforcement provides to anyone else. They may not be excluded or segregated from services, be denied services, or otherwise treated differently than other people." The ADA defines a person who has a disability as one who has a physical or mental impairment that substantially limits one or more major life activities, has a record of such an impairment, or is regarded as having such an impairment.

The Americans with Disabilities Amendments Act went into effect January 1, 2009, establishing new definitions of key terms, particularly the legal definition of a disability, and expanding on the definition of "substantially limits" by stating that the question of whether a major life activity is "substantially limited" should not be interpreted strictly. The act also broadens the group of individuals eligible for protection under the "regarded as" portion of the ADA: "The Amendments Act adds clarification providing that an individual who is 'regarded as' having a disability is one who has been subjected to discrimination based on an actual or perceived physical or mental impairment—whether or not the impairment limits or is perceived to limit a major life activity" (Collins 2009, 12).

Knowing who is disabled and, therefore, protected by ADA, is sometimes difficult. Some disabilities are obvious: paralysis and blindness, for example. Other disabilities, however, are not immediately apparent. Likewise, many conditions or diseases that impair speech are not immediately apparent and may be mistaken for intoxication or being under the influence of drugs. Nonetheless, officers must adhere to and abide by ADA requirements that prohibit discrimination against qualified individuals with disabilities in the delivery of government services, programs, or activities.

Blindness and deafness are two of the most common disabilities officers may encounter. The *visually impaired* comprise approximately 14 million Americans aged 12 years and older, according to the Centers for Disease Control and Prevention (CDC 2009). When interacting with people who are blind, police officers should identify themselves, and offer to let the people feel their badges as well. The *hearing impaired* are among those with "invisible" handicaps. Police officers will interact more effectively with citizens who are hearing impaired if they understand that most deaf people are not good lip-readers. In addition, the speech of individuals who have been deaf since birth may sound garbled and even unintelligible.

> The speech of a person who has been deaf since birth may be mistaken for that of one who is intoxicated or using drugs.

How deaf people communicate depends on several factors, including the type of deafness, the age at which the person became deaf, the individual's personality and intelligence, speech and speech-reading abilities, general language skills, and educational background. To communicate with an individual who is hearing impaired, officers should get the person's attention by gently tapping a shoulder or waving and speak slowly and clearly using short sentences. It is helpful to learn sign language. The services of a certified interpreter should be used whenever possible. In fact, several court cases have addressed when such services are required by law.

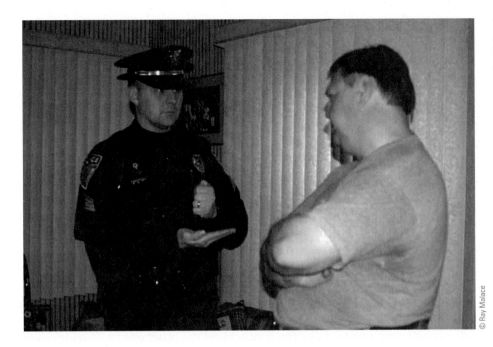

This officer's knowledge of sign language helps him communicate more clearly with a hearing-impaired person.

People with epilepsy also may present communication problems. Epilepsy is a disorder of the central nervous system in which a person tends to have recurrent seizures. It may alter behavior, movement, perception, and sensation. Some seizures impair consciousness and may last from a few seconds to several minutes.

> An epileptic seizure can look like intoxication or the influence of street drugs, as all may involve impaired consciousness, incoherent speech, glassy-eyed staring, and aimless wandering.

The person may be confused or need to rest after a seizure. A person having a seizure will generally regain his or her faculties within several minutes, whereas a drunk or high person will not.

Communicating with Individuals Who Are Mentally Ill

Historically, mentally ill individuals were locked away from society in insane asylums. Long-term institutionalization or hospitalization was the norm. Likewise, mentally retarded individuals were placed into special schools, usually hidden away from society. In the mid-1960s, however, a massive deinstitutionalization movement occurred, placing mentally disabled individuals into the community but without the support they formerly had. The continuing trend of deinstitutionalization has directly affected police, requiring them to acquire a new set of communication skills.

The National Institute for Mental Health (NIMH) estimates that in any given year, more than a quarter (26.2 percent) of adults and nearly one half (46.3 percent) of youths ages 13 to 18 in American suffer from a diagnosable mental disorder (NIMH n.d.). Many people with mental illness manage their conditions well and have little problem maneuvering through their daily activities and meeting their responsibilities. Some people, however, have insufficient social support and financial resources and may have difficulty receiving adequate care, getting to appointments, or maintaining treatment plans. As a result, they often stop refilling or taking needed medication, which eventually leads to behavior that brings them into contact with the law.

Although many proclaim the inappropriateness of using the criminal justice system to handle situations involving mentally disordered individuals, law enforcement officers need to know about mental illness nonetheless because of the high likelihood they will encounter people suffering from it as they work their beats. These contacts can be dangerous to the officer as well as to anyone involved in the contact, and training in crisis intervention and de-escalation techniques is essential to improve the chances that officer communication with mentally ill subjects will have a positive outcome. Even with training, these contacts can be virtual minefields regarding unpredictable subject behavior.

Only a few years ago, it was considered acceptable for a solo officer to attempt such contact and communication. Today, however, the recommended way to approach a scenario involving a mentally ill individual is to have two officers on scene, one to make the contact and the other one to provide cover for that officer. The police response to calls involving a mentally ill subject is discussed further in Chapter 6.

Communicating with Individuals Who Are Mentally Retarded or Autistic

The ADA ensures that people with developmental disabilities, such as mental retardation or autism, remain a part of our nation's increasingly diverse workforce. To avoid future potential litigation, officers need to be able to communicate effectively with those who are developmentally disabled.

Interacting with Individuals Who Are Mentally Retarded Recognizing mental retardation is the first step in dealing with it effectively. Often those who are retarded are adept at camouflaging their disability. When interacting with mentally retarded individuals, officers should try to find a quiet private setting, be patient, and speak slowly, using simple language and, if possible, visual aids, pictures, or diagrams. Officers should be aware that people who are mentally retarded often try to please others and may, therefore, make untruthful statements thinking it is what the officer, or someone else, wants to hear.

Interacting with Individuals Who Are Autistic Autism is a developmental disability that typically becomes apparent before a child reaches age 3. Some indicators that an individual may be autistic include the individual avoiding eye contact, lack of verbal response (many autistic people do not speak), speaking in monotone, repeating exactly what an officer says, engaging in repetitive physical actions, not responding to verbal commands or sounds, not understanding body language or recognizing a police uniform, dressing inappropriately for the weather, and not asking for help.

When responding to situations involving autistic individuals, officers should approach the person in a quiet, nonthreatening manner and talk in a moderate, calm voice. Instructions should be simple and direct, such as "stand up" or "go to the car now." Officers should understand that touching the autistic person or using a loud voice may startle the person and cause a protective "fight or flight response."

If a crime has been committed and an officer must take an autistic individual into custody, the suspect should be segregated until a mental health professional can evaluate him or her. Also, use caution when considering an autistic suspect's statements because they may confess to crimes they did not commit because of their desire to please and willingness to accept an authority figure's version of events.

Officers, particularly those without specialized training, often have difficulty recognizing when a subject has autism or another condition that warrants a shift in the "typical" police response. For this reason, some communities are trying an innovative approach in which such subjects, their parents, or their legal custodians voluntarily provide relevant medical information to law enforcement in advance, to facilitate any interaction that may occur at a later date between that citizen with special needs and the police. The Normal, Illinois, Police Department developed an early notification program (ENP) that collected this information from local citizens and provided a way for responding officers to access the information before arriving on scene, allowing the officers more time to develop an appropriate strategy, such as using less-lethal weapons or approach-and-contact techniques (Crutcher 2011). Such information, when made available to the responding officer ahead of time, can also explain what might otherwise be interpreted as suspicious behavior by the subject and help avoid a potentially fatal encounter (Crutcher 2011).

COMMUNICATING TO OBTAIN INFORMATION

A tremendous amount of time is spent communicating during police operations. Although much information officers receive may seem irrelevant to the law enforcement mission, it is important to the person conveying the information and should be treated accordingly. Officers who listen empathetically to citizens' concerns will promote public relations, enhance the department's image, and foster community policing. If they are truly "to serve and protect," officers must listen to their "clients."

The majority of officers' communicating time should be spent listening rather than speaking. Skillfully phrased questions can elicit a wealth of information. Active listening can greatly enhance the quality of the information obtained whether the communication involves a brief stop, a formal interview, or an interrogation.

THE FIELD INQUIRY AND AUTHORITY TO STOP

A **field inquiry** is the unplanned questioning of a person who has aroused a police officer's suspicions. It is not an arrest but could lead to one. Field inquiries are also referred to as "reasonable suspicion" investigatory stops or *field contacts*, and a card on which the information is recorded is called the *field contact card*.

Law enforcement officers are expected to stop and question people acting suspiciously. If an officer stops someone for questioning (a reasonable suspicion

field inquiry

The unplanned questioning of a person who has aroused a police officer's suspicions.

investigatory stop or field inquiry) and the officer believes the person may be armed, the officer can also pat down the person's outer clothing for weapons.

> The right to stop and question suspicious people was established in the landmark case of *Terry v. Ohio* (1968).

Briefly, this case involved Detective McFadden, an officer with 30 years of investigative experience, who observed three men who "just didn't look right" standing outside a jewelry store. After watching the men repeat a routine nearly a dozen times, McFadden suspected they were casing the store for a stickup and might be armed. Deciding to investigate their activity further, McFadden approached the men, identified himself as a police officer, asked for their names, and then decided to act.

He turned one man, John Terry, around, and made a quick patdown of Terry's outer clothing and felt a pistol in one pocket. Keeping Terry between himself and the others, McFadden ordered all three men to enter the store, where he asked the store owner to call for police while McFadden patted the outer clothing of the others. McFadden removed the revolver from Terry's pocket and another gun from the coat of a man named Chilton. Terry and Chilton were formally charged with carrying concealed weapons. When Terry and Chilton were brought to court, their lawyers moved that the guns could not be used as evidence, claiming they were illegally seized.

The trial judge disagreed, ruling that on the basis of McFadden's experience, he had reasonable cause to believe the defendants were conducting themselves suspiciously and some interrogation was warranted. For his own protection, the detective had the right to frisk the men whom he believed to be armed. The men were convicted, and both appealed their conviction to the U.S. Supreme Court. Before the Court's decision was handed down, Chilton died. Therefore, the Court's review applied only to Terry.

The Court recognized Detective McFadden as a man of experience, training, and knowledge and certainly "a man of reasonable caution." And as a man of "ordinary care and prudence," he waited until he had strengthened his suspicions, making his move just before what he believed would be an armed robbery. Given these facts, the Court upheld the trial court verdict, adding that McFadden had to make a quick decision when he saw the three men gathered at the store, and his actions were correct.

The *Terry* decision thus established protocol for one of the most fundamental aspects of police operations: in what has become known as a ***Terry* stop**, an officer with articulable reasonable suspicion that a crime is occurring, has occurred, or is about to occur may conduct a brief investigatory stop, including a patdown for weapons if the officer has reason to suspect the person is armed and dangerous. **Reasonable suspicion** is an objective and particularized basis, supported by specific and articulable facts, for suspecting an individual of criminal activity. For example, reasonable suspicion may be formed if a person fits the description of a suspect, doesn't "fit" the time or place, is acting strangely, is known to associate with criminals, is loitering, runs away, is present at a crime scene, and the area is a high-crime area. The stop may be all that occurs, it may lead to a patdown, or it may progress to an arrest,

***Terry* stop**

An officer with articulable reasonable suspicion that a crime is occurring, has occurred, or is about to occur may conduct a brief investigatory stop, including a patdown for weapons if the officer has reason to suspect the person is armed and dangerous.

reasonable suspicion

An objective and particularized basis, supported by specific and articulable facts, for suspecting an individual of criminal activity.

depending on the information received. The law of stop and frisk is examined in greater detail in Chapter 3.

Not every interaction between a police officer and a citizen amounts to a search or seizure requiring some kind of suspicion. Simply walking over to an individual and talking to him or her, as long as the officer does not block the person's way or order him or her to stay and talk, does not mean the person has been detained or require the officer to justify their contact. This was the ruling in *United States v. Mendenhall* (1980) when the Supreme Court held, "There is nothing in the Constitution which prevents a policeman from addressing questions to anyone on the streets."

More recently, in *Hiibel v. Sixth Judicial District Court of Nevada* (2004), the Supreme Court has upheld a Nevada law that makes it a crime for a person stopped for questioning, a *Terry* stop, to refuse to tell the police his name. In *Hiibel*, the Court said that asking questions is an important part of any police investigation and does not violate the Fourth Amendment. Citing a series of Supreme Court decisions, the Court stated that it is "clear that questions concerning a suspect's identify are a routine and accepted part of many *Terry* stops." Detaining a person for questioning is an important police function that easily generates hostility because people resent restriction of their freedom. Officers must be flexible. Some inquiries will be brief and simple; others extremely complex.

THE INTERVIEW

The interview is an important type of routine communication used by police officers. It differs from the impromptu field inquiry in that an **interview** is the planned questioning of a witness, victim, informant, or other person with information related to an incident or case. An interview is a "broad-based inquiry using open-ended questions to obtain facts, sequence of events, or alibis, which may or may not be true" (Sturman 2008, 44). To be effective, interviews should be based on specific goals and objectives.

A quality interview is often the deciding factor in solving a crime and having a successful prosecution. A successful investigator presents prosecutors with well-documented, detailed interviews of the victim, suspect, and all witnesses.

A quality interview promotes the victims' and public's confidence in law enforcement and increases the likelihood of guilty pleas. It reduces the hours often spent re-interviewing witnesses; directs investigators to additional suspects, evidence, and victims; and helps in recovering property. Quality interviews may also reduce false arrests and improve department morale.

interview

The planned questioning of a witness, victim, informant, or other person with information related to an incident or a case.

The Importance of Rapport

Building rapport is essential in successful interviewing. **Rapport** basically means a relationship of mutual trust, conformity, accord, and respect. It is a sense between two people that they can communicate comfortably and openly. This can be difficult to achieve between someone in a position of authority, such as a police officer, and someone under scrutiny, such as a suspect, or someone under emotional distress, such as a victim of a violent crime. Police rapport building is not always a quick and effortless endeavor, and different approaches

rapport

A relationship of mutual trust, conformity, accord, and respect; a sense between two people that they can communicate comfortably and openly.

work better with different suspects, as well with different police officer types. However, several basic suggestions may help facilitate the development of rapport between an officer and an individual the officer is interviewing.

Sturman (2008, 46) states, "A professional, yet friendly, approach to the person being interviewed is the most effective way to establish rapport. A quick way to do this is by finding some common ground or interest . . . By reading the suspect's personality, you can establish rapport by changing topics to discuss points of interest common to both of you. Try to connect with the suspect on one of the many similarities most people have. For example, common ground might be found in weather, family, work frustrations, bills, children, etc."

Rapport may also be fostered when an officer tries to fill a simple want or need the interviewee may have before getting into any details, particularly in the case of interrogations. For example, asking the person if he or she would like to use the rest room or have something to drink can help dissipate tension and get the interview off to a better start. Finally, when addressing the interviewee (whether victim, witness, or suspect) and throughout the duration of the contact, it is crucial to speak to interviewees with respect, regardless of what they are accused of having done.

Setting the Stage

The ideal setting for an interview can involve many factors, but the main thing is to keep the room simple and free of distractions, such as phones, clocks, magazines, and pedestrian traffic. The space should be relatively small (10 feet by 10 feet) and void of excess furniture. Barriers such as a desk or table between the interviewer and interviewee should be eliminated. The number of people in the room should also be limited. If there is a window in the room, the interviewee should be seated facing away from it.

Recording Interviews

Phillips (2008, 162) notes, "Law enforcement professionals conduct interviews with hundreds or perhaps even thousands of individuals every year, and each interview is as different as the background and personality of the interviewee. So, what happens when an interview turns into a case of 'he said, she said'?" One way to avoid this situation and to protect officers against false allegations is to record the interview. Some states, such as Minnesota, have mandated a policy of recording suspect interviews when feasible (Scales Law), and others strongly encourage departments to conduct such recordings.

closed question

Limits the amount or scope of information that a person can provide—for example, "What color was the car?" (the opposite of an open-ended question).

leading question

One that suggests an answer—for example, "You wanted your boss dead, isn't that correct?"

Types of Questions

Asking questions is a blend of art and science, and it takes practice to effectively extract the necessary information. Officers should distinguish between three types of questions: closed, leading, and open.

A **closed question** *limits* the amount or scope of information that the witness can provide—for example, "How many shots did you hear?" or "Did you see the suspect shove the victim?" Such questions may require a yes or no answer and should be avoided when seeking to obtain information. A **leading question** *suggests* an answer—for example, "You wanted your boss dead, isn't that correct?" Sumpter (2008b, 23) stresses, "It is important the officer maintains a neutral position, encouraging the interviewee to express the information developed in his head and not something created by the officer." An **open question** allows for an *unlimited* response from the witness in his or her own words. Usually open-ended questions are most effective in interviewing. For example: "Tell me what happened." Sumpter (2008b, 23) explains, "Open questions create a two-way conversation, allowing the interviewee to answer on his terms and take the answers into the conversational direction he prefers. Open questioning is the best indicator of the interviewee's cooperation. . . . Sometimes the answers to these questions are lengthy, but the interviewee must be allowed to answer without interruption."

Whether officers are seeking to comfort the victim of a crime while obtaining information or seeking to obtain information from a witness, certain techniques can make interviews more effective.

> **open question**
>
> One that allows for an unlimited response from the witness in his or her own words—for example, "What can you tell me about the car?" (the opposite of a closed-ended question).

INTERVIEWING TECHNIQUES

Interviews should be structured around the investigatory elements of the incident or crime. The need for careful planning and advance preparation cannot be overstated. In a preliminary interview at a crime scene, officers have extremely limited time for such planning. Consequently, they need to know their priorities in advance. They should obtain as much information as possible, identify and locate the offender(s), and broadcast the information or alert other officers and departments about the offense and identity of the offender(s).

Officers should not use police terminology when interviewing people because it will increase the incriminating atmosphere of the questioning. For example, use *take property* rather than *rob, have sex with* rather than *rape*, or *private use* rather than *embezzle*.

Phrasing Questions

Evidence shows that the phrasing of questions can definitely influence answers. In one study, for example, observers who were asked, "How tall was the basketball player?," estimated his height to be, on average, about 79 inches. Those asked, "How short was the basketball player?," responded with an estimated average of about 69 inches.

To minimize the inadvertent biasing of memory, witnesses should give an uninterrupted narration before being asked specific questions. Interrogation should also take place as soon as possible so that misleading information from various sources does not become part of the remembered event.

Follow-up questions can reduce or eliminate confusion and clarify statements that seem to contradict previously stated facts. Contradictory statements by an individual may be innocent, simply result from an error in memory, or may indicate deception. Skilled questioning can uncover lies told as part of a witness's or suspect's statement.

Avoiding Contaminating an Interview

Interviewing a person on a noisy, busy street with many onlookers may cause problems. Table 2.1 presents tips for avoiding interview contamination.

Table 2.1 Tips for Avoiding Interview Contamination

Focus on Interview Environment	
Questions to Consider	**Strategies to Use**
Where should the interview take place?	A location free of distractions
How should the room be configured?	Without barriers (e.g., desk or plants) between interviewer and subject
Who should conduct the interview?	One interviewer builds rapport and engenders trust more easily. Two interviewers should use a team approach; one asks questions and the other takes notes
Focus on Interviewer's Behavior	
Questions to Consider	**Strategies to Use**
How can interviewers encourage subjects to talk?	Use an open and relaxed posture, facing the subject; lean forward, make eye contact, nod, and occasionally say "uh huh" and "okay"
How can interviewers encourage subjects to listen?	Speak slowly, softly, and deliberately; avoid stressing or emphasizing one word over another
Focus on Interviewer's Questions	
Questions to Consider	**Strategies to Use**
What is a model for posing questions?	A funnel, with open-ended questions followed by closed-ended questions
What are the benefits of open-ended questions?	Gather complete information, minimize the risk of imposing views on subject, and help assess subject's normal behavior
What are the benefits of closed-ended questions?	Elicit specific details, ensure accuracy, and help detect deviations or changes in subject
How can interviewers ensure thoroughness?	Address the basics of who, what, when, where, how, and why
What are other cautions during questioning?	Never ask questions that disclose investigative information and lead the subject toward a desired response

Source: Vincent A. Sandoval, "Strategies to Avoid Interview Contamination," *FBI Law Enforcement Bulletin* (October 2003): 8.

Interviewing Witnesses and Victims: The Lifeblood of Criminal Cases

A witness is a person other than a suspect who is asked to give information about an incident or another person. A witness may be a victim, a complainant, an observer of an event, a scientific specialist who has examined physical evidence, or a custodian of official documents.

Officers must take accurate notes on what witnesses see, smell, or hear. Officers also must evaluate the witnesses' credibility on a number of intangible factors, such as their ability to articulate, their intelligence, their opportunity to observe, their sobriety, and their stress level at the time of observation.

Officers must realize that a crime of violence can put witnesses in shock. A **primary victim** is one actually harmed. A **secondary victim** is not actually harmed but suffers along with the victim—a spouse or parent, for example. Therefore, witnesses to a criminal event may also be considered victims of the crime. Effective interviewing helps officers obtain needed information and helps victims' and witnesses' future mental and emotional well-being. Officers should begin interviewing and questioning victims and witnesses only after establishing psychological and physical equilibrium. Insensitive questioning can compound the trauma.

primary victim

One who actually is harmed.

secondary victim

One who is not actually harmed but who suffers along with the victim—a spouse or parent, for example.

55

The Commission on Accreditation of Law Enforcement Agencies (CALEA) **Standard 55** "Victim/ Witness" states, "In its own best interests, law enforcement has a role to play in victim/ witness assistance, a role that no other component of the criminal justice system can effectively duplicate."

Source: Commission on Accreditation of Law Enforcement Agencies (CALEA) 2012. *Standards for Law Enforcement Agencies.* 5th ed. Fairfax, VA: Author.

55.2.2

Standard 55.2.2 specifically addresses the issue of victim and witness intimidation, requiring that an agency provide "appropriate assistance to victims/witnesses who have been threatened or who, in the judgment of the agency, express specific, credible reasons for fearing intimidation or further victimization."

Source: Commission on Accreditation of Law Enforcement Agencies (CALEA) 2012. *Standards for Law Enforcement Agencies.* 5th ed. Fairfax, VA: Author.

Bune (2008, 78) stresses, "Criminal victimization has a widespread impact, requiring extra attention and effective response strategies by agencies. . . . Law enforcement professionals and victim services personnel must be proactive in utilizing practical strategies and effective response mechanisms to ensure that crime victims are treated with the sensitivity, dignity and the respect they deserve." Crime victims who feel that the police are sensitive, fair, and respectful to them in the wake of their personal crisis, and not just there to get the "bad guy" and close the case, are far more likely to cooperate during the investigation.

Police officers should assure themselves that the witnesses they interview can and will testify. However, some information may be "off limits." **Privileged information** is information that need not be divulged to the police or the courts because of the existence of a special relationship, such as that between spouses or between lawyers and their clients. Two kinds of privileges exempt witnesses from testifying: absolute and conditional. An **absolute privilege** permits no exceptions. For example, conversations about social, business, and personal affairs are often private and privileged. Such conversations include communications between physicians and patients, lawyers and clients, husbands and wives, or others under a special obligation of fidelity and secrecy. A **conditional privilege** usually takes the form of the "official information privilege." An example is asking the court to not disclose an informant's identity.

Although witnesses may often be the only source of information available for solving a case, they are also fallible. One way to help witnesses recall events more accurately is the cognitive interview.

The Cognitive Interview

The **cognitive interview** puts witnesses mentally back at the scene of an incident and encourages them to tell the whole story without interruption. Most such interviews have five phases: (1) introduction to establish rapport; (2) open-ended questioning asking for a narrative of the event; (3) probing

privileged information

Information that does not need to be divulged to the police or the courts because of the existence of a special relationship, such as that between spouses or between lawyers and their clients.

absolute privilege

Information or testimony that cannot be received; there are no exceptions (see *privileged information*).

conditional privilege

The official information privilege—that is, the information can be received but the source of the information can be protected.

cognitive interview

Interviewing method that puts witnesses mentally back at the scene of an incident and encourages them to tell the whole story without interruption.

memory codes by asking the interviewee to close his or her eyes and concentrate on a specific portion of the narrative, again using open ended questioning; (4) reviewing the information obtained to be sure it is accurate and perhaps jogging the interviewee's memory more; and (5) closing, getting information about the witness—the background information usually collected first.

Interviewing Children

Officers may be particularly challenged when interviewing a child witness. Depending on the child's age, the witness may have a limited comprehension of what took place or may lack the vocabulary to adequately relate what was seen. These are among the main reasons why interviewing children requires a special skill set and interviewing techniques not commonly used with adults. Depending on the type of incident and type of interview taking place, officers may benefit from partnering with trained professionals such as social service agents or staff from private companies who are experienced in interviewing children. If time permits and circumstances allow, a responding officer may defer forensic interviewing of young children to a specially trained investigator. The National Children's Advocacy Center offers to law enforcement officers and others in related fields such training in the forensic interviewing of children.

A forensic interview of a child conducted by someone without specialized training may result in the evidence being held inadmissible in court. Special training can help ensure that the evidentiary results of child victim or witness interviews can stand up in court if a case goes to trial.

Interviewers of children should avoid leading questions, repeated interviews, and linguistically confusing questions. It is important the interview be conducted in a safe, child-friendly environment, preferably a room with child-sized furniture. Before the interview begins, however, the child and the adult who brought the child should be introduced to the interviewer and any others who will be present. Then, the child should be taken on a brief tour of the building, pointing out where the rest rooms are and where the accompanying adult will be waiting for the child, as well as explaining what will happen during the interview.

Interviewers should not wear a uniform or gun. The child should be praised indicating approval—for example, "You're doing a good job of telling me what happened." As with adult witnesses, officers should ask open-ended questions and avoid criticism.

Statements

statement

A legal, detailed account of events related to a crime.

If an interview yields important information, often a statement is taken. A **statement** is a legal, detailed account of events related to a crime. It begins with an introduction stating the date, time, place, and names of the people conducting and present at an interview and includes the name, address, and age of the person being questioned and providing the statement. The body of the statement is the person's account of the incident. A clause at the end states that the information was given voluntarily. The person making the statement reads each page, makes any needed corrections, initials each correction, and then signs the statement.

INFORMATION FROM INFORMANTS

An **informant** is a person who provides information in a criminal action and whose identity must be protected. Because of an informant's residence, occupation, associates, or lifestyle, that person may be in a better position than a police officer is to obtain information about a particular crime. Law enforcement commonly categorizes informants based on how reliable an informant has proven to be. Those who have previously worked successfully with law enforcement may be known as "credible informants" or CIs.

Often an informant's tip, along with some corroboration, can establish probable cause to arrest. The amount of corroboration needed to establish probable cause depends on the informant's credibility and source of information. And although officers often know informants' identities, having worked with them regularly, many times police receive information about crime from individuals who refuse to identify themselves, calling into question the reliability of the tip.

informant

A person who provides information in a criminal action and whose identity must be protected.

ANONYMOUS TIPS

Citizens are constitutionally protected through Fourth Amendment provisions from being forcibly detained by the government based solely on the false accusations of pranksters and those harboring grudges. In *Alabama v. White* (1990), the Supreme Court held that an anonymous tip can provide the foundation for reasonable suspicion if the tip predicts future activities the officer can corroborate.

Officers must use sound judgment in how they respond to anonymous tips, using court rulings as guidelines for what is legally allowed.

In *Florida v. J. L.* (2000), the Supreme Court held that an anonymous tip that a person is carrying a gun is not, without more information, sufficient to justify a stop and frisk of that person. An officer must have a reasonable suspicion that a suspect is engaged in criminal activity and may be armed.

THE INTERROGATION

The terms *inquiry, interview,* and *interrogation* are often confused. In police terminology, *inquiry* usually refers to conversations held with citizens during routine patrol. *Interviews,* as just discussed, are planned questionings of people having information about incidents. In contrast, an **interrogation** is the questioning of a hostile witness or suspect from whom officers try to obtain facts related to a crime as well as an admission or confession. An **admission** contains some information about the elements of the crime but falls short of a confession. A **confession** is information supporting the elements of a crime given by a person involved in committing that crime.

Interrogations carry an implied suspicion of criminal knowledge or involvement and must be handled differently from interviews. The Supreme Court has held that an interrogation "refers not only to express questioning, but also to any words or actions on the part of the police (other than those normally attendant to arrest and custody) that the police should know are reasonably likely to elicit an incriminating response from the suspect" (*Rhode Island v. Innis* 1980).

interrogation

The questioning of hostile witnesses or suspects from whom officers try to obtain facts related to a crime as well as admissions or confessions related to the crime.

admission

Statement containing some information concerning the elements of a crime, but falling short of a full confession.

confession

Information supporting the elements of a crime that is provided and attested to by any person involved in committing the crime; can be oral or written.

Investigators can make an interrogation appear to be a simple conversation that builds rapport and gains information and weakens the suspect's stance. Techniques known as mirroring, pacing, and leading can help achieve these goals. With mirroring, the interviewing officer mimics the suspect's verbal style. For example, the officer will raise and lower his or her voice to match that of the suspect's, swearing if the suspect swears, gesturing with hands if done so by the suspect. Pacing involves imitation of the suspect's nonverbal behavior, including shifts in posture, crossing of legs, folding of arms, leaning back or sitting forward in his or her chair, etc. These subtle emulations by the officer are intended to send a subconscious message to the suspect that compatibilities exist between the two parties. After the officer has spent some time mirroring and pacing the suspect, it is time to turn the table and try leading the suspect down a particular line of inquiry. During leading, the officer throws out nonverbal cues, such as a shift in posture or placing his or her hands in his or her lap, to see if the suspect unconsciously follows suit. If the suspect's behavior mirrors that of the officer, it is a sign that rapport has developed and the suspect is likely to cooperate with a particular line of questioning. If the suspect does not follow the officer's lead, the officer should go back to mirroring and pacing for awhile and try to build a stronger rapport before attempting further questioning (Sumpter 2008a).

Although interrogation is a vital law enforcement tool, it is susceptible to abuse and, consequently, is closely regulated by law. The landmark Supreme Court decision regulating police interrogation is *Miranda v. Arizona* (1966).

The *Miranda* Decision

In *Miranda v. Arizona*, 23-year-old Ernesto Miranda was arrested and interrogated about a rape and kidnapping. He confessed to the crimes but had not been told of his rights because police, aware Miranda had been arrested before, assumed he already knew his rights. The Supreme Court ruled (in a 5–4 decision) that the officers erred in not informing Miranda of those rights again: "The Fifth Amendment privilege is so fundamental to our system of constitutional rule and the expedient of being given an adequate warning as to the availability of the privilege so simple, we will not pause to inquire in individual cases whether the defendant was aware of his rights without a warning being given. Assessments of the knowledge the defendant possessed, based on information as to his age, education, intelligence, or prior contact with authorities, can never be more than speculation; a warning is a clear-cut fact."

In *Miranda v. Arizona* (1966), the Court established the following rights applied to custodial interrogations:
- The suspect has the right to remain silent.
- If the suspect gives up the right to remain silent, anything that the suspect says can be used in a court of law against him or her.
- The suspect has a right to speak to an attorney and to have an attorney present when being questioned by the police.
- If the suspect cannot afford one, an attorney will be appointed to represent the suspect *before* questioning begins.

Two key elements when deciding if *Miranda* applies are (1) the *custodial* nature of the questioning (i.e., Would a reasonable person in the suspect's position conclude that he or she is not free to go?) and (2) the *authority* of the person asking the questions (e.g., A private citizen or an agent of the law?). "Custodial" was defined as referring to the situation of a person who is "in custody" (under arrest) or *otherwise deprived of freedom of action in any significant way*. The Supreme Court ruled in *Yarborough v. Alvarado* (2004) that the *Miranda* custody standard is the same for juveniles as it is for adults. Furthermore, *Miranda* applies only to custodial interrogation by police. However, when police engage the help of a private citizen to get around *Miranda* requirements, that citizen has effectively become an agent of the police.

Many officers carry a card with the **Miranda warning** printed on it, clearly spelling out the suspect's rights, and read it verbatim to suspects. It is relevant to note that the Supreme Court has, to date, ruled more than once that no exact wording is required to satisfy *Miranda* (*California v. Prysock* 1981; *Duckworth v. Eagan* 1989; *Florida v. Powell* 2010). What is required is that the officer clearly convey the four different rights contained within *Miranda* and that the suspect understand each right as they have been presented to them. If, for example, a suspect speaks only Spanish, the warning might be read from a card bearing the warning in Spanish. When reading *Miranda* rights to juveniles, special care should be taken to ensure the suspect understands the warnings and that any request to speak to a parent or guardian before questioning is honored.

Miranda warning

A statement of a suspect's rights when that suspect is being questioned: the rights to remain silent, to talk to an attorney, and to have an attorney present during questioning, the attorney to be provided free if a suspect cannot afford one.

Waiving the *Miranda* Rights

An important facet of the *Miranda* decision is whether suspects are willing to give up these rights and talk to the police. If they do so, a signed waiver should be obtained. A **waiver** is a purposeful, voluntary giving up of a known right. If, after hearing a police officer read the *Miranda* warning, a suspect remains silent, the officer cannot interpret such silence as a waiver.

Although a detailed discussion is beyond the scope of this text, it is important to recognize the two distinct rights a suspect may invoke under *Miranda*: the right to remain silent and the right to counsel. Although a waiver applies to both, these two rights are distinct when invoked, and the police have different rules to follow depending on which right is invoked.

waiver

A purposeful, voluntary giving up of a known right.

Special care must be taken with individuals who do not speak English well, who are under the influence of drugs or alcohol, who appear to be mentally retarded, or who appear to be hampered mentally in any way. Many departments are now requiring officers to video record the notification of rights, the waiver, and the subsequent questioning of a suspect in major felony cases or instances where a suspect's competence to waive their rights might be called into question.

If at any time during an interrogation the suspect decides he or she wants a lawyer, either by direct request or through a comment such as, "Maybe I ought to have a lawyer," all questioning must end until legal counsel has been secured. The court has even held that a suspect's question, "Do you think I ought to have an attorney?" was an assertion of rights requiring an immediate cessation of the interrogation. It should be noted that the police should *never* give legal advice because this could be used against them later if the case goes to trial.

Which Comes First: *Miranda* Warning or Questioning?

Officers must be cognizant of the legal pitfalls surrounding questioning before *Mirandizing*. In *Missouri v. Seibert* (2004), Patrice Seibert was afraid she would be charged with neglect when her son, who had cerebral palsy, died in his sleep. Two of her other sons and their friends burned the mobile home to hide the circumstances of the son's death and left an unrelated mentally ill 18-year-old male to die in the fire so it would appear that the son was not left alone. Five days later, the police arrested her but did not read her rights.

At the police station, an officer questioned Seibert for 30 to 40 minutes until she eventually confessed to the fatal arson. The officer then gave her a 20-minute break from questioning. When he returned, he read her the *Miranda* rights and obtained a signed waiver to continue the questioning. The officer resumed questioning and was successful in getting Seibert to repeat her confession. At trial, the officer testified that he had purposely decided to question the suspect first to the point of obtaining a confession, then give the *Miranda* warning and repeat the questioning until he elicited from her the same information she had provided before being *Mirandized*. Seibert was convicted of second-degree murder. The case found its way to Missouri Supreme Court, which overturned the conviction saying that because the interrogation was nearly continuous, the second statement was clearly the product of the invalid first statement. The U.S. Supreme Court upheld this finding, suggesting that such tactics constituted a deliberate end run around the spirit and intent behind *Miranda*. Such deliberate questioning first and then *Mirandizing* and requestioning, sometimes referred to as **beachheading**, is unconstitutional.

When *Miranda* Is Not Required

It is not necessary to give a suspect the *Miranda* warnings if the officer does not intend to question the suspect, taking what is known as the *silent approach*. Other situations not involving "custodial interrogation" and, therefore, not invoking *Miranda* include brief on-the-scene questioning or investigatory questioning during a temporary detention, such as a *Terry* stop; roadside questioning following a routine traffic stop or other minor violation for which custody is not ordinarily imposed; routine booking questions attendant to arrest; nontestimonial identification procedures, such as fingerprinting, conducting a lineup, or taking voice, blood, or handwriting samples; conducting a sobriety test; volunteered, spontaneous statements by a suspect, even if in custody; and questioning by a private citizen.

Officers must distinguish between a *Terry* "detention" and a *Miranda* "custody." Although no bright-line rule exists for determining whether a particular police–suspect encounter is a *Terry* stop or an arrest, courts currently use the **totality of circumstances** test, that is, considering all relevant variables in a situation, including an individual's age, mentality, education, nationality, and criminal experience. During an interrogation, it also includes whether the *Miranda* warning was given, if basic necessities were provided, the length of the questioning, and the methods used during the interrogation.

Giving suspects the *Miranda* warning may inhibit suspects from talking by causing them to "lawyer up." FBI statistics show that the national clearance rate for violent crimes plunged 28 percent after the *Miranda* decision and has never

beachheading

Deliberate questioning first and then *Mirandizing* and requestioning— an unconstitutional interrogation strategy.

totality of circumstances

All relevant variables in an arrest, including an individual's age, mentality, education, nationality, and criminal experience, as well as the reason for the arrest and how it was explained to the individual being arrested. During an interrogation, it also includes whether basic necessities were provided and the methods used during the interrogation.

recovered: "Officers are not well-advised to give unnecessary *Miranda* warnings, risking the needless loss of a potential confession" (Rutledge 2009, 62). One way to avoid giving the *Miranda* warning is to ask a suspect to come to the station to be interviewed, voluntarily, without arrest. The admonitions might be worded, "You're not under arrest. You're free to leave anytime you want, OK?" Such a statement is known as a **Beheler admonition**, based on the Supreme Court ruling in *California v. Beheler* (1983). In this case, the Court ruled that no reasonable person in Beheler's position would have felt himself to be under arrest when he had been expressly advised that he was not, and when he came and went voluntarily without police restraints on his freedom (Rutledge 2009). Several factors that also indicate a lack of arrest or restraint in addition to giving a "Beheler admonition" are:

Beheler admonition

A statement given to a suspect who comes to the police station to be interviewed, voluntarily, without arrest, that conveys the message, "You are not under arrest. You are free to leave anytime you want."

▶ The suspect agrees to talk and brings himself in.

▶ No restraints or threats of detention or arrest are used.

▶ The suspect is questioned for an hour or two, with breaks allowed.

▶ The suspect is allowed to leave and is arrested sometime later (Rutledge 2009, 65).

The more of these factors that are present, the more likely the lack of a *Miranda* warning will be acceptable to the courts.

Providing Consular Rights Warnings to Foreign Nationals

Law enforcement officers must provide consular rights warnings to arrested or detained foreign nationals, that is anyone who is not a U.S. citizen. The U.S. State Department recommends the following notice be read to detained foreign nationals:

> As a non-U.S. citizen who is being arrested or detained, you are entitled to have us notify your country's consular representative here in the United States. A consular official from your country may be able to help you obtain legal counsel and may contact your family and may visit you in detention among other things. If you want us to notify your country's consular officials, you can request this notification now, or at any time in the future. After your country's consular officials are notified, they may call or visit you. Do you want us to notify your country's consular officials?

Under appropriate circumstances, law enforcement must also notify the foreign nationals' consular officials.

Ethical Considerations in Interrogation

The use of deception during interrogations is highly controversial. Many interrogators feel it is a vital tool to elicit information, but others hold deception to be highly unethical. Many types of deception have been used during interrogations:

▶ Misrepresenting the nature or seriousness of the offense—for example, telling a suspect that the murder victim was still alive

▶ Role-playing manipulative appeals to conscience—for example, projecting sympathy, understanding, and compassion; using the good cop/bad cop routine

▶ Misrepresenting the moral seriousness of the offense—for example, offering the suspect excuses, such as that a rape victim "asked for it"

▶ Using promises—for example, suggesting that a suspect's conscience will be eased

▶ Misrepresenting identity—for example, pretending to be a reporter or a cell mate

▶ Fabricating evidence

Considering the use of fabricated documents during interrogation, the Supreme Court has recognized that the duties of law enforcement may require limited officially sanctioned deception in the course of a criminal investigation, stating in *United States v. Russell* (1973), for example, "Criminal activity is such that stealth and strategy are necessary weapons in the arsenal of the police officer."

Playing arrestees against each other can also help investigators elicit a confession. With this strategy, interrogators typically start with the suspect most likely to waive his or her rights and confess: "This will often be the youngest, or the one with the cleanest record, or the one who looks most scared, or the person you believe has the least amount of involvement in the crime. . . . Even if the first suspect doesn't admit anything, you can return him to the cell with a big 'Thanks for everything, Danny,' right in front of his cell mate" (Rutledge 2008, 61).

Culhane, Hosch, and Heck (2008, 366) studied how current law enforcement, future law enforcement, and laypeople saw interrogation techniques and found that current law enforcement officers favored the use of "passive" interrogation techniques more than did the student and layperson groups and that all three groups minimally endorsed aggressive interrogation techniques such as the good cop/bad cop. Culhane, Hosch, and Heck (380) conclude, "The limited endorsement of aggressive techniques by all three groups suggests that there may be a concern for the well-being of suspects as well as a growing understanding of admissibility issues related to coerced confessions by those currently in law enforcement."

Use of Force or Coercion during Interrogation

In addition to giving the *Miranda* warning, officers must avoid any force or coercion during interrogation because any incriminating statements, admissions, or confessions that result from such tactics are likely to be of little use in building a case against the suspect. In 1944, the Supreme Court ruled to exclude from evidence confessions obtained by beating, threats, and promises, as well as those obtained under conditions that were "inherently coercive."

 Confessions obtained by force or under "inherently coercive" conditions are inadmissible in court.

The Court measured what is or is not inherently coercive by reviewing the totality of circumstances in each case where the admissibility of the confession was at issue.

Detecting Deception

Lies are generally told for one of the following reasons:

▶ Prosocial: to protect someone, to benefit or help others

▶ Self-enhancement: to save face or avoid embarrassment, disapproval, or punishment

▶ Selfish: to protect self or to conceal a misdeed

▶ Antisocial: to hurt someone intentionally or to gain something

Officers can detect subtle signs that a suspect is lying by watching the face and neck, particularly the eyes. An increase in the blinking rate or changes in pupil dilation are part of the fight-or-flight reaction and cannot be easily controlled. If this reaction is noticed, the officer should consider an aggressive line of questioning (Sumpter 2009). Researchers caution, however, that no empirical evidence exists to indicate that eye behavior or gaze aversion is a reliable gauge of truthfulness, nor is there a single indicator of lying (Matsumoto et al. 2011). Instead, investigators should consider a variety of verbal and nonverbal cues—clues to deception referred to as *leakage*—that occur across multiple channels and include facial expressions, gestures and body language, voice, verbal style, and the actual verbal statements made: "It is not the mere presence or absence of behaviors, such as gaze aversion or fidgeting, that indicates lying. Rather, it is how these nonverbal cues change over time from a person's baseline and how they combine with the individual's words" (Matsumoto et al. 2011, 3).

Studies have identified seven universal facial expressions of emotion that are independent of every demographic variable, including race, ethnicity, nationality, gender, age, and religious belief. In other words: "All people express emotions on their faces in exactly the same ways. Moreover, they are immediate, automatic, and unconscious reactions" (Matsumoto et al. 2011, 5). When investigators are trained to read and interpret these universal expressions, and combine those interpretations with statement analysis techniques, their ability to detect truthfulness and deception and, ultimately, assess credibility increases, thereby making their interrogations and interviews far more effective.

Many believe the ability to detect deception is greatly enhanced through use of technological instruments such as the polygraph and the voice stress analyzer (VSA).

Truth Detection Technology

A polygraph, which literally means "many writings," scientifically measures and records a subject's physiological reactions to specific questions in an effort to detect deception. As a polygraph operator asks a series of predetermined questions, changes in the subject's respiration, depth of breathing, blood pressure, pulse, and electrical resistance of the skin are measured and graphed for analysis.

A polygraph might be used to clear suspects; confirm victim, witness, and informant statements; or locate evidence. Polygraphs are sometimes used as part of an exploratory exam to further investigate the criminal involvement of someone already in custody for a different offense. Although the polygraph gives investigators another tool to use in their quest for information, the results are rarely admissible in court. Polygraph results can only be allowed into evidence if both prosecution and defense agree to its admissibility, which is unlikely as the results are likely to support only one side in a case. In addition, the Supreme Court, through several rulings, has failed to recognize the polygraph as a valid scientific instrument (*Frye v. United States* 1923; *Daubert v. Merrell Dow Pharmaceuticals, Inc.* 1993).

Some contend polygraph results violate hearsay rules because it is impossible to cross-examine a machine. However, even though polygraph results are not presently admissible in court, any confession obtained as a result of a polygraph test is admissible.

Another type of truth detection instrument is VSA, which is gaining popularity among law enforcement agencies, with departments across the country spending millions of dollars on VSA software programs in recent years (Damphousse 2008). Unlike the polygraph, the VSA does not limit the subject to only "yes" or "no" responses; it can analyze any spoken word. However, according to a study by the National Institute of Justice (NIJ), two of the most popular VSA programs being used by police departments were found to be no better than flipping a coin in detecting deception. On a positive note, the study also found that the mere presence of a VSA program during an interrogation may deter false answers (Damphousse 2008).

Before the terrorist attacks of September 11, 2001, research into deception and credibility assessment was minimal. Now, however, 50 such laboratories in the United States alone are undertaking such research: "Several universities and private companies are trying to develop the next generation of lie detection technologies by using functional magnetic resonance imaging, electroencephalography, near-infrared light, and other strategies to directly access brain function" (Gordon 2008, 73). However, most of this experimental research will not necessarily translate to an investigative role, and many such technologies will never be practical for police use. Noting that the polygraph remains the standard truth test for most law enforcement and government agencies, Gordon reports that the American Polygraph Association (APA) has a compendium of 80 research projects involving 6,380 examinations as well as 12 studies of the validity of field examination, providing an average accuracy of 98 percent (Gordon 2008).

No matter what type of technology is used, the results must always be used as an investigative aid, a supplement to a thorough investigation—never as a substitute for it.

Documenting Confessions

A confession can be given orally or in writing, but it must always be voluntary to be admissible. Documenting confessions is vital because a properly documented confession increases the likelihood of swift, successful prosecutions. Video recording of interrogations and confessions is becoming increasingly popular in law enforcement agencies nationwide to quell accusations of police brutality and reduce doubts concerning the voluntariness of confessions. Officers must be mindful, however, that even if a confession is obtained, it may later be revealed as untrue, or it may later be denied. Suspects may also claim that they confessed under duress or that their confessions were otherwise given involuntarily, claims that reinforce the value of video recording these conversations.

It is important to understand that a confession is only one part of the investigation. It must be corroborated by independent evidence. Usually such corroborating evidence is described in an officer's written report.

REPORT WRITING

Writing good reports is one of the most important communication skills law enforcement officers can possess. Murgado (2010), a 23-year veteran of law enforcement, observes, "As first responders, we consistently spend more time writing reports than on any other single task in law enforcement. The only thing that beats it is probably driving around patrolling our zones." Wilson and McLaren wrote more than three decades ago, "Almost everything that a police officer does must be reduced to writing. What is written is often the determining factor in whether a suspect is arrested in the first place, and if he is arrested, whether he is convicted and sentenced. The contents of written reports, in fact, often have a great bearing in life-and-death situations. To say that officers need to be proficient in report writing is an understatement" (1977).

Although investigative skills are important, they mean little if the report that synthesizes the investigation's findings crumbles under courtroom scrutiny. Cases can be made or lost on an officer's report alone. It has often been said that a good report is more important than a good arrest. Well-constructed police reports help expedite case processing and can alleviate the overall burden on the criminal courts because solid, effective reports are more likely to encourage plea bargaining. Indeed, plea bargaining is often considered a trial by police report. In addition, officers often are judged by their reports. A shoddy report makes the reader question the officer's intelligence, education, competence, or integrity—or perhaps all of these.

In today's litigious society, where anyone can sue anyone else for practically anything, law enforcement agencies and officers are not immune to becoming the target of a lawsuit. For this reason, well-written reports can reduce legal liability for both the officer and the department by clearly documenting the actions taken throughout the investigation.

■ AN OFFICER'S PERSPECTIVE ■
Well-Written Reports

Although you can get away with the minimum amount of pertinent information in relation to a case, it is important to record other relevant facts of the incident. If anything, it will refresh your memory when you reference the case if you ever end up testifying in court or are questioned by an administrator about it. I realize it is not feasible to record every detail of every incident, nor should you waste your time doing so. However, as an officer, you encounter many incidents on a day-to-day basis. Over time, without information written down, the details of a specific incident will blur together with many others. And there can be long stretches of time between when an event occurs and when you reference the case again, especially if it goes to court. It is beneficial to all who are involved, including your prosecuting attorney, if this information is there in the report. Good reports will also give you the reputation of being an officer who is thorough and well trained. Fellow officers, your bosses, prosecutors, judges, and defense attorneys will take note of that, and it can save you many headaches throughout your career.

—Sgt. Henry Lim Cho

Figure 2.2 shows the typical path of an investigative report. The number of times the report loops between the supervisor and the officer, or between the prosecutor and the officer, depends on how carefully (or carelessly) the officer constructs the report to begin with.

The Importance of Field Notes

Effective field notes are the basis for all types of reports and for further investigation of cases and incidents. Notes should be taken as soon after an incident as possible and should be kept in a notebook. Most officers prefer loose-leaf notebooks because they are easily organized, and notes can be removed and used as needed for writing reports or for testifying in court.

The ABCs of effective field notes are accuracy, brevity, clarity, and completeness. Accuracy is ensured by repeating information, spelling names, and verifying numbers. Brevity is accomplished by omitting the articles *a*, *an*, and *the*; by omitting all other unnecessary words; and by using common abbreviations. However, even common abbreviations can be misunderstood. For example, many people hear *P.C.* and think *personal computer* or *politically correct*. Police officers, however, are likely to think *probable cause* or *penal code*. Context often helps make the meaning obvious.

Clarity includes legibility. Notes that cannot be deciphered a few weeks later because of sloppy handwriting are worthless. A clear picture of what happened during an incident or at a crime scene depends on careful, complete notes that contain answers to six basic questions: who, what, where, when, why, and how. This is as true of misdemeanors as of felonies. Prosecutors contend that many police officers suffer from the **felony syndrome**; that is, they obtain complete information only on felony cases, deeming these to be "real" cases, with misdemeanors given much less time and attention. To the people involved, however, every incident or crime is important. Further, many more civil suits against police officers and departments arise from misdemeanor cases than from felony cases.

felony syndrome

Obtaining complete information only on felony cases, deeming them to be the only "real" police work.

Purposes of Reports

Police officers write many kinds of reports, including incident reports, continuation or supplemental reports, arrest reports, property and inventory reports, vehicle reports, missing-person reports, bias-motivated crime reports, domestic violence reports, police pursuit reports, and crash reports. These reports serve many important purposes.

> Reports are used to:
> - Permanently record facts.
> - Provide details of a criminal incident to be used in a follow-up investigation.
> - Provide a basis for prosecution.
> - Refresh an officer's memory when testifying in court.
> - Provide data for federal and state crime reporting systems.
> - Document the past and plan for future services.

Operations budgets and overall department budgets depend a great deal on accurate documentation of patrol activities.

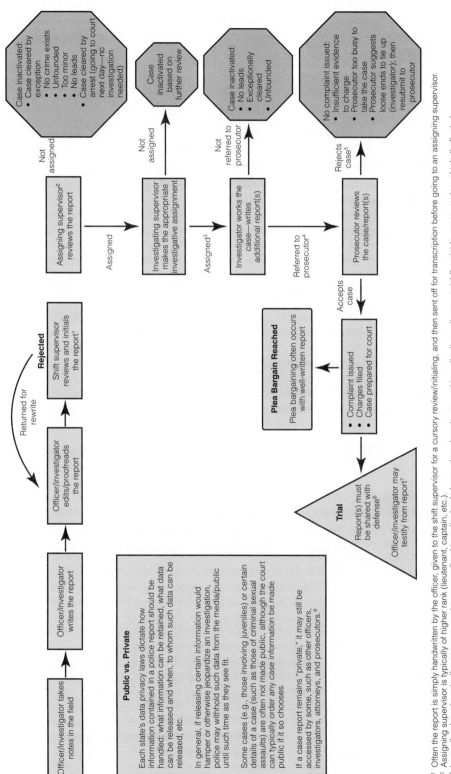

FIGURE 2.2 Typical Path of an Investigative Report

Note: Because this process varies from department to department, this flowchart illustrates a generalized oversimplification of one way an investigative report might travel from origination to final disposition.

Source: Hess/Hess/Orthmann, *Criminal Investigation*, 10E, © 2013 Cengage Learning.

1 Often the report is simply handwritten by the officer, given to the shift supervisor for a cursory review/initialing, and then sent off for transcription before going to an assigning supervisor.
2 Assigning supervisor is typically of higher rank (lieutenant, captain, etc.).
3 In smaller departments, the case may go to a generalized investigator. In larger departments, several investigative units may exist (homicide, arson, motor vehicle theft, etc.).
4 Case can proceed to prosecutor with or without an arrest having been made.
5 A rejection does not necessarily mean the case is not prosecutable at a later date. It means only that a complaint is not issued at that time.
6 Who has access to the report(s) at trial varies by state. For example, in Minnesota, the judge and jury do not automatically receive the report(s).
7 The report itself is not evidence, but any testimony the officer/investigator provides based on the content of a report becomes part of the trial record (testimonial evidence).
8 Check with your state's data privacy law. Laws vary from state to state regarding what can be retained, what must be released, and when information must be released. Consideration must also be given to whether or not release of information would hamper any ongoing investigations.

The Audience

A basic premise of effective writing is that it is reader based. All too often, writers try to *impress* their readers rather than to *express* their ideas clearly. They equate big words and long sentences with big brains and extensive education. WRONG. Reader-based writing avoids the tendency to impress.

 The audience for police reports includes other officers, supervisors, other professionals within the criminal justice system, and laypeople such as insurance investigators, social workers, and reporters.

reader-friendly writing

Communicates in plain, straightforward language; avoids police jargon and abbreviations; and considers its audience.

Reader-friendly writing communicates in plain, straightforward language; avoids police jargon and abbreviations; and considers its audience (Hess and Orthmann 2008).

Common Problems with Reports

The most common problems in police reports include misspelled words; unfamiliar abbreviations; confusing or unclear sentences; missing information, such as elements of the crime; missing work addresses and phone numbers; extreme wordiness and overuse of police jargon; missing or incomplete witnesses' names and addresses; and use of assumptions.

The Effective Report

The basic content of a police report includes an introduction, the body, and a conclusion. The information answers the same questions answered in field

■ PERSPECTIVE OF A FIRST-LINE SUPERVISOR
Written Reports

One of the most common problems with police reports from a first-line supervisor's perspective is a responding officer's timeliness in submitting a complete report. I know it sounds odd, so let me explain.

Officers can take many reports throughout their shift, some of which may seem unimportant to them. Officers may get busy as their shift continues, which can result in them having to stay past their shift and, consequently, deciding to complete what they consider their "less urgent" reports at a later time. They may also become lax in completing their reports on time or may just become forgetful.

In any case, no matter what priority the responding officer has given the report, it is probably very important to the person or people who were involved. Many times other officers in the department, as well as administrators, have no idea what the incident involved if a report has not yet been submitted. When individuals such as attorneys or members of the media inquire about those incidents, and the responding officer is not working or is otherwise unavailable to field questions, it leaves the agency looking unprofessional and embarrassed.

An untimely report has created avoidable headaches in countless other instances. The point is, as an officer, regardless how important (or unimportant) you feel a report may be, get it done in a timely manner or at least advise your direct supervisor of the incident and why you are not able to complete it at that time. This advice will surely help your career as well as your working relationship with your "road boss."

—*Sgt. Henry Lim Cho*

notes: who, what, where, when, why, and how. Good reports have the same characteristics as good field notes, plus several additional characteristics.

> Effective reports are accurate, brief, clear, complete, legible, objective, grammatically correct, and correctly spelled. Effective reports are also written in the past tense and in chronological order. They use verbs rather than nouns when possible, avoid sexist language, and can "stand alone."

Some police departments have their officers tape or dictate their reports. Increasing numbers of agencies throughout the country are moving toward digital dictation of reports, where an officer records his or her report verbally, and this dictation is later transcribed by clerical staff. The officer then signs off on the final report once it is drafted and appears accurate.

Computer-Assisted Report Entry

Many police departments use word-processing packages for report writing, and others go even further and use computer-assisted police report entry systems. Mobile technology is enabling officers to construct reports in the field, as information is obtained.

Before leaving the discussion of communication, one other important kind of communication should be considered—that between law enforcement and the media.

INTERACTION AND COOPERATION WITH THE MEDIA

Law enforcement needs the media, and the media needs law enforcement. Keys to success in dealing with the media include:

▶ Having a clear policy on what information is to be released to the press and what is not.

▶ Treating all reporters fairly.

▶ Being as sensitive to the need for the privacy of victims and witnesses as to the need of the public to know what is going on.

When Captain Sullenberger put US Airways Flight 1549 down in the Hudson River on January 15, 2009, US Airways CEO Parker provided an excellent example of dealing with the media by speaking with them right away, within two hours of the incident. He was empathetic, expressing concern about the victims and the community, and he dealt with facts and information, not with what he thought (Rosenthal 2009, 6).

Garner (2009, 54) offers the following guidelines for dealing with the media during a crisis:

▶ Tell the truth.

▶ Never say "No Comment."

▶ Keep consistent media rules during an incident.

▶ Do not hide; remain highly visible.

▶ Convey a sense of normalcy.

The police and the media have a symbiotic relationship, with each benefiting from the actions and efforts of the other. Here, North Miami Beach, Florida, Police Chief Rafael Hernandez talks to the media about the search for the killer of Miami police officer James Walker during a news conference. Hernandez is flanked by Miami Police Chief John Timoney, right, and members of several police agencies to his rear.

© AP Images/J. Pat Carter

▶ Do no harm.

▶ Stay calm and in control.

In addition to knowing what to do and not to do, officers must also be aware of the public's "right to know" and the privacy rights of victims and witnesses.

> Police departments must balance the public's "right to know" and reporters' First Amendment rights to publish what they know with the police's need to withhold certain information and to protect the privacy of victims and witnesses—Sixth Amendment rights.

Some larger departments have a public information officer (PIO) who is the only one authorized to release information to the media. Other departments allow those officers involved in specific cases to be interviewed by reporters interested in the cases. Media organizations should be told who their contacts will be. Whether a department has a PIO or permits individual officers to talk with the media, the department should always remember that most of what the public knows about law enforcement comes from the media. Their support for an agency is often directly related to the time and resources an agency spends on managing its message.

54 **CALEA Standard 54** on public information states, "Agencies have an obligation to inform the public and news media of events that affect the lives of citizens in the community with openness and candor. . . . Policies should be developed that govern what information should be released, when it should be released and by whom it should be released."

Source: Commission on Accreditation of Law Enforcement Agencies (CALEA) 2012. *Standards for Law Enforcement Agencies*. 5th ed. Fairfax, VA: Author.

Standards can ensure that the media is a friend rather than a foe of a police department. As with other areas of law enforcement, effective communication is the key.

SUMMARY

Effective communication can produce several positive outcomes and can be used to inform, persuade, diffuse, guide, motivate, reassure, and negotiate. Internal communication may be vertical (downward or upward) or horizontal (lateral). Among the valuable databases available to police officers are the National Crime Information Center (NCIC), the Law Enforcement National Data Exchange (N-DEx), the Law Enforcement Online service (LEO), the OneDOJ Initiative, the Regional Information Sharing System (RISS) Program, the Law Enforcement Information Exchange (LInX), CrimeCog, and the Intelligence Communications Enterprise For Information Sharing and Exchange (ICEFISHX).

Special problems encountered with communications technology include keeping police communications secure, interference on the line and dropped calls, lack of interoperability, and lack of a common language. The Department of Homeland Security recommends that first responders replace their 10-codes with plain language communications.

Special populations that may pose especially challenging communication issues include the elderly, individuals who speak little or no English or who have different cultural backgrounds, and those with disabilities or diseases that may impair their ability to communicate. An individual with Alzheimer's disease may have slurred, incoherent speech resembling intoxication. The speech of a person who has been deaf since birth may be mistaken for that of one who is intoxicated or using drugs. An epileptic seizure can look like intoxication or the influence of street drugs, as all may involve impaired consciousness, incoherent speech, glassy-eyed staring, and aimless wandering.

Effective communication in the field is critical to successful police operations and includes field inquiries, interviews, and interrogations. The right to stop and question suspicious people (field inquiries) was established in the landmark case of *Terry v. Ohio* (1968). In *Miranda v. Arizona* (1966), the Supreme Court established the following rights applied to custodial interrogations:

▶ The suspect has the right to remain silent.

▶ If the suspect gives up the right to remain silent, anything that the suspect says can be used in a court of law against him or her.

▶ The suspect has a right to speak to an attorney and to have an attorney present when being questioned by the police.

▶ If the suspect cannot afford one, an attorney will be appointed to represent the suspect before questioning begins.

Confessions obtained by force or under "inherently coercive" conditions are inadmissible in court.

In addition to verbal communication skills, police officers also need effective writing skills for both field notes and reports. Reports are used to permanently record facts, provide details of a criminal incident to be used in a follow-up investigation, provide a basis for prosecution, refresh an officer's memory when testifying in court, provide data for federal and state crime reporting systems, and document the past and plan for future services. The audience for police reports includes other officers, supervisors, other professionals within the criminal justice system, and laypeople such as insurance investigators, social workers, and reporters.

Effective reports are accurate, brief, clear, complete, legible, objective, grammatically correct, and correctly spelled. Effective reports are also written in the past tense and in chronological order. They use verbs rather than nouns when possible, avoid sexist language, and can "stand alone."

Police departments must balance the public's "right to know" and reporters' First Amendment rights to publish what they know with the police's need to withhold certain information and to protect the privacy of victims and witnesses—Sixth Amendment rights.

APPLICATION

As head of the public relations department, you have noticed an increase in complaints against officers who have mistaken a disability or physical problem as intoxication. Officers have no guidelines about how to determine whether what appears to be alcohol- or drug-induced intoxication is indeed alcohol- or drug-induced intoxication.

INSTRUCTIONS

Use the form in the Appendix to write a policy regarding communicating with individuals who *appear* to be under the influence of alcohol or drugs. Then write the procedures needed to carry out the policy.

AN EXERCISE IN CRITICAL THINKING

On April 13, Joel Powell's car was stopped, and he and a companion were arrested a few miles away from, and a few minutes after, the burglary of a supper club. The burglary had been reported by an eyewitness whose descriptions of the event and the car involved were transmitted by radio to area police officers. Powell's car matched the description of the car in which the burglars left the scene. It was also traveling in the same direction on the same road. After Powell and his passenger had been taken into custody, the car was sealed, towed, and searched. It contained two bank bags with about $500 in currency and coin, later identified as club property, and various tools, including pry bars, mauls, tire irons, and a hacksaw.

1. Must the factual basis for stopping a vehicle arise from the officer's personal observation?

   a. When stopping a vehicle, officers must have a warrant when they do not personally observe a felony being committed.

   b. Arresting officers may rely on any communicated information when a possible felony is to be investigated.

   c. The basis for stopping a vehicle may be supplied by information acquired from another person as well as other law enforcement officials.

   d. Arresting officers must have personal knowledge of the facts constituting probable cause.

   e. Six factors must be considered:

      1. The particular description of the offender or the vehicle in which the offender fled.

      2. The size of the area in which the offender might be found.

      3. The number of people in that area.

      4. The known or probable direction of the offender's flight.

      5. Observed activity by the particular offender.

      6. Knowledge or suspicion that the offender has been involved in other criminality of the type presently under investigation.

   Not all of these factors were clearly or completely communicated, so the stop is not supported.

DISCUSSION QUESTIONS

1. When you communicate with another person, are you aware of whether that person is really listening? How can you tell?

2. Do you feel the average citizen with whom you communicate is going to understand any legal language you may use to describe an offense?

3. What language barriers or other cultural barriers would you be likely to encounter in your community?

4. At night, you confront a suspicious man walking in an elite neighborhood. You stop to question the man, but he refuses even to

give his name. What are you going to do? Elaborate and justify your decision.

5. How would you warn a suspect of his rights if, while you were interviewing this person, he suddenly said, "I committed the crime"?

6. What are some positive outcomes of good incident reports?

7. How do the media affect police operations?

GALE EMERGENCY SERVICES DATABASE ASSIGNMENTS

▶ Use the Gale Emergency Services database (available for separate purchase) to answer the Discussion Questions as appropriate.

▶ Use the Gale Emergency Services database to research articles on *deception*. List the difficulties in detecting deception. State and support your opinion on whether deception is a viable tool in interrogation.

▶ Use the Gale Emergency Services database to research articles on *interoperability*. Outline the benefits realized and challenges faced to date and be prepared to share your findings with the class.

▶ Use the Gale Emergency Services database to find and outline one of the following articles:

- "Subtle Skills for Building Rapport: Using Neuro-Linguistic Programming in the Interview Room" by Vincent A. Sandoval and Susan H. Adams

- "When an Informant's Tip Gives Officers Probable Cause to Arrest Drug Traffickers" by Edward M. Hendrie

- "The Montgomery County CIT Model: Interacting with People with Mental Illness" by Rodney Hill, Guthrie Quill, and Kathryn Ellis

- "Law Enforcement and the Elderly: A Concern for the 21st Century" by Lamar Jordan

- "Strategies to Avoid Interview Contamination" by Vincent A. Sandoval

- "Criminal Confessions: Overcoming the Challenges" by Michael R. Napier and Susan H. Adams

- "Documenting and Reporting a Confession with a Signed Statement: A Guide for Law Enforcement" by Timothy T. Burke

- "The Americans with Disabilities Act: A Practical Guide for Police Departments" by Thomas D. Colbridge

- "Contact with Individuals with Autism: Effective Resolutions" by Dennis Debbaudt and Darla Rothman

- "Working with Informants: Operational Recommendations" by James E. Hight

- "The Psychological Influence of the Police Uniform" by Richard R. Johnson

- "Detecting Deception" by Joe Navarro and John R. Schafer

- "Offenders' Perceptual Shorthand: What Messages Are Law Enforcement Officers Sending to Offenders?" by Anthony J. Pinizzotto and Edward E. Davis

- "The Public Safety Wireless Network (PSWN) Program: A Brief Introduction" by Derek Siegle and Rick Murphy

REFERENCES

"About SAFECOM." n.d. Washington, DC: Department of Homeland Security. Accessed January 30, 2012. http://www.safecomprogram.gov/about/Default.aspx.

Ankerfelt, Jeff, Michael Davis, and Logan Futterer. 2011. "The Brooklyn Park, Minnesota, Police's Joint Community Police Partnership." *The Police Chief* (March): 22–31.

Basich, Melanie. 2009. "Wireless When You Need It." *Police* (January): 40–44.

Bune, Karen. 2008. "Focusing on What's Vital for Victims." *Law Enforcement Technology* (June): 78–85.

"Capital Wireless Information Net." 2010. College Park, MD: University of Maryland. Accessed January 30, 2012. http://www.capwin.org/.

Centers for Disease Control and Prevention. 2009 (September 28). "Vision Health Initiative." Atlanta, GA: Centers for Disease Control and Prevention. Accessed February 1, 2012. http://www.cdc.gov/visionhealth/data/national .htm.

Collins, John M. 2009. "Americans with Disabilities Amendment Act: What It Means for Law Enforcement Agencies." *The Police Chief* (January): 12–13.

Commission on Accreditation of Law Enforcement Agencies (CALEA). 2012. *Standards for Law Enforcement Agencies.* 5th ed. Fairfax, VA: Author.

Crutcher, Kent D. 2011. "The Early Notification Program." *FBI Law Enforcement Bulletin* (July): 12–15.

Culhane, Scott E., Harmon M. Hosch, and Cary Heck. 2008. "Interrogation Technique Endorsement by Current Law Enforcement, Future Law Enforcement, and Laypersons." *Police Quarterly* (September): 366–86.

Damphousse, Kelly R. 2008. "Voice Stress Analysis: Only 15 Percent of Lies about Drug Use Detected in Field Test." *NIJ Journal* (March): 8–13. (NCJ 221500)

Dorsey, Michael, and Douglas Smith. 2008 "Law Enforcement Information Exchange (LInX)." *Law and Order* (July): 44–48.

Galvin, Robert. 2009. "Getting with the Times." *Law Enforcement Technology* (February): 60–67.

Garner, Gerald W. 2009. "Surviving the Circus: How Effective Leaders Work Well with the Media." *The Police Chief* (March): 52–57.

Gavigan, Jennifer. 2011. "LightSquared Delivers Nationwide 4G-LTE Network." *Law and Order* (July): 32–33.

Gordon, Nathan J. 2008. "Today's Instruments for Truth Testing." *The Police Chief* (September): 70–78.

Haddad, Ronald. 2011. "Building Trust, Driving Relationships with the Dearborn, Michigan, Arab American Community." *The Police Chief* (March): 42–47.

Hess, Kären M., and Christine Hess Orthmann. 2008. *For the Record: Report Writing in Law Enforcement.* 6th ed. Rosemount, MN: Innovative Systems Publishers.

Holt, Greg. 2008. "Mobile Language Interpretation Program." *Law and Order* (July): 54–56.

Kanable, Rebecca. 2008. "ADA Compliance." *Law Enforcement Technology* (January): 68–75.

Kane, Kevin. 2009. "Radio Communication's Bandwidth Melting Pot." *Law Enforcement Technology* (February): 52–56.

"Law Enforcement Online." 2009 (August). Washington, DC: Federal Bureau of Investigation. Accessed January 30, 2012. http://www.leo.gov/leo_brochure_26.pdf.

Margetta, Rob. 2009. "Quest for Interoperability Applies to Talk, Not Just Technology." *CQ Homeland Security* (September). Accessed January 31, 2012. http://www .npstc.org/documents/CQ_Plain_Language_090918.pdf.

Matsumoto, David, Hyi Sung Hwang, Lisa Skinner, and Mark Frank. 2011. "Evaluating Truthfulness and Detecting Deception." *FBI Law Enforcement Bulletin* (June): 1–8.

Murgado, Amaury. 2010. "How to Master Report Writing." *Police* (November).

National Institute of Mental Health (NIMH). n.d. "Statistics—Prevalence: By Disorder." Rockville, MD: National Institutes of Health, National Institute of Mental Health. Accessed February 1, 2012. http://www.nimh.nih.gov/ statistics/index.shtml.

"N-DEx: Welcome to the Future." 2008 (April 21). Washington, DC: Federal Bureau of Investigation.

"NIMS and the Use of Plain Language." 2009 (September 10). *National Incident Management System ALERT.* Washington, DC: Department of Homeland Security, Federal Emergency Management Agency, NA: 06-09. Accessed January 31, 2012. http://www.fema.gov/pdf/ emergency/nims/NIMS_ALERT_06-09.pdf.

O'Toole, William C., and Eddie Reyes. 2008. "Making a Successful Transition to Common Radio Language." *The Police Chief* (May): 72–75.

Phillips, Amanda. 2008. "Bearing True Witness on Thy Neighbor." *Law Enforcement Technology* (October): 162–65.

Plain Language—Frequently Asked Questions (FAQs). 2010 (June). Washington, DC: Department of Homeland Security. Accessed January 31, 2012. http://www .safecomprogram.gov/SiteCollectionDocuments/ PlainLanguageFAQs.pdf.

Police Chiefs and Sheriffs Speak Out on Local Immigration Enforcement. 2008 (April). Washington, DC: Police Executive Research Forum.

Police Chief's Guide to Immigration Issues. 2007 (July). Arlington, VA: International Association of Chiefs of Police.

"Questions and Answers." n.d. Washington, DC: Federal Bureau of Investigation. Accessed January 30, 2012. http://www.fbi.gov/about-us/cjis/n-dex/ questionsandanswers#_What_is_OneDOJ?.

"Regional Information Sharing System." n.d. Washington, DC: Bureau of Justice Assistance. Accessed January 30, 2012. http://www.riss.net/.

Rosenthal, Rick. 2009. "Training the Media." *ILEETA Digest* (January/February/March): 6.

Rutledge, Devallis. 2008. "The *Bruton* Rule." *Police* (March): 61–63.

Rutledge, Devallis. 2009. "Non-Custodial Stationhouse Interrogations." *Police* (January): 62–65.

Schaefer, Robert, and Julie McNiff. 2011. "Awareness of Alzheimer's Disease." *FBI Law Enforcement Bulletin* (October): 12–16.

Sherwood, Mark. 2011. "Developing a Multifaceted Approach to Hispanic Outreach." *The Police Chief* (March): 54–55.

Sturman, Shane G. 2008. "Every Law Enforcement Officer Needs to Know How to Conduct a Criminal Interview and Interrogation." *Police* (October): 44–50.

Sumpter, J. L. 2008a. "The Art of a Conversation." *Law and Order* (July): 14–15.

Sumpter, J. L. 2008b. "Open and Closed Questioning." *Law and Order* (October): 23–24.

Sumpter, J. L. 2009. "Subtle Signs of Deception." *Law and Order* (January): 20.

U.S. Census Bureau. 2010. *2010 Census.* Suitland, MD: U.S. Census Bureau. Accessed January 31, 2012. http://2010.census.gov/2010census/.

"Websites and Social Media." 2012 (January). In *How Are Innovations in Technology Transforming Policing?*, pp. 4–12. Washington, DC: Police Executive Research Forum, Critical Issues in Policing Series.

"What Is ICEFISHX?" 2012. St. Paul, MN: Minnesota Joint Analysis Center. Accessed January 30, 2012. http://www.icefishx.org/.

Wilson, O. W., and Roy C. McLaren. 1977. *Police Administration.* 4th ed. New York: McGraw-Hill.

CASES CITED

Alabama v. White, 496 U.S. 325 (1990)

California v. Beheler, 463 U.S. 1121 (1983)

California v. Prysock, 451 U.S. 1301 (1981)

Daubert v. Merrell Dow Pharmaceuticals, Inc., 509 U.S. 579 (1993)

Duckworth v. Eagan, 492 U.S. 195 (1989)

Florida v. J. L., 529 U.S. 266 (2000)

Florida v. Powell, 559 U.S. ___ (2010)

Frye v. United States, 54 App. D.C. 46, 293 F. 1013 (1923)

Hiibel v. Sixth Judicial District Court of Nevada, Humboldt County, 542 U.S. 177 (2004)

Miranda v. Arizona, 384 U.S. 436 (1966)

Missouri v. Seibert, 542 U.S. 600 (2004)

Rhode Island v. Innis, 446 U.S. 291 (1980)

Terry v. Ohio, 392 U.S. 1 (1968)

United States v. Mendenhall, 446 U.S. 544 (1980)

United States v. Russell, 411 U.S. 423 (1973)

Yarborough v. Alvarado, 541 U.S. 652 (2004)

This available CourseMate has an interactive eBook and interactive learning tools, including flash cards, quizzes, and more. To learn more about this resource and access free demo CourseMate resources, go to www.cengagebrain.com, and search for this book. To access CourseMate materials that you have purchased, go to login.cengagebrain.com.

CHAPTER 3

Operational Skills:
Performing within the Law

DO YOU KNOW . . .

- What balance between freedom and order police officers must maintain?
- What two amendments restrict arrests and searches?
- What a stop-and-frisk situation involves?
- What constitutes an arrest?
- When officers may arrest someone?
- Why understanding and skill in making legal arrests are critical?
- How substantive and procedural criminal law differ?
- How officers arrest someone?
- What three use-of-force tests are established in *Graham v. Connor*?
- How much force can be used in making an arrest?
- If handcuffs should always be used in conjunction with an arrest?
- What less-lethal weapons police officers have available?
- What police activity can be an obstacle to community policing?
- When a search can be conducted?

CAN YOU DEFINE?

arrest
Carroll doctrine
compliance
continuum of contacts
curtilage
de facto arrest
due process of law
exclusionary rule
exigent circumstance
frisk
fruit of the poisonous tree doctrine
functional equivalent
good faith
"in the presence"
inevitable discovery doctrine

- How a search conducted with a warrant is limited?
- When a search warrant is *not* needed?
- How officers search a person and a building?
- What the exclusionary rule is and its relevance to police operations?

mere handcuff rule
patdown
plain view
positional asphyxia
probable cause
procedural law
reasonable suspicion
stop
stop-and-frisk situation
substantive law

INTRODUCTION

The basic skills discussed in this chapter—stopping and frisking, arresting, and searching—may be needed in a variety of situations. These skills are used often, and they are strictly governed by law and usually by department policies and procedures as well.

Police officers are expected to be familiar with the basic rules of criminal procedure. It is not the intent of this text to go into the details of any of these basic rules but rather to remind the reader of their critical importance in police operations. Chapter 2 discussed the importance of obtaining information legally. This chapter focuses on making legal arrests and searches.

> Law enforcement officers must maintain a balance between "freedom to" and "freedom from."

In a democracy such as ours, law enforcement has the awesome responsibility of ensuring that citizens have freedom *to* live, remain free, pursue happiness, and have due process of the law. Law enforcement has also been charged with protecting society—that is, giving citizens freedom *from* crime and violence as well as *from* unreasonable search and seizure by the government. The conflict between these two competing responsibilities is sometimes referred to as due process versus crime control. Police officers must strike a balance between the rights of individuals and those of our country and between the rights of law-abiding citizens and those of criminals. Officers must *act* to fulfill their responsibilities but always within the constraints of the law.

> Guarantees against unlawful arrests and searches are found in the Fourth and Fifth Amendments to the U.S. Constitution.

The Fourth Amendment states, "The right of the people to be secure in their persons, houses, papers and effects, against unreasonable searches and seizures, shall not be violated; and no warrants shall issue but upon probable cause, supported by oath or affirmation, and particularly describing the place to be searched, and the persons or things to be seized." The Fourth Amendment protects the fundamental right to privacy that lies at its core. Its guarantees extend to arrest warrants as well as to search warrants. It does *not,* however, prohibit arrests or searches without a warrant.

The Fifth Amendment provides that no person shall be "deprived of life, liberty, or property without due process of law" and protects those suspected of crime against self-incrimination (*Miranda v. Arizona* 1966). Both the Fourth and the Fifth Amendments should be kept in mind throughout this text and, indeed, throughout an officer's career.

This chapter begins with a look at the continuum of contacts, followed by an explanation of the common procedure of stopping and frisking someone acting suspiciously. Next, legal arrests are described, followed by a discussion of procedures for making legal arrests and the issue of use of force in making arrests. The chapter then turns to searches and how to conduct a legal search, including procedures for searching both people and places and using K-9s in searches. The chapter concludes with a discussion of the exclusionary rule as a mechanism to deter Fourth Amendment violations and the exceptions to this rule. This chapter contains more court cases than other chapters simply because of the topic: acting within the law while making arrests and conducting searches. The principles (and cases) discussed in this chapter will have relevance throughout the remaining sections of this text.

THE CONTINUUM OF CONTACTS

Police work involves much more than enforcing the law and catching criminals. As they work their shifts and carry out their duties to "serve and protect," police officers are in continuous contact with people from all corners of society, the vast majority of whom are not criminally involved. These contacts can be thought of as existing along a continuum, as shown in Figure 3.1. The **continuum of contacts** represents the almost limitless variation of contacts between the public and the police and illustrates how police action must correlate to an individual's actions to be constitutionally justified.

continuum of contacts

Almost limitless variations of contacts between the public and the police, ranging from no contact to incarceration or even the death penalty.

At one end of the continuum, contact consists of nothing more than an individual and an officer crossing paths and saying "hello" to each other—no governmental intrusion or police force is justified. As one moves up the continuum, police action becomes increasingly intrusive on individual freedom as the reasons for thinking criminal activity is afoot build. The first point on the continuum of contacts where police are constitutionally allowed to interfere with a person's freedom is the stop and frisk.

THE LAW OF STOP AND FRISK

Recall from Chapter 2 the discussion on police authority to stop and question people. If an officer stops someone for questioning (an investigatory stop or field inquiry) and believes the subject may be armed, the officer can also pat down the subject's outer clothing for weapons. This action *is* considered a search, albeit a very limited one.

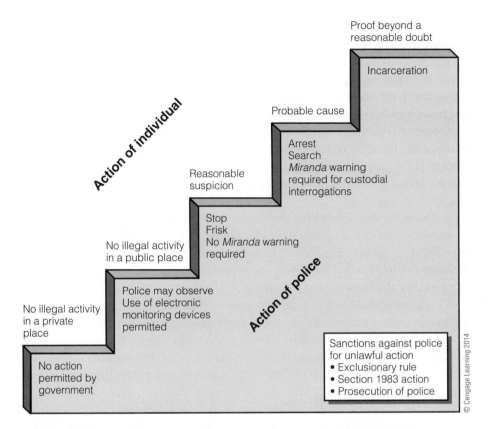

FIGURE 3.1 The Continuum of Contacts between Individuals and the Police

A **stop-and-frisk situation**, also called a *Terry* stop, is one in which law enforcement officers:

- Briefly detain (*stop*) a suspicious person for questioning (this is *not* an arrest).
- And *if* they reasonably suspect the person to be armed, they are allowed to pat down (*frisk*) the person's outer clothing (this *is* a limited search for weapons).

Although the words *stop* and *frisk* do not appear in the Fourth Amendment, the Supreme Court has ruled that these actions are tantamount to a search and seizure of the person. Consequently, it is vital that police officers understand how stops and frisks are regulated by the Fourth Amendment.

The Stop

The **stop** in a stop and frisk situation is a *seizure* of the person and, as such, must be *based on a reasonable suspicion* that the person detained is, or is about to be, engaged in criminal activity. **Reasonable suspicion** is more than a general hunch or "gut feeling" based on intuition; it is an objective and particularized basis for suspecting an individual of criminal activity,

stop-and-frisk situation

One in which law enforcement officers briefly detain a suspicious person for questioning and pat the person's outer clothing to ensure that the person is not armed.

stop

Brief detention of a suspicious person by law enforcement officers for questioning.

reasonable suspicion

More than a general hunch or "gut feeling" based on intuition; an objective and particularized basis for suspecting an individual of criminal activity that must be based on specific and articulable facts.

and it must be based on specific and articulable facts. In other words, for an investigatory stop to be constitutional, officers must be able to explain in detail (articulate) the specific facts that led them to become suspicious. The most common reasons for a stop were discussed in Chapter 2.

Several Supreme Court cases have set guidelines for law enforcement in determining when a stop is constitutional. In *United States v. Sokolow* (1989), the Court ruled, "In evaluating the validity of a stop such as this, we must consider the 'totality of the circumstances—the whole picture'." In *Alabama v. White* (1990), the Court held that reasonable suspicion is a less demanding standard than probable cause. Because the police made the stop on reasonable suspicion, it was legal.

In *Florida v. Bostick* (1991), the Supreme Court ruled that the location of a police–citizen encounter is only one factor to be considered in determining whether a seizure occurred: "In order to determine whether a particular encounter constitutes a seizure, a court must consider all the circumstances surrounding the encounter to determine whether the police conduct would have communicated to a reasonable person that the person was not free to decline the officers' requests or otherwise terminate the encounter."

The Supreme Court ruled in *Illinois v. Wardlow* (2000) that unexplained flight from the police is pertinent in developing reasonable suspicion necessary for a stop and frisk. In this case, officers patrolling an area of Chicago known for heavy narcotics trafficking observed Wardlow standing on the sidewalk holding an opaque bag. Wardlow looked in the direction of the officers and immediately fled, causing the officers to give chase. When they caught him, one officer conducted a patdown for weapons based on his experience that guns were commonly present during drug deals. A hard object in the shape of a gun was felt in the opaque bag. When the officer opened the bag, he found a loaded handgun. Wardlow was arrested for a weapons violation.

The trial court held that the officer's actions were a lawful stop and frisk. Two appellate courts, however, reversed, and the case eventually came before the Supreme Court. Noting that the officers were bound by the *Terry* (*Terry v. Ohio* 1968) standard of reasonable suspicion, the Court ruled that although Wardlow's presence in a high-crime area was insufficient, in and of itself, to justify reasonable suspicion of criminal activity, it was a relevant fact the officers could consider. Wardlow's unexplained flight was another pertinent factor, as Justice Rehnquist rationalized: "Headlong flight—whenever it occurs—is the consummate act of evasion: it is not necessarily indicative of wrongdoing, but it is certainly suggestive of such." This consideration of multiple relevant factors continued the long-standing totality of circumstances test for officers in justifying reasonable suspicion.

In *Hiibel v. Sixth Judicial District Court of Nevada* (2004), the Supreme Court ruled that police may properly request a person's name in a *Terry*-type stop. In this case, a Nevada rancher was stopped and asked for identification 11 times. He refused 11 times and was arrested and charged with the misdemeanor of refusing to identify himself. He was convicted and fined $250. Both the Nevada Supreme Court and the U.S. Supreme Court upheld his conviction. Jurisdictions differ on how they classify the crime of refusing to identify oneself or providing a false identity. In general, however, using someone else's real identity is more severe than making one up.

The stop may be all that occurs, it may lead to a patdown, or it may progress to an arrest, depending on the information received.

The Frisk

The **frisk** or **patdown** in a stop and frisk is conducted for the officers' safety and must be based on a reasonable suspicion that the person is armed. *Minnesota v. Dickerson* (1993) established that a frisk that goes beyond that authorized in *Terry* is invalid. The frisk cannot extend to a search for evidence. However, if during the frisk an officer feels what would reasonably be evidence, such as a packet of marijuana, the officer can retrieve the evidence under the "plain feel" doctrine discussed later in the chapter. If the stop turns into an arrest, a more thorough search can be conducted, also discussed later in the chapter.

Although a stop and frisk falls far short of an actual arrest and a full-blown search, it is *not* to be taken lightly, as the Supreme Court made clear in the *Terry* decision: "It is simply fantastic to urge that such a procedure [stop and frisk], performed in public by a police officer, while the citizen stands helpless, perhaps facing a wall with his hands raised, is a 'petty indignity.'" And, as noted, the stop might escalate into an arrest, depending on the specific circumstances.

frisk

A brief patdown following a stop to determine if a person is armed.

patdown

A brief feeling of a person's outer clothing to determine if a weapon is present; also called a *frisk*.

A stop-and-frisk situation is one in which officers briefly detain a suspicious person for questioning, and if they reasonably suspect the person to be armed, they may pat down the person's outer clothing.

© AP Images/Branimir Kvartuc

▌AN OFFICER'S PERSPECTIVE
Terry Stops and Officer Safety

This stage in the continuum of contacts is a potentially dangerous one for an officer. At this point, you have enough *reasonable suspicion* to conduct an investigatory stop on someone but do not yet have enough information to place the person under arrest. The articulable facts have been adding up. Perhaps the individual is giving you nonverbal cues, such as looking around nervously, which might indicate he is looking to retreat or attack. Perhaps he continues putting his hands in his pockets after you have told him several times not to. You are asking questions, the answers to which could mean his loss of freedom—but his hands and legs are still free at the moment. This is a period full of "unknowns" that, once turned into "knowns," will determine where the contact will lead. Because of those unknowns and the subject's freedom of movement, an officer must remain hypervigilant during this stage of contact and always be prepared for the worst-case scenario.

—Sgt. Henry Lim Cho

LEGAL ARRESTS

Making an arrest is one of the most important and extreme steps law enforcement officers take in their daily duties. The frequency of its occurrence, the nonserious nature of many offenses for which arrests are made, the poor character of many people subjected to it, and their lower socioeconomic status must never lull officers into forgetting the lofty place arrest holds in our law. The police responsibility in arrests is clearly defined.

Arrest Defined

The common meaning of *arrest* is simply "to stop." In a cardiac arrest, for example, the heart stops beating. Its meaning in the context of law enforcement is also generally known, that is, to seize and hold in jail or prison. The legal definition of *arrest* is somewhat narrower.

arrest

The official taking of a person into custody to answer criminal charges; involves at least temporarily depriving the person of liberty and may involve the use of force.

> An **arrest** is the official taking of a person to answer criminal charges. This involves at least temporarily depriving the person of liberty and may involve the use of force.

When Arrests Can Be Made

The Fourth Amendment stresses the importance of having an arrest warrant when making an arrest (or conducting a search). The law's ideal is for arrests to be made under an arrest warrant, where a neutral judge stands between the person to be arrested and the arresting officer and calmly determines that probable cause exists for the arrest. The courts have, nonetheless, recognized other circumstances in which an arrest can legally be made, acknowledging that the practical necessities of keeping the public peace often demand that police officers make arrests without a warrant.

An arrest can legally be made:

- With an arrest warrant.
- Without an arrest warrant
  - When any offense (felony or misdemeanor) is committed in an officer's presence.
  - When officers have probable cause to believe a person has committed a felony and no time is available to obtain a warrant.
  - For specifically enumerated misdemeanors, such as shoplifting in some jurisdictions.

Probable cause refers to a situation where it is more likely than not that a crime has been committed by the person whom a law enforcement officer seeks to arrest. An officer's probable cause to conduct an arrest depends on what the officer knew *before* taking action.

In the Presence **"In the presence"** does not refer to proximity, but rather to the officer's senses—that is, what the person making the arrest perceives through his or her senses. *Atwater v. Lago Vista* (2001) gave police the authority to arrest the driver of a vehicle for violations punishable only by a monetary fine, widening police authority in traffic-related stops. In this case, a police officer saw Atwater and her small children unrestrained in the front seat of her truck. The officer stopped the truck, confirmed that Atwater was violating the seat belt statute, handcuffed her, and drove her to the police station. There she had to surrender her personal property, was photographed, and placed in a jail cell for about an hour. Atwater sued the officer, the police chief, and the city, claiming her Fourth Amendment right to be free from unreasonable seizures had been violated. In deciding the case, Justice Souter stated, "If an officer has probable cause to believe that an individual has committed even a very minor criminal offense in his presence, he may, without violating the Fourth Amendment, arrest the offender."

"in the presence"

Perceived by an officer through his or her senses (does not refer to proximity).

Probable Cause Basic to lawful arrests is the concept of *probable cause.* **Probable cause** means it is more likely than not that a crime has been committed by the person a law enforcement officer seeks to arrest. An officer's *probable cause* to conduct an arrest depends on what the officer knew *before* taking action. Probable cause can be either observational (what the officer sees) or informational (what the officer is told). *Observational probable cause* includes suspicious conduct, being high on drugs, associating with known criminals, the existence of a criminal record, running away, presence in an unusual place or at an unusual time, presence in a high-crime area, presence at a crime scene, failure to answer questions, failure to provide identification, providing false information, and physical evidence. The more factors that are present, the greater the probable cause is. *Informational probable cause* consists of communications from official sources, such as wanted posters, statements from victims, and information from informants.

An often-quoted definition of probable cause is from *Brinegar v. United States* (1949): "Probable cause exists where the facts and circumstances

probable cause

That it is more likely than not that a crime has been committed by the person whom a law enforcement officer seeks to arrest: depends on what the officer knew *before* taking action.

within the officers' knowledge, and of which they had reasonably trustworthy information, are sufficient in themselves to warrant a man of reasonable caution in the belief that an offense has been or is being committed." In *Illinois v. Gates* (1983), the Supreme Court ruled that probable cause is a practical, nontechnical concept that should not be weighted in terms of "library analysis by scholars using tests." Rather, the test for probable cause under the Fourth Amendment should be a "totality of the circumstances test."

No precise formula for determining probable cause exists that can be applied to every case, just as no precise formula for determining reasonable suspicion for a stop exists. A stop and an arrest are both seizures regulated by the Fourth Amendment, and both must be determined from the individual facts and circumstances of each case. The intensity and scope of the seizure transforms a stop into an arrest. And although the Fourth Amendment does specifically use the term *probable cause*, the term *reasonable suspicion* is not constitutionally derived but rather an invention of the court to describe a level of suspicion that is lower than probable cause (Rutledge 2011b). Table 3.1 summarizes the basic differences between a stop and an arrest.

Several recent cases further clarify when a person can be arrested (seized) during a traffic stop. In *Brendlin v. California* (2007), police stopped a car to check its registration without reason to believe it was being operated unlawfully. One officer recognized Brendlin, a passenger in the car, as a parole violator and arrested him. A search of the car found, among other things, methamphetamine paraphernalia, and Brendlin was convicted. He appealed his conviction of violating parole, and the California Court of Appeals reversed the decision, saying suppression of the evidence was unwarranted because a passenger is not seized as a constitutional matter absent additional circumstances that would indicate to a reasonable person that he was the subject of the officer's investigation or show of authority. The Supreme Court, however, disagreed, and reversed the appellate court by stating, "When police make a traffic stop, a passenger in the car, like the driver, is seized for Fourth Amendment purposes, and so may challenge the stop's constitutionality." The *Brendlin* decision did not break any new legal ground regarding motor vehicle stops and passenger searches, but it did reinforce the fact that passengers may successfully have any evidence so obtained suppressed and may sue police for violating their constitutional rights while illegally stopping the driver (Collins 2007).

In a second case, *Virginia v. Moore* (2008), two police officers received a radio report alerting them that Moore was driving on a suspended license. They arrested him, and a search of his car turned up crack cocaine. Moore

Table 3.1 Stop versus Arrest

	Stop	Arrest
Justification	Reasonable suspicion	Probable cause
Warrant	None	Maybe
Officer's intent	To investigate suspicious activity	To make a formal charge
Search	Patdown for weapons	Full search for weapons and evidence
Scope	Outer clothing	Area within suspect's immediate control
Record	Minimal—field notes	Fingerprints, photographs, and booking

© Cengage Learning 2014

appealed his conviction to the Virginia Supreme Court, which reversed the decision, saying the officers should have simply issued a citation as state law required. The Supreme Court, however, disagreed, saying, "The police did not violate the Fourth Amendment when they made an arrest that was based on probable cause, but prohibited by state law, or when they performed a search subsequent to the arrest." Spector (2008, 12) contends, "It seems that in *Virginia v. Moore*, the U.S. Supreme Court has done a great favor to law enforcement officers and administrators in eliminating many of the concerns about violations of state statute arrest procedural rules." In other words, there is no Fourth Amendment violation even if an arrest violates state laws, as Rutledge (2008, 66) explains, "For federal civil liability purposes and to determine admissibility of evidence, the Supreme Court has ruled that state restrictions do *not* prevail over constitutional standards."

Sometimes the totality of the circumstances are such that the police bring someone in for questioning in a manner that is, in reality, an arrest, but in which the officers lack the requisite probable cause. This type of illegal seizure—a detention that is factually indistinguishable from an arrest but is without probable cause—is referred to as a *detention tantamount to arrest* or a **de facto arrest**. In *Kaupp v. Texas* (2003), the Supreme Court held that without probable cause for arrest, it is unlawful for law enforcement to transport a suspect against his or her will to the station for questioning.

de facto arrest

A detention without probable cause that is factually indistinguishable from an arrest.

The Importance of Lawful Arrests

"Almost every state limits police authority to arrest, especially without warrants—even when the officers have probable cause. Some of these statutory limitations are complicated, allowing arrest at certain time, with various jurisdictional limitations, and for particular crimes, and many of the statutes are peppered with a number of exceptions" (Spector 2008, 12). Although it is preferable to have an arrest warrant, it is not required to arrest a suspect on probable cause while in a *public place*. An arrest warrant is required, however, for a majority of situations where the suspect is in his or her own home. An exception to this requirement is when officers are in "hot pursuit" of an offender, with probable cause to arrest, and that individual flees into his or her own residence; in this situation, officers may lawfully enter that residence without a warrant to effect the arrest. Two other exceptions to this warrant requirement are consent and emergency situations.

Because arrests deprive individuals of their freedom, it is crucial that law enforcement officers be skilled at making *lawful* arrests.

Skill in making arrests is critical because:

- Fundamental rights to personal liberty and privacy are involved.
- The law of arrest is strict and technical.
- Arrest is often the first step in criminal proceedings.
- Illegal arrests may taint crucial evidence of guilt.
- Police performance quality is judged by arrests.
- Arrests may lead to civil suits and criminal prosecution of officers.
- Arrests may endanger officers' lives.

Arrests Involve the Fundamental Rights to Personal Liberty and Privacy In every arrest, the right to personal liberty is involved. This is the fundamental right to come and go or stay when or where one may choose—the so-called right to freedom of locomotion. This right is embodied in the common law of England and is protected by our state constitutions and the U.S. Constitution.

Although the essential nature of the right to personal liberty cannot be denied, it is, nevertheless, not absolute. It is limited by the fact that people do not live in a vacuum, isolated from others. Their survival demands that they live and work in a society whose well-being is also vital. Therefore, when people commit offenses against society's law, their right to personal liberty can be restrained for the common good. In other words, they can be arrested, and their arrest is justified if made according to **due process of law**, that is, the fundamental principles of justice embodied in the Fifth and Fourteenth Amendments. The power of arrest is inherent in the right of society to defend itself. It has long been recognized that offenders may be arrested on criminal charges and be detained for trial even though they may ultimately be proved innocent of wrongdoing.

The Law of Arrest Is Strict and Technical It severely limits the power of apprehension. It was formulated in England during the 17th and 18th centuries, when conditions as well as standards were far different from those of today. The professional police officer was unknown, and the fate of those arrested for crimes was fraught with danger.

In that era, people arrested on serious charges were rarely granted bail. Prisoners awaited court action in jails overrun with disease and corruption and where the dreaded jail fever was common. They were kept in irons for the jailers' safety. If they escaped from the easily breached lockups, their wardens were held personally responsible. Because the jails were run for profit and fees were charged for almost every aspect of prison life, a poor person who was locked up was in desperate straits.

This state of affairs led to the development of arrest laws greatly restricting the right to arrest. The courts, wanting a neutral judicial official to stand between the people being arrested and those doing the arresting, made it clear that an arrest was to be made only on the basis of a warrant issued by a judge. The courts also recognized the need to arrest without a warrant, but they spelled out the conditions under which such arrests could be made.

For example, the courts clearly distinguished between arresting without a warrant for a serious felony and arresting without a warrant for a minor misdemeanor. A warrantless arrest for a misdemeanor was limited to offenses committed in the arresting person's presence, whereas arrest for a felony without a warrant was not so limited. There was less justification for arresting people without a court order for minor offenses and subjecting them to the attendant dangers than for doing so for serious offenses that affected the whole community.

The ironclad law of arrest has survived the conditions that brought it about. Modern statutes and court decisions have remedied some technicalities of former times, but the old common law still controls many aspects of arrest,

due process of law

The fundamental principle of American justice that requires notice of a hearing or trial that is timely and that adequately informs the accused persons of the charges; it also gives the defendant an opportunity to present evidence in self-defense before an impartial judge or jury and to be presumed innocent until proven guilty by legally obtained evidence.

despite the arrival of professional police officers and vastly improved detention facilities and procedures. Legislatures and judges have hesitated to change concepts and procedures where the rights to personal liberty and privacy loom so large.

Arrest Is Often the First Step in Criminal Proceedings In the community's timeless attempt to keep the public peace through its criminal law, arrest by police officers is often the first step in criminal proceedings against wrongdoers. Despite the law's ideal that a court-issued warrant precedes an arrest, there is often no time in actual practice to apply for a warrant. The arrest must be made "now or never." Because police officers' duties often demand that they arrest people without the protection of a warrant, officers must know both the substantive and the procedural criminal law of their jurisdiction.

> **Substantive law** deals with content, or what behaviors are considered crimes. **Procedural law** deals with process, or how the law is applied.

substantive law

Deals with content, or what behaviors are considered crimes.

procedural law

Deals with process, or how the law is applied.

Substantive law defines the elements of crimes and the punishments for each crime. For example, premeditation is an element in first-degree murder, and the punishment upon conviction might be life imprisonment or even death. Crimes and their punishments are decided by elected bodies such as Congress and state legislatures.

Procedural law governs how the law is enforced and is perhaps of greater importance to law enforcement officers than is substantive law. Procedural law tends to be more controversial than substantive law. Although some laws are controversial (for example, those governing "victimless crimes" such as prostitution, gambling, and use of marijuana), other laws, such as those allowing criminals to "get off" because of a technicality, are even more controversial. It seems to many people that the criminals have all the rights and that victims' rights are ignored. This is largely because the framers of our Constitution had, themselves, experienced life under rule of a tyrannical government and believed it was better to risk letting the guilty go free than to risk recreating a society where the innocent suffered injustice at the hand of an arbitrary government.

Laws concerning crimes and arrest are complicated, and officers are allowed no margin of error in deciding whether the conduct, when not committed in the officers' presence, constitutes a felony and thus justifies arrest without a warrant. At one time, determining whether an offense was a felony or a misdemeanor was not difficult. The inherent seriousness or nonseriousness of the offense served as the guide. But this is no longer true. Legislatures have created felonies that are not inherently serious and misdemeanors that are. Officers must know the law.

The law will justify officers' actions if they proceed on the basis of probable cause or reasonable grounds. Yet, when they arrest without a warrant, they are responsible for exercising good judgment in hectic, fluid situations where mistakes are bound to occur.

Illegal Arrests May Taint Crucial Evidence of Guilt Although illegal arrests will not immunize defendants against criminal prosecution, such arrests may lead to the inadmissibility of crucial evidence of guilt. Physical evidence obtained by search and seizure incident to an illegal arrest, such as recovered stolen property or burglary tools, will be considered tainted and therefore suppressed under the exclusionary rule. This critical violation of the Fourth Amendment will be explored in greater depth at the end of the chapter.

The Quality of Police Performance Is Judged by Arrests The community's judgment of the quality of its police department frequently turns on the actions of officers in the more visible, dramatic areas of responsibility, such as apprehending felons. The public pays much less attention to officers' performance in the less colorful aspects of police work, even though extensive time and effort are necessarily required, for example, directing traffic.

Arrests May Result in Civil Suits or Criminal Prosecutions Lawsuits are an occupational hazard for police officers (del Carmen 2010). Claims of wrongful arrest or police brutality during an arrest are not uncommon in today's litigious society. However, if a lawsuit is not filed within the time specified by state statute, the claim can no longer be filed. The hazard of lawsuits against police officers is discussed in detail in Chapter 14.

Arrest Is Extremely Dangerous and Sometimes Life Threatening for Police Officers Arrests put police officers in jeopardy every time they take this drastic step. The peril exists with hardened criminals where possible violence is an obvious, ever-present concern, but also with people who do not have criminal records. Ordinary people often lose all sense of emotional and mental balance when arrested. They can react to their loss of freedom and the danger to their reputation in unexpected ways and may resist fiercely rather than submit to the command of the apprehending officers.

Arrests can also lead to dangers for the community at large. For example, an arrest that may seem particularly brutal and inhumane can bring about immediate and violent community reaction, as in the 1965 Watts riot.

PROCEDURES FOR MAKING LEGAL ARRESTS

The actual arrest is usually made by an officer stating to a person, "You are under arrest for…" The person being arrested should be told clearly—not in police jargon or legalese—the reason for the arrest. Officers should always be on guard when making arrests because people can react violently to being arrested, even those who appear meek and incapable of violence.

Depending on the circumstances, the person may first be handcuffed for the officer's safety. The arrested person should be searched for weapons and destructible evidence, as discussed later in this chapter. If the arrested person is to be questioned, the *Miranda* warning must be given before any questions are asked. However, "excited utterances," or things that suspects in custody spontaneously say in those initial moments surrounding an arrest, can still be used against them in a court of law under "hearsay" statutes, regardless of whether the arrestee has been *Mirandized* or not.

> In a typical arrest situation, officers should:
> - Announce the arrest and the reason for it.
> - Handcuff the person if warranted.
> - Search the arrested person for weapons and evidence.
> - Give the *Miranda* warning if questions are to be asked.

THE USE OF FORCE IN MAKING AN ARREST

One of the realities of police work is that force is sometimes required to obtain compliance from an individual. Indeed, police are legally authorized to use reasonable force, when necessary, to maintain public order or make an arrest. "No other enforcement task is more difficult or demanding personally and professionally than to use force only at the right time, in the right way, and for the right reasons" (Means and Seidel 2010, 18).

Police made an estimated 13,120,947 arrests nationwide in 2010, excluding traffic violations (*Crime in the United States* 2011). Results of several studies indicate that between 15 and 20 percent of all arrests may involve the use of force by police to control a resistant suspect (Smith et al. 2010). According to Eith and Durose (2011), individuals who the police suspected of wrongdoing or who have contact through a criminal investigation represent a relatively large percentage of the use-of-force incidents reported (16.6 percent) compared with all contacts with the public in which force is used or threatened (2.5 percent).

Force has been defined as the amount of effort required to gain compliance from an uncooperative subject. **Compliance** is a complete lack of physical resistance: A suspect willingly, although perhaps not enthusiastically, obeys the conditions and lawful orders of police. Many use-of-force incidents occur when the subject is intoxicated or under the influence of drugs.

compliance

A complete lack of physical resistance.

In *Graham v. Connor* (1989), the landmark case concerning police use of force, the Supreme Court acknowledged, "The reasonableness of a particular use of force must be judged from the perspective of a reasonable officer on the scene, rather than with the 20/20 vision of hindsight. The calculus of reasonableness must embody allowance for the fact that police officers are often forced to make split-second judgments—in circumstances that are tense, uncertain, and rapidly evolving—about the amount of force that is necessary in a particular situation."

> *Graham v. Connor* (1989) established a three-prong test for use of force: (1) the severity of the crime, (2) whether the suspect poses an immediate threat to the safety of law enforcement officers or others, and (3) whether the suspect is actively resisting arrest or attempting to evade arrest by flight.

Verbal Judo

Effective communication skills are critical to gaining compliance from subjects and managing the "intercalated" situations involving arrest, search and seizure, and use of force. In any use-of-force transaction, officers must use professional language so their communication becomes a tool for controlling the situation instead of a weapon used against the officer should the incident be reviewed. Training in verbal skills teaches officers to be assertive, not aggressive.

Many law enforcement professionals advocate learning what "Doc" Thompson, founder and president of the Verbal Judo Institute, teaches. Verbal Judo, or as some call it, tactical communication, is a skill that, like any other, can be learned. In contrast to deliberate tactical communication, "natural communication" is what we say without really thinking. Officers spend a great deal of time learning to fall and punch without hurting themselves but little time learning to communicate to enhance compliance rather than backing suspects into a corner where they are likely to become defensive and resistant to commands (Miller 2008).

▌AN OFFICER'S PERSPECTIVE ▐
Natural versus Tactical Communication

The noble goal of Verbal Judo is to maintain control. However, there is a persuasive argument against using this form of communication in that agencies that institute this style of communication as policy risk restricting or impairing an officer's natural communication skills, which may be, in many cases, a more effective form of communication. Although Verbal Judo can be valuable and highly successful at times, at other times it can make you sound "textbook" and unnatural and lead to a failure to properly empathize with those you come into contact with. Much like discretion in law enforcement, it is important to allow officers flexibility in communication styles and to give them a variety of tools to use when dealing with the many dynamic situations they will encounter. It is also important to allow officers to choose which tools to use in specific circumstances because the job has too many variables to be defined in black-and-white terms.

—*Sgt. Henry Lim Cho*

Usually communication is placed at the low level in use of force models.

Use of Force Models

Use of force applications must be broad enough to allow officers reasonable options in the field, yet specific enough to provide guidance. The Federal Law Enforcement Training Center (FLETC) Use of Force Model provides officers with various options categorizing the reasonable officer's perception to how a subject will or will not submit to arrest in one of five levels:

▶ Compliant level: Subject is cooperative and complies with the officer's commands.

▶ Resistive (passive) level: Subject directs no physical energy to the arrest, yet does not follow the officer's commands. An example is a protestor who sits on the ground and ignores an officer.

▶ Resistive (active) level: Subject directs energy and physical strength to resisting arrest but not directly at the officer—for example, grabbing a fence and refusing to let go. Verbal subject resistance can be included in this level. Compliance techniques include joint manipulation or restraints, leverage techniques, pressure points, or even pepper spray. Officers may warn the subject before using any of these techniques.

▶ Assaultive (bodily harm) level: A direct, physical attack on the officer. Use-of-force options include striking with hands, fists, elbows, and knees; kicking; baton strikes; and forcefully directing the subject to the ground.

▶ Assaultive (serious bodily harm or death) level: An attack where officers reasonably believe that they or others would be subject to serious bodily injury or death. The appropriate officer response is deadly force.

Guidelines for use of force when making an arrest:
- No resistance: Use no force[1]
- Resistance: Use as much force as is reasonable to gain control
- Threat or perceived threat to officer's life or the life of another: Use deadly force

Means and Seidel (2009b, 31) make an interesting point: "In a regularly lengthening series of decisions, federal courts have held that the Constitution does not require officers to use the least amount of force possible in a given situation. It requires only that the force used be 'reasonable.'"

Use-of-Force Continuums

Since the 1970s, use-of-force continuums have been used by police agencies to help guide officers in determining the appropriate level of force to use in various situations and under evolving circumstances (Fridell, Ijames, and Berkow 2011). Such continuums have necessarily changed over the years as the number and types of force options have increased to include chemical irritant sprays, impact weapons, and conducted energy devices (CEDs) such as the TASER (Means and Seidel 2009b). However, the basic structure of these models has remained the same, with "no force" at one end of the continuum and "deadly force" at the other, with numerous alternatives falling between these two extremes. Figure 3.2 presents one use-of-force continuum that depicts how force can escalate or de-escalate as a subject's response changes. It is important to recognize that the subject may enter the continuum at any level, meaning the officer may enter at any level that represents a reasonable response to the perceived threat posed by the subject. The continuum also goes in both directions, indicating that a step-down in police use of force is possible and appropriate when subjects lessen their resistance or increase their compliance.

Constructing a useful force continuum is challenging because of numerous important variables or "force factors" an officer must weigh during a use-of-force event: "No simple model can take into account the number or the relative importance of each force factor present during an incident" (Means and Seidel 2009b, 31). Among such variables are the suspect's known or apparent gender, age, size, strength, condition, and personal weapon proficiency, as well as the weapons available to the suspect and the suspect's known or

---

[1]Technically, mere "officer presence" is considered to be a use of force, albeit the extreme minimum level.

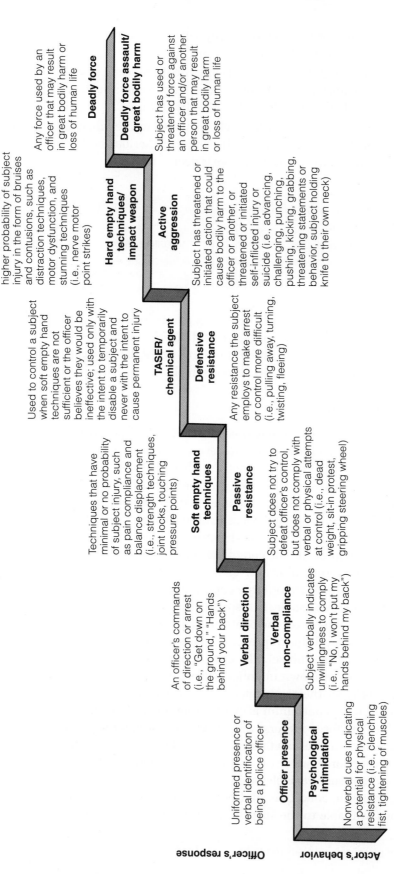

FIGURE 3.2 A Continuum in the Use of Force

Data source: Adapted from Owatonna (Minnesota) Police Department Use of Force Report.

NOTE: Subject may enter the continuum at any level. Officer may enter at any level that represents a reasonable response to the perceived threat posed by the subject.

apparent motivation to harm or escape, propensity for violence, and current state of mind. Every use-of-force situation is unique.

Use-of-force continuums are not without their critics, who point out that policing is not linear and that such continuums do not reflect the real world of confusion, fear, and sometimes an overwhelming sense of urgency that officers may face in violent confrontation with offenders. Force continuums may also cause hesitation and intensify officers' natural reluctance to use significant force even facing a serious threat. Furthermore, some continuum critics argue that the linear models imply that an officer must exhaust all options at one level before proceeding up or down the continuum to the next level. These critics suggest that if a use-of-force model is to be used, it should be circular and allow the officer to engage and disengage in force options at any point along the circle, according to the level of subject resistance met. Proponents of this type of force model note that a situation can jump, in a matter of seconds, from one in which minimal subject resistance exists to one in which deadly force is required, not allowing the officer time to "progressively" step up through the intermediate force levels.

In recent years, growing debate has surrounded the usefulness of and potential liability associated with force continuums, with some law enforcement scholars and practitioners advocating a move away from these models and toward a "just be reasonable" standard. Supporters of the "just be reasonable" approach contend that continuums are obsolete in the wake of *Graham v. Connor* because that decision set forth "clear force standards" directing officers to use force that is objectively reasonable given the totality of circumstances. Nonetheless, many other police practitioners and researchers believe the *Graham* Court's "reasonableness" standard is dangerously vague and that continuums fill a void in officer training by providing operational guidance regarding when and how much force an officer can apply in any given situation (Fridell, James, and Berkow 2011).

Using Forcible Entry to Arrest (or Search)

The right of law enforcement officers to use force to enter a building to make an arrest is more than 400 years old: "In all cases where the King is a party, the Sheriff, if the doors be not open, may break [into] the party's house, either to arrest him, or do other execution of the King's process, if otherwise he cannot enter. But before he breaks it, he ought to signify the cause of his coming and to make request to open the doors" (*Semayne's Case* 1603).

The use of forcible entry to arrest was firmly established early on in common law, even though a fundamental liberty of people includes protecting their homes. The home as a sanctuary and place of refuge is embodied in the Fourth Amendment to the Constitution and in state constitutions and protects homes against unjustified invasion. Even under common law, officers' authority to break the doors of a house to arrest was eventually drastically limited. It had to be shown that officers had reasonable cause to break and enter to arrest. They had to justify such extreme and drastic actions.

The Knock and Announce Rule   As a general rule, before crossing the threshold of a house in such emergency cases, officers must identify themselves, make known their purpose, demand admittance, and be refused. This requirement frequently is embodied in statutes. The rule was established to protect the right to privacy of citizens, to reduce the risk of possible violence to both police and occupants, and to prevent unnecessary destruction of private property. The rule applies equally to whether police are executing an arrest or a search warrant. Most of the cases discussed in this section apply to search warrants, but the basic rule applies to either.

The knock-and-announce notice is consistent with the presumption of innocence and lessens the danger arising from ambiguous conduct, bad information, mistaken identity, and other practical hazards of everyday police work. It makes clear to those within a dwelling what the object of the breaking is and prevents them from justifiably considering it an aggression to be resisted.

Guidance on how long officers must wait after the announcement and using force to enter is provided in *United States v. Banks* (2003), where the Supreme Court ruled that 15 to 20 seconds between an officer's knock and announcement of a search warrant and actual forced entry was "reasonable," overturning a lower court ruling: "The issue comes down to whether it was reasonable to suspect imminent loss of evidence after the 15 to 20 seconds the officers waited prior to forcing their way.... We think that after 15 or 20 seconds without a response, police could fairly suspect that cocaine would be gone if they were reticent any longer." In its unanimous ruling, the Court announced it would continue to take a case-by-case "totality of the circumstances" approach to deciding the constitutionality of police searches.

Three years later, the Court ruled 5–4 in *Hudson v. Michigan* (2006) that peace officers with search warrants may enter homes *without* knocking and *without* the risk of having any seized evidence thrown out at trial. In this case, Detroit officers approached Hudson's home, announced "Police, search warrant," but did not knock. Three to five seconds later, they opened the door and entered. The Supreme Court upheld the legality of the entry, even though it was made with only a 3- to 5-second delay. Justice Scalia noted that the negative social costs of allowing the exclusionary rule to be used in knock-and-announce violations would be considerable and would flood the courts with alleged claims, amounting, in many cases, to a "get-out-of-jail-free card" for criminals. Hilton (2007, 38) cautions, "Some police departments have interpreted the Supreme Court's recent *Hudson v. Michigan* (2006) ruling as a license to execute warrants without knocking, announcing, and waiting a reasonable amount of time for a resident to answer the door before entering. That interpretation is both wrong and dangerous. Failure to adhere to the requirements of the knock-and-announce rule can result in terrible tragedy and extremely expensive litigation."

One way to avoid claims of improper or illegal procedure is to conduct an audio/video recording of knock-notice announcements and entry, providing evidence of officers' compliance with knock notice and the time waited before forcing entry.

No-Knock Warrants Another way to avoid problems is to obtain a no-knock or quick-knock warrant, which provides a tactical advantage for law enforcement, especially in drug-related and other high-risk cases. Such warrants allow officers to enter without the requisite knock-announce-and-wait, instead allowing officers to announce who they are as they cross the threshold of the building, maximizing the element of surprise. However, when drafting and requesting this type of warrant, the officer must provide probable cause as to why this type of warrant is necessary. Possible justifications for a no-knock or quick-knock warrant include strong evidence of violent felons with weapons on the premises or individuals who have a history of violence with the police. Such circumstances can justify the necessity of this type of warrant that, once signed by a judge, can then be legally executed. Officers must be mindful that executing this type of warrant is likely to be extremely dangerous.

Level of Destruction If forcible entry is justified, the breaking must be done with the least amount of destruction. Only the slightest force is necessary to constitute a breaking. For example, pushing open an unlocked yet closed door constitutes forcible entry. In *United States v. Ramirez* (1998), the Supreme Court held, "Excessive or unnecessary destruction of property in the course of a search will violate the Fourth Amendment, even though the entry itself is lawful and the fruits of the search are not subject to suppression."

The Use of Handcuffs in Making an Arrest

Handcuffs have been used for more than 200 years to allow officers to restrict prisoners' mobility, thus offering some degree of safety. Agencies need a handcuffing policy that addresses handcuffing for all arrestees, with adaptations for special circumstances, such as people with physical injuries or disabilities.

The handcuffing process can be dangerous for officers because it brings them in close proximity with the suspect and necessarily requires officers to holster their sidearms to apply the cuffs. An officer who gets one cuff on and then loses control of the subject risks serious injury if that suspect decides to start swinging the handcuff. One technique some police trainers recommend is that before asking a suspect to put his arms behind his back, the officer grasp the suspect's upper arm, allowing the officer to more safely gauge a suspect's intent: "The *Lateral Arm Transitional Control Hold* (L.A.T.C.H.) places you in a position of relative safety while enabling you to anticipate suspect's resistance. In addition, it enables you to smoothly transition to familiar techniques to handcuff, create distance, or take the suspect to the ground" (Nance and Hallford 2008).

Many law enforcement agencies have a policy stating, "In the interest of officer safety, all persons arrested and transported shall be handcuffed." This policy has been called the **mere handcuff rule**. In stressing that everyone should be handcuffed, Rayburn (2011, 60) points out, "The ages of subjects that have feloniously killed law enforcement officers ranges from 12 years old to 82 years old. You have to have the mind-set that everyone, no matter the person's size, race, gender, or age, poses a possible threat." But such a rule, making mandatory the application of a form of force in all arrests, conflicts with the Fourth Amendment's "objective reasonableness" standard for use of force.

mere handcuff rule

A policy stating that in the interest of officer safety, all persons arrested and transported shall be handcuffed; it disregards the fact that handcuffing is a form of force and should be used only if the situation warrants.

Although handcuffing in some instances is vital to protecting an officer's life, to automatically handcuff every suspect arrested may leave the officer and the department open to a charge of objectively unreasonable handcuffing and a lawsuit.

© Henry Cho

 Whether an arrested person should automatically be handcuffed while being transported is controversial. Officer discretion may be advisable.

It is a common saying among law enforcement officers that "hands kill." This puts the emphasis on always watching a suspect's hands when dealing with suspects and is one of the primary justifications for using handcuffs. Although handcuffing in some instances is vital to protecting an officer's life, to automatically handcuff every suspect arrested may leave the officer and department open to a lawsuit charging objectively unreasonable handcuffing. Discretion might be used with the very young, the very old, and the physically disabled, always remembering, however, that these individuals can still pose a threat to officers' safety. In some scenarios, officers must use "creative handcuffing" to address an individual's specific physical needs and limitations while protecting themselves, as officer safety is primary.

Some courts have seen use of tight handcuffs as a violation of the Fourth Amendment. Using the *Graham v. Connor* standard on use of force, the reasonableness of the application and tightness of handcuffs should depend on the totality of circumstances of each case. Because tightness can be subjective, many academies and departments train officers to use a technique such as the two-finger rule, which is similar to the guideline used when placing a collar around a dog's neck. If an officer can comfortably fit the tips of the forefinger and middle finger between the cuff rim and the suspect's wrist, the handcuffs are generally deemed to be appropriately tight. The cuffs can then be double-locked to prevent further tightening. There are, of course, variations to this rule, and no absolute standard exists.

In some instances, officers go beyond handcuffs and use leg restraints or may even "hog-tie" extremely violent, unmanageable suspects. Be aware, however, this can pose an extreme hazard to the bound subject. **Positional asphyxia** may result if a person's body position interferes with breathing, as when a subject is in maximum restraints and placed prone on the ground or the back seat of a patrol car. Especially at risk of positional asphyxia are obese people whose weight can be displaced to the diaphragm, cutting off breathing; suspects who are acutely intoxicated from alcohol or drugs and, because of their state, may not realize they are suffocating; and suspects who have struggled violently before being restrained, making them susceptible to respiratory muscle fatigue.

Because of the dangers and liability associated with hogtying challenging subjects, many police departments are moving away from this method and replacing it with the use of hobble restraints, which are leg, ankle, knee, and elbow restraints designed for transporting prisoners in a upright sitting position.

positional asphyxia

A type of strangulation that results if a person's body position interferes with breathing.

Excessive Force

As officers carry out their daily duties, moving up and down the continuum of contacts and making countless, on-the-spot decisions regarding how much force to use, one hazard is ever-present: the possibility of going a fraction beyond the amount of force reasonably necessary to achieve a legitimate police objective. Stepping over that invisible line puts officers knee-deep into the area known as *excessive force*—that is, using an amount or frequency of force greater than that reasonably required to compel compliance.

Of the hundreds of thousands of police–citizen contacts that occur every day, the only ones that seem to receive media attention are those involving charges of excessive force, estimated to be less than 0.5 percent of all calls for service. Despite their relative infrequency, police misconduct, brutality, and excessive use of force do exist and are real problems for law enforcement.

CALEA Standard 1 "Law Enforcement Role and Authority" states, "Few issues outweigh the concern raised in a community when it is perceived that members of a law enforcement agency use inappropriate levels of force. A community rightfully expects that its law enforcement agency will issue weapons only to those agency members legally authorized to carry same as a condition of their duties, and that weapons and tactics are only utilized in conformance with sound policies, procedures, and training."

Source: Commission on Accreditation of Law Enforcement Agencies (CALEA) 2012. *Standards for Law Enforcement Agencies.* 5th ed. Fairfax, VA: Author.

In 1997 in a single police brutality claim in New York, the city and the police union paid $9 million to a Haitian immigrant, Abner Louima, who was tortured in a stationhouse bathroom. One officer, believing Louima had punched him during the arrest, sought revenge by sodomizing Louima with a broomstick. This was a clear case of police brutality (excessive force).

In *Scott v. Harris* (2007), Deputy Scott attempted to pull Harris over for speeding. When Harris fled, Scott pursued and attempted to stop him by ramming Harris's vehicle with his police cruiser. Harris crashed and was rendered a quadriplegic. Harris sued Scott, claiming he had used excessive force. The

Supreme Court, however, held, "Because the car chase respondent initiated posed a substantial and immediate risk of serious physical injury to others, Scott's attempt to terminate the chase by forcing respondent off the road was reasonable.... Viewing the facts in the light depicted by the videotape, it is clear that Deputy Scott did not violate the Fourth Amendment."

Consider this 10-item true-false quiz that addresses the issues typically raised in excessive force lawsuits. The answers are based on federal laws and the decisions of the Supreme Court and federal appellate courts, the primary sources of legal rules that govern police use of force (Plitt 2008):

1. There are constitutional limits on the types of weapons and tactics you can use on the street.

2. Your intent and your state of mind at the time you use force can be important factors in determining if your use of force was legal.

3. You must always retreat if possible before using deadly force.

4. You must first see a suspect's weapon before you can use force.

5. You must always use the least amount of force possible to gain control.

6. You cannot lawfully shoot a fleeing felon.

7. You may not use force to temporarily detain someone for purposes of a *Terry* stop.

8. Information you discover after force was used can be a factor in determining if the force you used was legally justified.

9. Courts and juries are permitted to evaluate your use of force by considering what you could have done differently.

10. Your uses of force in prior incidents can be considered in court in evaluating whether your use of force in the current situation was legally proper.[2]

All of the preceding *except* question 6 are false; item 6 is both true and false. Although *Tennessee v. Garner* (1985) held that officers could not shoot a fleeing felon who was simply fleeing to escape, if the suspect posed a danger to the officer or others, such a shooting may be justified.

The Use of Nonlethal or Less-Lethal Weapons in Making Arrests

Less-lethal weapons for use with violent, combative suspects include tear gas and other chemical irritant sprays, impact weapons, conducted energy devices (CEDs) such as the TASER, foams, nets, and K-9s.

Some of the most common nonlethal weapons are chemical irritant sprays, such as tear gas, chemical mace, and oleoresin capsicum (OC), more commonly

---

[2]Source: Plitt, Emory A. "Test Your 'Excessive Force' I.Q." *PoliceOne News*, February 28, 2008. Retrieved February 4, 2012, from http://www.policeone.com/legal/articles/1666240-Test-Your-Excessive-Force-I-Q/

called pepper spray. OC can be delivered in a cone-shaped spray, a fog, a directed stream, a splatter stream, or a foam.

Chemical irritants, in addition to being used in aerosol spray form, can be placed inside pellets and fired from a rifle, similar to paintballs. The PepperBall System, used by many police departments across the country, combines kinetic impact technology with OC pepper powder irritant. These devices are effective to about 30 feet but can also be deployed at point-blank range without causing great bodily harm.

As with all other impact or extended impact systems, certain target areas are off limits. For example, officers are not allowed to hit in the neck or head with a PR-24, or straight stick, and the same applies for the PepperBalls. However, most department policies also recognize that a suspect contact can escalate into a deadly force matter, at which time all restrictions on less-lethal targeting are off and deadly force with less-lethal weapons directed at typically restricted areas may be allowed.

Most conventional chemical agents work as either lacrimators, causing intense eye irritation and tearing, or as respiratory irritants, which make it difficult to breathe. Other less-lethal devices that use directed kinetic energy in projectile form are impact weapons such as bean-bag rounds and rubber bullets.

Although death and serious injury rarely result from use of these less-lethal impact projectiles, death has occurred, often caused by improper shot placement. Certain areas of the body are very vulnerable to impact injury, whereas others are relatively resistant.

Less-lethal devices that remove the need for accurate shot placement on a limited target area are CEDs, alternately called electronic control devices (ECDs), with the best known being the TASER™. An acronym for Thomas A. Swift Electric Rifle, the TASER is a conducted energy weapon that fires a cartridge with two small probes that stay connected to the weapon by high-voltage, insulated wire. Although prior generations of TASER stun technology have had limited success in stopping extremely motivated subjects or those under the influence of drugs or alcohol, the advanced TASER is able to incapacitate even the most focused combatants.

The TASER is not without critics. Several studies have linked TASER use with deaths; however, the *Study of Deaths Following Electro Muscular Disruption* (2008) by the National Institute of Justice reports, "Although exposure to CED is not risk free, there is no conclusive medical evidence within the state of current research that indicates a high risk of serious injury or death from the direct effects of CED exposure.... Therefore, law enforcement need not refrain from deploying CEDs, provided the devices are used in accordance with accepted national guidelines. (For example, *Electronic Control Weapons*, a model policy of the International Association of Chiefs of Police.)"

Other less-lethal alternatives include a "sticky foam" that hardens like taffy and can effectively immobilize a person. Another alternative is an aqueous (water-based) foam similar to that used by firefighters that incapacitates suspects by filling the space so the person cannot see or hear, although they can still breathe. Air bags in the rear seat of squad cars offer a third option to immobilize combative suspects.

A "tool" long used by law enforcement that is now gaining acceptance as an alternative means of force is the K-9. Police service dogs can enhance the safety of officers, bystanders, and suspects and help officers avoid resorting to deadly force. A source of K-9–related case law can be found on the Web site of Terry Fleck, an expert in the field of canine legalities.

Emphasis on CEDs and other less-lethal options may make handheld impact weapons obsolete because historically such handheld devices have filled a use-of-force gap between fisticuffs and firearms (Scoville 2009, 50). Scoville suggests that if you ask the average citizen what constitutes "police brutality," most would think of a cop with a baton or some other "club" beating on a suspect. Nonetheless, "Batons are probably one of the most valuable tools a police officer can have on his belt. They don't malfunction. They provide you with greater distance from the threat in lieu of having to use deadlier force. You will never hit a person harder with your hand than you will with your baton. The baton is the best equalizer, the best low technology weapon on a law enforcement officer's belt" (Scoville 2009, 51). The newer, telescoping batons can be an even more powerful persuader for compliance.

The general public is often confused about the risks of less-lethal weapons, with civil libertarians saying one thing and law enforcement agencies saying something else. Heal, Bovbjerg, and Kenny (2009) call most of the so-called research of libertarians "Voodoo Science," which they characterize as a catch-all term for any junk science that misleads or mischaracterizes the evidence (26–27): "Simply put, much of the 'science' cited by detractors of non-lethal options is either fundamentally flawed, misunderstood, mischaracterizes the evidence, or ignores influences beyond the control of the user. It is an exceedingly rare occurrence when any of this so-called science is subject to peer review by objective researchers, cited in reports by other researchers or scientists, used in supporting references, or corroborated with other research by bona fide scientific or academic institutions."

The Use of Deadly Force in Making Arrests

Using deadly force is perhaps the hardest decision a law enforcement officer faces. The use of such force is prescribed by state and federal statutes and basically requires that deadly force be used only in self-defense or in defense of another. Until 1985, it was legal in many states for officers to use deadly force to prevent a felon from escaping. This practice, however, terminated following *Tennessee v. Garner* (1985), when, as noted, the Supreme Court ruled that law enforcement officers cannot shoot "fleeing felons" unless they present an "imminent danger to life": "The use of deadly force to prevent the escape of all felony suspects, whatever the circumstances, is constitutionally unreasonable. It is not better that all felony suspects die than that they escape. Where the suspect poses no immediate threat to others, the harm resulting from failing to apprehend him does not justify the use of deadly force to do so."

The Duty to Warn

If a felon is fleeing, and an officer believes that the felon is a significant threat to the officer or others, the officer should shout a loud warning, "Stop or I'll

Table 3.2 Verbal Warning Requirements of Police Use of Force

Generic Police Force Continuum Levels	Force Description	Verbal Warning Requirement
Officer Command Presence	Police uniform, badge, or other visible identification displaying authority	None At this stage, there is no verbal interaction, only presence
Verbal Commands	Loud and clear verbal commands given by a police officer toward subject	Yes, if possible A warning is preferred in all states and U.S. territories
Soft Control Techniques	Escort holds, wrist locks, other physical techniques that do not require a large amount of force, OC pepper spray, CS gas	Yes, if possible A warning is preferred in all states and U.S. territories
Hard Control Techniques	Hard physical strikes, holds, tactical batons, PR-24, K-9, less-lethal devices (e.g., shotguns with bean-bag rounds), electro-muscular disruption devices (EMDs) (e.g., TASERs, flashbangs)	Yes, especially for passive aggressive and unlawful protestors in large groups of people A warning is preferred in all states and U.S. territories
Deadly Force	Firearm, any weapon used with lethal force	Yes

Created by Henry L. Cho—Cho Research & Consulting, LLC 2012.

© Cengage Learning 2014

shoot!" before firing. The warning should be loud enough that in addition to the fleeing felon, *everyone* who might be a witness to both the fleeing and the use of deadly force will hear the warning. It should be noted, however, that the "duty" to warn if possible is not legally required. Furthermore, circumstances may preclude an officer from providing such a warning, or the situation may be such that warning the fleeing felon actually presents an increased threat to the officer and others. Table 3.2 summarizes when a warning is preferred or required in using specific types of force.

Written Reports on Use of Force

An old law enforcement proverb says, "'If it's not in the report, it didn't happen'" and some officers intentionally leave out details, believing that the more detail they include in their report, the more a defense attorney can pick the incident apart. In actuality, "A well-written, detailed use-of-force report is the department and officer's best friend in post-incident reviews, whether in court or in internal administrative matters" (Means and Seidel 2009a, 29). Today, most defense attorneys do not ask for an internal affairs investigation but rather conduct a thorough investigation on their own (Means and Seidel 2009a). What commonly happens is several years after an incident, an officer is sued for excessive force. The plaintiff's case has been fully documented with evidence and statements gathered at the time of the incident. However, the defense side has no detailed use-of-force report, or possibly no report at all, and no internal investigation. The officer may not even remember the incident and is in about as bad a position as possible.

TECHNOLOGY IN POLICING

DOCUMENTING USE OF FORCE WITH BODY CAMERAS

They say a picture is worth a thousand words. In a case where an officer is accused of using excessive force, video technology is proving its worth by being able to document—far more effectively and definitively than the written report—whether the use of force was justified. Albuquerque, New Mexico, Police Chief Ray Schultz gives an example of such a case:

> On March 1 of [2011], we made it mandatory for our officers to wear a personal video camera.... Fifteen days after we went to the mandatory wear policy for the cameras, we had an in-custody death after use of an Electronic Control

Weapon. The officer's video camera captured the suspect apologizing for hitting the officer in the head with a crucifix. The suspect had gashed the officer's head open. Rescue personnel were at the scene taking care of the officer when the suspect fell over and had a medical episode. In this instance, the camera was able to exonerate the officers and show that they had done nothing wrong. ("Cameras." 2012, 20)

Source: "Cameras." In *How Are Innovations in Technology Transforming Policing?*, pp. 13–24, Washington, DC: Police Executive Research Forum, Critical Issues in Policing Series, January 2012.

The accuracy and completeness of force reports are extremely important. Officers need to be fluent in the language of force. Some practitioners suggest that agencies change the name *Use of Force Report* to *Subject Resistance Report*, focusing on the subject's actions (resistance) that led the officer to use force.

Use of Force and Community Policing

An integral part of the community policing philosophy is that the police must become *a part of* the community rather than stand *apart from* it. This places police in a somewhat difficult position as they try to become a part of the very entity over which they must exercise power and authority. Facing the potential dilemma of having to use force against the very citizens with whom they are seeking to form partnerships, this arrangement also presents a paradox—the ability of police to use force to secure a peaceful community.

 Use of force can be a serious obstacle to the community policing philosophy.

Adding to this challenge is the seemingly disproportionate use of force against minorities and those of lower socioeconomic status. Miller, Hess, and Orthmann (2011, 49) observe,

> Because police-enforcement efforts focus on common criminals, who are frequently poor, the most use of force by the police will be directed against this part of the population.

> Citizens in White suburban areas...may never see a police officer use force. The most negative experience they are likely to have with a police officer is receiving a traffic ticket.

> When people from these widely separated communities talk about the police, it seems as though they are speaking of entirely different entities. On the one

hand, police may be referred to as brutal, racist aggressors, whereas on the other hand, they may be described as professional, helpful, efficient protectors.

The public must be educated about the legitimate use of force required to maintain peaceful neighborhoods. They might also have input into policies on the use of force as well as incidents involving alleged excessive use of force.

LEGAL SEARCHES

The Fourth and Fifth Amendments also restrict police officers in when they can search and for what. As with an arrest, a search usually should be conducted with a *warrant*. Procedures for obtaining and executing search warrants vary by locality, but generally, search warrants may be issued if:

- ▶ The property was stolen or embezzled.
- ▶ Possession of the property is a crime.
- ▶ The property is in the possession of someone who intends to use it to commit a crime.
- ▶ The property was used in committing a crime.
- ▶ The items tend to show that a crime was committed or that a specific person committed the crime.

Three principal justifications have been established by the courts for the right to search.

> A search may be legally conducted if:
> - A search warrant has been issued.
> - Consent is given.
> - It is incidental to a lawful arrest.

Search Warrants

Ideally, all searches would be conducted with a search warrant. Typically, an officer or prosecutor drafts a search warrant explaining what is being searched for and where they expect to find such evidence, based on probable cause, and brings it before a judge. The judge reviews the warrant and either signs it to be active (if they believe probable cause exists) or denies it.

Wilson v. Arkansas (1995) held that the "knock and announce" requirements are part of the reasonableness inquiry and that officers must knock and announce *before* they enter. As with an arrest warrant, officers seeking to search premises under the authority of a search warrant can break down a door to gain admittance if they are denied entrance. Even with a search warrant, however, the search must be limited.

> A search conducted under the authority of a search warrant must be limited to the area specified in the warrant and for the items described in the warrant.

TECHNOLOGY IN POLICING

USING GPS TO TRACK SUSPECTS—*UNITED STATES V. JONES* (2012)

A 2011 Police Executive Research Forum (PERF) survey found that most of responding law enforcement agencies (83 percent) use global positioning system (GPS) technology to track the movements of criminal suspects ("PERF Survey Shows Widespread Use" 2012). A recent Supreme Court ruling makes it even more imperative that police understand the circumstances under which a warrant is required, lest their investigations lead to evidence that becomes inadmissible due to constitutional violations.

Such was the case in *United States v. Jones* (2012), in which federal investigators surreptitiously attached a GPS device to suspected drug trafficker Jones's vehicle as a way to monitor the vehicle's movements on public streets. Although a warrant had been obtained, the device was used beyond the approved scope of the warrant (the warrant authorized installation of the GPS in the District of Columbia and within 10 days, but agents installed it on the 11th day and in Maryland, and then proceeded to track the vehicle for 28 days). Investigators used the GPS data to have Jones indicted for drug trafficking conspiracy, and Jones was convicted in the district court, which ruled that the defendant held no expectation of privacy while driving on public streets. Jones appealed,

and the DC circuit court reversed, concluding that the warrantless use of the GPS device did, in fact, violate the Fourth Amendment. The U.S. Supreme Court affirmed, with Justice Scalia delivering the opinion of the Court:

> The Fourth Amendment provides in relevant part that "The right of the people to be secure in their persons, houses, papers, and effects, against unreasonable searches and seizures, shall not be violated." It is beyond dispute that a vehicle is an "effect" as that term is used in the Amendment.... We hold that the Government's installation of a GPS device on a target's vehicle, and its use of that device to monitor the vehicle's movements, constitutes a "search."
>
> It is important to be clear about what occurred in this case: The Government physically occupied private property for the purpose of obtaining information. We have no doubt that such a physical intrusion would have been considered a "search" within the meaning of the Fourth Amendment when it was adopted.

Source: *United States v. Jones*, 565 U.S. ___ (2012).

Exceptions to the Search Warrant Requirement

> Exceptions to the search warrant requirement are (1) execution of an arrest warrant, (2) frisks, (3) incident to arrest, (4) motor vehicles, (5) consent, (6) plain view or feel, (7) abandoned property, (8) open fields, (9) border searches, (10) inventory, and (11) exigent circumstances.

Arrest Warrant Execution Officers can search for a suspect in the suspect's home to execute an arrest warrant if they have probable cause to believe the suspect is there. This exception applies *only* to the suspect's home. They cannot conduct a search of any other location even though they have the arrest warrant. For other locations, a search warrant is generally required, although exceptions have been allowed by the courts. Officers *may* enter a third party's home to serve an arrest warrant without a search warrant under three circumstances: reason to believe the suspect lives at the third party's residence, consent, and exigency (Scarry 2009b). *Maryland v. Buie* (1990) established that officers may make a limited protective sweep of a home during an arrest if the circumstances warrant.

Frisks As previously discussed, *Terry v. Ohio* established that officers can conduct a patdown of an individual they have stopped if they believe the person is armed and dangerous. This is a protective search for weapons only. The Supreme Court has identified additional factors that could contribute to a reasonable suspicion that a suspect might be armed and dangerous and, thus, could justify a frisk for the officer's safety, including these:

- ▶ Violent nature of the suspected crime
- ▶ Visible bulges, holster, ammo, and so forth
- ▶ Menacing gestures or verbal threats
- ▶ Citizen tips of weapons or violence
- ▶ Information from bulletins or broadcasts
- ▶ Prior experience with the suspect
- ▶ Number of suspects and officers
- ▶ Size of suspects and officers
- ▶ Remote location of the encounter
- ▶ Obscure location lacking public visibility
- ▶ Late night or early morning hour
- ▶ Evasive conduct by the suspect
- ▶ Metallic clicking sounds
- ▶ Suspect's attempt to hide something
- ▶ Resistant or obstructive behavior
- ▶ Unprovoked flight on approach of police
- ▶ High-crime nature of the area
- ▶ Refusal to ID
- ▶ Suspicious clothing (such as a long coat on a warm day)
- ▶ The officer's training and experience (Rutledge 2007b, 38)

Such factors should be clearly stated in any report of the incident. These factors can also play a role in the other exceptions to the search warrant requirement, such as search incident to arrest.

Search Incident to Arrest *Chimel v. California* (1969) established that officers can search a person they have arrested for weapons and for evidence, but the search must be limited to the area within the arrested person's immediate control, sometimes referred to as the person's " wingspan." It is entirely reasonable for the arresting officer to search for and seize any evidence on the arrestee's person to prevent its concealment or destruction and the area from within which the arrestee might gain possession of a weapon or destructible evidence. The area within a person's control includes women's purses, chairs suspects are sitting on at the time of arrest, and the entire interior of an automobile if the person is in a car at the time of the arrest. (The trunk is not included in this exception.)

New York v. Belton (1981) provided broad justification to search a motor vehicle's interior after any passenger or recent passenger had been arrested: "When a policeman has made a lawful custodial arrest of the occupant of an automobile, he may, as a contemporaneous incident of that arrest, search the passenger compartment of that automobile." However, *Arizona v. Gant* (2009) has since narrowed the traditional bright-line rule under *Belton* and reduced law enforcement's authority to conduct warrantless vehicle searches incident to the arrest of one of its occupants. In this case, Tucson police officers arrested Rodney Gant in his driveway, after he had parked and exited his vehicle, for driving with a suspended license. After getting out of his car, Gant was arrested immediately, handcuffed, and placed into the back of a patrol car. Officers then returned to search his vehicle incident to the arrest and found a gun and a bag of cocaine in a jacket in the backseat. Gant was charged with and convicted of possession of narcotics for sale and possession of drug paraphernalia.

He appealed on the basis that the search of his vehicle incident to his arrest was a Fourth Amendment violation. The Arizona Supreme Court agreed that the warrantless search of Gant's vehicle was unreasonable because the scene was secure and out of Gant's reach, Gant was in custody and unable to pose a threat to the officers, and there was no reason to believe the car contained any evidence related to the crime for which Gant was arrested (driving with a suspended license). The U.S. Supreme Court affirmed this decision, rejecting a broad interpretation of *Belton* and replacing it with a two-prong test to articulate when police may conduct a warrantless search of a motor vehicle incident to a passenger's arrest:

1. If the arrestee is within reaching distance of the passenger compartment and can reach for a weapon or destroy evidence at the time of the search

2. If it is reasonable to believe the vehicle contains evidence of the offense of the arrest

Myers (2011, 25) explains, "*Gant* is an either/or proposition, meaning that only one prong of the test must be satisfied to be in compliance with the holding of the decision." The impact of *Gant* is that "a search incident to an arrest is no longer an entitlement" (Scarry 2009a, 20). And although *Gant* limits searches incident to arrest, it had no impact on the other exceptions, such as the consent exception, the exigent circumstances exception, the inventory exception, and the motor vehicle exception (Myers 2011).

Motor Vehicle Exception *Carroll v. United States* (1925) established that because automobiles are mobile, officers may search them without a warrant if they have probable cause to believe the car contains evidence of a crime. Known as the **Carroll doctrine**, this is the only exception allowing officers to search without a warrant even if they have time to get one. Probable cause alone supports the warrantless search. This exception includes the car's trunk, as well as suitcases within the trunk if the officers have probable cause to believe they contain evidence. This exception applies to all kinds of motorized vehicles, including mobile campers (*California v. Carney* 1985).

Consent The consent must be voluntary, and it must be given by a person who has the authority to do so. No threats can be used. The officers do not need to identify themselves as law enforcement officers. The consent can be withdrawn at any time during the search. Property owners cannot give consent to allow their tenants' apartments to be searched.

Carroll doctrine

Because automobiles are mobile, officers may search them without a warrant if they have probable cause to believe the car contains evidence of a crime; established in *Carroll v. United States* (1925).

Maryland State Police make a random vehicle check at the entrance ramp to the Baltimore Washington International Airport. Earlier in the day, police were stopping all vehicles entering the terminal area as part of a security check.

© Joe Giza/Reuters/CORBIS

If two occupants of a residence or apartment are present and one person consents but the other does not, no consent search can be conducted, as established by the Supreme Court's ruling in *Georgia v. Randolph* (2006): "A physically present co-occupant's stated refusal to permit entry renders warrantless entry and search unreasonable and invalid."

Plain View If officers are performing their duties and come across evidence or contraband that is easily seen—that is, it is in **plain view**—they may seize it. As the Supreme Court explained in *Katz v. United States* (1967), "The Fourth Amendment protects people, not places. What a person knowingly exposes to the public, even in his own home or office, is not a subject of Fourth Amendment protection." Officers can use a flashlight, provided they have a right to be at the location in the first place. The question of whether officers using binoculars or telescopic devices can seize evidence they discover under the plain view exception is controversial. Some courts have allowed it; others have not.

plain view

Term describing evidence that is not concealed, that is easily seen by officers while performing their legal duties.

Similar to not requiring an arrest warrant to allow officers to arrest someone they see committing a crime, a search warrant is not required for officers to seize contraband or other evidence that is in plain sight. Officers may not, however, act merely on reasonable suspicion and manipulate suspected evidence to determine its illegality. The evidence must be immediately recognizable as such.

In *Arizona v. Hicks* (1987), while conducting a lawful yet warrantless search of an apartment for a gunman immediately following a shooting, an officer noticed several pieces of expensive-looking stereo equipment that seemed out of place in the otherwise poorly furnished room. Suspecting the items were stolen, the officer recorded the equipment's serial numbers, moving some of the pieces in the process. A later check on the serial numbers revealed the items were indeed stolen. A search warrant was obtained, and the equipment was seized.

Suspect Hicks was charged with and convicted of robbery. Upon appeal, however, the Supreme Court reversed, ruling, "Moving the equipment... did constitute a 'search' separate and apart from the search for the shooter, victims, and weapons that was the lawful objective of [the officer's] entry into the apartment." The Court held that probable cause, not merely reasonable suspicion, to believe that items seen are contraband or evidence of criminal activity is required for the items to be seized under the "plain view" exception to the warrant requirement.

Plain Feel The *Minnesota v. Dickerson* case (1993) mentioned in the discussion of stop and frisk established the legitimacy of "plain feel" if probable cause is established. In this case, the Supreme Court ruled unanimously that a police officer may seize contraband discovered during a patdown search for weapons if it is immediately apparent to the officer that the object is an illegal substance. The officer may not, however, "manipulate" the object to determine whether it is actually contraband: "To this Court, there is no distinction as to which sensory perception the officer uses to conclude the material is contraband. An experienced officer may rely upon his sense of smell in DUI stops or in recognizing the smell of burning marijuana in an automobile. The sound of a shotgun being racked would clearly support certain reactions by an officer. The sense of touch, grounded in experience and training, is as reliable as perceptions drawn from other senses. 'Plain feel' therefore, is no different than plain view."

Despite this holding, the evidence against Dickerson was ruled inadmissible at trial because the police officer testified he had determined the lump contained cocaine only after squeezing, sliding, and manipulating it. The Court said such manipulation was a search, not a limited patdown for protection.

Abandoned Property *Abandoned property* refers to anything an individual throws away, including bags or purses discarded while being chased by the police. In *California v. Greenwood* (1988), the Supreme Court upheld the right of officers to search through an individual's garbage that had been placed on the curb. Some states, however, are more restrictive. New Jersey and Hawaii, for example, prohibit police from going through garbage without a warrant.

curtilage

A house and the area immediately surrounding it.

Open Fields The house and the area immediately surrounding it, called the **curtilage**, cannot be searched without a warrant. The curtilage is basically a person's yard and is protected by the Constitution. Open fields, however, are not. *Oliver v. United States* (1984) held that open fields are not protected by the Constitution and that, even if they are posted with "No Trespassing" signs, police can search them without a warrant. In this case, police were headed for a marijuana patch.

Border Searches In *United States v. Flores-Montano* (2004), Chief Justice Rehnquist stated, "Time and again, we have stated that searches made at the border, pursuant to the long-standing right of the sovereign to protect itself by stopping and examining persons and property crossing into this country, are reasonable simply by virtue of the fact that they occur at the border."

Routine searches are also allowed at places other than actual borders, under the **functional equivalent** doctrine. The functional equivalent doctrine refers to places other than actual borders where travelers frequently enter or exit the country, such as international airports.

functional equivalent

Refers to places other than actual borders where travelers frequently enter or exit the country, such as international airports.

Inventory Most police departments will automatically conduct an inventory of impounded vehicles. "Strictly speaking, an inventory search is not a targeted search for contraband or evidence but is an administrative procedure used to account for personal property found inside a vehicle that is impounded or parked and locked at the scene of arrest" (Rutledge 2010b, 69). An inventory search protects the owner's property, it protects the law enforcement agency against claims that property in its possession has been lost or stolen, and it uncovers any danger that may exist to police because of property in their possession, such as a bomb. Inventorying must be a standard department procedure for this exception to be used. In stressing the importance of police reports and testimony that clearly document that the impound inventory was conducted according to standard departmental policy, Rutledge (2011, 65) notes, "If you should encounter contraband or evidence while you are engaging in a routine inventory, it can be seized under the 'plain view' exception, and should then be admissible."

Exigent Circumstances **Exigent circumstances** occur when an emergency exists and there is no time for the officers to obtain a search warrant. That is, the evidence could be destroyed or gone by the time they obtained the warrant. This is a frequently used exception and the most difficult to justify. Once the right to search is established, officers should make certain they conduct the searches legally.

exigent circumstances

Conditions surrounding an emergency situation in which no time is available to secure an arrest or search warrant.

Situations Not Exempt from the Search Warrant Requirement

Despite these numerous situations in which the courts have upheld the exception to the search warrant requirement, other instances, such as luggage searches and the thermal imaging of a home from the outside, still do afford the individual an expectation of privacy and, as such, require a warrant based on probable cause.

Luggage Searches The Court's reasoning in *Dickerson* has been applied to searches of luggage. In *Bond v. United States* (2000), the Court extended its "look, but don't touch" policy when it ruled police officers can visually inspect travelers' luggage but not squeeze or physically manipulate a bag to determine whether it contains drugs or other contraband. To do so would constitute a warrantless search, thus requiring probable cause.

Thermal Imaging The use of technology that enables officers to see or listen into a subject's home has been heavily restricted by the law. Although wiretapping, electronic surveillance, and other sound-monitoring devices have been addressed by the court many times during the last few decades, a relatively recent issue involves the use of thermal imaging devices. In *Kyllo v. United*

States (2001), the Supreme Court ruled the use of technology-enhanced surveillance equipment is a "search" within the meaning of the Fourth Amendment if it reveals any information about the inside of a subject's home that police could otherwise know only by entering.

In this case, police were suspicious Kyllo was growing marijuana in his home, which was part of a triplex. Aware that indoor marijuana cultivation typically requires use of high-intensity lamps, agents used thermal imaging to monitor the amount of heat emanating from Kyllo's unit. The scan showed Kyllo's garage roof and a side wall were relatively hot compared with the rest of the home and noticeably warmer than the neighboring units. This evidence, combined with an offer made by Kyllo to a police informant to supply marijuana, was used to obtain a search warrant. The search netted 100 marijuana plants, weapons, and drug paraphernalia, and Kyllo was indicted on federal drug charges.

The lower court reasoned the thermal imaging technology did not reveal any intimate details about the activities inside the home, merely amorphous hot spots, and compared the level of intrusion to that involved in warrantless aerial surveillance. However, the majority of the Supreme Court disagreed, recalling the decision in *Katz v. United States* (1967) that individuals always retain the expectation of privacy in their homes and that police use of sense-enhancing technology constitutes a search that is presumptively unreasonable without a warrant.

PROCEDURES FOR LEGALLY SEARCHING PEOPLE

The least intrusive search is a patdown or frisk of a person's outer clothing as a protective search for weapons. In the case of arrest, the search is more thorough and includes a search for weapons. In a search incident to arrest, certain basic guidelines should be followed.

> When searching a person, officers should:
> - Handcuff the subject if warranted.
> - Be on guard, keeping themselves at arm's length from the person being searched.
> - Keep the subject facing away from the searching officer.
> - Be aware of where the service weapon is and keep it as far from the subject as possible.
> - Be systematic and thorough.
> - Keep the person under control, preferably off balance.
> - Use the back of the hand when patting down or searching the "private" areas of someone of the opposite sex (crotch area of both males and females; breast area of females).

The FBI and most police departments have a policy that individuals to be searched are handcuffed first for officer safety. If more than one suspect is to be searched, all except those currently being searched should be ordered to lie on the ground, facing away from the person being searched. If two officers are at the search scene, one conducts the search while the other officer stands guard.

PROCEDURES FOR LEGALLY SEARCHING BUILDINGS

Officers often must search buildings in response to either alarms or calls from citizens. Such searches are fraught with danger and require extreme caution.

Chimel v. California (1969) established that officers entering a structure to make a lawful arrest could look into areas within the arrestee's immediate control to deter the arrestee from obtaining a weapon or destroying evidence. In *Maryland v. Buie* (1990), the Supreme Court allowed the arresting officers to make a protective sweep of the immediately adjoining spaces where a potential assailant might be concealed. Such a *Buie* sweep does not require any suspicion that an assailant is present, but must be limited to immediately adjoining spaces, not through the entire premises.

Officers arriving at a building to search it should arrive as quietly as possible to preserve the element of surprise. To make certain no one escapes from within the building, observation posts should be set up and maintained while the search is being conducted. A thorough search depends on having enough officers to visually contain the building as well as to thoroughly and systematically search the inside.

The building search itself must be carefully planned. If time permits, the building's owner should be contacted to learn as much as possible about its layout and possible hiding places. The number of floors, including basements and attics, should be determined. Usually one door is selected as the entry and exit door for the search team. In some instances, however, officers enter the front and back of the building simultaneously.

Once inside the building, all officers must know what each is doing. Each should have a clear assignment to carry out. A system of communication should be established to maintain contact. Should a suspect be located, assistance should be called for immediately. The search should continue, however, as more than one suspect might be in the building.

As officers search the building, they should use proven techniques. For example, when entering a room or a building, they should look into the structure from both sides of the doorway without exposing any more of the body than necessary. They should always keep low and move rapidly. If the building is dark, they should use a flashlight without becoming a target.

One of the most dangerous moments in searching a building occurs when officers come to a *corner*. An armed suspect could be around that corner. In such instances, mirrors and periscopes can be invaluable.

When searching a building, officers should:
- Get as much information as possible before starting the search.
- Plan carefully: Set up an entry and exit point, learn the interior layout, and assign personnel to cover each area.
- Arrive quickly and quietly.
- Set up containment positions around the building.
- Make sure enough personnel are available.
- Make use of solid cover during the search.
- Use proper search techniques.

An aerial view of four customs officers and a K-9 checking cargo for bombs and other threats. A dog frequently lessens the dangers associated with such searches.

© Dennis Mac Donald/PhotoEdit

Officers also should take safety precautions when searching to avoid coming into contact with material that is contaminated and could result in acquiring hepatitis B or HIV. The risk factor in this area is ever increasing. Protecting against such hazards is discussed in-depth in Chapter 13.

USING K-9S IN SEARCHES

Dogs (K-9s) can be invaluable in conducting searches for suspects, evidence, drugs, and bombs. Numerous cases have addressed whether the use of detector dogs constitutes a search, with the court generally ruling that dog sniffs of inanimate items or in public locations are *not* searches. For example, in *United States v. Place* (1983), the Supreme Court held that a dog sniff of lawfully detained luggage in a public place does not constitute a search. In *City of Indianapolis v. Edmond* (2000), the Court extended this principle to the dog sniff of the exterior of a vehicle to which police have legitimate access. A dog sniff of the exterior of a warehouse or garage from a public location is not usually considered a search. The Supreme Court has never directly addressed the issue, but lower court cases generally consider a dog sniff of a person to be a search. Because state courts may find dog sniffs are searches under their own constitutions, officers should consult their state's laws related to using a dog to sniff items, locations, or people for the presence of contraband.

Despite the many benefits gained by using K-9s, officers must also be aware of some of the drawbacks and limitations. Some days a dog may not perform well, missing drugs or contraband.

THE EXCLUSIONARY RULE AND ITS EXCEPTIONS

As you have seen, the Fourth Amendment plays a prominent role in police operations with regard to searches and seizures. The authority of law enforcement to arrest and search individuals is not unlimited, and violating the Fourth Amendment through unlawful searches or seizures can have serious consequences. In addition to an officer facing internal sanctions as well as civil and criminal liability for procedural misconduct, there exists the very real consequence that crucial evidence will be excluded from court via the exclusionary rule. The exclusionary rule is not defined in the Constitution but, rather, is judge-made case law promulgated by the Supreme Court and designed to safeguard Fourth Amendment rights by deterring police misconduct (i.e., illegal searches and seizures).

> The **exclusionary rule** established that the courts cannot accept evidence obtained in illegal searches and seizures, regardless of how relevant the evidence is to the case (*Weeks v. United States* 1914).

exclusionary rule

Courts cannot accept evidence obtained in illegal searches and seizures, regardless of how relevant the evidence is to the case (*Weeks v. United States* 1914).

fruit of the poisonous tree doctrine

Evidence obtained as the result of an earlier illegality (e.g., an unconstitutional search or seizure) is inadmissible as evidence and must be excluded from trial.

This principle is also referred to as the **fruit of the poisonous tree doctrine**, meaning if the initial search or seizure is tainted because it is unconstitutional (the "poisonous tree"), anything that the subsequent search produces as evidence (the "fruit") will also be tainted and will be inadmissible in court.

Weeks v. United States applied only to federal cases. Nearly a half century later, *Mapp v. Ohio* (1961) established that the exclusionary rule applies to all state criminal proceedings under the Due Process Clause of the Fourteenth Amendment. Verbal evidence, such as incriminating statements obtained in the immediate aftermath of an illegal arrest, may also be barred from the jury's consideration. However, any evidence discovered during a search incident to a lawful arrest (i.e., one supported by probable cause) is presumed legally obtained and, thus, is not suppressible in most state courts.

The Court has recognized several exceptions to the exclusionary rule: the inevitable discovery doctrine, existence of a valid independent source, and good faith. Without going into great detail on the cases that led to these exceptions, the following is a brief summary of how these legal decisions have affected police operations.

Inevitable Discovery Doctrine

This exception was the result of two cases, *Brewer v. Williams* (1977) and *Nix v. Williams* (1984), in which murder suspect Williams made incriminating statements—obtained during an unconstitutional interrogation in which his right to counsel was violated—that led to the discovery of the victim's body. Although the defendant was convicted, the appellate court reversed and held that Williams's statements should not have been admissible during the original trial. The Supreme Court affirmed and granted Williams another trial in which his damaging statements were not allowed as evidence. The Court did, however, allow the victim's body to be introduced as evidence at the second trial because, at the same time Williams was providing information to officers

inevitable discovery doctrine

Created as an exception to the exclusionary rule to allow evidence to be admissible even if seized in violation of the Fourth Amendment when it can be shown that the evidence would have inevitably been found through lawful means.

about the location of the body, members of an independent search party was closing in on that very location and, the Court reasoned, would have inevitably discovered the evidence on their own. Thus, the **inevitable discovery doctrine** was created as an exception to the exclusionary rule to allow evidence to be admissible even if seized in violation of the Fourth Amendment when it can be shown that the evidence would have inevitably been found through lawful means. Williams was convicted of murder at the second trial.

Valid Independent Source

A second exception to the exclusionary rule concerns evidence obtained from a valid, independent source. One of the precedent cases for this exception is *Segura v. United States* (1984), in which evidence discovered during an illegal entry into an apartment was excluded, but evidence later found in the same apartment while a search with a warrant was being executed was admissible because the warrant was obtained with information completely unconnected with the illegal entry (Harr, Hess, and Orthmann 2012). In a second case, *Murray v. United States* (1988), the Court held that evidence initially seen during an illegal search but later recovered under a valid warrant is admissible. In *Murray*, the police initially entered a residence without a warrant but returned later with a valid warrant that had been obtained without using what they had seen during the initial entry to support the probable cause in the warrant.

Technology has brought new challenges to the interpretation of the independent source doctrine, including how the courts view searches of items containing digital content: "Eventually the U.S. Supreme Court will have to weigh in and settle the question of whether the Fourth Amendment applies differently to digital containers than to others" (Rutledge 2010a, 136). Because cell phones are included in the "digital container" category, it is suggested that until the Court rules on this issue, the "prudent move" for law enforcement officers is to keep the "independent source" doctrine in mind and try to establish other ways to justify cell phone searches in addition to searching incident to arrest (Rutledge 2010a).

Good Faith

good faith

Belief that one's actions are just and legal.

If officers are not aware that they are violating someone's constitutional rights, they are said to be acting in **good faith**, and the exclusionary rule may not apply: "The good faith exception often comes into play when the government is executing arrest or search warrants. If such warrants are later found to be invalid… the evidence obtained while the warrants are executed is still admissible because the officers were acting in 'good faith'" (Harr, Hess, and Orthmann 2012, 222). Objectively reasonable good faith circumstances that may prevent suppression and liability often occur in the following instances: search warrants, arrest warrants, misidentification, consent, and invalid statutes (Rutledge 2007a).

Massachusetts v. Sheppard (1984) established that if police were relying on a search warrant that had been approved by a magistrate but was later declared invalid, any evidence seized during that search would be admissible at trial. In a similar case, *United States v. Leon* (1984), the Court held, "Once the warrant issues, there is literally nothing more the policeman can do in seeking to comply with the law. Penalizing the officer for the magistrate's error, rather than his own, cannot logically contribute to the deterrence of Fourth Amendment violations."

In *Arizona v. Evans* (1995), the Supreme Court extended this logic to include information coming through "official channels," ruling that if officers reasonably rely on such information, and if the information turns out to be erroneous, any evidence developed from this information need not be suppressed because the officers themselves were not intentionally engaged in misconduct (Rutledge 2009).

SUMMARY

While conducting police operations involving arrests and searches, law enforcement officers must maintain a balance between "freedom to" and "freedom from." Guarantees against unlawful arrests and searches are found in the Fourth and Fifth Amendments to the U.S. Constitution.

A stop-and-frisk situation, also called a *Terry* stop, is one in which law enforcement officers briefly detain (stop) a suspicious person for questioning (this is *not* an arrest), and, *if* the officers suspect the person is armed, they are allowed to pat (frisk) the person's outer clothing (this *is* a limited search for weapons).

An arrest is the official taking of a person to answer criminal charges. This involves at least temporarily depriving the person of liberty and may involve the use of force. An arrest can legally be made with an arrest warrant or without an arrest warrant (1) for any offense (felony or misdemeanor) committed in an officer's presence, (2) when officers have probable cause to believe a person has committed a felony and no time is available to obtain a warrant, or (3) for specifically enumerated misdemeanors, such as shoplifting in some jurisdictions. Probable cause refers to a situation where it is more likely than not that a crime has been committed by the person whom a law enforcement officer seeks to arrest. An officer's probable cause to conduct an arrest depends on what the officer knew *before* taking action.

Skill in making arrests is critical because arrest involves fundamental rights to personal liberty and privacy; the law of arrest is strict and technical; arrest is often the first step in criminal proceedings; illegal arrests may taint crucial evidence of guilt; police performance quality is judged by arrests; arrests may lead to civil suits or criminal prosecution of officers; and arrests may endanger officers' lives.

To make lawful arrests, officers must know both substantive and procedural law. Substantive law deals with content, or what behaviors are considered crimes. Procedural law deals with process, or how the law is applied.

In a typical arrest situation, officers should announce the arrest and the reason for it, handcuff the person if warranted, and then search the person arrested for weapons and evidence. The person should be given the *Miranda* warning if any questions are to be asked. Use of force when making an arrest is always an issue. *Graham v. Connor* (1989) established a three-prong test for use of force: (1) the severity of the crime, (2) whether the suspect poses an immediate threat to the safety of law enforcement officers or others, and (3) whether the suspect is actively resisting arrest or attempting to evade arrest by flight. Keep in mind the following guidelines for use of force when making an arrest: If there is no resistance, no force should be used. If resistance occurs, officers may use as much force as is reasonable to gain control. If a threat to an officer's life exists, the use of deadly force is authorized in most departments. Handcuffing may be considered a use of force. Whether an arrested person should automatically be handcuffed while being transported is controversial. Officer discretion may be advisable.

Less-lethal weapons available for use with violent, combative suspects include tear gas and other chemical irritant sprays, impact weapons, conducted energy devices (CEDs) such as the TASER, foams, nets, and K-9s. Use of force can be a serious obstacle to the community policing philosophy.

A search may be legally conducted if a search warrant has been issued, consent is given, or it is incidental to a lawful arrest. A search conducted under the authority of a search warrant must be limited to the area specified in the warrant and for the items described in the warrant. Exceptions to the search warrant requirement are (1) execution of an arrest warrant, (2) frisks, (3) incident to arrest, (4) motor vehicles, (5) consent, (6) plain view/feel, (7) abandoned property, (8) open fields, (9) border searches, (10) inventory, and (11) exigent circumstances.

When searching a person, officers should handcuff the subject if warranted; be on guard, keeping themselves at arm's length from the person being searched; keep the subject facing away from the searching officer; be aware of where the service weapon is and keep it as far from the subject as possible; be systematic and thorough; keep the person under control, preferably off balance; and use the back of the hand when patting down or searching the private areas of individuals of the opposite sex (crotch area of both males and females; breast area of females).

When searching a building, officers should get as much information as possible before starting the search; plan carefully, including setting up an entry/exit point, learning the interior layout, and assigning personnel to cover each area; arrive quickly and quietly; set up containment positions around the building; make sure enough personnel are available; make use of solid cover during the search; and use proper search techniques.

The exclusionary rule established that the courts cannot accept evidence obtained in illegal searches and seizures, regardless of how relevant the evidence is to the case (*Weeks v. United States* 1914).

APPLICATION

You are a Bigtown patrol officer. You notice that transporting and booking a person arrested as a misdemeanant takes from one to three hours. This seems counterproductive because you are out of service during that time, not available for other calls, and the arrested person will usually be released from jail in a short time, often even before you finish the reports. You feel that issuing a citation to the person without formal procedures of arrest and booking would more than serve the purpose and would release you for more important duties. You approach your sergeant and pose your recommendations to her. She asks you to "put it in writing."

INSTRUCTIONS

Use the form in the Appendix at the end of this book to make your policy and procedure. The policy will include the following:

The policy of the Bigtown Police Department for releasing people from custody who have been arrested for a misdemeanor will change effective (date). Any person cited for a misdemeanor whom the officer feels will appear in court as promised may be given a written citation by the officer.

When a Citation May Be Issued. Give several circumstances or conditions that may exist whereby officers could issue a citation to such a person who also has no previous criminal record.

Justifications for Not Issuing a Citation. In completing this policy, you should insert what form is to be used when issuing a citation, what reports are necessary, and also that issuing a citation means suspects should be entered in the arrest log and assigned a log number and a case number. You should indicate what needs to appear in the citation notification form.

AN EXERCISE IN CRITICAL THINKING

At 7:40 a.m. on June 27, Officer Steve Sjerven was in the crossover preparing to turn south on Highway 65 to help the driver of an apparently disabled car. As he waited to turn, he saw a red pickup truck heading south on Highway 65 and made eye contact with the driver and sole occupant of the truck. The driver abruptly turned the truck right onto Tower Systems Road and appeared to immediately disappear. Not seeing the pickup truck or any dust that might be expected from a truck traveling down a gravel road, the officer concluded that the truck must have immediately pulled into a driveway. As the officer pulled up to assist the disabled car, he saw the pickup emerge and turn south onto Highway 65—a very short time after having turned onto Tower Systems Road. Inferring that the driver had turned off Highway 65 to avoid him, the officer motioned the driver of the pickup to stop. The driver did so, identified himself as Mark Johnson, and admitted that his license had been revoked.

1. As the U.S. Supreme Court's decisions require only that an officer have a "particular and objective basis for suspecting the particular person stopped of criminal activity," what is your judgment of Officer Sjerven's approach?

   a. Because Johnson's action can be explained as consistent with lawful activities, Officer Sjerven should not stop him.

   b. The officer's suspicion, though nothing more than a hunch, was later verified by the stop.

   c. Sjerven stopped Johnson on mere whim, caprice, or idle curiosity, and so should be disciplined for poor judgment in operational skills.

   d. Inferences and deductions might well elude an untrained person, but a trained police officer is entitled to draw inferences on the basis of "all of the circumstances."

   e. If the observed facts are consistent with innocent activity, then the stop is invalid.

DISCUSSION QUESTIONS

1. The Fifth Amendment provides that no person shall be "deprived of life, liberty, or property without due process of law." What does this really mean? Explain your answer as if you were giving a lecture to a high school class.

2. Substantive law is concerned with the content of the law. Criminal law defines what behaviors are illegal and imposes punishments for engaging in them. Name five types of behavior the law does not tolerate.

3. When officers make an arrest without a warrant, they act at their own peril and are allowed no margin of error. Why is this statement written so stringently?

4. Describe a good example of "reasonable grounds of suspicion."

5. What search situations are officers likely to find themselves in? How can they best prepare themselves?

6. Discuss how you felt when you read about the Abner Louima case. Do you think this incident could have been prevented?

7. Do you feel that given the awesome power police hold, they can ever be true partners with citizens in community policing?

GALE EMERGENCY SERVICES DATABASE ASSIGNMENTS

▶ Use the Gale Emergency Services database (available for separate purchase) to answer the Discussion Questions as appropriate.

▶ Use the Gale Emergency Services database to research recent incidents where *excessive force* was alleged against the police. Outline the characteristics that bring on alleged excessive force situations. Be prepared to share your outline with the class.

▶ Use the Gale Emergency Services database to find and outline one of the following articles:

- "Flight as Justification for Seizure: Supreme Court Ruling" by Michael E. Brooks
- "Reviewing Use of Force: A Systematic Approach" by Sam W. Lathrop
- "Using Drug Detection Dogs: An Update" by Jayme S. Walker
- "Deadly Force: A 20-Year Study of Fatal Encounters" by Larry C. Brubaker

- "U.S. Land Border Search Authority" by M. Wesley Clark
- "Inferring Probable Cause: Obtaining a Search Warrant for a Suspect's Home without Direct Information That Evidence Is Inside" by Edward Hendrie
- "Consent Searches: Factors Courts Consider in Determining Voluntariness" by Jayme Walker Holcomb
- "Obtaining Written Consent to Search" by Jayme Walker Holcomb
- "Consent Searches Scope" by Jayme Walker Holcomb
- "Use-of-Force Policies and Training: A Reasoned Approach" by Thomas D. Petrowski
- "Use-of-Force Policies and Training: A Reasoned Approach (Part Two)" by Thomas D. Petrowski
- "Force Continuums: A Liability to Law Enforcement?" by George T. Williams

REFERENCES

"Cameras." 2012 (January). In *How Are Innovations in Technology Transforming Policing?*, pp. 13–24. Washington, DC: Police Executive Research Forum, Critical Issues in Policing Series.

Collins, John M. 2007. "Recent Decision in *Brendlin v. California* Provides Good 'Law Review' on Seizures of Persons." *The Police Chief* (September): 10–11.

Commission on Accreditation of Law Enforcement Agencies (CALEA). 2012. *Standards for Law Enforcement Agencies.* 5th ed. Fairfax, VA: Author.

Crime in the United States, 2010. 2011 (September). Washington, DC: Federal Bureau of Investigation. Accessed February 4, 2012. http://www.fbi.gov/about-us/cjis/ucr/crime-in-the-u.s/2010/crime-in-the-u.s.-2010.

del Carmen, Rolando V. 2010. *Criminal Procedure: Law and Practice.* 7th ed. Belmont, CA: Wadsworth.

Eith, Christine, and Matthew R. Durose. 2011 (October). *Contacts between Police and the Public, 2008.* Washington, DC: Bureau of Justice Statistics. (NCJ 234599)

Fridell, Lorie, Steve Ijames, and Michael Berkow. 2011. "Taking the Straw Man to the Ground: Arguments in Support of the Linear Use-of-Force Continuum." *The Police Chief* (December): 20–25.

Harr, J. Scott, Kären M. Hess, and Christine H. Orthmann. 2012. *Constitutional Law and the Criminal Justice System.* 5th ed. Belmont, CA: Wadsworth Cengage.

Heal, Sid, Viktor Bovbjerg, and John Kenny. 2009. "Voodoo Science and Non-Lethal Weapons." *Tactical Response* (January/February): 24–28.

Hilton, Alicia M. 2007. "Clearing Up Knock-and-Announce Confusion." *Police* (August): 38–43.

Means, Randy, and Greg Seidel. 2009a. "Keys to Winning with the Use of Force: Avoiding Peripheral Poisonings." *Law and Order* (March): 28–30.

Means, Randy, and Greg Seidel. 2009b. "Maintaining Proportionality and Managing Force Escalations." *Law and Order* (February): 31–32.

Means, Randy, and Greg Seidel. 2010. "Keys to Winning with Use of Force: A Four-Step Plan." *Tactical Response* (March–April): 18–20.

Miller, Christa. 2008. "The Art of Verbal Judo." *Law Enforcement Technology* (August): 62–72.

Miller, Linda S., Kären M. Hess, and Christine H. Orthmann. 2011. *Community Policing: Partnerships for Problem Solving.* 6th ed. Clifton Park, NY: Delmar Cengage.

Myers, Kenneth A. 2011. "Searches of Motor Vehicles Incident to Arrest in a Post-*Gant* World." *FBI Law Enforcement Bulletin* (April): 24–32.

Nance, Richard, and David Hallford. 2008. "Cuffing with Useful Force." *Police* (May): 55–57.

Plitt, Emory A. 2008. "Test Your 'Excessive Force' I.Q." *PoliceOne News* (February 28). Accessed February 4, 2012. http://www.policeone.com/legal/articles/1666240-Test-Your-Excessive-Force-I-Q/.

"PERF Survey Shows Widespread Use of Many Technologies in Policing." 2012 (January). In *How Are Innovations in Technology Transforming Policing?*, pp. 1–3. Washington, DC: Police Executive Research Forum, Critical Issues in Policing Series.

Rayburn, Michael T. 2011. "Five Fundamentals of Making an Arrest." *Police* (April): 58–62.

Rutledge, Devallis. 2007a. "The 'Good Faith' Doctrine." *Police* (June): 70–71.

Rutledge, Devallis. 2007b. "How to Justify Officer Safety Searches." *Police* (October): 36–40.

Rutledge, Devallis. 2008. "Fourth Amendment Supremacy." *Police* (June): 66–70.

Rutledge, Devallis. 2009. "Official Misinformation." *Police* (March): 78–81.

Rutledge, Devallis. 2010a. "The 'Independent Source' Doctrine." *Police* (July): 134–37.

Rutledge, Devallis. 2010b. "Vehicle Searches: Where and When?" *Police* (December): 66–69.

Rutledge, Devallis. 2011a. "Impound Inventory." *Police* (April): 64–65.

Rutledge, Devallis. 2011b. "Probable Cause and Reasonable Suspicion." *Police* (June): 68–69.

Scarry, Laura L. 2009a. "The Searchers." *Law Officer Magazine* (June): 20–22.

Scarry, Laura L. 2009b. "Someone Else's Home: When an Arrest Warrant Isn't Enough." *Law Officer Magazine* (March): 20–24.

Scoville, Dean. 2009. "Do We Still Need Batons?" *Police* (March): 50–54.

Smith, Michael R., Robert J. Kaminski, Geoffrey P. Alpert, Lorie A. Fridell, John MacDonald, and Bruce Kubu. 2010 (July). *A Multi-Method Evaluation of Police Use of Force Outcomes: Final Report to the National Institute of Justice*. Washington, DC: National Criminal Justice Reference Service. (NCJ 231176)

Spector, Elliot B. 2008. "U.S. Supreme Court Diminishes Effect of Arrests That Violate State Procedural Rules." *The Police Chief* (November): 12–13.

Study of Deaths Following Electro Muscular Disruption: Interim Report. 2008 (June). Washington, DC: National Institute of Justice.

CASES CITED

Alabama v. White, 496 U.S. 325 (1990)

Arizona v. Evans, 514 U.S. 1 (1995)

Arizona v. Gant, 556 U.S. 332 (2009)

Arizona v. Hicks, 480 U.S. 321 (1987)

Atwater v. Lago Vista, 532 U.S. 318 (2001)

Bond v. United States, 529 U.S. 334 (2000)

Brendlin v. California, 551 U.S. 249 (2007)

Brewer v. Williams, 430 U.S. 387 (1977)

Brinegar v. United States, 338 U.S. 160 (1949)

California v. Carney, 471 U.S. 386 (1985)

California v. Greenwood, 486 U.S. 35 (1988)

Carroll v. United States, 267 U.S. 132 (1925)

Chimel v. California, 395 U.S. 752 (1969)

City of Indianapolis v. Edmond, 531 U.S. 32 (2000)

Florida v. Bostick, 501 U.S. 429 (1991)

Georgia v. Randolph, 547 U.S. 103 (2006)

Graham v. Connor, 490 U.S. 386 (1989)

Hiibel v. Sixth Judicial District Court of Nevada, Humboldt County, 542 U.S. 177 (2004)

Hudson v. Michigan, 547 U.S. 586 (2006)

Illinois v. Gates, 462 U.S. 213 (1983)

Illinois v. Wardlow, 528 U.S. 119 (2000)

Katz v. United States, 389 U.S. 347 (1967)

Kaupp v. Texas, 538 U.S. 626 (2003)

Kyllo v. United States, 553 U.S. 27 (2001)

Mapp v. Ohio, 367 U.S. 643 (1961)

Maryland v. Buie, 494 U.S. 325 (1990)

Massachusetts v. Sheppard, 468 U.S. 981 (1984)

Minnesota v. Dickerson, 508 U.S. 336 (1993)

Miranda v. Arizona, 384 U.S. 436 (1966)

Murray v. United States, 487 U.S. 533 (1988)

New York v. Belton, 453 U.S. 454 (1981)

Nix v. Williams, 467 U.S. 431 (1984)

Oliver v. United States, 466 U.S. 170 (1984)

Scott v. Harris, 550 U.S. 372 (2007)

Segura v. United States, 468 U.S. 796 (1984)

Semayne's Case, 5 Coke, 918 (1603)

Tennessee v. Garner, 471 U.S. 1 (1985)

Terry v. Ohio, 392 U.S. 1 (1968)

United States v. Banks, 540 U.S. 31 (2003)

United States v. Flores-Montano, 541 U.S. 149 (2004)

United States v. Jones, 565 U.S. _____ (2012)

United States v. Leon, 468 U.S. 897 (1984)
United States v. Place, 462 U.S. 696 (1983)
United States v. Ramirez, 523 U.S. 65 (1998)
United States v. Sokolow, 490 U.S. 1 (1989)

Virginia v. Moore, 553 U.S. 164 (2008)
Weeks v. United States, 232 U.S. 383 (1914)
Wilson v. Arkansas, 514 U.S. 927 (1995)

This available CourseMate has an interactive eBook and interactive learning tools, including flash cards, quizzes, and more. To learn more about this resource and access free demo CourseMate resources, go to www.cengagebrain.com, and search for this book. To access CourseMate materials that you have purchased, go to login.cengagebrain.com.

Getting the Job Done: Basic Police Operations

Most police operations books begin and end in this section. But a law enforcement officer must never forget that the actual operations themselves are only half the job.

To perform police operations professionally, officers must always keep in mind the content of the first section. They must consider the context in which they operate—the citizens they serve as well as the colleagues with whom they work. Law enforcement officers are an integral part of this context, not a separate entity. They do not operate in a vacuum. Officers must use effective communication skills, and they must do so while staying within the law.

With this solid foundation, now focus on the actual operations law enforcement officers perform. At the heart of police operations is patrol, often called the backbone of the police organization (Chapter 4). Activities conducted during patrol often include other functions performed by

SECTION II

Getting the Job Done: Basic Police Operations

officers, such as traffic enforcement (Chapter 5); responding to crime, disorder, and quality-of-life issues (Chapter 6); deterring violence (Chapter 7); dealing with emergencies (Chapter 8); and securing our homeland (Chapter 9). The next section focuses on specialized police operations.

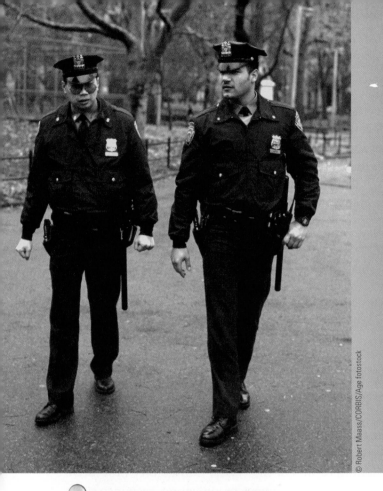
© Robert Maass/CORBIS/Age fotostock

CHAPTER 4

Patrol:
The Backbone of Police Operations

DO YOU KNOW . . .

- How patrol is typically described?
- What functions patrol typically performs?
- How the majority of patrol time is spent?
- How crowds can be classified?
- What methods of patrol have been used and the advantages and disadvantages of each?
- What type of patrol has the most mobility and flexibility and is usually the most cost effective?
- What the Kansas City Preventive Patrol Experiment found?
- What most affects the possibility of on-scene arrests?
- What two basic causes account for delays in calling for service?
- What basic change in perspective problem-oriented policing requires?
- What the SARA problem-solving process consists of?

CAN YOU DEFINE?

differential police response
  strategies
directed patrol
discovery crimes
impact evaluation
involvement crimes
preventive patrol
problem-oriented policing
  (POP)
process evaluation
proportionate assignment
proximate
random patrol
response time
routine patrol
saturation patrol
split-force patrol

INTRODUCTION

U sually the most complex, burdensome, and dangerous aspects of police service are performed by uniformed patrol officers. The work may be carried out in an atmosphere emotionally charged with hostility—an environment that breeds distrust and danger—and in situations that require officers to be clergy, psychologists, therapists, or many other types of professionals who deal with human problems.

 Patrol service has been described as the backbone of the police department.

Theoretically, patrol officers are the most valuable people in the organization. To a certain extent, all activity radiates from them. But such a concept is not totally supported by such measures as salary, working conditions, and authority.

This chapter begins with a brief overview of the importance of patrol and its historical organizational contradiction. This is followed by a look at the typical functions performed by patrol and the various methods of patrol, including foot, automobile, motorcycle, bicycle, Segway, mounted, air, water, special-terrain, K-9–assisted, and combined patrol. Next, patrol techniques and strategies are examined, including results of the classic Kansas City Preventive Patrol Experiment, area and shift assignment modification, response time, differential police response strategies, and use of split-force patrol, saturation patrol, and directed patrol. Then attention shifts to the critical role problem solving plays in patrol effectiveness. The chapter concludes with a discussion of patrol and community policing.

THE IMPORTANCE AND "PLACE" OF PATROL IN POLICING

"Officers working the beat are the most important members of any police organization" (Solar 2009). However, the identity and importance of patrol has long suffered from an organizational contradiction, with the most crucial people on the law enforcement team being lowest on the totem pole: "If patrol personnel are skeptical of their place in the law enforcement hierarchy, it is understandable. For while many a department still pays lip service to patrol constituting the backbone of law enforcement, empirical observations may lead one to conclude otherwise. For larger agencies, it is commonly accepted that the road to promotion is not via patrol, but through coveted positions along the administrative or investigative path" (Scoville 2008, 42).

A police department's ability to carry out its mission of providing public service and controlling crime depends greatly on the uniformed patrol officers' capabilities because these are the officers most likely to come in contact with the average citizen: "The most difficult, dangerous, complex job in the police department is the patrol officer that answers calls every day.

Everybody else is support to that patrol person" (Lansdowne 2007, 1). And although patrol officers are arguably a department's most valuable resource, they are often regarded as disposable: "Civilians and even some law enforcement brass have a tendency to judge the value of an officer by his or her rank" (Griffith 2008, 10).

Most of the country's police agencies are small, employing fewer than 20 officers. These departments assign almost all the officers to patrol, delegating additional special duties as needed. In a police agency with only one officer, that officer performs all roles from chief to records clerk, with the majority of the time spent serving a patrol function.

PATROL FUNCTIONS

41.1

CALEA Standard 41.1 states, "Patrol is considered to be a primary law enforcement function and embraces much more than the act of patrolling. It is defined as a generalized function in which officers may be engaged in a variety of activities which can range from traditional response to requests for service to alternate strategies for the delivery of police services."

Source: Commission on Accreditation of Law Enforcement Agencies (CALEA). 2012. *Standards for Law Enforcement Agencies.* 5th ed. Fairfax, VA: Author.

Every patrol division performs different tasks, although some are common to all. Patrol duties are not usually described in great detail, except when officers answer specific calls for service. "Routine" patrol means different things to individual officers, supervisors, and departments. For example, one officer on routine patrol may feel that if nothing is "happening," time can best be spent talking to citizens and getting to know the patrol areas. Another officer might feel the time should be spent looking into suspected gang activity. A third officer might feel this is the time to catch up on current events by reading the newspaper.

Among the important patrol functions are:
- Deterring or preventing crime and disorder
- Responding to crime calls for service
- Responding to noncrime calls for service
- Controlling traffic
- Assisting at the scene of a crime
- Conducting preliminary investigations
- Gathering intelligence
- Making arrests
- Patrolling public gatherings and special events
- Assisting at the scene of a fire and other medical calls
- Providing community service and general peacekeeping activities
- Partnering with others to solve problems related to crime and disorder

The patrol response to crime calls for service is the focus of Chapter 6. The following section of this chapter, however, will discuss the remaining basic functions of patrol, aside from the vital task of responding to criminal actions.

Deterring or Preventing Crime and Disorder

The police presence is intended to *deter crime and disorder* as well as give citizens a feeling of being protected. Officers on patrol can help reduce racial tensions in large-city ghettos; provide help to drunks, the mentally ill, street people, stranded motorists, or patrons of prostitution who may be at risk of robbery; disperse a group of juveniles who are lingering in parking lots looking to break into cars; and otherwise intervene to prevent or deter situations that contribute to crime and victimization. This general purpose, to thwart or deter crime and civil disorder through an ongoing police presence or *potential* presence, is the essence of **preventive patrol** and describes the function that arguably consumes the bulk of a patrol officer's time.

preventive patrol

Efforts to thwart or deter crime and civil disorder through an ongoing police presence or potential presence.

Noncrime Calls for Service

Responding to noncrime calls for service is an important function of patrol officers. Such calls are also known as civil complaints and may involve missing persons, damaged property, lost and found property, missing and stray animals, escort services, people locked out, disturbances, licensing, legal questions, mediating custody exchanges for people who are divorced or separated, inspections, city ordinance violations (e.g., open burning of leaves, noise complaints, etc.), and serving civil papers, including but not limited to protection orders, harassment orders, and court subpoenas.

Television programs have made the *missing persons* function of the police department seem routine. In actuality, however, unless foul play is suspected or the person missing is a juvenile, mentally handicapped, or in need of medication, the police often do not become involved in missing person cases. If no crime has been committed and the missing person's safety is not in jeopardy, the police department performs an administrative function, recording the information to be used in helping to identify individuals who are unconscious, who are found wandering (senility), or who are found dead and have no identification on them. The policy in some agencies may involve having an officer write a short report and submit a statewide alert, through dispatch, to check the welfare of the missing person if a police contact is made. Some agencies will only assist after a certain amount of time has passed and if there are certain suspicious variables involved, such as the person was intoxicated at the time he or she went missing. Also, if the missing person is a juvenile, a thorough report is done and a possible search-and-rescue plan enacted, along with the likely execution of an AMBER Alert (discussed in greater detail in Chapter 11). The National Crime Information Center (NCIC) includes a missing person file with four specific categories and criteria for entry: (1) disabled, (2) endangered, (3) involuntary (abducted, kidnapped), and (4) juvenile.

Citizens who experience *property damage* are likely to call the police. If the incident poses danger, the first priority of responding officers is to make sure the scene is safe to themselves and others, before proceeding to dealing with danger. If danger does exist, officers must act to remove the danger. For example, if a tree has fallen on power lines and hot wires are on the ground, police should rope off the area and call the power company. If no danger is inherent in the situation, officers should determine if the damage is the result of criminal or noncriminal actions. If it is criminal property damage—for example, the work of vandals—officers should conduct a thorough investigation. If it is a noncriminal (and nondangerous) situation—for example, a tree fallen on a home—police officers should advise the complainant of alternatives in taking care of the damage. The complainant usually should also be advised to notify his or her insurance agent.

The police department may also serve a *lost and found* function. People who find valuable property are likely to turn it in to the police department. Conversely, people who have lost items of value are likely to request assistance from the police department. In this situation, again, the police department plays primarily an administrative function, maintaining accurate records of lost or found property. In some cases, however, lost property does turn out to be stolen, and then a criminal investigation ensues.

Some police departments also have the responsibility for *missing and stray animals*, especially unlicensed dogs. And they may be called on to deal with dangerous animals, such as bears, or with trapped animals, such as a raccoon up a chimney of a home.

Police may be called on to provide *escort service* to celebrities and other public figures who are either extremely popular or unpopular. Police may also provide escort services for dangerous cargoes—such as those containing highly flammable materials, hazardous wastes, and the like—or for oversized cargoes. In addition, police may be asked to provide escort services for funeral processions or for very valuable cargoes, such as large sums of cash. Little agreement exists about when escort services are appropriate or how they should be provided—that is, should they include red flashing lights and sirens, or proceed as though on general patrol?

The police may also be called to assist *people locked out* of their cars or homes. In such instances, it is usually preferable to have the civilian call a locksmith. If this is not possible, officers should check the identity of the person requesting assistance. Imagine the predicament of a police officer who assists a burglar in breaking and entering.

The police department is sometimes involved in *licensing* handguns. It is to the department's advantage to know who owns what kind of weapons in its jurisdiction. In addition, the police are in a position to investigate applicants for a license and to determine if such a license should be granted. Police also may do background investigations on applicants for liquor licenses, taxi licenses, and tow truck licenses. The police department is also involved in other types of licensing, such as issuing animal licenses, licenses for holding parades, or for blocking off streets for community functions.

In addition, because officers routinely patrol the entire area over which the department has jurisdiction, many decisionmakers believe officers should be responsible for *inspections* to ensure adherence to fire codes, health codes, and building codes. This is another area of controversy because such activities are extremely time consuming. They do present the advantage of familiarizing officers with the people and buildings on their beats. However, such activities take officers off the street and into buildings where they are no longer on preventive patrol but rather are serving functions that could easily be carried out by inspectors specifically hired for the jobs, usually at less cost.

In many areas, police are also responsible for checking the weight of trucks. Police are used in this capacity because they must be on the scene anyway to issue tickets to overweight trucks or to stop trucks that bypass the scales completely. Some contend, however, that the patrol officers in the vicinity could be called in for either of the preceding situations and that it might be more practical not to use patrol officers in this capacity.

> Between 80 and 90 percent of all calls for police service are of a noncriminal nature.

Whether police officers should spend time in all these activities is somewhat controversial. Yet, proposals to eliminate such social service functions fail to recognize the relationship between social-service-type calls and more serious crime. For example, a domestic disturbance can end in a serious assault or even homicide.

In addition, police are the only agencies available 24/7 for immediate help, which is one reason they are so often called to intervene in *domestic disputes.* Such disputes usually occur at night and commonly involve people who have been drinking. Police officers often are expected to defuse such situations without making an arrest. And they frequently are called to the same scene time and again. Such calls may lull officers into complacency, making them vulnerable should a normally routine call turn out to involve crazed, weapon-wielding individuals. Dealing with domestic disputes is discussed in detail in Chapter 7.

Controlling Traffic

Patrol officers also serve a *traffic* function by directing traffic, responding to traffic crash calls, issuing tickets for traffic violations, and the like, as discussed in detail in Chapter 5.

Assisting at the Scene of a Crime

Responding to calls about *crimes in progress* or recently committed and conducting the *preliminary investigations* are other important functions of patrol officers. Because they are on patrol and readily available to respond, they are usually first on the scene. This is the type of call most officers consider to be "real" police work. On such calls, patrol officers are responsible for aiding injured victims, securing the scene, interviewing victims and witnesses, and arresting any suspects present at the scene. In smaller departments, patrol officers may also continue the investigation and *gather intelligence.* In larger departments, the investigation may be turned over to the detective division. The investigative function is discussed in Chapter 10.

Making Arrests

Making arrests is one of patrol officers' most serious and important responsibilities, as discussed in Chapter 3. Officers are commonly granted much discretion in this area, allowed to decide whether to arrest or not, and make decisions that can drastically change the futures of those engaged in unlawful activity. Frequently, a simple warning is the best alternative. However, in some situations, such as certain domestic violence incidents, officers are legally mandated to arrest, with statutory provision restricting their discretionary powers. Patrol officers deal with a wide variety of criminal and noncriminal situations; they also commonly deal with several such situations within a brief time, often without much background information.

Special Events

Many functions performed by patrol officers can also be required in handling *special events*. Patrol officers are often an essential part of large public gatherings, including sporting events, rock concerts, parades, celebrations, and political rallies. The presence of uniformed patrol officers helps ensure peaceful assembly and prevents unlawful actions. Patrol officers also help expedite the traffic flow of both vehicles and pedestrians. (Handling explosive crowds is discussed in Chapter 6.)

> Crowds may be classified as self-controlled, active, or explosive.

One trend is to hire off-duty patrol officers to perform the crowd-control function, particularly if the event is sponsored by private business or industry. Other alternatives include using volunteers or reserves to handle crowd-control problems.

Assisting at the Scene of a Fire

The patrol officer is often the first one to arrive at the scene at an *uncontrolled fire*. After either reporting the fire to the fire department or confirming that firefighters are en route, if the officer is aware that the life of someone is in immediate danger because of the fire, that officer may have to respond accordingly before the fire department arrives, despite not having the same tools and training as firefighters. And although officers should realize that their safety is paramount, they must also appreciate that the profession does pose a level of danger and that risk is simply expected as part of the job.

If no immediate danger to life is present and the fire department has not yet arrived, the officer may then attempt to control or suppress the fire. Other functions the police may serve include traffic control, ensuring that firefighting equipment can arrive quickly at the scene, and helping search for and rescue people trapped by the fire. If children are trapped in a burning home, rescuers should check under beds and in closets because children frequently try to hide from the smoke and flames. Police officers can also provide crowd control, assist with first aid, transport injured people to the nearest medical facility, and guard any personal property removed from the burning structure. Assisting with other emergency situations is the focus of Chapter 8.

▌AN OFFICER'S PERSPECTIVE
Responding to the Scene of a Fire

One night as a newer patrol officer, I was assigned to take a student ride-along who was interested in a law enforcement career. I was working dog shift and on regular patrol, driving through neighborhoods, and talking to my rider about the job.

While driving through a mobile home park, I saw white smoke billowing into the night sky. I rolled down my window and could smell a fire. Because it was around 2 a.m., I thought it was unusual that someone would be having a fire so late, so I drove around until I located the home where the smoke was coming from. Within minutes of my arrival, the back end of the home went up in flames, with fire coming out the rear windows. As I called the fire department in, I remembered the occupants of the mobile home from previous drug-related criminal contacts. I knew that the family had one infant child.

Because of how quickly the fire was spreading, I decided to make entry and attempt a search and rescue. I told my rider to stay in the squad, and I kicked the front of the mobile home trailer door in. As I entered, I felt extreme heat and what seemed like someone knocking the wind from my chest.

I got down low and ran toward the back of the trailer, yelling to see if anyone was in there.

The smoke inside was black, and I could not see anything, nor could I breathe well. As I got toward the far back of the home, all I could see was fire. At that time, I had to leave, knowing my limitations.

After I got out, the home was quickly engulfed in flames. I realized the poly thread on my uniform shirt had melted it was so hot! The fire fighters arrived on scene a short time later.

Fortunately, we learned that the family was gone from the home that evening and that it was unoccupied. I coughed up black stuff for the remainder of my shift, and I think my rider changed her mind about becoming a police officer.

Although the home was unoccupied at the time of the fire, I knew that a baby lived there, and that's what drove my decision to enter and make sure no one was inside before the home went up in flames. I knew it was going quickly and if there was anyone in there, the likelihood of survival would have been slim had I waited for the fire department to get there. Although officer safety is paramount, I know, too, that some level of danger is just inherent to the job.

—Sgt. Henry Lim Cho

The Community Service and Peacekeeping Function

In addition to their enforcement function, patrol officers also serve an important *peacekeeping function*. Although this function occupies the majority of the officers' time, it is largely unrecorded and unaccounted for. The public often misunderstands this function. When they see officers driving around simply observing the area, citizens often criticize the police for not chasing criminals or for not finding the "jerks" who "ripped off" their apartment when they were gone. Further, the peacekeeping function is seldom included in police training. The tendency is to think that all officers need is a little common sense. Consequently, texts, manuals, and training sessions seldom include this important patrol function, leaving officers to "play it by ear." Patrol functions are summarized in Table 4.1.

To serve these various functions, officers have a variety of patrol methods from which to choose.

Table 4.1 Patrol Officer Functions

Function	Situations
Noncrime calls for service (80–90 percent of calls for service)	Noise and party calls
	Domestic disturbances
	Property owner–tenant disputes
	Nuisance complaints
Traffic control	Traffic delays
	Pedestrian problems
	Crashes
	Traffic violations
	Drunken drivers
Preliminary investigations	Scene security
	Emergency first aid
	Evidence procurement
	Victim–witness statements
Arrests	Warrants
	Suspect transport
	Court testimony
Public gatherings	Sporting events
	Political rallies
	Rock concerts
	Parades
	Special events
Community service	Speeches and presentations
	Auto and home lockouts
	Babies delivered
	Blood transported
	Home and business security checks

Source: © Cengage Learning 2014

PATROL METHODS

The methods of patrol that departments use vary, depending on local needs. Most jurisdictions use some form of foot patrol in combination with automobile patrol.

 Patrol methods include foot, automobile, motorcycle, bicycle, Segway, mounted, air, water, special-terrain vehicle, K-9 assisted, and combination patrol.

Foot Patrol

Foot patrol is the oldest form of patrol. Its use declined with the introduction of the police squad car, but it has again gained prominence, largely because of the move toward community policing. The primary advantage of foot patrol is close citizen contact. Other advantages include the enhanced rapport between officers and the citizens and the proactive, rather than reactive, nature of foot patrol that seeks to address neighborhood problems before they become crimes: "By getting out and talking with people and business owners, you can establish relationships where citizens feel comfortable telling you about what and who concerns them. In time you will have your finger on the pulse of a neighborhood and be able to serve it better" (Wetzel 2011, 57).

One technique often used during foot patrol is the *knock and talk*, where an officer knocks on a resident's door and asks if they can talk. This technique is used to discover perceived crime and safety problems among the community's citizens as well as to gather information for police investigations. Be advised, however, that "chatting up the locals" can have a downside: "You do not want to endanger the residents who provide you with information. These citizens have to live and/or work in the neighborhood and talking to a cop could cause a problem for them. The intelligence you gather from them should be used judiciously and generally used to support other more formal information you've learned" (Wetzel 2011, 57).

Experiments conducted during the 1970s and 1980s—in Newark, New Jersey (1978–1979 and 1983–1984); Flint, Michigan (1979–1982); Oakland, California (1983); Houston, Texas (1983–1984); and Boston, Massachusetts (1983)—produced inconsistent results about the effectiveness of foot patrol in reducing crime or citizen fear of crime. Some of the studies found that foot patrol programs improved public relations between the police and the community, reduced citizens' fear of crime, and lowered the area's crime rates, but other studies found no effect on crime rates or citizens' fear of crime, and one study (Flint) actually reported an increase in citizen perceptions of the seriousness of the crime problem. Criticism was later leveled at these experiments for their flawed research designs and lack of rigorous statistical analysis.

Several recent studies have met with more encouraging results, as departments have begun to incorporate data analysis of crime types and locations into their foot patrol strategies (Craven 2009). The Philadelphia Foot Patrol Experiment has garnered attention lately for its focus on place-based policing, showing that when police resources are directed at hot spots, or those geographic locations where crime incidents tend to cluster, foot patrol can indeed have a net positive effect on reducing crime, particularly violent crime (Ratcliffe et al. 2011). The concept of spatial dosage, whether pertaining to the number of officers patrolling a certain area or the geographic extent of one patrol beat, was identified as a salient variable in whether foot patrol could effectively reduce violent crime.

The following key initiatives are suggested to help departments make foot patrol succeed (Craven 2009):

▶ Determine the date, time, and location of service calls by types and create representative maps to aid in efficient and effective deployment

▶ Complement statistical analysis with a community survey to obtain the opinions of residents and business owners regarding priority issues

▶ Invite the community to participate in planning sessions

▶ Recruit a range of individuals (both officers and civilians) to use various models of patrol, demonstrating that both police and civilians can address public expectations through a variety of approaches such as volunteer efforts with neighborhood watch programs and crime-prevention programming

Foot patrol is not without its disadvantages, however. It is relatively expensive, it may interfere with the officer's ability to communicate with dispatch or obtain information available from them, and it limits officers' ability to pursue suspects in vehicles as well as their ability to respond rapidly to calls for service in another area. However, technology has improved to the extent that officers are no longer tied to a patrol car for radio access and can request backup from a patrol car if needed. The geography of some jurisdictions, such as rural areas, makes the use of foot patrol highly impractical.

Automobile Patrol

Automobile patrol reverses the advantages and disadvantages of foot patrol. Unlike officers on foot, officers in squad cars can pursue suspects in vehicles and can respond rapidly to service calls in other areas. Officers also can transport equipment needed to process crime scenes as well as suspects they have arrested and have ready access to a variety of tools, such as their laptop computers, paperwork, additional weapons, emergency medical equipment and kits, and other valuable supplies. Officers in squad cars can patrol a larger area in less time, or the same area as an officer on foot can, but more frequently.

Communication with the citizenry, however, is greatly reduced. In addition, the physical act of driving requires much of the officers' attention, diverting it from attention to subtle signs that criminal activity may be taking place. A further disadvantage is that automobiles are restricted in the areas they can access. Despite these disadvantages, automobile patrol continues to be a mainstay of the patrol division.

> Automobile patrol has the greatest mobility and flexibility and is usually the most cost-effective patrol method.

To offset costs, many departments are buying refurbished highway patrol cars or using (and marking) vehicles seized from narcotics deals. Research on the effectiveness of the automobile patrol in preventing crime suggests that crimes prevented by a passing squad car are usually committed as soon as the police have gone.

41.3.1

CALEA Standard 41.3.1 states, "Conspicuously marked patrol cars are readily identified as law enforcement agency vehicles from every view and from a long distance, even at night. Conspicuous marking increases safety, serves as a warning to potential violators, and provides citizens with a feeling of security. Markings, if used, should include exterior mounted emergency lights, the agency's name, the emergency telephone number, and reflective materials placed on the sides and rear of the vehicle, such as reflective striping, lettering, or decals."

Source: Commission on Accreditation of Law Enforcement Agencies (CALEA). 2012. *Standards for Law Enforcement Agencies.* 5th ed. Fairfax, VA: Author.

Although most departments use vehicle patrol, departments vary in whether the vehicles are assigned to an officer or taken home when off duty, the number of officers assigned to each car, and the technology available in the vehicle.

Assigned Vehicle Programs Whether officers should be assigned their own patrol car and whether they should be able to take them home are disputed, often argued, emotionally charged issues. Many departments see such programs as a valuable recruiting tool. Numerous studies have been conducted on assigned/take-home police vehicles and car pool vehicles, and almost all support the use of take-home programs.

Research conducted on the Tacoma (Washington) Police Department's Assigned Vehicle Program (AVP), adopted in 1999, found that the benefits of assigning vehicles and allowing them to be taken home far outweigh costs and that police productivity was significantly enhanced through such a program (Lauria 2007). Numerous other evaluations of take-home vehicle programs by departments across the country have reached similar conclusions.

Such programs are not without their drawbacks, however. Departments with take-home vehicles usually require more police cars than do those that share vehicles; if only select officers are assigned cars, other officers may feel they are not being treated equitably; take-home cars make it obvious where officers live and are more easily stolen or vandalized than are those parked in a secured police lot; assigned vehicles might be used for personal gain; and it is arguable who should pay the commuting costs.

One-Officer versus Two-Officer Patrol Units Whether automobile patrol should have one or two officers per vehicle is controversial. Arguments can be made for either. One-officer units are more cost effective from a personnel point of view, allowing for twice the coverage and twice the power of observation. In addition, officers riding alone may be more careful and more attentive to what is happening around them because they have no one to distract them with conversation.

Two-officer units are more cost effective in the number of patrol vehicles required and may increase officer safety. Some unionized departments' contracts stipulate that two officers be assigned to each patrol car. Some departments use two-officer units only in high-crime areas or only at night.

Many studies have concluded that one-officer cars are more cost-effective, and nationwide, the majority of patrol assignments are to single-officer vehicles. But such economic savings may come at the expense of officer safety. Efficient communication among one-officer units on patrol and a clear policy on when to call for backup is one way to increase the safety of single officers on patrol (Scoville 2011). Other ways include K-9–assisted patrol and vehicle-mounted video.

In-Car Video (ICV) Increasingly popular are compact, high-resolution video cameras mounted by the squad car's rearview mirror. Although initially many officers were uneasy about having cameras record their actions, a

Police survey reports that an overwhelming majority (93 percent) of respondents whose agencies use in-car videos (ICV) now endorse the practice. They most often cite evidence and liability protection as the top benefits to law enforcement (Basich 2009). A 2011 Police Executive Research Forum (PERF) survey found that 71 percent of responding agencies currently use ICV, and 25 percent of those agencies equip all of their cars with the technology ("PERF Survey Shows" 2012).

ICV cameras can record whatever happens in front of the car through a wide-angle lens. The camera may be turned on and off by the officer or may be activated by automatic triggers, such as when the driver's door is opened or the lights are activated. The video is supplemented by a lightweight, wireless microphone worn by the officer. Most of the newer digital systems are always on and ready and are able to save video from as many as 30 seconds *before* activation of the camera. The actual recording unit is stored in a fireproof, bullet-resistant vault in the squad's trunk, inaccessible to suspects and officers alike. Therefore, any charges of tampering are avoided.

TECHNOLOGY IN POLICING

IN-CAR CAMERAS

In-car cameras are used to document exactly what is said and done during a police stop, be it a traffic violation or a driving while intoxicated (DWI) stop. Such recorded documentation helps officers write their incident reports, assists in internal affairs investigations, and helps settle court cases. Austin, Texas, Police Chief Art Acevedo, noting that his department averages three officer-involved shootings each year, shares how in-car video helped clarify the facts surrounding one of these controversial incidents:

> A 16-year-old burglary suspect was shot after aiming a gun at an officer while fleeing a store. Fortunately the camera in one of our police cars captured it all on video. We were able to tell the public that we had video that corroborated the officer's account of the incident. The citizens review panel, which typically requests an independent investigation after a shooting like this, didn't ask for one because they didn't see any policy violations. Once the investigation was completed, we released the video.

Source: "Cameras." In *How Are Innovations in Technology Transforming Policing?*, pp. 13–24. Washington, DC: Police Executive Research Forum, Critical Issues in Policing Series, January 2012.

One in-car camera captured the murder of a Texas police officer and was key in gaining a conviction. Often people who are stopped and are acting belligerently will change their attitudes completely when they learn they are being videotaped. In addition, the tapes serve a valuable training purpose.

41.3.8

CALEA Standard 41.3.8 states, "If in-car audio or video recording systems are used, a written directive establishes guidelines for situations for use; data security and access; and data storage and retention schedule."

Source: Commission on Accreditation of Law Enforcement Agencies (CALEA). 2012. *Standards for Law Enforcement Agencies.* 5th ed. Fairfax, VA: Author.

If officers need to leave their vehicles, they can still record what they encounter using VIDMIC, a shoulder microphone equipped with a video and audio recorder and a still camera. Data shows that when such video evidence is collected and a suspect alleges officer misconduct, the officer is exonerated 96.2 percent of the time (Garrett 2008).

Global Positioning and Information Systems (GPS/GIS) The global positioning system (GPS) is a satellite-based navigation system consisting of a network of 31 actively broadcasting satellites placed into orbit by the U.S. Department of Defense. The satellites circle the earth twice a day in precise orbits and transmit signal information to GPS receivers on the ground, which use triangulation to calculate the user's exact location. Many departments have added automatic vehicle location (AVL) software to their GPS systems to enhance officer safety by allowing dispatch and supervisors to monitor, via a secured server, real-time locations of all squads. A 2011 PERF survey indicated that 69 percent of all responding agencies used GPS to track police vehicles ("PERF Survey Shows" 2012).

GPS technology is vital for geographic information systems (GIS), which is also a vital police tool: "Every incident called in to a 911 center is associated with a real-world location where people need help. Immediate location awareness for dispatch and first responders during an incident can often mean the difference between life and death. Today the majority of law enforcement agencies use some degree of geographic information systems (GIS) mapping technology to locate callers and provide first responders with critical information before arriving on scene" (Wandrei 2007, 56). GIS as a crime analysis tool is discussed in Chapter 6.

Voice-Activated Patrol Car Equipment Patrol vehicles have a broad array of high-tech radios, computers, GPS, video cameras, radars, lights, sirens, and databases available to field officers. In many police vehicles, these can all be activated by voice commands—for example, engaging emergency lights and siren, accessing NCIC, activating radar, and the like. The ability to control in-car equipment through speech command frees officers' hands and allows officers to keep their eyes ahead, making patrolling easier and safer.

Motorcycle Patrol

Motorcycle patrol was first used more than 100 years ago by officers in Pittsburgh, Pennsylvania, to patrol the streets and enforce traffic regulations. Most police departments have their motorcycles marked with the same insignia as their patrol cars. Motorcycle patrol has many of the same advantages as automobile patrol, especially speed and maneuverability. Motorcycles have greater access than automobiles to some areas and are better suited to heavy traffic, narrow alleys, and rugged terrain.

Disadvantages include motorcycles' relatively high cost to operate; their limited use in bad weather; their inability to carry large amounts of equipment, evidence, or prisoners; and the danger involved in riding them. Proper protective clothing and helmets are a must. A motorcycle also offers officers much less protection than does a squad car should a person in a vehicle being pursued decide to start shooting.

Some departments, in their quest to improve their patrol division's efficiency and effectiveness, have begun exploring alternative vehicles for patrol. Here, a New York Police Department detective demonstrates the Vectrix eco-friendly electric motor scooter, which the department's motorcycle division will be trained to use.

© AP Images/Kathy Willens

Bicycle Patrol

Bicycle patrol is not new. In the 1880s, police in many large cities patrolled on bicycles. But automobile patrol displaced bicycle patrol for nearly 100 years until 1988 when bicycle patrol was reintroduced in Seattle, Washington. Bicycle patrol is growing in popularity.

A study by the Cincinnati, Ohio, Police Department compared activity of patrol officers on bikes with those in cars and found that bike patrol officers reported significantly more activity in many categories, including arrests, crimes discovered, warrants served, and motorist assists. Bicycle officers are also an important public relations tool, helpful in bringing citizens closer to the police (Menton 2007).

Another benefit to bicycle patrol is its cost effectiveness. For the cost of one police cruiser, several bicycle patrol officers can be outfitted. Bicycles are also very maneuverable and good for enforcing bicycle, motorized scooter, rollerblading, and skateboarding ordinances. On the Las Vegas (Nevada) strip, where most of the elite casinos are located, all patrol is on bicycle: on the streets, in the parking areas, and inside the casinos when officers respond to calls. Motor patrols go on the strip only when called for emergencies.

Additional advantages of bicycles include their stealth factor, allowing officers to sneak up on situations such as drug buys, and their green factor, referring to their environmentally friendly power source. Furthermore, bicycle patrol provides a good source of exercise and promotes the physical fitness of officers. Bicycles often are used in parks and on beaches and have many of the same advantages and disadvantages as motorcycles. Like motorcycles, bicycles leave the patrol officer extremely vulnerable. Officers should have the proper safety equipment and follow all basic safety practices while on bicycle patrol.

Bicycle patrols are becoming increasingly popular because of their ease in operation, their relatively low operational costs, and their acceptance by the public.

Segways

A newer method of patrol is the Segway Personal Transporter, commonly known as the "Segway PT" or simply a "Segway." Introduced in 2001, they are now being used by police departments throughout the country and for tasks ranging from patrol to hazardous material (hazmat) response. With only two wheels and a gyroscope balance system, the Segway was initially a hard sell as a viable patrol vehicle, but it has since caught on and now provides many law enforcement agencies with an enhanced, eco-friendly, and economical way to patrol.

Mounted Patrol

The greatest advantage of mounted patrol is that officers on horseback are usually more acceptable than K-9s as crowd-control instruments and are much

A Metropolitan Transportation Authority officer uses a Segway to patrol the Union Station in Los Angeles, California. Here, he is giving directions to a family on vacation.

Mounted patrol serves important symbolic and practical functions. Mounted patrols are especially good for crowd control: 1 horse and rider is equal to 10 foot-patrol officers in a crowd-control situation.

© AP Images/Ed Andrieski

more effective at controlling a disorderly crowd than are officers on foot or in any kind of vehicle (other than a tank). One horse and rider is equal to 10 foot-patrol officers in a crowd-control situation.

Mounted officers can often handle 911 calls and other emergencies with more speed and visibility than foot patrols can. In addition, mounted patrol members can help search for evidence at crime scenes, round up stray animals after a truck has tipped over, and search for lost children or bodies in tall corn or fields. Some mounted patrol units are beginning to use mobile data terminals (MDTs) that rest on the horse to allow officers a direct link to emergency dispatch and online databases.

Mounted patrol is decreasing in the United States but is still used in some large cities for crowd and traffic control and in some rural jurisdictions. Expense is one of the main disadvantages of mounted patrol.

Air Patrol

"The value of airborne law enforcement has been demonstrated since 1929, when the New York City Police Department started a fixed-wing (airplane) aviation unit to combat a growing menace of barnstormers" (Solosky 2009, 38). Air patrol is highly effective when large areas are involved. For example, searching for a suspect, an escaped convict, a lost child, or a downed aircraft can all be accomplished most efficiently by air. Using technology such as infrared or other heat sensory detectors can also help aerial surveillance be more effective in locating hidden or elusive suspects. Small airplanes and helicopters are used as eyes in the sky to report traffic tie-ups and to work along with police cars to conduct criminal surveillance or to detect, clock, and stop speeding vehicles and can reduce the hazards and costs associated with high-speed pursuits.

Helicopters are valuable in rescue efforts during disasters such as fires in tall buildings, floods, and earthquakes. Police aircraft and helicopters are also a cost-effective way to transport prisoners long distances. Air patrol, however, is quite expensive to operate and maintain. Other disadvantages include citizen complaints about the noise and about being spied on.

Nonetheless, "In the past 10 years, thanks in large part to the military surplus program, more law enforcement agencies are starting their own aviation units to take advantage of this strong and powerful asset. Today, there are approximately 800 U.S. law enforcement agencies flying aircraft" (Solosky 2009, 38).

Water Patrol

Water patrol units are extremely specialized and not in great use except in areas with extensive coasts or a great deal of lake or river traffic. Like aircraft, boats are expensive to buy, operate, and maintain. Further, those who operate them must have special training. Nonetheless, boats are the best means to effectively control violators of water safety regulations as well as to apprehend drug and gun smugglers. Boats are also valuable in rescue operations during times of flooding as well as in dragging operations for drowning cases.

A trend in water patrol is the use of personal watercraft (PWC) or Jet Skis, which have a very shallow draft, high maneuverability, and stability. They are also easy to operate. The front compartment provides storage for a ticket book, high-powered binoculars, and a portable breath test. Many are equipped with public-address systems, sirens, and lights.

In Miami Beach, Florida, for example, officers on PWC find they can approach areas not accessible by conventional patrol boats because of shallow water, low bridges, or other impediments. The watercraft have been used in search and recovery, in recovering drowning victims, in deterring boating law violations (including reckless operation and driving under the influence [DUI] violations), in checking fishing licenses and catch limits, and in improved public relations.

Special-Terrain Vehicles

Police departments responsible for areas with extensive coastlines may also rely on jeeps or amphibious vehicles to patrol the beaches. Those who must patrol where snow is common frequently rely on snowmobiles. Departments whose jurisdiction includes remote parts of the country, including hundreds of acres of desert, may also use jeeps or all-terrain vehicles (ATVs). An additional advantage of ATVs is that they can carry a substantial amount of support equipment. Special-terrain vehicles are useful for rescue missions as well as for routine patrol.

K-9–Assisted Patrol

The K-9–assisted patrol is becoming more popular, with even smaller departments beginning to establish K-9 units. The K-9 unit can be used to control crowds, break up fights, recover lost articles, or find evidence. In addition, dogs can provide protection for a one-officer patrol.

Detector dogs are specially trained to sniff out narcotics, explosives, or bodies (live and cadaver). Drug- and bomb-sniffing dogs are used extensively in international airports and border checkpoints. Tracker dogs can follow the scent of a fleeing suspect or a missing person. Search and rescue K-9s were used after the Oklahoma City bombing and the September 11, 2001, terrorist attack on the World Trade Center to locate trapped or deceased victims. Besides detection, canines can be trained and used for apprehension, chasing down and "holding" fleeing suspects until officers can gain physical control of such individuals. Dogs may be cross-trained in both detection and apprehension.

K-9 units are also an asset to public relations efforts. They can be used for demonstrations at state fairs or in local schools, showing how well trained and under control the animals are. According to a *Police* magazine survey, the majority of agencies (74 percent) use the "iconic American police dog," the German shepherd ("Almost 50% of Agencies" 2008). The second most popular breed used is the Belgian Malinois (44 percent). Like other forms of specialized patrol, K-9–assisted patrol has disadvantages. One drawback occurs when a police dog is trained to work with only one handler. Should that handler become ill or disabled or be killed, the dog must be retrained. Further, if a K-9 handler is wounded, the dog may not allow emergency personnel near the officer to help. To counter such problems, many departments are cross-training their dogs to work with two handlers. Another difficulty is that a K-9, like most dogs, is territorial, and its handler and its K-9 cruiser are part of its territory. It may become aggressive without being told to do so if its handler or cruiser is approached by strangers.

Because many dogs are donated, training generally constitutes the greatest expense of K-9 units. The training usually takes 10 to 12 weeks and can cost $1,000 to $2,000 per team, in addition to the officer's salary during this time. The other major expense is modifying the patrol car, removing the back seat and replacing it with a platform. Some units are equipped with a radio-controlled door or window opener that allows officers to release their K-9s from a distance. An alternative is for officers to leave a back window rolled down so the dog can get out of the car if called. Other costs of maintaining a canine unit include annual, routine veterinary care, and food.

Another factor to consider when implementing a K-9 program is the potential increase in vulnerability to lawsuits, particularly in cases involving searches and use-of-force issues. Because law enforcement officers use K-9s to find people, clear buildings, sniff out bombs, and locate evidence or contraband, their use implicates the Fourth Amendment. In *United States v. Place* (1983), the Supreme Court held that the exposure of luggage to a canine sniff in a public place did not constitute a search. However, courts are divided about when a dog sniff constitutes a search, and state courts may find dog sniffs are searches under their own state constitutions. Courts have also ruled police use of K-9s as a use of force, some going so far as to deem it lethal force. However, as one officer stated in defending the "lethality" of his K-9, "I can recall the dog. I can't recall a bullet." As noted in Chapter 3, one source of K-9–related case law is the Web site of Terry Fleck, an expert in canine legalities.

Combination Patrol

No single patrol method or combination of methods is best. Usually, the greater the variety of methods available, the more effective a department will be. Which methods of patrol to use will vary depending on the department's physical jurisdiction, the types of crimes occurring, the size of the department, the training of its officers, and its budget. Once a department knows which methods it has available, it can determine effective patrol techniques.

PATROL TECHNIQUES AND STRATEGIES

Patrol is, indeed, an essential function of law enforcement, yet it is not always as effective as it could or should be. To improve effectiveness, numerous patrol techniques and strategies have been tried and evaluated throughout the years, including routine or random patrol, rotating or fixed area and shift assignments, rapid response, differential police response, split-force patrol, saturation patrol, and directed patrol.

Routine Patrol and the Kansas City Preventive Patrol Experiment

Perhaps the most classic study of patrol as it is traditionally performed is the Kansas City Preventive Patrol Experiment. Although this study was conducted in 1972, it is still the most comprehensive study of the effects of routine patrol, also referred to as routine preventive patrol, a somewhat redundant term given that the primary purpose of routine patrol is to prevent crime. **Routine patrol** involves unstructured patrol throughout a beat, whether on foot, in a squad, or via some other method, in an effort to deter crime by creating a sense of police omnipresence. It is often considered synonymous with **random patrol**, a strategy based on the theory of probability in which an ongoing patrol presence is presumed to (1) increase the chances that an officer will detect and disrupt crime occurring in public places and (2) deter potential offenders because the unpredictable nature of patrol means there is a chance a squad car or foot patrol will come along at any minute. Random patrol does not have a specific focus or aim in enforcement, distinguishing it from directed or targeted patrol, as will be discussed shortly.

In the Kansas City Preventive Patrol Experiment, 15 beats in Kansas City were divided into three groups, each with five beats:

Group 1—Reactive Beats: No routine patrol, responding only to calls for service

Group 2—Control Beats: Maintained their normal level of routine preventive patrol

Group 3—Proactive Beats: Doubled or tripled the level of routine preventive patrol

---

routine patrol

Unstructured patrol throughout a beat in an effort to deter crime by creating a sense of police omnipresence; often considered synonymous with random patrol.

random patrol

A strategy based on the theory of probability in which an ongoing patrol presence is presumed to (1) increase the chances that an officer will detect and disrupt crime occurring in public places and (2) deter potential offenders because the unpredictable nature of patrol means there is a chance a squad car or foot patrol will come along at any minute.

> The Kansas City Preventive Patrol Experiment found that increasing or decreasing routine preventive patrol had no measurable effect on the following:
> - Crime
> - Citizens' fear of crime
> - Community attitudes toward the police on delivery of police services
> - Police response time
> - Traffic accidents

Says Klockars (1983, 130), commenting on the findings of the Kansas City experiment, "It makes about as much sense to have police patrol routinely in cars to fight crime as it does to have fire fighters patrol routinely in fire trucks to fight fire."

Although the Kansas City experiment demonstrated the limited effect that increasing or decreasing the number of officers engaged in unstructured random patrol appears to have, other studies have found changing area and shift assignments can have a significant effect.

Area and Shift Assignments

Many departments divide patrol into three 8-hour shifts to cover each 24-hour period, for example, 7:00 a.m. to 3:00 p.m., 3:00 p.m. to 11:00 p.m., and 11:00 p.m. to 7:00 a.m. (the dog shift). Some departments have gone to 10-hour shifts to provide overlap in personnel during peak incident times, and others offer a variety of shift lengths, to accommodate officers who prefer either 8-, 10-, or 12-hour shifts. It can be complicated for administrators to set up such schedules; however, computer software continues to improve to allow multiple shift strategies within one department.

Software can also make the assignment of beats easier and more effective. The municipality served by the department typically is divided into geographic areas—beats—on the basis of personnel available for patrol. Many departments rotate shifts, areas, or both. Other departments assign permanent shifts, areas, or both, believing this allows officers to become more familiar with their assignments and, consequently, more effective in patrolling. Regardless of whether an agency uses rotating or permanent beat assignments, having officers allocated to various beats tends to reduce disparities in how officers take calls, for example, having only one or a few officers who actively respond to calls throughout the jurisdiction while others are able to avoid responding at all.

The shifts and areas to which new officers are assigned depend on the supervisor's philosophy. Some departments assign rookies to high-crime areas and "fast" shifts to help them learn their new jobs more rapidly and to assess their performance. Other departments assign rookies to the slowest shifts and the lowest crime areas to allow them to ease into their new jobs. Two basic forms of shift scheduling are used. The first assigns equal numbers of patrol officers to each of the three shifts. The second assigns officers based on anticipated need.

As departments become more proactive, many are using *proportionate assignment*, which considers the number of calls and many other factors as well. In **proportionate assignment**, area assignments are based on the data available from requests for service, considering the amount and severity of crime occurring in various areas, population density, routes to the areas, and any special problems that might be involved, such as large groups of non-English-speaking citizens. Boundaries of the patrol beat are determined by considering how rapidly a responding car can cover the area, and assignments are made so that in normal circumstances police can respond within three minutes.

proportionate assignment

Determination of area assignments by requests for service based on available data; no area is larger than the time it takes a car to respond in three minutes or less.

Response Time

Patrol effectiveness is frequently measured in **response time**, the time elapsed between when the call is received and when the police arrive on the scene. One reason for rapid response is the opportunity to apprehend a person engaged in criminal activity. However, as Klockars (1983, 130) stresses, "Police currently make on-scene arrests in about 3 percent of the serious crimes reported to them. If they traveled faster than a speeding bullet to all reports of serious crimes, this on-scene arrest rate would rise to no higher than 5 percent."

Spelman and Brown (1991, 164) replicated the citizen reporting component of the Kansas City Experiment response time analysis and found, "In the cities we studied … *arrests that could be attributed to fast police response were made in only 2.9 percent of reported serious crimes*" [italics in original]. Spelman and Brown attribute this low response-related arrest rate largely to the fact that 75 percent of all serious crimes are **discovery crimes**; that is, they are completed before they are discovered and reported. This is in direct contrast to **involvement crimes**, in which the victim and suspect confront each other.

response time

The time elapsed from when the police are called to when they arrive on the scene.

discovery crimes

Offenses that have been completed and whose scenes have been abandoned before the crimes are noticed; in contrast to *involvement crimes.*

involvement crimes

Offenses in which the victim and the suspect confront each other; in contrast to *discovery crimes.*

> Citizen reporting time affects the possibility of on-scene arrests more than does police response time. Response time is often lengthened because citizens delay calling the police because of decision-making problems or problems in communicating with the police.

After citizens decide to call the police, they may encounter other problems: no phone available, not knowing what number to call, or not being able to communicate clearly with the person receiving the call. Response time is also increased when the department does not have enough patrol officers available for such duty at any particular time. Nonetheless, citizens often *expect* a rapid response when they call. This expectation can be modified, however. The response may not need to be immediate, and it may not have to be made by a sworn officer. An actual on-scene response may not even need to occur, given the increased availability of over-the-phone and online reporting capabilities in many jurisdictions. Surveys and studies have found that citizen satisfaction with police can be improved simply by having the department or dispatcher explain to a caller why an immediate response by a sworn officer may not occur and the reasoning behind the type of response selected. This type of triaging or sorting of calls is known as *differential police response.*

Differential Police Response

Differential police response strategies vary the rapidity of response as well as the responder based on the type of incident and the time of occurrence. Differential police response strategies replace the traditional first-come, first-served, and as-fast-as-possible response, depending on the type of incident and whether it is in progress, proximate, or cold. Usually, if a crime is in progress, the response will be immediate and made by a sworn officer. If it is **proximate**, that is, recently committed, response to the call may be put ahead of other, less urgent calls. If the incident is "cold," that is, it happened several hours before, the response may be "as time permits," by appointment, or over the phone.

The most common alternatives used in differential response strategies include response by sworn or nonsworn personnel and whether it is immediate, expedited, routine, or by appointment. Other alternatives for minor crimes include contact by telephone, mail, e-mail, referral, or no response. For example, a major personal injury would require an immediate response by sworn personnel, whereas a minor noncrime call might be handled by a referral or a direction to the caller to file a report online, if the department offers such a service.

differential police response strategies

Practice of varying the rapidity of response as well as the responder based on the type of incident and the time of occurrence.

proximate

Closely related in space, time, or order; very near.

Split-Force Patrol

Split-force patrol is a technique based on preventive patrol that maintains a continuous police presence to deter criminal activity. Although a traditional patrol strategy has units being diverted from proactive patrol to respond to calls, which takes officers off the streets and interrupts their crime detection and prevention efforts, **split-force patrol** assigns multiple units to a single geographical area or beat. While one unit responds to calls, the other unit continues to proactively patrol that beat. The clear advantage of split-force patrol is that there are officers dedicated solely to patrolling while other units handle calls, a strategy that maintains the police presence in the community as a deterrent to crime. The obvious disadvantage is that this patrol strategy requires a doubling, or more, of resources and can typically be managed only by larger departments that have enough personnel and other resources to provide duplicate coverage in some or all beats.

split-force patrol

Assigns multiple units to a single geographical area or beat; while one unit responds to calls, the other unit continues to proactively patrol that beat.

Saturation Patrol

Saturation patrol is a technique that uses a large number of patrol officers for specific enforcement in a concentrated area, such as a hot spot or high-crime corridor, or for enhanced enforcement during specific events, such as a "safe and sober" campaign. Examples of such enforcement include DWI checkpoints, speed enforcement, drug interdiction, and vice assignments. The goal of this form of enforcement is to deter these types of crimes by high visibility and targeted enforcement.

saturation patrol

A technique that uses a large number of patrol officers for specific enforcement in a concentrated area, such as a hot spot or high-crime corridor, or for enhanced enforcement during specific events, such as a "safe and sober" campaign.

Directed Patrol

If a department's goals are clear, and if the department has kept accurate records on calls for service and on crimes committed in the community, then based on this data, patrol time should be effectively structured to provide the best service and protection possible. It is usually much more productive to have officers' discretionary time directed toward accomplishing specific department objectives than to expect each officer simply to do his or her "thing." **Directed patrol**, sometimes called *targeted patrol*, uses officers' discretionary patrol time to focus on specific department goals. These goals are often identified through problem-oriented policing.

directed patrol

Use of officers' discretionary patrol time to focus on specific department goals.

PATROL AND PROBLEM-ORIENTED POLICING

problem-oriented policing (POP)

A proactive approach to patrol and policing that focuses on problems to be solved rather than incidents to be responded to.

Problem-oriented policing (POP)—a proactive approach to patrol and policing that focuses on problems to be solved rather than incidents to be responded to—was first formally introduced by Goldstein in 1979. Based on 20 years of research, this approach suggests a fundamental shift in perspective.

> Problem-oriented policing (POP) requires a shift in perspective from incident driven to problem driven; from reactive to proactive.

In this approach, police are trained to think not in terms of incidents but in terms of problems and to group calls for service in an effort to identify specific problems. According to Goldstein (1990, 33), "In handling incidents, police officers usually deal with the most obvious, superficial manifestations of a deeper problem—not the problem itself." He contends that "incidents are usually handled as isolated, self-contained events. Connections are not systematically made among them, except when they suggest a common crime pattern leading to identifying the offender." What is needed, suggests Goldstein (33), is a different approach—problem-oriented policing: "The first step in problem-oriented policing is to move beyond just handling incidents. It calls for recognizing that incidents are often merely overt symptoms of problems. This pushes the police in two directions: (1) It requires that they recognize the relationships between incidents (similarities of behavior, location, persons involved, etc.); and (2) it requires that they take a more in-depth interest in incidents by acquainting themselves with some of the conditions and factors that give rise to them."

Problem-oriented policing has been used to address many community problems, such as burglaries, graffiti, sex offenses, and trespassing. The SARA problem-solving technique has contributed greatly to its effectiveness.

The SARA Problem-Solving Process

> The problem-solving process called SARA consists of four stages:
> - Scanning: Identifying the problem
> - Analysis: Learning the problem's causes, scope, and effects
> - Response: Acting to alleviate the problem
> - Assessment: Determining whether the response worked

Excellence in Problem-Oriented Policing (2002, 2–3) describes each of these four stages:

Scanning

▶ Identify recurring problems of concern to the public and the police.

▶ Prioritize problems.

▶ Develop broad goals.

▶ Confirm that the problems exist.

▶ Select one problem for examination.

Analysis

▶ Try to identify and understand the events and conditions that precede and accompany the problem.

▶ Identify the consequences of the problem for the community.

▶ Determine how frequently the problem occurs and how long it has been taking place.

▶ Identify the conditions that give rise to the problem.

▶ Narrow the scope of the problem as specifically as possible.

▶ Identify a variety of resources that may assist in developing a deeper understanding of the problem.

Response

▶ Search for what communities with similar problems have done.

▶ Brainstorm interventions.

▶ Choose among the alternative solutions.

▶ Outline a response plan and identify responsible parties.

▶ State the specific goals for the response plan.

▶ Identify relevant data to be collected.

▶ Carry out the planned activities.

Assessment

▶ Determine whether the plan was implemented.

▶ Determine whether the goals were attained and collect pre- and post-response qualitative and quantitative data.

▶ Identify any new strategies needed to augment the original plan.

▶ Conduct ongoing assessment to ensure continued effectiveness.

Assessing Responses to Problems According to Eck (2002, 6), "You begin planning for an evaluation when you take on a problem. The evaluation builds throughout the SARA process, culminates during the assessment, and provides findings that help you determine if you should revisit earlier stages to improve the response." Figure 4.1 illustrates the problem-solving process and evaluation.

Two types of evaluations to conduct are **process evaluation**, to determine if the response was implemented as planned, and **impact evaluation**, to determine if the problem declined (Eck 2002). Table 4.2 provides guidance in interpreting the results of process and impact evaluation.

process evaluation

Assessment that determines if a response was implemented as planned.

impact evaluation

Assessment that determines if a problem declined.

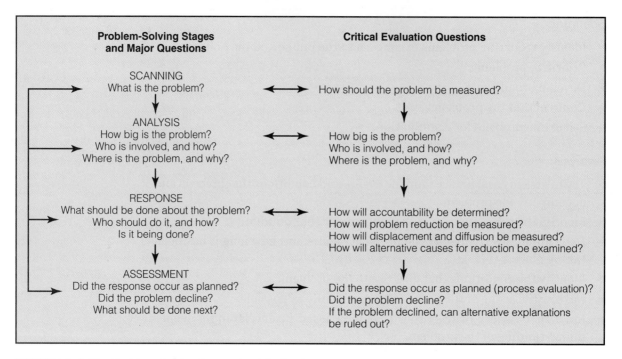

FIGURE 4.1 The Problem-Solving Process and Evaluation

John E. Eck, *Assessing Responses to Problems: An Introductory Guide for Police Problem-Solvers* (Washington, DC: Office of Community Oriented Policing Services, 2002), 6.

Table 4.2 Interpreting Results of Process and Impact Evaluations

	Process Evaluation Results	
Impact Evaluation Results	**Response implemented as planned, or nearly so**	**Response not implemented, or implemented in a radically different manner than planned**
Problem declined	A. Evidence that the response caused the decline	C. Suggests that other factors may have caused the decline, or that the response was accidentally effective
Problem did not decline	B. Evidence that the response was ineffective, and that a different response should be tried	D. Little is learned; perhaps if the response had been implemented as planned, the problem would have declined, but this is speculative

John E. Eck, *Assessing Responses to Problems: An Introductory Guide for Police Problem-Solvers* (Washington, DC: Office of Community Oriented Policing Services, 2002), 10.

Several nontraditional measures will indicate if a problem has been affected by the interventions (Eck 2002, 27):

▶ Reduced instances of repeat victimization

▶ Decreases in related crimes or incidents

▶ Neighborhood indicators: increased profits for legitimate businesses in target area, increased use of area/increased (or reduced) foot and vehicular traffic, increased property values, improved neighborhood appearance, increased occupancy in problem buildings, less loitering, fewer abandoned cars, less truancy

▶ Increased citizen satisfaction regarding the handling of the problem, which can be determined through surveys, interviews, focus groups, electronic bulletin boards, and the like

▶ Reduced citizen fear related to the problem

The SARA Model in Action

An example of problem solving in a situation facing most patrol officers is the Salt Lake City (Utah) Police Department's approach to dealing with false alarms. Their solution used the SARA model.

Scanning Scanning revealed the following problems:

▶ False alarm calls were draining patrol resources, making up 12 percent of all dispatched calls, contributing to a significant backlog of calls for service.

▶ Average police response time to alarm activations was up to 40 minutes, well beyond when police could hope to apprehend an intruder.

▶ More than 99 percent of all alarm calls were false, making responding officers increasingly complacent, risking injury.

▶ Nearly $500,000 of the budget (1.2 percent) was attributable to false alarms, but only $150,000 in alarm fines were collected.

▶ False alarms had three main causes: user errors resulting from insufficient training; inadequate verification by alarm company monitoring stations; and improper installation, inferior equipment, and application at the alarm site.

Analysis Analysis revealed that past efforts to reduce the volume of false alarms through permits, warnings, fines, and suspensions had only a modest effect. Examining other approaches tried elsewhere—from cost recovery to alarm industry regulation to outsourcing alarm administration—similarly proved only moderate effectiveness. Police response to alarms was most effective and efficient if the police had verification that an alarm activation indicated suspicious activity. Private security guards were ideally suited to make the initial verification. A legal opinion established that police were under no legal obligation to respond to all alarm activations.

Response The police department proposed to the city council that a verified alarm response ordinance be required in all alarm activations and that eyewitness verification of suspicious activity be identified by alarm company personnel or a private guard before notifying the police department. A campaign was then conducted to inform the public, elected officials, and the alarm industry about the purposes and advantages of verified response, and the police department conducted training for private security officers.

Assessment The police department experienced a 90-percent decrease in alarm-related calls for service during the first nine months, representing 6,338 fewer calls for service or the equivalent of five full-time patrol officers (valued at about $400,000). There were fewer backlogs of calls for service, and responses to high-priority calls for service dropped from 5 to 3 minutes.

Alarm owners benefit by achieving a 6- to 15-minute alarm activation response compared with the 40-minute average the police provided. The alarm industry benefited by now providing customers with a valued quick response.

By using problem-oriented policing and no longer attempting to manage a private sector problem, the Salt Lake City's verified response alarm ordinance provides a long-term solution to a problem the department had struggled with for 20 years.

PATROL AND COMMUNITY POLICING

Patrol officers can be catalysts for joint police and community problem-solving endeavors. Part of the evolution to community policing involves a shift in the patrol methods used, such as greater use of foot, bicycle, mounted, and K-9–assisted patrol. Community policing also involves the redeployment of patrol officers from vehicles into small, decentralized police posts. Some of the most effective community policing strategies used by patrol officers are quite simple and cost nothing. For example, the Burger King restaurant in Charles County, Maryland, was the first business in the country to set aside space as a "writing station" for officers. According to the owner, the main reason for setting up the writing stations was to help employees feel safer and to take an active part in community-police relations.

Another example is New York City's Cab Watch. The New York Police Department helped train Cab Watch taxi drivers to report incidents and provided the drivers with donated 911-direct wireless phones. In its first two years, Cab Watch expanded from the 50-driver pilot program to more than 1,700 who have alerted police to hundreds of incidents, as well as helping save lives in car crashes and building fires.

Other strategies are more complex and involve numerous partnerships with patrol officers. One such strategy is the Model Neighborhood Program, used in West Valley City, Utah, modeled after the Los Angeles Police Department (LAPD) Model Neighborhood Program. The program is a partnership of city, county, and federal agencies; the community; and the local police department. The local officer assigned to the area receives the names and addresses of property owners and then coordinates with U.S. Department of Housing and Urban Development (HUD) personnel and task force members of the police department to plan and conduct an area sweep serving arrest warrants, evicting problem tenants, and identifying specific hot spots needing extra attention. Coordination with local government agencies responsible for graffiti removal, abandoned cars impounding, and trash pickup is also undertaken. At the same time, the local city attorney or ordinance enforcement officer works with the police to contact owners of neglected property and invites them to participate in the program by evicting problem tenants, renovating their properties, and implementing screening procedures for new tenants. If owners are unwilling to improve their property, abatement procedures are initiated to confiscate and raze the property.

SUMMARY

Patrol service has been described as the backbone of the police department. Officers on patrol serve many functions. Among the important patrol functions are deterring or preventing crime and disorder; responding to crime calls for service; responding to noncrime calls for service; controlling traffic; assisting at the scene of a crime; conducting preliminary investigations; gathering intelligence; making arrests; patrolling public gatherings and special events; assisting at the scene of a fire and other medical calls; providing community service and general peacekeeping activities; and partnering with others to solve problems related to crime and disorder. Between 80 and 90 percent of all calls for police service are of a noncriminal nature. Patrol officers are often responsible for maintaining order with large groups of people. Crowds may be classified as self-controlled, active, or explosive.

Methods of patrol include foot, automobile, motorcycle, bicycle, Segway, mounted, air, water, special-terrain vehicle, K-9 assisted, and combination patrol. Automobile patrol has the greatest mobility and flexibility and is usually the most cost-effective patrol method.

Different patrol techniques have met with varying degrees of success. The Kansas City Preventive Patrol Experiment found that increasing or decreasing routine preventive patrol had no measurable effect on crime, citizens' fear of crime, community attitudes toward the police on delivery of police services, police response time, or traffic accidents. Regardless of the patrol strategy used, police effectiveness is greatly influenced by citizen involvement. Citizen reporting time affects the possibility of on-scene arrests more than does police response time. Response time is often lengthened because citizens delay calling the police because of decision-making problems or problems communicating with the police.

Problem-oriented policing (POP) requires a shift in perspective from incident driven to problem driven—from reactive to proactive. It often depends on the SARA technique. The SARA problem-solving technique has contributed greatly to policing effectiveness and consists of four stages:

▶ Scanning: Identifying the problem

▶ Analysis: Learning the problem's causes, scope, and effects

▶ Response: Acting to alleviate the problem

▶ Assessment: Determining whether the response worked

APPLICATION

The local chamber of commerce has asked that you assign an officer to foot patrol in the business district because of numerous problems, such as vandalism, shoplifting, boisterous conduct by young people, and general disruption of business because of gang activity.

You realize foot patrol is proactive, designed to prevent crime and deal with social problems before they become overtly criminal. The city council wants you to proceed; it will add an officer to your department to provide this service.

INSTRUCTIONS

Write a policy and procedure that would offer guidelines to an officer and satisfy the business community's request. Keep in mind that foot patrol is an important assignment with many advantages over automobile patrol: more person-to-person contact, high visibility, enhanced public relations, the potential to be proactive and solve problems, and increased community support.

Begin the policy with a statement of need. Consider that the officer, being highly visible, may need more supervision. Who will supervise the officer, and what will the officer's duties be? Some type of communication with the officer while on duty must be established, and a system of assignment decided on. Decide what parameters would be useful to officers on foot patrol when they employ the directed-patrol approach and problem-oriented policing. List expectations for the officer's conduct and responsibilities while serving this important function.

AN EXERCISE IN CRITICAL THINKING

At 2:04 a.m. on a Friday, a burglar alarm went off at Prior Lake Marine, a business located on the outskirts of Prior Lake, Minnesota. Officer Ferderer of the Prior Lake Police Department, responding to the dispatcher's request at 2:07 a.m. for assistance in investigating a burglary in progress, drove toward the burglary scene. The only car he saw was a red 2000 Honda Accord with three men in it proceeding on a residential street just two blocks from Prior Lake Marine and headed away from that area. Ferderer turned and stopped the car about a mile from the scene at approximately 2:15 a.m.

Ferderer waited until Officer Gliniany of the Savage (Minnesota) Police Department arrived to assist, then approached the car on foot. Another officer arrived a short time later. The three men in the car were all in short-sleeved shirts and jeans and were sweating heavily (their bodies were literally "soaked with sweat"). Although it was a warm night, the heavy sweating was obviously inconsistent with the men having just been driving around. Ferderer could see that the driver and the rear-seat passenger were wearing tennis shoes and that the front-seat passenger was barefooted. In fact, as Gliniany testified, the front-seat passenger's feet were muddy.

After telling the men in the front seat to put their hands on the dashboard, Ferderer asked the driver, Terry Theis, what he was doing in the area. He said he had stopped to "take a leak" and that he, Rolland Moffatt, and Gerald Moffatt were on their way to New Prague to visit a friend. Ferderer asked who the friend was, but apparently no name was given. Ferderer told the men there had just been a burglary in the area, and he was checking it out. He did not tell the men they were suspects.

A decision was made to separate the men from one another by placing them in separate squad cars. Ferderer did this by removing each man, one at a time, frisking him for weapons, and then placing him in a squad car.

After the three men were placed in separate squad cars, Officer Gliniany contacted Officer Brandt, who was with officers at the burglary scene, and asked Brandt if there were footprints at the scene. Brandt reported there were.

Under instructions radioed by a police sergeant at the burglary scene, the officers told each of the two men with shoes to take off one tennis shoe. At this point, Theis said he asked one officer if he was under arrest, and the officer said, "No, you're being detained." One officer got the third tennis shoe, that of the barefoot front-seat passenger, by reaching in and removing it from the floor of the front-seat passenger side, where it was in open view. It was then about 2:45 a.m. Officer Klegin of the Savage Police Department, who had been dispatched at 2:20 a.m., drove to the scene of the stop, arriving about 15 minutes after the shoes had been seized, picked up the three shoes, and drove them to the burglary scene. There he compared the distinctive treads of the tennis shoes, each a different brand, with the two different fresh tennis shoe footprints he found. He concluded that the pattern and size of each print had been made by two of the men.

Ten to 15 minutes after Officer Klegin picked up the shoes, Sergeant McColl contacted the officers, who then handcuffed the three men, told them that they were being taken into custody, gave them *Miranda* warnings, and impounded the stopped car. This occurred at 3:16 a.m., 61 minutes after the car was stopped.

A search warrant was obtained, and the car was searched. Three pairs of gloves, a box of tools, a crowbar, and other items were found in the trunk.

1. Did the police violate the Fourth Amendment rights of Rolland and Gerald Moffatt and Terry Theis in stopping their car a short distance from the burglary scene?

   a. Yes; before receiving a search warrant, neither the stop, the limited investigation, nor the seizing of shoes would be considered justified or proper.

   b. Yes; police obtained probable cause to arrest shortly before 2:45 a.m., but before that time a stop would not be lawful.

c. No; observing the only car in the area moments after the report of burglary justifies stopping the vehicle.

d. Yes; the observation that the three men were soaked with sweat and gave a lame reason for being in the area justified the stop.

e. Yes; the police have a right to stop any vehicle at any time as long as an officer has a hunch there is possible suspicious activity, so this stop was lawful.

2. Was the conduct of the police diligent and reasonable?

a. No; there are no good reasons for placing each man in a separate squad car, and no such action should occur before they are given a *Miranda* warning and told they are under arrest.

b. Yes; while conducting a limited investigation, officers must get all available information within half an hour, including any search.

Further, confiscating the shoes so they could be taken to the burglary scene for comparison with footprints requires a warrant.

c. No; once the officers frisked for weapons and put the three men in the squad cars, they converted what might have been a detention into an arrest for which there was no probable cause—no weapons were found.

d. Yes; this was diligent and reasonable police action because of the small police department, that it was a burglary investigation (not just a petty offense), and that there were three men involved; it was not in the interest of the police or public to release them quickly and allow them to get away with evidence of their guilt.

e. No; the 20-minute "bright line" rule by the American Law Institute, for the length of an investigative detention, makes this hour-long detention illegal.

DISCUSSION QUESTIONS

1. Which of the following is the most complex objective of patrol: crime prevention, crime repression, apprehending offenders, or recovering stolen property? Why?

2. What factors should be considered when using K-9–assisted patrol? What restrictions should be placed on such patrol?

3. Which is the most effective method of patrol: foot patrol, bicycle patrol, one-officer patrol vehicle, two-officer patrol vehicle, or some other method?

4. What factors should be considered in determining the most suitable patrol methods to use in a police agency? How do these factors affect the choice of patrol methods?

5. What are the relative strengths and weaknesses of foot patrol and automobile patrol? How can these two patrol methods be combined to enhance the effectiveness of patrol efforts?

6. Why do patrol officers' behaviors vary so widely from community to community?

7. How might the organizational contradiction embodied in the patrol function be reduced?

GALE EMERGENCY SERVICES DATABASE ASSIGNMENTS

▶ Use the Gale Emergency Services database (available for separate purchase) to answer the Discussion Questions as appropriate.

▶ Use the Gale Emergency Services database to research the *various incidents that occur on patrol* and *the various types of patrol* that agencies use. Can you determine a pattern or correlation in how the types of incidents handled influence the method of patrol used?

▶ Use the Gale Emergency Services database to find and outline one of the following articles:

- "Looking Inward with Problem-Oriented Policing" by Terry Eisenberg and Bruce Glasscock
- "Police on Horseback: A New Concept for an Old Idea" by John C. Fine
- "Using Drug Detection Dogs: An Update" by Jayme S. Walker

REFERENCES

"Almost 50% of Agencies Routinely Use K-9s." 2008. *Police* (March): 14.

Basich, Melanie. 2009. "Officers Overwhelmingly Approve of In-Car Video." *Police* (February): 18.

"Cameras." 2012 (January). In *How Are Innovations in Technology Transforming Policing?*, pages 13–24. Washington, DC: Police Executive Research Forum, Critical Issues in Policing Series.

Commission on Accreditation of Law Enforcement Agencies (CALEA). 2012. *Standards for Law Enforcement Agencies.* 5th ed. Fairfax, VA: Author.

Craven, Kym. 2009. "Foot Patrols: Crime Analysis and Community Engagement to Further the Commitment to Community Policing." *Community Policing Dispatch* (February). http://www.cops.usdoj.gov/html/dispatch/February_2009/foot_patrol.htm.

Eck, John E. 2002. *Assessing Responses to Problems: An Introductory Guide for Police Problem-Solvers.* Washington, DC: Office of Community Oriented Policing Services.

Excellence in Problem-Oriented Policing: The 2002 Herman Goldstein Award Winners. 2002. Washington, DC: National Institute of Justice, Office of Community Oriented Policing Services, and Police Executive Research Forum.

Garrett, Ronnie. 2008. "Smile, You're on VIDMIC." *Law Enforcement Technology* (June): 122–127.

Goldstein, Herman. 1990. *Problem-Oriented Policing.* New York: McGraw-Hill.

Griffith, David. 2008. "In Praise of the Patrol Officer." *Police* (January): 10.

Klockars, Carl B. 1983. *Thinking about Policing: Contemporary Readings.* New York: McGraw-Hill.

Lansdowne, William M. 2007. "'The Core of the Department Is Patrol': An Interview with San Diego Police Chief William M. Lansdowne." *Subject to Debate* (August): 1, 6.

Lauria, Donald T. 2007. "Cost-Benefit Analysis of Tacoma's Assigned Vehicle Program." *Police Quarterly* (June): 192–217.

Menton, Chris. 2007. "Bicycle Patrols versus Car Patrols." *Law and Order* (June): 78–81.

"PERF Survey Shows Widespread Use of Many Technologies in Policing." 2012. In *How Are Innovations in Technology Transforming Policing?*, pages 1–3. Washington, DC: Police Executive Research Forum, Critical Issues in Policing Series.

Ratcliffe, Jerry H., Travis Taniguchi, Elizabeth R. Groff, and Jennifer D. Wood. 2011. "The Philadelphia Foot Patrol Experiment: A Randomized Controlled Trial of Police Patrol Effectiveness in Violent Crime Hotspots." *Criminology* 49 (3): 795–831.

Scoville, Dean. 2008. "Working on the Front Lines." *Police* (July): 38–48.

Scoville, Dean. 2011. "Lone-Officer Patrols: Going Solo." *Police* (March): 54–61.

Solar, Patrick. 2009. "The Economics of Patrol Scheduling, Part 2." *Law and Order* (October): 74–79.

Solosky, Kenneth J. 2009. "Your Eye in the Sky." *Law Officer Magazine* (February): 38–43.

Spelman, William G., and Dale K. Brown. 1991. "Response Time." In *Thinking about Police: Contemporary Readings*, 2nd ed., edited by Carl B. Klockars and Stephen D. Mastrofski, 163–167. New York: McGraw-Hill.

Wandrei, Greg. 2007. "Instant Access to Vital Information: The Role of GIS." *Law Enforcement Technology* (November): 56–61.

Wetzel, Tom. 2011. "Surviving Foot Patrol." *Police* (November): 56–57.

CASE CITED

United States v. Place, 462 U.S. 696 (1983)

CHAPTER 5

© AP Images/EricAlbrecht

Traffic:
Policing in a Country on the Move

DO YOU KNOW . . .

- What three functional areas police traffic services include?
- What the basic purposes of traffic enforcement are?
- Who is responsible for traffic enforcement?
- How the problem of speeding in residential areas can be addressed?
- What the difference between aggressive driving and road rage is?
- What the number-one problem of traffic enforcement is?
- What strategies are being used to deter DUI?
- What balance must be maintained in an effective pursuit policy?
- What issues should be addressed in a pursuit policy?
- What a hazardous materials enforcement program should include?
- What the responsibilities of officers responding to a crash scene are?

CAN YOU DEFINE?

blood-alcohol concentration (BAC)
cruising
drug recognition expert (DRE)
drug recognition technician (DRT)
dual motive stop
enforcement index
implied consent law
nystagmus
pretext stop
racial profiling
road rage
scofflaws
traffic calming
vehicle pursuit

INTRODUCTION

The United States is truly a nation on the move. Citizens feel it is their *right* to drive vehicles, even though it really is a privilege, and they resent any limitations imposed on this "right." At the same time, they also expect city and state governments to keep the roadways in good condition and the police to keep traffic moving. Besides simply keeping traffic flowing, officers involved in this important aspect of police work are also charged with helping at and investigating crashes involving vehicles. Police also must deal with criminals who use vehicles in committing their crimes. This often involves high-speed chases. At the opposite end of the spectrum is law enforcement's responsibility to educate members of the driving public about their responsibilities and the rules and regulations they must obey.

More officer time is spent on traffic patrol than on any other police activity. Unfortunately, like patrol in general, traffic services are often perceived as unglamorous and rank low on the department's and community's priority list: "Addressing traffic-related concerns is increasingly challenging because of dwindling municipal budgets, competing resources, and rising crime rates. [Yet] the ease with which motorists can move about in a safe manner is an important attribute of a prosperous and livable community" (Maggard and Jung 2009, 46). Sweeney (2011b, 90) stresses that criminals continue to exploit the roadways of our nation, as they have since the automobile was invented, while they conduct their illegal activities: "This means the basic building block of police work remains proactive traffic enforcement. Society is more mobile than ever before and so, too, are the criminals and the terrorists who are never more vulnerable to police detection and arrest than when they are traveling from point A to point B in their motor vehicles. And as ordinary citizens travel these highways too, the only thing standing between them and criminals are troopers and patrol officers in their vehicles and on their motorcycles.... Traffic stops save lives and prevent and solve crimes. If law enforcement agencies neglect the basics, criminal activity can grow in prevalence. Traffic enforcement is first among the basics." Indeed, according to a past president of the International Association of Chiefs of Police (IACP), "I believe that it is no exaggeration to say that few duties of the law enforcement community affect the quality of life of our citizens as significantly as the rendering of quality police traffic services" (Marshall 2011, 6).

61.1

CALEA Standard 61.1 focuses on traffic, stating, "Activities undertaken by the agency that directly affect the movement and control of vehicles and pedestrians include point traffic control, traffic engineering, school crossing supervision, and other activities related to the design and implementation of plans and programs that expedite the movement of vehicles and pedestrians.... The agency may perform a variety of diverse, traffic-related services including providing general assistance, emergency assistance, public information, and directions; identifying and reporting roadway and roadside hazards; checking abandoned vehicles; and locating and recovering stolen vehicles."

Source: Commission on Accreditation of Law Enforcement Agencies (CALEA). 2012. *Standards for Law Enforcement Agencies.* 5th ed. Fairfax, VA: Author.

Directing traffic is a hazardous duty. Each year many officers are injured or killed by careless drivers.

© AP Images/Gregory Bull

Police traffic services (PTS) are divided into three major areas:
- Traffic direction and control
- Traffic enforcement
- Crash investigation

This chapter begins with a discussion of traffic direction and control. This is followed by a discussion of traffic enforcement and specific traffic violations, including failure to obey seat belt laws; speeding; red-light running; tailgating; aggressive driving and road rage; rolling domestics; and driving under the influence; as well as how selective traffic enforcement and the enforcement index influence which violations officers decide on which to focus. Next, the traffic stop is examined, including the use of automated citations and the issues surrounding pretext stops and racial profiling. This is followed by an in-depth look at recognizing and stopping drivers under the influence of alcohol and drugs. High-speed pursuits and hazardous materials enforcement are presented next. Then crash management and investigation are discussed. The chapter concludes with a look at the relationship between traffic, community policing and problem solving, and the benefits of an Area Traffic Officer (ATO) Program.

TRAFFIC DIRECTION AND CONTROL

Traffic direction and control (TD&C) is a planned assignment and may take place regularly at such places as schools before and after closing, major sporting events, parades, funerals, and the like. It may also take place during rush hour; during unexpected or emergency events, such as civil disturbances or natural disasters; or when a high-profile political figure or celebrity is in town. In addition, TD&C is part of an officer's responsibility at crash scenes.

TD&C requires great skill in nonverbal communication. The tools officers normally use are their hands, eyes, and a whistle. At night or in poor weather conditions, a vital tool is a flashlight or lighted cone. Seldom can verbal commands be issued. Officers get attention by short blasts on their whistles, use of their flashlights, and making eye contact with drivers. Officers provide direction with their hands, motioning drivers to stop, turn, or go straight.

Officers engaged in traffic direction and control should plan carefully how best to position themselves, considering both their visibility to oncoming traffic and their personal safety. Safety precautions include wearing reflective Day-Glo vests and, at night, using flashlights with cones attached. Officers must also consider in the overall plan how best to keep the traffic moving, including pedestrian traffic.

Whistles are great attention getters for traffic officers. One long whistle blast means stop all traffic, and two short blasts get the drivers started again. Officers should always be alert for distracted drivers—those talking on their phones, changing radio stations, looking at their GPSs, putting on makeup, or reading the newspaper—who may not be giving their full attention to the road and their driving and, consequently, to the officer standing in the street.

High Visibility

The Manual on Uniform Traffic Control Devices (2009) has mandated that highway workers wear high-visibility safety garments and apparel while working on or near the roadway, and this includes law enforcement. The Occupational Safety and Health Administration (OSHA) and many states are also mandating the use of "hi-viz" garments by all roadway workers, including law enforcement. Officers who are working special traffic enforcement details, such as Safe & Sober, Night Cap, and similar duties, are required to wear high-visibility traffic vests for the duration of their participation in such grant-funded events. And many departments require their officers to wear hi-viz traffic vests when working extended roadway assignments, such as a car crash scene.

The Cruising Problem

cruising

Driving around and around a predetermined, popular route, usually through the heart of a town or city; a social activity of teenagers.

Since the 1950s, cruising has been a favorite pastime of teenagers and young adults. **Cruising**—driving around and around a predetermined, popular route, usually through the heart of a town or city—gives young people a chance to see who is going out together and what kinds of cars other teenagers are driving, to pick up dates, and to spend their socializing hours in a relatively inexpensive way. When teenagers got out of hand in the 1950s and 1960s, police used existing curfew or loitering laws to send them home, a task easy to do in small towns.

By the 1970s, however, cruising had become a problem in major urban areas. Some cities passed cruising ordinances that prohibited a car from passing a specific point more than a certain number of times within a specific period. In addition, cruising is often associated with johns seeking prostitutes, drug addicts seeking drug buys, or potential robbers or burglars staking out possible targets. Further, it has become associated with drive-by shootings, certainly of grave concern to any community and its police.

TRAFFIC ENFORCEMENT

A primary responsibility of traffic services is enforcing a municipality's and state's traffic rules and regulations, which are enacted for the safety of all citizens: "There's nothing a law enforcement agency can do that has as much potential to save lives and prevent injury [as does traffic enforcement]" (Bolton 2009, 90).

> The two basic purposes of traffic enforcement are to control congestion and to reduce crashes. Enforcement can also detect criminal activity.

Enforcement action taken against traffic violators serves a dual purpose. First, it allows the court to evaluate the propriety of a motorist's conduct and administer appropriate punitive sanctions directly against that driver. Second, enforcement acts as a deterrent to other drivers in preventing future violations because citizens who know that traffic laws are enforced are more likely to comply with the rules of the road. Nonetheless, many drivers routinely break traffic laws, believing their minor infractions will not be noticed or result in tickets. Particularly troublesome are offenders who have had their driver's license permanently revoked because of continued traffic infractions and because their mentality is commonly one of "I can't lose something I've already lost."

Although most people respect the aims and efforts of police officers in traffic enforcement as applied to *other* drivers, many motorists turn critical of the same enforcement actions when they become the subject of a traffic stop. A common complaint of those ticketed for traffic violations is that the police should be focusing on catching real criminals instead of pulling people over for driving a little faster than the speed limit.

▌ AN OFFICER'S PERSPECTIVE ▌
Citizens: Be Careful What You Wish For

Police agencies may conduct traffic enforcement saturations that are based on community requests and citizen complaints. In one circumstance, several members of a residential area complained of speeders in their neighborhood, so our department arranged for a speed enforcement detail in the affected area. Ironically, most of the stops were of citizens who lived in that very same neighborhood. In fact, one of the original complainants was stopped and cited for the very infraction they had complained about.

—*Sgt. Henry Lim Cho*

Even some police officers do not regard traffic enforcement as "real" police work, contending that writing traffic citations could be done by nonsworn personnel. Indeed, nonsworn personnel are helpful in many areas, such as parking violations. However, stopping vehicles can be just as dangerous, if not more so, as responding to calls. In addition, a crucial, frequently unrecognized aspect of traffic enforcement is the potential apprehension of wanted suspects.

Someone willing to commit a serious criminal act usually has little reservation about breaking traffic laws. People who commit crimes are also often the ones driving with revoked licenses, expired tags, or burned-out taillights or headlights. Thus, the potential for exposure of other crimes during a traffic stop makes traffic enforcement a duty of all officers, not just those assigned to highway patrol or other specific traffic units.

> Even if a traffic enforcement unit exists, traffic enforcement is the responsibility of all officers.

A good example of the potential for traffic enforcement to lead to a criminal apprehension occurred when State Trooper Charles Hanger stopped Timothy McVeigh's car because it lacked license plates. Trooper Hanger, unaware of the driver's involvement in the day's earlier terrorist bombing of the Alfred P. Murrah Building, cited McVeigh for, among other things, the absence of license tags and carrying a concealed gun. While McVeigh sat in a jail cell being processed into the system for his offenses, investigators handling the bombing's aftermath were searching for suspects, including McVeigh. Their database search turned up a "hit," and the trooper was credited with apprehending the terrorist, McVeigh, who was later convicted and executed for his role in the bombing.

Traffic enforcement is a large part of proactive policing. Sanow (2009, 6) contends, "Traffic enforcement equals crime prevention," noting, "Aggressive traffic enforcement is a win-win. It reduces crime and increases safety. As a result of a focused traffic enforcement effort, Oklahoma County, Oklahoma, has already documented a 90-percent reduction in crashes and a 90-percent reduction in criminal activity."

The IACP Highway Safety Committee and the 3M Traffic Safety Systems Division have partnered for more than a decade in recognizing police officers who use license plates to solve serious, nontraffic crimes. The *Looking Beyond the License Plate* award substantiates and documents the importance of license plates as a critical law enforcement tool to track and identify offenders because an estimated 70 percent of all serious crime involves a motor vehicle ("*Looking Beyond the License Plate* Award Program" n.d.). Some state-level associations have devised similar incentive programs; for example, the Illinois Association of Chiefs of Police program, "Looking Beyond the Safety Belt," recognizes that law enforcement officers who initiate a traffic stop based solely on a safety-belt violation often discover other crimes or situations leading to an arrest.

Technology such as automated license plate recognition (ALPR) programs assists in efforts to check for suspicious vehicles, stolen vehicles or license plates, outstanding unpaid parking citations, and wanted felons.

Automated License Plate Recognition (ALPR)

ALPR or simply license plate recognition (LPR) systems were introduced in the United States in 2004 and have become a valuable tool for law enforcement. ALPR technology uses special cameras to photograph vehicle license plates and then uses optical character recognition (OCR) software to read the plate number and compare it with wanted vehicle databases that are updated every few minutes. This technology can read nearly 4,000 license plates an hour in real time (Easley and Wunk 2010).

TECHNOLOGY IN POLICING

LICENSE PLATE READERS

LPR can increase revenue related to traffic and parking citations and vehicle impounds, and such systems help officers and investigators solve crimes that go well beyond simple auto theft through the potential for plate "hits" to intersect in databases cross-referencing information on violent crimes, burglaries, or any other targeted criminal activities (Haug 2009). Consider the following examples of how LRP has recently helped police departments across the country ("License Plate Readers" 2012):

▶ In Washington, DC, LRP technology helped close two homicides and helped recover a vehicle connected to a third homicide.

▶ Minneapolis, Minnesota, has placed permanent and mobile LPRs on heavily trafficked bridges and was able to solve, with information stored in the license plate database, a domestic kidnapping case where a witness had only a partial plate number.

▶ Sacramento, California, has used LPR at a local shopping mall to reduce auto thefts at that mall by 66 percent and to identify homicide witnesses, robbery suspects, and stolen vehicles.

▶ Chicago, Illinois, uses LPR as an intelligence and investigative tool, to quickly and easily capture data near the scene of violent crimes, such as homicides and aggravated battery, which saves considerable manpower hours previously required to canvass the neighborhoods surrounding such crimes.

Some advocates of this technology argue that LRP "has the potential to be even more important to public safety and policing than DNA" (Stockton 2009, 8).

Traffic Violators and Violations

Most drivers stopped for traffic violations are not terrorist bombers or other wanted criminals—they will be average everyday people, most of whom are not necessarily actively refusing to conform to society's laws. They simply are not paying attention. Judging by the millions of traffic citations and parking tickets issued every year, operating a motor vehicle in compliance with all the laws is mastered by only a few motorists. Despite their good intentions and interest in community safety, hundreds of thousands of people—young and old, male and female, of all races, national origins, occupations, and religions—violate traffic laws.

Violations range from failing to wear a seat belt or put children in the proper child safety seats, to changing lanes or turning without signaling, to ignoring No Parking or No Turn on Red signs, to speeding or running red lights. The most serious traffic violations involve aggressive driving that may turn to road rage, or driving under the influence of alcohol or drugs. The reasons given for violations range from being late for an appointment; to "just keeping up with traffic"; to "getting away with something"; to being distracted by cell phones, radios, a steaming cup of coffee, screaming children, or conversation with other passengers; to being daydreamers whose thoughts are far away from the responsibilities of driving a vehicle.

Using a cell phone while driving has been determined so serious a distraction that it has become the subject of legislation. Currently, 10 states, the District of Columbia, and the Virgin Islands prohibit all drivers from using handheld cell phones while driving, permitting only hands-free calling, and more states are considering such legislation. Other states selectively impose this restriction on certain categories of drivers, such as those under age 18 (novice drivers) and school bus drivers. Text messaging by drivers—which

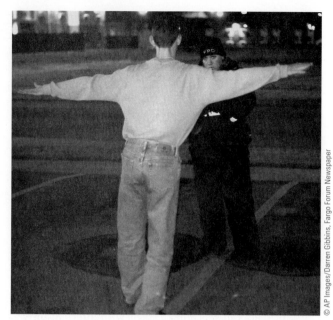

Being cited for a traffic violation is one of the most common ways citizens come in contact with the police. Here, a Fargo, North Dakota, police officer working a DUI checkpoint runs a motorist through a field sobriety test. The man was ultimately arrested on suspicion of driving under the influence. Such checkpoints are one method used to get impaired drivers off the roads.

© AP Images/Darren Gibbins, Fargo Forum Newspaper

includes composing, reading, or sending electronic messages when a vehicle is in motion or in traffic—is banned in 39 states, the District of Columbia, and Guam. Some states treat cell phone use and texting as part of a more comprehensive "distracted driving" issue. For example, in Utah, cell phone use is an offense *only* if a driver is also committing a moving violation other than speeding. A current list of which laws are in effect in the various states is available online at the Governor's Highway Safety Association Web site (www.ghsa.org). Additional information is available at www.distraction.gov, the official United States government web site for data regarding distracted driving.

In December 2011, the National Transportation Safety Board (NTSB) issued a report strongly recommending a complete ban on all cell phone use while driving, and the issue remains under debate at the federal level. Critics, however, argue that a complete ban is overreaching and that, if cell phones are really such a distraction, then perhaps all vehicle radios should be removed, passengers should not be allowed to talk, and drivers should be prohibited from eating or drinking while behind the wheel. These opponents contend that the focus should be on a driver's ability, or inability, to obey traffic laws, regardless of whatever else is occurring in the vehicle. Some drivers can observe the law while talking on the phone, especially when using hands-free equipment, whereas other drivers simply ignore the laws.

Seat Belt Laws

One of the most prevalent motor vehicle violations is the failure to buckle up. In 1994, because safety belt use stood at only 12 percent in New York, the state legislature approved a bill creating the nation's first mandatory seat belt law. That same year, an estimated 58 percent of vehicle occupants nationwide regularly wore their seat belts. By 2011, however, national seat belt use had climbed to 84 percent, accompanied by a steady decline in the number of passenger vehicle occupant fatalities during the daytime, which is defined as the period between 7 a.m. and 6 p.m. (*Seat Belt Use* 2011, 1). According to the survey, seat belt use continues to be higher in states in which vehicle occupants can be pulled over solely for not using seat belts ("primary law" states). An estimated 12,713 lives were saved in 2009 through use of seat belts in motor vehicles, and an estimated 72,000 lives were saved from 2005 through 2009 through such use (*Lives Saved in 2009* 2010). An additional 2,381 lives were saved by front-end air bags.

The leading cause of death for children ages 3 to 14 in the United States is motor vehicle crashes, with an average daily fatality rate of 4 children ages 14 and younger; another 529 children are injured (on average) in motor vehicle crashes each day (*Children* 2008). These deaths and injuries were largely caused by the nonuse or improper use of child seats and seat belts. Motor vehicle crashes are also the leading cause of death for 15- to 19-year-olds, accounting for more than one third of all deaths in this age group ("Teen Drivers: Fact Sheet" 2010). According to data from the Centers for Disease Control and Prevention (CDC), an estimated 3,000 teens ages 15 to 19 were killed in the United States in 2009 and more than 350,000 were treated in emergency rooms because of injuries sustained in motor vehicle crashes ("Teen Drivers: Fact Sheet" 2010). Furthermore, per mile driven, teen drivers ages 16 to 19 are four times more likely than older drivers are to crash. Yet, compared with other age groups, teens have the lowest rate of seat belt use. In addition, in 2008, nearly three of every four teen drivers killed in motor vehicle crashes after drinking and driving were not wearing a seat belt ("Teen Drivers: Fact Sheet" 2010).

Paralleling the institution of seat belt laws in 1994 was North Carolina's *Click It or Ticket Program* to increase use of seat belts, which has since become a national effort. The National Highway Traffic Safety Administration (NHTSA) Click It or Ticket (CIOT) Web site calls the program "the most successful seat belt enforcement campaign ever" ("Click It or Ticket" n.d.). The program uses heavy publicity and a solid public information and education campaign from mid-May to the beginning of June (Memorial Day). The primary audience continues to be men ages 18 to 34, whom research shows are less likely to wear seat belts.

Speeding

One of the most basic risk factors in traffic safety is speed: "Higher driving speeds lead to higher collision speeds and thus to severer injuries. Higher driving speeds also provide less time to process information and to act on it, and the braking distance is longer" ("Relation between Speed and Crashes" 2009, 1). According to the NHTSA, "Speeding is one of the most prevalent factors contributing to traffic crashes. The economic cost to society of speeding-related crashes is estimated by NHTSA to be $40.4 billion per year. In 2008, speeding was a contributing factor in 31 percent of all fatal crashes, and 11,674 lives were lost in speeding-related crashes" ("Speeding" 2008, 1).

Many drivers, particularly younger, less experienced ones, fail to anticipate hazards on the road and overestimate their ability to control their vehicle when the unexpected happens—another driver cuts in front of them, a dog runs across the street, a tire blows, or they hit an icy patch in the road. Some drivers subscribe to the philosophy that it is safer to "go with the flow" of traffic, even if it is 10 miles an hour over the posted speed limit, than to obey the traffic law and make other drivers maneuver their speeding vehicles through numerous lane changes to get around slower traffic. Still others, lost in thought or conversation, are completely unaware of the speed at which they are traveling. Sometimes, compliance with the speed limit can be obtained simply by reminding drivers to check their speedometers. Other times, aggressive ticketing campaigns are needed to get drivers to slow down.

The Problem of Speeding in Residential Areas Numerous studies have shown that traffic-related issues continue to be citizens' number-one complaint to police (Casstevens 2008). Speeding in residential areas makes citizens fear for children's safety; makes pedestrians and bicyclists fear for their safety; and increases the risk of vehicle crashes as well as the seriousness of injuries to other drivers, passengers, pedestrians, and bicyclists struck by a vehicle.

> Speeding can be addressed through engineering, education, and enforcement responses.

Engineering responses are preventative in nature and include posting warning signs and signals; installing cameras as deterrents; installing stop signs, speed limit signs, and computerized speed display boards; painting crosswalks; using turn prohibitions; designating streets as one-way; and using traffic calming alternatives. **Traffic calming** involves modifying road design and environmental conditions to make it more difficult for a driver to speed or to make drivers believe they should slow down for safety. Some traffic calming measures are speed bumps and humps, rumble strips, cul-de-sacs, narrowing the road, putting bends and curves in the road, permitting parking on both sides of residential streets, and timing traffic signals for vehicles traveling the desired speed. "Without traffic calming to intervene and prevent accidents, the number of traffic crashes and fatalities would rapidly escalate" ("World without Traffic Calming" 2009).

traffic calming

Describes a wide range of road and environment design changes that either make it more difficult for a vehicle to speed or make drivers believe they should slow down for safety.

Installing a radar speed display or speed trailer in a problem area is another engineering effort to reduce speeding. Such displays show the speed limit and the approaching motorist's speed, and are often set to flash when drivers exceed the posted speed limit. Some departments mount a speed display on the back of a patrol car that they park alongside a problem area.

Education responses include conducting anti-speeding public awareness campaigns, informing complainants about actual speeds, instituting neighborhood speed watch programs, and providing realistic driver training.

Enforcement responses include using photo radar, using laser/lidar (light detection and ranging) from a distance (this is different from squad radar), using speed display boards, ticketing speeders, deploying patrol saturation with a focus on speed enforcement, arresting the worst offenders, and training citizen volunteers to monitor speeding.

Measures to reduce speeding in residential areas that seem to have *limited effectiveness* include reducing speed limits, increasing fines and penalties, erecting stop signs, installing speed bumps and rumble strips, and reengineering vehicles. However, these measures used in conjunction with education and other engineering responses may prove to be effective.

Curbing Illegal Street Racing

Informally organized street races cause the deaths of numerous drivers and spectators every year. Strategies that may reduce street racing include using undercover officers and vehicles, videotaping or photographing the racing activities, developing interagency enforcement teams, working with the media to publicize the problem, developing an alternative site for racing, and making Internet contact through street racing groups' Web sites, and the department's own Web site. If these don't work, law enforcement should adopt a zero-tolerance policy: "Written enforcement action can be taken for careless driving, reckless driving, and racing on public streets. Nonparticipants (starters, timers, those who block street) can be charged with trespassing or obstructing public passage. Applicable curfew laws can be enforced to winnow crowds. And you can deprive the racers of their tracks by getting the local government to install speed bumps on particularly troublesome streets" (Petrocelli 2007, 21).

Officers are reporting seeing an increase in a particularly dangerous form of racing called "cutting the gap," speed contests in which racers weave in and out of traffic. Too often, the speed and power of the vehicles exceed the driving skills of the racers. Griffith (2007, 12) contends, "Cutting the gap is nothing short of attempted murder. It should be treated that way."

Using Decoy Patrols

Some jurisdictions are using decoy or dummy patrol vehicles to reduce speeding and traffic violations. These unmanned vehicles provide high visibility parked alongside the road in areas experiencing traffic problems. However, such squads may fall victim to vandalization, as happened in Durham, North Carolina, when a decoy highway patrol car left parked along Interstate 85 had its windows smashed and tires slashed. The deterrent effect of such decoys is also often only temporary, until the driving public recognizes that no officer is actually on-scene to issue citations. Nonetheless, decoy patrol vehicles have proven effective in many jurisdictions.

Speed Enforcement Technology

The conventional radar unit is the oldest electronic speed enforcement technology in use and is still the "tool of choice" for most traffic officers. A controversial new speed enforcement device is photo radar. Photo speed enforcement is also being used. These units are typically mounted in the rear of a sport-utility vehicle parked at roadside and aimed at a 22-degree angle at oncoming traffic. The radar detects a speeding car, records its speed, license number, and the driver's face. It then generates a ticket that is mailed to the driver.

Another type of speed enforcement is drone radar, which capitalizes on the fact that many motorists have radar detection units in their vehicles. (Radar detector use in cars is legal in most states, but its use in commercial vehicles was banned in all states by a directive of the U.S. Department of Transportation [USDOT] in 1995.) The sole purpose of drone radar is to trigger these radar detection units, thereby slowing their drivers in most instances. The units can be connected with speed display signs that announce, "You are going X miles" to alert drivers they are speeding. However, once drivers discover that a drone radar unit is operating and that no tickets are forthcoming, the effectiveness of the unit is lost, and the unit should be moved.

Red-Light Runners

When people are in a hurry and are speeding or are distracted, they are also more likely to run red lights and stop signs. Public awareness of the problems associated with red-light running might be raised through press conferences, billboards, and posters. Suggested engineering improvements include warning signs, pavement markings, skid resistance, bigger or brighter signs and signals, and timing of traffic signal phases. Another approach is to install automated red-light cameras.

For some people looking for faster ways to get from point A to point B, the stop sign or red stoplight has become a personal nemesis, seen not as a device to enhance traffic flow and safety but as an enemy to be beaten. Getting "caught" at the light is more than an inconvenience; it's a mild form of defeat. Some drivers, in their "battle" to triumph over such cameras, have tried placing covers or sprays over their plates. License plate sprays may foil traffic cameras by bouncing back the flash of the camera to overexpose the license plate, but these sprays do not work if flashless digital cameras are used.

Another potential concern is the availability of signal-changing devices. A mechanism called a mobile infrared transmitter, or MIRT, is the trigger device in traffic preemptions systems. Although no cities have reported this as a problem, several cities are urging their legislators to pass legislation specifically banning the use of MIRTs by unauthorized individuals.

Tailgating

Tailgating, or following too closely behind another car, is a factor in many crashes. However, as an increasingly common infraction, it has defied traffic officers for years. It is difficult for law enforcement to enforce the highway safety industry's 3-second rule—the guideline stating that the distance traveled in 3 seconds is the *minimum* distance a driver should be from the vehicle in front of him or her—because it is considered by many to be a subjective judgment (Galvin 2009). However, recently developed laser technology known as distance between cars (DBC) is allowing officers to calculate the time and distance between two moving vehicles traveling in the same lane, enhancing officers' ability to issue citations to tailgating offenders.

Aggressive Driving and Road Rage

Aggressive driving has become one of the leading safety hazards on our highways and, according to several studies, is considered more dangerous than are drunk driving and driving without seat belts. The NHTSA defines *aggressive driving* as occurring when "an individual commits a combination of moving traffic offenses so as to endanger other persons or property" (*Aggressive Driving Enforcement* 2004). The NHTSA distinguishes aggressive driving from road rage, saying that behaviors of aggressive drivers include tailgating, making erratic or unsafe lane changes, exceeding speed limits or driving too fast for conditions, weaving in and out of traffic, and ignoring traffic control devices such as stop lights and yield signs. Aggressive driving often precipitates road rage. The NHTSA defines **road rage** as "an assault with a motor vehicle or other dangerous weapon by the operator or passenger(s) of one motor vehicle on the operator or passenger(s) of another motor vehicle and is caused by an incident that occurred on the roadway."

road rage

"An assault with a motor vehicle or other dangerous weapon by the operator or passenger(s) of one motor vehicle on the operator or passenger(s) of another motor vehicle and is caused by an incident that occurred on the roadway."

> Aggressive driving is a traffic violation; road rage is a criminal offense.

Recognizing the danger posed by aggressive drivers, jurisdictions throughout the country are implementing special teams to tackle this growing threat.

Rolling Domestics

Rolling domestics pose another hazard on our nation's roadways. A *rolling domestic* is essentially a domestic situation that occurs in moving motor vehicle. Not only do these situations have the potential to become dangerous, full-fledged attacks on one or more occupants of the vehicle, but because they occur in traffic or on city streets, they can have extremely adverse effects on other vehicles driving nearby or on pedestrians, should the driver of the rolling domestic vehicle lose control.

Driving under the Influence

Another serious traffic violation that may earn a driver some jail time is driving under the influence of alcohol or drugs. Whether called *driving while intoxicated* (DWI), *driving under the influence* (DUI), *driving under the influence of liquor* (DUIL), or some other designation, those who do so are a critical problem for the community. Data from an NHTSA survey show that in 2008, 11,773 people died in the United States in motor vehicle crashes involving at least one driver with a BAC (blood alcohol concentration) of 0.08 or higher, a number representing 32 percent of all motor vehicle crash fatalities that year (Drew et al. 2010).

Law enforcement agencies take nearly 1.5 million drunk and drug intoxicated drivers off the road each year because of tougher laws, sobriety checkpoints, and saturation patrols. And yet, according to a CDC survey, approximately 4 million U.S. adults reported at least one episode of alcohol-impaired driving during 2010, for an estimated total of roughly 112 million alcohol-impaired driving episodes in a single year ("Vital Signs" 2011). The same survey estimated that the average drunk driver has made 80 alcohol-impaired driving trips before his or her first arrest.

The NHTSA position on drunk driving is echoed by police departments and sober driving advocates nationwide—that impaired driving is preventable and those people injured or killed by drunk drivers are not "accident" victims but rather victims of a violent crime (*Impaired Driving Prevention Toolkit* 2003).

> Nationwide, DUI is the number-one traffic law enforcement problem.

Yet police officers frequently simply issue a ticket and perhaps write a brief report, making prosecution extremely difficult. This is not to say that police do not want to see drunk drivers taken off the road. It only means that laws often make it extremely difficult and complex for an officer to charge an impaired driver with any significant offense. In some states, such as Minnesota, the first DWI offense, barring any aggravating factors, is only a misdemeanor crime and is citable. However, for every DWI offense after that, or if there are aggravating factors in the initial offense (e.g., excessive recklessness or speed, children in the vehicle, etc.), the offender is jailed. It is important to understand the various differences between state laws concerning DWI.

One reason officers may be detoured from enforcing DWIs is the weak punishments DWI offenders receive. Officers are commonly frustrated by how prosecutors treat DWI cases, often as just another traffic ticket. Offenders usually are able to bargain a weak punishment, frustrating officers because of all of the work and time it takes to process a DWI. A typical DWI from traffic stop to disposition lasts two hours, with many taking much longer, depending on the variables involved. Recognizing and stopping impaired drivers will be discussed in greater detail shortly.

enforcement index

A figure based on the ratio of tickets issued for hazardous driving violations to the number of fatal and personal injury crashes; standard suggests that for each fatal and personal injury crash, between 20 and 25 convictions for hazardous moving violations indicates effective traffic enforcement.

Selective Traffic Enforcement and the Enforcement Index

Officers cannot possibly stop and ticket every traffic violator. Consequently, most police departments rely on selective enforcement, the ability to decide when to impose legal sanctions on those who violate the law. Selective traffic enforcement plans allocation of police personnel and equipment by studying the violators and road conditions that contribute to collisions.

61.1.1

CALEA Standard 61.1.1 states, "The ultimate goal of selective traffic law enforcement is to reduce traffic collision. This may be achieved through the application of such techniques as geographic/temporal assignment of personnel and equipment and the establishment of preventive patrols to deal with specific categories of unlawful driving behavior. The techniques used should be based on collision data, enforcement activity records, traffic volume, and traffic conditions. The objective is to direct appropriate enforcement efforts toward violations, not only in proportion to the frequency of their occurrence in collision situations but also in terms of traffic-related needs identified in the agency's service community."

Source: Commission on Accreditation of Law Enforcement Agencies (CALEA). 2012. *Standards for Law Enforcement Agencies*. 5th ed. Fairfax, VA: Author.

Many police departments also use the **enforcement index**, a figure based on the ratio of tickets issued for hazardous driving violations to the number of fatal and personal injury crashes. The IACP and the National Safety Council suggest that an index of between 1:20 and 1:25 is realistic for most cities—that is, for each fatal and personal injury crash, between 20 and 25 convictions for hazardous moving violations indicate effective traffic enforcement. For some cities, the ratio may be higher; for others, lower. The index provides only a starting point for setting traffic enforcement goals and evaluating results.

Given the wide array of traffic violations and violators, it is critical that traffic enforcement be conducted fairly and uniformly. Departments must have clear policies on when motorists should be stopped and on the appropriate action to take.

THE TRAFFIC STOP

Police encounters with citizens involving traffic infractions will almost always be emotional, and drivers' reactions will vary greatly, from anxiety to remorse, fear, surprise, anger, or even hate. The first words officers say to violators set the tone for the rest of the contact. If officers are belligerent, the violators may be belligerent. If officers are pleasant, chances are the violators will be pleasant—but not always. Officers dealing with traffic violators should *never argue*. Motorists who want to debate their driving actions will never be convinced that they are wrong and the officer is right. Further, officers should not try to justify the enforcement action, as this only adds to the drivers' preconceived idea that the officer is wrong, prejudiced, or "picking on them."

Instead, officers should try to make the traffic contact an educational encounter for the driver, not a belittling or degrading experience. Motorists can be given information so they will be less likely to violate the law again. Studies have shown that many traffic stops by courteous, respectful officers have a positive effect on the citizens' perceptions of the police, even though a citation may be issued.

The stop should be made in a safe place, if possible, not necessarily the first available place. Dispatch should be notified of the stop and of the car's description and license number. After parking safely (many departments instruct officers to park behind the stopped vehicle and slightly to the left, leaving an alley of safety to protect the officer from passing traffic) and leaving the light bar flashing, the officer should approach the car cautiously and stand clear of the driver's door, which could be swung open unexpectedly. Data indicate that between 1993 and 2009, an average of one officer per month was struck and killed while performing a roadside stop. As a way to reduce this hazard, 49 states now have a *Move Over law* requiring motorists to change lanes or slow down when they approach an emergency vehicle (Batiste, Wagers, and Ashton 2011). Hawaii and the District of Columbia do not have a Move Over law.

Pennsylvania v. Mimms (1977) established that police officers may order the driver of a vehicle to exit the vehicle during a stop for a traffic violation. In some states, officers may also use a handheld fingerprint scanner, known as Identix Integrated Biometric Identification System (Identix IBIS), to identify wanted and missing people who are stopped. Officers can call into the National Crime Information Center (NCIC) database and remotely compare a suspect's fingerprints to that database.

Officers have great discretion in traffic enforcement. After making a stop, they usually do one of three things: (1) simply talk to the motorist and explain how the motorist has violated the law, perhaps warning the driver verbally, (2) issue a warning ticket, or (3) issue a citation. The third action may cause motorists to become irate and may lead them to act illogically. Motorists have been known to make ridiculous and profane statements, to tear up tickets, and to curse at officers. Sometimes such behavior stems from the fear of being discovered as "wanted" by the police and of being arrested on the spot.

Automated Citations

Automated citations have simplified the traffic stop process. With handheld, mobile, or tablet computers, which prompt officers for the information to be entered, citations can be issued on the spot and are legible and complete. Some handheld computers read the magnetic stripe on the driver's license in the same way magnetic tapes are read on credit cards. The information is saved and downloaded into the main processing unit at the end of the shift, or, in some jurisdictions, it can be uploaded into a server that includes all participating agencies.

Automated citations, electronic citations, or e-tickets usually allow the officer to choose from pull-down menus to input appropriate code, ordinance or statute violations, and other information. Multiple violations are easy to add, and the entire record can be saved with a paper copy printed for the driver. The entire process can be completed within 3 to 4 minutes, a great reduction from the standard 10 to 20 minutes needed to write out a citation, meaning officers can clear a traffic stop more quickly and reduce the risks faced while standing or parking on the roadside (Griffin 2009). Although this process is extremely convenient and efficient, like most computerized systems, it can experience technical problems. Thus, it is a good idea to keep a paper citation book handy for such instances.

Griffin (2009) describes the benefits of e-tickets:

▶ Eliminating handwritten tickets and the need to enter the same information into a separate database(s)

▶ Getting officers and drivers off the roadside more quickly

▶ Eliminating errors and duplicate entries by law enforcement, courts, clerks, and other staff

▶ Increasing the accuracy of information

▶ Giving officers more time to patrol by reducing paperwork

▶ Saving clerical time for clerks, courts, and agencies because data is transferred electronically

▶ Improving timeliness by making data available electronically

scofflaws

Persistent lawbreakers.

Handheld computers can also be used to deal with **scofflaws**—persistent lawbreakers. For example, when officers issue a parking ticket, they can run a check on the license and determine if other parking tickets are outstanding. If there are outstanding tickets, officers can have a boot put on one of the vehicle's tires so the vehicle cannot be moved before it can be towed to the impound garage. Handheld computers can also store and produce on command lists of stolen vehicles and revoked driver's licenses and can produce the daily logs that formerly required quantities of time and were tedious to complete.

As a final note, an officer who issues a traffic citation accepts the obligation to pursue that action through the courts by preparing evidence, obtaining witnesses, testifying, and performing the necessary functions to ensure a conviction.

Pretext Stops

A **pretext stop**, also called a **dual motive stop**, is one in which an officer stops a vehicle to investigate a traffic violation and because the driver looks suspicious. For example, an officer sees a suspicious-looking driver and follows the vehicle, hoping a violation occurs to justify a stop. The officer may then use the stop as a pretext to investigate the driver as well as the violation. Is such a stop legal? The states disagree. At the heart of the issue is the intent of the stop.

The question of pretext stops was clarified in *Whren v. United States* (1996). In this case, plainclothes officers patrolling a high-drug area in an unmarked vehicle saw a truck waiting at a stop sign for an unusually long time. The truck then turned suddenly without signaling and sped off at an "unreasonable" speed. The officers stopped the vehicle supposedly to warn the driver about the illegal turn and speed (traffic violations). When they approached the vehicle, they saw plastic bags of crack cocaine in the truck and arrested the driver.

The motion to suppress the evidence (cocaine) was denied, with the Supreme Court ruling, "The temporary detention of a motorist upon probable cause to believe he has violated the traffic laws does not violate the Fourth Amendment's prohibition against unreasonable seizures, even if a reasonable officer would not have stopped the motorist absent some additional law enforcement objective." In other words, the validity and constitutionality of a stop does not depend on whether police officers "would have" made the stop but rather whether the officers "could have" made the stop. The real purpose of a stop, even if ulterior, does not render the stop and subsequent search invalid if there was, in fact, a valid reason for the stop, such as traffic violations in this case.

Racial Profiling

Closely linked to the question of pretext stops is the issue of racial profiling. **Racial profiling** is the act of selecting an individual for further scrutiny or assessing the likelihood of criminal conduct or wrongdoing based solely on that person's race or ethnic background. This illegal, discriminatory enforcement of the law is part of a larger category of biased-based profiling, whereby an officer uses a common trait of a group—such as gender, sexual orientation, religion, economic status, or age—to suspect an individual of criminal conduct instead of assessing that person's behavior or actions. Racial profiling may be alleged when officers use discretionary authority in encounters with minority motorists, typically in the context of a traffic stop.

In October 2001, the Supreme Court refused to hear the only remaining case docketed for the year concerning an equal protection claim in a case where police officers stopped people based primarily on racial or ethnic descriptions—in effect upholding the ruling of the U.S. Court of Appeals for the Second Circuit in *Brown v. City of Oneonta*. In this case, the court held that when law enforcement officers have a description of a suspect that consists of the suspect's race and gender and have no evidence of discrimination, they can act on the description without violating the Equal Protection Clause of the Fourteenth Amendment.

The court noted that subjecting officers to an equal protection strict-scrutiny analysis in making investigative detentions or arrests could hinder police work. Officers fearful of personal liability might fail to act when they are

pretext stop

A stop in which the officer stops a vehicle to investigate a traffic violation but also because the driver looks suspicious; also called a *dual motive stop.*

dual motive stop

A stop in which the officer stops a vehicle to investigate a traffic violation but also because the driver looks suspicious; also called a *pretext stop.*

racial profiling

The act of selecting an individual for further scrutiny or assessing the likelihood of criminal conduct or wrongdoing based solely on that person's race or ethnic background; discriminatory enforcement of the law.

expected to. The court held, "Police work, as we know it, would be impaired and the safety of all citizens compromised.... The most vulnerable and isolated would be harmed the most. And, if police effectiveness is hobbled by special racial rules, residents of inner cities would be harmed most of all."

The Commission on Accreditation for Law Enforcement Agencies (CALEA) has added a prohibition against racial profiling. Although conceding that profiling can be a useful tool in law enforcement, bias-based profiling is prohibited (Standard 1.2.9).

In 1999, Connecticut became the first state to pass racial profiling legislation, requiring every municipal police agency and the state police to collect race data for every police-initiated traffic stop. Since that time, measures dealing with racial profiling have been introduced in many states. Data collection is a large issue in many departments. The Police Executive Research Foundation (PERF) has published *By the Numbers: A Guide for Analyzing Race Data from Vehicle Stops* (Fridell 2004). The purposes of this Community Oriented Policing Services–supported document are "(1) to describe the social science challenges associated with data collection initiatives so that agencies and other stakeholders can be made fully aware of both the potential and limitations of police–citizen contact data collection, and (2) to provide clear guidelines for analyzing and interpreting the data so that the jurisdictions collecting them can conduct the most valid and responsible analyses possible with the resources they have" (Fridell 2004, 2).

An innovative and low-cost approach to test for racial profiling in a department's traffic stop practices is the veil-of-darkness method, which uses changes in natural lighting to establish a benchmark for stop data. The basic premise of this method is that during nighttime hours, traffic officers possess a degraded ability to discern motorists' race; therefore, stop patterns at night represent a presumptively race-neutral benchmark. It can then be hypothesized that if a comparison of daytime stops to nighttime stops reveals no statistically significant difference regarding the race of the drivers involved, there is no racial bias by the traffic unit in determining which vehicles to pull over (Worden, McLean, and Wheeler 2012).

RECOGNIZING AND STOPPING DRIVERS "UNDER THE INFLUENCE"

Most police officers are familiar with the common physical symptoms of the person under the influence of alcohol or drugs: slurred speech, bloodshot or watery eyes, delayed reactions, lack of coordination, staggering, smell of alcoholic beverage on breath or clothing, confusion, dizziness, nausea, and exaggerated actions. Officers must be cautious, however, because many of these symptoms can be produced by medical conditions such as diabetes, epilepsy, heart attack, or concussion. Driving actions that tend to indicate a DUI suspect include:

▶ Unusually slow or excessive speeds for driving conditions or posted limits.
▶ Erratic starts and stops.
▶ Weaving or drifting between the center line and fog line in a lane, or straddling the center line.
▶ Failing to signal turns and lane changes.

▶ Problems making turns (either too wide or cutting across the curb).

▶ Driving the wrong direction on a roadway.

▶ Repeated use of horn in traffic.

Any one of these actions by itself may indicate only carelessness or haste, but a combination of such actions provides probable cause for an officer to stop the car. The officer must then determine if the driver is "under the influence."

Field and Chemical Tests for DUI

Common standardized field sobriety tests (SFSTs) include the heel-to-toe straight line walk, the finger-to-the-nose test, a balance test, a one-leg stand, counting backwards, and reciting the alphabet from a certain letter to another letter. One test used by most officers is the horizontal gaze nystagmus (HGN) test. **Nystagmus** is the involuntary jerking or bouncing of the eye, a possible cause of which is intoxication. In performing an HGN test, a thoroughly trained officer moves a pencil or fingertip in front of a driver's face and watches the driver's eyes for several things: equal tracking (making sure both eyes track the same) of the moving object, lack of smooth pursuit, distinct nystagmus ("bouncing" of the eye) at maximum deviation, and onset of nystagmus before 45 degrees. The officer may also check for vertical nystagmus. The way a driver performs on these various HGN tests can indicate to a trained officer the motorist's level of intoxication.

Chemical tests are also used. Because alcohol is absorbed directly into the bloodstream, its level of concentration can be tested. The **blood-alcohol concentration (BAC)** test represents the weight of alcohol in grams per milliliter of blood. A BAC of 0.08 represents 80 milligrams of alcohol per 100 milliliters of blood. (Some states use the term *blood-alcohol level [BAL]*.) States set specific blood-alcohol levels considered to indicate legal intoxication, with all 50 states setting the limit at 0.08.

A driver's blood-alcohol concentration can also be documented through a breath test, called a breath alcohol equivalent (BAQ) test. The same percentage should be obtained from both the breath and the blood test. Many squads carry a small, portable preliminary alcohol screening (PAS) device, also known as a preliminary breath test or PBT, that can display a BAC level after a person suspected of drunken driving blows into it.

A note about breath tests: If a PBT in the field indicates a driver is over the legal BAC limit, a more conclusive and accurate test is required. Devices such as the Intoxilyzer, a nonportable apparatus used by police departments nationwide, have, in recent years, been challenged by defense attorneys in several states because of technical issues with the machines' source codes or other operational problems. In Minnesota, for example, more than 4,000 DUI cases had been placed on hold during the six years it took for state and federal courts to determine whether the Intoxilyzer breath test for alcohol content was reliable. In June 2012, the Minnesota Supreme Court ruled that, although there were errors in the device's source code, the overall accuracy of the results were unaffected and the cases were placed back on the docket. In states where the pending legal status of the Intoxilyzer has yet to be decided by the courts, police officers are prevented from giving offenders the option of a breath test,

nystagmus

The involuntary bouncing or jerking of the eye, a possible cause of which is intoxication.

blood-alcohol concentration (BAC)

The weight of alcohol in grams per milliliter of blood.

thus restricting officer's choices to either a blood or urine sample only. If an offender requests a blood sample, he or she cannot be jailed because the results of the blood test are not immediate. In addition, it is costly, timely, and often dangerous to take blood from offenders. The status of this legal challenge is still being monitored in several states.

Recognizing the Driver under the Influence of Drugs

Often the symptoms of an individual impaired by drugs are very similar to those exhibited by an intoxicated person. This has given rise to a new specialty, the **drug recognition expert (DRE)** or **drug recognition technician (DRT)**. These experts are police officers with more than 80 hours of classroom training and 100 hours of field certification training, in addition to passing rigorous written and practical tests. Such specialists perform in the field, train other officers within the department, and can serve as expert witnesses in court cases requiring such testimony. Amid rising concern that drugged driving is an increasingly common factor in traffic crashes, and acknowledging that DRE training may be time- and cost-prohibitive for some departments, many are advocating the placement of the Advanced Roadside Impaired Driving Enforcement (ARIDE) program—a simplified yet effective mini-drug recognition program developed by the National Highway Traffic Safety Administration (NHTSA)—in all basic police academies (Sweeney 2011a).

Using speed or methamphetamine (meth) often results in changes in physical condition and appearance, conditions that commonly allow officers to identify such "speed freaks" and "meth heads" (Grossi 2009, 24). The first is *body odor*: "To put it plainly: speed freaks stink. Chronic meth use causes tweakers to sweat constantly. In addition to the odor of methamphetamine oozing from their pores, their hair and skin are usually greasy."

The second characteristic is *twitches*: "Speed freaks constantly move their heads and look around, left, right and behind. Their hands will be constantly busy too; they constantly touch themselves and their hair, and adjust their clothing. They'll also be continually shifting their weight from foot to foot."

The third characteristic Grossi (2009, 26) describes is a *rapid pulse*, noting that all people being stopped by the police may have rapid pulses because they are nervous. But speed freaks may have pulse rates in the mid-to-high 100s: "Sometimes the veins in their neck will be pulsing visibly." Other characteristics include dilated pupils and rapid, paranoid, disconnected speech.

People suspected of being under the influence of drugs or alcohol may be asked to take a blood, urine, or breath test. If they refuse, the consequences can be extremely negative because of the concept of implied consent.

Implied Consent

The **implied consent law** states that those who request and receive driver's licenses agree to take tests to determine their ability to drive. Refusal will result in license revocation. The implied consent law is based on the precept that driving an automobile is not a personal right but a privilege. Permission to drive a motor vehicle is given under whatever conditions and terms are considered reasonable and just by the granting state. Courts have uniformly upheld this principle.

---

drug recognition expert (DRE)

Specially trained individual who can determine if someone is under the influence of drugs; also called *drug recognition technician*.

drug recognition technician (DRT)

See *drug recognition expert*.

implied consent law

A law stating that those who request and receive driver's licenses agree to take tests to determine their ability to drive; refusal will result in license revocation.

In theory, no one is deprived of his or her constitutional rights by the implied consent law, nor is anything demanded of the driver that was not required before the law was enacted. The implied consent law gives drivers a choice: "If you wish to drive an automobile on the public highways of this state, you shall be deemed to have consented to submit to certain prescribed circumstances and conditions (such as breath tests). If you fail to submit to such tests, your privilege to drive on the state's highways will be revoked." Figure 5.1 illustrates how test refusal results in charges additional to the DWI, at least in the example state.

Videotaping Drivers

Many police departments have made it standard practice to videotape individuals stopped for DWI. This does not violate the person's constitutional rights. *Pennsylvania v. Muniz* (1990) is the leading case on Fifth and Sixth Amendment issues in videotaping drivers under the influence. The question before the Supreme Court was whether the police must give motorists suspected of DWI the *Miranda* warning before asking routine questions and videotaping them. The Court said, "No. The privilege against self-incrimination protects an accused from being compelled to testify against himself or otherwise provide the state with evidence of a testimonial or communicative nature, but not from being compelled by the state to produce real or physical evidence."

However, even though it is not a violation of a person's constitutional rights, videotaping a DWI stop may not be in the best interests of the prosecution. Unless the suspect is "falling down drunk," the videotape may actually work in the suspect's favor. Too often, an officer's word appears to contradict what a jury sees on videotape. This is not because the officer has embellished the facts. It is because the jury is untrained at detecting intoxication at levels as low as 0.08 BAC in a defendant viewed on a video monitor.

Strategies to Deter DUI

Traffic officers cannot do the job alone. Effective strategies to address the problem of impaired driving must include tougher laws, tougher judges, and frequent and ongoing awareness campaigns to keep impaired drivers out of the driver's seat.

> Strategies to deter DUI include educating drivers through awareness campaigns and establishing sobriety checkpoints and saturation patrols. Additional efforts aimed at repeat offenders include using ignition interlocks and enacting vehicle forfeiture programs.

Education and Awareness Campaigns Young people must be educated about the dangers of driving drunk and about the hazards of driving while high on pot, speed, cocaine, crack, or various other drugs used today for recreation, escape, and thrills. Two active national organizations committed to reducing drunk driving by raising awareness of the dangers it poses are Mothers Against Drunk Driving (MADD) and Students Against Drunk Driving (SADD).

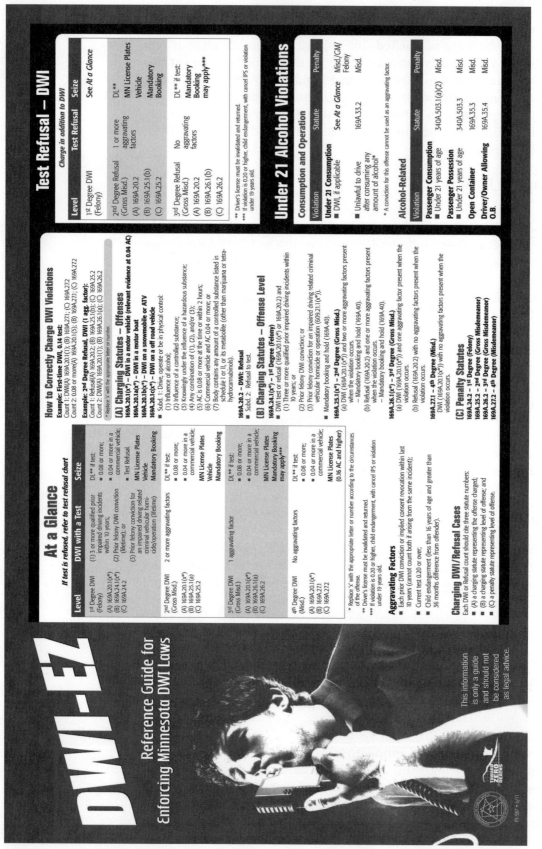

FIGURE 5.1 DWI-EZ Guide

Source: https://dps.mn.gov/divisions/ots/educational-materials/Documents/impaired-dwi-ez-poster.pdf.

Founded in 1980, MADD's purpose is "to stop drunk driving, support the victims of this violent crime and prevent underage drinking" (www.madd .org). SADD programs have been organized in many high schools throughout the country to help new teenage drivers acknowledge the serious responsibilities that accompany a license to drive. Common SADD activities include designated driver programs for "special" events where underage drinking is likely, such as homecoming and prom, and staging mock crashes and funerals for students to "witness" the deadly consequences of irresponsible driving.

Sobriety Checkpoints and Saturation Patrols Many states are using sobriety checkpoints to deter and detect drunk drivers. In *Michigan Department of State Police v. Sitz* (1990), the Supreme Court ruled, "Sobriety checkpoints are constitutional" because the states have a "substantial interest" in keeping intoxicated drivers off the streets and that the "measure of intrusion on motorists stopped at sobriety checkpoints is slight." The Court also cautioned against random stops, authorizing only well-conceived, carefully structured programs.

Drug Checkpoints In *City of Indianapolis v. Edmond* (2000), the Supreme Court ruled that police may not set up drug interdiction roadblocks because the Fourth Amendment requires that even a brief seizure of a motorist by the roadside requires a suspicion that the motorist committed a crime. As Justice O'Connor wrote, "We cannot sanction stops justified only by the generalized and ever-present possibility that interrogation and inspection may reveal that any given motorist has committed some crime."

61.1.10

CALEA Standard 61.1.10 suggests several countermeasures in various combinations in selective alcohol enforcement programs: "Selective assignment of personnel at the time when, and to the locations where analyses have shown that a significant number of violations and/or collisions involving incidence of drinking-driving collisions to ascertain the characteristic violation profile of the problem drinker who drives; selected alcohol related collision investigations and analyses of findings; selective roadway checks for deterrence purposes; and selective enforcement of drinking driving laws through concentration on existing laws and the expeditious processing of violators."

Source: Commission on Accreditation of Law Enforcement Agencies (CALEA). 2012. *Standards for Law Enforcement Agencies*. 5th ed. Fairfax, VA: Author.

Dealing with Repeat Drunk Drivers No matter how severe the consequences of drunk driving are, it seems some drivers are always willing to push their luck by continuing to get behind the wheel while intoxicated. *Ignition interlocks* are one solution aimed at the major problem of recidivism in DWI. An ignition interlock monitors how much a person has had to drink, and if the person has had too much, the vehicle will not start. To prevent someone other than the convicted DWI offender from using the system, a breath code is established.

Several states have *vehicle forfeiture* legislation permitting the permanent confiscation of vehicles of repeat DUI/DWI offenders—drive drunk, lose your car.

Legal Liability

The decision to arrest a drunk driver is not discretionary if the state has a law against drunk driving (which all states do). Arresting impaired drivers is an officer's *public duty*, a principle established in *Carleton v. Town of Framingham* (1994). In this case, an officer had spoken with an intoxicated driver inside a store but had put off taking him into custody, deciding instead to wait outside the store until the driver got into his car. When the officer then attempted a traffic stop for DUI, the intoxicated driver refused and continued driving, which resulted in a head-on collision and a lawsuit against the police.

ENFORCEMENT AND PURSUIT

Traffic officers must be prepared for the possibility that, when trying to effect a stop, drivers may have other ideas and try to flee, either in their cars or on foot. It is not the officer but rather the suspect who initiates a pursuit: "The officer must understand that when a suspect refuses to stop for the emergency lights and siren, a common encounter turns quickly into a high-risk and dangerous event where the 'show of authority' may negatively affect the suspect's [behavior]" (Schultz, Hudak, and Alpert 2010, 2).

Foot Pursuit

Pursuit is usually thought of as an officer in a police car pursuing a suspect in a vehicle; however, foot pursuits are also common and hazardous. Martinelli (2011, 54) notes, "Foot pursuits by their very nature are emotionally charged and dangerous events that occur frequently in police work. Law enforcement officers must balance their obligation to enforce laws and arrest perpetrators with their personal safety. Unfortunately, this rarely happens. More often than not, officers become emotionally captivated by the event and have an instinctive reaction, rather than a studied and planned response to resistance and chase without considering the inevitability of suspect capture. In other words, they chase the suspect until the suspect catches them."

Foot pursuits get the adrenalin flowing, which can make the unprepared officer toss safety tactics out the window. Officers may run headlong into a scenario full of unknowns that can seriously injure or kill them. Therefore, officers faced with a foot pursuit situation are strongly urged to consider a number of factors before chasing a suspect on foot, including what the suspect is wanted for; the possibility the suspect is armed or possesses martial arts skills; the likelihood the suspect is psychotic or under the influence of drugs (e.g., powerful stimulants or a hallucinogen such as phencyclidine [PCP, or angel dust]); where the suspect might be leading the pursuing officer—for example, a getaway car filled with accomplices ready to overwhelm you; if the suspect is in better physical condition than you; what environmental factors are involved; the time of day; and what communications are available for backup (Martinelli 2011).

Vehicle Pursuit

As with foot pursuit, vehicle pursuits can be extremely hazardous. A **vehicle pursuit** is "an active attempt by a law enforcement officer on duty in a patrol car to apprehend one or more occupants of a moving motor vehicle, providing

---

vehicle pursuit

"An active attempt by a law enforcement officer on duty in a patrol car to apprehend one or more occupants of a moving motor vehicle, providing the driver of such vehicle is aware of the attempt and is resisting apprehension by maintaining or increasing his speed or by ignoring the law enforcement officer's attempt to stop him."

the driver of such vehicle is aware of the attempt and is resisting apprehension by maintaining or increasing his speed or by ignoring the law enforcement officer's attempt to stop him" (Nugent et al. n.d., 1). This definition establishes four key points: (1) that the law enforcement officer is in a patrol car and, therefore, should be recognizable as a law enforcement officer; (2) that the driver is aware that the law enforcement officer is trying to stop him or her and resists the attempt; (3) that the reason for the pursuit may embrace traffic offenses, including speeding itself, and felonies; and (4) that the vehicle speed may vary (Nugent et al., n.d.).

One of the reasons vehicle pursuits are so dangerous is that innocent victims—other drivers or pedestrians—may become casualties of the chase, and data indicates that hundreds of civilians are killed or seriously injured every year because of police vehicle pursuits. One study found that 42 percent of people killed or seriously injured during police pursuits were innocent third parties (Schultz, Hudak, and Alpert 2010). Despite the dangers, the majority of agencies across the country have continued the practice of vehicle pursuits.

Pursuit Policies and Data In 2002, the IACP developed the national Police Pursuit Database, a user-friendly Web-based database for storing pursuit information enabling law enforcement leaders to set pursuit guidelines, make informed policy and training decisions, and generate statistical reports to assist in analysis and comparison with other jurisdictions. Analysis of the 7,737 policies currently in the database indicates that 94.8 percent of the policies allowed pursuit (Lum and Fachner 2008). Some departments have a "chase-them-all" policy. Others chase only those vehicles involved in felonies. And a few departments have a "no-chase" policy. Among the reasons given by officers for initiating a pursuit, traffic violations were the most common (42.3 percent), followed by a belief that the vehicle was stolen (18.2 percent), and the belief that the driver was intoxicated (14.9 percent). Felonies initiated pursuits more often than misdemeanors (Lum and Fachner 2008). Interestingly, one study of suspects who had fled from police revealed that 32 percent were driving a stolen vehicle, 27 percent had a suspended driver's license, 27 percent were trying to avoid arrest, and 21 percent were driving under the influence (drivers were allowed to give more than one reason for fleeing) (Schultz, Hudak, and Alpert 2010).

> An effective pursuit policy must balance crime-control efforts against the threat a pursuit poses to public safety and officer and department liability.

Pursuit policies can take several forms. One type of pursuit management can be viewed as a continuum, ranging from low-risk interdiction actions such as trailing of low-level offenders (those presenting a low-to-moderate public threat such as persons engaged in traffic offenses and less serious crimes), to high-risk interdiction involving vehicle contact maneuvers and possible discharge of firearms for offenders engaged in life-threatening felonies that justify the use of deadly force. Disengagement from the pursuit is always an option.

Lum and Fachner (2008, 8) stress, "The balance between crime control and safety/liability is a central framework in the discourse on police pursuits and is reflected in police policies, research, and practice. However, in addition to these ongoing concerns, two equally important and contemporary contexts should also motivate pursuit policy reform and data collection. These contexts include the advent of a new era of policing that emphasizes proactivity, prevention, and problem solving, accompanied by an increasing use and demand for information and analysis to support those innovations and hold officers and agencies accountable for the resulting outcomes."

> Issues that should be addressed in a pursuit policy include (Lum and Fachner 2008, 40) the following:
> - Supervision, monitoring, and accountability
> - Safety
> - Driving conditions
> - Vehicles involved
> - Situational context
> - Devices and tactics used

Pursuits were recorded by 89.0 percent of the departments; 84.9 percent kept in communication. Public safety was specifically mentioned in 95.9 percent of the policies; officer safety in 84.9 percent; suspect safety in 34.2 percent (Lum and Fachner 2008).

Driving conditions such as weather, visibility, and traffic variables are commonly included in pursuit policies—91.8 percent of the policies said both weather considerations and traffic considerations were discretionary; 57.5 percent said visibility considerations were discretionary. Relatively few policies allow pursuing officers to drive the wrong way during pursuit (19.2 percent) or go off road in their pursuit (5.5 percent). And only 4.1 percent placed limits on officer speed (Lum and Fachner 2008).

Regarding the number of vehicles involved, 84.9 percent of the policies allowed more than one vehicle to pursue, 54.8 percent allowed unmarked cars to pursue until a marked car was available, 53.4 percent allowed motorcycles to be used until a marked car was available, 28.8 percent mentioned air support, 15.1 percent said unmarked cars could not be used, and 11.0 percent said motorcycles could not be used (Lum and Fachner 2008).

Situational context includes the type of offense involved and whether the suspect is known. The type of offense limited pursuits in 47.9 percent of the policies—pursuit allowed for any offense (52.1 percent), misdemeanors or worse (21.9 percent), felonies only (12.3 percent), and no mention (8.2 percent). That suspect identification must end the pursuit was required in only 4.1 percent of the policies (Lum and Fachner 2008).

Various devices and tactics may be used during pursuit. Roadblocks and tire deflation could be used according to 61.6 percent of the policies, intentional collisions could be used in 57.5 percent, any contact was considered "deadly force" in 60.3 percent, and paralleling could be used in 32.9 percent (Lum and Fachner 2008).

Only 6 percent of the pursuits studied actually employed some form of termination method. Most pursuits ended when the suspect stopped (35.7 percent), the suspect crashed (18.4 percent), or the suspect eluded the police (17.9 percent). In only 0.8 percent was the officer involved in a crash

(Lum and Fachner 2008). When a termination method was used, the most common method was tire deflator (3.4 percent). Other methods used, which were identified in fewer than 1 percent of the policies, were roadblocks, rolling roadblocks, and the pursuit intervention technique (PIT) maneuver, also called the precision intervention technique, in which the violator is spun to a stop.

Since the U.S. Supreme Court held in *Brower v. County of Inyo* (1989) that compulsive, stationary roadblocks are akin to seizures, however, this pursuit intervention technique has been essentially abandoned by the vast majority of departments. And although rolling roadblocks, in which a minimum of three police cars are deployed to box in the suspect's vehicle, are more common today, they are not advised or condoned by most police departments because this form of intervention technique places multiple officers in harm's way: "A far safer method is the coercive roadblock. By positioning units to block exits and side streets, the suspect can be directed toward an area where the PIT maneuver or spike strip can be safely deployed, minimizing harm to officers, bystanders, and the suspect" (Scoville 2012, 48).

Should a suspect initiate a pursuit and an officer decide to engage, consideration must be given to how the chase will end. An officer's willingness to pursue is predicated on the belief that officers will apprehend the fleeing subject—otherwise, there is no reason to chase in the first place. However, if the pursuit reaches a point where the risk to public safety outweighs the need to capture the suspect, most policies require the officer to terminate the pursuit—the logic being that the suspect will return to safer driving behavior and, consequently, present a lower threat to the public, once the police end their chase. Although limited research exists, the little empirical data that is available indicates that approximately three-fourths of suspects report they would slow down within several miles after an officer disengages from a pursuit (Schultz, Hudak, and Alpert 2010).

TECHNOLOGY IN POLICING

IN PURSUIT OF SAFER PURSUITS

Scoville (2012, 52) describes four specific technology innovations being developed that aimed to safely end police pursuits or make them much shorter:

▶ OnStar by General Motors: Allows remote stoppage of a vehicle in which the system is installed if authorized by law enforcement.

▶ Launchable tracker by StarChase: A patrol-car-mounted launching device fires a tracker at a suspect's vehicle, which sticks to the car's bumper and allows police to surveil the suspect from a safe distance and at a safer speed.

▶ Pit-Bull by Pacific Scientific: A portable vehicle arresting device that looks like a speed bump but that actually releases a remote-fired net to capture the rear tire of a targeted vehicle. This technology improves officer safety by allowing them greater distance from the stopping device, reducing their chances of being struck by the suspect vehicle.

▶ PT1100 by PurTech LLC: A device that mounts to the front of a patrol car and deploys up to three stop sticks with the touch of a button. Again, this technology enhances officer safety by allowing them to stay in the vehicle.

Source: Dean Scoville, "Vehicle Pursuits." *Police* (January 2012): 46–52.

Whenever pursuit does occur, if damage results, officers and their departments may face lawsuits.

Liability Issues At issue usually is whether police officers violate the Fourteenth Amendment's guarantee of substantive due process by causing death through deliberate or reckless indifference to life in a high-speed automobile chase to apprehend a suspected offender. The Supreme Court, in *County of Sacramento v. Lewis* (1998), held, "In high-speed vehicle pursuit cases, liability in Section 1983 cases ensues only if the conduct of the officer 'shocks the conscience.' The lower standard of 'deliberate indifference' does not apply." Justice Souter noted that an officer's decision to pursue a fleeing suspect often is made in a "split-second... in circumstances that are tense, uncertain and rapidly evolving." Officers are forced to "balance on the one hand the need to stop a suspect and show that flight from the law is no way to freedom, and, on the other, the high-speed threat to everyone within stopping range, be they suspects, their passengers, other drivers, or bystanders."

More recently, in *Scott v. Harris* (2007), the Supreme Court ruled in favor of the police in a pursuit case. Victor Harris sued Officer Timothy Scott for pursuing his vehicle and ramming it, which left Harris a quadriplegic. In this case, the Court considered "whether a law enforcement official can, consistent with the Fourth Amendment, attempt to stop a fleeing motorist from continuing his public-endangering flight by ramming the motorist's car from behind. Put another way: Can an officer take actions that place a fleeing motorist at risk of serious injury or death in order to stop the motorist's flight from endangering the lives of innocent bystanders?' The Court's answer was "yes." Noting that it was Harris's actions, not the officer's, that initiated the pursuit, the Court ruled, "We are loath to lay down a rule requiring the police to allow fleeing suspects to get away whenever they drive *so recklessly* that they put other people's lives in danger. It is obvious the perverse incentives such a rule would create: Every fleeing motorist would know that escape is within his grasp, if only he accelerates to 90 miles per hour, crosses the double-yellow line a few times, and runs a few red lights. The Constitution assuredly does not impose this invitation to impunity-earned-by-recklessness. Instead, we lay down a more sensible rule: a police officer's attempt to terminate a dangerous high-speed car chase that threatens the lives of innocent bystanders does not violate the Fourth Amendment, even when it places the fleeing motorist at risk of serious injury or death."

An advance in technology that may help officers engaged in pursuits is the DriveCam. This is a black box recorder that automatically records everything a driver sees, hears, and feels for the 10 seconds before and after a crash, missed accident, abusive driving, or other event of interest.

TRAFFIC ENFORCEMENT AND TRANSPORTATION OF HAZARDOUS MATERIALS

In many states, traffic enforcement also includes enforcing truck weight limits, enforcing bicycle and pedestrian regulations, and regulating transportation of hazardous materials (HM or hazmat). The USDOT estimates that four billion tons of regulated hazardous materials move annually in America, much of it on highways, and police traffic officers are invariably the first responders to most hazmat incidents that occur on the roadway (*Highway Safety Desk Book* 2004). Data from the USDOT indicates that during the 10-year period from 2002 to 2011, 162,162 transportation-related hazmat incidents occurred, of which 140,634 (87 percent) occurred on the nation's highways. These highway hazmat incidents caused 109 fatalities (85 percent of transportation-related hazmat fatalities), 1,484 injuries (57 percent of total injuries), and more than $550 million in damages ("Incident Statistics" 2012). Yet traffic enforcement of transporting hazmat is often overlooked. Most traffic codes do not include dealing with the transportation of hazmat.

A hazardous materials enforcement program should consist of the following:
- Terminal audits
- Shipper and other audits
- Road enforcement
- Technical assistance and enforcement training
- Emergency response

The police should conduct periodic audits at transporters' hazmat terminals to ensure compliance with regulations, and they should conduct periodic audits of those who pack the materials to be transported. Police should conduct periodic inspections on the highway as well. In addition, training should be made available to carriers and shippers, as well as to other law enforcement agencies in the state.

Finally, law enforcement should have clearly established emergency response plans in case an accident or terrorist incident involving hazmat should occur. The Highway Safety Committee of the IACP recommends: "Every police vehicle used for traffic patrol should carry in it the latest edition of the federal USDOT *Emergency Response Guidebook.* This concise book contains a rapid reference by which officers can determine, from the numbers and other information on placards and shipping papers, the classification of hazardous materials being transported and the general cautions and instructions for containment of spills and evacuation of the public" (*Highway Safety Desk Book* 2004, 8–11). The emergency hazmat response is discussed in Chapter 8.

CRASH MANAGEMENT AND INVESTIGATION

Motor vehicle traffic crashes are a leading cause of death in the United States, although the data indicate that the number of fatalities attributed to such crashes during 2010 was the lowest it had been since 1949 (*2010 Motor Vehicle Crashes* 2011). According to the NHTSA, in 2010 there were an estimated 5,419,000 police-reported traffic crashes nationwide, in which 32,885 people were killed and approximately 2,240,000 people were injured. Roughly 3.8 million of the crashes involved property damage only (*2010 Motor Vehicle Crashes* 2011).

When a crash does happen, people are frequently in shock or disbelief. They may be dazed or seriously injured. They may be hysterical. They may be belligerent.

Officers called to major crashes often have multiple responsibilities, such as administering first aid to injured drivers, passengers, and possibly pedestrians, while keeping the traffic situation from causing further damage and injury. After the victims have been tended to and removed from the scene, investigation of the crash can commence.

© AP Images/Chuck Liddy

At a crash scene, officers are responsible for:
- Managing the scene, including protecting it, attending to injuries, keeping traffic moving, and restoring normal traffic flow.
- Investigating and reporting the cause(s) of the crash, including the possibility of a crime (e.g., criminal vehicular operation, etc.).

Formerly vehicle collisions were called *accidents*; however, this term implied a rather random, causeless chain of events that resulted in the crash of one or more vehicles. Recognizing that many, if not most, such incidents happen because of some identifiable factor(s) or reason(s), not by chance or coincidence, these collisions are now referred to as *crashes*.

Crashes Involving Pedestrians

Data from the NHTSA indicates that 4,092 pedestrians were killed in traffic crashes in the United States during 2009—a 7 percent decrease from 2008 and a 14 percent decrease from 2000 (*Pedestrians* 2010). Twenty percent of the children ages 9 and younger who were killed in traffic crashes in 2001 were pedestrians. Also during 2009, an estimated 59,000 pedestrians were injured because of a traffic crash, an average of one every nine minutes (*Pedestrians* 2010).

Responding to a Crash Call

Officers called to the scene of a crash usually must proceed as rapidly as possible, treating it as an emergency because injuries are often involved. However, be aware that in responding to a crash, your mindset can drastically change. Much like with a pursuit, the adrenaline starts to flow, heart rate and blood pressure rise, and tunnel vision can set in, leading to a dangerous loss of awareness of other things happening immediately around you: "*Bottom line*: You can't do any good unless you get there. Take the necessary time appropriate for the situation and get there safely" (Molnar 2008, 20).

Once there, officers should park to protect the scene but not to endanger other motorists coming on the scene. Once the scene is protected, the first responsibility is to attend to the victims. If injuries are serious, an ambulance or rescue squad should be called immediately. During this time, one officer should be keeping the traffic moving.

Crash scene management is critical because the more severe results of a crash can occur after the initial collision. This can include the injured not being properly or promptly cared for, other vehicles becoming involved in the crash, fires starting, hazmat leaking, or other matters that increase the probability of injury or property loss and increase congestion.

The National Incident Management System (NIMS) developed by the U.S. Department of Homeland Security has a traffic incident management system (TIMS) that adapts well to the control of traffic incidents. When an incident occurs, the incident commander is expected to do the following:

▶ Take immediate steps to stabilize the incident, provide for life safety, and establish traffic control. A perimeter for the scene needs to be established and evacuate persons as required.

▶ Evaluate the situation and call for needed assistance.

▶ Triage the injured and provide appropriate field treatment and emergency care transportation.

▶ Extend the area of operation to ensure safe and orderly traffic flow through and around the incident scene.

▶ Provide for the safety, accountability, and welfare of personnel, a responsibility that will be ongoing throughout the incident.

▶ Restore the roadway to normal operations after an incident has been cleared.

Sometimes problems arise at a crash scene when police, firefighters, and emergency medical services (EMS) personnel converge on the scene. For example, firefighters often arrive on the scene with a fire truck, and police officers may demand it be moved because it is obstructing traffic. What they should realize, however, is that fire trucks are brought to crash scenes for two very specific purposes: (1) the equipment officers may need is already on the truck, and (2) the truck provides good traffic control, protecting the crash scene and those responding to it.

Crash Investigation and Reconstruction

After victims have been tended to, officers should turn their attention to the crash investigation phase. In minor crashes, the so-called fender benders, a thorough investigation is seldom required. Officers should make certain the drivers involved exchange insurance information and complete the required forms. Many major crashes, including those involving disabling injuries and fatalities, are investigated by officers with specialized training. Such serious collisions often require a reconstruction of the crash, and the services of a crash reconstruction specialist may be required.

Crash investigation usually begins with taking statements from those involved and from any witnesses. It has been suggested that officers not ask bystanders if they are witnesses to the crash because they might not want to get involved. A better question is, What did you see happen? After statements are taken, a physical examination of the vehicles involved and the scene is conducted. Officers should measure the location of skid marks, the final position of vehicle(s), roadway widths, distances to bridge abutments, utility poles, and the like.

Photographs and careful notes are also critical in most serious crash investigations. A crash investigator should have a camera and be skilled in its use. Investigators should photograph debris showing approximate point of impact—for example, broken glass and dirt from the underside of the vehicles and tire imprints or skid marks in soft material such as mud, snow, and sand. Also, photographs should be taken of more permanent evidence: roadside objects, view obstructions, traffic signs, vehicular damage, road and tire marks, and the roadway environment.

Many law enforcement agencies are now using surveying techniques, such as those commonly used during construction planning and marking property boundaries, to map crash scenes, and numerous forensic mapping tools are available to help trained crash investigators piece together the circumstances of a crash. Precise measurements are generally desired when building cases for prosecutable fatalities, so it is important to have as much evidence as possible. Brown (2008, 44) observes, "Collision investigators no longer respond merely to gather information for insurance companies. These days, people are being tried for offenses ranging all the way up to murder for killing someone while behind the wheel. Furthermore, defense lawyers now hire highly educated engineering firms for their defense, and going up against an engineer can intimidate some officers. Having the training and technology to back up your investigations is imperative because no matter how many collisions your agency investigates each year, it's just a matter of time until you're hit with a potentially criminal fatal collision." In addition, the availability of surveying technique and mapping tools to crash investigations means law enforcement no longer needs to shut down roadways to take all the necessary measurements, saving the driving public much frustration, especially when crashes occurred during rush hour.

Of assistance in accident reconstruction might be the black box. These "black boxes" or event data recorders (EDRs) were designed to tell a car when to deploy its airbag, but the data contained has also been instrumental in determining the cause of a crash.

Crashes involving pedestrians are very different from those involving only vehicles and, thus, require different investigative techniques. Like vehicle crash investigations, however, photographs should be taken at all pedestrian-involved crash scenes, including photographs of the victim, the vehicle involved, and the roadway.

Fake Accidents

Staged auto crashes are always a possibility. Ambulance-chasing personal injury mills include a "capper" or "runner" who spreads the word that anyone involved in an auto collision can come to the capper's agency for help. Some crashes are arranged for insurance fraud purposes.

Crash Reports

Complete and accurate crash reports are critical to selective enforcement and other traffic safety measures. Some agencies are one to two months behind in manually entering data from traffic incidents, making the data no longer "real time." To combat this problem, many agencies are turning to electronic report forms.

Legal Liability

Crashes frequently result in lawsuits, so careful documentation of all facts is important. In addition, crash-scene management and investigation may also be the target of lawsuits, with the officers involved, their department, and their city being named as defendants. Accurate, complete documentation helps should a lawsuit be initiated and helps identify areas to be targeted for selective enforcement.

Legal liability in crash cases generally involves three areas of public duty: (1) to warn and protect other motorists, (2) to render assistance, and (3) to secure the scene.

TRAFFIC AND COMMUNITY POLICING

Not all traffic services involve enforcement or crashes. Much of it deals simply with keeping the traffic flowing smoothly. In many communities, traffic is considered a serious problem, one that plagues quiet residential communities and crime-ridden inner cities alike. Citizens want to see police on the street, and citizens don't want to see police ignoring traffic violations.

An approach to safety on our roadways emphasizing partnerships and citizen involvement is the Safe Communities program, sponsored by the USDOT. Increasing from a few sites in 1996, the 2011 directory lists 520 coalitions operating within 40 states, Indian Nations, the Pacific Territories, U.S. Virgin Islands, and Puerto Rico (*Safe Communities Directory* 2011). The program is based on the philosophy that communities are in the best position to effect improvements in motor vehicle and other transportation-related safety problems, and the Safe Communities objective is to promote community-based solutions to address transportation safety and other injury problems. According to its Web site ("About Safe Communities" n.d.), "A Safe Community expands resources and partnerships, increases program visibility, and establishes community ownership and support for transportation injury prevention programs. As the Safe Community concept addresses all injuries, transportation and traffic safety becomes positioned within the context of the entire injury problem." The Safe Communities Service Center is located at the NHTSA regional office in Fort Worth, Texas. In addition to services provided within its interactive Web site, the center provides one-stop shopping for a community's needs for information and resources related to constructing Safe Communities.

TRAFFIC AND PROBLEM-ORIENTED POLICING

The 2001 winner of the Herman Goldstein *Excellence in Problem-Oriented Policing* Award was the California Highway Patrol (CHP) for its *Corridor Safety Program: A Collaborative Approach to Traffic Safety* (2001). The program used the SARA model to address a high rate of fatal crashes on an infamous stretch of rural highway in California, the roadway where actor James Dean was killed in the late 1950s, dubbed "Blood Alley."

Although no traffic-specific initiatives have won the Goldstein award since 2001, hundreds of programs have been implemented across the country in the past decade, as revealed by a search of the Problem-Oriented Policing Web site (www.popcenter.org). A recent effort undertaken by the Cincinnati, Ohio, Police Department used a problem-oriented approach to address the high number of traffic crashes and fatalities, many of which were attributed to speeding, aggressive driving, impaired driving, and failure to wear a seat belt. A summary of their program follows (*Saving Lives with Traffic Safety* 2011).

Scanning

In 2005, the City of Cincinnati, Ohio, experienced its highest year for fatal traffic accidents in a decade with 36 fatal accidents and 37 people killed. In additional to the fatal accidents, Cincinnati had 18,519 traffic accidents for the year.

Analysis

Preliminary analysis revealed Cincinnati traffic accidents and fatalities were occurring as a result of speed/aggressive driving, operating a vehicle while impaired (OVI), and failing to wear a seat belt where one was available. Critically, the Cincinnati Police Department lacked a comprehensive strategy to proactively address either traffic-related problem causes or locations.

Response

Starting in 2006, the Cincinnati Police Department for the first time identified traffic safety as a core patrol strategy and developed a traffic safety business plan to guide traffic safety efforts across the department. Although the impetus for initial plan development was the theory of problem-oriented policing, various other theories including situational crime prevention and intelligence-led policing contributed to both its development and implementation throughout the department.

The crime prevention strategies were applied to three newly identified traffic safety focus areas: high visibility patrol, consistent enforcement, and analysis of hot spots. Specific interventions were developed for and implemented in each focus area. The interventions included partnership with the Ohio State Highway Patrol; the use of airspeed enforcement on all Interstate highways; OVI checkpoints; analysis of traffic data to determine high traffic accident locations, times, and causative factors; and the micro-grinding (texturing) of specific Cincinnati street and Interstate highway locations to improve vehicle traction in inclement weather.

The goal of the interventions was to achieve both a short- and long-term reduction in fatalities, serious injuries, and the overall number of traffic accidents within the city of Cincinnati corporate limits. It was theorized that by having Cincinnati Police Department Officers patrol along the busiest high traffic accident locations during peak periods a reduction in the number of traffic accidents would occur in all three categories.

Assessment

Since the incremental rollout of the traffic safety interventions, the Cincinnati Police Department has achieved significant reductions in the number of fatalities, serious injuries, and overall traffic accidents. Time-series analysis demonstrated roughly a 15 percent statistically significant decline in overall traffic accidents between the pre- and post-intervention periods; additional analyses demonstrate that the reduction in Cincinnati was greater than the reductions experienced in the remainder of the county, state, and country during the same period.[1]

AN AREA TRAFFIC OFFICER (ATO) PROGRAM

An innovative program that combines community policing and a focus on problem solving was recently instituted in Irvine, California. The Irvine Area Traffic Officer (ATO) Program is aimed at implementing problem-solving strategies with an emphasis on long-lasting solutions using community input and is intended to:

▶ Identify and resolve traffic problems through a single point of contact.

▶ Increase monitoring of areas of concern.

▶ Build close-knit relationships with community residents, business owners, and school administrators.

▶ Establish proactive, long-term solutions that consider input from other city departments and key personnel.

▶ Explore innovative methods of moving vehicles more effectively through the city in a safe and efficient manner.

▶ Affirm a commitment to increasing reliable two-way communication, which the community expects from its local government. (Maggard and Jung 2009, 46)

The program has divided Irvine into three areas, each assigned an ATO responsible for investigating and resolving complex traffic-related issues in his or her respective geographic area: "The ATOs work hand-in-hand with area motor officers, patrol officers, traffic engineers, land use planners, and key personnel from Irvine Public Works Department to address traffic issues in a comprehensive and collaborative manner" (Maggard and Jung 2009, 46).

The ATOs have achieved significant results. They have improved school safety by making improvements to school parking/loading areas to enhance overall safety and maximize traffic flow, determined the need for additional crosswalks, revised access plans, and determined the need for additional speed limit and cautionary signs. ATOs have also addressed the issue of abandoned vehicles, which can become unsightly and be targets for vandalism and other criminal activity. In addition, the ATOs have worked closely with major retail shopping centers and business owners to improve circulation and safety issues by enhancing directional signage and have increased parking enforcement.

---

[1]Source: Daniel Gerard. *Saving Lives with Traffic Safety.* Cincinnati Police Department, 2011. Reprinted by permission of the author.

Another area of concern that has been addressed is construction traffic. ATOs work well ahead of development projects in collaboration with construction superintendents to address such issues as the delivery of building supplies, truck routes, roadway closures, detour barriers, roadway excavation, and appropriate construction signage. Residential traffic has also been a focus, especially speed enforcement. ATOs frequently deploy radar speed boards throughout the city that post the legal speed limit and inform drivers of their speed.

Maggard and Jung (2009, 50) conclude, "The benefits of establishing an ATO program far outweigh those of the traditional approach of addressing traffic management issues." Such a program can stretch existing law enforcement resources—the Irvine Police Department's three area commanders previously assigned to resolve chronic circulations issues now have time to address their primary responsibilities while ATOs focus exclusively on traffic-related inquiries. Maggard and Jung also note that since the inception of the ATO program, traffic accidents have decreased by 6 percent. "A program that improves safety and communication while reducing the strain on law enforcement resources should be viewed as a success by any measure" (50).

SUMMARY

Police traffic services (PTS) are divided into three functional areas: traffic direction and control, traffic enforcement, and crash investigation. The two basic purposes of traffic enforcement are to control congestion and to reduce crashes. Enforcement can also detect criminal activity. Even if a traffic enforcement unit exists, traffic enforcement is the responsibility of *all* officers. Speeding can be addressed through engineering, education, and enforcement responses.

Some of the more challenging and hazardous motorist behaviors involve aggressive driving, road rage, and driving under the influence. Aggressive driving is a traffic violation; road rage is a criminal offense. Nationwide, DUI is the number-one traffic law enforcement problem. Strategies to deter DUI include educating drivers through awareness campaigns and establishing sobriety checkpoints and saturation patrols. Additional efforts aimed at repeat offenders include using ignition interlocks and enacting vehicle forfeiture programs.

Another problem area for traffic officers is pursuit. An effective pursuit policy must balance crime-control efforts against the threat a pursuit poses to public safety and officer and department liability. Pursuit policies should address such issues as supervision, monitoring, and accountability; safety; driving conditions; vehicles involved; situational context; and devices and tactics. A frequently overlooked area in traffic enforcement involves transportation of hazardous materials. A hazardous materials enforcement program should consist of terminal audits, shipper and other audits, road enforcement, technical assistance and enforcement training, and emergency response.

Dealing with motor vehicle crashes is another function of traffic services. At a crash scene, officers are responsible for managing the scene, including protecting it, attending to injuries, keeping traffic moving, and restoring normal traffic flow. Officers are also responsible for investigating and reporting the cause(s) of the crash, including the possibility of a crime (e.g., criminal vehicular operation, etc.).

APPLICATION

The chief of police in your agency approaches you over concern with the inconsistency of written crash reports in your department. Officers have been writing accident reports for incidents that have occurred on both public and private properties. Although no law prohibits writing state accident reports on private property, your chief is concerned that having no consistent policy may expose your agency to liability. Currently, officers are allowed discretion regarding whether to write the accident reports on private property. Your chief has asked you as a supervisor to create a policy for writing accident reports that meet local, state, and national criteria along with remaining consistent for the public you serve.

INSTRUCTIONS

With current local, state, and national criteria in mind, draft a policy for your agency outlining what criteria need to be met to write a state accident report. In addition, make the policy consistent, stating whether all accidents are required to be written up as long as they meet the criteria, or if only certain accidents are required to be written up. Also, in the event that an accident does *not* need to be reported, what is required of the officer responding to that call? Officers should also consider legal liability and refer to other local agencies' policies regarding this matter.

EXERCISES IN CRITICAL THINKING

On July 15 at 2:14 a.m., Officer Geasone was working patrol and pulled into a gas station in his marked squad car. As he pulled in, he observed a lone driver, who was already parked in the lot, get out of his vehicle from the driver side and enter the gas station. Geasone entered the gas station and made small talk with the driver while waiting in line with him to buy refreshments. In speaking with the driver, Geasone noticed the odor of an alcoholic beverage on the driver's breath. He further observed the driver to have bloodshot, watery eyes and slurred speech. Geasone did not actually observe the driver driving the vehicle, nor did he conduct a traffic stop on him. When he engaged the driver in conversation, his intent was not to inquire if the driver was intoxicated.

1. Does Officer Geasone have probable cause to pursue a DWI investigation?

   a. No, because Officer Geasone did not at anytime observe the driver driving, and therefore did not observe any driving conduct. Because there was no development of probable cause from driving conduct, Geasone cannot pursue a DWI investigation at this point.

   b. Yes, because Officer Geasone observed the driver get out of the driver seat of the vehicle as he arrived at the gas station. He further observed that the driver was alone at the time. Although he did not conduct a traffic stop, based on that information Geasone has probable cause to continue this investigation.

   c. No, because Officer Geasone cannot use general conversation with the driver while in the gas station as usable probable cause that the driver was driving under the influence. Geasone further cannot go back for an initial stop since he did not have any reason to suspect that the driver was drinking until he spoke to him in the gas station.

   d. Yes, because Officer Geasone does not need driving conduct alone to continue with a DWI investigation. The time of day and all the other factors that Officer Geasone became aware of while making contact with the driver, along with Geasone observing the driver in control of the vehicle in the parked position, is probable cause enough to continue an investigation.

e. No, because Officer Geasone's contact with the driver in the gas station was not directly related to looking to develop further probable cause if the driver was intoxicated. The conversation was general, and therefore has no correlation to probable cause.

On March 10 at 9:00 p.m., Officer Wagon received road and driving complaints from multiple complainants regarding one driver who was "all over the road." Dispatch was able to get a license plate that listed the registered owner's address near the area of the complaints. The vehicle was also described as a unique classic collector Corvette. The record on the registered owner of the vehicle came back with several previous DWI convictions on record. Wagon was not able to respond to the area quickly enough to observe the vehicle driving but did, however, arrive at the registered owner's address shortly after the call. Wagon did not observe the driver driving at anytime. Upon arrival, Wagon observed, by peering through a garage window, that the suspected vehicle was parked inside the residential garage. Officer Wagon knocked on the door of the residence and made contact with the registered owner of the vehicle.

Wagon could clearly observe that the registered owner was intoxicated. Wagon observed the odor of an alcoholic beverage emitting from the man's breath; bloodshot, watery eyes; slurred speech; and inability to stand up. The registered owner would not exit his residence, did not admit to driving, and insisted he had been home for a long time. The registered owner continued speaking with Wagon through his open front door but would not cooperate in answering questions related to the complaints. Wagon was not able to get hold of any of the complainants. The registered owner stated that he was not the only one home at the residence, but Wagon did not observe anyone else. The registered owner eventually grew tired of speaking with the officer and closed his door.

1. Could Officer Wagon take the registered owner from his residence because he was actively speaking with him with an open door to his residence? Could Officer Wagon then continue with a DWI investigation and conduct field sobriety tests based on multiple complainant reports and a previous history?

a. Yes. Officer Wagon was not able to make contact with any of the complainants and was not able to get a description of the actual driver of the vehicle but does not need it when responding to a road and driving complaint. The complaint alone is enough probable cause to continue with a DWI investigation in this situation.

b. Yes. Officer Wagon did not observe the registered owner drive or in control of the vehicle at any time and only made contact with the registered owner when he was already in his residence. However, once Wagon made contact with the registered owner, the officer developed more probable cause.

c. No, because there is no probable cause to indicate that the registered owner of the vehicle was driving at the time of the reports. Officer Wagon did not have probable cause to pursue a DWI investigation. Furthermore, Wagon did not observe the driver of the vehicle between the time he had parked and went inside his residence, which left a time where he plausibly could have consumed alcohol, even though it was a matter of minutes between the call and the response to the residence. There was also no hot pursuit in this incident.

d. No, because it does not matter who the registered owner of the vehicle was or if he was home alone, even if Officer Wagon had that information. The registered owner was inside his residence the entire time he was speaking with the officer. He did not invite the officer into his residence and would not cooperate in answering questions about driving recently. There is nothing the police could do about it either way.

DISCUSSION QUESTIONS

1. What should be the top priority in a traffic program? Justify your selection.

2. Your municipality has an ordinance stating that it is against the law to drink and drive. Obtain a copy of that ordinance and bring it to class. What is the legal limit for intoxication? Do you feel the legal limit justifies the penalty if one is convicted? Would you suggest some modifications in the law as you see it enforced?

3. Three tests are usually given to determine if a person is under the influence of alcohol while driving: a breath test, a urine test, and a blood test. From evidence that might be presented in court, which test would you favor if you were a police officer? What are the advantages and disadvantages in administering each test?

4. Is a pursuit policy justified in a police department, or should officers be allowed to make a discretionary decision to chase without the benefit of a specific policy?

5. Should officers expose those they are pursuing to hazardous roadblock conditions or be given permission to ram cars? If so, what restrictions should apply, if any?

6. Radar detectors used by motorists are a source of irritation to most traffic officers. Do you feel they should be declared illegal to possess and use, as they have been in some states?

7. Most warning tickets issued by officers are never formally recorded on a driver's record. Are such tickets an effective tool in obtaining compliance to traffic laws?

GALE EMERGENCY SERVICES DATABASE ASSIGNMENTS

▶ Use the Gale Emergency Services database (available for separate purchase) to help answer the Discussion Questions as appropriate.

▶ Use the Gale Emergency Services database to research *road rage*. Write a brief (two- to three-page) report on the characteristics of this type of driver and the effects of aggressive driving.

▶ Use the Gale Emergency Services database to read and outline one of the following articles to share with the class:

● "The Role of Race in Law Enforcement: Racial Profiling or Legitimate Use?" by Richard G. Schott

● "Collecting Statistics in Response to Racial Profiling Allegations" by Karen J. Kruger

● "High-Speed Police Pursuits: Dangers, Dynamics and Risk Reduction" by John Hill

● "Alexandria CARES and BABY-1: Protecting the Future" by Dianne Gittins

● "Battling DUI: A Comparative Analysis of Checkpoints and Saturation Patrols" by Jeffrey W. Greene

REFERENCES

"About Safe Communities." n.d. Washington, DC: National Highway Traffic Safety Administration. Accessed February 22, 2012. http://www.nhtsa.gov/Driving+Safety/Safe+Communities/About+Safe+Communities.

Aggressive Driving Enforcement: Evaluations of Two Demonstration Programs. 2004 (March). Washington, DC: National Highway Traffic Safety Administration. (DOT HS 809 707)

Batiste, John R., Michael L. Wagers, and Richard J. Ashton. 2011. "Preventing Traffic-Related Line-of-Duty Deaths." *The Police Chief* (July): 52–55.

Bolton, Joel. 2009. "Why Are Traffic Laws Enforced?" *The Police Chief* (February): 90.

Brown, Weston. 2008. "Collision Investigation: Know and Use the Tech behind Vehicle Crashes." *Law Officer Magazine* (February): 44–47.

Casstevens, Steven. 2008. "Traffic Enforcement Is Real Police Work." *Law and Order* (August): 44–46.

Children. 2008. Washington, DC: National Highway Traffic Safety Administration, Traffic Safety Facts. (DOT HS 811 157)

"Click It or Ticket." n.d. Washington, DC: National Highway Traffic Safety Administration Web site. Accessed February 17, 2012. http://www.nhtsa.gov/CIOT.

Commission on Accreditation of Law Enforcement Agencies (CALEA). 2012. *Standards for Law Enforcement Agencies.* 5th ed. Fairfax, VA: Author.

Corridor Safety Program: A Collaborative Approach to Traffic Safety. 2001. Sacramento: California Highway Patrol. Accessed February 23, 2012. http://www.popcenter.org/library/awards/goldstein/2001/01-09(W).pdf.

Drew, Lisa, Dawn Royal, Benjamin Moulton, Anne Peterson, and Dar Haddix. 2010 (August). *National Survey of Drinking and Driving Attitudes and Behaviors: 2008.* Washington, DC: National Highway Traffic Safety Administration. (DOT HS 811 342)

Easley, Richard B., and Thomas Wunk. 2010. "How New Parking Technologies Help Law Enforcement Fight Crime, Control Traffic, and Boost Revenues." *The Police Chief* (May): 62–64.

Fridell, Lorie A. 2004. *By the Numbers: A Guide for Analyzing Race Data from Vehicle Stops.* Washington, DC: Police Executive Research Forum.

Galvin, Bob. 2009. "Laser Device Takes on Tailgating." *Law Enforcement Technology* (January): 70–73.

Griffin, Michelle. 2009. "Going Mobile: Building a Case for e-Ticketing." *Law Officer Magazine* (February): 30–33.

Griffith, David. 2007. "Death Race." *Police* (November): 12.

Grossi, Dave. 2009. "Night Crawlers: How to Spot Speed Freaks and Meth Heads." *Law Officer Magazine* (February): 24–28.

Haug, Scot. 2009. "Kootenai County Goes High Tech: A Case Study in License Plate Recognition." *Law Officer Magazine* (January): 64–68.

Highway Safety Desk Book. 2004 (September). 2nd ed. Alexandria, VA: International Association of Chiefs of Police, Highway Safety Committee.

Impaired Driving Prevention Toolkit. 2003 (January). Washington, DC: National Highway Traffic Safety Administration. (DOT HS 809 552)

"Incident Statistics." 2012 (February 22). Washington, DC: U.S. Department of Transportation, Pipeline and Hazardous Materials Safety Administration, Hazmat Intelligence Portal. Accessed February 22, 2012. http://www.phmsa.dot.gov/hazmat/library/data-stats/incidents.

"License Plate Readers." 2012 (January). In *How Are Innovations in Technology Transforming Policing?,* 28–34. Washington, DC: Police Executive Research Forum, Critical Issues in Policing Series.

Lives Saved in 2009 by Restraint Use and Minimum-Drinking-Age Laws. 2010 (September). Washington, DC: National Highway Traffic Safety Administration, Traffic Safety Facts. (DOT HS 811 383)

"*Looking Beyond the License Plate* Award Program." n.d. Alexandria, VA: International Association of Chiefs of Police. Accessed February 17, 2012. http://www.theiacp.org/About/Awards/LookingBeyondtheLicensePlateAwardProgram/tabid/343/Default.aspx.

Lum, Cynthia, and George Fachner. 2008 (September). *Police Pursuits in an Age of Innovation and Reform: The IACP Police Pursuit Database.* Arlington, VA: International Association of Chiefs of Police.

Maggard, David L., and Daniel Jung. 2009. "Irvine's Area Traffic Officer Program." *The Police Chief* (March): 46–50.

The Manual on Uniform Traffic Control Devices, 2009 Edition. 2009 (December). Washington, DC: U.S. Department of Transportation, Federal Highway Administration.

Marshall, Mark A. 2011. "'The Great Threat' to Public Safety." *The Police Chief* (July): 6.

Martinelli, Ron. 2011. "To Chase or Not to Chase?" *Police* (December): 54–55.

Molnar, J. P. 2008. "Crash Investigation." *Law Officer Magazine* (November): 20–21.

Nugent, Hugh, Edward F. Connors, J. Thomas McEwen, and Lou Mayo. n.d. *Restrictive High-Speed Police Pursuits.* Washington, DC: U.S. Department of Justice. (NCJ 122025)

Pedestrians. 2010. Washington, DC: National Highway Traffic Safety Administration, Traffic Safety Facts, 2009 Data. (DOT HS 811 394)

Petrocelli, Joseph. 2007. "Street Racing." *Police* (April): 20–21.

"The Relation between Speed and Crashes." 2009 (April). Leidschendam, the Netherlands: Institute for Road Safety Research. Accessed February 17, 2012. http://www.swov.nl/rapport/Factsheets/UK/FS_Speed.pdf.

Safe Communities Directory: 2011 Coalitions and Partners Database. 2011. Fort Worth, TX: National Highway Traffic Safety Administration.

Sanow, Ed. 2009. "Traffic Enforcement Equals Crime Reduction." *Law and Order* (March): 6.

Saving Lives with Traffic Safety. 2011. Cincinnati, OH: Cincinnati Police Department. Accessed February 23, 2012. http://www.popcenter.org/library/awards/goldstein/2011/11-39.pdf.

Schultz, David P., Ed Hudak, and Geoffrey P. Alpert. 2010. "Evidence-Based Decisions on Police Pursuits: The Officer's Perspective." *FBI Law Enforcement Bulletin* (March): 1–7.

Scoville, Dean. 2012. "Duty Dangers: Vehicle Pursuits." *Police* (January): 46–52.

Seat Belt Use in 2011—Overall Results. 2011 (December). Washington, DC: NHTSA Traffic Safety Facts. (DOT HS 811 544)

"Speeding." 2008. Washington, DC: National Highway Traffic Safety Administration, Traffic Safety Facts. (DOT HS 811 166)

Stockton, Dale. 2009. "New Year, New Challenges: Synergy, Technology & Video." *Law Officer Magazine* (January): 8.

Sweeney, Earl M. 2011a. "Four Emerging Traffic Safety Problems." *The Police Chief* (January): 78.

Sweeney, Earl M. 2011b. "Traffic Enforcement Faces Interesting Times." *The Police Chief* (June): 90.

"Teen Drivers: Fact Sheet." 2010 (October 18). Atlanta, GA: Centers for Disease Control and Prevention, National Center for Injury Prevention and Control. Accessed February 17, 2012.

http://www.cdc.gov/MotorVehicleSafety/Teen_Drivers/teendrivers_factsheet.html.

2010 Motor Vehicle Crashes: Overview. 2011 (December). Washington, DC: National Highway Traffic Safety Administration, Traffic Safety Facts, Research Note. (DOT HS 811 552)

"Vital Signs: Alcohol-Impaired Driving Among Adults—United States, 2010." 2011 (October 4). *Morbidity and Mortality Weekly Report.* Atlanta, GA: Centers for Disease Control and Prevention. Accessed February 19, 2012. http://www.cdc.gov/mmwr/preview/mmwrhtml/mm6039a4.htm.

Worden, Robert E., Sarah J. McLean, and Andrew P. Wheeler. 2012. "Testing for Racial Profiling with the Veil-of-Darkness Method." *Police Quarterly* 15 (1, March): 92–111.

"A World without Traffic Calming." 2009. *The Traffic Calmer Newsletter* (January).

CASES CITED

Brower v. County of Inyo, 489 U.S. 593 (1989)

Brown v. City of Oneonta, 221 F.3d 329 (2nd Cir.2000), cert. denied, 534 U.S. 816 (2001)

Carleton v. Town of Framingham, 640 N.E. 2d 452 (1994)

City of Indianapolis v. Edmond, 531 U.S. 32 (2000)

County of Sacramento v. Lewis, 523 U.S. 833 (1998)

Michigan Department of State Police v. Sitz, 496 U.S. 444 (1990)

Pennsylvania v. Mimms, 434 U.S. 106 (1977)

Pennsylvania v. Muniz, 496 U.S. 582 (1990)

Scott v. Harris, 550 U.S. 372 (2007)

Whren v. United States, 517 U.S. 806 (1996)

This available CourseMate has an interactive eBook and interactive learning tools, including flash cards, quizzes, and more. To learn more about this resource and access free demo CourseMate resources, go to www.cengagebrain.com, and search for this book. To access CourseMate materials that you have purchased, go to login.cengagebrain.com.

CHAPTER 6

Crime, Disorder, and Quality-of-Life Issues:
Responding to the Call

© AP Images/Lewiston Tribune, Kyle Mills

DO YOU KNOW . . .

- What the official sources of information about crime are?
- What index offenses the FBI compiles statistics on?
- What technologies assist law enforcement in addressing crime and disorder issues?
- What the responsibilities of officers responding to a criminal action call are?
- What the preliminary investigation of a crime consists of?
- What issues may lead to civil disobedience in the 21st century?
- How police departments should be prepared to deal with demonstrations and violence?
- What crisis situations police officers may face?
- What the number-one rule is when dealing with hostage situations, barricaded subjects, or attempted suicides?

CAN YOU DEFINE?

chain of custody
chain of possession
civil disobedience
collective efficacy
flashbangs
geographic information systems (GIS)
hot spots
incivilities
preliminary investigation
property crimes
routine activity theory
Stockholm syndrome
Uniform Crime Reports (UCRs)
violent crimes

INTRODUCTION

Responding to calls about crime is a basic function of law enforcement and has been a defining priority throughout the history of policing. Many believe this is the only true function of the police and that in a perfect world, one free of all crime, police would be unnecessary. Of course, police operations involve more than just handling crime. By the same token, the response to crime is not new, nor has it always been solely the responsibility of law enforcement.

The English citizenry, beginning with the reign of Alfred the Great (871–899), were expected to catch criminals under the frankpledge system. If a crime was committed, everyone in the community was to raise a "hue and cry." Failing to catch an offender meant paying a fine, which forced the entire realm to engage in law enforcement. Modern policing has returned to the idea of engaging the community to help combat crime because crime is not just a law enforcement problem. It is everyone's problem.

Preliminary data from the Federal Bureau of Investigation (FBI) Uniform Crime Reports (UCR) show that both violent and property crime decreased in the United States during the first six months of 2011 when compared with crime data for the same time in 2010, with a decrease of 6.4 percent in reported violent crime and a drop of 3.7 percent in reported property crime (*Preliminary Semiannual Uniform Crime Report* 2011). Data from the Bureau of Justice Statistics (BJS) National Crime Victimization Survey (NCVS) show that the rate of total violent crime victimization dropped by 13 percent in 2010, and violent and serious violent victimization declined by one-third (nearly 34 percent) between 2001 and 2010 (Truman 2011).

Many contend the added "eyes and ears" of the citizenry has contributed to the stable or declining crime rate. Paradoxically, some citizens have grown increasingly fearful of crime and victimization. Some studies have found those who watched the most local television news reported the highest levels of fear of crime. Media accounts of crime usually focus on the most serious, sensational cases, which may help explain why the levels of citizens' fear of crime appear to be unrelated to the actual levels of crime in their neighborhoods. Study after study shows that the media focuses on crime and violence to the neglect of other aspects of law enforcement.

This chapter begins with a look at how crimes are classified and measured, including a discussion of the Uniform Crime Reports, the National Incident-Based Reporting System, and the National Crime Victimization Survey. Next is a look at how technology is helping police move from measuring crime to predicting crime in their quest to be more proactive, followed by a discussion of how police respond to calls about crimes. The chapter then examines the police response to disorder and civil disobedience and crisis situations involving hostages, barricaded individuals, and suicide attempts. The chapter concludes with a look at how crime and disorder are related to both community policing and problem-oriented policing.

CLASSIFYING AND MEASURING CRIME

The U.S. Department of Justice administers several statistical programs to measure the magnitude, nature, and impact of crime in America. The FBI collects and disseminates crime statistics through its UCR Program and the National Incident-Based Reporting System (NIBRS). The BJS collects detailed crime information via its NCVS.

> The official sources of information about crime are the Uniform Crime Reports (UCR), the National Incident-Based Reporting System (NIBRS), and the National Crime Victimization Survey (NCVS).

Although the UCR and NCVS programs each have unique strengths, they are conducted for different purposes and use different methods. Therefore, caution is needed in comparing crime trends presented by the UCR and NCVS because each examines the nation's crime problem from a unique perspective, so their results are not comparable. Nonetheless, the information they produce provides a more comprehensive view of crime in the United States together than either could produce alone.

Uniform Crime Reports

The FBI gathers statistics on reported crimes from local, county, and state law enforcement agencies throughout the country and reports the findings annually in its **Uniform Crime Reports (UCRs),** called *Crime in the United States.* According to the FBI (*Crime in the United States* 2010), the law enforcement agencies active in the UCR Program during 2010 represented 17,000 law enforcement agencies serving nearly 95 percent of U.S. citizens.

When the UCR program was launched in 1929, seven offenses were chosen to serve as an index for gauging fluctuations in the overall volume and rate of crime reported to law enforcement. These crimes—known as Part I offenses—included the **violent crimes** of murder and nonnegligent manslaughter, forcible rape, robbery, and aggravated assault and the **property crimes** of burglary, larceny/theft, and motor vehicle theft. A 1979 congressional mandate added arson, a property crime, as the eighth Part I offense captured in the annual UCR counts.

>
> The FBI's Uniform Crime Reports contain statistics on violent crimes (murder and nonnegligent manslaughter, aggravated assault causing serious bodily harm, forcible rape, and robbery) and property crimes (burglary, larceny/theft, motor vehicle theft, and arson).

Figure 6.1 shows the relative frequency of violent and property crime offenses in 2010. This graphic does not imply regularity in the commission of the Index offenses. Rather, it shows the annual ratio of crime to fixed time intervals. Figure 6.2 shows the relative distribution of the offenses in 2010.

Uniform Crime Reports (UCRs)

The FBI's national crime reporting system, published annually as *Crime in the United States.*

violent crimes

Offenses in which physical contact with the victim occurs, including assault, murder, rape, and robbery; sometimes called *crimes against persons.*

property crimes

Offenses in which no physical contact with the victim occurs, including arson, auto theft, burglary, and larceny/theft.

2010 Crime Clock

One violent crime	Every 25.3 seconds
One murder	Every 35.6 minutes
One forcible rape	Every 6.2 minutes
One robbery	Every 1.4 minutes
One aggravated assault	Every 40.5 seconds

One property crime	Every 3.5 seconds
One burglary	Every 14.6 seconds
One larceny/theft	Every 5.1 seconds
One motor vehicle theft	Every 42.8 seconds

FIGURE 6.1
2010 Crime Clock
Source: *Crime in the United States, 2010.* Washington, DC: Federal Bureau of Investigation, 2010. http://www.fbi.gov/about-us/cjis/ucr/crime-in-the-u.s/2010/crime-in-the-u.s.-2010/offenses-known-to-law-enforcement/crime-clock

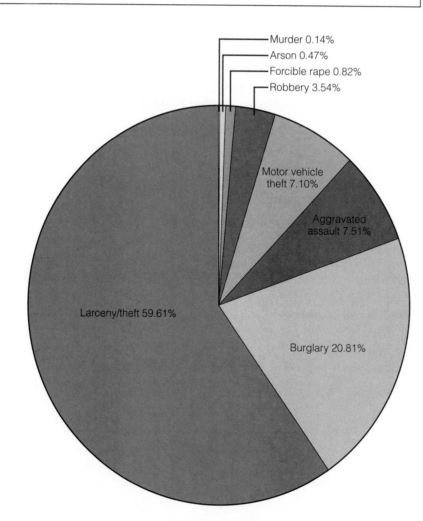

Murder 0.14%
Arson 0.47%
Forcible rape 0.82%
Robbery 3.54%
Motor vehicle theft 7.10%
Aggravated assault 7.51%
Burglary 20.81%
Larceny/theft 59.61%

FIGURE 6.2 Percent Distribution of Part I Offenses—2010
Data sources: http://www.fbi.gov/about-us/cjis/ucr/crime-in-the-us/2010/crime-in-the-us/2010/tables/10tbl01.xls, and Arson Table 2: http://www.fbi.gov/about-us/cjis/ucr/crime-in-the-u.s/2010/crime-in-the-u.s.-2010/tables/10arsontbl2.xls

One of the major criticisms of the UCR program, from a data resource perspective, is that it uses the hierarchy rule in the collection of crime statistics, meaning only the most serious offense in a multiple-offense situation is recorded. For example, if a forcible rape victim is also robbed and assaulted by the same assailant during the same attack, only the rape is counted because it comes above the other offenses on the hierarchy of seriousness. Exceptions to the hierarchy rule involve the offenses of justifiable homicide, motor vehicle theft, and arson. Nonetheless, the UCR reporting method has been criticized as providing an underrepresentation of the true nature and extent of crime in the country. To address this shortfall, the FBI has been transitioning to a more comprehensive, detailed reporting system—the NIBRS.

National Incident-Based Reporting System (NIBRS)

Although the UCR counts incidents and arrests for the eight Part I offenses and arrests only for other offenses, NIBRS provides detailed incident information on 48 Group A offenses representing 22 categories of crimes. NIBRS also distinguishes between attempted and completed crimes:

> NIBRS data can be directly traced back to original information collected by the local agency to allow for data quality checks that were impossible under the Summary Program. Now, with the advances in technology and computing resources, leveraged by incident-based crime reporting, the information relayed to law enforcement can be monitored from the initial response until its final report to the FBI. These capabilities in combination with a state program designed to foster quality control can substantially increase the chance of identifying effort in the data and improving the quality of those data.[1]

Table 6.1 shows the NIBRS Group A offenses, comparable to the UCR Part I offenses. Table 6.2 shows the Group B offenses—the "other" offenses, or Part II offenses.

National Crime Victimization Survey (NCVS)

Conducted by U.S. Bureau of the Census personnel and reported through the BJS, the NCVS is an ongoing survey of a nationally representative sample of approximately 49,000 households to collect information on crimes suffered by individuals and households, whether or not those crimes were reported to law enforcement. All household members ages 12 and older (about 101,000 people) are interviewed every 6 months for 3 years. New households are continuously rotated into the sample.

Since its inception in 1973, the NCVS has been the primary source of information on the characteristics of criminal victimization and on the number and types of crimes *not* reported to law enforcement authorities. Following are some of the highlights from the 2010 NCVS (Truman 2011):

---

[1]Source: Barnett-Ryan, Cynthia, and Swanson, Gregory. "The Role of State Programs in NIBRS Data Quality." *Journal of Contemporary Criminal Justice*, February 2008, pp.18–31. Reprinted by permission of SAGE Publications.

Table 6.1 The NIBRS Group A Offenses

Arson	Kidnapping/abduction
Assault offenses	Larceny/theft offenses
Aggravated assault	Pocket picking
Simple assault	Purse snatching
Intimidation	Shoplifting
Bribery	Theft from building
Burglary/breaking and entering	Theft from coin-operated machine
Counterfeiting/forgery	Theft from motor vehicle
Destruction/damage/vandalism of property	Theft of motor vehicle parts/accessories
Drug/narcotic offenses	All other larceny
Drug/narcotic violations	Motor vehicle theft
Drug equipment violations	Pornography/obscene material
Embezzlement	Prostitution offenses
Extortion/blackmail	Prostitution
Fraud offenses	Assisting or promoting prostitution
False pretenses/swindle/confidence game	Robbery
Credit card/ATM fraud	Sex offenses, forcible
Impersonation	Forcible rape
Welfare fraud	Forcible sodomy
Wire fraud	Sexual assault with an object
Gambling offenses	Forcible fondling
Betting/wagering	Sex offenses, nonforcible
Operating/promoting/assisting gambling	Stolen property offenses
Gambling equipment violations	Weapon law violations
Sports tampering	
Homicide offenses	
Murder/nonnegligent manslaughter	
Negligent manslaughter	
Justifiable homicide	

Source: Brian A. Reaves, *National Incident-Based Reporting System: Using NIBRS Data to Analyze Violent Crime* (Washington, DC: Bureau of Justice Statistics Technical Report, October 1993), 1.

Table 6.2 The NIBRS Group B Offenses

Bad checks	Nonviolent family offenses
Curfew/loitering/vagrancy	Peeping Tom
Disorderly conduct	Runaway
Driving under the influence	Trespassing
Drunkenness	All other offenses
Liquor law violations	

Source: Brian A. Reaves, *National Incident-Based Reporting System: Using NIBRS Data to Analyze Violent Crime* (Washington, DC: Bureau of Justice Statistics Technical Report, October 1993), 2.

▶ Males and females had similar rates of violent victimization during 2010, 15.7 per 1,000 and 14.2 per 1,000 respectively.

▶ The percentage of victims of violent crimes who were injured during the victimization increased from 24 percent in 2008 to 29 percent in 2010.

▶ From 2001 to 2010, approximately 6 to 9 percent of all violent victimizations were committed with a firearm, a figure that has remained stable since 2004.

▶ Only about 50 percent of violent victimizations and 40 percent of property victimizations in 2010 were reported to the police.

These various data collection programs—UCR, NIBRS, and NCVS—have created a documented history of crime problems throughout our country and have helped the national law enforcement community gain better insight into trends regarding criminal activity and victimization in the United States. And although these programs continue to be beneficial, many departments have moved beyond simply measuring crime to using data and technology to help them predict crime.

FROM MEASURING CRIME TO PREDICTING CRIME—USING TECHNOLOGY TO BECOME PROACTIVE

Law enforcement's ability to understand the extent of crime and patterns to its occurrence is continuously evolving. Increasingly sophisticated technology is now enabling police at the local level to track and analyze crime directly affecting their community. In addition to real-time capabilities, technology also has forward-looking capabilities, meaning it affords agencies a degree of predictability in forecasting future crime in their community, allowing the department to become more proactive. A 2011 Police Executive Research Forum (PERF) survey found that 70 percent of responding law enforcement agencies had already implemented some form of *predictive policing*, which was defined as "the advanced use of information/technology to predict and prevent crime" ("PERF Survey Shows" 2012, 1). In addition, 90 percent of respondents indicated a plan to increase their use of predictive policing by 2016.

15 CALEA Standard 15 states, "Crime analysis represents a system utilizing regularly collected information on reported crimes and criminals to prevent and suppress crime and to apprehend criminal offenders. Crime analysis is a scientific process in the sense that it involves the collection of valid and reliable data, employs systematic techniques of analysis, and seeks to determine, for predictive purposes, the frequency with which events occur and the extent to which they are associated with other events. The collection, analysis, and distribution of readily available crime data information to affected personnel will enhance agency effectiveness."

Source: Commission on Accreditation of Law Enforcement Agencies (CALEA). 2012. *Standards for Law Enforcement Agencies.* 5th ed. Fairfax, VA: Author.

Tactically, the fundamental function of crime analysis is to provide law enforcement and its support staff with crime series patterns and trends and to help develop information to improve chances of apprehending criminals and preventing crimes (Paletta and Belledin 2008). Crime analysis combines geographic data with local crime and administrative data to give police a more comprehensive picture of *why* crime happens where it does (or does not), rather than simply identifying locations of where crime does and does not happen (Peed, Wilson, and Scalisi 2008).

> Technologies that greatly assist law enforcement in analyzing and responding to crime and disorder issues include mapping, geographic information systems, geospatial statistical analysis, and CompStat.

Mapping Crime

Mapping crime has evolved from using color-coded pushpins to using user-friendly mapping software, designed for examining and predicting crime and criminal behavior. Traditional density mapping allows departments to visualize how crime is distributed across the landscape and to detect patterns or trends along various corridors, within certain neighborhoods or as associated with other geographical features. Such mapping allows departments to more readily identify **hot spots**, or areas where incidents of crime and disorder tend to cluster in close proximity to one another. Mapping can also reveal *hot dots*, or specific addresses of persistent calls for police service. These maps help law enforcement administrators direct patrols to areas where they are most needed—putting "cops on the dots."

hot spots

Clusters of crime in certain geographic areas.

When the PERF surveyed police agencies in 2005 and 2006 to identify the most widely used antiviolence strategy, the highest-ranking program cited by 63 percent of the respondents was hot spot enforcement: "In general, hot spot enforcement refers to police efforts to identify the location—a residence, a store, a nightclub, or other particular address; a street corner; a city block; a neighborhood—that generates the most calls to 911 or other indicators of criminal activity. Then, police analyze the types of crimes being committed at each hot spot and devise ways of reducing the crime.... Nearly 9 out of 10 agencies use hot spot enforcement efforts directed either at larger hot spot areas like neighborhoods, smaller hot spot places like intersections, or both" (*Violent Crime in America* 2008, 3). Given that prevention is one of the primary goals of proactive policing, hot spot enforcement may provide police with a new way to break the vicious cycle of crime: "Hot spots policing may be to the new millennium what problem-oriented policing was to the 1990s" (Wexler 2008, 29).

Hot spot policing and incident-based deployment has also been used to address public safety issues such as traffic crashes. One jurisdiction with several miles of major interstate highway running through the city used mapping to identify the specific corridor of hot spot crash activity that was costing millions of dollars and several hundred injuries every year. Armed with that data, the department mobilized a unit for interstate traffic enforcement and crash reduction and was able to remedy a problem area in their community (Hoelzer and Gorman 2011).

Recognizing that the majority of calls for police service—about 70 percent by some estimates—are for noncriminal matters, some departments have begun to use mapping to address, assess, and enhance the police response to other types of issues, such as locating lost children or elderly residents suffering from Alzheimer's disease, and improving surveillance and protection efforts around critical infrastructure in the post–9/11 era (Markovic and Scalisi 2011). Many departments map field contacts in addition to locations at which officers provide services such as "well-being checks."

Geographic Information Systems (GIS)

In addition to identifying hot spots, mapping is also routinely used to track registered sex offenders in communities. **Geographic information systems (GIS)** enhance traditional mapping by adding information from various other databases. For example, modern GIS software can generate maps that correlate crime with vacant housing units, schools, or parks; income level of a census tract; patterns of car thefts; and locations of chop shops:

> Because police solutions to crime are necessarily about where crime takes place, the ability to visualize and analyze geographic patterns becomes paramount.... Continuing improvements in GIS software have made it possible to better assemble, integrate, and create new ways of analyzing data. Not only can analysis, with the help of GIS software, assemble multiple and disparate sets of demographic, economic, and social data; they can also create new units of analysis that more accurately model human behavior. (Peed, Wilson, and Scalisi 2008, 24)

Geospatial Statistical Analysis

Geospatial statistical analysis takes GIS technology a step further by allowing analysts to identify areas within the community that are statistically similar to locations where prior incidents have occurred and, thus, at increased risk for future incidents:

> Geospatial statistical analysis...characterizes the locations associated with past events and creates a model that incorporates environmental factors statistically associated with past incidents. This model can then be used to identify similar locations where future incidents are likelier to occur. Ultimately, this approach enables law enforcement to act proactively to prevent crime and influence outcomes. (McCue 2011, 4)

Drawing on environmental criminology and the principle set forth in the **routine activity theory**—that crime occurs at the intersection of a motivated offender, a suitable target, and an absent or ineffective guardian—geospatial statistical analysis can help law enforcement understand and identify the specific jurisdictional characteristics associated with their local crime and disorder problems: "Certain environmental factors attract or enable crime, while other features may serve as deterrents. These factors can be ranked based on their relative contribution to the likelihood of future incidents and used for analysis. This factor analysis provides unique opportunities for information-based or 'tailor-made' crime prevention" (McCue 2011, 5). This information-based response represents a game-changing shift in police operations by allowing law enforcement to create customized solutions to particular crime problems and, ultimately, keep their communities safer.

geographic information systems (GIS)

Enhance traditional mapping by adding information from various other databases.

routine activity theory

Principle of environmental criminology that states crime occurs at the intersection of a motivated offender, a suitable target, and an absent or ineffective guardian.

CompStat

Many departments have enhanced their crime analysis by using CompStat, short for "computer comparison statistics." First implemented in 1994 in New York City under then-police commissioner William Bratton, CompStat is a progressive, goal-oriented, information-driven police management strategy based on four core components: (1) accurate and timely collection of crime data and intelligence analysis, (2) rapid deployment of personnel and other resources, (3) effective tactics and strategies to address crime and disorder problems, and (4) relentless follow-up, assessment, and accountability (Jang, Hoover, and Joo 2010).

The crime control strategies that form the foundation of CompStat policing include hot spot policing, problem-solving approaches and broken windows enforcement (Jang, Hoover, and Joo 2010). The CompStat model embraces the broken windows philosophy by taking a zero-tolerance approach to even minor infractions and offenses, under the premise that a police focus on improving social disorder and quality of life issues can ultimately affect and reduce serious crime. Research has found, however, that while the CompStat approach can be effective in reducing property crime and total index crime rates, it does not significantly reduce violent crime rates (Jang, Hoover, and Joo 2010).

Beyond Crime Analysis

Effective crime analysis can use several processes, including the traditional crime analysis process, the SARA model, the intelligence cycle model, and others, but the most difficult aspect of preventing crime and arresting criminals is the transition between analysis and response: "It is here that the analyst loses direct control over the process and must pass the baton to the operational units" (Bruce and Ouellette 2008, 30). Building on routine activity theory, Bruce and Ouellette point out that although directed patrol is a "default response" to a crime pattern, hot spot, or problem, it can be effective for some issues and can result in both suppression and apprehension. Agencies have many more potential responses beyond directed patrol at their disposal: apprehending offenders, hardening potential targets, and suppressing underlying opportunities for crime.

Issues Related to Disseminating Crime Information to the Public

As beneficial as this technology is for police operations, it has raised some legitimate concerns. For example, given communities' growing desire for access to timely information about crime and disorder in their neighborhoods, how much of this crime data should be made so readily available? Although technically such data is public information, and citizens do have a right to know about crime in their communities, how do law enforcement agencies address victims' right to privacy?

The National Center for Victims of Crime has published *Beyond the Beat: Ethical Considerations for Community Policing in the Digital Age* (2008). The publication describes how recent advances in one-way communications such as online crime statistics, crime maps, and sex offender registries can help combat crime but may also present ethical challenges. Other concerns involve the possible revitalization of informal redlining methods used by some insurance and banking companies. Although a neighborhood identified as a high-crime area could benefit from positive local interventions, it could also be flagged (i.e., redlined) as undesirable, resulting in residential flight and causing more damage to an already disadvantaged area. Real estate agents and homeowners may become concerned about decreasing property values if crime maps lead to the perception their neighborhoods are unsafe.

RESPONDING TO CALLS ABOUT CRIME AND DISORDER

Despite great advances in detecting crime and apprehending criminals, crimes will continue to be committed, and when crime and disorder problems surface, law enforcement must respond. How police officers respond to calls about committed crimes depends on several important variables:

▶ What specific crime is involved?

▶ Is the crime still in progress?

▶ How many suspects are involved?

▶ Do we know their identity?

▶ Are weapons involved?

▶ Are there other aggravating circumstances regarding the suspect(s), for example, are they intoxicated, mentally imbalanced, and so forth?

▶ Are there victims involved or injured?

▶ Is there a danger to the public?

▶ Could a hostage situation develop?

▶ What weather and environmental factors can affect a response?

▶ How many officers are needed to respond?

▶ How many officers are available?

▶ Where are they?

Sometimes answers to all these questions are available. More often, however, responding officers lack much of this information.

> Responsibilities of officers responding to a call regarding a criminal act include:
> - Arriving as rapidly, yet as safely, as possible.
> - Assessing safety procedures.
> - Providing emergency care for any injured people at the scene.
> - Securing and controlling persons at the scene.
> - Establishing and preserving scene boundaries.
> - Transferring control of the scene to the investigator(s) in charge or conducting the preliminary investigation.

Arriving at the Scene

Whether the police arrive with red lights and sirens will depend on the nature of the information to which police are responding. The element of surprise may be important if the crime is believed to be still in progress. At other times, such as in assault cases, the siren may be desirable because it may frighten off the attacker. Each specific call must be assessed for whether the added speed of response available through the use of red lights and siren is an advantage. Recall the Kansas City Preventive Patrol Experiment, which showed that rapid response time did not greatly improve chances of making an arrest at the scene. In addition, the more rapid the response, the greater the likelihood of a crash en route involving the responding squad or citizens who happen to be in the way.

The National Institute of Justice (NIJ) has produced a reference guide for law enforcement officers (*Crime Scene Investigation* 2004, 9–10), suggesting that officers follow these steps when making their initial response at a crime scene:

1. **Note all information received from dispatch, via direct citizen complaint or through personal onsite observation:** Address, location (e.g., storefront, second floor rear, mile marker), time, date, type of call, parties involved, weapons involved, ongoing, and/or dangerous scene.

2. **Be aware of any persons or vehicles leaving the crime scene:** Note arrival time and describe vehicles (make, model, color, condition, license plate number, age) and individuals (height, weight, race, age, clothing, sex, distinguishing features). Note direction of travel from first observation.

3. **Approach the scene cautiously:** Scan the entire area and note any possible secondary crime scenes (e.g., different areas where evidence/activity is observed) as well as any persons or vehicles in the vicinity that may be related to the crime.

4. **Assess the scene for officer safety:** Look, listen, smell (e.g., downed power lines, animals, biohazards, chemicals, weapons). Unreasonably dangerous scenes should *not* be entered (e.g., anthrax, bomb scene).

5. **Remain alert and attentive:** Assume crime is ongoing until determined to be otherwise (e.g., keep looking, listening, smelling).

6. **Treat location(s) as a crime scene until determined to be otherwise:** Use all information initially received, use all senses. *NOTE: The scene may not be what it initially appears to be. Anticipate the unexpected.*[2]

Assessing Safety Procedures

The actual arrival may be fraught with danger; consequently, officers should make use of cover if it is thought the suspect might still be at the scene. If the element of surprise is important, officers should have a system of hand signals to coordinate their arrival and approach to the scene. Communication with other officers is critical and is typically done via radio, although alternatives to using the main channel include switching over to a tactical talk-around channel on the radio or using push-to-talk cell phones. The NIJ suggests the following steps when assessing the safety of a scene (*Crime Scene Investigation* 2004, 11):

1. **Evaluate the scene for safety concerns:** Scan the area for dangers (look, listen, smell); check for hazardous materials (e.g., gasoline, natural gas, electrical lines, biohazards), weapons, and *radiological* or

---

[2]Source: *Crime Scene Investigation: A Reference for Law Enforcement Training* (Washington, DC: Department of Justice, National Institute of Justice, June 2004), 9–10. (NCJ 200160)

chemical threats. Notify appropriate support agencies to render the scene safe prior to entry (e.g., fire department, hazmat, bomb squad).

2. **Approach the scene with caution:** Ensure officer safety and reduce risk to victim(s), witnesses, and others.

3. **Survey the scene for dangerous persons and control the situation:** Be aware of violent persons and potentially escalating conflicts. *NOTE*: Officers' actions can contribute to the escalation or de-escalation of the situation. Apply communication and defensive training skills.

4. **Notify supervisory personnel and call for assistance/backup:** Follow departmental guidelines.[3]

Note: The next two responsibilities, providing emergency care to injured people and securing persons at the scene, may occur in reverse order, depending on the situation. If the injuries are not life threatening and the suspect is considered dangerous, apprehending that suspect will take precedence over attending to the injuries.

Providing Emergency Care

Once dangerous situations or people have been brought under control, the responding officer's next responsibility is to ensure that medical attention is provided to injured persons while awaiting the arrival of emergency medical services (EMS) personnel. Furthermore, the officer must act to minimize contamination of the scene and loss of evidence. Assisting, guiding, and instructing medical personnel during the care and removal of injured persons will help in this endeavor. Suggested steps to follow are these (*Crime Scene Investigation* 2004, 12–13):

1. **Assess the victim(s) for injury:** Evaluate medical needs and signs of life. Administer emergency first aid if needed.

2. **Call for medical personnel:** Follow department procedure for notifying EMS personnel and continue to assist the victim(s) as necessary.

3. **Guide medical personnel to the victim(s) at the scene:** Choose a pathway to minimize *contamination* or alteration of the crime scene and direct EMS personnel along this route. Remain with EMS personnel, if possible.

4. **Point out potential physical evidence to medical personnel:** Instruct EMS personnel to avoid contact with items of evidence and to preserve all clothing, taking care to avoid altering (by cutting, tearing or ripping through) bullet holes, knife tears, etc. in the clothing. Document the movement of injured persons and any scene items (e.g., furniture, blankets, weapons) by EMS personnel.

5. **Instruct emergency medical personnel not to "clean up" the scene:** Avoid removal of *trace* and other physical *evidence* by adherence to EMS equipment and personnel cleaning the victim's skin surface. Avoid altering items originating from the scene or adding items *to* the scene by EMS personnel.

---

[3]Source: *Crime Scene Investigation: A Reference for Law Enforcement Training* (Washington, DC: Department of Justice, National Institute of Justice, June 2004), 11. (NCJ 200160)

6. **Document emergency medical responder(s) at the scene:** Obtain each individual's name, unit, agency name, and business phone number for future investigative purposes (e.g., information about scene alteration or to obtain *elimination* and/or *standard/reference samples*). Also obtain the name and location of the medical facility to which the victim(s) is being transported.

7. **Obtain "dying declaration" as appropriate:** If the victims' levels of injury are life threatening, record any statement they make. *NOTE*: Review jurisdictional law regarding *dying declarations.*

8. **Document statements and comments:** Record statements and comments made by victims, suspects, and witnesses, including to whom and under what circumstances statements/comments were made.

9. **Document statements and comments made during transport:** If possible, accompany the injured person(s) to the medical facility and record any statements and comments they make during transport. If law enforcement is unavailable, request that EMS personnel who accompany the injured person(s) to the medical facility document statements and comments.[4]

As a final reminder, instruct EMS personnel to preserve evidence and follow up with them to retrieve any items they may have obtained.

Securing and Controlling Persons at the Scene

As soon as emergency matters are tended to, the primary responsibility of the police is to secure and control persons at the crime scene, including the suspect. Keep in mind some of the following steps may have already occurred, preceding the rendering of first aid if injuries were non–life threatening and someone at the scene posed an imminent threat to the officer or others. But once emergencies have been dealt with, the following steps should be taken to secure and control all other people at the scene (*Crime Scene Investigation* 2004, 14)

1. **Control all persons at the scene:** Restrict movement of people at the scene to prevent them from altering or destroying physical evidence. Continue to control the scene by maintaining officer presence.

2. **Identify all persons at the scene:** Identify bystanders and remove them from the scene. Obtain verifiable personal information from suspects (secure and separate them), witnesses (secure and separate them), and victims, family members, and friends (control their movement but show compassion). Identify medical and assisting personnel.

3. **Exclude unauthorized/nonessential personnel from the scene:** This includes law enforcement officials not working the case, politicians, media, and other nonessential personnel (e.g., any persons not performing investigative or safety functions at the scene).[5]

[4]Source: *Crime Scene Investigation: A Reference for Law Enforcement Training* (Washington, DC: Department of Justice, National Institute of Justice, June 2004), 12–13. (NCJ 200160)

[5]Source: *Crime Scene Investigation: A Reference for Law Enforcement Training* (Washington, DC: Department of Justice, National Institute of Justice, June 2004), 14. (NCJ 200160)

When taking a suspect into custody, "Remember the contact and cover principles: firm, clear and concise verbal commands given by only one officer; watch the suspect's hands; hands kill; and 'no' people belong on the ground" (Grossi 2007b, 25). A "no" person is considered one who resists an officer's commands, in contrast to "yes" people who comply, surrender, and are able to be taken into custody while remaining standing. Defiance and failure to comply is a danger to officers; thus, "no" people must be immobilized by commanding them to get down on the ground before an officer can safely approach, handcuff, and search the individual.

Establishing and Preserving Crime Scene Boundaries

The first officer to arrive on the crime scene automatically incurs the critical responsibility of securing the crime scene from unauthorized intrusion or other contamination. If more than one officer responds to the call, the scene can be secured immediately by one officer while the other officer handles any emergency situation.

Officers should consider any crime scene as highly dynamic and make the preliminary survey of the layout carefully while preserving crime scene integrity. Sometimes securing the scene is as simple as closing a door, but other times it is more complex. In a bank robbery, for example, the entire lobby is usually secured and closed for business until the preliminary investigation is completed. Outdoor crime scenes are generally roped off or barricaded. Only those individuals with official business should be allowed into the crime scene. In many cases, authorized personnel such as other police officers who are curious, or administrators who arrive on scene to "check things out," are responsible for compromising or contaminating a crime scene. As a general rule, no one should be allowed on the scene other than those who are actually investigating or processing it (after the incident has been secured).

A way to deter curiosity seekers is to require all personnel who enter the scene, from the chief of police down through patrol officers, to write a detailed report stating their reason for being there and what they did on the scene. This requirement serves as a reminder that anyone entering a crime scene can be called into court to testify about what they saw and did—a clear deterrent to those who are present for no good reason—and makes personnel think twice before entering a scene where their actions may compromise any evidence.

The NIJ suggests that setting well-defined, liberal, and controllable boundaries is a critical aspect in preserving the integrity of evidentiary material (*Crime Scene Investigation* 2004, 15–16):

1. **Establish scene boundaries by identifying the focal point(s) of the scene and extending outward:** Secure areas where the crime occurred, areas that are potential points and paths of entry/exit of suspects/ witnesses, and areas where victim(s) and evidence may have moved or been moved. Initially secure a larger area, since it is easier to contract than to expand the boundaries. *NOTE*: Be aware of trace and *impression evidence* during scene assessment.

2. **Set up physical barrier(s):** Set the physical perimeter for established scene boundaries with crime scene tape, rope, cones, vehicles, personnel, etc., or by using existing structures, such as walls, rooms, gated areas, etc.

3. **Document entry of all people entering and exiting the scene:** Record their names.

4. **Maintain integrity of the scene:** Control the flow of personnel and animals entering and exiting the scene.

5. **Attempt to preserve/protect evidence at the scene:** Protect evidence from humanmade intrusions (e.g., shoe or tire impressions), mechanical devices (e.g., sprinklers, helicopters), animals, and if possible, environmental elements.

6. **Document the original location of the victim(s) or objects at the scene that were observed being moved:** Document point of origin of the victim(s) or items at the scene as well as alternate location. *NOTE*: Care should be taken to use nondestructive techniques to document locations.

7. **Follow jurisdictional laws related to search and seizure:** Determine the need to obtain consent to search or a search warrant.[6]

In many cases, crime scene investigators will set up two boundaries, one that expands well beyond the scene and another that is just at the border of the scene. This dual barrier creates a buffer zone that gives authorized personnel a work space just outside and around the actual crime scene, thereby improving scene integrity. It also acts as an added buffer for the media and public onlookers by keeping such individuals beyond the outermost boundary.

Transferring Control of the Scene to the Investigator(s) in Charge or Conducting the Preliminary Investigation

In some departments, this is where the responsibilities of the responding officers end. They keep the scene secure until investigators or detectives arrive to conduct the investigation, especially in crimes such as murder, as discussed in Chapter 10. The NIJ guidelines regarding this "changing of the guard" are (*Crime Scene Investigation* 2004, 17):

1. **Brief the investigator(s) taking charge of the scene:** Introduce yourself, explain your role, and relay information regarding the incident, including roles and identities of the parties, facts of the incident, observations, comments by the parties, and information by *other responders.* Point out scene boundaries and chosen pathway to minimize contamination.

2. **Assist in controlling the scene:** Check with the lead investigator for instruction.

3. **Transfer control of entry/exit documentation:** Relinquish responsibility for continued documentation to a designated person and ensure this responsibility is understood.

4. **Remain at the scene until relieved of duty:** Contact the *investigator(s) in charge* for instruction and document your scene departure time.[7]

---

[6]Source: *Crime Scene Investigation: A Reference for Law Enforcement Training* (Washington, DC: Department of Justice, National Institute of Justice, June 2004), 15–16. (NCJ 200160)

[7]Source: *Crime Scene Investigation: A Reference for Law Enforcement Training* (Washington, DC: Department of Justice, National Institute of Justice, June 2004), 17. (NCJ 200160)

In many departments, particularly smaller agencies that lack the resources for a designated crime scene unit, the responding officers may conduct the preliminary investigation and, perhaps, the entire investigation. If the crime itself is complicated and severe, even larger local departments may enlist assistance or additional support from state-level law enforcement agencies. Keep in mind: The more information and evidence that can be obtained immediately after a crime has been committed, the better the chances of identifying the person responsible and of successfully prosecuting the case. The officers initially responding to the call are usually in the best position to obtain this information and evidence.

preliminary investigation

The on-the-scene interviews of victims and witnesses, interrogations of suspects, and search of the crime scene itself.

> The **preliminary investigation** of a crime involves on-the-scene interviews of victims and witnesses, interrogation of suspects, and a search of the scene itself.

The preliminary investigation is not so much an "investigation" in the traditional sense, where days, weeks, months, even years of tracking leads, developing suspects, and refining theories go into the eventual solving of a crime. (The complete investigation itself is discussed in Chapter 10.) Compared with this level of examination, the preliminary investigation is a rather superficial on-site assessment and collection of evidentiary details observed by the initial responding officer(s) and relayed by witnesses.

Obtaining Information on the Scene from Victims, Witnesses, and Suspects In larger departments, if a suspect is apprehended at the scene, interrogation is usually done at the police department by experienced, trained investigators. Interviewing and interrogating were discussed in Chapter 2. Witnesses should be separated and their statements recorded.

Curiosity seekers can destroy valuable evidence and contaminate a crime scene, so it is necessary to cordon off the area.

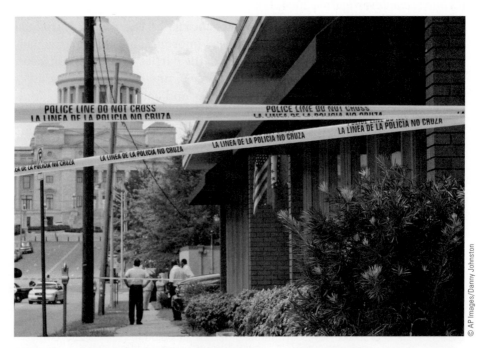

© AP Images/Danny Johnston

Recognizing and Collecting Physical Evidence Officers arriving at the scene are often responsible for recognizing and gathering evidence as part of the preliminary investigation. Therefore, officers must know the elements of each crime and what evidence will prove them. The crime-scene search is, for certain offenses, the most important part of the investigation. A large part of the preliminary investigation centers around whether officers can obtain evidence that a crime has been committed and been committed by a particular person. Evidence may be the turning point determining whether a case can be made and a criminal convicted.

Although some crimes—such as forgery, embezzlement, identity theft, and credit-card fraud—have no crime scenes and yield little to no physical evidence, many crimes do have crime scenes and provide physical evidence. The value of any physical evidence used in court to verify that a crime has been committed, to identify the person(s) who did it, and to obtain a conviction often depends on the officers who arrive first at a crime scene. In most cases, the officers who protect and search a crime scene play a critical role in determining whether a case can be made.

Experienced officers anticipate finding certain types of evidence in specific crimes. In many offenses, criminals contact the physical surroundings and leave evidence linking themselves to victims and crime scenes. Violent crimes, for example, often involve a struggle and frequently yield evidence such as blood, skin, saliva, semen, or other DNA evidence; hairs; fibers; fingerprints; and weapons. Property crimes, in contrast, commonly yield evidence such as tool marks on doors, windows, safes, money chests, cash registers, and desk drawers, as well as fingerprints. Recognizing and collecting evidence are examined in greater depth in Chapter 10.

All preliminary investigations must be systematic and thorough. The finding of some answers does not mean that all answers have been uncovered. Likewise, the finding of some evidence does not mean that more may not exist. One is mindful of the question once considered the epitome of the obvious, "Who's buried in Grant's tomb?" Those who answer "General Ulysses S. Grant" are only half right. His wife, Julia, is buried with him. Professional police officers must get *all* the facts and information, not just the obvious.

When evidence is found, it must be carefully marked (often with the officer's badge number), placed in a secure container, sealed, tagged, recorded in the officer's notebook, and, as soon as practical, placed in the property or evidence room. It must be kept secure until it is needed for trial. The **chain of possession**, or **chain of custody**, documents who has had control of the evidence from the time it is discovered until it is presented in court. Any time evidence is taken from the property room, it must be signed for. When it is returned, it is examined to be sure that it has not been altered in any way.

chain of possession

See *chain of custody*.

chain of custody

Documented account of who has had control of evidence from the time it is discovered until it is presented in court; also called *chain of possession*.

Crime-Scene Units

Because most local police departments have fewer than 20 sworn officers, they seldom have special teams of criminal investigators. In such cases, a crime-scene team consisting of patrol officers assigned crime-scene duty as a collateral duty is often of value.

The crime-scene unit, after conducting a preliminary survey of the crime scene, determines the actual crime-scene perimeter and search area. They set the search objectives as well as the equipment and personnel needed and develop a theory of the crime. In addition, they identify and protect transient evidence and prepare a narrative description of the scene.

In some departments, after these functions are performed, the work of the crime-scene unit is complete, and the case is turned over to an investigative or detective division. In smaller departments, however, the crime-scene unit may conduct the entire investigation.

RESPONDING TO CALLS REGARDING DISORDER AND QUALITY-OF-LIFE ISSUES

Closely associated with the problem of crime is the problem of disorder and quality-of-life issues. When disorder occurs, police are expected to deal with it. In 1989, Wilson and Kelling set forth their classic broken windows theory, writing,

> At the community level, disorder and crime are usually inextricably linked, in a kind of developmental sequence. Social psychologists and police officers tend to agree that if a window in a building is broken *and is left unrepaired*, all the rest of the windows will soon be broken. This is as true in nice neighborhoods as in run-down ones. Window-breaking does not necessarily occur on a large scale because some areas are inhabited by determined window-breakers whereas others are populated by window-lovers; rather, one unrepaired broken window is a signal that no one cares, and so breaking more windows costs nothing. (It has always been fun.)…
>
> The citizen who fears the ill-smelling drunk, the rowdy teenager or the importuning beggar is not merely expressing his distaste for unseemly behavior; he is also giving voice to a bit of folk wisdom that happens to be a correct generalization—namely, that serious street crime flourishes in areas in which disorderly behavior goes unchecked. The unchecked panhandler is, in effect, the first broken window. [8]

collective efficacy

Cohesion among neighborhood residents combined with shared expectations for informal social control of public space that inhibits both crime and disorder.

incivilities

Subtle signs of a community not caring about disorder, including rowdiness, drunkenness, fighting, prostitution, and abandoned buildings.

The link between disorder and crime, and whether social and physical disorder lead directly to more serious offenses, has been debated. However, collective efficacy may help explain this link. **Collective efficacy** refers to cohesion among neighborhood residents along with expectations of informal social control in public places that inhibits both crime and disorder. "Broken windows and smashed cars are visible signs of people not caring about their community. Other less subtle signs include unmowed lawns, piles of accumulated trash, and graffiti, often referred to as **incivilities**. Incivilities include rowdiness, drunkenness, fighting, prostitution, and abandoned buildings" (Miller, Hess, and Orthmann 2010, 64–65). The community can be enlisted to deal with the physical incivilities.

[8]Source: Wilson, James Q., and Kelling, George L. "Making Neighborhoods Safe." *The Atlantic Monthly*, February 1989, pp.46–52.

Jones (2009) describes a dramatic increase (14 percent) in calls for service in Suwanee, Georgia, that was forcing the department to operate strictly reactively, no longer able to maintain its traditional open communication and positive relationship with the community. Analysis of the department's calls-for-service data revealed that the vast majority of calls were from neighborhoods, not businesses or public areas. Residents in one neighborhood called the department every day to complain about speeders, potholes, and many other quality-of-life issues. The department decided to use community outreach through the homeowners associations already in place in the community.

In 2002, the department established the Police and Citizens Together (PACT) program to encourage community residents to work together to maintain the quality of life in their own neighborhoods. The first year focused on the neighborhood that had been calling every day. Through PACT, each homeowners association has its own police officer with whom they can become familiar and build a relationship. The officers hold meetings at least three times a year.

PACT achieved its major goal of halting the spiraling increase in calls for service, actually reducing such calls even though the community was growing rapidly. Officers were given time to work proactively, problem solving with residents to address issues of concern: "Officers are empowered to assist directly and residents do not feel the need to make repeated calls for service" (Jones 2009, 26). A further goal was also reached—keeping Suwanee's crime rate low, with the crime rate not keeping pace with the population growth.

Disorderly or troublesome people may include panhandlers, prostitutes, inebriates, and individuals who are mentally ill or homeless.

Panhandlers

The public has two vastly different views on panhandling: Some, including many civil libertarians and homeless advocates, sympathize, believing that panhandling is essential to destitute people's survival and should not be prohibited by the government. Some even see panhandling as an expression of the plight of the needy, and an opportunity for those more fortunate to help. Others, however, see panhandling as a blight that contributes to community disorder and crime, as well as to panhandlers' shame as their basic problems go unaddressed. Those with the latter view believe the government should regulate panhandling.

Two types of panhandling are passive and aggressive: "Passive panhandling is a silent solicitation; the panhandler generally lets his appearance speak for itself. Aggressive panhandling involves some type of verbal interaction usually accompanied by a physical action.... Passive panhandling plays on a citizen's sense of generosity; whereas aggressive panhandling plays more on a citizen's sense of fear" (Petrocelli 2007, 20). Police are more apt to take action against aggressive panhandlers, but according to one study, police made arrests for panhandling in about 1 percent of all encounters (Petrocelli 2007).

Unfortunately, laws prohibiting panhandling seldom control the problem, nor does "shooing" them away. One suggestion is for officers to build a strong file on a chronic offender, so that if an arrest is made, the case is strong. Video surveillance, officer decoys, and citizen complaints also help build a case. Restraining orders might forbid a panhandler to frequent certain areas or establishments. Some departments use a voucher system by which concerned citizens buy vouchers from area merchants good only for basic necessities, not for liquor or cigarettes. This system allows sympathetic citizens to donate, knowing their contribution will be used as intended (Petrocelli 2007).

Prostitutes

Petrocelli (2009, 20) asserts, "For as long as there have been men and women, there has been the exchange of valuables for sexual favors, though there rarely have been societies that allowed prostitution. Sanctions have varied from fines to death, yet prostitution has flourished in every stratum of society in every part of the world. Prostitution takes many different forms from high-priced call girls who meet clients in hotel rooms to street prostitutes who ply their trade in public." A closely related crime, and much more serious, is human trafficking. Of all alleged human trafficking incidents reported by task forces between January 2008 and June 2010, roughly 82 percent involved allegations of sex trafficking—adults or children forced into prostitution (Banks and Kyckelhahn 2011).

Street-level prostitution can directly affect a neighborhood's quality of life, attracting strangers to an area and providing opportunities for other street-level crimes. However, enforcement often simply displaces the problem: "As police officers, we recognize that arresting streetwalkers and their customers is like squeezing a balloon. When the heat (the squeeze) is on, prostitutes and their customers just move to another area" (Jetmore 2008, 96). Street sweeps are largely ineffective. Law enforcement in many jurisdictions has shifted from attacking the supply to targeting the demands, but this strategy alone does not reduce the problem: "Any effective policy is going to incorporate a balanced attack against the suppliers and those who demand it" (Petrocelli 2009, 20). Although street prostitution accounts for only 10 to 20 percent of the prostitution problem, it has the greatest negative impact on the community. It also has a negative impact on the prostitutes themselves.

Many prostitutes are homeless, and most have limited education and few ties with the community. Most did not choose prostitution as a career but sell themselves to survive, often as a result of addiction to drugs or alcohol and a lack of skills or resources. Departments might consider setting up programs presenting opportunities for offenders to get out of the business, serve restraining orders to prohibit them from returning to certain high-risk areas, or place curfews to ensure they do not work during peak hours. Proposed solutions include having all "johns" make the court appearance on the same date, allowing the judge and public to see the magnitude of the problem, shaming offenders by publishing their names, sending them warning letters, or sending them to "john schools" where they learn about the legal and health consequences of their behavior (Petrocelli 2009). Other strategies involve distributing pamphlets to the public outlining the dangers of paying for sex, especially in cities that host conventions. Reporting abandoned buildings and working to restrict or eliminate motel rooms available by the hour can also help in reducing opportunities for prostitution. Often prostitutes find their "johns" in bars.

Problems around Bars

Bars can present yet another challenge for law enforcement. It is common knowledge that alcohol lowers inhibitions. Alcohol makes many people feel powerful and unconcerned about the consequences of their actions. Individuals who drink too much often get into fights and may commit an assault or become a victim of assault. Generally speaking, certain "problem" bars account for the majority of violent incidents, including bars that tolerate disorderly conduct, yelling, and profanity and whose clientele includes drug users, drug sellers, and prostitutes (Petrocelli 2008). Other characteristics of bars where violence is likely to occur are those that do not sell food, are overcrowded, and are poorly ventilated.

Law enforcement should work with the bar owners association in the community, attend their meetings, and have a police representative at any alcohol licensing procedures. Drink servers should be trained to identify those who have had too much to drink and who are acting aggressively. Because much of the violence in and around bars occurs at closing, departments might consider adding supplemental patrols to trouble spots during this relatively brief time. Some bars serve nonalcoholic drinks and food for an hour after normal closing time, allowing an hour-long "cooling off" or "sobering up" period as well as staggering the exodus from the bar.

The New York Police Department, in an effort to address the crime and disorder often associated with bars and nightclubs, partnered with the New York Nightlife Association to jointly consider how to address the problem (Kelly 2008). The working group adopted a series of 60 best practices, 47 of which applied to security, employees, age verification, club policies, and police-community relations. The remaining 13 related to reporting crimes, including physical and sexual assaults.

Individuals Who Are Mentally Ill

The most common call, where mentally ill persons are involved, is disturbing the peace. As discussed in Chapter 2, it is recommended that agencies maintain a database of incidents involving mentally ill citizens as well as a list of mental health services available 24 hours per day. Recall also that it is now recommended that two officers respond to calls involving a subject with mental illness—one to make the contact and the other one to provide cover for that officer.

Many agencies now provide crisis incident team (CIT) training to help officers identify individuals who need mental health treatment, thereby preventing such individuals from ending up in jail for "disturbing the peace"—or dead. A CIT is more than a law enforcement initiative; many other players are involved. Two main components of the CIT model—also called the Memphis Model for where it was developed—are (1) *a collaborative framework* comprising members of the mental health community, citizens who receive services from the mental health system, policymakers, and local law enforcement agencies; and (2) *specialized training* for CIT officers so that they may recognize and understand the signs and symptoms of mental illnesses, know about pharmacological interventions and their common side effects, develop crisis intervention and de-escalation skills, and become familiar with user-friendly mental health resources available in their community (Tucker et al. 2011).

Some community-based programs partner mental health practitioners from local government and private practice with local law enforcement to conduct officer safety and de-escalation training. In most departments, however, calls involving mentally ill subjects fall to all patrol officers, not just to a specialized unit of CIT officers.

In some cases, unfortunately, use of force is necessary. The courts have held that in certain situations police use of force against a mentally ill person is justifiable and necessary for the protection and safety of the officer and public. Only after safety is established should officers attempt to achieve a relationship with a mentally ill subject. Many of those who are mentally ill are also homeless as a result of the deinstitutionalization that occurred in the 1960s and 1970s.

The Homeless

The homeless constitute an ever-increasing social problem in the 21st century: "Prior to the foreclosure crisis and economic recession, homelessness was already a national crisis, with 2.5 to 3.5 million men, women and children experiencing homelessness each year, including a total of 1.35 million children and over a million people working full or part time—but unable to pay for housing. Since then, homelessness has increased dramatically" (National Law Center 2011, 6). In general, communities simply do not want the homeless around. Citizens clamor for their city councils to pass laws against sleeping in the street. And when city councils oblige, the social problem becomes a law enforcement problem that poses a dual challenge for police: Some homeless people break the law, and some become victims.

Although it is not against the law to be homeless, many people living on the streets, by virtue of their lack of residence, do engage in illegal activity or otherwise contribute to a community's level of disorder. With no place to sleep, use the bathroom, keep their belongings, dump their trash, get drunk, or take care of other private matters, the homeless have to conduct such "business" in public.

A large percentage of homeless adults are unemployed and, without income, many resort to panhandling or stealing just to be able to eat. National data indicate 20 percent of homeless people eat one meal a day or less. Addicts often turn to crime to support their habits or engage in crime while under the influence of alcohol and other drugs. Nearly half of all homeless people suffer from chronic health problems such as high blood pressure, arthritis, diabetes, or cancer, and more than half lack medical insurance. Many homeless people suffer from mental illness and, if unable to pay for medication, can present erratic behavior that can bring them into contact with law enforcement. Another problem is that those who advocate for the homeless sometimes break the law—for example, taking over unoccupied private homes as well as unoccupied public buildings and demanding that these buildings be made into homeless shelters.

The homeless are also frequently *victims* of crime and violence, being vulnerable because of their inability to lock themselves and their possessions, if any, safely away from those who would cause them harm. Furthermore, because they have no home, most homeless cannot simply pick up the phone to call for help when needed. Many, in fact, have lost the privilege of voting because they lack a permanent residence. Nonetheless, they are citizens to whom law enforcement is responsible for protecting against those who want to take advantage. One of the most important challenges is reducing violent attacks against homeless people, which data indicate have increased substantially over the past decade. Jurisdictions across the country have begun modifying their statutes to designate crimes against the homeless as hate crimes.

Thus, although homelessness may begin as a social service issue, with entire families living on the streets or in cars, when it becomes combined with the economic factor of unemployment, the medical factors of mental illness or substance abuse, and the increased risk of victimization, it can quickly become a criminal justice issue. Police must first see the homeless as individuals and as possible victims and then do all they can to protect them from victimization. Police must also consider the reality that, many times, the homeless are offenders and need appropriate diversion and treatment alternatives to prevent further criminal behavior.

Law enforcement should be aware of what kinds of assistance are available for the homeless and make this information known, including helping them obtain services. Some departments are providing sensitivity training to educate officers about the specific needs and concerns of homeless people. Other agencies have formed alliances between officers, city officials, local businesses, homeless shelters, and human services outreach workers to provide a coordinated response to the multiple issues surrounding homelessness.

CIVIL DISOBEDIENCE

The challenges to law enforcement when responding to troublesome people can be much greater when the situation is not one-on-one but instead involves a crowd bent on civil disobedience. **Civil disobedience** consists of breaking a law to prove a point or to protest something. Civil disobedience occurs daily around the world, from the fight against apartheid in South Africa, to the quest for autonomy of ethnic groups in Europe, to the antiwar protests across America following the U.S.–led invasions in Iraq and other Middle East countries, to the Occupy movement that began on Wall Street in September 2011 and has since spread throughout the United States in protest of the unprecedented and deepening economic inequality between corporate leaders (that is, the 1%) and the vast majority of employees beneath them (the other 99%). Our society, like many others around the globe, is filled with dissension. And law enforcement officers are called on to control or suppress these demonstrations.

The purpose in most cases of civil disobedience is to protest some governmental or institutional policy. Although most protests start out lawfully and are relatively peaceful demonstrations, emotions may become inflamed, legal barriers are crossed, and a classic civil disobedience situation develops. A civilly disobedient person breaks the law to prove a point. The act is done openly. A law is violated because people feel the law violates their sense of what is right, and they are willing to accept punishment for their actions supporting their beliefs. The United States was born through the efforts of dissenters, and some of our greatest Americans, now regarded as heroes, were lawbreakers in their time. George Washington, Benjamin Franklin, John Adams, and

civil disobedience

Intentional breaking of a law to prove a point or to protest something.

Alexander Hamilton were all civilly disobedient and considered traitors until success crowned their efforts.

Nonviolent lawbreaking begins when participants are willing to be punished by the courts for their lawbreaking. From there, demonstrators may become violent lawbreakers, frequently disregarding the rights of others. The extreme result of this type of action is anarchy, chaos, revolution, and bloodshed. The police generally agree that nonviolent protest is one thing to contend with, but violent protest—which can result in property damage, looting, personal injuries, and, in some cases, death—infringes on the rights of police officers as well as of other citizens.

Whether demonstrations are violent or nonviolent, police have been designated by our society as the correct vehicle for coping with the various kinds of demonstrations occurring in the 21st century.

Issues Leading to Civil Disobedience

Issues leading to civil disobedience include:
- Overt racism and bias.
- Human rights concerns.
- Environmental concerns.
- Animal rights concerns.
- Pro-life and pro-choice conflicts.
- Economic inequality—the Occupy movement.

Racism and Other Biases Historically, the Ku Klux Klan has been the epitome of violent racism. However, other groups are now contending for this dubious title. A group known as the skinheads poses a threat to minorities of several types, including homosexuals, Jews, and "people of color." Skinheads get their name from their practice of shaving their heads, although some have let their hair grow out so they are not as easily recognized by police. Acting in groups, they attack ruthlessly, often beating or stomping their lone victims. Skinheads often display patches bearing American flags, German swastikas, and such slogans as "White Supremacy" and "WAR," an acronym for White Aryan Resistance.

Most states have enacted some type of hate crime penalty-enhancement statute that allows courts to issue more severe sentences for people convicted of criminal actions motivated by bigoted, prejudiced, and hateful beliefs. Hate crimes are discussed in depth in Chapter 10.

Human Rights Concerns Violent civil rights protests swept the country in the 1950s and 1960s and are being seen again. Gay rights issues, the rights of individuals with communicable diseases such as AIDS, and the right to die are among the most hotly debated controversies.

Environmental Concerns Environmental protest issues include nuclear waste disposal and logging versus forest preservation. Activist groups such as Earth First have forced municipal police and rural police into thinking about dealing with protests and the unique circumstances they present. One key problem with the rural protests and demonstrations is that most of the law enforcement officers who have to deal with them know the protesters.

Animal Rights Concerns

Campaigns to protect certain species of animals have been around for decades and usually are confined to fund-raising efforts and massive informational mailings. However, one group, the Animal Liberation Front (ALF), has been described as a terrorist group because of the extreme measures its members undertake for their "cause." For example, the ALF has been associated with more than 80 break-ins since 1977, including one that caused $3.8 million in damages to a University of California, Davis, animal research facility.

Pro-Life and Pro-Choice Conflicts

Conflicts between pro-life and pro-choice groups are common and often make headlines as groups of pro-lifers seek to shut down abortion centers and pro-choicers seek to stop them. What may begin as a relatively peaceful march around an abortion center or clinic may escalate rapidly into a violent, destructive confrontation resulting in property damage and personal injuries. Political careers have been made and destroyed on this single issue. The courts also have become involved in the controversy. And police officers are likely to have their own views on this highly personal issue.

Pro-life demonstrators and others involved in the harassment of doctors and patients feel it is their moral obligation to protest the taking of unborn human lives. These demonstrators assert their First Amendment rights in such protests. However, the U.S. Supreme Court ruled in *Madsen v. Women's Health Center, Inc.* (1994) that a Florida statute establishing a 300-foot zone around clinics to protect them from abortion protesters was constitutional. In addition, it was constitutional to restrict excessive noisemaking within the earshot of, and the use of images observable by, patients inside the clinic, and to create a 300-foot buffer zone around the residences of clinic staff.

Economic Inequality—The Occupy Movement

The most recent issue to sweep the nation is the Occupy movement, a leaderless group of protestors who set up camps on public land in communities across the country to remonstrate the corporate greed and corruption that has led to extreme inequity in the distribution of the nation's wealth: "The earnings gap between the CEOs of major corporations in the U.S. and their rank-and-file employees has widened steadily and dramatically to level of about 500 to 1. The result is that the richest 1% of Americans now holds almost as much wealth as the bottom 99%—an unprecedented disparity" (Pontell and Black 2012, 3).

The occupiers have foregone the traditional nine-to-five picketing and protest parades in favor of an attempted 24/7 occupation of public venues, a tactic that has law enforcement facing new challenges in crowd control and protest response: "Protestors have been victims of sexual assaults and batteries, often by fellow protestors. Within the shadows of one camp, a man was murdered; others have been found dead in their tents, as a result of carbon-monoxide poisoning. In Houston, a police officer shot and wounded a gunman who threatened Occupy Houston protestors. Occupiers also hurt the very working people whose causes they are ostensibly trumpeting" (Scoville 2012, 32). For example, pedestrians on their way to work have been

An Occupy Wall Street activist is detained by police officers during a demonstration in New York's Grand Central Station on January 3, 2012. About one hundred Occupy Wall Street protesters rallied in New York City's Grand Central Station to call attention to the National Defense Authorization Act signed by President Barack Obama on New Year's Eve—a law protestors say represses civil liberties and that civil rights groups criticize as seeming to grant to the military extraordinary powers to detain U.S. citizens indefinitely without trial.

© AP Images/Mary Altaffer

engulfed by crowds of protestors and arrested as part of the pack. The chaos surrounding camps hurts nearby businesses by driving away customers and fiscally erodes local income and infrastructure. The overtaxing of local police and other city resources while the camps are occupied, as well as the resources required to clean up the trash and human waste left behind when camps are dismantled, puts additional strain on already financially strapped communities (Scoville 2012).

Another challenge presented by the Occupy movement is that among the sincere members of the protest group are other disenfranchised members of society—namely, hackers and anarchists—who have insinuated themselves into the masses only because they want to be part of a more substantial unit of social disorder and find the camps an easier place to cloak their existence (Scoville 2012). These infiltrators may tend to be more violence-prone than the general occupiers and may be more intent on causing injury to officers who are assigned to camp detail.

Responding to Demonstrations and Civil Disturbances

"Perhaps there is no greater challenge for police officers in a democracy than that of managing mass demonstrations. It is here, after all, where the competing goals of maintaining order and protecting the freedom of speech assembly meet" (Wexler 2006, i). A key to responding to demonstrations is advance planning and preparation. Although officers may not know exactly when they may need to intervene, they can anticipate what types of intervention might be necessary depending on their locality. A police department responsible for a jurisdiction in which animal research is being conducted or in which an abortion clinic is located should be prepared for demonstrations that might turn violent.

> To deal with demonstrations and possible violence, police departments should
> - Assess their risks.
> - Develop contingency plans.
> - Have a call-out system for off-duty officers.

One of the challenges presented to law enforcement by the Occupy movement is the protestors' proclivity for spontaneous action, making it difficult for police to effectively plan ahead to mobilize resources. Brian Muller of the Los Angeles County Sheriff's Department explains, "There is a difference between an 'event' and an 'incident.' An event is pre-planned. There is time to gather intel, exploit open source information sources such as Facebook and Twitter, and decide what personnel and gear you want in place ahead of time.... But an incident is something that is spontaneous. You don't have as much lead time to get your resources in place. And unfortunately, much of law enforcement's responses to the Occupy movement protests have been the results of an incident type behavior" (Scoville 2012, 34).

One key to effectively handling civil disorder incidents is a coordinated response among agencies, including police, fire, and corrections personnel. Police departments should know what additional emergency medical personnel might be available and how to contact them. Police departments might also coordinate with corrections personnel regarding the handling and transportation of arrestees.

Some departments use a cross-arm carry to remove arrestees; others use stretchers. Whatever the method, departments must have a sound policy on use of force during demonstrations, and officers should use only as much force as is necessary to control the crowd. Because many, if not most, demonstrations involve citizens' exercising their freedoms of speech and expression, any police action taken to reduce or stop that activity necessarily falls under court scrutiny. The Supreme Court has stated, "Freedom of individuals to oppose or challenge police action without risk of arrest is one of the principal characteristics by which we distinguish a free nation from a police state."

Videotaping a demonstration and the police response can counter any claims of police brutality. If a demonstration gets big enough and violent enough, a jurisdiction may call on the National Guard for help. This request usually has to be made by the sheriff to the governor.

Vernon (2008, 64–65) describes an annual ritual at a university when, on the first hot day of spring, the fraternity students engage in a massive water fight. A large bucket of water was thrown into an open window of a vehicle, distracting the driver who bumped into the curb, shaking up his pregnant wife who seemed to be going into labor. Vernon was called to the scene and summoned the three available units. When the biggest officer and Vernon approached the crowd, they were met with whistles and cat calls and saw one frat boy mixing mud with the water in his bucket. Vernon held his hand up, palm forward and shouted with a smile, "I come in peace. Before I am executed, take me to your leader." They presented a "massive, Viking-like fraternity member" and identified him as their leader. Vernon asked to speak before getting doused. He shouted, "You know this is your street. We in the police department know this is your street." Then he told them how they may have unknowingly put a life in danger. Visibly shocked by this news, they agreed to return to their rooms and send a delegation with him to the dean's office. Vernon points out, "All situations have their own unique factors, so there is no cookie-cutter strategy. Dealing with crowds can be very volatile and dangerous. There are, however a few basic principles to consider:

1. Assess the crowd's motives.
2. Select the appropriate posture or emotion—ranging from a strong command presence to a show of force.
3. Consider crowd psychology, including allowing them to save face.
4. Target leadership.
5. Make a swift decision." (Vernon 2008, 65)

He cautions that just as a small fire can turn into a firestorm in minutes, an unruly crowd can turn into a full-blown riot very quickly. Officers have a window of opportunity of just a few minutes to prevent this.

The Occupy movement has challenged law enforcement to refine their crowd control tactics to counter this new form of protest more effectively. One of the tactics most criticized by Occupy supporters is the placing of undercover officers into the camps to thwart criminal activity and victimization (Scoville 2012). Another response has been to deploy sonic blasters, long-range acoustic devices (LRADs) that emit a painfully loud sound and have proven highly effective in dispersing an unruly crowd. However, the majority of tactics employed at Occupy camps are those commonly included in the police arsenal of riot control devices: TASERS, pepper spray, water cannons, mounted patrol, K-9 units, and armored fighting vehicles (Scoville 2012).

TECHNOLOGY IN POLICING

LONG-RANGE ACOUSTIC DEVICES (LRADs)

Sonic blasters, or long-range acoustic devices (LRADs), have been used previously to communicate with unruly crowds, such as those encountered by Pittsburgh (Philadelphia) police during the G-20 summit and attendant protest rallies. LRADs are also being increasingly deployed to coerce occupiers to vacate their camps: "Emitting beams of sound with laser-like intensity, a 'low end' model is capable of generating 137 decibels [dB]. Higher-end models such as the LRAD's 500X model can reach 149 decibels"

(Scoville 2012, 35). For comparison purposes, consider that normal conversation between two people standing 3 feet apart is around 60 dB, a home lawn mower produces 95 to 100 dB, a loud rock concert averages 110 dB, a jet aircraft at takeoff registers 130 dB 65 feet away from the engine, and a shotgun blast emits about 165 dB. The level at which hearing loss can result from sustained exposure is between 90 and 95 dB, pain begins around 125 dB, and permanent hearing loss even with short-term exposure occurs around 140 dB.

Police Management of Mass Demonstrations: Identifying Issues and Successful Approaches (Narr et al. 2006) provides detailed information on planning and preparation, training, intelligence and information management, roles and responsibilities, crowd control and use of force, and media relations. This report concludes,

Over the past fifteen years, mass demonstrations have created significant challenges for law enforcement agencies. From spontaneous disorder after athletic events to highly organized protests against international monetary policies, local law enforcement agencies have encountered demonstrations that require seemingly every available resource to contain. In addition, police actions seem to be the subject of increased monitoring by third parties, including news agencies, amateur reporters and civil rights organizations, all of whom are armed with video cameras.... (Narr et al. 2006, 73–74)

Agencies must balance a number of conflicting demands when managing demonstrations. These include allowing legitimate groups to express their First Amendment rights, protecting innocent bystanders, safeguarding municipal and private property, ensuring unimpeded commerce and traffic, containing unruly protestors with the appropriate type and amount of force, preventing injuries to officers—projecting professionalism and proficiency all the while.

CRISIS SITUATIONS

Another form of disorder law enforcement officers must be prepared to deal with is that accompanying crisis situations. Frequently, negotiation techniques are called on to prevent such crises from escalating to violence. In some critical incidents, such as hostage taking, barricaded suspects, snipers, terrorist acts, and other high-risk incidents, special weapons and tactics (SWAT) teams may be used.

> Police officers may face crises that include hostage situations, barricaded individuals, and suicide attempts.

Hostage Situations

When police respond to a call about a crime in progress or a terrorist group in action, they may encounter a hostage situation. The FBI and most police departments divide hostage takers into four distinct categories: (1) the criminal trapped at the crime scene or escaping from the crime scene who uses bystanders as shields or bargaining tools, (2) terrorists, (3) prisoners, and (4) mentally unstable individuals. Category 1 is considered the "traditional" hostage situation. The most dangerous hostage situation is usually one involving terrorists; terrorists are usually willing to die for their cause and have little problem killing others. The most prevalent and usually least dangerous hostage situation involves the mentally disturbed. A somewhat different classification method places hostage takers into three categories: revenge seekers, power seekers, and attention seekers (Grossi 2007a). Whatever the motivation, it is important to recognize which type of hostage situation is involved because the negotiation process is directly affected.

The first two hours of a hostage situation are usually the most dangerous. Stress and anxiety are high in the hostage taker, hostage, and rescue personnel. As time passes, the hostage and captor may emotionally bond in a phenomenon called the **Stockholm syndrome** whereby, through the process of

Stockholm syndrome

In a hostage situation, the process of transference, with the hostages feeling positively toward their captors (and negatively toward the police) and the captors returning these positive feelings.

transference, hostages begin to feel positively toward their captors and negatively toward the police, and the captors return these positive feelings. This syndrome makes it less likely that the hostage taker will harm the hostages.

Because the first few hours of a hostage incident are so volatile, it is important for those responding to the high-anxiety situation to *slow everything down* in an effort to avoid "tunnel vision." Beyond allowing time for captors and hostages to calm down, other benefits to stalling include having enough time to adequately contain and isolate the scene, being able to call in the appropriate personnel for the response, and allowing enough time to devise a plan.

> The number-one rule in hostage situations is to slow things down.

If a strategy that involves negotiation of some type is selected, it is critical that someone skilled in hostage negotiations should be available to talk with the hostage holder. The FBI hostage negotiator course emphasizes, "Negotiators don't command; commanders don't negotiate." To have the person in command of the containment of the situation also conduct the negotiations is usually not the best approach. The commander at the scene should devote full attention to the entire situation. In addition, if the hostage taker knows the negotiator is also the person in command, the hostage taker also knows that individual has the authority to grant requests. With the commander as negotiator, the advantage of stalling while waiting for authorization is lost.

Because many hostage situations involve mentally unstable captors, hostage negotiation teams typically include mental health professionals. In addition to mentally disturbed hostage takers, police may need to deal with those under the influence of alcohol.

SWAT members may attempt to facilitate the victim's rescue and the perpetrator's apprehension by distracting the hostage holder so a tactical plan can be implemented. In hostage situations and in some high-risk entries, some police departments have used **flashbangs**, devices that explode with a loud bang and emit a brilliant, temporarily blinding light. Flashbangs should not, however, be used when the elderly or small children are a part of the situation because they may panic. Flashbangs also may create a lot of smoke, reducing visibility, and they may set off smoke alarms.

flashbangs

Devices that explode with a loud bang and emit brilliant light; used by police as a diversion.

The Officer as Hostage An officer being held hostage should first calm himself down and then use verbal defusing skills, as would be used with an emotionally disturbed person, to calm the hostage taker and to find out who and what the officer is dealing with (Grossi 2007a). As in other hostage situations, it is important to slow things down and try to get the hostage taker to see the officer as a human, rather than as a law officer.

Officers should practice escape techniques such as having a cutting tool within reach in the event of being duct-taped, hiding a handcuff key on your body and being able to retrieve and use it, and if, policy allows, carrying a back-up gun (Grossi 2007a). The three best times to attempt an escape are (1) during the early stages of the incident when the scene is still disorganized, (2) when the suspect

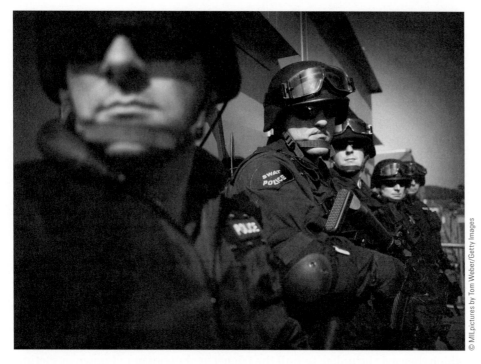

SWAT officers stand ready during a hostage rescue operation.

relaxes a bit thinking you aren't going to fight back, and (3) any time the captor is distracted or you can create a distraction (Grossi 2007a). Perhaps most important is to have a plan for such a situation beforehand and train for it.

Many techniques used in hostage situations are also appropriate when responding to a situation in which an individual is barricaded or threatening suicide.

Barricaded Individuals and Suicide Attempts

"Crisis negotiation is a complex discipline. Negotiating with an armed barricaded person holding hostages can be a prolonged and stressful event. When a uniformed officer responds to an event that becomes a barricade incident, he may not have the luxury of patiently waiting the 45 to 60 minutes for the tactical team and crisis negotiators to arrive. Negotiations by one of the first responders may not be just an option, it may be an absolute necessity" (Massock 2008, 39).

In these scenarios, officers must first ensure their own safety and obtain as much information about the subject and incident as possible. Massock (2008) recommends against using a bullhorn or loudspeaker to make contact, and suggests either telephone or voice-to-voice as better alternatives. The first responder should introduce himself as an officer and ask the subject for his or her name, the conditions of the others with the subject (do not refer to them as hostages), and the subject's own condition. The subject should be allowed to talk uninterrupted, even if yelling and screaming. Being a good listener is critical for successful negotiations. It is recommended that officers not respond to demands or a timeline and that honesty is the best approach. The first responder is key to gathering intelligence about the situation, information that will be used to brief the negotiator when he or she arrives, and thus holds immense value for resolving the incident (Massock 2008).

Police departments need clear guidelines about how to handle life-threatening situations such as those involving barricaded individuals and those who are threatening suicide. Of prime importance are the lives of those involved. If no danger exists for the police or the public, it is often best to talk the situation out or simply wait it out.

> The number-one rule in barricaded-individual or suicide-attempt situations is to slow things down.

In some instances, negotiations fail and the barricaded subject takes his or her own life. Or there may be no hostage or barricaded situation; the person simply commits suicide. Although some suicidal individuals come to police attention through an acute episode of crisis behavior, others are suffering from the more chronic condition of mental illness.

If officers respond to a successful suicide, they must secure the scene and conduct a thorough investigation, keeping in mind that, to many people, suicide is a stigma. Family members may hide or destroy evidence of a suicide, including a note that may have been left. This may be done so that insurance can be collected. Sometimes those intent on dying set up a situation in which they get the police to pull the trigger, a phenomenon known as victim-precipitated homicide or, more commonly, suicide by cop.

PERSPECTIVE OF A FIRST-LINE SUPERVISOR
Barricaded Suicidal Individual

Responding to a barricaded suicidal call can be one of the most dangerous calls an officer faces. The officer can assume that a suicidal person has nothing to lose, is not in his or her right mind, and, thus, poses an extreme danger to public safety.

As a first-line supervisor, I would expect a responding patrol officer to consider several things when dealing with this situation. First and foremost is the safety of the officer and others around the suicidal person. If a suicidal person wielding a deadly weapon has barricaded himself or herself alone inside a house, a responding officer can secure the area and make a plan. However, if that same person has innocent victims trapped inside as well, an officer may have to make a split-second decision that presents risk to gain control of the suspect or get innocent victims to safety.

In the case that the suspect is alone, some of the immediate planning that involves responding officers may include these elements:

- A perimeter with an officer who has "eyes" on the suspect, if possible
- A person who is the point of contact (this may also be the responding officer) until a trained negotiator comes on the scene
- A reactionary team in case things turn from bad to worse and the suspect decides to come out with guns blazing
- Considerations for both less-lethal and deadly force coverage

Communication and teamwork results in the best chance for a safe diffusion of this type of incident. It is not a bad idea to go through scenarios with other teammates during a shift to plan how these incidents might be addressed and the expectations of each other. There is no doubt that if you work patrol long enough, you will encounter this type of scenario.

—*Sgt. Henry Lim Cho*

Suicide by Cop (SBC) Suicide by cop (SBC) is a well-recognized phenomenon and a troubling trend. As with other crisis incidents, officers should attempt to slow down the situation when possible. However, the pacing of the event ultimately rests in the hands of the subject, and in the end, there is often little an officer can do once someone has set his or her mind on dying this way. One study of officer-involved shootings (OIS) found that 36 percent of OIS incidents resulted from SBC situations. Furthermore, of all SBC incidents examined, the subject was killed 97 percent of the time. Even more troubling is data showing a one-in-three chance that someone other than the suicidal individual will be injured or killed during an SBC incident (Scoville 2010).

Many departments have begun to use CITs when faced with suicide-by-cop situations. Although the ideal is to have specialized units staffed by expressly trained officers to respond to calls involving emotionally compromised individuals, the reality is, "Often it is the first responder's initial approach to the situation that will dictate its conclusion" (Scoville 2010, 36).

It is important to note that the California Court of Appeals ruled, in *Adams v. Fremont* (1998), that officers are not legally obligated to intervene on behalf of a suicidal individual if officers feel their own safety is in jeopardy: "We hold that police officers responding to a crisis involving a person threatening suicide with a loaded firearm have no legal duty under tort law that would expose them to liability if their conduct fails to prevent the threatened suicide from being carried out."

Line officers responding to an attempted suicide by cop will need to do the following:

▶ Contain the problem to the best of their abilities

▶ Have a realistic sense of their mission

▶ Adopt the requisite mindset: "Treat everyone like Mother Teresa, but have a plan to kill her if she turns against you"

▶ Rely on the best tactics and personnel available (Scoville 2010)

For their part, departments must train officers to deal with these types of crisis situations and make the necessary resources available (Scoville 2010). Furthermore, departments must stand behind and support their officers in the aftermath of a SBC.

For officers involved in an SBC incident that ends in the subject's death, the officer must recognize the range of emotions that may follow the shooting and receive timely critical incident stress debriefing. Officers involved in SBC shootings have reported feeling angry at and used by the perpetrator, guilty for shooting someone who was not necessarily dangerous but in dire psychological pain, and a sense of failure for not recognizing the "set up." When officers do not work through these emotions, their ability to respond effectively to future incidents is severely compromised, making the officer vulnerable to potentially fatal errors in judgment and leaving the department susceptible to lawsuits. The mere instant it takes an officer to second-guess a course of action is all the time a subject needs to pull the trigger. Furthermore, officers unable to resolve the incident in their own minds may succumb to overwhelming feelings of guilt and failure and become, themselves, suicidal.

Officer Suicide Police work is, without question, stressful. Officers who fail to deal with stress in a positive way risk depression, burnout, and suicide. Sanow (2008, 6) says of police officers, "We kill ourselves by a 3 to 1 ratio more than we are killed by others. The ratio may actually be much higher because many police suicides are purposefully misclassified on death certificates as accidents or undetermined deaths. The rate of police suicide is also more than three times that of the general population. And those rates are increasing compared with a decade ago."

One trigger that appears to precipitate officer suicide appears to be retirement, with retired law enforcement personnel being 10 times more likely to commit suicide than are age-matched peers (Honig and White 2009). Officers who retired because of a disability had a suicide rate of 2,616 per 100,000 compared with age-matched peers having a rate of 34 per 100,000.

Many officer suicides are made to look accidental or duty-related because of the stigma attached to the act; an officer killed in the line of duty receives a hero's funeral and has his or her name memorialized on a wall at the National Law Enforcement Officers Memorial Fund in Washington, DC, whereas officers who commit suicide get no such honor. Additional factors are emotional and financial implications associated with the different causes of death, with survivors of officers killed "in the line of duty" being better emotionally supported, better able to accept the death, and typically eligible for financial compensation from the federal government as well as college scholarships for their children.

Negotiating with another officer is extremely difficult and presents both advantages and disadvantages for the negotiation (Christol 2009). The advantages include that rapport is often already built because they may know one another, there is a common bond as police officers, it is easier to empathize because the negotiator knows what the officer may be going through, and background information is usually easier to obtain. The disadvantages are that the negotiator represents an agency that may be the cause of the situation, the suicidal officer knows police tactics and skills, and he or she may blame other officers for not recognizing his or her situation. Christol (2009) recommends not conducting negotiations alone and using extreme caution, as anyone willing to kill himself or herself may also be willing to kill you.

CRIME, DISORDER, AND COMMUNITY POLICING

An effective police response to crime and disorder requires community mobilization and active citizen involvement because, in the long run, vibrant neighborhoods are the best defense against crime. The law enforcement community has recognized this principle in embracing community policing and seeking to address and solve local problems through partnership with residents.

As discussed, since the advent of community policing, many departments across the country have focused on the aggressive enforcement of disorder offenses. These aggressive strategies are popularly known as "zero-tolerance," "order-maintenance," and "quality-of-life" policing. Following their seminal article, "Broken Windows," Wilson and Kelling (1989, 49) contend, "Like it or not, the police are about the only city agency that makes house calls around the clock. And like it or not, the public defines broadly what it thinks of as public order, and holds the police responsible for maintaining order. Community-oriented policing means changing the daily work of the police to include investigating problems as well as incidents. It means defining as a problem whatever a significant body of public opinion regards as a threat to community order. It means working with the good guys, and not just against the bad guys."

Some agencies, such as the San Diego (California) Police Department, have taken community policing "up a notch," to a strategy called *neighborhood policing*. Numerous examples of communities coming together to deal with problems of crime and disorder using problem-oriented policing are available.

CRIME, DISORDER, AND PROBLEM-ORIENTED POLICING

"Reducing Crime and Disorder at Motels and Hotels in Chula Vista, California" was the 2009 Herman Goldstein Award winner for excellence in problem-oriented policing. The following summary explains how the Chula Vista police, in cooperation with other city stakeholders, used the SARA model to address a public safety concern surrounding the local overnight lodging establishments:

> Chula Vista is a city of 233,000, located seven miles south of San Diego and seven miles north of the Mexican border. The City is perfectly situated to accommodate tourists visiting both the San Diego area and Baja, Mexico. However, for many years, the City's overnight lodging industry consisted primarily of cheap motels that were havens for serious crime, drug dealing, parolees, and prostitutes. Efforts to bring tourist dollars to such Chula Vista attractions as the U.S. Olympic Training Center, Knott's Soak City, and Coors Amphitheatre, were inhibited by the lack of safe and clean lodging in the City. Olympic Training Center athletes were actually housed in San Diego hotels, because none of the motels in Chula Vista were deemed safe enough for the athletes.

Scanning

> In the mid-1990s, business organizations asked for the City's help in improving the quality and safety of Chula Vista's motels. In response, police increased enforcement at motels and implemented a new law requiring all motel guests to show photo ID at check-in. Despite these efforts, police continued to respond to a high number of calls for service at motels, which remained platforms for criminal activity and inhibited efforts to bring tourist dollars to the City. With a mandate for improvement, police staff, along with other City staff and business groups, began working on a problem-oriented policing project to improve public safety levels at motels.

Analysis

> The problems at motels were analyzed in a variety of ways, including motel user interviews; motel manager interviews; environmental surveys; analysis of calls for service (CFS), crime, and arrest data; and a comprehensive review of the literature pertaining to crime and disorder at motels. Project staff tested and rejected a number of hypotheses regarding the cause of the problems at

Chula Vista motels. Ultimately, the project team concluded that motel managers and owners could effectively control crime and disorder on their properties through good management practices—if they chose to do so.

Response

Working together, Police, Code Enforcement, and Chamber of Commerce staff spent several years reaching out to motel managers and owners, offering information on the nature and level of problems at motels and ways those problems could be reduced. Code Enforcement staff began an annual motel inspection program in 2003, to ensure that the properties met state and local housing codes. However, these efforts did not substantially reduce public safety problems at motels. In 2005 and 2006, police worked with staff from the City Attorney's Office, Planning & Building, Community Development, Finance, and Fire Departments to develop an ordinance that enabled the city to hold motels accountable for meeting a CFS-based public safety performance standard.

Assessment

- ▶ CFS to Chula Vista motels declined 49 percent.
- ▶ Violent crimes and crimes against persons at motels declined 49 percent; Part I and Part II crimes at motels went down 70 percent.
- ▶ Drug arrests at motels decreased 66 percent.
- ▶ The quality and appearance of several motels improved dramatically.
- ▶ Motel management practices improved.
- ▶ The number of motel rooms that did not meet basic safety standards declined from at least 378 to 0.
- ▶ Aggregate transient occupancy tax reported to the City increased.[9]

SUMMARY

The official sources of information about crime are the Uniform Crime Reports (UCR), the National Incident-Based Reporting System (NIBRS), and the National Crime Victimization Survey (NCVS). The FBI's Uniform Crime Reports contain statistics on violent crimes (murder and nonnegligent manslaughter, aggravated assault causing serious bodily harm, forcible rape, and robbery) and property crimes (burglary, larceny/theft, motor vehicle theft, and arson). Technologies that greatly assist law enforcement in analyzing and responding to crime and disorder issues include mapping, geographic information systems, geospatial statistical analysis, and CompStat.

One major function of law enforcement is to respond when a crime has been committed. Responsibilities of officers responding to a call regarding a criminal act include arriving as rapidly, yet as safely, as possible; assessing safety procedures; providing emergency care for any injured

---

[9]Source: Schmerler, Karin. "Reducing Crime and Disorder at Motels and Hotels in Chula Vista, California." Reprinted by permission of the Chula Vista Police Department, Chula Vista, California.

people at the scene; securing and controlling persons at the scene; establishing and preserving scene boundaries, and transferring control of the scene to the investigator(s) in charge or conducting the preliminary investigation. The preliminary investigation of a crime involves on-the-scene interviews of victims and witnesses, interrogation of suspects, and a search of the scene itself.

In addition to dealing with crime, police officers are also often called on to deal with situations involving disorder and civil disobedience. Civil disobedience consists of breaking a law to prove a point or to protest something. Issues leading to civil disobedience include overt racism and bias, human rights concerns, environmental concerns, animal rights concerns, pro-life and pro-choice conflicts, and economic inequality—the Occupy movement. To deal with demonstrations and possible violence, police departments should assess their risks, develop contingency plans, and have a call-out system for off-duty officers.

Police officers may face crises that include hostage situations, barricaded individuals, and suicide attempts. Sometimes when police respond to a call regarding a crime, a hostage situation develops. The number-one rule in hostage situations, as well as in crisis situations involving barricaded individuals or those threatening to commit suicide, is to slow things down.

APPLICATION

The chief of police of the Bigtown Police Department notices there is no policy or written procedure to guide patrol officers when they receive a call to a crime scene. Past analysis of reports indicates that many officers have made their own policies about what their responsibilities are. No uniformity exists. The chief calls you in as the head of the patrol division and instructs you to formulate a policy and procedure for all officers when responding to a crime.

INSTRUCTIONS

Use the form in the Appendix at the end of this book to make the policy and procedure. The overall policy of how such calls are to be regarded and the specific procedures to be followed, including priorities, should be addressed.

AN EXERCISE IN CRITICAL THINKING

On June 13 at 10:00 p.m., Officers Cha and Ericsen responded to a report of a suicidal male who was believed to be intoxicated. The call came out with details of unknown weapons. Cha and Ericsen had previous dealings with this suspect, having responded to the residence several times before, and were aware that he had fought and resisted arrest with the police in the past. The officers were also aware that the suspect was an alcoholic. The officers responded to the residence and made contact with the suspect, who was intoxicated. The suspect had admitted to drinking and stated he was feeling "down" but stated that he did not want to kill himself. The suspect cooperated with the officers and spoke with a mental health representative, who believed that the suspect was okay to be released. A neighbor friend agreed to watch him for the night as he was still extremely intoxicated. The officers cleared the residence.

Shortly afterward, the officers received another call back to the residence. Dispatch again stated the suspect threatened suicide. The officers arrived on scene and saw the suspect in his backyard; he requested that the officers come meet him there. As Officers Cha and Ericsen approached him in the low light, they observed the suspect reaching into his jacket with his right hand in a motion suggesting that he was pulling out a gun. The suspect also yelled, "Kill me!" several times, and refused to show his hands after several loud verbal commands by both officers.

1. If you were responding as a back-up officer, how would you assist your partners in this situation?

   a. Set up a perimeter around the incident to prevent innocent bystanders from accidentally or intentionally entering a dangerous zone.

   b. Back up the officers until the situation was under control.

   c. Wait for more officers, or officers with special training such as SWAT, to respond.

   d. Attempt to apprehend the suspect alone.

   e. Start interviewing neighbors and possible witnesses.

2. After several loud verbal commands, the suspect eventually complied and pulled his hands out (empty) very quickly. The officers did not observe any weapons and placed the suspect in custody while holding adequate cover.

   a. Was deadly force justified in this situation? Why, and what are the guidelines?

   b. What other types of force would be justified in this situation?

   c. After taking the suspect into custody, what would be your procedure? Would you just jail him?

DISCUSSION QUESTIONS

1. What forces spark crime and disorder in our streets?

2. Select a recent popular movie you have seen that contains scenes of crime, disorder, or quality-of-life issues. Compare your reactions with those of other students. Discuss its effects on the general population who may see it.

3. Does your community have more or less crime and disorder than average? On what do you base your opinion?

4. Have you ever participated in a demonstration? If so, what was the cause? How did you feel about participating? Was it peaceful?

5. Is homelessness a problem in your community? If so, how does your police department deal with it?

6. Have there been any instances of the police having to interact with the mentally ill in your community? Were they handled well by the police?

7. Have there been instances of suicide by cop in your community? If so, what were the circumstances and were the police justified in using deadly force?

GALE EMERGENCY SERVICES DATABASE ASSIGNMENTS

▶ Use the Gale Emergency Services database (available for separate purchase) to help answer the Discussion Questions as appropriate.

▶ Use the Gale Emergency Services database to find and outline one of the following articles:

   • "The Montgomery County CIT Model: Interacting with People with Mental Illness" by Rodney Hill, Guthrie Quill, and Kathryn Ellis

   • "CompStat Design" by Jon M. Shane

   • "CompStat Implementation" by Jon M. Shane

   • "Hostage/Barricade Management: A Hidden Conflict within Law Enforcement" by Gregory M. Vecchi

REFERENCES

Banks, Duren, and Tracey Kyckelhahn. 2011 (April). *Characteristics of Suspected Human Trafficking Incidents, 2008–2010.* Washington, DC: Bureau of Justice Statistics Special Report. (NCJ 233732)

Barnett-Ryan, Cynthia, and Gregory Swanson. 2008. "The Role of State Programs in NIBRS Data Quality." *Journal of Contemporary Criminal Justice* (February): 18–31.

Beyond the Beat: Ethical Considerations for Community Policing in the Digital Age. 2008. Washington, DC: National Center for Victims of Crime.

Bruce, Christopher W., and Neil F. Ouellette. 2008. "Closing the Gap between Analysis and Response." *The Police Chief* (September): 30–34.

Christol, Tim. 2009. "Negotiating with a Fellow Officer." *Tactical Response* (January–February): 34–38.

Commission on Accreditation of Law Enforcement Agencies (CALEA). 2012. *Standards for Law Enforcement Agencies.* 5th ed. Fairfax, VA: Author.

Crime in the United States 2010. 2010. Washington, DC: Department of Justice, Federal Bureau of Investigation. Accessed February 25, 2012. http://www.fbi.gov/about-us/cjis/ucr/crime-in-the-u.s/2010/crime-in-the-u.s.-2010.

Crime Scene Investigation: A Reference for Law Enforcement Training. 2004 (June). Washington, DC: Department of Justice, National Institute of Justice. (NCJ 200160)

Grossi, Dave. 2007a. "Officer-as-Hostage: Survival Tips." *Law Officer Magazine* (February): 30–33.

Grossi, Dave. 2007b. "Responding to In-Progress Crimes." *Law Officer Magazine* (December): 24–25.

Hoelzer, Gary, and Jim Gorman. 2011. "Incorporating Hot-Spots Policing into Your Daily Patrol Plan." *FBI Law Enforcement Bulletin* (November): 10–15.

Honig, Audrey L., and Elizabeth K. White. 2009. "By Their Own Hand: Suicide among Law Enforcement Personnel." *Community Policing Dispatch* (April). http://www.cops.usdoj.gov/html/dispatch/April_2009/suicide.htm.

Jang, Hyunseok, Larry T. Hoover, and Hee-Jong Joo. 2010. "An Evaluation of CompStat's Effect on Crime: The Fort Worth Experience." *Police Quarterly* 13 (4, December): 387–412.

Jetmore, Larry F. 2008. "The Oldest Profession: Investigating Street-Level Prostitution." *Law Officer Magazine* (October): 92–96.

Jones, Michael. 2009. "Police and Citizens Together: The Suwanee PACT Program." *The Police Chief* (April): 20–26.

Kelly, Raymond W. 2008. "Formulating Best Practices for Nighttime Establishments." *The Police Chief* (May): 52–58.

Markovic, John, and Nicole Scalisi. 2011. "Full Spectrum Use of GIS by Law Enforcement: It's Not Just about Mapping Crime." *Geography and Public Safety* (A Quarterly Bulletin of Applied Geography for the Study of Crime & Public Safety) 3 (1, October): 2–4.

Massock, Bill. 2008. "Negotiations for First Responders." *Law and Order* (December): 39–42.

McCue, Colleen. 2011. "Proactive Policing: Using Geographic Analysis to Fight Crime." *Geography and Public Safety* (A Quarterly Bulletin of Applied Geography for the Study of Crime & Public Safety) 2 (4, March): 3–5.

Miller, Linda J., Kären Matison Hess, and Christine Hess Orthmann. 2010. *Community Policing: Partnerships for Problem Solving.* 6th ed. Clifton Park, NY: Delmar.

Narr, Tony, Jessica Toliver, Jerry Murphy, Malcolm McFarland, and Joshua Ederheimer. 2006. *Police Management of Mass Demonstrations: Identifying Issues and Successful Approaches.* Washington, DC: Police Executive Research Foundation.

National Law Center on Homelessness and Poverty. 2011 (June). *"Simply Unacceptable": Homelessness and the Human Right to Housing in the United States 2011.* Washington, DC: The National Law Center on Homelessness and Poverty.

Paletta, Kevin, and Stacy Belledin. 2008. "Finding Out What You Don't Know: Tips on Using Crime Analysts." *The Police Chief* (September): 36–39.

Peed, Carl, Ronald E. Wilson, and Nicole J. Scalisi. 2008. "Making Smarter Decisions: Connecting Crime Analysis with City Officials." *The Police Chief* (September): 20–28.

"PERF Survey Shows Widespread Use of Many Technologies in Policing." 2012 (January). In *How Are Innovations in Technology Transforming Policing?*, 1–3. Washington, DC: Police Executive Research Forum, Critical Issues in Policing Series.

Petrocelli, Joseph. 2007. "Patrol Response to Panhandling." *Police* (November): 20–21.

Petrocelli, Joseph. 2008. "Patrol Response to Violence around Bars." *Police* (November): 16–18.

Petrocelli, Joseph. 2009. "Patrol Response to Street Prostitution." *Police* (February): 20–22.

Pontell, Henry N., and William K. Black. 2012. "White-Collar Criminology and the Occupy Wall Street Movement." *The Criminologist* 37 (1, January/February): 1, 3–6.

Preliminary Semiannual Uniform Crime Report, January–June, 2011. 2011. Washington, DC: Federal Bureau of Investigation.

Sanow, Ed. 2008. "Use CIT Two Ways." *Law and Order* (May): 6.

Scoville, Dean. 2010. "Suicide by Cop." *Police* (April): 32–41.

Scoville, Dean. 2012. "Tales of the Occupation." *Police* (February): 32–36.

Truman, Jennifer L. 2011 (September). *Criminal Victimization, 2010.* Washington, DC: Bureau of Justice Statistics, National Crime Victimization Survey. (NCJ 235508)

Tucker, Abigail S., Vincent B. Van Hasselt, Gregory M. Vecchi, and Samuel L. Browning. 2011. "Responding to Persons with Mental Illness." *FBI Law Enforcement Bulletin* (October): 1–6.

Vernon, Bob. 2008. "Unruly Crowd or Riot?" *Law Officer Magazine* (January): 64–65.

Violent Crime in America: What We Know about Hot Spots Enforcement. 2008 (May). Washington, DC: Police Executive Research Forum.

Wexler, Chuck. 2006. "Foreword." In *Police Management of Mass Demonstrations: Identifying Issues and Successful Approaches*, edited by Tony Narr, Jessica Toliver, Jerry Murphy, Malcolm McFarland, and Joshua Ederheimer, i–ii. Washington, DC: Police Executive Research Foundation.

Wexler, Chuck. 2008 (May). "Conclusion." In *Violent Crime in America: What We Know about Hot Spots Enforcement*, 29–30. Washington, DC: Police Executive Research Forum.

Wilson, James Q., and George L. Kelling. 1982. "The Police and Neighborhood Safety: Broken Windows." *The Atlantic Monthly* (March): 29–38.

Wilson, James Q., and George L. Kelling. 1989. "Making Neighborhoods Safe." *The Atlantic Monthly* (February): 46–52.

CASES CITED

Adams v. Fremont, 80 Cal. Rptr. 2d 196 (1998)

Madsen v. Women's Health Center, Inc., 512 U.S. 753 (1994)

This available CourseMate has an interactive eBook and interactive learning tools, including flash cards, quizzes, and more. To learn more about this resource and access free demo CourseMate resources, go to www.cengagebrain.com, and search for this book. To access CourseMate materials that you have purchased, go to login.cengagebrain.com.

© Dan McCoy - Rainbow/Science Faction/Corbis

CHAPTER 7

Violence:
At Home, in the Classroom, on the Job

DO YOU KNOW . . .

- Who is at risk of being a victim of domestic violence?
- What law enforcement's responsibility is when domestic violence occurs?
- How dangerous police response to a domestic violence call is?
- What the Minneapolis experiment established?
- What *Thurman v. City of Torrington* (1984) established?
- Whether incidents of school violence can be anticipated or are always a surprise?
- What three-pronged approach is an effective response to the issue of school violence?
- What controversial measures have been taken to make schools safer?
- What similarities exist between school and workplace violence?

CAN YOU DEFINE?

battered woman syndrome
battering
bullying
elder abuse
expressive violence
instrumental violence
lockdown
stake-in-conformity variables
zero-tolerance policies

239

INTRODUCTION

Violence has accompanied every stage of our country's existence from its birth to the present and is often involved in ensuring law and order. Violence is connected with some of the most positive events of U.S. history: independence from England through the Revolutionary War, the emancipation of slaves and preservation of the Union following the Civil War, and the expansion and stabilization of frontier society via vigilante violence. Some of the nation's most violent criminal figures—such as Al Capone, John Dillinger, Jesse James, and Bonnie and Clyde—were popular folk heroes. Even today, our nation is drawn into a violent fight for the preservation of its values, including the freedom to live in peace. A statement made by Martin Luther King Jr., more than 50 years ago seems eerily prophetic in light of recent events: "The choice today is no longer between violence and nonviolence. It's between nonviolence and nonexistence."

Many fear violence is becoming a way of life in the United States, and there exists among the public a common perception that violent crime is spinning out of control. True, violence occurs throughout the United States and directly touches the lives of millions of people. However, the reality is that violent crime has decreased, as discussed in Chapter 6.

The dominant expression of violent behavior in the United States involves acts of *interpersonal* violence that occur nearly everywhere, every day. Domestic violence is a major challenge for law enforcement. In addition, bar fights, street fights, beatings, slashings, stabbings, and shootings are the types of violent transactions most likely to require a police response. These "garden-variety" acts of violence require police officers to possess excellent communication skills. Police may also have to resort to violence themselves. Indeed, one of the paradoxes of modern law and order is that police are granted authority to use force to achieve a peaceable society.

Children are also demonstrating an increased capacity for violence, which has crept into our schools and made students fearful of victimization by their classmates. Metal detectors, surveillance cameras, and drug- and weapons-detector dogs are a growing presence on school campuses nationwide. When the final bell rings and the class day is over, the violence is carried onto the extracurricular activities fields, where kids are taught to compete and win at all costs. Aggression is rewarded and even modeled by the parents who, in front of their own children, shamelessly hurl more than words at coaches, umpires, and parents of the opposing team.

Workplace violence also captures headlines, as the media report more murder-suicide stories involving disgruntled employees who return to the office seeking vengeance against the "higher ups" or workplace bullies who wronged them. Stress at home, in the classroom, and on the job moves with people as they go from point A to point B, sometimes manifesting as road rage. Drivers run each other off the road, assault each other during postcrash confrontations, and shoot each other for taking the parking spot they had been waiting for.

While reading this chapter, keep in mind that because the police have a monopoly on the *legitimate* use of force, they have the authority to impose themselves on conflicts as third-party agents of social control. Therefore, police–citizen encounters are *always* potentially coercive relationships. This is a particularly important factor when considering the role of the police in controlling "typical" violent encounters. The dangers implicit in these encounters, for both the police and the citizens involved, are thoroughly documented in research on violence.

This chapter begins with an overview of domestic and family violence and the various forms of partner abuse, including battered women, battered men, gay domestic violence, and teen dating violence. Next is a look at the police response to calls of domestic violence and the challenges presented by incidents of stalking. Then child abuse and neglect, often referred to as *maltreatment*, is looked at very briefly—it is discussed in detail in Chapter 11. The section on domestic and family violence concludes with abuse of the elderly and cooperative efforts. Next, the chapter examines the increasingly publicized issue of school violence and how police are expected to respond in efforts to keep our nation's students and teachers safe. The final domain of violence presented in this chapter concerns that found in the American workplace. The chapter concludes with problem-oriented policing and violence.

VIOLENCE: AN OVERVIEW

Violent crime rates do not remain static—they rise and fall from year to year, with gradual trends noticeable in hindsight. Violent crime in the United States reached an unprecedented high in 1994 and then began a 10-year decline. However, there was a slight uptick in violent offending during the middle of the first decade of the new millennium, sparking fears that our nation was on the brink of another long-term bout of rising crime and violence. Newscasts and headlines such as the following painted a grim outlook:

- ▶ "Startling New Stats Show Cross-Country Crime Spike," *ABC News*, October 2006
- ▶ "Report Outlines Rising Crime Wave," *CBS News*, October 2006
- ▶ "FBI Stats Show Spike in Violent Crime," *ABC News*, December 2006
- ▶ "Violent Crime Is Up for 2nd Straight Year," *Washington Post*, December 2006
- ▶ "Spike in Violent Crime Creates Fears for the Future," *CBS News*, January 2007
- ▶ "PERF Releases Violent Crime Report Showing 24 Months of Alarming Trends," *Subject to Debate*, March 2007

Many feared we were headed for a new long-term surge in violent offending, but in 2007, violent crime rates once again began to decrease. They have since continued on a downward trend, with the 2010 violent crime total 13.2 percent below the 2006 level and 13.4 percent below the 2001 level (*Crime in the United States* 2010). Preliminary 2011 data also indicate a continued downward trend in violent crime rates. Nonetheless, according to the FBI's

2010 Crime Clock, one violent crime occurred every 25.3 seconds (*2010 Crime Clock* 2010). Particularly troubling is when violent crimes are perpetrated not by strangers but by people who know one another, whether they are family, school friends, or coworkers.

DOMESTIC AND FAMILY VIOLENCE

It seems contradictory that the social unit people depend on for love and support can also foster violence. But this is true in hundreds of thousands of homes. Although people who live together usually form close relationships, they may also take their hurts and frustrations out on others within the family. The psychology around this is that those we love the most can also hurt us the most. An intergenerational cycle of violence is taught by parents who use physical force to discipline their children. Some parents even say, while administering a spanking or beating, "This hurts me more than it hurts you," truly believing it is their responsibility to physically punish children who misbehave. Many parents also teach their children to defend themselves and to "fight their own battles." Children then come to learn that "might makes right."

Risk Factors for Domestic Violence Victimization

Domestic violence knows no bounds. It occurs in families of all races, ethnicities, and religions and across all socioeconomic and educational levels, although it is more likely to involve law enforcement at the lower economic levels. A comprehensive review of current research on domestic violence reveals a high correlation between alcohol and substance abuse and domestic violence by abusers and an increased likelihood of domestic abusers being involved in other criminal activity, findings that have direct implications for law enforcement. Officers responding to an incident of domestic violence are well advised to check the involved parties' status regarding outstanding warrants, probationary or parole status, and other concurrent criminal justice involvement (Klein 2008).

The tensions of our complex society, the prevalence of drug and alcohol abuse, and the fact that people are living longer, often creating an emotional and economic strain, all contribute to the problem of domestic violence.

 Wives, husbands, significant others, children, and elders—in fact, anyone within a family unit—may be at risk of becoming a victim of domestic violence.

Such violence may be threatened or actual; it may be physical, sexual, or psychological/emotional.

The Extent of the Problem

Research shows that domestic violence-related police calls constitute the single largest category of calls received by police, accounting for between 15 and more than 50 percent of all calls. Such data emphasize the need for law enforcement agencies to commit as much time, resources, and attention to the problem of domestic violence as they do to other major types of crime (Klein 2008).

Many criminal justice scholars speculate "family" violence is the most widespread form of violence in the country (Sherman n.d.). However, domestic violence is often viewed by others, including those in law enforcement, as a family matter. Even victims may hold this perception, agonizing over the decision to report abuse to authorities. The victim wrestles with feelings of fear, loyalty, love, guilt, and shame; often there is a sense of responsibility for other victims in the household. A victim may fear retaliation and not want to give up the abuser's income or companionship. The victim also knows that reporting is a risk. All too often police or prosecutors minimize or ignore the problem, and the victim is left alone to face an attacker who will respond with anger at being reported or incarcerated.

Victims often do not want to press charges and do not want the victimizers to be put in jail. All victims want is for the violence to stop. It seldom does, however, and instead continues in an increasingly frequent and severe three-stage cycle of abuse shown in Figure 7.1.

The cycle theory of violence was developed by Dr. Lenore Walkers, whose research in the 1970s established the concept of the "battered woman syndrome." According to this theory, domestic violence continues to cycle because of the delay commonly experienced in bringing domestic violence cases to court. Police are generally called during the acute battering phase, and by the time the case is processed for prosecution, the honeymoon phase has set in and the victim is ready to forgive the batterer (Hill 2008). Such violence tends to be self-perpetuating; it can also be passed from one generation to the next. The National Coalition against Domestic Violence (NCADV) cautions that witnessing domestic violence between one's parents, guardians, or caretakers is the strongest risk factor of transmitting violent behavior from one generation to the next, and that boys who witness domestic violence are twice as likely to abuse their own partners and children as adults ("Domestic Violence Facts" 2007).

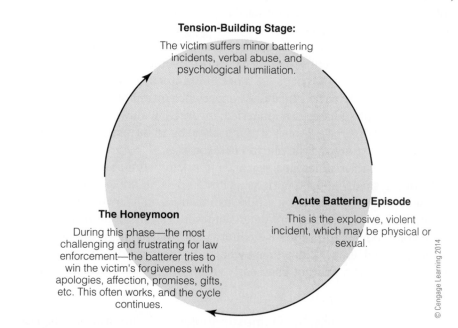

Tension-Building Stage:
The victim suffers minor battering incidents, verbal abuse, and psychological humiliation.

Acute Battering Episode
This is the explosive, violent incident, which may be physical or sexual.

The Honeymoon
During this phase—the most challenging and frustrating for law enforcement—the batterer tries to win the victim's forgiveness with apologies, affection, promises, gifts, etc. This often works, and the cycle continues.

© Cengage Learning 2014

FIGURE 7.1 Three-Stage Cycle of Abuse

INTIMATE PARTNER VIOLENCE

According to the Centers for Disease Control and Prevention (CDC), "Intimate partner violence (IPV) is a serious, preventable public health problem that affects millions of Americans. The term *intimate partner violence* describes physical, sexual, or psychological harm by a current or former partner or spouse. This type of violence can occur among heterosexual or same-sex couples and does not require sexual intimacy. IPV can vary in frequency and severity. It occurs on a continuum, ranging from one hit that may or may not impact the victim to chronic, severe battering" ("Intimate Partner Violence" 2010).

Data from the National Crime Victimization Survey (NCVS) indicates there were 407,700 female and 101,530 male victims of IPV in the United States during 2010 (Truman 2011). However, these numbers underestimate the extent of the problem because many incidents of IPV go unreported to the police. The CDC estimates that the cost of IPV, which includes medical care, mental health services, and lost productivity—exceeds $8 billion annually ("Understanding Intimate Partner Violence" 2012).

Battered Women

battering

The use of physical, emotional, economic, or sexual force to control another person.

Under English common law, a woman was her husband's property, and he could beat her with a stick as long as the stick was no larger in diameter than his thumb—hence, the well-known phrase "rule of thumb." Unfortunately, many modern-day relationships suffer under this archaic concept, but today it is called **battering**—the use of physical, emotional, economic, or sexual force to control another person. Whether the batterer is consciously applying his "rule of thumb" to keep "the little woman" in line, or whether he is merely continuing a cycle of abuse witnessed as a child that later came to define how relationships "worked," the behavior of battering is about power and control. It is violence, and it can take many forms. It happens among married and unmarried couples. It may surface after a once-happy relationship takes a wrong turn, or battering may have actually been an element of a relationship as it was forming. Battering tends to worsen over time, sometimes ending in death.

Leaving an abusive marriage does not guarantee the battering will end. Women separated from their husbands experience intimate partner violence at rates significantly higher than married, divorced, widowed, or never married women, and divorced women are victimized by an intimate partner at the second highest rate among the marital categories.

Separate research studies have reached remarkably similar findings: "Being sexually or physically abused both as a child and as an adolescent is a good predictor of future victimization. Child sexual abuse on its own, however, did not predict adult victimization. Women who were victims of both sexual and physical abuse before adulthood were more likely to become adult victims of physical or sexual abuse than women who had experienced only one form of abuse or women who had not been early victims of abuse" (*Violence against Women* 2004, ii).

"Special Needs" Victims of Domestic Violence In addition to the risk factors already discussed, several types of "special needs" victims of domestic violence have been identified. An estimated 17 percent of *pregnant women* are battered, with the abuse either beginning or intensifying during pregnancy. Battered *immigrant women* face the triple threat of being held in isolation by their batterers, being isolated by language barriers, and often being fearful and distrusting of the police and government in general. As society becomes more culturally and ethnically diverse, law enforcement must be aware that women are still viewed as property in many different cultures, where it is acceptable within the family to treat women this way. Battered women of these cultures also face the additional threat of being ostracized by their own family and community and, thus, are extremely unlikely to cooperate with our criminal justice system's efforts to bring their batterers to justice.

Women with disabilities are also more vulnerable to physical, emotional, and sexual abuse. Physical disabilities resulting from injury (e.g., paralysis, amputation), disease (e.g., multiple sclerosis), or a congenital condition (e.g., cerebral palsy) can prevent victims from escaping violent situations. Abusers may also withhold mobility-assisting apparatuses, such as prosthetic devices or wheelchairs. Sensory disabilities, such as vision and hearing impairments, may severely hinder abused women's ability to seek help because, although they may be able to physically escape the violent environment itself, they often face communication and mobility challenges once outside. Mental impairments, including mental retardation, mental illness, and cognitive disabilities caused by head trauma also increase a woman's risk of abuse because they may limit victims' ability to physically defend themselves and diminish their problem-solving capacity such that they do not know how to seek or where to go for help.

Finally, some research suggests that violence may occur more frequently in police families than among the general public; thus *women married to police officers* face the difficulty of seeking help from their abuser's colleagues, some of whom may even be the batterer's close friends (Gallo 2004). It is sometimes a "don't ask, don't tell" situation—ignored, hidden, or denied, protected by the "blue wall of silence."

Despite officers' sworn duty to uphold the law, they are susceptible to the same stresses that spark abuse in others' relationships, perhaps even to a greater degree. The abused intimate may also struggle with the added consequence of a complaint leading to the officer's loss of employment. If the officer is the sole breadwinner in the family and the only source of health insurance and other benefits, a loss of employment could financially devastate a family with young children or those with chronic medical conditions. A 1997 federal law known as the Lautenberg Amendment to the Gun Control Act prohibits any person with a misdemeanor domestic violence conviction from possessing or purchasing a firearm. Unable to carry a weapon, officers are not likely to keep their jobs. Thus, a victimized police spouse wishing only to have the violence stop, not to get the batterer fired, may choose not to report the abuse, or may recant a previous statement of abuse because of financial considerations.

The International Association of Chiefs of Police (IACP) has issued a policy statement, *Domestic Violence by Police Officers* (effective in 2003), which begins, "This policy recognizes that the profession of law enforcement is not immune from members committing domestic violence against their intimate partners.... This policy offers a comprehensive, proactive approach to domestic violence by police department employees with an emphasis on victim safety. It delineates a position of zero tolerance by the department" (2003, 1).

Theories about Why Men Batter Four theories generally explain why some men batter in intimate relationships (Sampson 2007, 7–8):

Psychological theory: Battering is the result of childhood abuse, a personality trait (such as the need to control), a personality disturbance (such as borderline personality), or a psychological disorder or problem (such as post-traumatic stress, poor impulse control, low self-esteem, or substance abuse).

Sociological theory: Sociological theories vary but usually contain some suggestion that intimate violence is the result of learned behavior. One sociological theory suggests that violence is learned within a family, and a partner-victim stays caught up in a cycle of violence and forgiveness. If the victim does not leave, the batterer views the violence as a way to produce positive results. Children of these family members may learn the behavior from their parents (boys may develop into batterers and girls may become battering victims). A different sociological theory suggests that lower income subcultures will show higher rates of intimate abuse because violence may be a more acceptable form of settling disputes in such subcultures. A variant on this theory is that violence is inherent in all social systems and people with resources (financial, social contacts, prestige) use these to control family members, and those without resources resort to violence and threats to accomplish this goal.

Feminist or societal-structural theory: According to this theory, male intimates who use violence do so to control and limit the independence of women partners. Societal traditions of male dominance support and sustain inequities in relationships.

Violent individuals theory: Although the full extent of violence batterers perpetuate is unknown, evidence indicates that many batterers are violent beyond domestic violence, and many have prior criminal records for violent and nonviolent behavior. This suggests that domestic violence batterers are less unique and are more accurately viewed as violent criminals, not solely as domestic batterers.

Battered Men

Men are not the only intimate partners who batter. The reverse is sometimes true. Some women are much larger and stronger than their husbands or boyfriends and may beat them at will. Others are physically inferior to the men in their lives, but the men, when hit, will not hit back. Further, women tend to use weapons as equalizers; therefore, the physical harm may be greater. Data indicate that women are twice as likely as men are to use a knife or other sharp object and three times more likely than men are to use a blunt object during an IPV incident (Smith and Farole 2009).

Husbands and boyfriends can also be emotionally abused through belittling, name-calling, ridiculing in public, and the like. In extreme cases, some battered women use their abuse as justification to kill their batterers, a phenomenon known as **battered woman syndrome**, now recognized as a legal defense by the courts. Some studies suggest a trend in young women becoming more aggressive in domestic relationships. For example, a longitudinal study involving 360 couples found,

> Many young women believe they can hit male partners with impunity; significantly more young women than young men believed that their hitting would not injure their partner, that the police would not intervene, and that their partner would not hit back. However, these beliefs are misguided, as women's abuse does have consequences...Women inflict a substantial minority of domestic injuries and deaths,...women make up as many as one quarter of police arrests for abuse in some jurisdictions,...and men do abuse women who abuse them. (Moffitt, Robins, and Caspi 2001, 23)

Regarding the limited research thus far on the subject, Sampson (2007, 8) states, "Less is known about women who use violence in relationships, particularly the extent to which it may be in self-defense, to fight back, or to ward off anticipated violence." She also notes, however, "Clearly there are women who use violence in relationships provocatively outside the context of fighting back or self-defense" (9). Another study that examined whether men and women who commit IPV are different from other violent offenders found that men are generally more reluctant than women to use violence against a partner unless that partner had previously used violence against them (Felson and Lane 2010).

Men are less likely to report acts of violence against them by their intimate partner, fearing negative reactions of others. Men who endure abuse often let it go unreported because such victimization is not socially or culturally acceptable, nor is it often believed by the general public. This is true for men who are sexually assaulted by woman as well. And although there are many resources now for battered and abused woman and children, similar resources for battered men are exceedingly rare because they are still an extreme minority.

Gay Domestic Violence

Although calls involving battered men are generally not considered the "traditional" type of domestic call, police responding to calls of domestic violence between gay or lesbian partners may find themselves in even more unfamiliar territory. Nonetheless, partner abuse among the lesbian, gay, bisexual, transgender, and queer (LGBTQ) community does exist and is increasingly being brought to the attention of law enforcement. Data from the National Coalition of Anti-Violence Programs (NCAVP) indicates that 3,419 incidents of IPV involving lesbians, gays, bisexuals, transgender, or queer people were reported in 2008, and 9 of these incidents resulted in murder (*Lesbian, Gay, Bisexual, Transgender, and Queer* 2009). Regarding these IPV incidents in 2008, 51 percent of the LGBTQ victims were women, 42 percent were men, and 5 percent were transgender.

As with other types of IPV, it is believed the reported incidents of LGBTQ domestic violence are an undercount of the true extent of the problem. The reasons given for not reporting a victimization to the police include fear of retaliation, fear of loss of emotional support, a desire to avoid embarrassment or shame, fear of being "outed," a distrust of law enforcement, and a lack of confidence in the courts.

battered woman syndrome

Defense used by women who have been beaten by their husbands and who then kill those husbands, apparently while completely sane and in control.

Teen Dating Violence

The CDC classifies dating violence as a type of intimate partner violence because it occurs between two people in a close relationship, despite the participants' youthful age ("Understanding Teen Dating Violence" 2012). Three common types of teen dating violence are physical, emotional, and sexual. Dating violence can occur in person or by electronic means, via computer or text messages. Negative effects of dating violence include depression, poor school performance, drug and alcohol use, development of eating disorders, and thoughts of or attempted suicide. Research shows that people who harm their dating partners are more depressed, have lower self-esteem, and are more aggressive than their peers. Among adult victims of physical abuse, rape, or stalking by an intimate partner, 22.4 percent of women and 15.0 percent of men report first experiencing some type of partner violence between the ages of 11 and 17 ("Understanding Teen Dating Violence" 2012).

RESPONDING TO DOMESTIC VIOLENCE CALLS

Legislative bodies have placed the burden of settling domestic disputes largely on the shoulders of the police. The police response to calls of domestic violence must be unbiased and executed without regard to the victims' gender or the gender of their abusers. An effective response to domestic disputes requires special skills, especially communication and negotiating skills, by law enforcement. Family violence has a strong tendency to repeat itself, and officers often are called back several times—sometimes in the same evening. It also tends to escalate. Effective handling of the first few calls can greatly decrease the number of further calls.

In most crimes, the responsibilities of the responding officers are clear-cut: gather evidence supporting the elements of the crime, determine who is responsible, and make an arrest. Responsibilities in domestic violence calls are much less clear-cut. Often, it is not obvious who is responsible. Frequently, both parties are at fault, but the violence must still be ended. Even if one party is clearly to blame, it is usually a mistake for officers to take sides in a domestic dispute. They must maintain their objectivity.

Police responding to a call in which the man claims to be the victim often have difficulty believing a woman can physically abuse a man. Officers may downplay the seriousness of the call and may actually blame the man for being weak or cowardly. As with any other assault, one involving a woman battering a man must be investigated thoroughly. If probable cause exists to believe an assault has occurred and the woman did it, she should be arrested. It may also be difficult to sort out who the primary aggressor is when police respond to a domestic call and find both partners disheveled, bruised, and hostile.

Police responding to a domestic violence call involving a fellow officer may find it particularly challenging to remain objective, yet they must adhere to department policy regarding the handling of such calls because of ethical and professional obligations and because the integrity of the policing profession and the community's trust are at stake. The IACP policy states, in the section on patrol response, "Upon arrival on the scene of a domestic violence call or incident involving a police officer, the primary patrol unit shall immediately notify dispatch and request a supervisor of higher rank than the involved officer report to the scene, regardless of the involved officer's jurisdiction" (*Domestic Violence by Police Officers* 2003, 4). Furthermore, if probable cause exists that the involved officer committed an assault, the responding officer shall make an arrest.

Responsibilities at the scene of domestic violence include these:

- ▶ Stop the violence.
- ▶ Separate those in conflict.
- ▶ Administer medical assistance if required.
- ▶ Determine if assault has occurred.
- ▶ If no probable cause for an arrest exists, mediate the situation. Get them to talk it out, to stop shouting and fighting and to start talking and thinking about their situation.
- ▶ If mediation is not possible, order the abusive spouse out of the house.
- ▶ Suggest possible solutions and sources of assistance to the abused person.
- ▶ If probable cause supporting the crime of assault does exist, make an arrest.

Dual arrest occurs when officers arrest both parties in a domestic violence incident. Research indicates that approximately 2 percent of IPV incidents result in dual arrests, and officers are more likely to make dual arrests in incidents involving same-sex couples (Hirschel 2009). However, dual arrest usually has limited effectiveness because there is almost always one primary aggressor. The victim may feel safe expressing anger against the batterer when the police are there, making it appear as though it is a "mutual combat" situation. Consequently, more than 20 states have enacted primary aggressor or "predominant aggressor" laws. Although the specific phrasing of primary aggressor statutes vary from state to state, many do contain similar language regarding the factors responding officers must consider when determining whether one or both parties should be arrested, such as any history of domestic abuse between the parties, the relative severity of the injuries inflicted on each person, the likelihood of future injury to each person, whether one of the persons acted in self-defense, evidence from the persons involved in the domestic abuse, and evidence from witnesses of the domestic abuse.

▌AN OFFICER'S PERSPECTIVE
Dual Arrests

Sometimes dual arrests occur when a victim suffers from "battered partner syndrome." In such cases, the police respond to a domestic situation and arrest the aggressor. But the victim then obstructs the legal process in an attempt to protect his or her abuser and, consequently, may end up being placed under arrest for separate offenses that stem from the original domestic assault. The psychology behind why this occurs is complex, but officers should be aware that arresting the primary aggressor may set off a defensive response by the victim.

—*Sgt. Henry Lim Cho*

Police officers responding to a domestic violence call are responsible for investigating it thoroughly as an assault and for making an arrest if probable cause exists.

A comprehensive, collaborative response strategy is one that considers the response to a domestic violence incident and includes action before and after an incident as illustrated in Table 7.1.

The importance of an effective law enforcement response to a domestic violence call is clear. Research has shown that although police actions such as follow-up home visits after incidents can encourage victims to report further incidents of domestic violence, victims who thought the criminal justice response was insufficient were less likely to report future incidents (Klein 2008). Studies have found that victim dissatisfaction generally includes four basic "themes": (1) an adverse personal outcome (victim arrested, child protection called), (2) the police made assumptions or did not listen, (3) the police took sides, and (4) nothing happened (absence of a strong court sanction) (Klein 2008). In summary, the research concludes, "The single, most appreciated service officers can deliver to the greatest number of victims is arresting their abusers" (Klein 2008).

Additional strategies for responding to domestic violence include educating potential victims and offenders, encouraging domestic violence victims and witnesses to call the police, encouraging other professionals to screen for

Table 7.1 Matrix of Responses to Domestic Violence

Strategic Focus	Strategic Times for Responses	Goal	Police Role	Other Agencies, Organizations, Group
At-risk population	Before incidents	Prevention; persuade those at risk that, if abused, call the police	Alert and educate at-risk victim population; educate/warn at-risk offending population	Public health organizations, domestic violence coalitions, schools and educators, medical professionals
Peers and neighbors of at-risk individuals	Ongoing	Getting peers and neighbors to call the police if they learn of domestic abuse	Educate these groups about the importance of calling the police to reduce the violence	Public health organizations, domestic violence coalitions, educators
Injured women and men	During medical care	Screen the injured for domestic violence; raise awareness of available services; provide medical care	Engage the medical profession and link medical professionals with appropriate referral organizations	Medical professionals
Individual incident	During	Violence cessation	Stop the violence; identify primary aggressor; accurately identify abuse history	Medical and public health professionals
Immediately after incident	After, ongoing	Prevent revictimization	Assist with victim safety; develop tailored strategies for victim and offender based on risk/physical violence history; increase focus on high-risk offenders; ensure victim is linked with needed resources; increase focus on high-risk victims; ongoing monitoring	Domestic violence victim advocates, victims' friends and family, shelters, victim services, criminal justice system, treatment services

Source: Rana Sampson, *Domestic Violence* (Washington, DC: Office of Community Oriented Policing Services, Problem-Oriented Guides for Police, Problem-Specific Guides Series, Guide No. 45, 2007), 25.

domestic violence victimization and make appropriate referrals, providing victims with emergency protection and services after an assault, assessing the threat of repeat victimization, arresting offenders, issuing and enforcing restraining orders, aggressively pursuing criminal prosecution of severe domestic violence cases and publicizing convictions, establishing special domestic violence courts, and providing treatment for batterers (Sampson 2007).

The Danger of Domestic Calls

It is commonly thought that a domestic call can be one of the most dangerous calls police officers receive. Indeed, some calls are extremely dangerous, even fatal, for the responding officer(s).

> Responding to a domestic violence call is hazardous, but not as hazardous as is often thought.

Because researchers originally did not separate domestic disputes from other types of "disturbance" calls, using data from *all* disturbance calls

A hearse carrying the body of fallen Capitol Police Officer John Gibson turns off Memorial Drive and into Arlington Cemetery in Arlington, Virginia, during his funeral procession. Officers who are called on to deal with violence can become victims of that violence themselves.

© AP Images/Stephan Savoia

"stretched the findings beyond what they reasonably meant" (Sampson 2007, 1). Furthermore, the frequency of domestic disturbance calls likely adds to the exaggerated claims of dangerousness regarding such calls in terms of injury to officers.

Documenting Evidence of Domestic Violence

After the abuser has been arrested and removed from the scene, a thorough investigation is needed, including comprehensive interviews with the victim and any witnesses. Information should be obtained about the frequency and intensity of the domestic violence as well as any previous police contacts.

Photographs should be taken of injuries and of indications of the level of violence, such as tipped-over or broken furniture, smashed objects, and the like. Any evidence of the violence should be properly collected. Keep in mind bruises often do not show up until several hours after a battering, perhaps even a day or two later. Furthermore, many victims change their minds within 24 hours of filing a complaint of abuse and try to drop charges against their batterer. As with videotaping statements, photographing evidence may be necessary insurance in cases where victims are uncooperative in seeing the case through to prosecution and can help remind victims why they must stand firm in pressing charges.

Arresting Batterers

Traditionally, the police response to a domestic call regarding wife battering has been to try to mediate the situation or to simply get the batterer out of the house for the night. Unless the police were threatened or actually assaulted, arrests seldom were made. Today, arrests are not made because often the police do not have the legal authority to do so unless they actually witness the assault or unless the victim presses charges. Sometimes, making an arrest only adds to the violence as the batterer seeks to avoid being arrested. Other times, the victim changes his or her mind and refuses to cooperate with the police. In addition, such cases are often not prosecuted vigorously.

For several decades, researchers have sought to assess the effects of arrest on intimate partner violence and how such a response compares with more informal, therapeutic intervention methods such as on-scene counseling and temporary separation. Although many studies throughout the years have produced inconsistent findings, researchers have now come to a general consensus about the benefit of arrest.

The Minneapolis Domestic Violence Experiment In 1981, the National Institute of Justice (NIJ) and the Minneapolis Police Department conducted what many now consider one of the most influential social science studies ever completed. The study, led by Lawrence W. Sherman (Sherman and Berk 1984), examined three police responses to domestic violence calls and their effects on reducing future abuse:

▶ Arrest the suspect.
▶ Give only advice to the suspect.
▶ Order the suspect to leave the premises.

Instances of repeat violence were examined through a review of police records and interviews with the victims. Although the effectiveness of advising compared with separating is inconclusive from this study, the effectiveness of arrest is clear.

> In the Minneapolis experiment, arrest was clearly more effective in reducing future violence than was advice or sending the suspect away.

The finding—that police should arrest suspects in domestic violence cases, rather than giving them on-the-spot counseling or other types of more lenient treatment, because arrests reduce recidivism—affected police policies nationwide and led Congress to fund grant programs encouraging law enforcement agencies to establish "pro-arrest" policies.

Other Studies on the Effects of Arrest Follow-up studies replicating the Minneapolis experiment, however, yielded less conclusive results. In some cases, offenders who were arrested had higher levels of recidivism than did those who were not arrested. Such findings led some, including Sherman, to call for the repeal of mandatory arrest laws. After further research examining the dynamics between socioeconomic status, domestic violence, and the likelihood of repeated abuse, Sherman developed a community-specific law enforcement policy advocating mandatory arrest of batterers in neighborhoods with low unemployment and discretionary arrest in those with high unemployment. His reasoning was based on findings that arrest increased recidivism among unemployed suspects by 52 percent but reduced subsequent violence by 37 percent among batterers who were employed. Sherman's conclusion: Officers should be allowed discretion in deciding whether to make an arrest.

More recent research has provided mixed results. According to Klein (2008, 16), "A major reexamination of a series of fairly rigorous experiments in multiple jurisdictions finds that arrest deters repeat abuse." A further finding was that no site showed evidence that arrest was associated with increased re-abuse. A major study reported by the NCVS based on 2,564 partner assaults reported between 1992 and 2002 found that police involvement, whether arrest occurred or not, had a strong deterrent effect: "The positive effects of police involvement and arrest are not dependent upon whether or not the victim or a third party reported the incident to law enforcement. Nor are they dependent upon the seriousness of the incident assault, whether a misdemeanor or felony" (Klein 2008, 16). However, a meta-analysis by Garner and Maxwell (2010) concluded that the use of criminal sanctions against perpetrators of intimate partner violence had no effect, one way or the other, on repeat offending—the arrest, prosecution, and conviction of abusers neither increased nor decreased their tendency to commit future IPV.

Arrest Policies States laws fall into one of three policy categories regarding arrests in domestic violence cases (Hirschel 2008):

▶ Arrest is mandatory (22 states and the District of Columbia).
▶ Arrest is preferred (6 states).

> ▶ Arrest is at the officer's discretion (22 states).
> ▶ These laws also delineate the circumstances in which officers can make an arrest. For instance, the law might state an officer can make an arrest *only*
>   - In cases of felonies.
>   - Within a certain number of hours of the incident.
>   - If the couple is married, blood related, living together, or has a child together.

The policies of a jurisdiction govern whether officers can decide to arrest or whether they are required to do so. In addition, the policy in a jurisdiction may require more of the police than state law. For example, a state law may say that an arrest is preferred in domestic violence cases, but a jurisdiction may choose to make an arrest mandatory (Hirschel 2008).

instrumental violence

That used to exert control.

expressive violence

That resulting from hurt feelings, anger, or rage.

In formulating a response, police might consider the difference between **instrumental violence** (that used to control) and **expressive violence** (that resulting from hurt feelings, anger, or rage). Arrest may work best for batterers who use instrumental violence, but other methods, such as learning to mediate differences, may work better with batterers who use expressive violence. Again, however, this difference may not matter depending on state law and jurisdictional policies, where officers have no choice but to arrest.

"Failure to Protect" Lawsuits In many states, officers who have evidence that an assault has occurred have no choice but to make an arrest. The case largely responsible for this change in approach is *Thurman v. City of Torrington* (1984), in which Tracey Thurman, over a period of 8 months, contacted Torrington (Connecticut) police on at least 11 separate occasions to report threats on her life and the life of her child made by her estranged husband, Charles Thurman.

Between October 1982 and June 1983, Charles's threatening behavior became more violent, and after he smashed Tracey's windshield while she was inside the vehicle, he was placed on probation and ordered to stay away from her. However, Charles, ignoring the conditions set for his probation, continued to threaten Tracey, and the police continued to respond to her calls with an "oh, no, not again" attitude. On May 6, 1983, she obtained a court-issued restraining order forbidding Charles from assaulting, threatening, and harassing her. And on June 10, 1983, when Charles went to her house demanding to see her, Tracey called the police asking he be picked up for violating his probation. About 15 minutes later, expecting police to arrive shortly, Tracey went outside to talk to Charles, who then stabbed her 13 times in the chest, neck, and throat. Ten minutes later (25 minutes after her call), a single officer arrived on the scene to witness Charles drop a bloody knife and kick Tracey in the head as she lay on the ground. Tracey Thurman sued the police department for "failure to protect."

At the trial, the department defended its "hands off" response as a means of promoting domestic harmony by refraining from interference in marital disputes. The jury, however, decided the police response had been less than adequate, evidencing a pattern of deliberate indifference by the police department to the complaints of the plaintiff Tracey Thurman and to its duty to protect her. The court added an officer may not "automatically decline to make an arrest simply because the assaulter and his victim are married to each other."

Tracey was awarded $2.6 million dollars. The case resulted in the passage of the Family Violence Protection and Response Act in Connecticut and has resulted in more than 60,000 arrests. The message in the law is clear: Domestic violence is a crime.

> *Thurman v. City of Torrington* (1984) established that domestic violence is an assault rather than simply a family affair. Officers and departments can be sued for "failure to protect."

Police departments that develop and implement pro-arrest policies in domestic assaults can substantially reduce the risk of being sued for federal civil rights violations alleging discrimination. Another way to reduce liability and exposure to lawsuits is to require officers responding to domestic assault calls to document when and why no arrest was made—for example, there was a lack of probable cause because no injuries were visible on the victim, no signs of a struggle, and the like.

Batterer Intervention Programs (BIPs)

Batterer intervention programs (BIPs) are also known as spouse abuse abatement programs or SAAPs. Several studies have found little or limited support for court-ordered treatment for batterers. Some studies have found the batterer's "stake-in-conformity" as the most significant factor in rehabilitation. **Stake-in-conformity variables** include marital status, employment, and residential stability—all variables offenders might lose if convicted for a repeat offense. The batterer's age has also been found to be a factor, when linked to residential stability, in whether abuse occurs or reoccurs, with younger men lacking a stable residence being significantly more likely to self-report committing acts of severe intimate partner violence than are older, more residentially stable men.

stake-in-conformity variables

Include marital status, employment, residential stability, and age—all variables offenders might lose if convicted for a repeat offense.

Most BIP programs are based on the Duluth Model, which was designed in 1981 to be a coordinated community response of law enforcement, the criminal and civil courts, and human service providers to hold offenders accountable for their behaviors. The program helps offenders understand how their beliefs about women, men, and marriage contribute to their abusive behavior and that intentional violence is a choice used to control an intimate partner. However, numerous evaluations of BIPs indicate that most programs show little or no effect on re-offense rates and have no impact on batterers' attitudes about domestic violence (Jackson et al. 2003).

For example, in one study where misdemeanor domestic violence offenders were randomly assigned to either a batterer program or not, and to either monthly or graduated judicial monitoring, with the latter involving reduced court appearances for compliance and increased appearances for noncompliance, the researchers found that neither approach reduced the rearrest rates for any offense, for domestic violence, or for domestic violence with the same victim (Labriola, Rempel, and Davis 2008). A follow-up one year later revealed similar results, with victim interviews showing that neither program assignment nor monitoring schedule significantly affected re-abuse (Labriola, Rempel, and Davis 2008).

Nonetheless, a 2009 roundtable discussion that brought together practitioners, researchers, policymakers, and other stakeholders to discuss challenging issues related to batterer intervention revealed that, despite negative research findings, BIPs continue to play a significant role in the response to IPV, if for no other reason than that no better alternatives exist. One of the key results to come from the roundtable meeting was the critical need for BIPs to be linked to other interventions and the assertion that these programs cannot operate successfully in isolation (Carter 2010).

Helping Victims Deal with the Assault

Besides arresting the abuser, officers responding to calls of domestic assault can help battering victims by making them aware of the many resources available to them. Support groups, counseling programs, and shelters have been established throughout the country to help victims of domestic violence. Other strategies that also may effectively address the problem include establishing programs to rehabilitate those who commit domestic violence and using protective and restraining orders and ensuring that such orders are adhered to.

Restraining Orders A civil restraining order (RO), also called a temporary restraining order (TRO) or order for protection (OFP), is a legally enforceable document that limits physical contact between abuser and abusee. Furthermore, a TRO is valid anywhere a victim might go within the country. Article IV, Section 1 of the U.S. Constitution contains the phrase, "Full faith and credit shall be given in each state to the public acts, records, and judicial proceedings of every other state." This provision allows such things as marriage licenses and driver's licenses to have nationwide validity, regardless of which state issued them.

Federal law requires officers to honor out-of-state protection orders, and given the technology and information-sharing databases now prevalent in law enforcement, agencies and their officers are no longer excused for remaining ignorant of such orders. In fact, officers may be held liable for not checking for any existing protection orders when encountering these situations; failure to check may be considered a dereliction of duty.

Some states differentiate between orders that protect individuals involved domestically and orders that have no domestic involvement. This difference may confuse victims as to which order they should apply for. Harassment orders may cost a court fee; however, restraining order fees are often waived because of the domestic violence it may stem from.

Using GPS to Track Abusers Thirteen states have passed legislation expanding the use of global positioning devices to include domestic abusers and stalkers who have violated orders for protection. Thousands of domestic abusers are being tracked nationwide, but it is still challenging to protect families who live in rural areas or where there are not enough police officers to respond quickly.

In cases of extreme violence, judges have been known to order global positioning system (GPS) use before trial, as a condition of bail or as a sentence, but this measure often leads to complaints by the American Civil Liberties

Union and other critics that it allows too much leeway for judges. With the economic downturn, states have cut funding previously allocated for training police and judges in GPS use. Jurisdictions must be mindful of the Supreme Court ruling in *United States v. Jones* (2012), discussed in Chapter 3, in which the use of a GPS device to track a suspect was held to constitute a search under the Fourth Amendment and, as such, required a warrant. In other words, using GPS to monitor individuals is legal but comes with strict warrant requirements.

STALKING

Another type of domestic violence requiring an enhanced awareness by and response of law enforcement is stalking. If the goal of domestic abuse is to exert power and control over a victim, often through fear, stalking certainly qualifies as such abuse. In fact, strong connections exist between stalking and other crimes, such as domestic violence and sexual assault (*Model Stalking Code Revisited* 2007).

Current data indicate an estimated 3.4 million persons age 18 or older are victims of stalking each year (Baum et al. 2009). The most common types of stalking behavior reported are receiving unwanted phone calls (66 percent), receiving unsolicited letters or e-mail (31 percent), or having rumors spread about oneself (36 percent). About half (46 percent) of stalking victims experienced at least one unwanted contact per week, and 11 percent had been stalked for 5 years or more (Baum et al. 2009). The risk of stalking victimization is highest for individuals who are divorced or separated—34 per 1,000 individuals. Women are at greater risk than men, but women and men are equally likely to report their victimization to police. About 1 in 4 stalking victims reports some form of cyberstalking such as e-mail (83 percent) or instant messaging (35 percent).

Nearly 3 in 4 stalking victims know their offender in some capacity. Most stalking cases involve a male offender and a female victim who had a prior intimate relationship with each other. In addition to this primary category of intimate or former intimate stalking, two other categories exist: acquaintance stalking, where the stalker and victim may know each other casually and may even have dated once or twice but were never intimate; and stranger stalking, commonly found in cases involving celebrities and other public figures, where no prior relationship between the stalker and victim exists.

California passed the first anti-stalking law in 1990, and since then, the federal government, all 50 states, the District of Columbia, and U.S. territories have enacted criminal laws to address stalking. Although *stalking* is generally defined as "a course of conduct directed at a specific person that would cause a reasonable person to feel fear," the legal definition for *stalking* varies across jurisdictions (Baum et al. 2009, 1):

> State laws vary regarding the element of victim fear and emotional distress, as well as the requisite intent of the stalker. Some state laws specify that the victim must have been frightened by the stalking [the *actual fear* standard], while others require only that the stalking behavior would have caused a reasonable person to experience fear [the *reasonable person* standard]. In addition states vary regarding what level of fear is required. Some state laws require prosecutors to establish fear of death or serious bodily harm, while others require

only that prosecutors establish that the victim suffered emotional distress. Interstate stalking is defined by federal law 18 U.S.C. § 2261A.[1]

An effective police response to stalking requires that officers understand the nature of the crime, its legal definition, its various forms, its relationships with other crimes, and its impact on victims (Velazquez, Garcia, and Joyce 2009). Stalking behavior often escalates over time, and an inability or unwillingness of the criminal justice system to promptly and effectively intervene may allow some stalkers the opportunity to engage in increasingly violent acts (*Model Stalking Code Revisited* 2007).

Thus, it is important that law enforcement agencies recognize the seriousness of stalking and develop specific protocols and procedures to guide their response to stalking cases. A first step is to understand that stalking differs from many other crimes in two important ways: "First, because it involves repeat victimization of a targeted individual, stalking is, by its very nature, a series of acts rather than a single incident. Second, this crime is defined at least partly by its effect on the victim" (Velazquez, Garcia, and Joyce 2009). To document these two elements and help prosecutors build a stronger case, stalking victims should be instructed to keep a log of specific incidents and to include their initial, visceral reactions. Officers should also obtain as much information about the stalker as possible and then make an effort to talk with the suspect, recording the conversation if possible. It should be made clear that stalking is a crime and must stop or an arrest will be made.

The National Center for Victims of Crime's *Model Stalking Code Revisited* (2007) provides recommendations to help legislators, criminal justice and victim assistance professionals, and others expand their awareness of the range of options available to them and of the impact that legislative language and structure can have on the enforcement of the law.

CHILD ABUSE AND MALTREATMENT

Because child abuse and maltreatment commonly occur within a family setting, it can be considered a special subtype of domestic violence. But such abuse can also be perpetrated by people outside the family, and now, with the Internet reaching into homes across the country, strangers many miles away are able to victimize children online, creating new challenges for law enforcement and the criminal justice system as a whole. Because of the unique dynamics involved in interacting with child victims and the technical issues surrounding such incidents as Internet crimes against children, we will save the bulk of this discussion for Chapter 11, the chapter devoted to issues concerning youths and juvenile justice.

For now, however, it is enough to acknowledge that, in families where spousal abuse is occurring, it should also be considered a possibility that child abuse is occurring, or may occur in the future. At the very least, child endangerment exists. Millions of children witness violence in their homes; even when they are not themselves the direct targets of abuse, children may

[1] Source: Katrina Baum, Shannan Catalano, Michael Rand, and Kristina Rose, *Stalking Victimization in the United States (NCVS)* (Washington, DC: Bureau of Justice Statistics Special Report, January 2009). (NCJ 224527)

be victimized through continued exposure to abusive relationships. Officers responding to a domestic call involving adults must remain aware of the "invisible victimization" suffered by children who witness violence in the home and tend to these young victims as well. Often, when adults are arrested for domestic violence, additional charges of *endangering children* should be made if children were present during the abuse, and those children should also be taken into protective custody.

Children themselves may become perpetrators of family violence, when they are grown and turn abusive to their elderly parents. Thus, the elderly may be as vulnerable to violence as children are.

ELDER ABUSE

In 1900, the average life expectancy of U.S. residents was only 47 years. A century later, that figure has nearly doubled, and the elderly—those age 65 and up—will soon outnumber children for the first time in our country's history. The U.S. Bureau of the Census projects that by 2030, the U.S. population older than age 65 will number about 72 million, more than double the number of seniors in 2000. Census data also reveals the fastest-growing segment of the elderly population is occurring among Americans age 85 and older.

With the increasing number of elderly come an increasing number of elder abuse cases. In the 1990s, elder abuse was criminalized including the creation of mandatory-reporting legislation and increased penalties for elder abusers. Although the definition of *elder abuse* and the laws against it vary from state to state, **elder abuse** is generally considered to include the physical, sexual, or emotional abuse; financial exploitation; neglect; or abandonment of a person aged 65 or older. Elder abuse affects people of all races and ethnicities, religions, socioeconomic groups, and educational levels.

elder abuse

The physical, sexual, or emotional abuse; financial exploitation; neglect; or abandonment of a person aged 65 or older.

Findings from the oft-cited *National Elder Abuse Incidence Study* (1998) suggest that more than 500,000 Americans aged 60 and older were victims of domestic abuse in 1996. This study also found that only 16 percent of the abusive situations are referred for help—84 percent remain hidden. A more recent survey of elderly Americans found that 11 percent of respondents reported some type of mistreatment or abuse during the previous year, 1.2 percent reported two forms of mistreatment or abuse, and 0.2 percent reported three forms of abuse (Acierno et al. 2009).

The *2004 Survey of State Adult Protective Services* (APS), the "most rigorous national study of state-level APS data conducted to date," showed a 19.7 percent increase in the combined total of reports of elder and vulnerable adult abuse and neglect and a 15.6 percent increase in substantiated cases in the 4 years since the last survey was conducted in 2000 (Teaster et al. 2006). In the overwhelming majority of cases (89.3 percent), the alleged abuse was reported to have occurred in a domestic setting. Types of maltreatment substantiated included self-neglect (37.2 percent), caregiver neglect (20.4 percent), financial exploitation (14.7 percent), emotional/psychological/verbal abuse (14.8 percent), physical abuse (10.7 percent), sexual abuse (1 percent), and other (1.2 percent) (Teaster et al. 2006, 1).

Just as it is difficult to understand how parents could abuse their children, it is difficult to understand how adult children could abuse their elderly parents.

Literature suggests multiple causes of abuse and that most instances are not intentional and preconceived but are the result of the accumulation of stress and limited knowledge and resources for the person providing care. There are instances, however, where adult children who abuse their parents are dependent on their victims for financial assistance, housing, and other forms of support. Often, the abusers need this support because of personal problems, such as mental illness, alcohol or drug abuse, or other dysfunctional personality characteristics. The risk of elder abuse seems to be particularly high when these adult children live with the elder. Elderly victims often allow the abuse to continue, being either unwilling or unable to report it. For example, an elderly parent being "cared for" at home by a grown child may fear that reporting the abuse will lead to the caretaker's arrest and incarceration, thus forcing the elderly victim into a nursing home. However, if the elder reports the abuse and the caretaker is not arrested, the elder may end up in an even more violent situation with an abusive caretaker seeking retaliation for being "told on."

Elderly parents may choose not to report abuse because they feel guilty, ashamed, and embarrassed that their own children are mistreating them. It is very common for individuals of this older generation to consider it inappropriate to discuss these matters with anyone outside of the family, and many do not view such treatment as a police issue. Sometimes elderly parents either do not know who to report abuse to or are physically unable to report it, perhaps because they are bedridden with no access to a telephone or they have no visitors. Other times, the abused elders are so disoriented, confused, or otherwise impaired they do not recognize their mistreatment as abusive.

Elderly residents in nursing homes also have been abused, physically and sexually, by caregivers and sometimes even by other residents. As with the elderly parents living with their children, nursing home residents may have no way to contact help and may fear retribution if they claim they are being abused.

Many other elderly people are not physically abused; they are simply neglected, deprived of all but the most basic necessities. Still others are financially exploited, targeted by unscrupulous scam artists and bilked out of their life savings, or defrauded by caregivers or relatives.

It is important to acknowledge that spouses make up a large percentage of elder abusers, and that a substantial proportion of these cases are domestic violence grown old: partnerships in which one member of a couple has traditionally tried to exert power and control over the other through emotional abuse, physical violence and threats, isolation, and other tactics.

Warning Signs and Symptoms of Elder Abuse

Barriers to a successful response to and prosecution of elder abuse include the inability of responding officers to identify injuries as signs of abuse or neglect, the assumption that the death of an elderly person is simply the result of "old age," and a hesitation to take elderly victims at their word, knowing that some older people suffer from dementia and may make claims that are highly exaggerated or entirely untrue (Bulman 2010). A crucial step to overcoming these barriers is to raise awareness among the public and among law enforcement: "Police...need to recognize elder abuse and treat it as potentially criminal and something that should be investigated. The key to this is...education and training—teaching officers and other first responders to identify and respond to signs of abuse and neglect among the elderly" (Berson 2010, 9). The National Center on Elder Abuse ("Major Types of Elder Abuse" 2011) lists warning signs that there could be an elder abuse problem:

▶ Bruises, pressure marks, broken bones, abrasions, and burns may be an indication of physical abuse, neglect, or mistreatment.

▶ Unexplained withdrawal from normal activities, a sudden change in alertness, and unusual depression may be indicators of emotional abuse.

▶ Bruises around the breasts or genital area can occur from sexual abuse.

▶ Sudden changes in financial situations may be the result of exploitation.

▶ Bedsores, unattended medical needs, poor hygiene, and unusual weight loss are indicators of possible neglect.

▶ Behavior such as belittling, threats, and other uses of power and control by spouses are indicators of verbal or emotional abuse.

▶ Strained or tense relationships, frequent arguments between the caregiver and elderly person are also signs.

One NIJ study that followed a group of elderly individuals for 16 months to document the difference between accidental and intentional bruising found that accidental bruising occurred in predictable locations in the geriatric population, with 90 percent of all bruises occurring on the extremities. No accidental bruises were seen on the ears, neck, genitals, buttocks, or soles of the feet (Wigglesworth et al. 2009). Other characteristics of bruising were noted in the study as potential forensic markers for physical elder abuse: "Bruises that occur as a result of physical elder mistreatment are often large (greater than 5 cm) and on the face, the lateral right arm, or the posterior torso. Older adults with bruises should be asked about the cause of the bruises to help ascertain if physical abuse occurred" because even those individuals with dementia or other memory problems are able to remember incidents with an emotional content, such as abuse by a family member or other trusted individual, as opposed to an accidental bruise in which there is no emotional association (Wigglesworth et al. 2009, 2).

Factors Associated with Elder Abuse

Both living with someone else and being socially isolated have been associated with higher elder abuse rates. These seemingly contradictory findings may turn out to be related in that abusers who live with the elder have more opportunity to abuse and yet may be isolated from the larger community themselves or may seek to isolate the elders from others so that the abuse is not discovered. Further research needs to be done to explore the relationship between these factors.

Many other theories about elder abuse have been developed. Few, unfortunately, have been tested adequately enough to definitively say whether they raise the risk of elder abuse or not. It is possible each of the following theories will ultimately be shown to account for a small percentage of elder abuse cases.

▶ **Caregiver stress** This commonly stated theory holds that well-intentioned caregivers are so overwhelmed by the burden of caring for dependent elders that they end up losing control and striking out, neglecting, or otherwise harming the elder. Much of the small amount of research that has been done has shown that few cases fit this model.

▶ **Personal characteristics of the elder** Theories that fall under this umbrella hold that dementia, disruptive behaviors, problematic personality traits, and significant needs for assistance may all raise an elder's risk of being abused. Research on these possibilities has produced contradictory or unclear conclusions.

▶ **Cycle of violence** Some theorists hold that domestic violence is a learned problem-solving behavior transmitted from one generation to the next. This theory seems well established in cases of domestic violence and child abuse, but no research to date has shown that it is a cause of elder abuse.

The Police Response

Albrecht (2008, 44) contends, "It's in your best interest (and your duty as a mandated reporter in nearly all states) to respond, ask questions, investigate all potential crimes, and check on the health and viability of any elderly person under the care or control of someone." Most elder abuse does not happen in retirement or nursing homes; it occurs in the home of the senior citizen, with the most common perpetrator being the spouse. Responding officers must proceed with respect and caution and must be aware of the laws governing elder abuse in their state. The skills used in dealing with domestic violence and abused children apply to investigating elder abuse. Special consideration and training is required for dealing with victims of elder sexual abuse, as their needs are different from both the younger sexual abuse victims officers are perhaps more used to dealing with and from victims suffering from elder physical abuse (Payne 2010).

Elder abuse should be defined and documented as a crime separate from assault, battery, burglary, murder, or some other category. This would accomplish two purposes: raise awareness of the problem and help outline a proper police response to the problem. Law enforcement should first try to prevent such abuse by empowering the elderly with information about how to protect themselves. Police should identify the at-risk population such as those elderly dependent on others for some or all of their basic daily needs. Officers should also recognize and understand why the elderly are abused and develop a strategy to meet their needs.

Officers investigating a report of elder abuse in a residence should observe the general condition of the residence (Petrocelli 2007). Has the garbage been taken out? Has the mail been brought in? Are there dirty dishes in the sink? How does the house smell? After assessing the living conditions, officers should interview the alleged victim, paying attention to nonverbal cues such as whether the victim makes or avoids eye contact during the conversation. Be aware of others nearby, particularly if a suspected perpetrator is hovering in the area and interfering with the question-and-answer process. Officers should also evaluate the victim's mental state by asking if the victim knows what day or month it is, who the president is, or what the answer to a simple math problem (such as 2 + 3) is (Petrocelli 2007).

Because physical evidence of assault or neglect is vital to establishing a charge of elder abuse, officers responding to a call where physical abuse is suspected should examine the elderly victim for indicators such as fractures, bruises, burns, lacerations, and punctures. Officers should look for the presence of old and new wounds and be alert to difficulties the elderly victim has with walking or sitting, recognizing that mobility impairment is also a normal part of aging. Evidence of psychological abuse is more difficult to detect but may manifest as depression, a change in personality, a loss of interest in themselves and their surroundings, anger, or agitation.

Law enforcement must also respond to financial abuse of the elderly including stealing, embezzling, or misusing money or possessions, savings, or stocks; misusing the person's property or other resources; and denying the elderly a home. Sometimes the grown children are responsible for financially exploiting their elderly parents, a relatively easy crime to commit if the adult child is the victim's guardian, has power of attorney for the elderly parent, or has been given other rights over the victim's estate and person.

Elder abuse also includes neglect that may take the form of abandonment or denial of food, shelter, clothing, basic hygiene practices, and medical attention. Often abusers rely on overmedicating their victims to control them.

Although interviewing abused elders directly is a preferred police response, often the victim is confused or unable to grasp what has happened. Elderly victims may have impaired mental abilities or memories. In such instances, information provided by other people becomes extremely important. If elderly victims live at home, all those who have contact with the victims should be interviewed. If elderly victims live with one of their children, all family members should be interviewed. If elderly victims live in a nursing home, other residents of the home as well as the care providers should be interviewed. The past record of the institution should be looked into, including any violations of licensing standards reported to the state department of human services or whatever agency issues licenses to nursing homes.

Cooperative Efforts

As with other areas of domestic violence, cooperative efforts in responding to elder abuse are critical and can include social workers, mental health workers, elder protective services, hospital workers, shelters for the elderly, and transportation services. As stressed throughout this text, multiagency partnerships and a focus on community policing have been shown to increase the effectiveness of police response to crime. The application of such collaborative efforts to the issue of domestic violence is as promising as it is to any other police operation, yet it faces the same challenges found with other areas involving partnerships.

SCHOOL AND COLLEGE VIOLENCE

Although incidents of school and college violence are to be taken seriously and have received much media attention in recent years, such publicity has also generated a widespread, baseless fear that today's schools are teeming with youths more valueless and violent than ever before. Current research suggests differently. Analysis of data submitted to the FBI's National Incident-Based Reporting System (NIBRS) from 2000 to 2005 indicates that, of the more than 17 million incidents reported during this period, only 3.3 percent occurred at schools and colleges (Noonan and Vavra 2007). In these incidents of school violence, most (38.0 percent) of the offenders were 13- to 15-year-olds, followed by those age 19 or older (18.2 percent). The majority (76.7 percent) of offenders were males and White (71.1 percent). The relationship between offender and victim most often reported was "acquaintance," which, when combined with "otherwise known," were 3.3 times more likely to occur than were other relationships. Personal weapons (hands, fists, feet) were 3.4 times more likely to have been reported than was any other weapon type. Knives and other cutting instruments were used as weapons more often than were guns, by a ratio of 3.2 to 1.

Data from *Indicators of School Crime and Safety: 2011* (Robers et al. 2012) indicate that our nation's schools are relatively safe but that crime and violence still occur. During the July 2009 to June 2010 school year, there were 49,373,307 students enrolled in prekindergarten through 12th grade and:

▶ There were 17 homicides of school-age youth (ages 5–18) at school (1 homicide per 2.9 million enrolled students)—less than 2 percent of all youth homicides nationwide during this period.

▶ There was 1 suicide of a school-age youth (ages 5–18) at school—less than 1 percent of all youth suicides nationwide during the same time period.

▶ Students ages 12 to 18 were victims of about 828,000 nonfatal crimes, including 470,000 thefts and 359,000 violent crimes.

▶ Four percent of students ages 12 to 18 reported being victimized at school during the previous 6 months. Less than half of a percent reported serious violent victimization.

▶ Ten percent of male students in grades 9 to 12 reported being threatened or injured with a weapon on school property compared with 5 percent of female students.

▶ A greater percentage of teachers in city schools reported being threatened with injury or physically attacked than did teachers in suburban, town, or rural schools.

▶ Seventy-four percent of public schools reported that one or more violent incidents of crimes had occurred.

▶ Twenty-three percent of public schools reported that student bullying was a daily or weekly problem.

▶ Twenty percent of students ages 12 to 18 reported there were gangs at their schools.

▶ Twenty-eight percent (ages 12–18) reported having been bullied at school, and 6 percent (ages 12–18) reported being cyberbullied.

▶ Thirty-nine percent of sixth graders reported being bullied at school.

▶ Eleven percent (grades 9–12) said they had been in a fight on school property.

▶ Six percent (grades 9–12) reported they had carried a weapon on school property during the previous 30 days.

▶ Five percent (grades 9–12) reported using marijuana on school property, and 4 percent reported having at least one alcoholic drink on school property.

▶ About 4 percent of students (ages 12–18) reported being afraid of attack or harm at school.

▶ Five percent (ages 12–18) reported avoiding a school activity or one or more places in school in the previous 6 months because of fear of attack or harm.

▶ The majority of students (ages 12–18) reported that their school had a student code of conduct (96 percent) and a requirement that visitors sign in (94 percent).

▶ Sixty-eight percent reported the presence of security guards or an assigned police officer, and 11 percent reported the use of metal detectors at their schools.

LAW ENFORCEMENT IN SCHOOLS AND COLLEGES

Law enforcement has become increasingly involved in maintaining safe environments for learning at all levels of education. At the K–12 level, the most common form of law enforcement involvement is the school resource officer or SRO. At the college/university level, the most common form of law enforcement is a campus-based police department.

The School Resource Officer (SRO)

A police–school liaison program was developed in 1958 in Flint, Michigan, with the cooperation of school authorities, parents, social agencies, juvenile court officials, businesses, and the police department. The foundation for the police–school liaison program established a workable relationship with the police department and the public school system. This program gradually evolved into what is today the SRO program.

Part Q of Title I of the Omnibus Crime Control and Safe Streets Act of 1968 defines the SRO as "a career law enforcement officer, with sworn authority, deployed in community-oriented policing, and assigned by the employing police department or agency to work in collaboration with school and community-based organizations." According to the National Association of School Resource Officers, school-based policing is the fastest growing area of law enforcement.

Although SROs have traditionally educated students about topics such as pedestrian safety and the dangers of substance abuse through programs such as Drug Abuse Resistance Education (D.A.R.E.), their role has greatly expanded. SROs do not enforce school regulations, which are the responsibility of the school superintendent and staff. Instead, officers typically enforce all violations of law that occur on school property or have school staff involved. This includes all crimes, including status violations such as tobacco use, involving students who attend school. This also includes crimes such as fraud or assault that may be committed by school staff. SROs also work with students, parents, and school authorities to apply preventive techniques to problems created by antisocial youths including counseling children and their parents, referring them to social agencies to treat the root problems, referring them to drug and alcohol abuse agencies, and being in daily contact in the school to check their progress. Some of the disorder and misbehavior that occurs in educational institutions is an extension of pressures and problems children experience outside of school. For example, SROs might find themselves having to deal with difficult situations involving children living in poverty or youth who come from abusive homes. SROs may also find themselves dealing with irate parents and disgruntled school faculty: "Policing in an educational setting truly is a unique responsibility. It presents special challenges because the school environment differs so greatly from the jurisdiction of most other law enforcement agencies. To understand how to police this unique environment, law enforcement personnel need to receive training to sensitize them to the needs of the students, faculty, and staff" (Rudick 2011, 21).

SROs may patrol elementary school areas until school starts in the morning, during the noon hour, and after school, watching for suspicious people or automobiles and for infractions of safety rules. SROs also check the middle school areas for anyone loitering around the building or grounds trying to pick up students in the area. These officers are an invaluable resource to the police department because they usually have an opportunity to build rapport with the youth in the community because the SRO position is usually a long-term one, if not indefinite. SROs are often aware of rumors of crimes that will happen or have happened involving students. They know the kids in the community and who they are all connected to. If the youths are considered "problem kids," the officer may already have established a relationship with the child and his or her parents.

Another important area SROs are involved in is *liaison work with other interested agencies*, including juvenile courts, social agencies, mental health agencies, other schools, and private organizations. Officers often coordinate their efforts with these other agencies to better treat children. Finally, *recreational participation* is a type of interaction with youths that breaks down many walls of resentment. Officers who participate in organized athletics with youngsters build a rapport that carries over into their other contacts with those youths.

Campus Law Enforcement

The first official campus police force was formed at Yale University in 1894. In 1968, a New York study of campus police found that most chiefs and officers had not completed high school and had little or no training or background in law enforcement; most departments worked out of the boiler room, reporting to the maintenance department; and more than one-third of all the officers were more than 60 years old (Peak, Barthe, and Barcia 2008). In reviewing the evolution of campus policing in America during the past 20 years, the following summary can be made:

> What is most evident is that these contemporary organizations have generally experienced a marked increase in the use of the title "Police Department" (with a concomitant decline in the designation of "Security Department"), the nature of reporting lines (they now typically report to the central administration as opposed to a head of campus buildings and grounds), and greater diversity among administrative-level personnel. There also have been slight increases in the number of administrators having graduate degrees. Furthermore, today

more campus police agencies have full police powers, statewide jurisdiction, and greater numbers of full-time sworn personnel, agency ranks, and activities/responsibilities. They also report more positive relations with local area police agencies, a more detailed hiring process, and higher levels of mandatory annual in-service training; and they are generally very much engaged in disaster planning and terrorism readiness. (Peak, Barthe, and Barcia 2008, 258)[2]

During the 2004–2005 school year, 74 percent of the 750 law enforcement agencies serving 4-year universities and colleges with 2,500 or more students employed sworn law enforcement officers having full arrest powers. The other campuses hired nonsworn security officers. Two-thirds (67 percent) of campus law enforcement agencies used armed patrol officers (Reaves 2008).

One of campus law enforcement's major responsibilities is adhering to the crime reporting requirements of the Crime Awareness and Campus Security Act of 1990, which amended the Higher Education Act (HEA) of 1965 and requires all postsecondary institutions participating in HEA's Title IV student financial assistance programs to disclose campus crime statistics and security information. Because the law is tied to federal student financial aid programs, it applies to most institutions of higher education, both public and private. It is enforced by the U.S. Department of Education.

The law was amended in 1992 to add a requirement that schools afford the victims of campus sexual assault certain basic rights and was amended again in 1998 to expand the reporting requirements. The 1998 amendments also renamed the law the *Jeanne Clery Disclosure of Campus Security Policy and Campus Crime Statistics Act* in memory of 19-year-old university freshman Jeanne Ann Clery, who was raped and murdered while asleep in her residence hall room on April 5, 1986. The law is now generally referred to simply as the *Clery Act*. Subsequent amendments in 2000 and 2008 added provisions dealing with registered sex offender notification and campus emergency response, respectively. The 2008 amendments also added a provision to protect crime victims, "whistleblowers," and others from retaliation. Violators can be fined as much as $27,500 per nonreported incident (Ward and Mann 2011). The revised and comprehensive *Handbook for Campus Safety and Security Reporting* is a valuable resource that emphasizes compliance as a whole system of developing policy statements, gathering information from a variety of sources and translating it into the appropriate categories, issuing alerts, disseminating information, and, finally, keeping records (Ward and Mann 2011).

Responsibilities of law enforcement officers in schools and on college campuses can be quite varied. Consider, as an example, the responsibilities of officers at the Fort Hays State University (Kansas) Police Department, which employs nine full-time, armed, state-certified police officers: "The officers are responsible for a full range of public safety services, including criminal investigations, enforcement of criminal statutes and city ordinances, collection of data for the required statistical crime reports, motor vehicle

---

[2] Source: Peak, Kenneth J.; Barthe, Emmanuel P.; and Barcia, Adam. "Campus Policing in America: A Twenty-Year Perspective." *Police Quarterly*, June 2008, pp. 239–260. Reprinted by permission of SAGE Publications.

accident investigations, civil commitments for persons in need of care, traffic and parking enforcement, emergency management, enforcement of FHSU rules and regulations, and the security of the university's physical assets" (Howell et al. 2008, 20).

Bullying

Research suggests that many of the roots of crime and violence may stem from what is often ignored throughout the educational system—incidents of bullying and harassment. According to Olweus's (1992) groundbreaking study, former school bullies in Norway had a fourfold increase in the level of relatively serious, recidivist criminality as young adults.

Although some parents, other adults, and even students tend to dismiss schoolyard bullying as a "rite of passage," a simple cycle of the big kids "picking on" the little kids, who in turn grow up to be the big kids who pick on the little kids, and so on, the U.S. Department of Education asserts that **bullying** is more than just big versus small: It is a repeated pattern of aggressive behavior that involves an imbalance of power and that purposefully inflicts harm on the bullying victim (Stuart-Cassel, Bell, and Springer 2011). Bullying also indicates a behavior pattern that may worsen over time, as numerous studies have found evidence that bullies are more likely to engage in antisocial and criminal behavior as they progress through adolescence into adulthood (Moon, Hwang, and McCluskey 2011). Bullying may be any of the following:

bullying

Repeated pattern of aggressive behavior that involves an imbalance of power and that purposefully inflicts harm on the bullying victim.

- ▶ Physical: hitting, kicking, spitting, pushing, punching, poking, hair-pulling, biting
- ▶ Verbal: name-calling, taunting, gossip, malicious teasing, making threats
- ▶ Psychological/emotional: rejection, humiliation, ostracism, intimidation, extortion, spreading rumors, manipulating social relationships, berating personal characteristics such as perceived sexual orientation
- ▶ Sexual: harassment and actual abuse

Bullying is a serious concern in the issue of school violence because of its far-reaching and long-lasting impacts beyond a specific "episode" between bully and victim. The evolution of cyberbullying, or using electronic devices to harass victims from a distance, has enabled bullying to spread far beyond the traditional school yard and into youths' homes and anywhere they go online or receive cell phone calls and texts. Cyberbullying also provides a degree of anonymity to perpetrators, emboldening those who might otherwise not be able to directly confront a victim.

Results of a recent study revealed that verbal bullying was the most prevalent form of bullying (53.6 percent), followed by relational (51.4 percent), physical (20.8 percent), and electronic (13.6 percent), with some students reporting being victimized by more than one type of bullying (Wang, Iannotti, and Nansel 2009). Gender differences in bullying involvement were also noted, with boys more involved in the physical and verbal forms of bullying and girls more involved in the relational form. Regarding cyberbullying, boys were more likely to be perpetrators and girls more like to be victims. Roughly one-fourth (23 percent) of public schools report that bullying occurs among students on a daily or weekly basis (Robers et al. 2012).

Most students do not report bullying to adults (teachers or parents), fearing retaliation, that they would not be believed, or that their teacher would tell the bully who told on him; feeling shame at not standing up for themselves; or thinking it was worse to be thought of as a snitch (Sampson 2009). Because of this reluctance to tell, teachers and school resource officers may not think they have a problem. Sampson (2009, 19–23) suggests the following approaches to address bullying:

▶ Enlist the school principal's commitment and involvement.

▶ Use a multifaceted, comprehensive approach including establishing a schoolwide policy addressing bullying and providing guidelines for teachers, other staff, and students on actions to take if bullying occurs, educating and involving parents, adopting strategies to deal with bullies and victims, and encouraging students to report bullying and to be helpful to classmates.

▶ Increase student reporting of bullying by setting up a bully hot line or having a "bully box" where students can drop a note about bullying.

▶ Develop activities in less-supervised areas such as schoolyards, lunchrooms, and lavatories.

▶ Reduce the time students can spend with less supervision such as recess, lunch breaks, and class changes.

▶ Stagger recess, lunch, and/or class-release times.

▶ Monitor areas where bullying can be expected.

▶ Assign bullies to a particular location or to particular tasks during release time.

▶ Post classroom signs prohibiting bullying and listing the consequences for it.

Approaches that do *not* appear to be effective include training students in conflict resolution and peer mediation, adopting a "zero-tolerance" policy, providing group therapy for bullies, and encouraging victims to simply "stand up" to bullies (Sampson 2009).

Attention must also be paid to victims of bullying. Some victims of bullying suffer such humiliation and loss of self-esteem they become violent toward themselves. Other bullying victims turn their anger and frustration outward, sometimes with lethal results. Consider the following excerpt from a 15-year-old boy's journal: "I hate being laughed at. But they won't laugh after they're scraping parts of their parents, sisters, brothers and friends from the wall of my hate." These words were written by Kip Kinkel, who later killed both of his parents and then went on a shooting spree at his high school in Springfield, Oregon, killing two students and wounding two dozen more.

School Shootings

"Statistically, shootings and other homicides are a rare event in U.S. schools.... [However] school shootings can be a very real and very frightening part of school violence in this country. Each attack has a terrible and lasting effect on the students, school and surrounding community—and on the nation as a whole" (Schuster 2009, 42). Consider the 1999 tragedy at Columbine High School in Littleton, Colorado, where two shooters killed a dozen students and

Seventeen-year-old T. J. Lane is led from juvenile court by Sheriff's deputies in Chardon, Ohio, following his arraignment in the shooting of five high school students Monday, February 27, 2012. Three of the five students died. Lane, who is being tried as an adult, has pleaded not guilty.

© AP Photo/Mark Duncan

a teacher and wounded 23 others before turning their guns on themselves. Further investigation revealed the shooters had been plotting for a year to kill at least 500 and blow up their school.

In response to the Columbine event, the U.S. Secret Service developed the *Safe School Initiative*, the objective of which was to attempt to identify information that could be obtainable, or "knowable," before a targeted school attack. (A targeted attack is one in which the school is purposefully selected as the site for violence rather than being a random site of opportunity.) Such information would then be analyzed and evaluated to produce a factual, accurate knowledge base, which could then, in turn, be used to help public policymakers, school administrators, police officials, and parents in communities across the country formulate policies and strategies aimed at preventing school-based attacks (Vossekuil et al. 2002).

The *Safe School Initiative* study identified the following 10 key findings (Vossekuil et al. 2004, 11–12):

▶ Incidents of targeted violence at school rarely were sudden, impulsive acts.

▶ Prior to most incidents, other people knew about the attacker's idea or plan to attack.

▶ Most attackers did not threaten their targets directly prior to advancing the attack.

▶ There is no accurate or useful "profile" of students who engaged in targeted school violence.

▶ Most attackers engaged in some behavior prior to the incident that caused others concern or indicated a need for help.

▶ Most attackers had difficulty coping with significant losses or personal failures. Moreover, many had considered or attempted suicide.

▶ Many attackers felt bullied, persecuted, or injured by others prior to the attack.

▶ Most attackers had access to and had used weapons prior to the attack.

▶ In many cases, other students were involved in some capacity.

▶ Despite prompt law enforcement responses, most shooting incidents were stopped by means other than law enforcement intervention.[3]

Although some school shooters were described as socially isolated, others have been quite popular. Some were bullied, some were not. They came from both intact and broken families, and academic performance ranged from excellent to failing. It is important to avoid overgeneralizing or making faulty assumptions based on backward logic. Although the majority of school shooters may have experienced bullying, it cannot be said that the majority of kids who are bullied will become violent or go on shooting rampages.

Following traditional law enforcement protocol, many have tried profiling the shooters and victims involved in school violence, searching for a pattern that may help predict or prevent similar events in the future. Teachers and others should avoid relying on profiles or checklists of danger signs to identify the next youth likely to bring lethal violence to a school.

> School violence almost never occurs without warning.

Although use of profiles and checklists is strongly discouraged, early warning signs of violent behavior have been recognized that, when presented in combination, might aid in identifying and referring children who may need help. Such early warning signs include social withdrawal and isolation; depression; impulsive and uncontrollable behavior; poor coping skills; low frustration tolerance; history of physical assault; grudges, delusions, hallucinations, or bizarre thoughts; victim or perpetrator of bullying; substance abuse; rebellion against authority; low school interest and poor performance; expression of violence in writings and drawings; uncontrolled anger; discipline problems; suicidal ideation, wishes of death, or a desire to kill others; boastfulness about weapons; abusive language; and threats of violence (Booth, Van Hasselt, and Vecchi 2011).

Of particular importance is the finding that youths who eventually commit school homicide had previously exhibited behavior leakage: "This refers to a student's intentional or unintentional disclosure of thoughts, fantasies, feelings, and possible intentions.... Leakage can also take the form of a fascination with violence and violent entertainment. It appears that nearly 50 percent of school

---

[3] Source: Bryan Vossekuil, Robert Fein, Marisa Reddy, Randy Borum, and William Modzeleski, *The Final Report and Findings of the Safe School Initiative: Implications for the Prevention of School Attacks in the United States.* (Washington, DC: U.S. Secret Service and the U.S. Department of Education, May 2002).

homicide perpetrators exhibit some type of warning sign, including leaving notes or making a verbal threat" (Booth, Van Hasselt, and Vecchi 2011, 4).

The Police Response

As the nature of school and campus violence has changed over the years, so too has law enforcement's response to such incidents. The tragic events at Columbine fundamentally changed how police react to school shootings. During the Columbine rampage in 1999, the police did what they were trained to do—contain the situation and wait for a special weapons and tactics (SWAT) team. However, it took the SWAT team 45 minutes to assemble and get there; during that time, Eric Harris and Dylan Klebold shot 10 of the 13 people who were killed that day. One victim bled to death. Since then, police across the country have established "active-shooter" protocol, in which responding officers rush toward gunfire to stop the gunman (the "active shooter") first and foremost. This response is considerably different from that expected of police in other highly volatile or dangerous situations, where they are trained to take cover and wait for backup. A basic premise of the active-shooter response is that there is not enough time to wait for backup because it is assumed that the shooters will continue killing and have already committed themselves to dying in the altercation rather than surrendering by way of negotiation or communication.

This active-shooter response was used by the Virginia Tech police, fire, and emergency medical services (EMS) responders during the deadliest school shooting in U.S. history, when Seung-Hui Cho "methodically murdered" 32 students and faculty and wounded 23 more:

> At 9:41, the first 9-1-1 call of the shooting went to the Blacksburg (Virginia) police department, which when it learned the shooting was on the Virginia Tech campus, immediately transferred the call to the VTPD. Within a minute, VTPD dispatched all available officers to an active shooting at Norris Hall and requested all county EMS units to respond. Police arrived at 9:45 and heard shots. They hesitated briefly to make sure they were not being fired upon and then rushed to the entrances, which Cho had chained shut. At 9:50, officers used a shotgun to shoot open the lock of an entrance Cho had not chained and followed the sounds to the second floor. At 9:51 Cho shot himself in the head just as police reached the second floor. The second floor was secured by 9:52 and medics entered to begin triage. In those 11 minutes, Cho had fired 174 rounds, and as noted, had plenty of additional ammunition to continue his deadly shooting spree had the approach of the police not caused him to shoot himself. (Larson 2008, 40–42)

Another trend, particularly among smaller departments, is toward more cross-training and pooling of resources. A comprehensive, step-by-step discussion of police response to school violence is beyond the scope of this text; however, several other publications focus in their entirety on this subject. A particularly useful document published by the IACP, based on the input of more than 500 experts and 15 focus groups with a diverse range of disciplines addressing school violence, is the *Guide for Preventing and Responding to School Violence* (2009).

IN SEARCH OF SAFER SCHOOLS

Beres (2008) suggests, "A combination of community policing, school resource officers, and physical security can go a long way toward guaranteeing a safe school environment. This combination should have as its basis a well-thought-out and practiced plan for any crisis, natural or manmade."

 An effective three-pronged approach to school security encompasses crisis planning, security technology, and school/law enforcement/community partnerships.

Crisis Planning

Every agency and institution affected or involved during an episode of school violence must decide in advance how they plan to respond, knowing that no two situations will be exactly the same and that even the best-laid plans will require on-the-spot, last-minute adjustments. For police, the first step is generally to obtain blueprints or floor plans and to conduct walk-throughs of local schools. The next step is to actually train the response and to make such training exercises routine. Some departments stage mock disasters to test their emergency preparedness for acts of school violence and to identify areas that need improving. Such drills often highlight the importance of collaboration and communication with other agencies to an effective response.

Security Technology

A second prong in the effort to achieve safer schools involves security technology, such as weapons screening programs, entry control systems, and surveillance cameras. Recognizing that a significant proportion of school violence is perpetrated by those who neither attend nor work at the school, many districts are implementing entry control systems, such as mandatory sign-in for all visitors and photo ID cards, to make it easier to spot outsiders. Video surveillance cameras are also being installed as a way to curb school violence. Most cameras are not actively monitored but, rather, tape on a continuous loop and are reviewed only when an incident is reported.

Although many schools have found positive benefits in using video cameras and other security devices, technology cannot replace the human factor.

Partnerships

It cannot be emphasized enough that, as with so many other areas of police operations, partnerships are a vital component in an effective response to school violence. Partnerships to address the issue of school violence can take many forms and involve numerous entities.

The Safe Schools Pyramid developed by the North Carolina Department of Juvenile Justice and Delinquency Prevention's Center for the Prevention of School Violence, and illustrated on the Center's website (http://www .ncdjjdp.org/cpsv/safe_schools_pyramid.html), reflects the importance of the community policing concept in school safety. The community sits at the pyramid's base because the school environment often mirrors what's happening in the community. Community problems can disrupt the school environment and impede learning. The SRO is the first level of the pyramid itself, depicting the SRO's function as an integral connection between the school and the community.

Moving up the pyramid, the next level is composed of law-related education and programs that teach students what types of behavior our society deems lawful and unlawful. The level above law-related education and programs is conflict management and peer mediation, strategies that have been found to dissipate early tension in schools—tension that, if left unchecked, can escalate and lead to violence.

The fourth level in the Safe Schools Pyramid is Students against Violence Everywhere (S.A.V.E.), a student-driven program that teaches youth about alternatives to violence and how to put this knowledge into practice through participation in school and community service projects. In addition to teaching kids conflict management skills and crime prevention strategies, the S.A.V.E. program educates students about the value of good citizenship and civility.

Teen and student courts, at the next higher level of the pyramid, are intervention programs used primarily for first-time offenders in misdemeanor, nonviolent cases such as shoplifting/theft, alcohol possession, criminal mischief, vandalism/property damage and traffic offenses. Teen courts are also used for school disciplinary issues. Youth volunteer roles in teen court hearings commonly include the defense attorney (youth advocate), prosecuting attorney (community advocate), clerk, bailiff, juror and sometimes judge. Teen courts provide an effective intervention in jurisdictions where the enforcement of misdemeanor charges is given low priority because of heavy caseloads of more serious offenses. Youth courts turn peer pressure into a positive tool by letting offenders know, through other teens, that their behavior was wrong.

At the peak of the school safety pyramid is the physical design and technology implemented in the school structure itself, which serve important roles in enhancing the overall safety of students, staff and visitors on school property.

All of the strategies identified in the School Safety Pyramid are proactive, student-focused approaches that mix the philosophies of prevention and intervention to create safe, secure learning environments and empower students to address safety problems that may arise in their schools.

The SRO plays an important part in threat assessment and crisis planning: "In times of crisis, having an SRO in the school decreases response time and increases student and staff perceptions of safety. The SRO also can educate students about the consequences of their behavior and identify peer conflicts" (Booth, Van Hasselt, and Vecchi 2011, 6).

Threat assessment task forces are one example of how partnerships can enhance school and campus security. Since the widely publicized and tragic shooting incidents at Virginia Tech in April 2007 and Northern Illinois University in February 2008, several organizations and task forces have recommended that campuses create behavioral threat assessment/behavioral intervention teams as a key measure for preventing violence before it can occur (Margolis and Healy 2009). The *Virginia Tech Special Task Force Report* calls for implementation of systems that link "troubled students to appropriate medical and counseling services either on or off campus, and to balance the individual's right with the rights of all others for safety." The report also recommends,

"Incidents of aberrant, dangerous, or threatening behavior must be documented and reported immediately to a college's threat assessment group, and must be acted upon in a prompt and effective manner to protect the safety of the campus community" (Margolis and Healy 2009).

OTHER EFFORTS TO PREVENT SCHOOL VIOLENCE

Some schools have supplemented their violence prevention efforts with programs, policies, and procedures aimed at problematic student behavior. Intervention and behavior modification programs have proven successful in some jurisdictions. Another approach to preventing school violence is for those involved with students, particularly law enforcement officers, to have the skills to de-escalate juvenile aggression. For youths who pose no immediate danger but whose aggression appears to be manifestly deliberate, de-escalation tactics include reminding, warning, or confronting the student; verbally removing the student (telling the student to leave); and physically removing or restraining the youth. In cases where no immediate danger is perceived and the youth's aggression might stem from an underlying emotional status, de-escalation strategies include giving the student space and time, listening reflectively to what is on the student's mind, and counseling positively (Golden 2004, 34).

> Some schools have adopted controversial measures to prevent school violence, including zero-tolerance policies and school security procedures known as *lockdowns*.

Zero-Tolerance Policies

Zero-tolerance policies mandate predetermined consequences for specific offenses. Most such policies and procedures focus on the possession of weapons and other contraband on school property. And although it seems to make good sense that schools, in fulfilling their duty to maintain a safe learning environment, should restrict what students are allowed to carry on campus, policies and procedures aimed at achieving the goal of safety are not without controversy.

Consider, for example, a case from Fort Myers, Florida, where school officials saw a knife on the floor of the passenger's side of an honor student's car while she was in the school. The knife, which had a 5-inch blade, had been left in the car after she moved some possessions over the weekend. The girl, 18, spent Monday in jail on a felony charge of possession of a weapon on school property. Further, the girl was not allowed to participate in her graduation ceremony because the principal insisted, "A weapon is a weapon." In thinking about these words, recall the data presented earlier in the chapter indicating that "personal" weapons, such as hands, fists, and feet, were used more than three times as often in incidents of school violence than were any other type of weapon. Students cannot be expected to check their hands, fists, and feet at the door, so common sense must prevail when implementing and interpreting school policies.

zero-tolerance policies

School policies that mandate predetermined consequences or punishments for specific offenses—for example, suspension or expulsion for possession of drugs or a weapon.

Proactive Lockdowns

Another controversial effort aimed at preventing school violence is the planned but unannounced lockdown. Some schools are taking a **lockdown** approach not as a reactive response to a crisis, but rather as a proactive step to avoid a crisis.

Many legal issues must be considered when planning such a lockdown, so collaboration with the district attorney's office is usually required. An "amnesty time" is announced during which students can turn over any illegal substances or weapons without penalty and can list such items in their lockers. While part of the lockdown team searches the campus for contraband, another part meets with students to discuss what is occurring.

Although some criticize such lockdowns as being frightening or intimidating to students, and some students complain they feel threatened when their day is interrupted by the police, this approach has, thus far, not been challenged in court or before a school board. In addition to curbing the possession of drugs and weapons in the public schools, these lockdowns demonstrate the cooperation between law enforcement and the school system.

Proactive lockdowns may be effective in locating and securing weapons that might be used in incidents of school violence, but they are used very infrequently in very few schools. Zero-tolerance policies fall dangerously short in their effectiveness if students believe any prohibited items they bring to school will go unnoticed. In fact, many weapons are discovered only after they have been used in a violent episode. Metal detectors, again, are used rather infrequently, especially in smaller schools and in smaller communities, despite statistics showing these jurisdictions are also vulnerable to fatal school violence.

So although these efforts are seen as luxuries for those schools able to afford them, they cannot be relied on alone and are no substitute for the power of partnerships between students, teachers, officers, parents, and other community members.

WORKPLACE VIOLENCE

The third major setting for violence for which law enforcement must prepare a response is the workplace. Workplace violence is a serious health and safety issue and has been identified as the third leading cause of death for people at work (Stelter 2011). Preliminary data indicate there were 521 workplace homicides during 2009, a slight drop from the 526 workplace homicides reported in 2008 (Harrell 2011).

Workplace homicides, while making for sensational headlines, actually represent a very small fraction of workplace violence incidents. Data from the NCVS and the Census of Fatal Occupational Injuries (CFOI) show that approximately 572,000 nonfatal violence crimes occurred in the workplace during 2009, with simple assault comprising the largest portion (77.8 percent of incidents) (Harrell 2011). More than one-third of workplace violence incidents (38 percent) went unreported to police— 22 percent of victims said they did not report the incident because it was considered a "personal matter," and 24 percent of workplace violence victims felt the incident was not important enough to be reported to law enforcement (Harrell 2011).

Similarities between School and Workplace Violence

Researchers have noted some striking similarities between school and workplace violence: "It is critical to understand that workplace violence does not happen at random or 'out of the blue.' Rather, perpetrators usually display some behaviors of concern" (Romano et al. 2011, 3). Such concerning behaviors include aggressive outbursts, inability to handle criticism, hypersensitivity to perceived slights, poor coworker relations, decreased work productivity, depression, threats, verbal abuse and references to weaponry (Romano et al. 2011). As with school violence, it must be stressed that no single behavior should be taken to signal impending violence; a cluster of behaviors, however, might suggest increased vigilance is warranted. The perpetrators are frequently loners with poor social skills, often obsessed with violence and weapons. The targets include authority figures and peers who are in conflict with the perpetrators. The perpetrators often bring an arsenal of weapons and kill all who get in their way. The common motive is revenge, believing they have been treated unjustly. Many are suicidal and feel they have nothing left to lose.

> As with school violence, workplace violence rarely occurs without warning. Similarities between school and workplace violence include the perpetrators' profiles, the targets, the means, and the motivation.

Precipitating events for workplace violence might include problems at home, use of drugs or alcohol, missed promotions, and terminations.

The Police Response

Although no two incidents of workplace violence are exactly the same, a general multipronged approach of prevention and control is used as a starting point for most cases. Part of an emergency preparedness effort should include steps to make blueprints or floor plans of the premises available to law enforcement, should an episode of workplace violence turn into a barricaded subject incident, one where hostages are involved, or an active-shooter situation.

Officers can work with a company's crisis response team to train staff in how to detect signs of violence and procedures for reporting them to the threat management team. Prescreening programs are also strongly recommended. Because workplace violence can strike anywhere, thorough background checks are a first line of defense.

Other preventive measures include a no-weapons policy, drug and alcohol testing, and alternative dispute resolution (ADR) programs. Access control is another area businesses may consider when addressing the issue of workplace violence. Some companies have developed scripts and step-by-step instructions for on-site security personnel for managing violent employees and visitors, including how to summon and advise law enforcement. In cases where an abuser enters the workplace to victimize an employee, security or another member of the crisis management team must call police immediately.

If prevention efforts fall short and a "flash point" occurs—the moment when an intense episode of workplace violence erupts—employees must be prepared to react quickly for their own safety and survival, as research shows many of these situations last only a few terrifying minutes and are over before law enforcement arrives (Romano et al. 2011). In taking a community policing approach to the problem of workplace violence, officers may also educate and inform local businesses of resources available to help employees who are victims of domestic violence.

PROBLEM-ORIENTED POLICING AND VIOLENCE

The Urban High School Disorder Reduction Project in Dayton, Ohio, was one of the 2011 Herman Goldstein Award finalists for excellence in problem-oriented policing.

For the past 10 years, Belmont High School, an urban high school located in southeast Dayton, had been the number-one violent crime location in the city and diminished the Dayton Police Department's capacity to answer calls for service in other areas of the district. Negative network and print media coverage highlighted problems. As a result, the Dayton Police Department created a partnership with Dayton Public Schools and the Montgomery County Juvenile Court to focus on high-rate offenders. Police worked in collaboration with Belmont High School staff and, as a result of their efforts, reduced crimes significantly at the school and surrounding neighborhoods. Neither extra staffing nor overtime was used by the Dayton Police Department for this project.

Scanning

In November 2008, the Dayton Police Department assigned a new commander to its 2nd District. At the time, 2nd District was responsible for approximately 59,000 citizens and more than 46,000 calls for service per year. While preparing for a monthly status meeting in December 2008, Belmont High School was identified as using a large portion of police resources, such as calls for service and numbers of crimes in and around the area of the high school. This prompted an investigation into the underlying cause of calls and crimes in and around the high school. In addition, residential neighbor complaints and complaints from the Belmont Business Association supported initial data suggesting the problem was growing beyond the school grounds.

From September 8 through April 4 of the 2008–2009 school year, Belmont High School registered nearly twice the number of calls for service (98) as the next highest urban high school in the same school district and almost half of all calls for service at all five of the high schools in the district (203). Of arrests made at all of the high schools, Belmont High School accounted for two-thirds of the total (33 arrests out of 50 arrests for all schools). The highest call categories were assaults, drug activity, disturbances/disorderly juveniles, and threats. High-frequency arrest categories included assault, possession of drugs, and robbery.

Analysis

The problem was statistically evaluated through standard crime analysis, including a review and comparison of calls for service, reported crimes, and arrests. An intuitive analysis was conducted by meeting with patrol officers to collect more background information on the nature of the problem and specific incident stories. Additionally, meetings were held with the former and current principals of Belmont High School, Dayton Public Schools security, and Dayton Police crime analysts to examine the impact of crime and disorder on academic performance and quality-of-life issues in the student population.

Many factors could have played a part in the problem. The City of Dayton has been experiencing a very long and sustained economic downturn. A dwindling tax base coupled with population loss has manifested into a host of economic and social problems affecting nearly every aspect of the inner-city environment. Subsequent to classic inner-city issues such as urban blight and staffing cuts, Belmont High School's environment began to slowly mirror societal problems. Overcoming larger societal issues by addressing specific identifiable problems in and around the high school was the challenge.

Although 45 violent crimes occurred in the 2008–2009 school year, a more in-depth analysis showed the problem actually began in the year 2001 and appears to have grown slowly in intensity and frequency, affecting many different groups. The participants were identified as offenders of various types, victims, students, Dayton Public Schools as an organization and as individual employees, the Dayton Police Department, neighbors, and businesses. Offender types ranged from low level disorderly behavior to opportunistic misdemeanor crimes to violent felonies. Interviews with school officials revealed that student and teacher/staff victims were motivated by basic survival. They simply wanted to endure the school day without repeat victimization by school bullies and criminal behavior. With a focus on basic survival, they were distracted from attempting or achieving academic excellence. The academic harms affected the offenders and victims, as well as the bystander students, teachers, and the school district as a whole.

Before the problem-solving project, crime and disorder at the school was addressed with traditional policing methods. Officers responded to calls, which were treated as isolated incidents. Where appropriate, crime reports were completed, citations were issued, and arrests were made. The result of those responses was an increase in calls, crimes, citations, and arrests. The traditional policing response provided short-term solutions to immediate problems, which were actually symptoms of the larger underlying issues. But the root causes of disorder and crime were not treated, so responding to the symptoms failed to improve the overall and growing problem.

The intuitive analysis revealed significant factors in the causes and underlying conditions precipitating the problem. The assignment of classrooms inside the school building was not organized in a manner that was conducive to order; rather, it contributed to the disorder. Students were running from one end of the building to the opposite end between classes. This led to collisions between students and confrontations between students of different age groups and academic classes. The unnecessary interactions led to many of the assaults and robberies. Students were not always monitored after school as they left the building and walked to public bus stops and nearby alleys. They enjoyed relative anonymity because no responsible stakeholders were there to identify them and correct or witness their behavior.

The nature of the problem was largely a place management issue. Therefore, the best opportunity to manage the problem was to manage the place. In studying Belmont's incidents, certain behaviors were found to be common to numerous incidents; assaults made up 78% of violent crimes. Offenders can sometimes be controlled by handlers. In this case, handlers could be identified as parents, teachers, administrators, and even the juvenile court system with its vast array of services including holding parents accountable for their children's behavior.

Hot spots of activity were identified as alleyways, bus stops, bathrooms, and even the hallways. Addressing such a diverse area required the combined approach of the Dayton Police Department and Dayton Public Schools. One of the problems was identified as bus stops and the transportation of students, so Regional Transit Authority (RTA) was contacted early on in the analysis phase.

A large majority of the offenders were juveniles, so the input and guidance of the Common Pleas Court, Juvenile Division, of Montgomery County, was quickly sought. The assessment of offenders and their handlers referred to the Juvenile Division was an extremely important component of the intervention. Some of the goals of the Juvenile Court System—such as holding accountable those who fail to meet their obligations as parents, guardians, or custodians—fit well with holistic approach in addressing the "handler/offender" portion of the crime triangle.

The juvenile court's abilities in assessing a myriad of issues such as mental health, alcohol, and drugs, coupled with identifying abused, dependent, and neglected children, was beneficial to short- and long-term intervention for troubled students and their families. The juvenile court was a willing and sympathetic partner to the cause and provided a breakdown totaling 178 juveniles, 262 cases, and 306 referrals for all Belmont High School students for the school year 2008–2009. These numbers were used as one of the benchmarks in the assessment phase.

Response

The primary project goals were to reduce crime and disorder in and around the school while improving quality of life for the students, staff, neighborhood, and businesses and to improve the academic environment. The corresponding measurable objectives were a decrease in calls for service, decrease in reported crimes, decrease in juvenile arrests, improvement in academic standings, and improvement in grade-to-grade promotion rates for Belmont High School.

The available resources to help solve the problem were existing patrol officers assigned to the affected patrol district, Dayton Public Schools management, Belmont High School staff, and the Montgomery County Juvenile Court. Additionally, alternative schools were offered to some troubled students who had been identified as possessing special skills or interests. Furthermore, local business leaders pushed for culture change in the school and supported project efforts by both the school and the police department.

Before implementing the response plan, the project committee and a police lieutenant held meetings with all stakeholders and continuously communicated with project partners. The lieutenant conducted extensive follow-up meetings with all partners to review the plan and ensure every member was engaged and committed to the plan, goals, and objectives. Only one major difficulty was encountered in response implementation and that was to elicit a complete and total agreement among the stakeholders that the problem was so large that it had to be addressed from multiple angles. From the perspective of the police department, the school, and the community, doing nothing or maintaining the status quo was ethically and morally unacceptable.

Ultimately, the project committee and stakeholders agreed on the following strategy:

	Key Finding	Resolution Strategy
1.	Increasing number of calls for service in and around Belmont resulting in numerous issues and affecting numerous groups	Meetings and continuous communication with all community partners
2.	Small number of students were influencing or directly causing large number of crimes, especially assaults	Identify students for special intervention who were responsible for crime and disorder through arrest records
3.	Unnecessary interaction among students between classes was causing assaults and additional crimes	Reassign classrooms to group students by grade level as much as possible within the school building
4.	Many problem students were juveniles	Develop vertical prosecution/special response from Juvenile Court and Juvenile Division prosecutors to emphasize a no-tolerance policy for violations and crimes committed on and around school property while making appropriate referrals and addressing individual needs
5.	Outside of class, students had insufficient supervision	Assign school staff members to monitor the lunch period as well as the school grounds and nearby hot spots (routes to bus stops) after school
6.	The problem was not isolated to just school grounds, but extended to nearby student bus stops	Assign patrol officers to assist with monitoring hot spots and address violations in 2-week periods until order is restored (10 weeks—no overtime used)
7.	Vague rules allowed students to find excuses for bad behavior	Remove excuses by establishing clear rules for student behavior in and around the school
8.	There was minimal enforcement of rules once violated	Reinforce rules by making arrests for criminal activity, issuing citations for disorder violations, and subjecting students off school grounds to discipline

Source: "The Urban High School Disorder Reduction Project." Dayton, OH: Dayton Police Department, 2011. Retrieved March 10, 2012 from http://www.popcenter.org/library/awards/goldstein/2011/11-40(F).pdf

Assessment

The first preliminary assessment after response implementation (August 2009) showed a significant improvement of the problem. The method of evaluation was primarily statistical analysis of calls for service and crimes in a multiyear comparison. The evaluation was conducted by Dayton Police Department crime analysts, Lieutenant Williams, and the crime prevention officer.

Dayton Public Schools and Belmont High School offered internal data that accurately reflected the incremental improvements necessary to saving the whole school, specifically promotion rates, or the numbers of students who graduate from one class to the next each year. They reported a 54% increase in the 9th-grade promotion rate and a 38% increase in the 10th-grade promotion rate from 2008 to 2011. In addition, the number of 11th-grade students who took the ACT for college admission increased from 8% in 2008–2009 to 80% in 2010–2011.

Juvenile courts statistics showed a massive drop in numbers, cases, and referrals of Belmont High School students yearly based by school years 2008–2009, 2009–2010, and 2010–2011. This was an expected positive result based on the intervention of the Dayton Police and Belmont High School. Additional results of the project, comparing 2008–2009 and 2009–2010 school years were the following:

- ▶ Crimes at Belmont dropped from 66 to 16, a 76% decrease.
- ▶ Crimes around Belmont dropped from 90 to 21, a 77% decrease.
- ▶ Simple assaults at Belmont dropped from 38 to 2, a 95% decrease.
- ▶ For the entire calendar year, crimes around Belmont averaged 18 crimes per quarter in 2009 versus only 8 crimes per quarter in 2010.

All the response goals were accomplished, and in addition, there was one unanticipated secondary accomplishment. Nearly all of the displaced students returned to Belmont High School, and since their return, there has been no noticeable increase in crime or disorder. One of the students who was removed for bad behavior and low academic performance was transferred to an alternative trade and technology school. That student, identified at Belmont as a poor performer with little chance of success, graduated from the new school and was the valedictorian of her class.

The positive results of the project led to the National Education Association visiting Belmont High School to study its restructured learning environment for possible use or replication in other school districts or communities. With the continued efforts of the Dayton Police Department and Dayton Public Schools, the police and school officials believe the significant reductions can be maintained and replicated to ensure the safety of the schools.

SUMMARY

Wives, husbands, significant others, children, and elders—in fact, anyone within a family unit—may be at risk of becoming a victim of domestic violence. Police officers responding to a domestic violence call are responsible for investigating it thoroughly as an assault and for making an arrest if probable cause exists. Responding to a domestic violence call is hazardous, but not as hazardous as is often thought. In the Minneapolis experiment, police officers responding to domestic violence calls found that arrest was clearly more effective in reducing future violence than was advice or sending the suspect away. *Thurman v. City of Torrington* (1984) established that domestic violence is an assault rather than simply a family affair. Officers and departments can be sued for "failure to protect."

School violence is of growing concern to law enforcement and almost never occurs without warning. An effective three-pronged approach to school security encompasses crisis planning, security technology, and school/law enforcement/community partnerships. Some schools have adopted controversial measures to prevent school violence, including zero-tolerance policies and school security procedures known as *lockdowns.*

As with school violence, workplace violence rarely occurs without warning. Similarities between school and workplace violence include the perpetrators' profiles, the targets, the means, and the motivation.

APPLICATION

With the addition of several new elderly care facilities and homes in your community, you have noticed an increase in elderly related crimes, a crime that has begun to rapidly increase in other jurisdictions as well. Deputies within your agency are not yet well experienced in dealing with these incidents, including the investigation that is required of these cases. As a supervisor, your sheriff has approached you and requested that you draft a policy on dealing with elder abuse in your community. This policy should have guidelines that the deputies responding to these types of incidents can reference. In addition to the policy, you are also tasked with implementing elder abuse training for your deputies. Detail how you would train your deputies and what sources you would use.

INSTRUCTIONS

Write a policy for your sheriff's office detailing deputies' response to elder abuse crimes. The policy should contain the needs statement first. It should also include procedures for domestic violence, resources, and referrals to social services and related agencies. The statement should include the sheriff's office's expectations of deputies in dealing with these types of calls. This policy should also include special needs and considerations toward this demographic in the community.

The training outline should include a goals statement. It should also include what topics and issues should be covered in the training to make it successful for both the elderly community and the sheriff's deputies.

EXERCISES IN CRITICAL THINKING

A. On November 22, Officers David Miller and Peter Kelly were called to investigate a disturbance of the peace at 1131 Selby Avenue, St. Paul, Minnesota, reported by Jeanne McDowell, a neighbor. In the past month, several domestic disturbances had been reported and investigated at this address, which officers knew was the residence of Eddie and Donna Konkler.

While approaching 1131 Selby, the officers heard a loud male voice shouting obscenities, the sound of breaking glass, two loud thumps, and the muffled sounds of children crying. Officer Miller knocked loudly on the door and called out to Eddie, who opened the door. He held a revolver in his right hand, and his breath smelled of an alcoholic beverage. Donna was sitting on the floor leaning against a wall. She had a bloody nose and several red marks on her face. Broken glass was scattered around the room.

Officer Miller was successful in talking Eddie into relinquishing the revolver and in quieting him, but for 15 minutes, Eddie and Donna continued shouting and cursing at each other and at the officers. During this time, Officer Kelly assisted Donna in stopping the bleeding, and she became subdued. Eddie continued his verbal abuse, so the officers requested that Eddie leave the house until he became calm. Eddie then told the police he was sorry and would not cause any more trouble. The officers gave suggestions for possible agencies that could help and suggested specific places where Donna could receive assistance if future repetitions of abuse were to occur.

1. What mistake did Officers Miller and Kelly make?

   a. Because of the cold weather in Minnesota, Eddie should not be removed from his residence; a firm warning and threat of arrest would be sufficient.

   b. Police should not approach a domestic disturbance by letting an abusive person know who they are. The abuser should not be given a chance to then draw a dangerous weapon.

   c. Police should not allow the parties to refuse to talk to one another. Police should make the two stop fighting and shouting, and then insist that they talk and think about their situation so that mediation can bring about a solution to their problem.

  d. Repeated domestic abuse and an assault involving the display of a dangerous weapon justifies an arrest for second-degree assault.

  e. The officers should issue a ticket for disturbing the peace, but cases of domestic problems do not involve an arrest for criminal sexual conduct, kidnapping, terroristic threats, or second-degree assault.

B. William Mosby, age 34, had known the mother and family of N.D., age 7, for seven years. Immediately before the events in question, Mosby had lived with N.D.'s family for three weeks. At the end of the third week, N.D.'s mother gave permission for N.D. to go grocery shopping with Mosby while she went to work.

After going to the cleaners, grocery store, and liquor store, Mosby took N.D. back to the apartment building. There, Mosby had N.D. scrub a shower stall. He gave her a robe to change into, saying he would wash her clothes with his laundry. N.D. reported that Mosby, who had been drinking beer, had N.D. sit on his lap. N.D. reported that Mosby said, "I want to have a baby by you." But N.D. said she was not ready for that. After taking a shower, Mosby came and stood naked in front of N.D. He then put on some boxer shorts, sat on the bed, and asked N.D. to comb his hair. Mosby then told her to lie down and asked if she "ever had a dicky before." He then put his finger in her vagina and touched her chest. N.D. began crying, and Mosby slapped her, telling her to shut up, and tried to get the robe off. When she ran to unlock the door, Mosby told her to lock the door, or he was going to beat her. However, N.D. unlocked the door and ran screaming to the caretaker's apartment.

The caretaker testified that Mosby, wearing only boxer shorts, came running after N.D. and asked the caretaker if he believed N.D. N.D. told the caretaker to look at her, opened the robe, and said, "Look at what I've got on." Mosby kept closing the door to the caretaker's apartment, and the caretaker kept opening it. A next-door tenant came and said she had called the police. Mosby looked excited, jumped up, and left the apartment building. The next-door tenant took N.D. to the tenant's apartment. N.D. threw up while there. The police let N.D. go home without being given a medical examination.

1. What is the responsibility of the police who arrive on the scene?

   a. Having made sure that physical violence has ceased, the police are responsible to advise the mother on her rights and responsibilities.

   b. Police should require the caretaker to notify them if Mosby returns and again causes trouble.

   c. Police must interview all witnesses, determine if there is a substantial basis for finding probable cause for criminal sexual conduct, procure an arrest warrant, and go out to search for Mosby.

   d. As no probable cause for arrest exists, mediate so that emotions can calm down, and help the mother and N.D. start talking about their situation by suggesting possible solutions and sources of assistance.

   e. Instead of letting N.D. go home without being given a medical examination, medical assistance should be sought.

2. Why are cases of domestic violence or criminal sexual conduct difficult to prosecute?

   a. Evidence is usually insufficient to establish beyond a reasonable doubt that one is guilty of domestic violence or criminal sexual conduct in either the first or second degree.

   b. Testimony is insufficient to establish sexual penetration.

   c. Victims have tendencies, because of emotional trauma, to fabricate charges resulting in evidence of dubious credibility that, upon close examination, is filled with discrepancies.

   d. Victims are fearful of future retaliation and continue to hope the offender will change his ways.

   e. Adult males are more believable than children or women.

3. If N.D.'s mother obtains an order for protection (OFP),

   a. The police can arrest Mosby even if he had done nothing to N.D. or her mother *if* he comes to their home after having been ordered to stay away, and N.D.'s mother calls the police.

b. Mosby can have no further contact with the victim at her home but can make contact only on neutral ground.

c. Police can and should make an arrest only if additional assault or threat of bodily harm is made.

d. A police officer will be assigned to protect N.D. for 24 hours.

e. It will be voided if N.D.'s mother lets the abuser into her home or allows visitation with her children.

DISCUSSION QUESTIONS

1. Before reading this chapter, did you know about the extent of domestic violence? If yes, what have you read, seen, or known about the problem?

2. Do you think parents have the right to discipline their teenage children? What do you think about hitting, slapping, yelling, restricting youths to their rooms, or imposing monetary penalties on dependent adolescent children?

3. Much controversy exists in the schools regarding punishing children through the use of physical force. What is your position on allowing school officials to use physical force against students?

4. Do you think zero-tolerance policies in schools have gone too far? Why or why not?

5. Why should law enforcement be knowledgeable about workplace violence?

6. What has been your experience with bullying?

7. Does your local police department have an SRO? If so, in what schools does the officer work, and what are some of the typical functions they perform within those schools?

GALE EMERGENCY SERVICES DATABASE ASSIGNMENTS

▶ Use the Gale Emergency Services database to help answer the Discussion Questions as appropriate.

▶ Use the Gale Emergency Services database to search one of these topics for an article to review: *stalking psychology*, *intimate partner violence*, *elder abuse*, *workplace violence*, *school shootings*, *bullying*. Be prepared to share and discuss your outline with the class.

▶ Use the Gale Emergency Services database to read and outline one of the following articles:

- "The School Shooter: One Community's Experience" by William P. Heck
- "Addressing School Violence: Prevention, Planning and Practice" by Francis Q. Hoang
- "Safe Harbor" by Steven C. Bahls and Jane Easter Bahls

- "Murder at Work" by Jane McDonald
- "Nonfatal Workplace Violence Risk Factors: Data from a Police Contact Sample" by Mario J. Scalora, David O'Neil Washington, Thomas Casady, and Sarah P. Newell
- "Intimate Partner Violence in Pregnancy" by Tracey Fox-Bartels
- "A Study on Cyberstalking: Understanding Investigative Hurdles" by Robert D'Ovidio and James Doyle
- "Stalking-Investigation Strategies" by George E. Wattendorf
- "Stalking the Stalker: A Profile of Offenders" by Robert A. Wood and Nona L. Wood
- "Law Enforcement and the Elderly: A Concern for the 21st Century" by Lamar Jordan

REFERENCES

Acierno, Ron, Melba Hernandiz-Tejeda, Wendy Muzzy, and Kenneth Steve. 2009 (March). *The National Elder Mistreatment Study.* Washington, DC: National Institute of Justice, unpublished study. (NCJ 226456)

Albrecht, Leslie. 2008. "Elder Abuse Investigations: Police Response to Abuse, Neglect, Theft and Scams." *Law Officer Magazine* (April): 44–46.

Baum, Katrina, Shannan Catalano, Michael Rand, and Kristina Rose. 2009 (January). *Stalking Victimization in the United States (NCVS).* Washington, DC: Bureau of Justice Statistics Special Report. (NCJ 224527)

Beres, Judith. 2008. "Ensuring a Safe School Environment." *Community Policing Dispatch* 1 (8, August). http://cops. usdoj.gov/html/dispatch/August_2008/school_safety. htm.

Berson, Sarah B. 2010. "Prosecuting Elder Abuse Cases." *NIJ Journal* 265 (April): 8–9.

Booth, Brandi, Vincent B. Van Hasselt, and Gregory M. Vecchi. 2011. "Addressing School Violence." *FBI Law Enforcement Bulletin* (May): 1–9.

Bulman, Philip. 2010. "Elder Abuse Emerges from the Shadows of Public Consciousness." *NIJ Journal* 265 (April): 4–7.

Carter, Lucy Salcido. 2010. *Batterer Intervention: Doing the Work and Measuring the Progress. A Report on the December 2009 Experts Roundtable.* San Francisco, CA: Family Violence Prevention Fund.

Crime in the United States 2010. 2010. Washington, DC: Federal Bureau of Investigation. Accessed March 5, 2012. http:// www.fbi.gov/about-us/cjis/ucr/crime-in-the-u.s/2010/ crime-in-the-u.s.-2010.

Domestic Violence by Police Officers: A Policy of the IACP Police Response to Violence against Women Project. 2003 (July). Arlington, VA: International Association of Chiefs of Police. Accessed March 5, 2012. http://www.theiacp.org/ LinkClick.aspx?fileticket=p3MQ8yU3EZY%3d&tabid=87.

"Domestic Violence Facts." 2007 (July). Washington, DC: National Coalition against Domestic Violence. Accessed March 5, 2012. http://www.ncadv.org/files/Domestic ViolenceFactSheet(National).pdf.

Felson, Richard B., and Kelsea Jo Lane. 2010. "Does Violence Involving Women and Intimate Partners Have a Special Etiology?" *Criminology* 48(1): 321–338.

Gallo, Gina. 2004 (June). "Airing Law Enforcement's Dirty Laundry." *Law Enforcement Technology* 31(6): 132–137.

Garner, Joel H., and Christopher D. Maxwell. 2010 (September). *The Crime Control Effects of Criminal Sanctions for Intimate Partner Violence.* Washington, DC: National Institute of Justice (unpublished report). (NCJ 236959)

Golden, Jeffrey S. 2004. "De-Escalating Juvenile Aggression." *The Police Chief* (May): 30–34.

Guide for Preventing and Responding to School Violence. 2nd ed. 2009. Alexandria, VA: International Association of Chiefs of Police.

Harrell, Erika. 2011 (March). *Workplace Violence, 1993–2009.* Washington, DC: Bureau of Justice Statistics, Special Report. (NCJ 233231)

Hill, Rodney. 2008. "Domestic Violence and the Reluctant Victim: Prosecuting without the Victim's Cooperation." *Subject to Debate* (March): 3, 6.

Hirschel, David. 2008 (July). *Domestic Violence Cases: What Research Shows about Arrest and Dual Arrest Rates.* Washington, DC: U.S. Department of Justice. (NCJ 222679)

Hirschel, David. 2009 (June). *Making Arrests in Domestic Violence Cases: What Police Should Know.* Washington, DC: National Institute of Justice. (NCJ 225458)

Howell, Ed. L., Paul Morin, Paul Cell, Maureen S. Rush, and Vicky M. Stormo. 2008. "College and University Policing." *The Police Chief* (March): 20–30, 33.

"Intimate Partner Violence: Definitions." 2010 (September 20). Atlanta, GA: Centers for Disease Control and Prevention. Accessed March 5, 2012. http://www.cdc. gov/ViolencePrevention/intimatepartnerviolence/ definitions.html.

Jackson, Shelly, Lynette Feder, David R. Forde, Robert C. Davis, Christopher D. Maxwell, and Bruce G. Taylor. 2003 (June). *Batterer Intervention Programs: Where Do We Go from Here?* Washington, DC: National Institute of Justice. (NCJ 195079)

Klein, Andrew R. 2008 (April). *Practical Implications of Current Domestic Violence Research.* Washington, DC: U.S. Department of Justice.

Labriola, Melissa, Michael Rempel, and Robert C. Davis. 2008. "Do Batterer Programs Reduce Recidivism? Results from a Randomized Trial in the Bronx." *Justice Quarterly* (June): 252–282.

Larson, Randall D. 2008. "The Shooting at Virginia Tech: The View from the 9-1-1 Center." *9-1-1 Magazine* (January/ February) 38–55.

Lesbian, Gay, Bisexual, Transgender, and Queer Domestic Violence in the United States in 2008. 2009. New York: National Coalition of Anti-Violence Programs. Accessed March 6, 2012. http://www.avp.org/documents/2008NC AVPLGBTQDVReportFINAL.pdf.

"Major Types of Elder Abuse." 2011 (September 21). Washington, DC: National Center on Elder Abuse. Accessed March 7, 2012. http://www.ncea.aoa.gov/Main_ Site/FAQ/Basics/Types_Of_Abuse.aspx.

Margolis, Gary J., and Steven J. Healy. 2009. "Campus Threat Assessment Training: A Multidisciplinary Approach." *Community Policing Dispatch* 2 (4, April). http://www. cops.usdoj.gov/html/dispatch/April_2009/campus_ threat.htm.

The Model Stalking Code Revisited: Responding to the New Realities of Stalking. 2007. Washington, DC: National Center for Victims of Crime.

Moffitt, Terrie E., Richard W. Robins, and Avshalom Caspi. 2001. "A Couples Analysis of Partner Abuse with Implications for Abuse-Prevention Policy." *Criminology and Public Policy* (November): 5–36.

Moon, Byongook, Hye-Won Hwang, and John D. McCluskey. 2011. "Causes of School Bullying: Empirical Test of a General Theory of Crime, Differential Association Theory, and General Strain Theory." *Crime and Delinquency* 57 (6, November): 849–877.

National Elder Abuse Incidence Study. 1998 (September). Prepared by the National Center on Elder Abuse at the American Public Human Services Association in collaboration with Westat, Inc. Accessed March 7, 2012. http://aoa.gov/AoARoot/AoA_Programs/Elder_Rights/Elder_Abuse/docs/ABuseReport_Full.pdf.

Noonan, James H., and Malissa C. Vavra. 2007 (October). *The CARD Report—Crime in Schools and Colleges: A Study of Offenders and Arrestees Reported via National Incident-Based Reporting System Data.* Washington, DC: Federal Bureau of Investigation.

Olweus, Dan. 1992. "Bullying among Schoolchildren: Intervention and Prevention." In *Aggression and Violence throughout the Life Span*, edited by Ray D. Peters, Robert J. McMahon, and Vernon L. Quinsey. Newbury Park, CA: Sage.

Payne, Brian K. 2010. "Understanding Elder Sexual Abuse and the Criminal Justice System's Response: Comparison to Elder Physical Abuse." *Justice Quarterly* 27 (2, April): 206–224.

Peak, Kenneth J., Emmanuel P. Barthe, and Adam Barcia. 2008. "Campus Policing in America: A Twenty-Year Perspective." *Police Quarterly* (June) 239–260.

Petrocelli, Joseph. 2007. "Patrol Response to Elder Abuse." *Police* (February): 16–17.

Reaves, Brian. 2008 (February). *Campus Law Enforcement, 2004–2005.* Washington, DC: Bureau of Justice Statistics Special Report. (NCJ 2193740)

Robers, Simone, Jijun Zhang, Jennifer Truman, and Thomas D. Snyder. 2012 (February). *Indicators of School Crime and Safety: 2011.* Washington, DC: National Center for Education Statistics and Bureau of Justice Statistics. (NCES 2012-002/NCJ 236021)

Romano, Stephen J., Micòl E. Levi-Minzi, Eugene A. Rugala, and Vincent B. Van Hasselt. 2011. "Workplace Violence Prevention: Readiness and Response." *FBI Law Enforcement Bulletin* (January): 1–10.

Rudick, Gary D. 2011. "Policing in Public Schools: Beyond the Active Shooter." *FBI Law Enforcement Bulletin* (November): 16–21.

Sampson, Rana. 2007 (January). *Domestic Violence.* Washington, DC: Office of Community Oriented Policing Service, Problem-Oriented Guides for Police, Problem-Specific Guides Series, Guide No. 45.

Sampson, Rana. 2009 (January). *Bullying in Schools.* Washington, DC: Office of Community Oriented Policing Service, Problem-Oriented Guides for Police, Problem-Specific Guides Series Problem-Oriented Guides for Police, Problem-Specific Guides Series, Guide No.12.

Schuster, Beth. 2009. "Preventing, Preparing for Critical Incidents in Schools." *NIJ Journal* (262, March): 42–46. (NCJ 225765)

Sherman, Lawrence W. n.d. "Domestic Violence." In *Crime File Study Guide, National Institute of Justice.* Washington, DC: U.S. Government Printing Office.

Sherman, Lawrence W., and Richard A. Berk. 1984. *The Minneapolis Domestic Violence Experiment.* Washington, DC: Police Foundation Reports.

Smith, Erica L., and Donald J. Farole, Jr. 2009 (October). *Profile of Intimate Partner Violence Cases in Large Urban Counties.* Washington, DC: Bureau of Justice Statistics, State Court Processing Statistics. (NCJ 228193)

Stelter, Leischen. 2011. "Report Finds Workplace Violence Still a High Risk, But Awareness Growing." *Security Director News* (April 26). Accessed March 10, 2012. http://www.security-directornews.com/?p=article&id=sd201104yISdk7.

Stuart-Cassel, Victoria, Ariana Bell, and J. Fred Springer. 2011 (December). *Analysis of State Bullying Laws and Policies.* Washington, DC: U.S. Department of Education, Office of Planning, Evaluation and Policy Development, Policy and Program Studies Service.

Teaster, Pamela B., Tyler A. Dugar, Marta S. Mendiondo, Erin L. Abner, Kara A. Cecil, and Joanne M. Otto. 2006 (February). *The 2004 Survey of State Adult Protective Services: Abuse of Adults 60 Years of Age and Older.* Washington, DC: National Center on Elder Abuse, Administration on Aging. Accessed March 6, 2012. http://www.ncea.aoa.gov/Main_Site/pdf/021406_60PLUS_REPORT.pdf.

Truman, Jennifer L. 2011 (September). *Criminal Victimization, 2010.* Washington, DC: Bureau of Justice Statistics, National Crime Victimization Survey. (NCJ 235508)

2010 Crime Clock. 2010. Washington, DC: Federal Bureau of Investigation. Accessed March 5, 2012. http://www.fbi.gov/about-us/cjis/ucr/crime-in-the.u.s/2010/crime-in-the.u.s.-2010/offenses-known-to-law-enforcement/crime-clock.

"Understanding Intimate Partner Violence." 2012. Atlanta, GA: Centers for Disease Control and Prevention, Fact Sheet.

"Understanding Teen Dating Violence." 2012. Atlanta, GA: Centers for Disease Control and Prevention, Fact Sheet.

Velazquez, Sonia E., Michelle Garcia, and Elizabeth Joyce. 2009. "Mobilizing a Community Response to Stalking: The Philadelphia Story." *The Police Chief* (January): 30–37.

Violence against Women: Identifying Risk Factors. 2004 (November). Washington, DC: NIJ Research in Brief. (NCJ 197019)

Vossekuil, Bryan, Robert Fein, Marisa Reddy, Randy Borum, and William Modzeleski. 2004 (June). *The Final Report and Findings of the Safe School Initiative: Implications for the Prevention of School Attacks in the United*

States. Washington, DC: U.S. Secret Service and the U.S. Department of Education.

Wang, Jing, Ronald J. Iannotti, and Tonja R. Nansel. 2009. "School Bullying among U.S. Adolescents: Physical, Verbal, Relational and Cyber." *Journal of Adolescent Health* 45 (4, October): 368–375.

Ward, Diane, and Janice Lee Mann. 2011 (February). *The Handbook of Campus Safety and Security Reporting.*

Washington, DC: U.S. Department of Education, Office of Postsecondary Education.

Wigglesworth, Aileen, Raciela Austin, Maria Corona, and Laura Mosqueda. 2009 (March). *Bruising as a Forensic Marker of Physical Elder Abuse.* Washington, DC: National Institute of Justice, unpublished report. (NCJ 226457)

CASES CITED

Thurman v. City of Torrington, 595 F. Supp. 1521 (D. Conn. 1984)

United States v. Jones, 565 U.S. _____ (2012)

This available CourseMate has an interactive eBook and interactive learning tools, including flash cards, quizzes, and more. To learn more about this resource and access free demo CourseMate resources, go to www.cengagebrain.com, and search for this book. To access CourseMate materials that you have purchased, go to login.cengagebrain.com.

CHAPTER 8

© AP Images/Mark Schiefelbein

Emergency Situations:
When Disaster Strikes

DO YOU KNOW . . .

- What emergencies a police department should plan for?
- What should be included in a pre-disaster plan?
- What FEMA's mission is?
- What two major difficulties police face during disasters?
- What the "pulse" of the government's response to an emergency is?
- What the four phases of an emergency usually are?
- What posttraumatic stress disorder is and why it is important to police officers who respond to emergency calls?
- Who should conduct a critical-incident stress debriefing and when, and who should attend?
- What emergency conditions require special considerations and contingency planning?
- What the prime consideration in any emergency is?
- What the two post-emergency "killers" may be?
- What other emergencies contingency plans must be made for?
- What the policy of most police departments is regarding the handling of suspected bombs?
- How important the police are during a pandemic?

CAN YOU DEFINE?

critical-incident stress debriefing (CISD)
emergency management
emergency operations center (EOC)
FEMA
hazmat incident
incident management
pandemic
posttraumatic stress disorder (PTSD)
swatting
triage

INTRODUCTION

Emergencies may be natural or caused by people. Natural emergencies include floods, fires, tornados, hurricanes, typhoons, tidal waves, landslides, avalanches, volcanic eruptions, extreme temperatures, blizzards, leaking natural gas, and earthquakes. People-caused emergencies include civil disturbances; industrial and transportation accidents; hazardous-materials spills; water contamination; radiological and arson incidents; explosions; biological, chemical, and nuclear attacks; and terrorist attacks. Emergencies may involve individuals, neighborhoods, communities, counties, or even larger areas.

Historically, many police departments have placed low priority on emergency management, believing that mass disasters were unlikely to happen in their jurisdictions. However, this is no longer realistic. Considering the increasing population and corresponding development of infrastructure along our nation's coastal regions, the negative effects of hurricanes and floods can reach immense proportions with long-lasting impacts. A case in point: The devastation caused in 2005 by Hurricane Katrina is still being felt today in those areas hardest hit. And since the terrorist attacks of September 11, 2001, the United States itself has been forever changed. (Terrorism and homeland security are the focus of Chapter 9.)

This chapter begins by discussing what an agency must do *before* an emergency occurs—construct a pre-disaster plan and give thought to how communication and coordination needs will be met once a disaster develops. Next, the four phases of an emergency are briefly described, and the guidelines for dealing with emergencies are examined. The discussion then focuses on special considerations in dealing with specific kinds of natural and person-made emergencies and with pandemics. The chapter concludes with a brief look at the relationship between emergency situations and community policing.

PRE-DISASTER PLANS

Every police agency should have a carefully formulated, periodically updated plan for responding to an emergency, and that plan should be practiced. In our post–9/11 society, agencies with high-risk terrorist attack targets within their jurisdiction must devise specific emergency action plans (EAPs) for possible incidents at such locations and facilities. Similarly, departments in regions geographically vulnerable to certain weather events or natural disasters (hurricanes, tornadoes, earthquakes, tsunamis, avalanches, volcanic eruptions) need to anticipate how they will respond to such events.

 Police departments should have pre-disaster plans for those emergencies likely to occur within their jurisdictions.

Unanticipated emergencies should, however, also be included in a comprehensive pre-disaster plan. For example, blizzard-like conditions can paralyze southern states precisely because such weather is not expected there.

Departments should be mindful that an emergency response, in many cases, is the same or, at the least, involves many overlapping skills and tactics whether the disaster is one brought about by natural forces or one set off by human activity. For example, an assessment of the response to Hurricane Katrina found that the lessons learned could be important in helping law enforcement prepare for future hurricanes and in formulating a response to other natural disasters and possible terrorist strikes, especially those involving weapons of mass destruction (Rojek and Smith 2007).

Federal grants are available to help fund the training and tools needed to properly address emergency response planning in locations that contain high-risk areas. Those departments *not* prepared to handle emergencies may fail to protect property and life and may face expensive, time-consuming lawsuits as well as adverse political decisions.

Pre-disaster plans should include:
- What emergencies to prepare for.
- What needs to be done in advance (supplies on hand, agreements with other agencies, etc.).
- What specific functions must be performed during the emergency and who is responsible for performing them, including outside organizations and agencies that might help.
- How continuity of operations and governance will be maintained.
- How personnel and their families will be protected.
- How to keep the media informed.
- What steps need to be taken to restore order after the emergency is ended.
- How the response is to be evaluated.

A 2006 assessment of the emergency plans of all states and territories of the United States, *Nationwide Plan Review Phase 2*, by the Department of Homeland Security (DHS) found that 59 percent of states and 65 percent of urban areas did not have sufficient continuity of operations (COOP) or continuity of government (COG) plans (Cashen 2008). A COOP "facilitates the performance of essential functions during an emergency situation that disrupts normal operations, and it provides for the resumption of normal operations once the emergency has ended" (Cashen 2008). A COG refers to preserving, maintaining, or reconstituting civil governments' ability to carry out its constitutional responsibilities. However, the more recent 2010 assessment reports significant improvement in the preparedness of states and urban areas and a higher level of confidence that their overall basic emergency operations plans are well suited to meet the challenges presented during a large-scale or catastrophic event: "Since the 2006 Review, participants have worked tirelessly to update and exercise plans. More than 80 percent of states and more than 75 percent of urban areas have updated their basic plans since the last Review. Most important, many of these updates occurred in the last two years. Additionally, nearly 95 percent of all states and urban areas have exercised their basic plans since the 2006 Review" (*Nationwide Plan Review* 2010, iii).

An emergency plan should also identify the levels of emergencies that might occur and the level of response required. Many jurisdictions use a three-level approach, with Level 1 including minor events that can usually be handled by on-duty personnel. A Level 2 event is a moderate-to-severe situation that requires aid from other agencies and perhaps other jurisdictions. A Level 3 event refers to catastrophes in which a state of emergency is proclaimed and county, state, and even federal assistance is requested. In such instances, the National Guard is often called for help.

46.1

CALEA Standard 46.1 states, "The planning function is vital to the success of the critical incident plan. Preparation of a documented incident action plan is one of the first responsibilities of the planning function. This function is also responsible for collecting and evaluating information about the incident, the status of resources and anticipated equipment and manpower needs. The planning function is typically tasked with assembling information on current and alternative strategies, identifying needs for special resources, providing periodic predictions on incident potential, and preparing recommendations for release of resources."

Source: Commission on Accreditation of Law Enforcement Agencies (CALEA). 2012. *Standards for Law Enforcement Agencies.* 5th ed. Fairfax, VA: Author.

The plan should *not* be developed solely by top management, but also by those who would be involved in implementing it, including government officials, fire department personnel, health care personnel, and the like. Jurisdictions may seek assistance in developing their pre-disaster plan from the Federal Emergency Management Agency (FEMA).

The Federal Emergency Management Agency (FEMA)

FEMA

The Federal Emergency Management Agency, a federal agency charged with building and supporting the nation's emergency management system. Its mission is to reduce loss of life and property and protect our nation's critical infrastructure from all types of hazards through a comprehensive, risk-based, emergency management program of mitigation, preparedness, response, and recovery.

The Federal Emergency Management Administration (**FEMA**) was founded in 1979 and charged with building and supporting the nation's emergency management system. By October 8, 2011, FEMA had 7,474 full-time and standby disaster assistance employees available to help after disasters, a sizable increase from the approximately 6,600 employees reported in 2008 ("About FEMA" 2012). FEMA has replaced the American Red Cross as the agency in charge of coordinating the provision of shelter, food, and first aid to disaster victims. This change in the federal emergency plan was partially the result of criticism regarding the lack of cooperation between FEMA and Red Cross leaders after Hurricane Katrina as well as of a new law bolstering FEMA's role in providing emergency housing, human services, case management, and financial help.

The mission of FEMA is to reduce the loss of life and property and protect the nation from all hazards, including natural disasters, acts of terrorism, and other human-made disasters, by leading and supporting the nation in a risk-based, comprehensive emergency management system of preparedness, protection, response, recovery, and mitigation.

On March 1, 2003, FEMA became part of the Department of Homeland Security and, in its most recently published five-year plan, has identified five strategic goals:

1. Lead an integrated approach that strengthens the nation's ability to address disasters, emergencies, and terrorist events.

2. Deliver easily accessible and coordinated assistance for all programs.

3. Provide reliable information at the right time for all users.

4. Invest in people, and have people invest in FEMA, to ensure mission success.

5. Build public trust and confidence through performance and stewardship. (*FEMA Strategic Plan* 2008, iii)

FEMA has published a comprehensive preparedness guide (*Developing and Maintaining Emergency Operations Plans* 2010) to help planners at all levels of government develop and maintain a viable, integrated, and coordinated all-hazards, all-threats emergency plan. Of particular importance to police operations is the National Response Framework (NRF), a guide to how the nation conducts all-hazards incident response:

> The NRF emphasizes the concept of resilient communities. Resiliency begins with prepared individuals and depends on the leadership and engagement of local government, civic leaders, and private sector businesses and organizations. Local police, fire, emergency medical services (EMS), emergency management, public health and medical providers, public works, and other community agencies are often the first to be notified about a threat or hazard or to respond to an incident. These entities should work with individuals, families, and service providers for people with disabilities and others with access and functional needs to enhance their awareness of risk levels and specific threats, develop household emergency plans that include household pets and service animals, and prepare emergency supply kits. (*Developing and Maintaining Emergency Operations Plans* 2010, 2–3)[1]

The NRF has designated 15 Emergency Support Functions (ESFs) that communities need to address in their disaster plans, and the police response intersects with many, if not most, of these functions:

ESF #1: Transportation

ESF #2: Communication

ESF #3: Public works and engineering

ESF #4: Firefighting

ESF #5: Emergency management

ESF #6: Mass care, emergency assistance, housing, and human services

ESF #7: Logistics management and resource support

ESF #8: Public health and medical services

ESF #9: Search and rescue

---

[1]Source: *Developing and Maintaining Emergency Operations Plans: Comprehensive Preparedness Guide (CPG) 101, Version 2.0.* Washington, DC: Department of Homeland Security, Federal Emergency Management Administration, November 2010.

ESF #10: Oil and hazardous materials response

ESF #11: Agriculture and natural resources

ESF #12: Energy

ESF #13: Public safety and security

ESF #14: Long-term community recovery

ESF #15: External affairs

Specific Elements to Consider in an Emergency Response Plan

Among the many issues an agency must give thought to when anticipating an emergency response is how to get large numbers of citizens out of harm's way quickly and safely and how to handle the inevitable media scrutiny.

Planning for Evacuation In any disaster requiring evacuation, traffic control becomes a major challenge. FEMA's *Mass Evacuation Incident Annex* to the NRF provides an overview of functions, agency roles and responsibilities, and overall guidelines for the evacuation of large numbers of people in incidents requiring a coordinated federal response (*Mass Evacuation Incident Annex* 2008, 9):

> State and local law enforcement agencies have primary responsibility for providing for public safety and security during an incident that requires a mass evacuation. During a mass evacuation, State, tribal, and local law enforcement agencies will be conducting operations in accordance with their respective plans and protocols. However, State, tribal, and local public safety and security agencies and private-sector entities could rapidly become overwhelmed and require logistics or operational support from within their States, from other States pursuant to mutual aid and assistance compacts, or from the Federal Government through ESF #13.

> ESF #13 may involve assisting State, tribal, and local governments with the following evacuation-related functions:

> ▶ Security assessments of pre-identified transportation facilities

> ▶ Site security at designated evacuation locations

> ▶ Traffic control and/or transportation security duties

> ▶ Screening of evacuees for prohibited weapons

> ▶ Force protection

> ▶ General planning and technical assistance[2]

Planning to Interact with the Media "During a critical incident requiring police action, one of the last things the police think about is public perception. All critical incidents have the potential to be a world-watched event, forcing us to have to rely on the media to help shape the public's perception

---

[2]Source: *Developing and Maintaining Emergency Operations Plans: Comprehensive Preparedness Guide (CPG) 101, Version 2.0.* Washington, DC: Department of Homeland Security, Federal Emergency Management Administration, November 2010.

of our actions. Unfortunately in the media world, perception equals reality" (Donlon-Cotton 2007, 24).

During an incident such as a natural disaster, the media will be concerned with the quality of the officers' immediate and initial actions. In most disasters, the media are not officially notified and have to "go on the prowl for information. This results in automatically placing the law enforcement agency on the defensive and immediately sets the stage for a media disaster" (Donlon-Cotton 2007, 24). First responders need to respond to the media during such incidents rather than referring them to someone else or saying they can't take time to talk. Donlon-Cotton suggests responses such as, "The rescue effort is going well, and all officers are doing their best. Our primary concern is making sure everyone is safe, and then we'll focus on what comes next."

Consider the example of the crash of US Air flight 1549 into the Hudson River on January 15, 2009, and the way Doug Parker, the company's chief executive officer (CEO), handled the media relations portion of that crisis[3] (Rosenthal 2009, 6):

▶ Rule #1: Deal with the media right now! Never ignore the media or refuse any comment because you don't have all the facts. Do that and you lose control of your story and lose essential credibility as well. You should deliver your first statement to the media within two hours after the crisis hits, and that's exactly what US Airways' Parker did.

▶ Rule #2: Be empathetic. Express your concern about the incident, your caring for the victims/citizens/community, and your commitment to making things right. Parker expressed his concern for the passengers and announced the airline had already set up a response team and a hotline to help them and their families.

▶ Rule #3: Always deal in facts and information. Tell what you know, not what you think you know … Give the media what you can early on; then follow up with frequent updates. Never speculate. Parker not only refused to speculate, in his first statement he urged the media to avoid speculation, too.

Police and media representatives should meet and draw up agreements that respect the presses' First Amendment right to freedom of the press, but also the Sixth Amendment rights of others to privacy and law enforcement's need for safety and successful management of critical incidents. Effective message management must be based on mutual trust that can be built over time for the price of a cup of coffee, an occasional lunch, and visits to the local media offices. But remember, it is in the department's best interest to work *with* the media. If you do not provide them with something, they will fill in the gaps themselves. If dealt with correctly, the media can be a great asset to the police.

COMMUNICATION AND COORDINATION DURING AN EMERGENCY

Whether by voice or through data transmissions, well-planned interoperable communications can mean the difference between life and death for citizens and first responders, as discussed in Chapter 2. Yet, unfortunately, many

---

[3]Reprinted with permission of author Rick Rosenthal, President, RAR Communications, Inc.

departments fail to plan ahead how they will communicate and coordinate with other responding agencies, adding unnecessary operational challenges to their response efforts when emergency situations arise in their jurisdictions.

> Lack of communication and coordination are the major problems during disasters.

The National Incident Management System (NIMS)

A key to effective communication and coordination is found in the National Incident Management System (NIMS), which is a comprehensive, national approach to incident management developed by the DHS that applies at all jurisdictional levels and across functional disciplines:

> Incidents typically begin and end locally, and are managed on a daily basis at the lowest possible geographical, organizational, and jurisdictional level. However, there are instances in which successful incident management operations depend on the involvement of multiple jurisdictions, levels of government, functional agencies, and/or emergency responder disciplines. These instances require effective and efficient coordination across this broad spectrum of organizations and activities.

NIMS uses a systematic approach to integrate the best existing processes and methods into a unified national framework for incident management. **Incident management** refers to how incidents are managed across all homeland security activities, including prevention, protection, response, mitigation, and recovery.

This framework forms the basis for interoperability and compatibility that will, in turn, enable a diverse set of public and private organizations to conduct well-integrated and effective emergency management and incident response operations. **Emergency management** is the coordination and integration of all activities necessary to build, sustain, and improve the capability to prepare for, protect against, respond to, recover from, or mitigate threatened or actual natural disasters, acts of terrorism, or other human-made disasters [bold added]. (*National Incident Management System* 2008, 5)[4]

At the heart of NIMS is the Incident Command System (ICS), which is a vital tool in designating clear roles and responsibilities for any type of disaster.

incident management

Refers to how incidents are managed across all homeland security activities, including prevention, protection, response, mitigation, and recovery.

emergency management

The coordination and integration of all activities necessary to build, sustain, and improve the capability to prepare for, protect against, respond to, recover from, or mitigate against threatened or actual natural disasters, acts of terrorism, or other human-made disasters.

---

[4]Source: *National Incident Management System*. Washington, DC: Department of Homeland Security, Federal Emergency Management Agency (December 2008). (FEMA Publication P-501) Accessed March 5, 2012. http://www.fema.gov/pdf/emergency/nims/NIMS_core.pdf

46.1 | **CALEA Standard 46.1**, the critical incident section, follows the NIMS, noting, "The Incident Command System (ICS) has proven very effective in federal and fire services emergencies over the past two decades. This system permits a clear point of control and can be expanded or contracted with ease to escalating or diminishing situations.... With responders using a common language and standardized procedures, they will all share a common focus, and will be able to place full emphasis on incident management when a critical incident occurs."

Source: Commission on Accreditation of Law Enforcement Agencies (CALEA). 2012. *Standards for Law Enforcement Agencies.* 5th ed. Fairfax, VA: Author.

Specific multilevel benefits of NIMS include a more efficient, effective incident response through the ICS, the ability to collect and share information during an incident via a multiagency coordination systems, and the capability to notify the public before and during an incident through a public information system. Currently FEMA and the Federal Communications Commission (FCC) jointly administer a nationwide emergency alert system (EAS) involving radio and television broadcasters, cable, satellite, and wire line providers across the country. The system underwent its first nationwide test in November 2011 to assess its readiness and effectiveness in the event the president needs to address the public during a time of extreme national emergency. Although successful in many regards, the test revealed several technical areas in need of improvement. FEMA is also developing the Integrated Public Alert and Warning System (IPAWS) to incorporate leading-edge technologies that allow it to relay alerts to a wider variety of communications devices, such as Internet Protocol (IP)–enabled communications (Moore 2010).

The Emergency Operations Center (EOC)

A key to effective emergency management is the EOC, which is the "heart and soul of an agency's operations" (Moore 2009, 10).

The **emergency operations center (EOC)**, the location from which personnel operate during a natural disaster or other type of emergency, is the "pulse" of the government's response to an emergency and helps reduce the problems of lack of communication and coordination.

emergency operations center (EOC)

The location from which personnel operate during a natural disaster or other type of emergency.

Whereas an incident command center (ICC) is a physical location that administers the on-scene incident command and the other major incident management functions, an EOC is a physical location positioned separately from the on-scene ICC that supports the on-scene response by providing external coordination and securing of additional resources. Sometimes the incident will dictate the location of the EOC. Often an existing site in a government building works well. Ideally, the center is located close to police, fire, and government officials. Mobile ICCs or EOCs—typically large recreational-type vehicles or buses converted and equipped with the necessary tools and devices—may also be available.

The needs of officers are met by an efficient and effective emergency operations center. Here, officials from various law enforcement agencies work in the New York Police Department Emergency Operations Center preparing for the Republican National Convention held in New York City in August 2004.

© Mary Altaffer/Pool/Reuters/CORBIS

TECHNOLOGY IN POLICING

INCIDENT COMMAND AND EMERGENCY OPERATIONS VEHICLES

In some instances, the incident command or emergency operations may be done remotely. For example, in the event a natural disaster destroys a stationary command center, the EOC may become mobile. In some cases, one vehicle may act as both EOC and ICC.

Portable technology is now enabling almost any vehicle to become a mobile command and operations center. One example is the NOMAD Incident Command Platform: "Cross-breed a Hummer H2 with a top-of-the-line laptop, add a satellite phone, fax machine, digital printer, and broadband Internet access, and you can begin to picture the NOMAD's capabilities and ruggedness. This unit is a shining example of the future of crisis communication equipment for first responders" (Ross 2009, 68). Measuring roughly 22 × 18 × 10 inches and weighing 56 pounds, NOMAD is an expandable kit of critical tools and

technology to support mobile communication needs and can be deployed by a single user in less than 5 minutes. Capabilities and features of the NOMAD include the ability to support hundreds of users over a large geographic area; a combination of technology, durability, and portability that allows it to be deployed to any part of the country in minutes; being small enough and light enough to haul in fire trucks or in the back of police cruisers; a power supply able to run as long as 24 hours of mission support on a single charge; and having passed rigorous field testing (Ross 2009). The NOMAD is currently deployed to every FEMA region across the country and is used in other countries as well. In 2007, NOMADs were deployed to California to help battle the blazing wildfires, and in 2008 NOMADs were used by 17 states across the nation to assist with incident command during other natural disasters.

Dispatchers are key people in the communications center, taking calls and sending officers to respond. One problem they face is a phenomenon called **swatting**, an emerging trend by pranksters involving communication centers in which a false report is filed, via the Internet, to the emergency dispatch center to deploy special weapons and tactics (SWAT) teams to a residence where the occupants are oblivious to the situation (Garrett 2009). The potential for violence, injury, and death is "huge" with such calls, and some suggest the offense not be treated as a prank, a misdemeanor, but rather that perpetrators be charged with filing a false report as well as what they caused SWAT team members to do: assault with a deadly weapon and false imprisonment of the innocent victims (Garrett 2009).

swatting

An emerging trend by pranksters involving communication centers in which a false report is filed, via the Internet, to the emergency dispatch center to deploy SWAT teams to a residence where the occupants are oblivious to the situation.

The Emergency Management Assistance Compact (EMAC)

Jurisdictions may also incorporate into their pre-disaster plans a procedure to request response aid from other states, when the emergency is of such magnitude that it overwhelms local or state resources. The EMAC is a congressionally ratified organization managed by the National Emergency Managers Association (NEMA) to provide form and structure to interstate mutual aid. Whenever there is a governor-declared state of emergency, EMAC facilitates the sending of personnel, equipment, commodities, and other resources from one state or territory to help in another state or territory. For example, following Hurricanes Katrina and Rita, EMAC helped deploy more than 6,880 sheriff's deputies and police officers from 35 states and countless local jurisdictions to those areas in Louisiana and Mississippi needing additional disaster relief resources, which accounted for 35 percent of all deployed resources during those emergency responses ("Tips for Law Enforcement Deployments" n.d.). All 50 states, the District of Columbia, Puerto Rico, the U.S. Virgin Islands, and Guam have enacted legislation to become EMAC members.

Having looked at what a police department needs to do in anticipation of an emergency, consider next the typical phases in which an emergency unfolds.

THE FOUR PHASES OF AN EMERGENCY

Most emergencies happen in four phases: (1) the *warning* period, (2) the *impact* period, (3) the *immediate reaction* after impact, and (4) the period of *delayed response*.

Usually as much *warning* as possible is desirable. Sometimes, however, warnings are impossible, as is the case, for example, with earthquakes and train derailments. In addition, advance warning might have an adverse effect on some individuals, who may panic and become completely helpless, as though the emergency had already occurred. Their panic may spread to others. For example, this reaction sometimes occurs following the posting of a hurricane warning when the eye of the storm is projected to make landfall over a heavily populated area.

During the *impact period*, when the emergency is actually happening, different people will react differently. Many will react with stunned inactivity, a paralysis of sorts, with people unable to act effectively. Others, fueled by adrenaline, may act with determination, purpose, and strength. Some report going "on automatic pilot." The period *immediately following the disaster* is the most crucial from the standpoint of rescue operations. Effective performance can save property and lives. A *delayed response* may occur once the immediate danger is past. Those who were functioning effectively may cease to do so, and vice versa.

GUIDELINES FOR DEALING WITH EMERGENCIES

Every emergency will present a unique challenge to responding officers. Nonetheless, several guidelines can help ensure the most effective response possible at each phase of the disaster.

Before the Emergency

▶ Be prepared. Be proactive. Anticipate the immediate problems and the personnel needed to deal with them.

▶ Identify the equipment and resources required, and make certain they are either available or immediately accessible. To deal with disasters, departments should have, at minimum, lighted traffic batons, barricades, reflective signs for vehicles, safety vests for traffic officers, and special vehicle-mounted lights and sirens. First aid kits, gloves, and blankets are also imperative. It is recommended departments also have ready access to gas masks and hazardous materials (hazmat) suits.

▶ Establish and maintain good relationships with the media. They are among the first on the scene of emergencies and have a job to do. They can be invaluable in getting messages out to the general public and keeping panic to a minimum. They can also be a terrible liability if a good relationship does not exist.

▶ Establish a system so that police officers can know that their own families are safe during an emergency. As discussed previously, first responders must be confident their own families—their first priority—are being taken care of before they can fulfill their sense of duty to other citizens and the community at large.

During the Emergency

▶ Take time to assess the situation. Do not make the situation worse by acting without thinking.

triage

Prioritizing, sorting out by degree of seriousness, as in medical emergencies.

▶ Make saving lives a top priority. Establish a **triage** area where surviving victims can be separated according to the severity of their injuries. Those with critical medical needs should be tended to immediately and, once stabilized, transported to medical facilities. A morgue area for those who have died in the crisis should also be established.

▶ Do not broadcast a general call for help. Carefully but quickly assess what is needed and call for that.

▶ Keep the channels of communication open and the information flowing as required to those who need it.

▶ Keep as many options open as possible. Avoid either/or thinking that limits problem solving.

▶ Do not get sidetracked by personal, individual requests for help but, rather, focus on the big picture, routing individual requests to the appropriate source of assistance.

▶ Accept the fact that the police cannot do everything. The emergency manager must prioritize and delegate responsibilities quickly. Mistakes will probably happen.

▶ Involve key personnel as rapidly as possible. Do not let other agencies shirk their responsibilities.

▶ Keep top city officials fully informed of progress and problems.

▶ Ensure that someone is tending to normal business.

After the Emergency

▶ Get back to "normal" as soon as possible, but understand that sometimes this just does not happen, or does not happen as quickly as desired.

▶ Expect that victims of the disaster or emergency may have very emotional reactions, including posttraumatic stress disorder. This is also true of the officers who have dealt with the disaster or emergency.

▶ Also expect that lawyers will become involved. *Document* everything that was done.

▶ Evaluate the response after the situation has returned to normal. Prepare an after-action report (AAR) detailing what happened, why it happened, and how it can be done better. Look on "mistakes" as the "least effective alternatives" as well as learning opportunities.

▶ Modify emergency-preparedness plans as needed based on what has been learned.

Posttraumatic Stress after Large-Scale Disasters The American Psychological Association defines **posttraumatic stress disorder (PTSD)** as "an anxiety problem that develops in some people after extremely traumatic events, such as combat, crime, an accident or natural disaster" ("Post-Traumatic Stress Disorder" 2012). The symptoms of PTSD include these:

▶ Reexperiencing the event, either while awake or in recurrent dreams

▶ Detachment and lack of involvement, diminished interest in formerly important activities, detachment from other people

▶ At least two other of the following symptoms not present before the event:

- Hyper-alertness
- Sleep disturbance
- Guilt about surviving when others did not

posttraumatic stress disorder (PTSD)

A debilitating stressful reaction to a trauma that may last for months or years; can be experienced by victims and by those who help the victims.

- Memory impairment or trouble concentrating
- Avoiding activities that remind the person of the event

Many disaster victims experience PTSD, but so do many of those involved in helping them, especially if deaths have been particularly gruesome or have involved children. Police officers *are* susceptible to PTSD and should have support groups available to them.

> Posttraumatic stress disorder (PTSD) is a debilitating stressful reaction to a traumatic event; PTSD may last for months or years. It can be experienced by those who help the victims as well as by victims.

Jetmore (2008, 63–64) cautions, "The emotional exhaustion resulting from continuous exposure to stress-related trauma can ultimately cause an officer to change from a positive, service-oriented, care-giving person to one who is uncaring, negative, and callous." Providing for medical care and for psychological care for first responders is a crucial, yet often overlooked, element of an emergency plan (Rojek and Smith 2007). The likelihood that PTSD will occur in responding police officers can be reduced by having contingency plans that require them to mentally rehearse probable disaster situations, thus lowering their anxiety. It can be reduced further by practicing these plans, assigning each officer a specific task, maintaining order during the emergency, requiring that officers get some break periods during the emergency if it lasts longer than 10 hours, and having a thorough debriefing following the emergency.

critical-incident stress debriefing (CISD)

Officers who experience a critical incident, such as a mass disaster or large accident with multiple deaths, are brought together as a group for psychological debriefing soon after the event.

The Critical-Incident Stress Debriefing An important consideration following a disaster is to conduct a **critical-incident stress debriefing (CISD)**, proven to be a powerful tool in preventing posttraumatic stress disorder.

> A critical-incident stress debriefing (CISD) should be conducted by a trained team, which includes a professional mental health practitioner and peer supporters, approximately 24 to 72 hours after the incident, and should be available to all personnel involved in the incident. Individual department policy, however, may dictate whether such a debriefing includes peer support or if it is mandatory versus voluntary.

A CISD conducted before 24 hours has passed is likely to be ineffective because the full impact may not yet be felt. These debriefings should be mandatory to avoid anyone feeling it is not macho to attend. The FEMA search and rescue teams located throughout the country are trained to do debriefings if an agency needs assistance in this area.

Identifying Fatalities A comprehensive disaster plan should include how fatalities will be identified. Help in identifying fatalities is available through the FBI Identification Division's Disaster Squad, which has aided in such disasters as the volcanic eruption of Mount St. Helens, in the 1978 mass murder–suicides at Jonestown, Guyana, and in the 1986 space shuttle explosion. The Disaster Squad also provided assistance during Operation Desert Storm. The squad's free identification services are available 24 hours per day. In addition to cost-free fatality identification services offered by the Disaster Squad, the FBI provides assistance to law enforcement and civic agencies in formulating emergency response plans.

Restoring Order When emergencies have been controlled and their urgency has diminished, police services are still needed. The constant threat of looting and malicious damage will continue until the area again becomes functional and the residents return to their homes or emergency workers are no longer present. When extra police are required following an incident, supervisors should conduct a gradual phase-out rather than allowing an abrupt return to normal duty.

Also, following any emergency situation, there is usually a steady flow of curiosity seekers that will tend to taper off as interest diminishes and the area returns to normal. This process may take several hours, days, or weeks, depending on the emergency's magnitude.

NATURAL DISASTERS

Some emergencies are so severe they are declared disasters. Just as general guidelines can be specified for emergencies, general guidelines and considerations can be made in advance for specific kinds of natural emergencies, thus reducing the loss of property and lives.

> In addition to general pre-disaster plans, contingency plans should be made for such natural disasters as floods, fires, cyclones, earthquakes, and tsunamis. In all such emergencies, saving lives is top priority.

Floods

A flood, although damaging and usually predictable, demands a coordinated response and implementation of a previously thought-out plan. Normally, police will assist residents and merchants in the affected areas to evacuate their homes and their businesses. As soon as a police department receives notice of an impending flood, the regular and reserve officers are usually called to duty. In some instances, they may be put on alert or on standby in case they are needed.

During an evacuation and while the emergency is in progress, the police must seal off the affected area to prevent looting and vandalism. Special passes can be issued to residents who have legitimate business in the area. All others not living or having business in the flood area should be excluded.

Fires

Fires are usually the fire department's primary responsibility, although some police departments have a combined public safety service. Such departments have trained officers to assist firefighters. One police responsibility is to protect firefighters from harassment. Some sections of cities are plagued with spectators who taunt firefighters and try to disrupt firefighting. In these cases, police officers must protect firefighters and also control spectators, protect fire equipment, and regulate traffic drawn to the scene.

When the Bandelier National Monument started a "controlled burn" west of Los Alamos, New Mexico, in 2000, high winds spread the fire eastward, destroying structures in Los Alamos and threatening the Los Alamos National Laboratory. The area's 18,500 residents were evacuated without a single death or serious injury. The police department had long had a plan in place because of the sensitivity of the work at the National Laboratory, which conducts classified nuclear weapons development.

Utility agencies shut off gas and water. A reverse-911 system notified many residents by telephone, delivering instructions on the evacuation. The local radio station switched to 24-hour coverage of the evacuation, and loudspeaker announcements from emergency vehicles reached residents who had not heard the news. To prevent looting, National Guard personnel patrolled the town along with state and local police. In addition, the police held two press briefings a day to accommodate the hundreds of media people on the scene.

Cyclones: Hurricanes and Tornados

In strict meteorological terminology, a cyclone is an area of low atmospheric pressure surrounded by a wind system blowing, in the Northern Hemisphere, in a counterclockwise direction. When this weather system develops over water, it is called a *hurricane* or, in the western Pacific, a *typhoon*. A hurricane is a very strong tropical cyclone involving heavy rains and sustained winds stronger than 74 miles per hour (mph). It may also be accompanied by a strong storm surge, with large waves causing extensive damage to coastal property and near-shore structures.

Cyclones occurring over land are tornados—dark, funnel-shaped clouds containing violently rotating air that twists, rises, and falls and, where it reaches the earth, causes great destruction. A tornado's diameter can range from a few feet to more than a mile, with winds circulating between 200 and 300 mph. The length of a tornado's path on the ground varies from less than a mile to several hundred miles. In an average year in the United States, some 800 tornadoes injure more than a thousand people. Again, preparedness is the key to limiting the amount of destruction. Tornado warning systems are an integral part of preparedness, as is education of the public about steps to take, where to seek shelter, and the like.

Many of the emergencies already discussed may also occur during a hurricane or tornado, including flooding, fires, and explosions, accompanied by looting and vandalism. In addition to the tragic loss of life and damage to property, those responding to the disaster may face communication and mobility problems. Regular phone lines may be down, two-way radio communications may be unavailable because of damaged repeaters, and cellular communications networks may be overwhelmed by ongoing use. Getting around may be difficult because road signs and other landmarks may be gone, street lights may be out, and many roads may be blocked by such obstacles as fallen trees, live utility wire, and other debris. Some low areas may be flooded and impassable. Highways and other main travel arteries may become gridlocked during the evacuation efforts, and debris scattered across roadways may cause numerous flat tires and other traffic mishaps involving citizens and first responders.

Eventually, things will come under control, but time, and perhaps lives, may be saved if a pre-disaster plan is in place. Citizens should be educated about the steps to take, such as evacuating if advised to do so, boarding up windows or closing shutters if not evacuating, and having ample potable water and flashlights or candles available.

In the aftermath of such natural disasters, many departments find their most significant problem is not, as might be expected, the cleanup but rather the quick depletion of their yearly overtime budgets and completion of the massive amount of paperwork required by FEMA so the jurisdiction can be reimbursed for expenses resulting from the disaster.

> Post-emergency "killers" may be overruns in overtime and excessive paperwork.

Earthquakes and Tsunamis

Although floods and hurricanes usually can be predicted, earthquakes strike with no warning. Areas in which earthquakes are likely to occur must have pre-established plans to deal with such emergencies. Included within these plans should be measures to deal with collapsed buildings and bridges, downed power lines, fires, explosions, injuries, and deaths. As in other kinds of emergencies, traffic problems, vandalism, and looting must also be anticipated.

Earthquakes that occur beneath the ocean floor can set off a tsunami, as happened in Japan in March 2011. The initial earthquake caused considerable damage to certain locations in northeastern Japan, but the secondary incident of the tsunami caused widespread devastation and loss of life. As with the tidal surge that can accompany strong hurricanes making landfall at high tide, tsunamis can wreak major havoc in jurisdictions in coastal regions, particularly along the Pacific Ocean. Unlike the tidal surges of hurricanes, however, tsunamis come with relatively little warning, making mass evacuations impractical.

ACCIDENTAL OR INTENTIONAL EMERGENCIES

Jurisdictions must also be prepared for catastrophic accidents and deliberate acts that can lead to loss of life or injury and destruction of property.

> Contingency plans also must be made for other emergencies such as bridge collapses, plane crashes, hazardous materials spills, bomb threats, actual bombings and explosions, and terrorist attacks involving chemical, biological, and nuclear weapons of mass destruction (WMDs). Regardless of the cause, saving lives is the top priority in all such emergencies.

Terrorism and securing our homeland are the topic of Chapter 9 and, thus, the following discussion will not address the police response to WMDs.

Bridge Collapses

Our country's aging and, in many cases, ailing infrastructure poses a growing danger to the public. For example, a comprehensive assessment of the nation's 600,000 bridges confirmed that many of them are in serious trouble: "In almost all cases, structurally deficient bridges remain operational. They may have reduced weight limits posted, but they generally stay open. The I-35W bridge had a structurally deficient rating, and short-term repairs were being done at the time of the collapse" (Eggers 2007, 94).

The collapse of the I-35W bridge over the Mississippi River in Minneapolis, Minnesota, occurred at 6:05 p.m., August 1, 2007, during rush hour, leaving 13 people dead and more than 100 injured, dozens critically. The response effort required the full resources of the Hennepin County (Minnesota) Sheriff's Office and the resources of more than 100 additional agencies, most notably the Minneapolis police and fire departments. The rescue and recovery of victims and their vehicles took three weeks, involved the importation of ultra-high-tech equipment, and required the respectful handling of information for both the press and the families of those killed. The remarkable response of all responding was praised throughout the country (Moore 2008). The incident commander for the bridge collapse response noted several lessons learned from the tragedy. First: Expect the unexpected. Second: Plan, train, and prepare incessantly. He noted that his agency had previously worked and trained with many of the 100-plus law enforcement agencies that came to assist ("Minneapolis Area Police Officials" 2007).

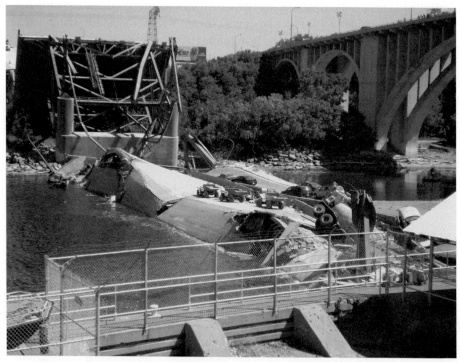

The scene of the I-35W bridge collapse over the Mississippi River in Minneapolis, Minnesota. On August 1, 2007, during the evening rush hour, the bridge suddenly collapsed, killing 13 people and injuring 145. The rapid response to the collapse of a state bridge into a county river between two banks of a city was exceptionally efficient and effective because city, county, and state employees at all levels knew their roles and had practiced them as a result of having received FEMA emergency management training the year following the 9/11 terrorist attacks.

© Henry Cho

Plane Crashes

Although often accidental, plane crashes may also occur at the hands of terrorists in their effort to cause death and fear, as discussed in the next chapter. Two accidental crashes—the 1996 crash of TWA Flight 800 off Long Island into the Atlantic and the November 2001 crash of American Airlines Flight 587 into a residential neighborhood in Queens, New York—and the terrorist hijacking and subsequent crash of United Flight 93 into a rural Pennsylvania field on September 11, 2001, highlight the extreme destruction and tragedy such an emergency can cause. A plane crash carries very heavy responsibilities because loss of life usually is associated with the crash. Upon notification of a plane crash, the police department must notify the Federal Aviation Administration (FAA), which has jurisdiction over and responsibility for such investigations. The National Transportation Safety Board (NTSB) also has jurisdiction if a death is involved. In the case of a military aircraft, the military service involved must be notified. The security of the aircraft and its scattered parts then becomes the responsibility of the military police.

The initial responsibility of the police department is to seal off the area surrounding any parts that may have been separated from the plane. Frequently, other jurisdictions may become involved, as parts of the aircraft may be found several blocks or miles away from the main crash site. If large numbers of people are injured, the ambulance services and the fire department rescue units may become overburdened. When this occurs, the hospital may send several of its staff members to the scene to assist. Police officers must provide easy access to and from the scene for those hospital personnel.

Hazardous Materials (Hazmat) Incidents

Some emergencies to which police are called may involve hazardous materials—known as a **hazmat incident**—and other dangerous goods: derailed trains, overturned chemical-laden tank trucks, incidents at industrial plants, or other scenes where toxic substances are present. Modes of transportation of hazardous materials include truck, rail, pipeline, water, and air, and each mode presents its own unique challenges to hazmat responders.

hazmat incident

An incident involving hazardous materials.

The U.S. Department of Transportation reports that 13,453 hazmat incidents have occurred in the past decade, with 1,274 occurring in 2008 ("Hazardous Materials Safety" 2008). Most hazmat incidents were caused by human error, followed by dropping, improper preparation for transportation, and a defective component or device. For the past decade, the vast majority of incidents occurred on a highway, as did the bulk of fatalities and injuries. In addition, the greatest amount of damage sustained occurred on our highways.

An example of an accidental hazmat emergency was the derailment in North Dakota of a train with four cars carrying anhydrous ammonia that leaked following the crash. One person died and hundreds were evacuated, with many requiring hospitalization.

Hazmat events may also be intentional, such as the dispersal of anthrax using the U.S. mail system. The law enforcement response to such deliberate releases involves actions directed toward the hazmat incident itself and toward the follow-up criminal investigation.

Whatever the origin, the increasing number of hazardous materials in commercial use has significantly raised the likelihood of law enforcement officers being called to a spill, and they must be trained to respond appropriately. Some law enforcement agencies have their own hazmat teams, but others have a regional team.

Short of any specialized training, officers should know some basic guidelines for responding to hazmat emergencies. When hazardous cargo is being transported, federal law requires the haulers to carry a manifest specifically detailing what they are carrying, how much, and the shipment destination. Many manifests also provide a material safety data sheet (MSDS), with information on handling, containing, and neutralizing the hazardous materials or dangerous goods in the event of a spill, leak, or other inadvertent release. Haulers are also required to display a colored placard and symbol identifying the hazardous nature of their shipment. The most familiar warnings are the colored placards on the sides and rear of the trailer or shipping container, generally visible from a greater distance than the symbol, thereby allowing first responders to tailor their approach accordingly. The standard placard colors and what they represent are:

▶ Flammable: red

▶ Corrosive: black and white

▶ Explosive: orange

▶ Poison: black and white

▶ Nonflammable gas: green

▶ Oxidizer: yellow

Officers should have binoculars in their vehicles so they can read, from a safe distance, the placards and markings on trucks or railroad cars involved in accidents. Because the danger of explosion, fire, or toxic fumes is always present, officers should stay as far away as possible but also try to identify what the truck or railroad car was transporting.

General safety precautions and other basic guidelines for first responders to a hazmat accident scene include:

▶ Respond upwind and upgrade, when possible, and anticipate changes in wind direction.

▶ Park vehicles heading away from the incident, then approach on foot.

▶ The first priority is to isolate and secure the scene. Use barrier tape, traffic cones, or barricades, *not* flares.

▶ Keep contaminated, ill, or injured people away from others.

▶ If necessary, initiate an evacuation.

▶ Do not eat, drink, or smoke at any hazardous materials incident.

▶ Do not touch any container, and avoid contact with liquids or fumes.

▶ Treat all hazardous materials as if they were toxic or explosive. Always consider the possibility of more than one hazard being present.

▶ Latex (surgical type) and leather gloves are *not* adequate protection against most hazardous materials.

▶ Keep your dispatcher informed of all actions you take at the scene.

▶ Be cautious about keying up the microphone on your handheld radio or squad radio because the transmission might ignite chemicals present in the air.

A useful resource is the Chemical Transportation Emergency Center (CHEMTREC), established in 1971 by the chemical industry as a public service hotline for firefighters, law enforcement, and other emergency responders. An integral part of the American Chemistry Council, CHEMTREC maintains a state-of-the-art communication center and a high-end MSDS document storage and retrieval system, containing nearly 2.8 million MSDSs. These documents enable CHEMTREC to supply information on a product's known hazards and what to do and not do in case of a spill, a fire, or exposure to the substance.

CHEMTREC can also provide immediate advice by telephone for the on-scene commander at a hazmat emergency. Its personnel will promptly contact the shipper of the hazardous material(s) involved in the incident for detailed assistance and relay an appropriate response back to the on-scene incident commander. In some situations, a segment of the chemical industry or even a company may have a hazmat team that will respond. CHEMTREC can alert such teams if they exist. The CHEMTREC 24-hour Emergency Call Center, located in Arlington, Virginia, may be accessed toll-free by first responders.

Bombs, Bomb Threats, and Explosions

"Bombs and explosive incidents have consistently, if slowly, grown in numbers. Whether initiated by terrorists, criminals, juveniles, or emotionally disturbed individuals, bombings may occur in any jurisdiction. Police will often be on the leading edge encountering devices and their makers" (Laska 2011, 73). Any business or establishment can be the victim of a bomb threat or bombing. Among the most common targets are airlines, banks, educational institutions, government buildings, hospitals, industrial complexes, military installations, office buildings, and utilities. According to the Bureau of Alcohol, Tobacco, Firearms and Explosives (ATF), the top three motivating factors for bombings are vandalism, revenge, and protest.

The February 26, 1993, bombing of the World Trade Center in New York, which killed six and injured more than a thousand, and the April 19, 1995, bombing of the Alfred P. Murrah Federal Building in Oklahoma City, which left 169 people dead and nearly 500 injured, were not just disasters resulting in loss of life but were also major crime scenes—the sites of the mass murders of innocent civilians.

Although most law enforcement officers will never encounter an actual bomb, it is probable that they will have to deal with suspicious packages and bomb threats. Even though 98 percent of bomb threats are hoaxes, the threats are costly and emotionally charged, and may be dangerous if people panic. Having a well-established procedure to handle a bomb-threat call is imperative. It should be written, kept in plain view of those who answer the phone, and practiced. If a threat is received, the person who receives it should know exactly what to do. Receivers of bomb threats should:

▶ Keep the caller talking as long as possible.

▶ Try to learn as much as possible about the bomb, especially when it will go off and where it is located.

▶ Try to determine the caller's sex, age, accent, and speech pattern, and whether he or she is drunk or drugged.

▶ Listen for any background noises.

▶ Immediately notify the appropriate person(s) of the call.

It is critical that individuals who answer telephones know to whom they should report a bomb threat. This person then determines what action to take. Alternatives include ignoring the threat, searching for the possible bomb, or evacuating the premises. No matter what alternative is selected, the police should be called.

A command post should be established as soon as the decision is made to treat the bomb threat as real. The entire building should then be diagrammed and areas crossed off as they are searched. A system of communicating among searchers must be established, but it must not involve the use of portable radios because they may detonate the bomb. All searchers should be cautioned not to turn on lights because this might also detonate the bomb. Searchers should move slowly and carefully, listening for any ticking sounds and watching for tripwires. Laska (2011, 70) suggests the following technique to identify tripwire triggers: "Extend your collapsible baton, hang a four-foot length of crime scene tape from the end, and let it walk ahead, where it will drape over any hidden wires.... Particularly dangerous is the 'tanglefoot' style of tripwire.... a loose tripwire that lies on the ground and is designed to get tangled about a walker's feet. If you suspect a tanglefoot, look hard for it. Use your light. If you carry an alternate color light (many tactical lights include an ultraviolet, blue, or red source), switch between colors."

Sometimes metal detectors are used to assist in the search. Many police departments are using bomb-sniffing dogs with great success. Such dogs are trained to move quietly and to not bark when a bomb is located, but rather to simply "point" to it. Explosives-detecting dogs are especially valuable in searching cluttered or inaccessible areas. Officers who respond to bombs (threatened or actual) should have available bomb suits, hazmat protection, and robots.

Remotely operated vehicles have been used for various tasks by SWAT teams and bomb squads for many years. A more recent application is using unmanned aerial vehicles (UAVs) for domestic emergency services that operate under the same standards required of remote controlled model aircraft, not operating within 3 miles of an active airport and only at or below 400 feet above ground level.

Areas that are usually unlocked and unwatched are the most common sites for bombs—for example, restrooms, lobbies, lunchrooms, elevators, and stairs. Officers should look for anything out of place or foreign to the area, for example, a briefcase in the restroom. Bombs can be hidden in lunch pails, briefcases, shopping bags, candy boxes, and any number of other types of containers.

Bombings with potentially disastrous effects are remarkably simple to perform. Several underground newsletters give detailed instructions on how

TECHNOLOGY IN POLICING

ROBOTICS FOR BOMB SQUADS

The use of robots has become increasingly common in the response to bombs and bomb threats, and the technology applied to these robots has been advancing steadily. For example, the Remotec Andros F6A robot has many valuable features including the ability to go up and down stairs, operate in difficult terrain such as thick mud, and drag an injured person from the danger zone. It is heavily equipped with cameras for enhanced surveillance and reconnaissance use, and their placement allows technicians the versatility to look under cars or over fences. The zoom capability of the cameras is good enough to allow the robot operator to read the label on a pill bottle inside a vehicle. The Andros F6A has night vision and external scene lighting capabilities and can carry an X-ray machine or air quality monitoring equipment to a suspicious package for threat assessment. Finally, the robot can fire laser-guided rounds at suspicious containers and objects to render them safe. A 1,200-foot long fiber optic cable permits the robot operator to control the Andros F6A from a safe distance, and the video images can be uplinked to a larger screen, such as at a command center, so multiple people can view the scene simultaneously (Marks 2012).

to make improvised explosive devices (IEDs) using common materials. A quick search on the Internet can also reveal easy instructions for making a bomb.

Many indicators should alert law enforcement officers to suspicious packages: lopsidedness, protruding wires, oily stains on the wrapper, a strange odor, no return address, excessive weight, visual distractions, foreign mail, air mail, special delivery, restrictive markings such as confidential or personal, postage not canceled, excessive security tape or string, and handwritten or poorly typed addresses. Officers should be suspicious of any plastic bottle emitting a gas or causing the ground around it to discolor.

If a bomb is found, the police should be prepared to deal with it themselves or know who to call to deal with it.

> The policy of most police departments when dealing with a suspected bomb is *do not touch*—move the people away from the bomb, not the bomb away from the people. A 300-foot radius is a good general rule to follow.

It is usually not necessary for officers to act immediately other than to evacuate the immediate area and to then call the fire department or a bomb disposal unit, which are better equipped to handle such situations. If a military installation is close by, its bomb demolition team may help. When a suspicious object or bomb is located, doors and windows in the area should be opened, and all fire extinguishers should be readied and in position to combat any fires caused by the explosion. The bomb should be surrounded with sandbags or similar shock-absorbing objects. Valuable and irreplaceable documents, files, computer disks, and other items should be removed from the vicinity and, if time allows, so too should highly flammable material.

A recoilless disrupter might also be used. This is a device that uses gunpowder to fire a jet of water or a projectile at a particular component of an explosive to render it safe.

Explosions may be accidental or purposeful. Accidental explosions may result from earthquakes, natural fires, plane or train crashes, or natural gas leaks. Purposeful explosions include those caused by arsonists and by terrorists. Department policies and procedures should be developed for dealing with all types of explosions. Regardless of whether the explosion originates from an accidental source or an intentional bombing, as with other emergency responses, collaboration among many agencies is required during and immediately following the incident. This was certainly true on September 11, 2001. Explosive technicians and special investigators worked side by side with clean-up crews, around the clock, seven days a week, sifting through hundreds of tons of debris. The army of response and rescue workers included law enforcement officers, firefighters, sheriff's deputies, dog handlers, emergency medical teams, hospital personnel, engineers, heavy equipment operators, chaplains, National Guard members, Red Cross staff and volunteers, and social service workers from across the country.

PANDEMICS

pandemic

An infectious disease that occurs over a large geographic area and affects a significantly high percentage of the population.

A potential crisis that does not fit into the natural, accidental, or human-made crisis categories but that is gaining increasing attention among law enforcement agencies is the pandemic. A **pandemic** is an infectious disease that occurs over a large geographic area and affects a significantly high percentage of the population. Between 1918 and 1919, the "Spanish flu" killed 50 million people worldwide, 650,000 of them in the United States. From 1968 to 1969, the "Hong Kong flu" killed 34,000 people in the United States. The 21st century has raised concerns about the "Avian (bird) flu" and "Swine flu" becoming pandemics. Although a pandemic might seem like a public health problem, it is also a concern to law enforcement:

> Police may be called upon to enforce quarantines, to provide security in hospitals swamped with patients, and to ensure that vaccines—when they become available in limited quantities—could be delivered to those with the greatest need for them.

> But perhaps the biggest reason why a flu pandemic would be a police problem lies in the answer to this question: Whenever anything bad happens, whom do people call? The local public health agency? How many people even know the name of their public health agency, much less its phone number?

> When bad things happen, people call the police. Public health agencies would take the leading role in dealing with a flu pandemic, but police would be involved from start to finish, if only because the public always looks to the police to answer their questions and solve their problems. (Wexler 2007, ii)

 Police are vital in maintaining order and providing services should a pandemic occur. People look to the police first when things go wrong.

The Police Executive Research Forum (PERF) has published *Police Planning for an Influenza Pandemic: Case Studies and Recommendations from the Field* (Luna, Brito, and Sanberg 2007, 1), which states in its introduction, "A pandemic flu has the potential to cause more death, illness, and social and economic disruption than most other threats faced by law enforcement." This document (8) states, "In every site, plans call for police to maintain public order *and*

▶ Provide security for vaccine/treatment transport and vaccine distribution sites,

▶ Be prepared to assist in executing public health orders,

▶ Provide initial site security as needed at medical facilities and similar venues, and

▶ Assist with handling mass fatalities."

Because the police are first responders and, as such, have a high likelihood of exposure, it is important that they be among the first to be vaccinated. If officers believe their own safety and the safety of their families are at risk, they may not respond to incidents, regardless of whether their jobs depend on it.

In a pandemic, as in all the previously discussed emergency situations, an agency that has incorporated the community policing philosophy into its operations is likely to be much more effective than are those agencies that are more reactive.

EMERGENCIES AND COMMUNITY POLICING

One difficulty frequently encountered by departments seeking to implement community policing is that no sense of community exists. In times of crisis, such as that following the terrorist attacks of September 11, this "sense of community" may either be strengthened or weakened. The "upside" of emergencies and disasters, be they natural or not, is how the community often pulls together for survival, support, and recovery. Walls come down, the circle of trust expands, and people look past their differences to focus on their common ground—as Americans in need of help from one another. The other side to this, of course, is that some people may react just the opposite—walls go up, trust in others diminishes, and suspicion and fear grow toward citizens who share any characteristics with those deemed responsible for the crisis.

SUMMARY

Police departments should have pre-disaster plans for those emergencies likely to occur within their jurisdictions. Such plans should include what emergencies to prepare for; what needs to be done in advance (supplies on hand, agreements with other agencies, etc.); what specific functions must be performed during the emergency and who is responsible for performing them, including organizations and agencies that might help; how continuity of operations and governance will be maintained; how personnel and their families will be protected; how to keep the media informed; what steps need to be taken to restore order after the emergency is ended; and how the response is to be evaluated.

Jurisdictions may seek assistance in developing their pre-disaster plan from the Federal Emergency Management Agency, or FEMA, an independent federal agency charged with building and supporting the nation's emergency management system. The mission of FEMA is to reduce loss of life and property and protect the nation from all hazards, including natural disasters, acts of terrorism, and other human-made disasters, by leading and supporting the nation in a risk-based, comprehensive emergency management system of preparedness, protection, response, recovery, and mitigation.

Lack of communication and coordination are the major problems during disasters. The emergency operations center (EOC), the location from which personnel operate during a natural disaster or other type of emergency, is the "pulse" of the government's response to an emergency and helps reduce the problems of lack of communication and coordination. Most emergencies happen in four phases: (1) the *warning* period, (2) the *impact* period, (3) the *immediate reaction* after impact, and (4) the period of *delayed response.*

Any particularly devastating event can have long-range emotional effects, including post-traumatic stress disorder (PTSD), a debilitating stressful reaction to a traumatic event. PTSD may last for months or years. It can be experienced by those who help the victims as well as by victims. A powerful tool in preventing posttraumatic stress disorder is the critical-incident stress debriefing (CISD), which should be conducted by a trained team, which includes a professional mental health practitioner and peer supporters, approximately 24 to 72 hours after the incident,

and should be available to all personnel involved in the incident. Individual department policy, however, may dictate whether such a debriefing includes peer support or if it is mandatory versus voluntary.

In addition to general pre-disaster plans, contingency plans should be made for such natural disasters as floods, fires, cyclones, earthquakes, and tsunamis. Common post-emergency "killers" include overruns in overtime and excessive paperwork. Contingency plans also must be made for other emergencies such as bridge collapses, plane crashes, hazardous materials spills, bomb threats, actual bombings and explosions, and terrorist attacks involving chemical, biological, and nuclear weapons of mass destruction (WMDs). Regardless of the cause, saving lives is the top priority in all such emergencies.

The policy of most police departments when dealing with a suspected bomb is *do not touch—* move the people away from the bomb, not the bomb away from the people. A 300-foot radius is a good general rule to follow.

Police are vital in maintaining order and providing services should a pandemic occur. People look to the police first when things go wrong.

APPLICATION

As your department's emergency management officer, you have been directed to establish a policy and procedure to respond to a natural disaster likely to threaten your jurisdiction.

INSTRUCTIONS

Using the form in the Appendix, develop a policy on your jurisdiction's anticipated response to a natural disaster (you can select one that has a high likelihood of occurring in your geographic area). Specify the procedures to be taken before, during, and after the emergency, including training needed, equipment allocation, and other resource considerations. Also include the roles of local, state, and federal agencies in your policy and procedure.

AN EXERCISE IN CRITICAL THINKING

On July 8 at 3:35 a.m., two police officers in separate squad cars received a call reporting a multiple-vehicle crash on the eastbound lanes of Interstate Highway 94 three miles east of Twin Lakes at the crossing of the Kinnickinnic River. There were patches of fog approaching the area, reducing visibility in the location of the collisions to 100 feet. Seven vehicles had collided.

Four were in the ditch to the right side of the road, one was on the left shoulder facing toward the ditch, one was on the right shoulder with the front left tire four feet into the right lane, and one vehicle was straddling the two lanes with its front tires in the right lane and its back tires in the left lane.

1. As no headlights of approaching traffic can be seen,
   a. Both officers should leave their squad cars, with lights flashing as warnings, and survey damages to vehicles and personal injuries.
   b. One officer should stop all approaching traffic at a point west of the patches of fog while the other officer surveys the scene to call for the appropriate assistance.
   c. One officer should act as an emergency manager and prioritize and delegate responsibilities.
   d. The officers should immediately broadcast a general call for help—obtain ambulance and medical help, wreckers, and clean-up assistance, then stand aside to direct traffic.
   e. The first to arrive on the scene should attempt to give first aid to individuals requesting help, and the second should begin an investigation to see if gross misdemeanors for aggravated driving violations are in order.

2. If one person is observed leaving the scene of the crash,
   a. The officer arriving second should pursue and arrest that individual and place him or her in the back seat of the squad car for later interrogation and sobriety tests.
   b. The first officer to arrive should call for K-9 backup to track down the individual for interrogation.
   c. Both officers should ignore this departure unless the individual appears to pose a threat to others. After the initial traumatic shock, this person will probably recover emotional balance and return without coercion.
   d. Action should be taken only if the emergency manager assesses it to be necessary and timely.
   e. Officers should request an ambulatory survivor who is physically able to chase down this individual and bring him or her back to the scene of the crash.

3. In addition to three injured people who were removed in ambulances and two who were given medical attention but not hospitalized, Reginald Jones was found slumped behind the wheel of the vehicle found in the middle of the highway. Others stated that they had braked and swerved to miss this vehicle, which along with the poor visibility had caused the onset of the multiple-vehicle collision. One officer walked up just as Jones was about to be removed from the vehicle by ambulance attendants. The attendants turned Jones over to the officer, who noticed indications of intoxication. Jones refused to take field sobriety tests, stating the officer had no right to ask him because an acquaintance named "Arel" had been driving the car all evening until it stalled at the spot where police found it. Jones did not request an attorney.
   a. Jones should be arrested for an aggravated driving violation.
   b. Insufficient evidence exists for Jones to be tested or arrested.
   c. Only if other witnesses can corroborate that no other person was in the vehicle with Jones should he be interrogated.
   d. If Jones can give "Arel's" full name and address, then he should be released; otherwise, he should be arrested and interrogated.
   e. As Jones is the prime suspect who has caused the entire emergency, he should be arrested, searched, handcuffed, and taken to police headquarters for interrogation.

DISCUSSION QUESTIONS

1. What types of emergencies are most likely to occur in your community? Least likely?

2. Assume that the potential for flooding exists in your community. What type of training would you recommend for the police department?

3. What should be the foremost concern of police officers when dealing with a natural disaster?

4. In dealing with a bomb threat, what are the most important considerations?

5. How might the media be of help during an emergency situation?

6. Have you ever been involved in an emergency situation yourself? How well was it handled? What could have been done differently?

7. Does your local law enforcement agency have an emergency preparedness plan? If so, what does it consist of?

GALE EMERGENCY SERVICES DATABASE ASSIGNMENTS

▶ Use the Gale Emergency Services database (available for separate purchase) to answer the Discussion Questions as appropriate.

▶ Find and read the article "The Manageable Future" by Charles S. Heal. Pay special attention to the two figures. Summarize what each figure graphically depicts.

▶ Find and read the article "Nationwide Application of the Incident Command System" by Michael D. Cardwell and Patrick T. Cooney. Write a brief report explaining what the acronym FIRESCOPE stands for, what it is intended to do, and why the authors suggest it should be adopted nationwide.

REFERENCES

"About FEMA." 2012 (July 18). Washington, DC: Federal Emergency Management Agency. Accessed March 5, 2012. http://www.fema.gov/about/index.shtm.

Cashen, Kevin. 2008. "Elements for Continuity of Operations." *Law and Order* (May): 67–72.

Commission on Accreditation of Law Enforcement Agencies (CALEA). 2012. *Standards for Law Enforcement Agencies.* 5th ed. Fairfax, VA: Author.

Developing and Maintaining Emergency Operations Plans: Comprehensive Preparedness Guide (CPG) 101, Version 2.0. 2010 (November). Washington, DC: Department of Homeland Security, Federal Emergency Management Administration.

Donlon-Cotton, Cara. 2007. "Critical Incidents: Dealing with the Media." *Law and Order* (September): 24–28.

Eggers, Ron. 2007. "America's Ailing Infrastructure Poses Dangers." *9-1-1 Magazine* (November/December): 94.

FEMA Strategic Plan: Fiscal Years 2008–2013. 2008 (January). Washington, DC: Department of Homeland Security, Federal Emergency Management Administration. (FEMA P-422).

Garrett, Ronnie. 2009. "Sighting in Swatting." *Law Enforcement Technology* (May): 26–32.

"Hazardous Materials Safety." 2008. Washington, DC: U.S. Department of Transportation.

Jetmore, Larry F. 2008. "Post Traumatic Stress Syndrome." *Law Officer Magazine* (May): 62–66.

Laska, Paul R. 2011. "Suspicious Packages and Booby Traps." *Police* (May): 68–73.

Luna, Andrea M., Corina Sole Brito, and Elizabeth A. Sanberg. 2007 (October). *Police Planning for an Influenza Pandemic: Case Studies and Recommendations from the Field.* Washington, DC: Police Executive Research Forum.

Marks, Kathy. 2012. "Robotics for Bomb Squads." *Tactical Response* (January–February): 52–56.

Mass Evacuation Incident Annex. 2008 (June). Washington, DC: Department of Homeland Security, Federal Emergency Management Agency. Accessed March 5, 2012. http://www.fema.gov/pdf/emergency/nrf/nrf_massevacuation-incidentannex.pdf.

"Minneapolis Area Police Officials Describe 'Lessons Learned' from Bridge Collapse." 2007. *Subject to Debate* (October): 1, 4–5.

Moore, Carole. 2008. "An Accident Waiting to Happen." *Law Enforcement Technology* (January): 8–14.

Moore, Carole. 2009. "Telling Your Officers Where to Go—and How to Get There." *Law Enforcement Technology* (May): 10–16.

Moore, Linda K. 2010 (December 14). *The Emergency Alert System (EAS) and All-Hazard Warnings.* Congressional

Research Service, Report for Congress. Accessed March 5, 2012. http://www.fas.org/sgp/crs/homesec/RL32527.pdf.

National Incident Management System. 2008 (December). Washington, DC: Department of Homeland Security, Federal Emergency Management Agency. (FEMA Publication P-501). Accessed March 5, 2012. http://www.fema.gov/pdf/emergency/nims/NIMS_core.pdf.

Nationwide Plan Review: Fiscal Year 2010 Report to Congress. 2010 (July 15). Washington, DC: Department of Homeland Security, Federal Emergency Management Agency.

Nationwide Plan Review: Phase 2 Report. 2006 (June 16). Washington, DC: Department of Homeland Security in cooperation with the U.S. Department of Transportation.

"Post-Traumatic Stress Disorder." 2012. Washington, DC: American Psychological Association. Accessed March 5, 2012. http://www.apa.org/topics/ptsd/index.aspx.

Rojek, Jeff, and Michael R. Smith. 2007. "Law Enforcement Lessons Learned from Hurricane Katrina." *Review of Policy Research* 24 (6): 589–608.

Rosenthal, Rick. 2009. "Media Relations Lessons from Flight 1549." *ILEETA Digest* (January/February/March): 6.

Ross, David Anthony. 2009. "Reliable Communications in Unreliable Conditions." *Law Enforcement Technology* (May): 68–70.

"Tips for Law Enforcement Deployments." n.d. Lexington, KY: National Emergency Management Association, Emergency Management Assistance Compact. Accessed March 5, 2012. http://www.emacweb.org/index.php?option=com_content&view=article&id=201&Itemid=292.

Wexler, Chuck. 2007 (October). "Foreword." In *Police Planning for an Influenza Pandemic: Case Studies and Recommendations from the Field,* edited by Andrea M. Luna, Corina Sole Brito, and Elizabeth A. Sanberg. Washington, DC: Police Executive Research Forum.

CHAPTER 9

Terrorism:
From Hometown Security to Homeland Security

©AP Images/Charles Dharapak

DO YOU KNOW . . .

- What most definitions of terrorism include?
- How the FBI classifies terrorist acts?
- What motivates most terrorist attacks?
- What domestic terrorist groups exist in the United States?
- What methods terrorists might use?
- What federal office was established as a result of 9/11 and what its purpose is?
- What the lead federal agencies are in responding to acts of terrorism and handling consequence management?
- How the USA PATRIOT Act enhances counterterrorism efforts by the United States?
- What the first line of defense against terrorism in the United States is?
- What three obstacles to intelligence effectiveness are?
- What the Law Enforcement Officer's Safety Act authorizes?
- What two concerns are associated with the current "war on terrorism"?
- What balance law enforcement must maintain in the "war on terrorism"?

CAN YOU DEFINE?

agroterrorism
asymmetric war
bioterrorism
contagion effect
cyberterrorism
deconfliction
ecoterrorism
estimative language
fusion center
jihad
sovereign citizens
terrorism

INTRODUCTION

Terrorism was a concern for the United States long before September 11, 2001. However, the horrific events of that day pulled together and unified the American people in a way most had never seen. Patriotism was immediately popular. Thousands of volunteers helped search for victims and donated blood and money. The American flag flew everywhere. In addressing the nation, President George W. Bush stated, "Tonight we are a country awakened to danger and called to defend freedom. Our grief has turned to anger, and anger to resolution."

In addition to galvanizing the nation, the 9/11 tragedy had other ramifications, such as changing how our nation viewed its security and thrusting local law enforcement onto the front lines of a new war: "[The] 9/11 attacks… inaugurated a war on terror that continues to this day. And this war is different than any other in our history. It is fought by soldiers abroad and law enforcement officers at home. A decade on, it is not unusual to see officers patrolling subways and metro rails with automatic rifles and K-9s…. Whatever appraisal history eventually accords America's response to the catastrophic events of 2001, its dramatic impact on law enforcement during the last decade would be difficult to exaggerate" (Scoville 2011, 28).

In this post–9/11 world, our country has embarked on a new era of policing. However, the heightened focus and increased attention placed on terrorism has not absolved local law enforcement of its duties to prevent and investigate more traditional types of crime and disorder. The need to balance crime-fighting efforts with counterterrorism efforts should be kept in mind while reading this chapter.

This chapter begins with a brief discussion of homeland security in context, noting that terrorism, and efforts to prevent and respond to it, is but one facet of this multidimensional endeavor. The challenge of defining terrorism is discussed next, followed by how it is classified as domestic or international. Next is a look at the various ideologies behind and motivations for terrorism, the new type of war that law enforcement is engaged in, the methods used by terrorists, how terrorism is funded, and valuable targets for terrorism. This is followed by a look at the federal response to terrorism, including the formation of the Department of Homeland Security (DHS) and passage of the USA PATRIOT Act. Next is a discussion of the critical role of local law enforcement in responding to terrorism and efforts to detect, prepare for, prevent, protect against, respond to, and recover from terrorist attacks. Then initiatives to assist in the fight against terrorism and the role of the media in this fight are discussed, followed by two major concerns related to that war: erosion of civil liberties and retaliation against people of Middle Eastern descent. The chapter concludes with a discussion of community policing and homeland security.

HOMELAND SECURITY IN CONTEXT

When people think of *homeland security*, it is very likely that the first image that comes to mind is of thick, black smoke billowing from the twin towers, or of a deep scar cut through the Pennsylvania landscape by a commercial aircraft whose heroic passengers kept the plane from reaching its intended target:

> The story of homeland security is inextricably linked to the story of 9/11. The vivid images of the World Trade Center, the Pentagon, and smoldering fields in Shanksville, Pennsylvania, portrayed a Nation obviously shaken by the catastrophic surprise attacks that had occurred on its soil. Yet on that same day there were other images—of firefighters racing up the stairs of the Twin Towers, of police and first responders rushing aid to those in need at the Pentagon, and of ordinary Americans, indeed total strangers, coming together to help each other cope with challenges large and small. These images of American resilience portrayed a Nation determined to do whatever it might take to recover from this disaster and to prevent such attacks from occurring again.
>
> In the closing days of 2001, the first narrative describing homeland security began to take shape: that despite the dramatic changes since the end of the Cold War, the world was still very much a dangerous place....Our Nation believed that it needed to improve its vigilance, increase its preparedness, reduce its vulnerabilities, and strengthen its guard against any future attack in order to confront this threat.
>
> The Federal Government began to institutionalize these priorities with a series of initiatives under the banner of *homeland security*....
>
> In the years since 9/11, homeland security has become commonly and broadly known as both a term and as a Federal department. Less well understood, however, has been its ongoing purpose and function. What is homeland security? Is it more than preventing terrorism? If so, what else does it take to achieve a safe and secure homeland? What risks are we willing to accept? Who has the responsibility, authority, capabilities, and resources to do all that needs doing? (*Quadrennial Homeland Security Review Report* 2010, 1)[1]

The various threats and hazards identified by the government as falling under the umbrella of homeland security include high-consequence weapons of mass destruction; global violent extremism; high-consequence or wide-scale cyber attacks, intrusions, disruptions, and exploitations; pandemics, major accidents, and natural hazards; illicit trafficking and related transnational crime; and smaller-scale terrorism (*Quadrennial Homeland Security Review Report* 2010). Thus, "Homeland security describes the intersection of evolving threats and hazards with traditional governmental and civic responsibilities for civil defense, emergency response, law enforcement, customs, border control, and immigration. In combining these responsibilities under one overarching concept, homeland security breaks down long-standing stovepipes of activity that have been and could still be exploited by those seeking to harm America. Homeland security also creates a greater emphasis on the need for joint actions and efforts across previously discrete elements of government and society" (viii).

---

[1]Source: *Quadrennial Homeland Security Review Report: A Strategic Framework for a Secure Homeland* (Washington, DC: Department of Homeland Security, February 2010). Accessed March 18, 2012. http://www.dhs.gov/xlibrary/assets/qhsr_report.pdf.

So although homeland security is built on critical law enforcement functions, it is not about preventing all crimes or administering our country's judicial system. Although homeland security is deeply embedded in trade activities, it is neither trade nor economic policy. And although homeland security requires international engagement, it is not responsible for foreign affairs: "Rather, homeland security is meant to connote a concerted, shared effort to ensure a homeland that is safe, secure, and resilient against *terrorism and other hazards* where American interests, aspirations, and way of life can thrive" (emphasis added) (*Quadrennial Homeland Security Review Report* 2010, 13).

Thus, the authors wish to remind readers that, although this chapter focuses on terrorism, homeland security encompasses far more than the nation's collective efforts to prevent and respond to terrorist acts.

TERRORISM DEFINED

There is no single, universally accepted definition of *terrorism.* The Federal Bureau of Investigation (FBI) uses the guidelines set in the U.S. Code of Federal Regulations, which defines **terrorism** as "the unlawful use of force and violence against persons or property to intimidate or coerce a government, the civilian population, or any segment thereof, in furtherance of political or social objectives" (28 C.F.R. § 0.85).

terrorism

"The unlawful use of force and violence against persons or property to intimidate or coerce a government, the civilian population, or any segment thereof, in furtherance of political or social objectives."

Most definitions of terrorism have common elements, including the systematic, criminal use of physical violence, either actual or threatened, against noncombatants to create a climate of fear and to cause some religious, political, or social change.

CLASSIFICATION OF TERRORIST ACTS

The FBI classifies terrorism as either domestic or international, depending on the origin, base, and objectives of the terrorist organization or individual.

The FBI categorizes terrorist acts in the United States as either domestic or international terrorism.

Domestic Terrorism

"Domestic terrorism is the unlawful use, or threatened use, of force or violence by a group or individual based and operating entirely within the United States or Puerto Rico without foreign direction committed against persons or property to intimidate or coerce a government, the civilian population, or any segment thereof in furtherance of political or social objectives" (*Terrorism 2002–2005* n.d., v). Domestic terrorists—Americans who, because of their extreme right- or left-wing ideologies or special interest beliefs, attack other Americans—is a growing concern for law enforcement at all levels. The following events highlight the threat of domestic terrorism:

A shell of what was once part of the twin towers of New York's World Trade Center rises above the rubble that remains after both towers were destroyed in a terrorist attack September 11, 2001. The 110-story towers collapsed after two hijacked airliners carrying scores of passengers slammed into the symbols of American capitalism.

© David Turnley/CORBIS

- ▶ The 1995 bombing of the Murrah Federal Building in Oklahoma City
- ▶ The 2002 Beltway sniper attacks in Washington, DC, Maryland, and Virginia
- ▶ The 2009 shooting of a guard at the Holocaust Museum in Washington, DC
- ▶ The 2009 shooting at Fort Hood in Texas
- ▶ The 2010 flight of a small airplane into the Internal Revenue Service (IRS) building in Austin, Texas

Many domestic terrorists are antigovernment and antitaxation and engage in survivalist training to perpetuate a White, Christian nation. The right-wing militia or patriot movement is a law enforcement concern because of the potential for violence and criminal behavior. Some states have passed legislation limiting militias, including types of training they can undergo. Domestic terrorism is examined in-depth under the discussion of motivation for terrorism.

International Terrorism

"International terrorism involves violent acts or acts dangerous to human life that are a violation of the criminal laws of the United States or any state, or that would be a criminal violation if committed within the jurisdiction of the United States or any state. These acts appear to be intended to intimidate or coerce a civilian population, influence the policy of a government by intimidation or coercion, or affect the conduct of a government by assassination or kidnapping. International terrorist acts occur outside the United States or transcend national boundaries in terms of the means by which they are accomplished, the persons they appear intended to coerce or intimidate, or the locale in which their perpetrators operate or seek asylum" (*Terrorism 2002–2005* n.d., v). The FBI divides international terrorism into three categories: (1) foreign state sponsors of international terrorism using terrorism as a tool of foreign policy, for example, Iraq and Afghanistan; (2) formalized terrorist groups, such as al

Qaeda and Revolutionary Armed Forces of Columbia (FARC); and (3) loosely affiliated international radical extremists who have a variety of identities and travel freely in the United States, unknown and undetected by law enforcement or the government.

Immediately following the 9/11 attacks, al Qaeda became the top threat most feared by Americans. Although al Qaeda's notorious leader, Osama bin Laden, was assassinated by U.S. special forces in a May 1, 2011, raid on the Pakistani compound in which he had been hiding for several years, the terror group has implemented new leadership under Ayman al-Zawahiri and continues to answer its call to holy war (**jihad**) and its mission to organize mass-casualty attacks against "infidels." Al Qaeda, which is currently planning to produce Disney-like animated cartoons aimed at recruiting young children into the terror network, remains intent on attacking U.S. interests worldwide and is likely to focus on prominent political, economic, and infrastructure targets to produce mass casualties, significant economic disruption, and fear among American citizens. However, many experts currently believe al Qaeda in the Arabian Peninsula (AQAP), the organization behind the attempted Christmas Day 2009 attack of a U.S. airliner, is now the greatest single terrorist threat to the United States (Boucek 2011).

The director of national intelligence regularly examines the evolving threat of terrorism to our country, which is presented in the *Worldwide Threat Assessment of the US Intelligence Community for the Senate Select Committee on Intelligence* (Clapper 2012), a report that uses **estimative language**, or language based on analytical assessments and judgments rather than on facts or hard evidence. The report uses terms such as *we assess*, *we expect*, and *we judge* synonymously and outlines the following key judgments:

jihad
A holy war.

estimative language
Language based on analytical assessments and judgments rather than on facts or hard evidence.

▶ "The next two to three years will be a critical transition phase for the terrorist threat facing the United States, particularly from al-Qa'ida and like-minded groups, which we often refer to as the 'global jihadist movement.' During this transition, we expect leadership of the movement to become more decentralized, with 'core' al-Qa'ida—the Pakistan-based group formerly led by Usama bin Ladin—diminishing in operational importance; regional al-Qa'ida affiliates planning and attempting terrorist attacks; multiple voices providing inspiration for the movement; and more vigorous debate about local versus global agendas" (1).

▶ "We assess that with continued robust counterterrorism (CT) efforts and extensive cooperation with our allies and partners, there is a better-than-even chance that decentralization will lead to fragmentation of the movement within a few years. With fragmentation, core al-Qa'ida will likely be of largely symbolic importance to the movement; regional groups, and to a lesser extent small cells and individuals, will drive the global jihad agenda both within the United States and abroad" (1).

▶ "We assess that a mass attack by foreign terrorist groups involving a chemical, biological, radiological or nuclear (CBRN) weapon in the United States is unlikely in the next year, as a result of intense counterterrorism pressure" (2).

▶ "Although we assess that a mass attack is unlikely, we worry about a limited CBR attack in the United States or against our interests overseas in the next year because of the interest expressed in such a capability by some foreign groups" (2).

▶ "We do not assess that al-Qa'ida's new leader, Ayman al-Zawahiri, will change al-Qa'ida's strategic direction, but most al-Qa'ida members find Zawahiri's leadership style less compelling than bin Ladin's image as a holy man and warrior, and will not offer him the deference they gave bin Ladin" (2).

▶ "The death or capture of prominent al-Qa'ida figures since bin Ladin's death has shrunk the layer of top lieutenants directly under Zawahiri. These losses, combined with the long list of earlier losses since CT operations intensified in 2008, lead us to assess that core al-Qa'ida's ability to perform a variety of functions—including preserving leadership and conducting external operations—has weakened significantly" (2).

▶ "We judge that with its degraded capabilities al-Qa'ida increasingly will seek to execute smaller, simpler plots to demonstrate relevance to the global jihad, even as it aspires to mass casualty and economically damaging attacks, including against the United States and U.S. interests overseas" (3).[2]

The Dual Threat

In fighting terrorism, all law enforcement—local, state, and federal—must keep as close an eye on domestic terrorists as they do on the international variety. And sometimes the line between the two is blurred. For example, during the past several years, more than a dozen young men, nearly all of Somali descent, have left their homes in the Minneapolis–St. Paul (Minnesota) area to travel to Somalia in hopes of joining al Shabab, a terrorist group with links to al Qaeda (Stanek 2011). In most cases, family members and leaders in the Somali community were unaware that these young men held radical views and were being recruited into terrorism. Such homegrown violent extremists (HVEs) present an evolving and complex threat to the security of the United States (O'Brien 2011).

Homegrown terrorists or HVEs are typically described as radicalized Western citizens or local residents who have adopted extremist political or religious ideologies that are hostile to Western social values. Although the term *radicalization*, like many other concepts in criminology, has various definitions among intelligence and law enforcement communities, the FBI has defined it as "the process by which individuals come to believe their engagement in or facilitation of nonstate violence to achieve social or political change is necessary and justified" (Hunter and Heinke 2011, 25–26).

IDEOLOGY AND MOTIVATIONS FOR TERRORISM

One approach to understanding terrorism is to examine the ideology, or organizing principles that provide the motive and framework for action, behind it.

---

[2]Source: James R. Clapper, *Worldwide Threat Assessment of the US Intelligence Community for the Senate Select Committee on Intelligence: Statement for the Record* (Washington, DC: Office of the Director of National Intelligence, January 31, 2012). Accessed March 17, 2012. http://www.dni.gov/testimonies/20120131_testimony_ata.pdf.

> Most terrorist acts result from dissatisfaction with a religious, political, or social system or policy and frustration resulting from an inability to change it through acceptable, nonviolent means.

Religious motives are seen in Islamic extremism. Political motives include such elements as the Red Army Faction. Social motives are seen in single-issue groups such as antiabortion groups, animal rights groups, and environmentalists.

> Terrorist groups within the United States with specific motivations include right-wing extremists (White supremacists, Black supremacists, and militia groups), left-wing extremists, pro-life extremists, animal rights activists, and environmental extremists.

Right-Wing Extremists

Right-wing extremism began in the early 1980s and has remained active since then, perhaps motivated by the government's actions at Ruby Ridge and Waco. The Ruby Ridge incident involved an attempt to arrest Randy Weaver, a White supremacist charged with selling illegal firearms to undercover Bureau of Alcohol, Tobacco, Firearms and Explosives (ATF) agents. A shootout ensued, resulting in the death of a U.S. marshal and Weaver's young son. The FBI laid siege to Weaver's Ruby Ridge cabin and killed his pregnant wife before Weaver surrendered.

The federal siege of the Branch Davidian compound near Waco, Texas, began in 1993 when ATF agents, trying to serve a search warrant, were met with gunfire that killed four agents and wounded several others. After a three-month siege, FBI agents moved in with tear gas, not knowing the compound was laced with gasoline. The compound burned, killing more than 70 people, including several young children.

The most violent right-wing groups, White supremacists, have strengthened their recruiting and rhetoric since 9/11. White Supremacists include one of the original American terrorist organizations, the Ku Klux Klan, formed following the Civil War to terrorize Blacks and exert political influence over the Reconstruction South. The Klan is still a threat, burning churches and intimidating and harassing minorities and minority advocates. Neo-Nazi groups such as the Skinheads also espouse White supremacy. On June 10, 2009, 88-year-old neo-Nazi James von Brunn shot to death a security guard at the U.S. Holocaust Memorial Museum. Responding officers shot and critically wounded von Brunn, and a search of his car after the attack revealed a list of other intended targets, including the White House. Among Black Supremacists is the Black Panther Party for Self-Defense, established in 1966 during a time of racial turmoil.

Another right-wing extremist group is the militia movement. Most militia groups are heavily armed and practice shooting. Many militia members are frustrated, overwhelmed, and socially unable to cope with the rapid pace of change in the modern world. Militia groups commonly provide the rhetoric for violence. In March 2010, nine members of the Hutaree Militia were arrested in raids conducted in Michigan, Ohio, and Indiana and charged with seditious conspiracy and attempted use of weapons of mass destruction. The group had allegedly planned to kill a Michigan police officer and then deploy bombs and homemade missiles to murder other officers attending the funeral, the ultimate goal being to ignite a war with the government. A year later, in March 2011, six members of the Alaska Peacemakers Militia were arrested and charged with plotting to kill or kidnap state troopers and a local judge. The group was in possession of a large weapons cache, including a .50-caliber machine gun, grenades, and a grenade launcher. The group's leader had identified himself as a "sovereign citizen."

sovereign citizens

A loose network of individuals scattered across the United States who believe that the original citizens of the United States were free from all government control and that the federal, state, and local governments today operate illegally.

Sovereign citizens—a loose network of individuals scattered across the United States who believe that the original citizens of the United States were free from all government control and that the federal, state, and local governments today operate illegally—are a growing domestic threat to law enforcement: "The FBI considered sovereign-citizen extremists as comprising a domestic terrorist movement.... Sovereign citizens do not represent an anarchist group, nor are they a militia, although they sometimes use or buy illegal weapons. Rather they operate as individuals without established leadership and only come together in loosely affiliated groups to train, help each other with paperwork, or socialize and talk about their ideology" (FBI Counterterrorism Analysis Section 2011, 21). The tactics of sovereign citizens are designed to harass, mock, and intimidate government entities, including law enforcement and the courts, as well as financial institutions. In protest of what they see as an illegal government, sovereign citizens often do not pay taxes and commonly create their own license plates, driver's licenses, and currency. Although these crimes seem minor and are nonviolent in nature, there is certainly reason for concern: "If someone challenges (e.g., a standard traffic stop for false license plates) their ideology, the behavior of these sovereign-citizen extremists quickly can escalate to violence. Since 2000, lone-offender sovereign-citizen extremists have killed six law enforcement officers" (FBI Counterterrorism Analysis Section 2011, 20).

▌AN OFFICER'S PERSPECTIVE ▬▬▬
Not Every Citizen Recognizes the Authority of Your Badge

During my time working as a police officer in a relatively suburban area of Minnesota, I have conducted traffic stops and made contact with several people who have identified themselves as "Posse Comitatus," an antigovernment militia group that does not believe in the authority of any law enforcement other than the actual sheriff elected by the people for the county. They also do not believe in paying taxes, and I have stopped a few with license plates that they have created on their own. Although these people told me that they did not believe in my power of authority as a law enforcement official, I still held them accountable to the law. Fortunately, the ones that I have had contact with ended up cooperating, but that is not always the case. It is also important to note that these individuals are not only secluded in small rural areas; they are around the suburbs and cities as well.

—*Sgt. Henry Lim Cho*

Left-Wing Extremists

Left wing extremists take a pro-Marxist stance, believing the rich must be brought down and the poor raised up. As left-wing terrorist groups regenerate over the coming years, they will continue to pose a threat to economic and law enforcement targets, with violent protests against the perceived effects of trade globalization on human rights, labor rights, and the environment continuing and likely escalating (*Strategic Plan* 2004). Examples of left-wing "anarchist movement" activity include the large-scale destructive protests at the World Trade Organization as well as some of the anarchist propaganda occurring at Occupy camps across the country.

Pro-Life Extremists

Although many pro-life, antiabortion advocates stay within the law in promoting their beliefs, some groups do not. One such group is an active terrorist organization called the Army of God, and its crimes range from arson to assault to assassination. The 2009 murder of abortion provider Dr. George Tiller is being recorded by those in the law enforcement community as an act of domestic terrorism.

Animal Rights Activists

An active domestic terrorist group is the Animal Liberation Front (ALF), which has claimed credit for attacks on meatpacking plants, furriers, and research labs. Founded in England in 1976, ALF's influence spread to the United States in 1982. Since then, the group has caused millions of dollars in damage and medical research setbacks through its acts of vandalism, arson, and freeing of laboratory animals. Leaders of this underground movement often seek free speech protections under the First Amendment while leading criminal lifestyles to maintain both themselves and the group: "The ALF's ultimate objective is to eliminate animal euthanasia and the use of all animals in laboratory testing in universities and science centers. In the pursuit of these objectives, elements of the group have become more violent" (Downing 2009, 35).

Environmental Extremists

Environmental extremists are often referred to as ecoterrorists, with *eco* being derived from *ecology*—the study of the interrelationships of organisms and their environment. **Ecoterrorism** seeks to inflict economic damage on those who profit from the destruction of the natural environment. The FBI considers ecoterrorism to be the No. 1 domestic terror threat in the United States and defines it as "the use or threatened use of violence of a criminal nature against innocent victims or property by an environmentally oriented, subnational group for environmental-political reasons, or aimed at an audience beyond the target, often of a symbolic nature" (Jarboe 2002).

ecoterrorism

Seeks to inflict economic damage on those who profit from the destruction of the natural environment.

One ecoterrorist group is the Earth Liberation Front (ELF), which often works with the ALF. Arson is a favorite weapon, responsible for tens of millions of dollars of property damage, including a U.S. Department of Agriculture building, a U.S. Forest Service ranger station, and a Colorado ski resort.

The group claims responsibility for releasing 5,000 mink from a Michigan fur farm, releasing 600 wild horses from an Oregon corral, and burning the Michigan State University's genetic engineering research offices. In 2000, ELF claimed responsibility for torching a $2 million home in Colorado. Ecoterrorists commit many crimes as they fight to save nature, including equipment vandalism, package bombs or pipe bombs, destruction of research data, arson of buildings, obliteration of experimental plants and animals, and the like.

A NEW KIND OF WAR—AN ASYMMETRIC WAR

asymmetric war

One in which a much weaker opponent takes on a stronger opponent by refusing to confront the stronger opponent head on or to adhere to proscribed "rules of engagement."

Although motivations for terrorists both within the United States and outside our borders might differ, they have in common the tactic of using an entirely different type of warfare. This new kind of war has been called an **asymmetric war**, in which a much weaker opponent takes on a stronger opponent by refusing to confront the stronger opponent head on or to adhere to proscribed "rules of engagement." The strategy also differs in that those seeking to harm the United States and its people do not envision the country's downfall as the result of a single spectacular act of terror but rather as a gradual wearing down of defenses and resources and will brought about by a series of smaller, unpredictable yet economically and psychologically damaging attacks—the philosophy of "death by a thousand cuts."

Although discussions of asymmetric warfare have previously been applied primarily to our military, the concept of this new kind of war must be understood by those on the front lines of this new war—local law enforcement. Attacks on American soil have caused a blurring of war and crime and drawn law enforcement directly into the war on terrorism. Because of this, local law enforcement is expected to be knowledgeable about the various methods terrorists use.

METHODS USED BY TERRORISTS

The *2010 Report on Terrorism* (2011) notes that, for the third consecutive year, most terrorist attacks used fighting methods such as armed attacks, bombings, and kidnappings, but in unconventional ways. Armed attacks continued to be the most prevalent form of attack, accounting for more than one-third of all attacks in 2010 (see Figure 9.1). However, bombings, including suicide attacks, were far more lethal and caused nearly 70 percent of all fatalities. Suicide bombings in particular continued to be the most lethal type of terrorist attack, resulting in approximately 13.5 percent of all terrorism-related deaths. Sunni extremists carried out 93 percent of all suicide attacks in 2010.

 Terrorists use arson, explosives and bombs, weapons of mass destruction (biological, chemical, or nuclear agents), and technology to carry out attacks.

Explosives and Bombs

Bombs and bomb threats were discussed from the perspective of an emergency in Chapter 8. This discussion looks at explosives as a method of terrorism. From

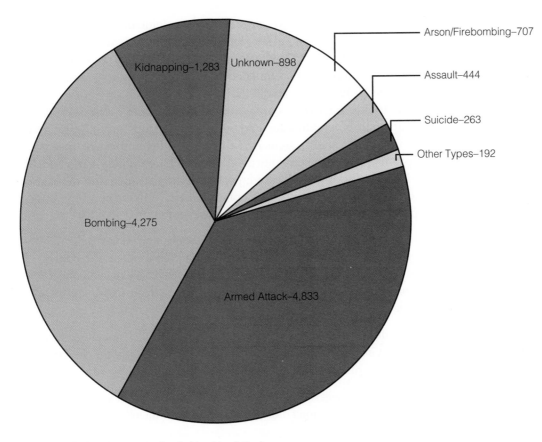

FIGURE 9.1 Primary Methods Used in Attacks
Note: 11,604 total attacks; some double counting occurred when multiple methods were used.
Source: *2010 Report on Terrorism* (Washington, DC: National Counterterrorism Center, April 30, 2011),
13. http://www.nctc.gov/witsbanner/docs/2010_report_on_terrorism.pdf.

1978 to 1996, Theodore Kaczynski terrorized the country as the Unabomber, through a string of 16 mail bombings that killed three people apparently in a protest against technology. Ramzi Ahmed Yousef, found guilty of masterminding the first World Trade Center bombing in 1993, declared that he was proud to be a terrorist and that terrorism was the only viable response to what he saw as a Jewish lobby in Washington, DC. The car bomb used to shatter the Murrah Federal Building in 1995 was Timothy McVeigh's way to protest the government and the raid on the Branch Davidians in Waco. In 2002, Lucas Helder terrorized the Midwest by placing 18 pipe bombs, accompanied by antigovernment letters, in mailboxes across five states. Six of the 18 bombs exploded, injuring four letter carriers and two residents. And the most horrific act of terrorism against the United States occurred on September 11, 2001, when two airplanes were used as missiles to explode the twin towers of the World Trade Center, and another plane was used as a missile to attack the Pentagon. A fourth plane crashed in a Pennsylvania field before it could reach its intended target.

Suicide Bombers Many terrorists believe sacrificing themselves makes them martyrs and ensures them a place in their version of heaven. Their families are held in reverence and taken care of. Suicide bombers try to kill as many people as possible: "The 9/11 hijackers were the ultimate suicide bombers. They used commercial aircraft as bombs rather than devices that fit inside a backpack. But at their core, their motivations were the same—they believed that political or religious ideology justified murdering innocent bystanders and killing themselves in the process" (Wexler 2007, i).

Potential suicide terrorists come from different backgrounds and age groups and are male or female, educated or uneducated, upstanding citizens or deviants. Among the warning signs revealing a suicide bomber are unseasonable garb; profuse sweating; obvious disguises (such as a police uniform with a security badge); and a well-dressed, perfumed appearance and demeanor fitting for one who is going to meet his or her maker. A suicide bombing attack typically progresses through a certain series of stages:

> The operational cycle for suicide bombing attacks can be viewed as a nine-phase process that begins with identification and recruitment of bombers; continues through their training, target selection, purchase of components, fabrication of devices, final preparation, and movement to the target; and ends with the detonation of the device....

> Interdiction during the last two phases is extremely difficult. Law enforcement agencies must be proactive, taking advantage of opportunities for detection and effective interdiction during the initial seven stages....

> There is evidence to suggest that recruiting initiatives may be under way in U.S. prison populations and among radicalized extremists—including U.S. citizens in a number of U.S. communities....

> Perhaps the best opportunities for detection and successful interdiction occur when terrorist organizations are selecting targets and conducting reconnaissance against them as well as when they are purchasing explosives components and fabricating explosive devices. (Priem, Hunter, and Polisar 2007, 35)[3]

Car Bombs A significant challenge to law enforcement is stopping the terrorists' low-tech, lethal weapon of choice, the car bomb or vehicle-borne improvised explosive device (VBIED), whose simplicity and stealth make them complex adversaries. It is impossible to screen all the cars and trucks that drive past critical buildings or other infrastructure, so authorities now use simple tools, such as restricting parking and traffic and putting up concrete median barriers and security checkpoints. However, the May 2010 attempted bombing in New York's Times Square illustrates how easily a VBIED may be hidden in plain sight. Fortunately, in this case, a street vendor observed smoke coming from the dark green Nissan Pathfinder and summoned a nearby officer, who correctly assessed the scene as volatile and potentially deadly and, with the assistance of backup, quickly evacuated the area around the vehicle and called for a bomb squad. The IED found inside was crudely constructed from propane tanks, gasoline, and fireworks, with two battery-operated clocks intended as a timing device and, although it had begun to detonate, a malfunction apparently occurred.

---

[3]Source: Priem, Richard G.; Hunter, Dennis M.; and Polisar, Joseph M. "Terrorists and Suicide Tactics: Preparing for the Challenge." *The Police Chief*, September 2007, pp.32–36.

There is no one standard type of vehicle associated with VBIEDs, and vehicle selection likely depends on several factors, such as the ability of the vehicle to blend in with the normal traffic at the target, the availability of the vehicle availability, and the security surrounding the intended target: "For instance, 'hardened' facilities with good physical security measures (including barriers to ensure significant standoff distances) may require the terrorist to use trucks with large, enclosed cargo areas. A vehicle of this size provides increased explosives capacities capable of generating damaging air blast effects over a large distance" (Doherty 2009, 3–4).

Weapons of Mass Destruction (WMDs)

Terrorist organizations have shown increasing interest in the acquisition and development of weapons of mass destruction (WMDs) (*Strategic Plan* 2004). The acronym CBR includes all potential terrorist threats that can have consequences for the health of large numbers of people, including chemical agents (C), biological agents (B), and radiation exposure (R). Nuclear, biological, or chemical agents are also referred to as NBC agents. Biological WMDs have been used since the 1300s. The 20th century saw the first use of artificially produced WMDS—or chemical agents—during World War I. Today, the means and recipes for developing nuclear, radiological, biological, and chemical weapons are well known and documented.

Some experts suggest that bioterrorism is the third most likely terrorist act to occur. Incendiary devices and explosives are most likely to be used because they are easy to make. Chemical devices are next in likelihood because the raw materials are easy to get and easy to use. But whatever form such weapons take, "FBI officials have been quoted as saying there is a 100 percent chance of a WMD attack on America in the near future" (Griffith 2011, 41).

Biological Agents **Bioterrorism** involves using viruses, toxins, or fungi—classes of organism that include anthrax, botulism, and smallpox—as weapons of mass destruction. The letters laced with anthrax sent to television news anchor Tom Brokaw (NBC News), Senators Patrick Leahy and Tom Daschle, and the *New York Post* generated hundreds of calls to *America's Most Wanted*.

Especially susceptible to bioterrorism are the nation's food and water supply, which might also be attacked using chemical agents. **Agroterrorism**, which is a subset of bioterrorism, is the intentional release of animal or plant toxins to generate widespread public fear and economic loss and undermine social stability: "Agriculture may not represent terrorists' first choice of targets because it lacks the shock factor of more traditional attacks; however, it comprises the largest single sector in the U.S. economy, making agroterrorism a viable primary aspiration. Such terrorist groups as al Qaeda have made economic and trade disruption key goals. They believe that by imposing economic hardship on America, its citizens will tire of the struggle and force their elected leaders to withdraw from commitments abroad" (Olson 2012, 8). This low-tech attack method can also cause widespread, long-term social panic as the U.S. population loses confidence in the safety of the food and water supply as well as the ability of the government to keep them safe.

bioterrorism

Involves using viruses, toxins, or fungi—classes of organism that include anthrax, botulism, and smallpox—as weapons of mass destruction.

agroterrorism

A subset of bioterrorism, it is the intentional release of animal or plant toxins to generate widespread public fear and economic loss and undermine social stability.

Chemical Agents The four common types of chemical weapons are nerve agents, blood agents, choking agents, and blistering agents. One agent, ricin toxin, is both a biological and a chemical weapon and is 1,000 times more poisonous than cyanide. In its purest form, a particle of ricin no bigger than a grain of table salt can kill an adult. Reportedly, detailed procedures for ricin extraction and use were found in al Qaeda's military manuals seized in safe houses and caves in Afghanistan.

The Aum Shinrikyo attack in the Tokyo subway in 1995 occurred when members of the religious cult released a poisonous gas, sarin, into the crowded subway system. The incident confirmed that a nonstate entity could manufacture a viable chemical agent and deliver it in a public location. Unfortunately, anyone with access to the Internet can obtain the chemical formula for sarin in less than 40 minutes through a Web search and can produce it inexpensively.

One chemical agent receiving increased attention is chlorine gas. Although a chlorine gas attack requires perfect conditions and a poor emergency response to cause heavy casualties, "if properly released in a well-populated area, chlorine gas has the potential to cause tens of thousands of casualties" (Harwood 2007, 18).

The DHS has released interim rules to streamline federal security regulations for high-risk chemical facilities nationwide (Edwards 2007). Efforts are ongoing to screen more than 15,000 chemical facilities and require those with certain quantities of specified chemicals to complete an assessment to determine a risk level. A company found to pose greater risk will be required to conduct a vulnerability assessment and submit site security plans that meet the DHS performance standards (Daniels 2007). Failure to comply could result in penalties as high as $25,000 a day and an order to cease operations.

Nuclear Terrorism Goodwyn (2008, 48) notes, "Terrorists' attraction to nuclear weapons is due to the destructive capability of the weapons, the horrific effects it would have on life and property, and also the economic impact on all U.S. citizens as well as the entire world." The International Atomic Energy Agency (IAEA) categorizes radionuclides into five categories based on the relative hazard posed by the radioactivity they contain, with Category 1 being most hazardous. According to the U.S. Nuclear Regulatory Commission (NRC), approximately 4,593 radioactive sources were reported lost, abandoned, or stolen between 2001 and 2010, and 2,429 were not recovered (Smith and Sant 2011). However, of all sources not recovered, only 5 were considered "significant," falling within the first three categories (Smith and Sant 2011). Nonetheless, that left 2,424 sources of lower radioactivity unaccounted for during that 10-year period.

The successful detonation of a low-yield nuclear device or radiological dispersion device (RDD), also called a dirty bomb, would be more devastating than the terrorist attacks on September 11, 2001. It is likely that the most destruction and disruption from such a dirty bomb would be caused by public panic, rather than radiation: "Even though a dirty bomb incident would be unlikely to cause many deaths, its real purpose would be to create instant terror in the form of mass panic, with lingering psychological damage" (Page 2009, 50). Such a dirty bomb, if detonated in a crowded sports arena or shopping mall, would make the decontamination and treatment of perhaps thousands of panic-stricken victims a severely daunting, expensive task.

Technological Terrorism

A method of terrorist attack that is much more difficult for law enforcement to recognize and respond to is technological terrorism. The United States is susceptible to two methods of technological terror. The first involves the conversion of an industrial site, such as a chemical plant, into a lethal instrument through sabotage. The second is an attack on a source that supplies technology or energy. Either method could be catastrophic. Any interruption of energy supplies could be a national security threat.

The term *cyberterrorism* was coined in the 1980s by Barry Collin to describe a variant of terrorism that transcended the traditional, physical realm and occurred in the virtual realm. The Center for Strategic and International Studies (CSIS) defines *cyberterrorism* as "the use of computer network tools to shut down critical national infrastructures (e.g., energy, transportation, government operations) or to coerce or intimidate a government or civilian population" (Lewis 2002, 1). A working definition of **cyberterrorism** is the use of high technology to disable or delete critical infrastructure data or information as a means of promoting a religious or political ideology and that targets innocent civilians, elements of the business sector, or government agencies (Tafoya 2011). These last two criteria—the *context* of promoting an ideology and the *targeting* of innocent civilians—is what sets cyberterrorism apart from information warfare (a military context and target) and cybercrime, which is generally committed for either personal gain or revenge (Tafoya 2011). The technological tools, techniques, and skills used by cyberterrorists and cybercriminals are the same.

cyberterrorism

The use of high technology to disable or delete critical infrastructure data or information as a means of promoting a religious or political ideology and that targets innocent civilians, elements of the business sector, or government agencies.

FUNDING TERRORISM

It takes money to carry out terrorism—for general operating expenses, as well as for weapons. Terrorist groups commonly collaborate with organized criminal groups to deal drugs, arms, and, in some instances, humans. To finance their operations, terrorist groups smuggle stolen goods and contraband, forge documents, profit from the diamond trade, and engage in extortion and protection rackets (White 2012). Many terrorist operations are financed by charitable groups and wealthy Arabs sympathetic to the group's cause. Information about local and national charities is available from the Wise Giving Alliance through the Better Business Bureau, a resource that evaluates charities against 20 rigorous accountability standards in an effort to boost donor confidence and strengthen trust in the charitable sector.

VALUABLE TARGETS FOR A TERRORIST ATTACK

Targets considered valuable for a terrorist attack include high-occupancy structures or any site where a significant number of lives are affected; a structure containing dangerous substances; any vital, high-use portion of the infrastructure; any item of significant historical, symbolic, strategic, defensive, or functional value; and a structure holding highly sensitive, rare, or irreplaceable artifacts or documents. Terrorists also seek to attack so-called "soft targets," or those locations not significantly fortified or guarded. Although terrorists most often plan their attacks with great purpose and focus directed at a specific, predetermined target, they might also select targets of opportunity if that target has significant symbolic value (White 2012).

THE FEDERAL RESPONSE TO TERRORISM

In 1996, the FBI established a Counterterrorism Center to combat terrorism. Also in 1996, the Antiterrorism and Effective Death Penalty Act was passed, including several specific measures aimed at terrorism. It enhanced the federal government's power to deny visas to individuals belonging to terrorist groups and simplified the process for deporting aliens convicted of crimes.

In 1999, the FBI announced the prevention of terrorism as its top priority by adding a new Counterterrorism Division with four subunits: the International Terrorism Section, the Domestic Terrorism Section, the National Infrastructure Protection Center, and the National Domestic Preparedness Office. But this was not enough to avert the tragic events of 9/11. It took a disaster of that magnitude to make the war on terrorism truly the first priority of the United States. One of the first federal initiatives was the establishment of the Department of Homeland Security.

The Department of Homeland Security

On October 8, 2001, President Bush signed Executive Order 13228 establishing the Department of Homeland Security (DHS).

> As a result of 9/11, the Department of Homeland Security (DHS) was established, reorganizing the departments of the federal government. The DHS facilitates collaboration between local and federal law enforcement to develop a national strategy to detect, prepare for, prevent, protect against, respond to, and recover from terrorist attacks within the United States.

The five-point mission of the DHS is as follows (*Quadrennial Homeland Security Review Report* 2010, x):

Mission 1: Preventing terrorism and enhancing security

Goal 1.1: Prevent terrorist attacks

Goal 1.2: Prevent the unauthorized acquisition or use of chemical, biological, radiological, and nuclear materials and capabilities

Goal 1.3: Manage risks to critical infrastructure, key leadership, and events

Mission 2: Securing and managing our borders

Goal 2.1: Effectively control U.S. air, land, and sea borders

Goal 2.2: Safeguard lawful trade and travel

Goal 2.3: Disrupt and dismantle transnational criminal organizations

Mission 3: Enforcing and administering our immigration laws

   Goal 3.1: Strengthen and effectively administer the immigration system

   Goal 3.2: Prevent unlawful immigration

Mission 4: Safeguarding and securing cyberspace

   Goal 4.1: Create a safe, secure, and resilient cyber environment

   Goal 4.2: Promote cybersecurity knowledge and innovation

Mission 5: Ensuring resilience to disasters

   Goal 5.1: Mitigate hazards

   Goal 5.2: Enhance preparedness

   Goal 5.3: Ensure effective emergency response

   Goal 5.4: Rapidly recover[4]

> At the federal level, the FBI is the lead agency for responding to acts of domestic terrorism. The Federal Emergency Management Agency (FEMA) is the lead agency for consequence management (after an attack).

The DHS had previously established a five-level color-coded threat system that it used to communicate with public safety officials and the public at large. However, in April 2011, DHS Secretary Janet Napolitano announced that a two-level National Terrorism Advisory System would replace the five-tiered color-coded security advisory system:

▶ Elevated threat: Warns of a credible terrorist threat against the United States.

▶ Imminent threat: Warns of a credible, specific, and impending terrorist threat against the United States.

The *National Terrorism Advisory System Public Guide* (2011, 4) explains that the basic difference between the two threat levels is that *elevated* applies to situations when there is "no specific information about the timing or location" of a credible threat, whereas *imminent* applies when it is believed the "threat is impending" or will occur "very soon."

The USA PATRIOT Act

Another effort to enhance national security was passage of the USA PATRIOT Act. On October 26, 2001, President George W. Bush signed the Uniting and Strengthening America by Providing Appropriate Tools Required to Intercept and Obstruct Terrorism (USA PATRIOT) Act into law, giving police unprecedented ability to search, seize, detain, or eavesdrop in their pursuit of possible terrorists. The law expands the FBI's wiretapping and electronic surveillance authority and allows nationwide jurisdiction for search warrants and electronic surveillance devices, including legal expansion of those devices to e-mail and the Internet.

---

[4]Source: *Quadrennial Homeland Security Review Report: A Strategic Framework for a Secure Homeland* (Washington, DC: Department of Homeland Security, February 2010). Accessed March 18, 2012. http://www.dhs.gov/xlibrary/assets/qhsr_report.pdf.

> The USA PATRIOT Act significantly improves the nation's counterterrorism efforts by:
> - Allowing investigators to use the tools already available to investigate organized crime and drug trafficking.
> - Facilitating information sharing and cooperation among government agencies so they can better "connect the dots."
> - Updating the law to reflect new technologies and new threats.
> - Increasing the penalties for those who commit or support terrorist crimes.

Using Tools Already in Use in the War on Drugs   The war the United States has waged on illicit drugs can provide lessons in the war against terrorism because both wars have several commonalties in their delivery and control. For example, drugs and terrorism involve covert illegal activities that use sophisticated undercover operations. Both have a domestic component, but the organized and international component of each is far more devastating. In addition, some terrorist cells and networks have structures similar to those of drug cartels. Finally, both "wars" require coordination among various law enforcement agencies and cooperation and information sharing with other partner countries and an overall policy weighing global strategies.

Facilitating Information Sharing   The importance of this provision of the act can be seen in the case of an al Qaeda cell in Lackawanna, New York:

> This case involved several residents of Lackawanna, who traveled to Afghanistan in 2001 to receive training at an al Qaeda–affiliated camp near Kandahar. The investigation of the "Lackawanna Six" began during the summer of 2001, when the FBI received an anonymous letter indicating that these six individuals and others might be involved in criminal activity and associating with foreign terrorists. The FBI concluded that the existing law required the creation of two separate investigations in order to retain the option of using FISA [Foreign Intelligence Surveillance Act]: a criminal investigation of possible drug crimes and an intelligence investigation related to terrorist threats. Over the ensuing months, two squads carried on these two separate investigations simultaneously, and there were times when the intelligence officers and the law enforcement agents concluded that they could not be in the same room during briefings to discuss their respective investigations with each other.

The USA PATRIOT Act, however, took down the "wall" separating these two investigations by making clear that the sharing of case-sensitive information between these two groups was allowed. As a result of key information shared by intelligence investigators, law enforcement agents were able to learn that an individual mentioned in the anonymous letter was an agent of al Qaeda. Further information shared between intelligence and law enforcement personnel then dramatically expedited the investigation of the Lackawanna Six and allowed charges to be filed against these individuals. Five of the Lackawanna Six pleaded guilty to providing material support to al Qaeda, the sixth pleaded guilty to conducting transactions unlawfully with al Qaeda. These individuals were then sentenced to prison terms ranging from seven to ten years. (*Report from the Field* 2004, 3)[5]

Updating the Law to Reflect New Technologies and New Threats Those who defend the constitutionality of roving wiretaps note that the act is not asking the law to expand, but rather to grow as technology grows. Terrorists are trained to change cell phones frequently and to route e-mail through different Internet computers to defeat detection.

Increasing the Penalties for Terrorism The PATRIOT Act also includes money laundering provisions and sets strong penalties for anyone who harbors or finances terrorists. The 1984 Act to Combat International Terrorism (ACIT) established a monetary reward program for information involving terrorism and increased the amount of money offered or paid to an informant. The PATRIOT Act also established new punishments for possessing biological weapons and made it a federal crime to commit an act of terrorism against a mass transit system.

Controversy over the USA PATRIOT Act

Some members of Congress and civil liberties groups say the act gives federal agents too much power to investigate suspected terrorists, threatening the civil rights and privacy of Americans. Those who defend the law argue that repealing it would endanger American lives and help terrorists achieve their mission. Expanding the powers of federal agents to use wiretaps, surveillance, and other investigative methods and to share intelligence has given them the tools they need to adapt and outthink terrorists. Attempts to strip law enforcement agents of their expanded legal powers could open the way to further terrorist attacks.

The PATRIOT Act was passed as an immediate response to the 9/11 attacks to provide federal law enforcement with better means to defend against terrorism. However, federal officials recognized the importance of local officers in defense against terror, and in October 2001, President Bush signed Executive Order 13231, calling for federal agencies to reach out to state and local agencies. The concern about local involvement was later incorporated into the Homeland Security Act (HSA) in November 2002. But again, this act focused on reorganizing 22 agencies to defend against terrorism. Unquestionably, the efforts of local law enforcement agencies are critical in the fight against terrorism.

The Renewal of the USA PATRIOT Act

This legislation has undergone several renewals amid continued debate between those who believe our national security depends on its renewal and those who believe that increased government powers are no longer needed, especially because no further attacks have occurred since the immediate threat that spurred the drafting of the act in the first place.

---

[5]Source: *Report from the Field: The USA PATRIOT Act at Work* (Washington, DC: Department of Justice, July 2004).

After an extension from its expiration at the end of 2005, President Bush signed into law on March 9, 2006, the USA PATRIOT Improvement and Reauthorization Act, which was almost unchanged from the original PATRIOT Act. Again, proponents asserted that the law would help keep America safe from threats while opponents feared the real threat was from a nearly unbridled government armed with this law. The reauthorized PATRIOT Act included new tools to combat the manufacture and distribution of methamphetamine. Other than two provisions—the sections dealing with business and library records and roving wiretaps, which were set to expire at the end of 2009—the revised version of the PATRIOT Act was intended to be permanent and would not expire, with changes occurring only through legislation. On May 26, 2011, President Barack Obama signed a 4-year extension on the USA PATRIOT Act, which included three key provisions addressing roving wiretaps, surveillance, and searches of business records.

Changes in the FBI following 9/11

Since September 2001, the FBI has "dramatically" strengthened its ability to combat terrorism by realigning resources, shifting agents to counterterrorism, doubling the number of intelligence analysts, and tripling the number of linguists. It has also increased the number of multiagency joint terrorism task forces (JTTFs) to 103, 71 of which have been created since 9/11 ("Protecting America from Terrorist Attack" n.d.). These JTTFs include more than 4,400 members nationwide—more than four times the pre–9/11 total—from more than 600 state and local agencies and 50 federal agencies. The FBI's effectiveness in counterterrorism, however, ultimately depends on the vigilance of and information from local law enforcement.

THE CRITICAL ROLE OF LOCAL LAW ENFORCEMENT IN HOMELAND SECURITY

Every terrorist act committed in the United States occurs in some local law enforcement agency's jurisdiction. That agency is closer to the activities in its community and has the responsibility and authority to protect that community. Law enforcement personnel now realize that their duties have expanded considerably and that our nation cannot rely solely on federal agencies and the military as the sources of our county's protection: "On 9/11 cops became a vital component of the homeland security mission. And the majority of the responsibility for this additional requirement came to rest squarely on the shoulders of the uniformed patrol officer, America's first line of defense in the war on crime, the war on drugs, the war on gangs, and now, the war on terror" (Lovette 2008, 34).

 The first line of defense against terrorism is the patrol officer in the field.

U.S. Attorney General Eric Holder, speaking at the National League of Cities Conference, stressed the importance of cities, particularly their law enforcement agencies: "Our cities are, in a very real sense, on the front lines in our fight

46.3

CALEA Standard 46.3 requires, "The agency maintains liaison with other organizations for the exchange of information relating to terrorism. The exchange of information should facilitate information sharing and multi-jurisdictional preemption of terrorist acts or events. Private agencies should be considered for participation in information sharing as necessary for various situations."

Source: Commission on Accreditation of Law Enforcement Agencies (CALEA). 2012. *Standards for Law Enforcement Agencies.* 5th ed. Fairfax, VA: Author.

against terrorism. Your police officers are often the first to see a threat and the first to report it. And information reported by a cop on the street in Omaha can make a difference in thwarting an attack in San Francisco. We are making a big mistake if we don't find ways to partner with urban law enforcement to multiply our forces in the fight against terrorism" (Holder 2009).

The local police have the powers of search, seizure of evidence, and arrest; an increasing ability to manage, share, and analyze information; skill in identifying and interpreting suspicious behaviors; and skill in carrying out investigations from beginning to end. They also add the "critical elements of speed, resources, and numbers" (Downing 2009, 30). The crimefighting model used to investigate organized crime gangs and drug trafficking organizations can apply equally to investigating terrorist networks: "Police hold the key to mitigating and ultimately defeating terrorism in the United States" (40).

AN OFFICER'S PERSPECTIVE
How 9/11 Affected Hometown Security

Post–9/11, all police officers in my agency [a suburban metropolitan department] are required to read and complete several online Homeland Security Courses put out by universities and the federal government. These courses involve several hours of required reading and the completion of several tests at the end of the course. A passing score is required; otherwise, you must retake the course. The courses outline what our roles as first responders are if a terrorist attack or a disaster were to occur in our community. One of the benefits of this training, beyond the obvious one of preparedness, is the eligibility to receive federal grants.

In addition to new terrorism/disaster training, there have been other changes implemented at the patrol level. Since 9/11, we have now outfitted each of our squad cars with a "Terrorism/Disaster" bin, placed

in the trunk, that includes a bio-hazard protective or hazmat suit, latex gloves, and boot covers. Officers are also fitted for a gas mask on an annual basis. Several other emergency items in this bin include a medical kit, flares, cones, a blanket, and more.

Responding to calls has changed as well. In the city I work in, a refinery has been identified as a sensitive target for a possible terrorist attack. Before 9/11, if an individual were to stop in the area to photograph the facility on public area, there was no issue. Post–9/11, however, private security along with law enforcement attempt to make contact and identify the suspicious activity. That information is then passed on through a joint terrorism task force (JTTF) agency that works in cooperation with local law enforcement.

—*Sgt. Henry Lim Cho*

Savelli (2004, 65–66) stresses, "Keep in mind, any law enforcement officer can potentially come in contact with a terrorist at any time, whether investigating an unrelated crime, conducting normal duties, or responding as a backup for another law enforcement officer. Also, keep in mind how many of the 9/11/01 hijackers had contact with law enforcement officers in various parts of the country and how many unsuspecting law enforcement officers, in any capacity, may have such contact with terrorists today or in the future." For example (Savelli 2004, 65–66):

▶ September 9, 2001, Ziad Jarrah, hijacker of the plane that crashed in Shanksville, Pennsylvania, was stopped by police in Maryland for speeding. He was driving 90 mph in a 65-mph zone. He was issued a ticket and released.

▶ August 2001, Hani Hanjour, who hijacked and piloted the plane that crashed into the Pentagon, killing 289 persons, was stopped by police in Arlington, Virginia. He was issued a ticket for speeding and released. He paid the ticket so he would not have to show up in court.

▶ April 2001, Mohammed Atta, who hijacked and piloted the plane that crashed into the north tower of the World Trade Center, was stopped in Tamarac, Florida, for driving without a valid license and issued a ticket. He didn't pay the ticket so an arrest warrant was issued. A few weeks later, he was stopped for speeding but let go because police did not know about the warrant.

Agencies and cities across the country have increased their security-related spending to purchase items such as surveillance cameras, security gates, bulletproof glass, filters for building ventilation systems, security badges, outdoor lighting, gas respirators, concrete planters, body armor, biohazard suits, metal detectors, fences, motion detectors, caller-ID technology, alarms, vehicle-tracking systems, electronic door locks, guardhouses, and bomb-sniffing dogs.

Understanding the Typical Stages in a Terrorist Attack

Terrorist attacks typically have three stages. The first stage is research, including surveillance, stakeouts, and local inquiries. This is the stage during which local law enforcement officers can best serve the counterterrorism effort because the terrorists are out in public, watching us, studying our habits, discovering our vulnerabilities, and reporting back to their handlers with prospective targeting data to begin the planning stage. (Recall the nine-stage process used by suicide bombers, discussed previously, and the need for law enforcement to detect and intervene during the earliest stages possible.)

The second stage is planning, usually conducted behind closed doors. The average planning cycle for international terrorists is 92 days, compared with 14 days for environmental terrorists (Smith 2008). The third stage is execution, the actual attack, and possible escape.

Understanding and Identifying the Enemy

An important step in preparedness is learning about, understanding, and identifying the enemy. To successfully fight terrorism in the United States, law enforcement must have a clear understanding of the adversary—who the enemy is, their thinking processes, their tactics, and their mindsets. For example, local law enforcement working in jurisdictions with large Arab and

Muslim communities might strive to develop trusting relationships with these immigrants citizens in an effort to obtain information about local discontent, anti-government rhetoric or propaganda, travel activity of local residents to international locations known to provide training and other support to the terrorist ideology, and similar indicators that members of the local population may be involved in terrorism.

One critical dimension of this knowledge is differentiating the street criminal from the terrorist. Officers who are trained and equipped to deal with traditional crimes are now expected to apprehend individuals operating with different motivations and who usually use much deadlier weapons than traditional criminals do. It should be recognized, however, that terrorists also engage in criminal behavior and have been found to commonly commit mail theft, coupon fraud, sale of illegal cigarettes, identity theft, credit card scams, ATM fraud, counterfeit food products and postage stamps, money laundering, and video/audio piracy (Savelli 2004). Nonetheless, criminals and terrorists demonstrate practical behavioral differences, including these (White 2012, 44):

▶ Criminals are unfocused. Terrorists focus their actions toward a goal.

▶ Criminals may live in a criminal underworld, but they are not devoted to crime as a philosophy. Terrorists are dedicated to a cause.

▶ Criminals will make deals to avoid punishment. Terrorists rarely cooperate with officials because they do not wish to betray their cause.

▶ Criminals usually run when confronted with force. Terrorists tend to attack.

▶ Criminals strike when the opportunity to do so is present. Terrorists strike against symbols after careful planning.

▶ Criminals rarely train for crime. Terrorists prepare for and rehearse their operations.[6]

Another important dimension of understanding and identifying the enemy is an awareness of terrorist indicators, such as negative rhetoric and possession or dissemination of anti-American literature, excessive physical training, or a disregard for U.S. laws (Savelli 2004).

Identification can be aided by a familiar tool of law enforcement—profiling. Such profiling must hinge on behavioral characteristics, however, because racial profiling is illegal. This is not say, however, that law enforcement should not consider appearances; it means that appearance cannot be the sole factor in profiling. The typical appearance of an al Qaeda terrorist is a young (20 to 30) Middle Eastern–appearing male of average height and weight with prominent facial hair and a foreign accent. Few use alcohol or smoke cigarettes, although many terrorists intentionally shave their beards, wear western style clothes, frequent bars, and smoke cigarettes to avoid detection. Law enforcement must also be aware that al Qaeda is actively recruiting westerners who are better able to evade suspicion because of their physical appearance.

---

[6]Source: From White. *Terrorism and Homeland Security*, 7E. © 2012 Wadsworth, a part of Cengage Learning, Inc. Reproduced by permission. www.cengage.com/permissions

Behavior pattern recognition (BPR) can also help in identifying terrorists. BPR is based on two activities: observation of irregular behaviors for a given location and targeted conversations with suspects. The community can also be instrumental in providing information, especially those areas in which community policing is used, as discussed later in the chapter.

If several individuals within one jurisdiction are identified as being terror-linked, there exists the possibility they belong to the same *cell*, the most basic unit of a traditional terrorist organization. A cell is a tactical group that has its own distinct mission and operates in virtual isolation from other cells in the same organization (White 2012). A cell that has been integrated into a community such that its members blend in with the local population is often referred to as a *sleeper cell*, a unit that essentially lies in wait until dispatched into action by those higher in command. The challenge, and key to disrupting these cells, is identifying its members.

Intelligence Gathering and Sharing

Officers can improve their ability to detect a potential terrorist attack in their communities by gathering intelligence just as they would on any investigative encounter. Many of the day-to-day duties of local law enforcement officers bring them into proximity with sources of information about terrorism. Traffic patrol can track down information related to terrorism if properly trained in what to look for and what questions to ask when interacting with citizens. When making a traffic stop, ask questions such as "Where are you from? Where do you work? Why are you here?" Note that these questions are not specific to profiling possible terrorists but are standard policing methods used by officers attempting to gather information on possible criminal activity, regardless of whether it has to do with homeland security.

The intelligence process focuses on knowing what you don't know, asking for what you don't know, finding the answers, and then making sure the answers get to the right people (*Strategic Plan* 2004). Finding intelligence gaps should lead to specific intelligence collection or production tasks. Then information needs to be collected to fill these gaps in intelligence. The information gathered should be used for briefings, reports, and studies that are then disseminated to all interested parties and partners.

> Three obstacles to intelligence effectiveness are technological, political, and ethical.

The most challenging technological issue, as discussed previously, is *interoperability*, the ability to exchange information seamlessly. Political obstacles include finances (who pays for what) and turf wars, including relationships with the FBI and with the state police. The ethical obstacles include the issues of profiling and open records legislation.

Withholding Information Counterterrorism efforts are made more difficult by the operational style that exists at almost every level of policing and in most agencies—withholding, rather than sharing, information—often referred to as "working in silos." Reluctance to share information in a multijurisdictional capacity is also known as "stovepiping" or creating a "stovepipe" of information that travels only in a narrow upward column without spreading outward or laterally to other agencies that might find such information useful or valuable. Sometimes information cannot be shared, such as classified information. Rules of federal procedure and grand jury classified material are two other limitations to what or how much information can be shared.

Noting how law enforcement officers may err on the side of caution in not sharing information that might compromise a terrorism investigation, Savelli (2004, 43) suggests, "The best way to avoid compromising an existing investigation, or conducting conflicting cases, is to develop a local networking module with local, state, and federal law enforcement agencies to discuss investigative and enforcement endeavors to combat terrorism.... These networking modules should have built-in deconfliction protocol. **Deconfliction**, in essence, means avoiding conflict. Deconfliction can be deployed with declassified and confidential investigations."

deconfliction

Avoiding conflict.

The National Criminal Intelligence Sharing Plan (NCISP) A subtitle of the Homeland Security Act of 2002, called the Homeland Security Information Sharing Act, required the president to develop new procedures for sharing classified information as well as unclassified but otherwise sensitive information with state and local police. This charge was fulfilled in May 2002 when the International Association of Chiefs of Police (IACP), the Department of Justice, the FBI, the DHS, and other representatives of the federal, state, tribal, and local law enforcement communities endorsed the NCISP, which increases cooperation and communication among local, state, and federal partners to an unprecedented level, strengthening the abilities of the justice community to detect threats and protect American lives and liberties.

Intelligence Reform and Terrorism Prevention Act of 2004 In December 2004, President Bush signed into law the Intelligence Reform and Terrorism Prevention Act to enhance public safety communication operability at all levels of government. It requires the president to facilitate sharing terrorism information among all appropriate federal, state, local, tribal, and private security entities through the use of policy guidelines and technology.

Fusion Centers An initiative aimed at promoting and facilitating information and intelligence sharing among federal and local law enforcement agencies is the development of fusion centers throughout the country. A **fusion center** manages and facilitates the flow of information and intelligence across all levels and sectors of government and private industry, turning information and intelligence into actionable knowledge:

fusion center

Manages and facilitates the flow of information and intelligence across all levels and sectors of government and private industry, turning information and intelligence into actionable knowledge.

> Fusion centers contribute to the Information Sharing Environment (ISE) through their role in receiving threat information from the federal government; analyzing that information in the context of their local environment; disseminating that information to local agencies; and gathering tips, leads, and suspicious activity reporting (SAR) from local agencies and the public.

Fusion centers receive information from a variety of sources, including SAR from stakeholders within their jurisdictions, as well as federal information and intelligence. They analyze the information and develop relevant products to disseminate to their customers. These products assist homeland security partners at all levels of government to identify and address immediate and emerging threats.

Beyond serving as a focal point for information sharing, fusion centers add significant value to their customers by providing a state and local context to help enhance the national threat picture. Fusion centers provide the federal government with critical state and local information and subject matter expertise that it did not receive in the past—enabling the effective communication of locally generated threat–related information to the federal government. Integrating and connecting these state and local resources creates a national capacity to gather, process, analyze, and share information in support of efforts to protect the country. ("National Network of Fusion Centers" 2012)[7]

Fusion centers help law enforcement detect, prevent, investigate, and respond to terrorist activity and to violent crime, weapons violations, and drug trafficking (Lambert 2010). By March 2012, there were 72 fusion centers throughout the country.

TECHNOLOGY IN POLICING

EGUARDIAN

Information sharing became a top priority after 9/11. The National Strategy for Information Sharing (NSIS) directed the FBI to share more information—specifically that related to terrorism—with law enforcement agencies and led to the creation of the eGuardian system, which provided three critical and unprecedented functions related to information sharing (Durner 2012, 12–13):

> First the system allows local law enforcement agencies to put terrorism-related information in a database where it has a direct electronic path to the FBI's Joint Terrorism Task Force (JTTF)....

Second, eGuardian allows the FBI to share its unclassified terrorism information with the rest of the domestic law enforcement community....

Third, information entered into eGuardian can be seen nationwide by all law enforcement entities with system access.

During its first three years, eGuardian has demonstrated substantial success in facilitating the exchange of terrorism-related information among federal, state, local, and tribal law enforcement agencies. The system has enabled the FBI to open 106 new terrorism cases and enhance 388 cases the FBI was already working on (Durner 2012).

RESPONDING TO A TERRORIST ATTACK OR ATTEMPT

Just as local law enforcement is the first line of defense in preventing a terrorist event in their jurisdiction, they are also most likely to be the first ones to respond to any attempts or actual attacks.

---

[7]Source: "National Network of Fusion Centers Fact Sheet." (Washington, DC: Department of Homeland Security, page reviewed February 3, 2012). Accessed March 20, 2012. http://www.dhs.gov/files/programs/gc_1296484657738.shtm.

Responding to Suicide Bombers

The Police Executive Research Forum (PERF) has developed guidelines for a patrol-level response to a suicide bomb threat, stressing that any protocol should be consistent with the agency's policies and procedures for use of force, active shooter situations, and bomb threats. A suggested tactic for first responders facing a potential suicide bomber is to issue a clear verbal command: "Do not move," because any movement might trigger the explosives (Chudwin 2007). Live-fire shooters should stand ready to make a head shot, preferably with a long gun able to deliver a high-velocity round or 12-gauge slug. Officers should not let their guard down with "presumed compliance." Officers should establish a perimeter around the suspected bomber, considering that the blast radius for explosive devices attached to the body can easily cover 100 yards.

Responding to WMD Incidents

In most instances, patrol officers will be dispatched to a WMD event. Terrorists might attempt to interfere with the emergency response by detonating secondary explosives, creating additional events requiring emergency resources and unauthorized entrance to restricted areas. First responder responsibilities include rescuing the injured and trapped victims and calling for medical assistance if needed: "In a WMD incident, this process must occur, but with strict attention to preserving the health and safety of responders. This implies that emergency responders without protective personal equipment (PPE) should not perform such duties" (Carlson 2008, 3). Table 9.1 illustrates the level of protection, description, type of protection afforded, and circumstance for use of each level of equipment.

After the injured have been attended to, the responsibilities of first responders turn to containing, protecting, assisting, and investigating (Carlson

Table 9.1 Personal Protective Equipment

Level	Description	Protection	Circumstance
D	Work uniform	Provides no respiratory protection and minimal skin protection	Should not be worn on any site where respiratory or skin hazards exist
C	Full facepiece, air-purifying, canister-equipped respirator, and chemical-resistant clothing	Same skin protection as level B, but a lower level respirator	Worn when airborne substance is known, concentration is measured, criteria for using air-purifying respirators are met, and skin and eye exposures are unlikely
B	Chemical-resistant clothing (overalls and long sleeves) and self-contained breathing apparatus (SCBA)	Provides splash protection	When the highest level of respiratory protection is needed but a lesser level of skin and eye protection is sufficient
A	Fully encapsulating chemical-resistant suit and SCBA can be worn for only 15 to 30 minutes due to overheating; special training is required	Provides full protection	When the highest level of respiratory, skin, eye, and mucous membrane protection is needed

Source: Melissa Reuland and Heather J. Davies. *Protecting Your Community from Terrorism: Strategies for Local Law Enforcement.* Vol. 3, *Preparing for and Responding to Bioterrorism.* Washington, DC: Community Oriented Policing Services (COPS) and the Police Executive Research Forum, September 2004.

2008). Unified command might be achieved by using the National Incident Management System (NIMS) discussed in Chapter 8. The incident command post should establish a joint information center to handle all public and media releases. Carlson concludes, "The possibility of a terrorist attack using weapons of mass destruction poses a challenge unlike any other facing today's law enforcement profession. Beyond dealing with the death and destruction brought about by such an event, agencies must ensure the safety and survival of their personnel and their families" (2008, 5–6).

A major catastrophe might be beyond a police agency's capability to handle and could require assistance from many law enforcement organizations, public safety departments, other government services, and the private sector: "Protecting the public, treating the injured, and protecting other responders will require just about all of the fire, EMS, HazMat, and police resources in the community that gets hit" (Griffith 2011, 42). Many law enforcement agencies have formed WMD teams to be ready if needed.

A WMD Team In addition to responding to dirty bombs, the toxic dust at Ground Zero, or the anthrax-laced letters sent to government building, first responders are also trained to respond to suspected meth labs, all involving situations immediately dangerous to life or health (IDLH). Hazardous materials (hazmat) training, discussed in Chapter 8, will be of tremendous benefit in such situations. In IDLH situations, federal agencies, including the Occupational Safety and Health Administration (OSHA), have established standards emergency responders must adhere to, which apply to tactical officers as well as to fire department and the hazmat team (Perin 2009). Thus, it makes sense for departments to combine hazmat and special weapons and tactics (SWAT) training for tactical operations. Although both entities are first responders and bound by OSHA standards, SWAT team operators' mission differs from that of a hazmat team when responding to potential hazards. Nonetheless, personnel from each team might benefit from training together and learning how to assist each other in numerous situations. "HAZSWAT" teams might be the strategy of the future.

The Federal Protective Services (FPS), which is part of the DHS, operates a CBRNE (chemical, biological, radiological, nuclear, and high-yield explosives) program to handle credible CBRNE threats or incidents involving federal properties. If a WMD incident occurs, FPS coordinators will work with local law enforcement to get more "boots on the ground" for an effective response. However, local agencies must understand that deploying external resources takes time and that help may not be instantaneous, meaning they must be prepared to handle the initial response alone: "In reality when we deal with a WMD event, it will be a local event; it will be a local problem. It will start at the local level and end at the local level" (Griffith 2011, 44).

Detecting Radiation and Other Bioterrorism Agents A variety of technologies is available to help investigators detect radioactive and other hazardous agents. Dosimeters are small, lightweight devices that use silicon diode technology to instantaneously detect and display the accumulated radiation exposure dose and dose rate. They can identify the specific radionuclide(s) involved and let investigators calculate how long they can safely remain on the scene.

Another tool used to detect hazardous agents is the *electronic nose*, which is already used to select fragrant wines and diagnose diseases. Electronic nose technology is designed to detect all chemicals within an aroma or fragrance and miss nothing. Some electronic noses use wireless technology, allowing an investigator more than a mile away from the device to use a computer to remotely monitor the vapors, smells, odors, and chemistry of the air.

Robotic detection and identification technology can warn responders of NBC agents' presence and strength. Global positioning systems (GPS) can be applied to determine the coordinates of an NBC release relative to the position of responders, residential or other civilian centers, or other critical location information. GPS can also track vehicles charged with transporting NBC materials to and from the site. Finally, weather data—such as wind direction and speed, barometric pressure, relative humidity, and so forth—is critical to responders at NBC scenes.

Law enforcement officers must be prepared to manage CBRNE threats through detection devices, although such devices are relatively new and used mainly by larger metropolitan agencies seen as potential terrorist targets (Trudeau 2009). One such detection device, the RadTruck, is equipped with adaptable radiation area monitors (ARAMs) mounted in the back cargo areas of sports utility vehicles (SUVs) (Page 2009). The ARAMs can detect a radiation source no larger than a grain of sand and determine, in an instant, if it is a lethal substance or the harmless potassium found in a banana, all while cruising past a person, vehicle, or building at street speed in a police SUV. The ARAMs are built to detect illicit low-energy gamma rays and neutron emissions characteristic of weapons-grade plutonium and highly enriched uranium. They can provide accurate, positive warning and identification if suspicious materials come within detection range or if a RadTruck comes within the range of the suspicious material.

Of course, law enforcement should not overlook the low-tech options of K-9s, which are increasingly being trained to detect various scents associated with agents used to make a variety of explosives. Such bomb dogs are commonly used at airports and other mass transit hubs.

Lessons Learned from Mumbai

Theodore Roosevelt once said, "Americans only learn by disaster." Considering, in retrospect, how much has changed since 9/11, this assessment certainly seems accurate. Our knowledge continues to grow with each event endured, and numerous valuable lessons were learned in the wake of the terrorist attacks in Mumbai, India, in November 2008.

The first lesson is to *heed the warning signs.* The United States had warned India's government of a coming attack, probably on luxury hotels, but the message was not communicated from the top down (Chudwin 2009).

The second lesson is that *leadership must be proactive, responsive, and adaptive.* Law enforcement exists as hierarchical organizations geared toward making the big decisions. But in critical incidents, leaders must be willing to allow line-level decision making: "In attacks like those in Mumbai, patrol supervisors will be the generals of the street, and individual initiative will rule the moment" (Chudwin 2009, 51).

Third, the key to stopping terrorist attacks is keeping in touch to have an opportunity at *prevention and deterrence*. The intelligence function is the foundation of this effort.

Fourth, *system capability and officer response* are vital. In Mumbai, the home-field advantage was lost to the terrorists, who had done reconnaissance and knew their target better than the police and follow-on military did. To maintain the home-field advantage, officers should study building plans; do walk-throughs of potential targets; liaise with security directors of hotels, airports, and other likely targets; and plan ahead of an attack what should be done. Officers should be aware of and make use of the intelligence fusions centers around the country and get to know members of the JTTF in the local FBI office.

Last, *stand ready and prepared to fight*. There will be no time to wait for special teams. If terrorists are allowed time to set defenses, blockade entrances, and set explosives, it will be Mumbai again. The bottom line is, "Police must be capable and ready to fight. This is the core mission of law enforcement: protect our citizens and residents from threats to their lives. There's a time to talk and a time to fight. Administrators and street officers must know the difference." Chudwin (2009, 55) suggests that each officer have at-the-ready a "go bag" that contains extra ammunition, radio and flashlight batteries, wound bandages, a tourniquet, binoculars, and other combat essentials: "We have skilled men and women in uniform on the street and in command positions. It only takes the willingness to accept that the threat is real, imminent, and coming to your hometown. In the end, it's not enough to be willing to fight. There must be a total commitment to win" (55).

In assessing a jurisdiction's target attractiveness and vulnerability, law enforcement should keep in mind these lessons learned from Mumbai (Monahan and Stainbrook 2011):

▶ Tourism destinations (theme parks, cruise lines) and the hospitality industry (hotels, resorts) continue to be attractive and vulnerable targets to terrorists.

▶ Venues with a high human density (sporting events, concerts) are attractive targets because they maximize the potential number of casualties while minimizing required terrorist resources (ammunition, number of operatives required to carry out the attack).

▶ Selection of landmark and iconic targets will ensure media coverage, which is a prime objective of terrorists.

▶ The terrorists who conduct the preoperational surveillance and reconnaissance will likely not be the same individuals who conduct the attack.

▶ The taking of hostages is effective in delaying a police counterattack, which allows terrorists time to fortify their position; hostages also make the event more likely to receive continuous media coverage.

▶ Fire is an efficient, inexpensive, and portable weapon for causing mass casualties and giving terrorists a strategic and tactical advantage—most first responders (fire, EMTs, police) are ill-prepared to simultaneously fight fires and provide emergency medical assistance in active combat environments: "Cross-training and properly equipping local police, fire, and emergency medical personnel is the only way to neutralize this advantage" (Monahan and Stainbrook 2011, 32).

INITIATIVES TO ASSIST IN THE FIGHT AGAINST TERRORISM

Several initiatives have been undertaken to help in the fight against terrorism. One such initiative is production of the *FBI Intelligence Bulletin*, a weekly online publication containing information related to terrorism in the United States. Recipients include duly authorized members of all law enforcement agencies who have registered with a law enforcement network.

Another initiative that indirectly supports the fight against terrorism was drafting of the Community Protection Act of 1997, or H.R. 218, a bill that was finally signed into law seven years later by President Bush. In 2004, H.R. 218 became Pub. L. 108–277, the Law Enforcement Officer's Safety Act of 2004, amending Title 18, U.S. Code, to exempt qualified current and former law enforcement officers from state laws prohibiting the carrying of concealed handguns.

> The Law Enforcement Officer's Safety Act of 2004 gives off-duty as well as qualified retired police officers the right to carry their concealed firearms in all 50 states.

Other initiatives include increased security at our borders, the Community Vulnerability Assessment Methodology, the Terrorist Center, the National Infrastructure Protection Plan (NIPP), fusion centers, the Memorial Institute for the Prevention of Terrorism (MIPT), the Center for Food Protection and Defense, and the National Incident Management System.

Increased Border Security

The terrorist attacks in Mumbai, India, brought to the forefront the vulnerability of our nation's ports because the United States has no central port authority

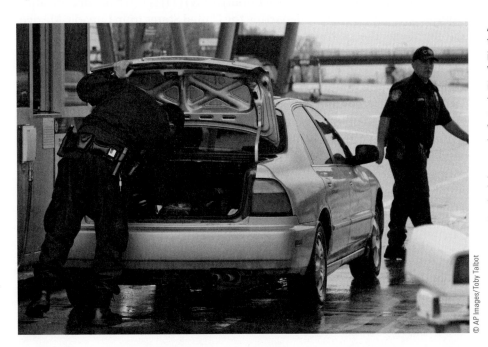

Agents check a vehicle at the U.S. border crossing in Highgate Springs, Vermont, as part of increased efforts to screen for terrorist activity. Implementation of the Western Hemisphere Travel Initiative also now requires all Canadian and American citizens entering the United States by land to have passports or other special driver's licenses.

© AP Images/Toby Talbot

to oversee security (Taylor and Kaufman 2009). Approximately 8,000 ships with foreign flags make 51,000 calls on U.S. ports each year, and 90 percent of overseas commerce comes by ship. In addition, more than 6.5 million passengers from cruise ships pass through the nation's ports each year, along with about 9 million cargo containers—about 26,000 cargo containers a day: "If terrorists used a cargo container to conceal a weapon of mass destruction and detonated it upon arrival at a U.S. port, the impact on global trade and the world economy could be immediate and devastating" (Taylor and Kaufman 2009, 32).

Research on security measures currently in place at our nation's ports found that many have created physical barriers, limited access, installed detection equipment, increased law enforcement activity, and coordinated strategies among agencies (Taylor and Kaufman 2009). Some of the best systems combined closed-circuit television (CCTV) and video analysis to analyze video proactively based on observed behavior. One simple strategy used by most of the ports stacked empty shipping containers with their doors facing each other to block entry to terrorists, stowaways, or smugglers. Other border security programs are aimed at those seeking illegal entry into the United States.

The Department of Homeland Security's program, U.S. Visitor and Immigrant Status Indicator Technology (US-VISIT), seeks "to enhance the security of our citizens and visitors; facilitate legitimate travel and trade; and ensure the integrity of our immigration system." The program requires visitors to submit to inkless finger scans and digital photographs to allow Customs and Border Protection officers to determine whether the person applying for entry is the same one who was issued a visa by the State Department. Biometric and biographic data will also be checked against watch lists of suspected foreign terrorists and databases of sexual predators, criminals wanted by the FBI, and people deported previously from the United States.

The Western Hemisphere Travel Initiative (WHTI) set stricter identification requirements for entering or departing the United States from Canada, Mexico, and Bermuda. The air travel requirement phase took effect January 23, 2007, and the land and sea requirement went into effect June 1, 2009. This initiative requires all travelers, including children, to present a passport or other WHTI-compliant document when entering the United States. The goal is to facilitate entry for U.S. citizens and legitimate foreign visitors while reducing the possibility of people entering the country using fraudulent documents. Another new development is the electronic passport (e-passport), which is the same as a regular passport but with a small computer chip embedded in the back cover as an upgraded security feature. Since August 2007, the United States has issued only e-passports.

Community Vulnerability Assessment Methodology

The Community Vulnerability Assessment Methodology (C-VAM) identifies a community's weaknesses by using a detailed, systematic analysis of the facilities and their relationship to each other. By considering a community as individual structures, a department can focus its resources on the areas where they are most needed.

The Terrorist Screening Center

The Terrorist Screening Center (TSC) maintains the government's Terrorist Watchlist—a single database of identifying information about those known or reasonably suspected of being involved in terrorist activity. According to the FBI, the Terrorist Watchlist is one of the most effective counterterrorism tools for the U.S. government. While distributing information about encounters with known or suspected terrorists, the TSC is also "dedicated to ensuring that data is maintained in a manner consistent with protecting privacy and civil liberties" ("Safeguarding Civil Liberties" n.d.).

The National Infrastructure Protection Plan (NIPP)

The NIPP is a comprehensive risk management framework defining critical infrastructure protection roles and responsibilities of federal, state, local, tribal, and private security partners. The goal of the NIPP is to "Build a safer, more secure and more resilient America by enhancing protection of the nation's critical infrastructure and key resources (CI/KR) to prevent, deter, neutralize, or mitigate the effects of deliberate efforts by terrorists to destroy, incapacitate, or exploit them; and to strengthen national preparedness, timely response and rapid recovery in the event of an attack, natural disaster, or other emergency" (*National Infrastructure Protection Plan* 2009, 9). The NIPP (2009, 4) describes sector-specific agencies and assigned critical infrastructure and key resources sectors in Table 9.2.

The cornerstone of the NIPP is the risk management framework, shown in Figure 9.2. This framework establishes the process for combining consequence, vulnerability, and threat information to produce a comprehensive, systematic, and rational assessment or national or sector-specific risk that drives CI/KR-protection activities.

The Memorial Institute for the Prevention of Terrorism (MIPT)

The MIPT, which originated from the 1995 bombing of the Alfred P. Murrah Federal Building, is a counterterrorism center focused on training, analysis, and information sharing in preventing terrorist attacks. Its name and mission are identical—preventing terrorism. Members of the institute do so by delivering training on site or remotely, creating exercises and teaching tools, advising government and private enterprise, and sharing knowledge through their library ("About MIPT" n.d.).

In April 2009, the MIPT hosted a round-table discussion with law enforcement officers from the Middle East, including Afghanistan, Bangladesh, Egypt, Kuwait, Maldives, Pakistan, Qatar, and the West Bank. The objective was to share lessons learned from fighting terrorism as well as to examine the roles, responsibilities, and cooperative efforts of key law enforcement institutions (Manos 2009).

The Center for Food Protection and Defense

The mission of the National Center for Food Protection and Defense, an effort led by the University of Minnesota, is to safeguard the security of the food system through research and education. Its goals are to reduce the vulnerability of the nation's food system to terrorist attack by contamination with biological,

Table 9.2 Sector-Specific Agencies and Assigned CIKR Sectors

Sector-Specific Agency	Critical Infrastructure and Key Resources Sector
Department of Agriculture[a]	Agriculture and Food
Department of Health and Human Services[b]	
Department of Defense[c]	Defense Industrial Base
Department of Energy	Energy[d]
Department of Health and Human Services	Healthcare and Public Health
Department of the Interior	National Monuments and Icons
Department of the Treasury	Banking and Finance
Environmental Protection Agency	Water[e]
Department of Homeland Security Office of Infrastructure Protection	Chemical
	Commercial Facilities
	Critical Manufacturing
	Dams
	Emergency Services
	Nuclear Reactors, Materials, and Waste
Office of Cybersecurity and Communications	Information Technology Communications
Transportation Security Administration	Postal and Shipping
Transportation Security Administration United States Coast Guard[f]	Transportation Systems[g]
Immigration and Customs Enforcement, Federal Protective Service	Government Facilities[h]

[a] The Department of Agriculture is responsible for agriculture and food (meat, poultry, and egg products).

[b] The Department of Health and Human Services is responsible for food other than meat, poultry, and egg products.

[c] Nothing in this plan impairs or otherwise affects the authority of the Secretary of Defense over the Department of Defense (DoD), including the chain of command for military forces from the President as Commander in Chief, to the Secretary of Defense, to the commander of military forces, or military command and control procedures.

[d] The Energy Sector includes the production, refining, storage, and distribution of oil, gas, and electric power, except for commercial nuclear power facilities.

[e] The Water Sector includes drinking water and wastewater systems.

[f] The U.S. Coast Guard is the SSA [Sector-Specific Agency] for the maritime transportation mode.

[g] As stated in HSPD-7 [Homeland Security Presidential Directive 7], the Department of Transportation and the Department of Homeland Security will collaborate on all matters relating to transportation security and transportation infrastructure protection.

[h] The Department of Education is the SSA for the Education Facilities Subsector of the Government Facilities Sector.

Source: *National Infrastructure Protection Plan* (Washington, DC: Department of Homeland Security, 2009), 3.

chemical, or radiological agents at any point along the food supply chain; to strengthen the food system's preparedness and resiliency to threats, disruption, and attacks; and to mitigate the potentially catastrophic public health and economic effects of food system attacks ("Program Summary" n.d.).

The National Incident Management System (NIMS)

In 2004, the NIMS became the country's first standardized management approach unifying federal, state, and local governments for incident response. NIMS establishes standardized incident management processes, protocols, and procedures that all responders—federal, state, tribal, and local—use to coordinate and conduct response action, as discussed in Chapter 8.

Continuous improvement to enhance protection of CI/KR

FIGURE 9.2 NIPP Risk Management Framework
Source: *National Infrastructure Protection Plan* (Washington, DC: Department of Homeland Security, 2009), 4.

THE ROLE OF NEWS MEDIA IN THE WAR ON TERRORISM

As already discussed, terrorism and the news media seem to have a symbiotic relationship, with each benefiting from the actions of the other. The media gain tremendous viewership with coverage of terrorist events, which pleases sponsors and brings more revenue to the media. Terrorists, in turn, rely on the news media to spread information about their efforts, bring attention to their cause, and generate a climate of fear among the public: "An Algerian terrorist once said he would rather kill one victim in front of a news camera than one hundred in the desert where the world would not see them. His point should be noted: Modern terrorism is a media phenomenon" (White 2012, 104).

Some analysts and scholars contend that media coverage can result in the **contagion effect**, that is, the coverage of terrorism inspires more terrorism. It is, in effect, contagious. For example, an article in *The Police Chief* states, "The media attention and public reaction to the Mumbai attacks could possibly prompt other terrorist incidents" ("Need for Homeland Security" 2009, 25). White (2012, 122) notes, "There may be a contagious relationship between a terrorist event and the level of violence in later events. On March 11, 2004, terrorists set off a series of bombs on commuter trains in Madrid. The attack was intended to kill as many people as possible in a spectacular fashion." Some have speculated that this type of attack is a product of mass media reporting, with international terrorists coming to believe that their attacks must be spectacular in magnitude if they are to achieve international media coverage: "In this sense, the level of violence is contagious" (White 2012, 122). This controversial issue leads to discussions about censorship in the war on terrorism.

contagion effect

Media coverage of terrorism inspires more terrorism—it is, in effect, contagious.

CONCERNS RELATED TO THE WAR ON TERRORISM

"We have learned that it is not possible to secure the American homeland simply with physical protections or through strategies that reinforce fear or isolation. Nor is this country made safe by substantially curtailing the very rights and liberties that define the free and diverse society we seek to protect, or by excluding visitors and lawful immigrants. Indeed, homeland security is as much about protecting the American way of life as it is about protecting this country from future attacks. Thus, a safe and secure homeland must... ensure that the liberties of all Americans are assured" (*Quadrennial Homeland Security Review Report* 2010, 2).

> Two concerns related to the "war on terrorism" are that civil liberties might be jeopardized and that people of Middle Eastern descent might be discriminated against or become victims of hate crimes.

Concern for Civil Rights

Civil libertarians are concerned that valued American freedoms will be sacrificed in the interest of national safety. For example, the Justice Department has issued a new regulation giving itself the authority to monitor inmate–attorney communications if "reasonable suspicion" exists that inmates are using such communications to further or facilitate acts of terrorism. However, criminal defense lawyers and members of the American Civil Liberties Union (ACLU) have protested the regulation, saying it effectively eliminates the Sixth Amendment right to counsel because, under codes of professional responsibility, attorneys cannot communicate with clients if confidentiality is not ensured. The ACLU has vowed to monitor police actions closely to see that freedoms protected under the Constitution are not jeopardized.

> A difficult challenge facing law enforcement is balancing the need to enhance security with the need to maintain freedom.

Retaliation or Discrimination against People of Middle Eastern Descent

Another concern is that some Americans might retaliate against innocent people of Middle Eastern descent, many of whom were either born in the United States or are naturalized citizens. We must remember the Japanese internment camps during World War II and make sure we do not repeat that mistake. Four significant obstacles to improved relations between police and Arab American communities are the following (Henderson et al. 2008):

▶ Distrust between Arab American communities and law enforcement
▶ Lack of cultural awareness among law enforcement officers
▶ Language barriers
▶ Concerns about immigration status and fear of deportation

Community policing efforts can do much to overcome these obstacles.

Closely related concerns are the rights of citizens detained as enemy combatants and the rights of detained foreign nationals. In *Hamdi v. Rumsfeld* (2004), the Supreme Court ruled that a citizen detained in the United States as an enemy combatant must be afforded the opportunity to rebut such a designation. Petitioner Hamdi was captured in an active combat zone in

Afghanistan following the September 11, 2001, attack on America and surrendered an assault rifle. The U.S. District Court found that the declaration from the Defense Department did not support Hamdi's detention and ordered the government to turn over numerous materials for review. The U.S. Court of Appeals for the Fourth Circuit reversed, stressing that, because it was undisputed that Hamdi was captured in an active combat zone, no factual inquiry or evidentiary hearing allowing Hamdi to rebut the government's assertions was necessary. A 6–3 Supreme Court vacated and remanded, concluding that Hamdi should have a meaningful opportunity to offer evidence that he was not an enemy combatant.

In *Rasul v. Bush* (2004), the Supreme Court ruled that U.S. courts have jurisdiction to consider challenges to the legality of the detention of foreign nationals captured in Afghanistan in a military campaign against al Qaeda and the Taliban regime that supported it. The petitioners, 2 Australians and 12 Kuwaitis, were being held in Guantanamo Bay, Cuba, without charges. These and other legal issues regarding civil rights will be debated as the country seeks to balance the need for security with civil rights.

Lively controversy surrounds the future of Guantanamo Bay (aka GITMO), where a detainment facility run by the U.S. military houses "enemy combatants" captured in the war on terrorism (Note: In March 2009 the Obama administration officially dropped the label "enemy combatant" in referring to those detained at Guantanamo Bay). President Barack Obama is committed to closing the facility but is facing criticism and challenges from Congress, the public, and other sources for possible ramifications of releasing dangerous individuals who are intent on causing harm to our country and its citizens. It is impossible to predict what might result from such a dismantling of this facility, but this will undoubtedly be a topic of discussion for future editions of this text.

COMMUNITY POLICING AND HOMELAND SECURITY

"Individual citizens and cohesive communities are key partners in the homeland security enterprise and have an essential role to play in countering terrorism. Mechanisms for identifying and reporting suspicious activities must be made clear and accessible. Moreover, enhanced public preparedness and effective warning systems can empower communities, help minimize fear, and diminish the effectiveness of terrorist tactics" (*Quadrennial Homeland Security Review Report* 2010, 39).

Police departments wanting to mobilize their community in counterterrorism efforts should (Vernon 2008, 57):

1. Establish a liaison with DHS.
2. Formulate a policy statement that will guide community mobilization efforts.
3. Educate community members about the significant differences between reporting sought-after information (proper) and conducting covert investigations or other quasi-police actions (improper).
4. Emphasize the importance of reporting information without making assumptions about a person's guilt.

Citizen Corps, a component of the USA Freedom Corps, focuses on opportunities for people across the country to participate in a range of measures to make their families, homes, and communities safer from the threats of terrorism, crime, and disasters of all kinds ("Citizen Corps Programs" 2007). In addition, Citizen Corps brings together a community's first responders, firefighters, emergency health care providers, law enforcement, and emergency managers with its volunteer resources. Other sources of information in the community include Neighborhood Watches, hotels, real estate agents, storage facilities, religious groups, social and civic clubs, colleges and universities, print shops, business managers, transportation centers, tourist attractions, major industrial enterprises, schools, office building custodians, health care providers, bars and liquor stores, and inspectors and code enforcers.

In July 2010, the DHS launched a national "If You See Something, Say Something™" public awareness campaign to engage citizens as extra eyes and ears in detecting indicators of terrorism and violent crime, and to emphasize the importance of reporting suspicious activity to the appropriate state and local law enforcement authorities. The campaign was originally used by New York's Metropolitan Transportation Authority (MTA), which has licensed the use of the slogan to DHS for antiterrorism and anticrime efforts.

Because a critical element of the DHS mission is ensuring that the civil rights and civil liberties of persons are not diminished by our security efforts, activities, and programs, the "If You See Something, Say Something™" campaign emphasizes the importance of *behavior*, rather than appearance, in identifying suspicious activity. Extralegal factors such as race, ethnicity, national origin, or religious affiliation alone are not suspicious. Thus, the public is reminded to report only suspicious behavior and situations (e.g., an unattended backpack in a public place or someone trying to break into a restricted area) rather than beliefs, thoughts, ideas, expressions, associations, or speech unrelated to terrorism or other criminal activity. Only reports that document *behavior reasonably indicative of criminal activity related to terrorism* will be shared with federal partners.

The "If You See Something, Say Something™" campaign is being launched in conjunction with the rollout of the Nationwide Suspicious Activity Reporting Initiative (NSI), an administration-wide effort to develop, evaluate, and implement common processes and policies for gathering, documenting, processing, analyzing, and sharing information about terrorism-related suspicious activities. Both the "If You See Something, Say Something™" campaign and the NSI underscore the concept that homeland security begins with *hometown security*, where an alert public plays a critical role in keeping our nation safe.

SUMMARY

The threat of terrorism has become a reality in America. Most definitions of terrorism have common elements, including the systematic, criminal use of physical violence, either actual or threatened, against noncombatants to create a climate of fear and to cause some religious, political, or social change. The FBI classifies terrorist acts in the United States as either domestic or international terrorism. Most terrorist acts result from dissatisfaction with a religious, political, or social system or policy and frustration resulting from an inability to change it through acceptable, nonviolent means. Terrorist groups within the United States with specific motivations include right-wing extremists (White supremacists, Black supremacists, and militia groups), left-wing extremists, pro-life extremists, animal rights activists, and environmental extremists. Terrorists might use arson, explosives and bombs, weapons of mass destruction (biological, chemical, or nuclear agents), and technology to carry out attacks.

As a result of 9/11, the Department of Homeland Security (DHS) was established, reorganizing the departments of the federal government. The DHS facilitates collaboration between local and federal law enforcement to develop a national strategy to detect, prepare for, prevent, protect against, respond to, and recover from terrorist attacks within the United States. At the federal level, the FBI is the lead agency for responding to acts of domestic terrorism. The Federal Emergency Management Agency (FEMA) is the lead agency for consequence management (after an attack).

The USA PATRIOT Act significantly improves the nation's counterterrorism efforts by:

▶ Allowing investigators to use the tools already available to investigate organized crime and drug trafficking.

▶ Facilitating information sharing and cooperation among government agencies so they can better "connect the dots."

▶ Updating the law to reflect new technologies and new threats.

▶ Increasing the penalties for those who commit or support terrorist crimes.

The first line of defense against terrorism is the patrol officer in the field.

Three obstacles to intelligence effectiveness are technological, political, and ethical. The Law Enforcement Officer's Safety Act of 2004 gives off-duty as well as qualified retired police officers the right to carry their concealed firearms in all 50 states.

Two concerns related to the "war on terrorism" are that civil liberties might be jeopardized and that people of Middle Eastern descent might be discriminated against or become victims of hate crimes. A difficult challenge facing law enforcement is balancing the need to enhance security with the need to maintain freedom.

APPLICATION

You are a public safety administrator with an agency that has several high-risk terrorism target locations, as identified by the FBI, in your city. Among the targets identified are a large oil refinery and a nationally recognized water park that draws hundreds of thousands of tourists and local visitors annually. Your agency is large and well prepared for general public safety; however, it seems that the city does not have the funds to properly outfit your agency with all of the items needed to respond to a terrorist attack or a large-scale disaster. Your agency is eligible to receive grants because of the recognized terrorist targets within your community and because the potential for attack is high, and your chief administrator has requested that you research and write some federal or state grants. Your objective is to receive funding to alleviate some of the financial burden for items that need to be purchased to respond to a terrorist incident.

INSTRUCTIONS

Draft a grant requesting the items you need for your city and provide a detailed explanation of why you need them. Your application should include the details of your agency and a purpose statement. Furthermore, research what federal or state agencies might have available grant money for homeland security–specific funding such as this.

AN EXERCISE IN CRITICAL THINKING

You are a police officer with Big City Police Department who has been assigned to a specialized Terrorism Task Force Unit and Retail Liaison with a large mall that operates in your city. This mall is a major international tourist attraction and has a worldwide reputation that embodies much of what the United States represents in terms of free trade and capitalism. Your assignment includes working closely with the mall's company administration and security, as well as with federal agents from the DHS and the FBI. Your duties include gathering intelligence and investigating suspicious activity that could be terrorism related.

While conducting foot patrol around the mall, you notice a man of Middle Eastern descent walk toward a restricted corridor in the building. You follow him to make contact. When you approach him, you see he has a high-quality digital camera and is taking pictures of the inside of the restricted area. When he sees you, he appears startled and quickly takes the memory card out of his camera and places it in his pocket. Upon questioning, he tells you his name, shows you a state-issued identification document, and states he just got lost because the building was so large. A check comes back to a valid and clear person. He is cooperative until you ask him why he was taking pictures in the restricted area. At that time, he becomes nervous and no longer wishes to speak with you.

1. How would you handle the situation?
   a. Arrest the man for suspicious activity and being in a restricted area on private property. Then bring him to an area where you can attempt a detailed interrogation and take his property as a search incident to arrest and trespass him from the property.
   b. Confiscate his camera and memory card on scene and release him since you have already identified who he is.
   c. Accept the man's excuse as reasonable, log his information, and pass it on as intelligence. Inform the man that his information is on file and that he is not allowed to take further pictures of restricted areas. Then escort him off the property.
   d. Because he is suspicious, arrest him. Then draft a search warrant and legally retrieve the pictures for intelligence purposes.
2. What follow-up would you do as a result of your decision?
   a. Nothing. You have already gained his information and identity.
   b. Ensure that the suspect's information was passed on to mall administration, security, and federal officials.
   c. Post the suspect's information publicly as well as contact the media over the incident.
   d. Attempt to contact the suspect later on, to see what he is up to.

DISCUSSION QUESTIONS

1. Which is the greater threat—domestic or international terrorism? Why?
2. Does your police department have a counterterrorism strategy in place? If so, what is it?
3. What type of terrorist attack do you fear most? Why?
4. Do you feel Americans have become complacent about terrorism?

5. What provisions of the PATRIOT Act do you think are most important?

6. What barriers to sharing information among the various local, state, and federal agencies do you think are most problematic?

7. Does media coverage of terrorist acts lead to more terrorism—that is, do you think the contagion effect is in operation?

8. Should Americans expect to give up some civil liberties to allow law enforcement officers to pursue terrorists?

9. Do you think a terrorist sleeper cell could operate in your community? What signs might indicate that such a cell exists?

10. What means might terrorists use to attack the United States in the future? Are we more or less vulnerable at home or at our interests abroad?

GALE EMERGENCY SERVICES DATABASE ASSIGNMENTS

▶ Use the Gale Emergency Services database to help answer the Discussion Questions as appropriate.

▶ Use the Gale Emergency Services database to determine how many countries in the world have been exposed to terrorism and the specific nature of terrorist acts, if any distinguishing trends are noted.

▶ Use the Gale Emergency Services database to find and outline one of the following articles:

- "State and Local Law Enforcement: Contributions to Terrorism Prevention" by William McCormack

- "The FBI Joint Terrorism Task Force Officer" by Brig Barker and Steve Fowler

- "One of These Things Is Not Like the Others: Customizing Terrorism Preparedness to Meet L.A. County's Unique Needs" by Linda Spagnoli

- "Demands on Police Services in a WMD Incident" by Joel A. Carlson

- "Law Enforcement and Hazmat/WMD Emergency Response: NFPA 472 As a Tool for Compliance" by Ed Allen and Steve Patrick

- "Countering Violent Islamic Extremism: A Community Responsibility" by Carol Dyer, Ryan E. McCoy, Joel Rodriguez, and Donald N. Van Duyn

- "Words Make Worlds: Terrorism and Language" by Angus Smith

REFERENCES

"About MIPT." n.d. Oklahoma City, OK. Accessed March 20, 2012. https://www.mipt.org/AboutMIPT.aspx.

Boucek, Christopher. 2011. "Terrorist Threat to the U.S. Homeland—Al-Qaeda in the Arabian Peninsula." *Homeland Security NTARC News* (March 2). Accessed March 13, 2012. http://www.carnegieendowment.org/2011/03/02/terrorist-threat-to-u.s.-homeland-al-qaeda-in-arabian-peninsula/1yt.

Carlson, Joel A. 2008. "Demands on Police Services in a WMD Incident." *FBI Law Enforcement Bulletin* (March): 1–6.

Chudwin, Jeff. 2007. "Homicide Bombers: Tactics for First-Responders." *Law Officer Magazine* (January): 62–64.

Chudwin, Jeff. 2009. "Terror, Again: First-Responder Lessons from the Attacks in India." *Law Officer Magazine* (January): 50–55.

"Citizen Corps Programs Ensure Everyone Is Prepared in the Event of a Disaster." 2007. *NCJA Justice Bulletin* (March): 8–9.

Clapper, James R. 2012 (January 31). *Worldwide Threat Assessment of the U.S. Intelligence Community for the Senate Select Committee on Intelligence: Statement for the Record.* Washington, DC: Office of the Director of National Intelligence. Accessed March 17, 2012. http://www.dni.gov/testimonies/20120131_testimony_ata.pdf.

Commission on Accreditation of Law Enforcement Agencies (CALEA). 2012. *Standards for Law Enforcement Agencies.* 5th ed. Fairfax, VA: Author.

Daniels, Rhianna. 2007. "Chemical Facilities Secure DHS Standards." *Security Director News* (February): 8.

Doherty, Ruth. 2009 (May 4). *Counter Improvised Explosive Devices (C-IED).* Washington, DC: U.S. Department of Homeland Security, Science and Technology Directorate, Version 1.0. Accessed March 16, 2012. http://www.dhs.gov/xlibrary/assets/st_detect_and_defeat_vbied.pdf.

Downing, Michael P. 2009. "Policing Terrorism in the United States: The Los Angeles Police Department's Convergence Strategy." *The Police Chief* (February): 28–43.

Durner, Colin. 2012. "eGuardian Gains Momentum." *FBI Law Enforcement Bulletin* (January): 12–15.

Edwards, Al. 2007. "DHS Reveals Chemical Guidelines." *Security Director News* (May): 1.

FBI Counterterrorism Analysis Section. 2011. "Sovereign Citizens: A Growing Threat to Law Enforcement." *FBI Law Enforcement Bulletin* (September): 20–24.

Goodwyn, Al. 2008. "Minimizing the Nuclear Threat: A Local Law Enforcement Strategy." *The Police Chief* (February): 45–59.

Griffith, David. 2011. "9/11: WMD Preparedness Now." *Police* (September): 40–45.

Harwood, Matthew. 2007. "Assessing Chlorine Gas Bombs." *Security Management* (June): 18–19.

Henderson, Nicole J., Christopher W. Ortiz, Naomi F. Sugie, and Joel Miller. 2008 (July). *Policing in Arab-American Communities.* Washington, DC: National Institute of Justice. (NCJ 221706)

Holder, Eric. 2009 (March 16). "Remarks as Prepared for Delivery by Attorney General Eric Holder at the National League of Cities Conference." *Public Radio News.*

Hunter, Ryan, and Daniel Heinke. 2011. "Radicalization of Islamist Terrorists in the Western World." *FBI Law Enforcement Bulletin* (September): 25–31.

Jarboe, James F. 2002 (February 12). *Testimony before the House Resources Committee, Subcommittee on Forests and Forest Health.* Washington, DC: Federal Bureau of Investigation. Accessed July 25, 2012. http://www.fbi.gov/news/testimony/the-threat-of-eco-terrorism/.

Lambert, David. 2010. "Intelligence-Led Policing in a Fusion Center." *FBI Law Enforcement Bulletin* (December): 1–6.

Lewis, James A. 2002 (December). *Assessing the Risks of Cyber Terrorism, Cyber War and Other Cyber Threats.* Washington, DC: Center for Strategic and International Studies. Accessed March 17, 2012. http://csis.org/files/media/csis/pubs/021101_risks_of_cyberterror.pdf.

Lovette, Ed. 2008. "Anti-Terrorism Intel for the Patrol Officer." *Police* (February): 32–37.

Manos, Christi. 2009 (April 28). "MIPT Engages in Open Exchange with Law Enforcement Officials from the Middle East." Oklahoma City, OK: Memorial Institute for the Prevention of Terrorism. Accessed March 20, 2012. http://mipt.publishpath.com/mipt-engages-in-open-exchange-with-law-enforcement-officials-from-the-middle-east.

Monahan, Tom, and Mark Stainbrook. 2011. "Learning from the Lessons of the 2008 Mumbai Terrorist Attacks." *The Police Chief* (February): 24–32.

National Infrastructure Protection Plan. 2009. Washington, DC: Department of Homeland Security.

"National Network of Fusion Centers Fact Sheet." 2012 (February 3). Washington, DC: Department of Homeland Security. Accessed March 20, 2012. http://www.dhs.gov/files/programs/gc_1296484657738.shtm.

National Terrorism Advisory System Public Guide. 2011 (April). Washington, DC: Department of Homeland Security. Accessed March 18, 2012. http://www.dhs.gov/xlibrary/assets/ntas/ntas-public-guide.pdf.

"The Need for Homeland Security: Greater than Ever." 2009. *The Police Chief* (February): 24–25.

O'Brien, Lauren B. 2011. "The Evolution of Terrorism since 9/11." *FBI Law Enforcement Bulletin* (September): 3–10.

Olson, Dean. 2012. "Agroterrorism: Threats to America's Economy and Food Supply." *FBI Law Enforcement Bulletin* (February): 1–9.

Page, Douglas. 2009. "The RadTruck Stops Here." *Law Enforcement Technology* (May): 50–55.

Perin, Michelle. 2009. "HAZSWAT Changed?" *Law Enforcement Technology* (May): 20–25.

Priem, Richard G., Dennis M. Hunter, and Joseph M. Polisar. 2007. "Terrorists and Suicide Tactics: Preparing for the Challenge." *The Police Chief* (September): 32–36.

"Program Summary." n.d. St. Paul, MN: University of Minnesota, National Center for Food Protection and Defense. Accessed March 20, 2012. http://www.ncfpd.umn.edu/index.cfm/about/program-summary/.

"Protecting America from Terrorist Attack: Our Joint Terrorism Task Forces." n.d. Washington, DC: Federal Bureau of Investigation. Accessed March 18, 2012. http://www.fbi.gov/about-us/investigate/terrorism/terrorism_jttfs.

Quadrennial Homeland Security Review Report: A Strategic Framework for a Secure Homeland. 2010 (February). Washington, DC: Department of Homeland Security. Accessed March 18, 2012. http://www.dhs.gov/xlibrary/assets/qhsr_report.pdf.

Report from the Field: The USA PATRIOT Act at Work. 2004 (July). Washington, DC: Department of Justice.

"Safeguarding Civil Liberties." n.d. Washington, DC: Federal Bureau of Investigation, Terrorist Screening Center. Accessed March 19, 2012. http://www.fbi.gov/about-us/nsb/tsc/tsc_liberties.

Savelli, Lou. 2004. *A Proactive Law Enforcement Guide for the War on Terrorism.* Flushing, NY: Looseleaf Law Publications.

Scoville, Dean. 2011. "10 Years After." *Police* (September): 28–33.

Smith, Brent. 2008. "A Look at Terrorist Behavior: How They Prepare, Where They Strike." *NIJ Journal* (July): 2–7.

Smith, Thomas W., and Robert L. Sant. 2011 (February). *Nuclear Material Events Database—Annual Report: Fiscal Year 2010.* Washington, DC: U.S. Nuclear Regulatory Commission. Accessed March 16, 2012. http://nmed.inl.gov/AnnualReports/NMEDFY10%20Annual.pdf.

Stanek, Richard W. 2011. "It Can and Does Happen Here: Somali Youth with Terrorist Ties in the Twin Cities." *The Police Chief* (February): 48–52.

Strategic Plan 2004–2009. 2004. Washington, DC: Federal Bureau of Investigation.

Tafoya, William L. 2011. "Cyber Terror." *FBI Law Enforcement Bulletin* (November): 1–7.

Taylor, Bruce, and Pat Kaufman. 2009. "Protecting America's Ports." *NIJ Journal* (262, March): 32–36.

Terrorism 2002–2005. n.d. Washington, DC: Federal Bureau of Investigation.

Trudeau, Scott. 2009. "Managing 21st-Century Threats with Chemical, Biological, Radiological, Nuclear, and Explosives Detection Devices." *The Police Chief* (February): 44–50.

2010 Report on Terrorism. 2011 (April 30). Washington, DC: National Counterterrorism Center.

Vernon, Bob. 2008. "Reliable Sources: The Right Way to Mobilize Your Community to Increase Security." *Law Officer Magazine* (June): 56–57.

Wexler, Chuck. 2007 (April). "Foreword." In *Patrol-Level Response to a Suicide Bomb Threat: Guidelines for Consideration,* edited by Lisa L. Spahr, Joshua Ederheimer, and David Bilson, i–ii. Washington, DC: Police Executive Research Forum.

White, Jonathan R. 2012. *Terrorism and Homeland Security.* 7th ed. Belmont, CA: Wadsworth.

CASES CITED

Hamdi v. Rumsfeld, 542 U.S. 507 (2004)

Rasul v. Bush, 542 U.S. 466 (2004)

HELPFUL RESOURCES

Centers for Disease Control and Prevention: www.cdc.gov

The Counterterrorism Training and Resources Web site: http://www.counterterrorismtraining.gov

Federal Emergency Management Agency: http://www.ready.gov

Federal Bureau of Investigation: http://www.fbi.gov

U.S. Department of Homeland Security: http://www.dhs.gov

This available CourseMate has an interactive eBook and interactive learning tools, including flash cards, quizzes, and more. To learn more about this resource and access free demo CourseMate resources, go to www.cengagebrain.com, and search for this book. To access CourseMate materials that you have purchased, go to login.cengagebrain.com.

Specialized Police Operations

The previous section described the basic police operations within any law enforcement agency: patrol; traffic; dealing with crime and disorder; dealing with violence at home, in school, and on the job; dealing with emergencies; and fighting the war on terrorism—protecting the homeland. In addition to these basic functions, law enforcement agencies also perform highly specialized operations. In smaller departments, the patrol officer performs these specialized operations. In larger departments, they may be assigned to specific officers or even to specialized departments.

This section discusses the specialized operations that may be required of law enforcement agencies, including investigation (Chapter 10), dealing with juveniles (Chapter 11), and dealing with gang and drug problems (Chapter 12). Even when the specialized operations are performed by nonpatrol officers, they still will require patrol officers' input and cooperation and, indeed, that of the entire community for maximum effectiveness.

CHAPTER 10

Criminal Investigation

© Henry Cho

DO YOU KNOW . . .

- What the primary goals of a criminal investigation are?
- What the most critical phase in the majority of criminal investigations is?
- What AFIT is and how it helps solve crimes?
- What two forms of positive identification may be available in criminal investigations?
- What the major violent crimes are, what their elements are, and what special considerations might be involved in each?
- What the focus of the homicide investigation should be after priority matters are addressed?
- How homicide is classified and what the various degrees of murder and manslaughter are?
- What some special problems in homicide investigations are?
- What the major property crimes are, what their elements are, and what special considerations might be involved in each?
- What two key characteristics of computer crime are?
- What victimless crimes are?
- When surveillance, undercover assignments, raids, and stings might be necessary?
- When undercover assignments are used?

CAN YOU DEFINE?

accelerants
Advanced Fingerprint Identification Technology (AFIT)
contamination
covert investigations
CSI effect
DNA profiling
equivocal death investigation
forensics
igniters
Locard's principle of exchange
overt investigations
parallel proceedings
phishing
premeditation
proxy data
spoofing
victimless crimes

INTRODUCTION

One of the most important functions of law enforcement agencies is criminal investigation. This is largely carried out by detectives, and everyone knows what a detective is because of television programs such as *Blue Bloods, CSI,* and *Law & Order.* To the public, detectives and criminal investigators have the "glamour jobs" within law enforcement. Actually, this same view is held by many officers who, at some point in their careers, desire promotion to the detective division.

The criminal investigative function—the process by which officers collect evidence, interview people, and compile facts for the purpose of supporting a prosecution—has long been viewed as the most challenging role in police work. This chapter describes the real-life challenges of criminal investigation, an exceedingly complex field that can be only briefly introduced here. The chapter begins by discussing the primary goals, the investigation process, the preliminary investigation, *who* is responsible for investigating crimes, and the follow-up. Next is a look at the types of evidence to look for, and the role of forensics and crime analysis in criminal investigations. Then the discussion turns to investigating specific crimes, including the violent and property crimes classified as Index offenses and other serious crimes, as well as the special considerations involved in each type of investigation. This is followed by a quick look at the problem of false reports and the challenges of investigating so-called victimless crimes. Next surveillance, undercover assignments, raids, and stings are explored, including the use of informants. The chapter concludes with a look at the relationship between criminal investigation and community policing, including problem-oriented policing.

GOALS OF CRIMINAL INVESTIGATION

Although the public often perceives that the solitary goal of criminal investigation is to solve cases—to discover "whodunit"—in reality, the myriad goals of criminal investigation are not quite so simple.

The primary goals of criminal investigation are to

- Determine whether a crime has been committed.
- Legally obtain information and evidence to identify the responsible person.
- Arrest the suspect.
- Recover stolen property.
- Present the best possible case to the prosecutor.

Above all else, the criminal investigation seeks to establish the factual truth surrounding an event.

Secondary goals of investigation include surveillance, crime prevention, crime scene investigation, background investigations, and sexual offender tracking.

An investigation can be considered successful if it follows a logical sequence and legally obtains all available physical evidence and information from witnesses and suspects, if all leads are thoroughly developed, and if all details of the case are accurately and completely recorded and reported. Successful investigation involves a balance between scientific knowledge acquired by study and experience and the skills acquired by the artful application of learned techniques.

THE INVESTIGATIVE PROCESS

A criminal investigation is usually initiated by an officer's personal observation of an incident or by information from a citizen through a call for service. In other words, patrol officers may see a suspicious action or person, or a citizen may report suspicious actions or people. Such information is received at police headquarters by telephone, fax, e-mail, radio, or direct report when a person steps up to a police complaint desk. A police dispatcher relays the information to a patrol officer by radio or phone, and the officer responds. However the incident becomes known to police, this reporting of a crime sets the investigative wheels in motion and is the first stage in a criminal investigation.

Unless the incident is complicated, dynamic, time-consuming, or potentially high profile, the case is generally not referred to a special criminal investigations unit, and the responding patrol officer is typically the one who investigates the matter. The various stages of the investigative process, as well as the personnel involved, the official reports generated, and the victim's role, are described in Table 10.1.

Table 10.1 A Brief Summary of the Investigative Process

Stage of Investigation	Police Role	Stage of Reports	Victim's/ Complainant's Role	Suspect's Role
Initial report	Dispatched to call for service.	Recording of initial call/ report.	Report the incident, request police response.	Sometimes interferes with the call.
Initial investigation/ police contact	Arrive on scene and acquire information. May collect evidence.	Incident reports and all applicable forms.	Provide interviews and information about the incident and suspect. May provide evidence.	Provides interviews and information about the incident. May provide evidence.
Incident review	After a review of the case, it is determined if further investigation is required.	Police supervisor reviews the case for approval.	Sometimes informed of case status.	None.
Follow-up investigations	Gather remaining information and evidence required for the case.	Additional reports, additional interviews, and evidence.	Verify and confirm information.	Provides additional interviews and interrogations if cooperative and warranted.
Case preparation and approval	Review the reports, coordinate the case with prosecution.	Ready to submit for formal charging or court processing.	None.	None.
Prosecution and charging of crime	Be available for court and testimony.	Prosecution and court reports.	Be available for court and testimony.	Is in custody or present for court. If not present, has legal representation.
Conclusion	Clear reports, release or purge evidence, and close case with a disposition.	File all complete reports into Records.	Retrieve any property used as evidence in the case.	None.

THE PRELIMINARY INVESTIGATION

Most criminal investigations have two phases: the preliminary investigation and the follow-up investigation. Chapter 6 stressed the importance of the preliminary investigation and outlined the duties and responsibilities typically encountered.

 The most critical phase in most criminal investigations is the preliminary investigation.

A brief review of the typical steps of a preliminary investigation is warranted:

▶ Attend to any existing emergencies, such as an injured person or a fleeing suspect.

▶ Secure the scene.

▶ Make necessary arrests.

▶ Measure, photograph, videotape, and sketch the scene.

▶ Search for evidence.

▶ Identify, collect, examine, and process physical evidence.

▶ Interview victims, witnesses, and suspects.

▶ Record all statements and observations in notes to be later transformed into a report.

The order in which these tasks are performed will depend on the specific circumstances. Questioning witnesses, which is a procedural *must*, may also include canvassing the neighborhood, which is warranted in certain types of incidents. The last task, recording all information into a pocket notebook or onto a digital recorder, is vital.

Documentation and creating an evidence chain of custody is crucial throughout an investigation. Most people who go into law enforcement are amazed at the amount of paperwork and writing that is required—as much as 70 percent of an investigator's job is consumed by these functions. In addition, photography plays an important role in documenting evidence and presenting cases in court.

Start taking notes as soon as possible after receiving a call to respond, and continue recording information as it is received throughout the investigation. Enter general information first: the time and date of the call, location, officer assigned, and arrival time at the scene. Police departments using centrally dispatched message centers may automatically record date, time, and case numbers. Even if this is done, make written notes of this initial information because recorded tapes may not be kept for extended periods or may become unusable. The tapes and notes corroborate each other. Record all information that helps answer the questions, Who? What? Where? When? How? and Why?

Take notes describing the physical scene, including general weather and lighting conditions. Record everything you observe in the overall scene: all services rendered, including first aid, description of the injured, location of wounds, and who transported the victim and how. Record complete, accurate information regarding all photographs taken at the scene. As the search is conducted, record the location and description of evidence and its preservation. Record information to identify the type of crime and what was said and by whom. Include the name, address, and phone number of every person present at the scene and all witnesses.

In addition, investigative photographs and videotapes are essential to proper crime scene documentation. The basic purpose of crime scene photography is to record the scene permanently. Photos and video taken immediately, using proper techniques to reproduce the entire crime scene, provide a factual record of high evidentiary value. The time that elapses between the commission of a crime and when a suspect in that crime is brought to trial can stretch into years, during which time the crime scene will undoubtedly change. Thus, photos and videos are a way to preserve the crime scene.

Finally, sketch all serious crime and crash scenes after photographs are taken and before anything is moved. Sketch the entire scene, the objects, and the evidence. The crime scene sketch accurately portrays the physical facts, establishes the precise location and relationship of objects and evidence at the scene, helps create a mental picture of the scene for those not present, and is usually admissible in court. Computer software programs, such as computer-aided dispatch (CAD) crime scene applications, have become essential tools for investigators to diagram complex crime scenes.

WHO INVESTIGATES?

Exactly *who* is responsible for the preliminary and follow-up investigations varies by department, although most officers are expected to be trained and competent in performing basic investigative operations. Although many local police departments lack special criminal investigative units, with line personnel bearing responsibility for crime scene duty, some departments, particularly those in larger jurisdictions, have specialized teams of detectives to perform investigative functions. Some agencies also have specialized units within the investigations unit to handle different types of cases, such as sex crimes or crimes against children. Although most detectives are crime scene investigators, many agencies have a separate crime scene unit (CSU) that conducts this portion of the investigation (processing the scene). In these instances, it is important that the investigator is still involved and has open communication with the CSU's findings and reports.

Popular television series such as *CSI, Cold Case*, and *Without a Trace* have brought the role of the crime scene investigator and the importance of forensic evidence into the limelight. These shows have also, however, created fictionalized, unrealistic expectations regarding how quickly and easily such evidence is obtained. A survey of 1,000 jurors asked what forensic evidence they expected the prosecution to present and found that jurors expected *in every criminal case* to see the following (Shelton 2008, 3):

- ▶ Some kind of scientific evidence (46 percent)
- ▶ DNA evidence (22 percent)
- ▶ Fingerprint evidence (36 percent)
- ▶ Ballistic or other firearms laboratory evidence (32 percent)

Jurors also expect crime lab results and an entire investigation to be completed in a matter of a few hours, followed by a nice graphically designed portrayal of the incident presented on video that ties the entire incident together—much like they view on TV. These expectations have been referred to collectively as the *CSI effect*, "where unrealistic portrayals of the science have translated to equally unrealistic expectations from not only the public but also other professions that operate within the justice system who now apparently believe in magic" (Fantino 2007, 26). These are, of course, impractical expectations.

CSI effect

"Where unrealistic portrayals of the science have translated to equally unrealistic expectations from not only the public but also other professions that operate within the justice system" who have unrealistic expectations about what crime scene investigators can do.

THE FOLLOW-UP INVESTIGATION

In many cases, the preliminary investigation does not yield enough evidence or information to close a case. In such instances, a follow-up investigation is needed, again performed either by the patrol officer who responded to the original call or by a detective, depending on the case and the size of the agency. If investigators take over a case begun by patrol officers, coordination is essential.

The follow-up phase builds on what was learned during the preliminary investigation. Investigative leads that may need to be pursued include checking the victim's background; talking to informants; determining who would benefit from the crime and who had sufficient knowledge to plan the crime; tracing weapons and stolen property; and searching modus operandi (MO), mug shot, and fingerprint files. Specific follow-up procedures for the major offenses are presented later in the chapter.

42.2.2

CALEA Standard 42.2.2 requires that a follow-up investigation include at a minimum:
- Reviewing and analyzing all previous reports prepared in the preliminary phase, departmental records, and results from laboratory examinations.
- Conducting additional interviews and interrogations.
- Seeking additional information (from uniformed officers, informants).
- Planning, organizing, conducting searches, and collecting physical evidence.
- Identifying and apprehending suspects.
- Determining involvement of suspects in other crimes.
- Checking suspects' criminal histories.
- Preparing cases for court presentation

Source: Commission on Accreditation of Law Enforcement Agencies (CALEA). 2012. *Standards for Law Enforcement Agencies*, 5th ed. Fairfax, VA: Author.

Regardless of who is charged with conducting a criminal investigation and whether it is preliminary or follow up, the types of evidence to look for remain the same, and maintaining the integrity and subsequent admissibility of such evidence is as vital a role for the line officer as it is for the special crime scene investigator.

EVIDENCE

The successful resolution of a criminal investigation most often hinges on the availability of irrefutable, relevant, and admissible evidence. Even when a suspect confesses, evidence is still required because the confession may later turn out to be untrue, it may later be denied, or there may be claims it was coerced or involuntary and is, therefore, inadmissible. A confession is only one part of an investigation. It must be corroborated by independent evidence.

Criminal investigators and forensic scientists work often with proxy data. **Proxy data** are not seen as they are created but are, rather, the remnants left behind of an event. This is based on the theory of transfer developed by Edmund Locard, a 20th-century French forensic microscopist who posited, in what is now known as **Locard's principle of exchange**: When two objects come into contact, information or material, however minute, is exchanged. The result of such a transfer or exchange is known as proxy data. Once criminal activity stops, any transfers that take place are considered **contamination**, that is, an undesired transfer of information between items of evidence.

Advances in technologies for detecting and distinguishing evidence hold promise for speeding up evidence collection, limiting contamination, and facilitating analysis. Among the advancements are a variety of alternative light sources (ALS) being used to enhance evidence.

Classification of Evidence

Evidence is generally categorized as one of four types: testimonial, documentary, demonstrative, or physical. *Testimonial evidence* is information obtained through interviewing and interrogating individuals about what they saw (eyewitness evidence), heard (hearsay evidence), or know (character evidence). *Documentary evidence* typically includes written material, audio recordings, and videos. *Demonstrative evidence* includes mockups and scale models of objects or places related to the crime scene and helps juries visualize more clearly what they are unable to view personally. Most commonly, investigators deal with *physical evidence* that is anything real or tangible—that is, which has substance—that helps to establish the facts of a case. It can be seen, touched, smelled, or tasted; is solid, semisolid, or liquid; and can be large or tiny. It may be at an immediate crime scene or miles away; it may also be on a suspect or a victim.

Physical evidence may be further classified as direct and indirect evidence. *Direct evidence* establishes proof of a fact without any other evidence. *Indirect evidence* merely tends to incriminate a person—for instance, a suspect's footprints found near the crime scene. Indirect evidence is also called *circumstantial evidence*, or evidence from which inferences are drawn. Extremely small items, such as hair or fibers, are a subset of direct evidence called *trace evidence*. Evidence established by law is called *prima facie evidence*. For example, 0.08 blood alcohol content (BAC) is *prima facie* evidence of intoxication in some states. *Associative evidence*—such as fingerprints, footprints, bloodstains, and hairs—links a suspect with a crime.

Corpus delicti evidence establishes that a crime has been committed. Contrary to popular belief, the corpus delicti ("body of the crime") in a murder case is not the dead body but the fact that death resulted from a criminal act. Corpus delicti evidence supports the elements of the crime. Pry marks on an entry door are corpus delicti evidence in a burglary.

Probative evidence is vital to the investigation or prosecution of a case, tending to prove or actually proving guilt or innocence. Also of importance to the

---

proxy data

Pieces of evidence not seen as they are created but which are only the remnants of an event left behind.

Locard's principle of exchange

When two objects come into contact, information or material, however minute, is exchanged.

contamination

An undesired transfer of information between items of evidence.

investigator is *exculpatory evidence*, which is physical evidence that clears one of blame—for example, having a blood type different from that of blood found at a murder scene. *Best evidence*, in the legal sense, is the original evidence or highest available degree of proof that can be produced.

Kinds of Evidence

Evidence found at crime scenes may include fingerprints; blood, hair, and other DNA-rich substances such as semen, skin, and fingernails; digital/electronic evidence; bite marks; shoe and tire impressions; soil; tool fragments; glass; paint; safe insulation; fibers; insects; documents; and firearms.

Fingerprints Fingerprints, the study of which is called *dactyloscopy*, are among the most common and useful types of evidence found at crime scenes because they are a positive form of identification. If latent prints are found, they can be entered into a city's or state's *automated fingerprint identification system* (AFIS) or into the Federal Bureau of Investigation's (FBI) *Integrated Automated Fingerprint Identification System* (IAFIS), which contains millions of prints. IAFIS provides to local, state, and federal criminal justice agencies nationwide access to electronic 10-print identification services, latent fingerprint databases, subject search and criminal history databases, document and image services, and remote search service. Figure 10.1 illustrates the submission of an electronic 10-print.

In 2011, the FBI introduced Advanced Fingerprint Identification (or Information) Technology (AFIT) as part of its broader technology initiative called Next Generation Identification (NGI). AFIT provides faster, more efficient IAFIS processing, and it can incorporate biometric data such as latent palm prints and facial recognition technology. The new system reduces the time it takes to analyze fingerprints, from hours or even days with IAFIS to minutes with AFIT, and is more than 99 percent accurate, compared with the older system's 92 percent accuracy rate.

> **Advanced Fingerprint Identification Technology (AFIT)** is the next generation of IAFIS and provides faster, more accurate identification of prints than previous systems did.

Advanced Fingerprint Identification Technology (AFIT)

The next generation of IAFIS; provides faster, more accurate identification of prints than previous systems did.

Live scan is an advance in fingerprinting technology that reduces the chance that prints will be disqualified because of poor quality. In this method, a computer analyzes the prints in progress and will not allow the process to move forward until it captures a passing print, which is identified from the computer itself. The information is then stored in a digital format, making it easy to send or share the files.

Blood and Hair *Blood* may be valuable as evidence in assaults, homicides, burglaries, hit-and-run cases, and rape. Blood is classified as A, B, AB, or O. Although blood cannot be used to identify a particular individual's race or sex, it can help *eliminate* suspects.

Hair from victims and suspects can be found on clothing, weapons, blankets, sheets, seat covers, and the undercarriage of vehicles. Microscopic

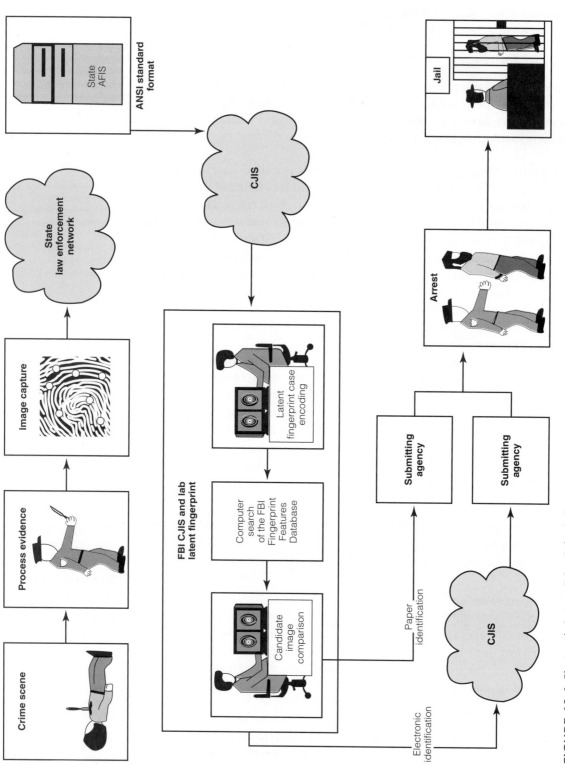

FIGURE 10.1 Electronic Latent Print Submission

Source: http://www.fbi.gov/hq/cjisd/iafis/efts71/section_3.htm

A forensics officer collects evidence by dusting a car window for fingerprints at a crime scene.

examination can identify hair as human or animal, but it cannot be identified as coming from a specific person. Microscopic examination of hair can usually identify the person's race, but not the person's sex or age, except in the case of infants. Microscopic examination can also tell if the hair was pulled out forcibly and which part of the body it is from. If the root is still attached to the hair, DNA from that portion can be analyzed.

DNA Blood, hair, and other body tissues and fluids—such as semen, saliva, skin, and fingernails—contain DNA—the "blueprint of life"—wherein genetic sequences unique to each individual can be located and analyzed through **DNA profiling**. Whereas other tests of human tissues and secretions can only eliminate suspects, DNA can positively identify an individual. New research is showing that even identical twins, who are born with identical DNA sequences, may experience divergence in genetic markers as they age (Lei 2008).

DNA profiling

Use of the unique genetic structure of an individual for identification; blood, hair, and other body tissues and fluids may be used in this process.

Forensic technology has become advanced enough to extrapolate DNA evidence from fingerprints or other microscopic amounts of cellular material left behind on evidence—"touch" or "trace" DNA. Thus, instead of lifting prints, investigators will eventually just swab the prints for the DNA and submit the sample for analysis.

Investigators need to know where DNA evidence is likely to be located. Table 10.2 describes the possible location and source of DNA evidence.

Even with no suspect, DNA can be helpful because it can be entered into the FBI's Combined DNA Index System (CODIS), also called the National DNA Index System (NDIS), and searched against an ever-growing collection of DNA profiles. This national database and searching mechanism had more than 7 million offender profiles and 268,404 forensic profiles by May 2009. More than 100 crime laboratories nationwide have installed the CODIS system.

Table 10.2 Location and Sources of DNA Evidence

Evidence	Possible Location of DNA on the Evidence	Source of DNA
Baseball bat	Handle	Skin cells, sweat, blood, tissue
Hat, bandanna, or mask	Inside surfaces	Sweat, hair, skin cells, dandruff, saliva
Eyeglasses	Nose or ear piece, lens	Sweat, skin cells
Facial tissue, cotton swab	Surface	Mucus, blood, sweat, semen, ear wax
Dirty laundry	Surface	Blood, sweat, semen, saliva
Toothpick	Surface	Saliva
Used cigarette	Cigarette butt (filter area)	Saliva
Used stamp/envelope seal	Moistened area	Saliva
Tape or ligature	Inside or outside surface	Skin cells, sweat, saliva
Bottle, can, or glass	Mouthpiece, rim, outer surface	Saliva, sweat, skin cells
Used condom	Inside or outside surface	Semen, vaginal or rectal cells
Bed linens	Surface	Sweat, hair, semen, saliva, blood
"Through and through" bullet	Outside surface	Blood, tissue
Bite mark	Surface of skin	Saliva
Fingernail/partial fingernail	Scrapings	Blood, sweat, tissue, skin cells

Note: When reviewing evidence, it is important to maintain chain of custody, consult with laboratory personnel, and take all appropriate precautions against contamination, including wearing gloves and changing them between handling of different pieces of evidence.

Source: *Using DNA to Solve Cold Cases* (Washington, DC: NIJ Special Report, July 2002), 21.

Although DNA fingerprinting has been heralded as a major breakthrough for criminal investigation, some courts still do not accept it. In *California v. Simpson* (1995), DNA played a pivotal role. The defense focused on procedures rather than the scientific validity of DNA analysis to discredit and have thrown out the DNA evidence. In several states, legal challenges have been *unsuccessfully* raised that DNA collection constitutes an invasion of an individual's right to privacy. The privacy issue relates to the controversy regarding when DNA should be collected and whether those of preconviction status should be exempt.

Research is helping counter some of this criticism, however. A study done in Chicago that followed the criminal histories of eight convicted felons concluded that if officials had collected DNA at these felons' first felony arrests, officials would have prevented 60 violent crimes, including 30 rapes and 22 murders (Garrett 2009b, 31–32). Using such data to support their actions, 16 states have passed legislation requiring law enforcement to collect DNA for most felony arrests and upload it to the state DNA databank (Garrett 2009b, 31).

Yet another controversial issue related to DNA collection is for what offenses DNA should be sought as evidence. Traditionally, DNA analysis has been reserved for violent crimes such as murder and rape. However, law enforcement agencies across the nation are beginning to recognize the value of DNA evidence in solving high-volume property crimes such as burglary and automobile theft (Wilson, McClure, and Weisburd 2010). Considering that property crime offenders commonly have high recidivism rates and commit many more offenses than those for which they are arrested, and considering the research that shows burglary offenders often graduate to more serious crimes, the analysis of DNA evidence in property crimes has considerable potential to prevent and reduce the incidence of more violent crimes in the future (Geoghegan 2009).

Research shows that burglary investigations that incorporate DNA analysis are 2½ times more likely to result in a suspect identification compared with traditional investigations that use only fingerprint evidence. Arrest and prosecution rates doubled as well when DNA evidence was included (Johns and Rushing 2009).

Critics argue that adding DNA testing for property crimes would completely clog the already critically overburdened forensic laboratories. For example, according to the FBI, there were more than 9 million property crimes brought to the attention of the police in 2010 (*Crime in the United States 2010* 2010). Nonetheless, the research indicates that this technology greatly assists in clearing property crimes cases.

> Physical fingerprints and DNA fingerprinting are the two forms of positive identification available to investigators.

As technology improves, police are turning to older, smaller degraded DNA samples to help solve cases. For example, researchers have used DNA fingerprinting to make identifications from a 4-year-old bloodstain and from semen stains that were several weeks old. Also as the result of advances in DNA analysis, many cold cases are being reinvestigated, as discussed later in the chapter.

Digital/Electronic Evidence With the proliferation of electronic devices that hold information, digital evidence has become increasingly important in many investigations. Most investigators are not educated in examining digital evidence, but they should recognize sources for such evidence at a crime scene, including computers, external hard drives, flash drives, cell phones, iPods, PDAs, digital cameras, global positioning systems (GPS) units, and game units. Many criminals fail to consider their electronic gadgets as digital storage devices containing potentially incriminating evidence (Garrett 2009a).

Patrol officers commonly run across cell phones containing a wealth of information. In one case involving a California gang shooting, where rival gangs rolled into a parking lot and fired hundreds of rounds at each other with automatic weapons, responding officers were met with claims by those involved that they had not seen anything. However, when officers confiscated and searched the gang members' cell phones, they found photos, text messages, and other information about the shootings (Garrett 2009a).

Investigators must manage digital evidence appropriately if it is to be of any value in court (Cameron 2011). This means adhering to a well-documented standard operating procedure (SOP) for evidence collection and preservation, maintaining the chain of custody, and applying requisite access controls and security (McNeil 2009). In many cases, local departments lack the base knowledge and internal technical capability to analyze every digital device or computer involved in every investigation, thus requiring such evidence to be submitted to a task force or larger agency that has the resources and training to process it (Garrett 2009a).

In addition to evidence found on a suspect's electronic devices, a wealth of information can be found on the Internet, by performing an Internet search for an area of interest, and on social network sites such as MySpace, Facebook, and Twitter.

Other Kinds of Evidence *Bite marks* are sometimes significant in child and adult abuse cases, rape and homicide cases, and assault and battery cases. They may also be left on the perpetrator by the victim. Bite marks have individual characteristics that match the size and configuration of the teeth. Bite marks helped convict Ted Bundy of murder in Florida. The key is successfully preserving the tissue. Marks on the body may last for several weeks. Bite marks can also be found at a crime scene on inanimate objects such as pencils, Styrofoam cups, gum, candy bars, apples, and other partially eaten soft foods (Page 2007). Forensic orthodontologists can help investigators analyze tooth-related evidence (Jetmore 2007).

Shoe or *tire impressions* often are found where suspects have entered or left a crime scene hastily. Shoe and tire prints are of two types: contamination prints and impressions. Contamination prints are left when a shoe or tire has on it a substance such as dirt or blood, which then leaves a print on a hard surface. Impressions are imprints left in soft surfaces such as mud or sand. Shoe or tire impressions can place a suspect at a crime scene.

Soil is also analyzed in some cases The composition of various soils and other ground substrates can be unique and distinguishable, thus providing evidence that a suspect (or his or her shoes or tires) crossed over a particular stretch of land at some point in time.

Tool fragments also may be found at a crime scene and later matched to a broken tool in a suspect's possession. *Tool marks* are found most often in burglaries and in malicious-destruction-of-property crimes. Tool marks may be found on windowsills and frames, doors and frames, cash register drawers, file cabinets, and cash boxes. Tool marks often are left when windows have been forced open with screwdrivers or pry bars; when locks have been snipped with bolt cutters; or when safes have been opened with hammers, chisels, or punches. These tools leave marks that often can be identified as definitely as fingerprints.

Glass from windows, automobiles, bottles, and other objects often is used as evidence in assaults, burglaries, murders, and many other crimes. When a person breaks a window, tiny pieces of glass are usually found in the clothing, pant cuffs, or pockets or on the clothing's surface. Glass is excellent evidence because two different pieces of glass rarely contain the same proportions of sand, metal oxides, or carbonates. In addition, police usually can determine whether the glass was broken from inside or outside a building by observing the fracture marks and the location of the fragments.

Paint frequently is transferred from one object to another during the commission of a crime. During burglaries, it may be chipped off surfaces. During hasty getaways, it may flake off automobiles. Paint has provided a strong link in the chain of circumstantial evidence because it can associate an individual with the crime scene. It also can eliminate innocent suspects.

Safe insulation can be identified microscopically by composition, color, mineral content, and physical characteristics. Particles of safe insulation or fireproof insulation on a suspect's clothing or shoes are strong indications of guilt.

Fibers from clothing are often found where burglars have crawled through a window or opening. Clothing fibers are also often found adhering to the fenders, grill, door handles, or undercarriage of hit-and-run vehicles. Fingernail scrapings and weapons also may contain fiber evidence. Examination of the fibers can identify the type of fabric: wool, cotton, rayon, nylon, and so on. Sometimes the type of garment from which the fibers came can be identified.

Insects on a body or present at a scene can provide high evidentiary value, particularly when they are not normally present in such a location. The developmental stage of insects found on a body can provide significant information to investigators regarding a death. Criminal investigators increasingly rely on the field of forensic entomology for assistance in solving crimes.

Documents may contain fingerprint evidence and may be examined for handwriting characteristics or for typewriter or printer characteristics. If a document has been handwritten, experts can do a side-by-side comparison of the document and samples of the suspect's handwriting to determine if both were done by the same person. Testimony of handwriting experts has been accepted in our courts for several years. Documents produced on a typewriter or printer can be examined to determine the manufacturer, make, model, and age of the machine.

Firearms left at a crime scene may be traced to their owner through the serial number, the manufacturer's identification, or the dealer who sold the gun. Firearms also may contain fingerprints or other marks that could lead to identification. The weapon's make usually is determined by the barrel rifling, spiral grooves cut into the gun barrel in its manufacture. The rifling varies considerably from manufacturer to manufacturer and imparts a "signature" on bullets passing through, which can help investigators link weapons to shootings. Gunshot residue (GSR) may also be present on the shooter and anyone located within a 3-foot radius of the weapon when it was fired (Trimpe 2011).

In the 1990s, the Bureau of Alcohol, Tobacco, Firearms and Explosives (ATF) and the FBI had competing systems, with the FBI being interested in cartridge cases through its DrugFire program and the ATF being interested in bullets through its Integrated Ballistics Information System (IBIS). In 1999, however, the directors of the ATF and the FBI signed a memorandum of understanding to create a unified ballistics evidence system, using the basic technology of the IBIS machine and combining it with functions specific to the DrugFire system, creating the National Integrated Ballistics Information Network (NIBIN).

An innovative new ballistics technology is called *microstamping*, a process in which a weapon's serial number is stamped onto each cartridge it fires, helping police determine from which weapon a shell was fired (Page 2008).

An often-overlooked tool in discovering ballistic evidence is the metal detector. Investigators using standard search patterns with a metal detector can ensure that the crime scene is completely covered.

The Chain of Custody

Whatever evidence investigators deal with, they must be certain to document the chain of custody. The importance of the chain of custody is evidenced in the Commission on Accreditation of Law Enforcement Agencies (CALEA) standards.

83 **CALEA Standard 83** states, "For physical evidence to be accepted by the court at time of trial, it is essential that the chain of evidence be maintained. The initial step in this process is marking or labeling the item at the time it is collected, seized, or received. Items should be marked so as not to damage or contaminate the evidence. Items that cannot be marked should be placed in an appropriate container, sealed, and the container labeled.

For all items of evidence gathered at a crime scene, the investigator and/or processor should prepare a list containing a description of the item collected, the source (person or location obtained from), and the name of the person collecting the item.

If the evidence is transferred to another person prior to being logged in with the agency, documenting the transfer is critical to maintaining the chain of custody. The record of transfer of evidence should include the following: date and time of transfer; receiving person's name and functional responsibility; reason for the transfer; name and location of the laboratory; synopsis of the event; examinations desired; and date of transfer to a laboratory not within the agency."

Source: Commission on Accreditation of Law Enforcement Agencies (CALEA). 2012. *Standards for Law Enforcement Agencies*, 5th ed. Fairfax, VA: Author.

FORENSICS

forensics

The application of scientific processes to solve legal problems, most notably within the context of the criminal justice system.

Law enforcement has benefited greatly from the many advances in **forensics**— the application of scientific processes to solve legal problems, most notably within the context of the criminal justice system. However, television programs have given the viewing public the mistaken notion that crime laboratories can provide results quickly when, in truth, most crime laboratories have large case backlogs ("Increasing Efficiency in Crime Laboratories" 2008).

The National Academy of Sciences (NAS) has released a report citing serious deficiencies in the United States' forensic science system (*Strengthening Forensic Science* 2009). The report calls for major reforms, new research, and stronger standards and protocols for analyzing and reporting on evidence. There is also a scarcity of peer-reviewed studies establishing the scientific bases and reliability of many forensic methods. The report further notes that, with the exception of DNA analysis, "No forensic method has been rigorously shown able to consistently, and with a high degree of certainty, demonstrate a connection between evidence and a specific individual or source" (Feigin 2009, 3). This despite the ruling in *Daubert v. Merrell Dow Pharmaceuticals* (1993) that established the essential factors in scientific testimony, including empirical testing, peer review, error rate, and acceptability in the scientific community.

The University of Tennessee's National Forensic Academy (NFA) provides one possible approach to improving the country's forensic system (Blakely 2009). This 10-week, in-residence training program holds three sessions each year, each involving 170 hours of classroom instruction and 230 hours of field practice. The instructors are nationally known experts, both academically and as practitioners. The facility includes an interactive classroom, a laboratory, photography lab, and specially designed clean experiment rooms where crime scene investigators (CSIs) can learn to better evaluate blood evidence and practice casting tire and footwear impressions.

The FBI is also engaged in improving our country's forensic capabilities. The FBI now has nine Regional Computer Forensics Laboratories (RCFL) that provide accreditation to computer forensic laboratories: "The accreditation process is an intensive assessment which evaluates the qualifications of all laboratory personnel; the laboratory's operational and technical policies, practices, and procedures; and the laboratory's quality management system" ("FBI's Regional Computer Forensics" 2009).

In addition to well-trained computer forensic examiners and CSIs, criminal investigation is greatly enhanced by experts in crime analysis, as discussed in Chapter 6.

CRIME MAPPING AND ANALYSIS

Before computers, investigators relied on pin maps, wall charts, and other such devices to analyze facts related to a crime. This has changed considerably, and computers are being used to determine where to focus investigative resources. Artificial intelligence (AI) programs being used in several police departments help structure investigations by using software to help determine which cases are most likely to be cleared by arrest.

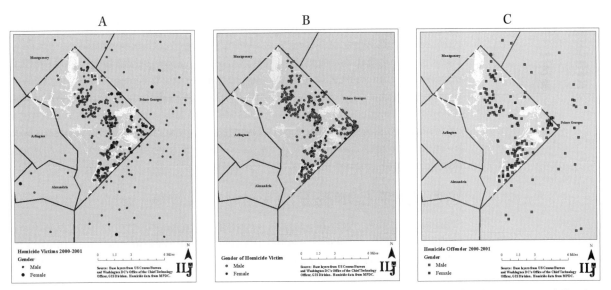

Crime mapping and analysis have become powerful tools to help police solve local problems related to chronic crime and disorder. Exhibit A shows the home locations for victims killed in one jurisdiction over a 2-year period, the map reflecting the fact that a significant number of victims resided outside the city's borders. Exhibit B maps the locations of the homicides for the two years, showing several concentrations, including areas just north of the center of the city and the southeast area along the county border. Finally, Exhibit C shows the home locations of offenders for the 2-year period.

A: Map of Home Location of Homicide Victims
Source: Institute of Law and Justice, Groff and McEwen, *Exploring the Spacial Configuration of Places Related to Homicide Events, Final Report*, March 2006. Used with permission.
B: Map of Homicide Locations for Victims
Source: Institute of Law and Justice, Groff and McEwen, *Exploring the Spacial Configuration of Places Related to Homicide Events, Final Report*, March 2006. Used with permission.
C: Map of Home Locations of Offenders
Source: Institute of Law and Justice, Groff and McEwen, *Exploring the Spacial Configuration of Places Related to Homicide Events, Final Report*, March 2006. Used with permission.

Chapter 6 introduced crime mapping as a way to identify hot spots of crime. Geographic profiling takes crime mapping techniques and turns them inside out. Geographic profiling can help prioritize suspect lists, direct stakeouts, and conduct neighborhood canvasses. In March 2008, the Office of Community Oriented Policing Services (COPS) and the National Institute of Justice (NIJ) launched the first issue of *Geography and Public Safety*, dealing with applied geography for the study of crime and public safety and providing a valuable new resource for law enforcement in all capacities and ranks, from patrol to special investigations, from frontline officers to police chiefs.

Other technology is being used to help map human behavior in an effort to identify criminal suspects. Some say that cell phone data has become the new technological version of DNA. Cell phone data taken from cell towers along with social media geolocators and photo mapping can be analyzed to see suspect patterns, which can help law enforcement investigate crimes and locate individuals. In one homicide investigation, investigators were able to obtain a first-degree murder conviction using the call and text patterns between the suspect and victim as evidence (Paige 2011). Mapping information can show the suspect in the vicinity of a crime during specific times. Data embedded into photographs taken by cell phones can also be traced, and that data often includes dates and location of where the pictures were taken.

Regardless of the highly sophisticated technologies available to criminal investigators, to respond effectively and appropriately to a crime, officers must first know what defines the crime.

INVESTIGATING SPECIFIC CRIMES

Some actions and activities may seem "wrong" and unjust but are not technically criminal. Someone took something? Was it robbery, burglary, larceny/theft, or simply a misunderstood "borrowing"? Following is a brief examination of some specific crimes and how they are generally investigated. This section begins with the FBI's eight Part I Index offenses and their general definitions, including the specific elements of each offense that must be proven during a criminal investigation. Then investigating other serious crimes is discussed, including crimes against children, bias/hate crimes, environmental crimes, and computer-related crimes.

VIOLENT CRIMES

Statistically, violent crimes do not occur as often as property crimes. However, violent crime investigations generally result in higher quantity and quality of information and evidence than do property crime investigations because of the personal contact that occurs between victim and suspect. In violent crimes, the victim is also an eyewitness and can be an important key to identifying the suspect. The victim and other witnesses can often provide important information about how and by what means the attack was made; what the attacker's intent or motive was; descriptive information about the attacker, weapon, and any getaway vehicle; and what words may have been spoken. Weapons may provide physical evidence, as may any injuries suffered by the victim. Typically, violent crimes yield a considerable amount of physical evidence, with the type of evidence to anticipate directly related to the type of crime committed. Officers could expect to find such evidence as a weapon, blood, hair, fibers, fingerprints, footprints, and the like, depending on the specific crime. Consequently, the clearance rate for violent crimes is relatively high.

Violent crime investigations have been enhanced by the establishment of the Violent Criminal Apprehension Program (VICAP) at the FBI National Police Academy in Quantico, Virginia. The goal of this program is to coordinate major violent crime cases, regardless of their location, in the United States. Information considered viable is published in the FBI's *Law Enforcement Bulletin*. If the case merits interagency cooperation, a major case investigation team of investigators from all involved agencies may be formed.

> The major violent crimes are homicide, rape, assault, and robbery.

Keep in mind that entire books and courses are devoted to criminal investigation and, because of space and time limitations, what follows is necessarily only a cursory look at what is involved in investigating criminal offenses.

Homicide

Homicide is the killing of one person by another. Homicide receives extensive public attention as well as intensive police attention. Unfortunately, the homicide clearance rate has declined steadily, dropping from 92 percent in 1961 to 64.8 percent in 2010 (*Crime in the United States 2010* 2010). This decrease may be attributed to an increase in the more difficult to solve "stranger-to-stranger" homicides, reduced cooperation from witnesses, the release of hundreds of thousands of inmates yearly, and increases in illegal immigrants who fear police and, thus, make poor sources of information as crime victims or witnesses.

Homicide investigations frequently require all investigative techniques and skills. A primary requirement is to establish that death was caused by a criminal action. The four basic types of death are death by natural causes, accidental death, suicide, and homicide. Although technically officers are concerned only with homicide, frequently they do not know at the start of an investigation what type of death has occurred. Therefore, any of the four types of death may require investigation.

> Homicide is classified as criminal (felonious) or noncriminal. The various degrees of murder and manslaughter are criminal homicide, noncriminal homicide (which includes excusable homicide—the unintentional, truly accidental killing of another person), and justifiable homicide (killing another person under authorization of law).

The elements present in a criminal homicide determine whether the act is charged as murder in the first, second, or third degree, or as voluntary or involuntary manslaughter. The "weapon" used also influences the charge, as in the case of criminal vehicular homicide, aka vehicular manslaughter. All states except Alaska, Montana, and Arizona have vehicular homicide statutes, and most statutes state this crime involves the death of an individual from the negligent operation of a vehicle (including driving while intoxicated [DWI]), which is generally a lesser charge than manslaughter. The Model Penal Code has no specific category for vehicular homicide, and the offense is generally categorized under negligent homicide. In those states without specific vehicular homicide statutes, offenders can still be charged with murder or manslaughter depending on the circumstances.

> A common element in every charge is "causing the death of another human being." Other elements in homicide include premeditation, malicious intent, adequately provoked intent resulting in heat of passion, while committing or attempting to commit a crime that is not a felony, when forced or threatened, culpable negligence or depravity, or simple negligence. **Premeditation**, the deliberate, precalculated plan to cause death, is the essential element of first-degree murder, distinguishing it from all other murder classifications.

premeditation

The deliberate, precalculated plan to cause death; the essential element of first-degree murder, distinguishing it from all other murder classifications.

Heat of passion homicides are often the culmination of intimate partner violence. In addition, "An overwhelming proportion of intimate partner homicide perpetrators are under the influence of substances when the crime occurs, and alcohol consumption is a strong indicator of intimate terrorism of women" (Roberts 2009, 67).

The first priority in a preliminary homicide investigation is to determine that death has occurred—provided the suspect is not at the scene. Signs of death include lack of breathing, lack of heartbeat, lack of flushing of the fingernail bed when pressure is applied and then released, and failure of the eyelids to close after being gently lifted. In some instances, police can enter a premise without a warrant if they believe a person is in need of medical assistance or if they believe the premises may contain a victim or a killer, as established in *Flippo v. West Virginia* (1999). The Supreme Court "acknowledged that police may make warrantless entries onto premises if they reasonably believe that a person is in need of immediate aid or may make a prompt warrantless search of a homicide scene for other victims or a killer on the premises."

> After priority matters are completed, the focus of the homicide investigation is to identify the victim, establish the time of death, establish the cause of death and the method used to produce it, and develop a suspect.

Homicide victims are identified by their relatives, friends, or acquaintances; by personal effects, fingerprints, DNA analysis, skeletal studies including teeth and dental records, clothing and laundry marks; or through missing-persons files.

Determining the time of death is one important part of any homicide investigation. General factors used to estimate time of death are body temperature, rigor mortis, postmortem lividity, appearance of the eyes, stomach contents, stage of decomposition, and evidence suggesting a change in the victim's normal routine.

Currently, if a body is found within a day, investigators can determine the time of death quite accurately based on lividity, appearance of the eyes, rigor mortis, and the like. After a day has passed, it becomes much more difficult to determine time of death. A project at the Oak Ridge National Laboratory is developing a device to wave over a body to determine how long a person has been dead. The project is based on the fact that as a body decomposes, proteins break down into amino acids and progressively smaller molecules. By studying whether there is a constant rate at which the large molecules of the body break down, researchers can correlate the percentage of larger molecules to small ones within a number of days.

Another aid in homicide investigations comes from forensic entomology. Insects, particularly flies, are attracted to the nose, eyes, ears, and mouth of dead bodies and lay eggs, which emerge or "hatch" into maggots. Interpreting entomological evidence at a crime scene can help establish time of death, season of death, geographic location of death, movement or storage of the remains following death, specific sites of trauma on the body, sexual molestation, and even drug use.

A medical examination or autopsy provides legal evidence as to the cause and time of death and corroborates information obtained during the investigation. It may also reveal evidence that may otherwise have gone undetected and that may link the victim to a suspect. Suspects are developed by determining a motive for the killing and by circumstantial evidence.

Physical evidence in a homicide includes a weapon, a body, blood, hairs, and fibers. The type of evidence available will depend on the nature of the homicide and the type of scene involved. For example, a hit-and-run crime scene may have numerous kinds of physical evidence, including hairs, fibers, blood and other biological fluids, and materials from the vehicle, including broken plastic or glass from lights.

The initial police response to a homicide call and their subsequent degree of involvement and thoroughness in the follow-up investigation directly affect the outcome of the case and whether it is cleared. Some homicide investigations are relatively straightforward and free of complication. Others, however, pose one or more challenges.

> Special problems in homicide investigations include pressure by the public and the media; difficulty in establishing that it is homicide, rather than suicide or an accidental or natural death; handling serial murders; and, in some cases, reopening cold cases.

Among the most common causes of unnatural death are gunshot wounds; stabbing and cutting wounds; blows from blunt instruments; asphyxia induced by choking, drowning, hanging, smothering, strangulation, gases, or poisons; poisoning and drug overdoses; burning; explosions; electric shock; and lightning. An **equivocal death investigation** may have two or more meanings and may be presented as either a homicide or a suicide, depending on the circumstances. The facts may be purposefully vague or misleading or appear suspicious or questionable. For example, one type of equivocal death is autoerotic asphyxia, the intentional cutting off of oxygen to the brain for sexual

equivocal death investigation

May have two or more meanings and may be presented as either a homicide or a suicide, depending on the circumstances.

arousal. The difficulty in investigating such cases is determining if the death is accidental or suicide. In rare instances, murder might be suspected.

In equivocal death investigations, any weapon tightly clutched in the victim's hand as the result of cadaveric spasm indicates suicide rather than murder, but this cannot always be assumed. The victim's background also provides information about whether the death was accidental, suicide, or homicide. This background and evidence on the victim's body often provide leads to a suspect.

Occasionally, investigators find themselves handling multiple homicide cases with key similarities. Such cases may be linked merely by coincidence or may be the signature of a serial killer. The FBI held a 4-day symposium attended by 135 experts on serial murder (*Serial Murder* 2008). The report from the symposium cited the following myths and facts about serial killers. First, serial killers are not all dysfunctional loners: "The majority of serial killers are not reclusive, social misfits who live alone" (3). The Green River Killer, Gary Ridgeway, who killed 48 women during a 20-year period, was married, employed, and attended church. A second myth is that all serial killers travel interstate when, in fact, most operate in a defined geographic area, staying within their comfort zone. Those who do travel are either itinerants, homeless, or have jobs that involve interstate travel (4).

A third myth is that all serial killers are White males when the reality is that they span all racial groups, reflecting the racial makeup of the country, and have included women (*Serial Murder* 2008, 4). Fourth, a widely believed myth is that all serial killers are motivated by sex, when many are actually motivated by anger, thrill, financial gain, or attention seeking. The Washington, DC, snipers killed primarily out of anger and for the thrill. In the end, they sought financial gain (4).

A fifth myth is that serial killers cannot stop killing. BTK killer Dennis Rader murdered 10 victims from 1974 to 1991 but did not kill again. He was captured in 2005, stating that he used autoerotic activities as a substitute (*Serial Murder* 2008, 4–5). A sixth myth is that all serial killers are insane or are evil geniuses: "As a group, serial killers suffer from a variety of personality disorders.... Most, however are not adjudicated insane. Their intelligence ranges from borderline to above average levels" (6). A final myth is that serial killers want to be caught: "As serial killers continue to offend without being captured, they can become empowered, feeling they will never be identified" (6).

The experts agree that there is no generic profile of a serial killer, but some traits are commonly observed, including sensation seeking, lack of remorse or guilt, impulsivity, the need for control, and predatory behavior.

The FBI has launched a new initiative focused on highway serial killings, with the bodies of murdered women being dumped along the Interstate 40 corridor in Oklahoma, Texas, Arkansas, and Mississippi ("Highway Serial Killings" 2009). Most victims lived high-risk, transient lifestyles, often involving substance abuse and prostitution, and were picked up at truck stops or service stations, predominantly by long-haul truck drivers.

Commonly, cases involving serial killers have been put on hold because of lack of evidence. The NIJ defines a cold case as a case whose probative investigative leads have been exhausted. A case that is only a few months old may be classified as "cold." More attention has been focused on cold cases because of the popular television series and the increased involvement and public visibility of family members as well as recent advances in DNA technology (Heurich 2008). In other instances, the perpetrator may be known but his or her whereabouts is unknown.

Sexual Assault

Sexual assault (rape) is sexual intercourse with a person against the person's will. It is classified as forcible (by use or threats of force) or statutory (with a minor, with or without consent).

 Most states have in common the following elements for the crime of rape or sexual assault: (1) an act of sexual intercourse, (2) committed without the victim's consent, (3) against the victim's will and by force.

All sexual assault reports should be considered valid unless evidence indicates otherwise because strong sexual assault cases require strong, thorough written reports with a high level of detail (Kurash 2009). Failing to adhere to this principle opens an agency up to liability and can result in offenders avoiding accountability for their crimes.

Special problems in investigating rape include the sensitive nature of the offense, social attitudes, and the victim's embarrassment and feelings of shame. The victim's age can also present a challenge, and those who investigate sexual assaults on children and young juveniles typically receive special training. Culture can also be a hindrance, as can language barriers. A rape investigation requires great tact. A sexual assault response team (SART) consisting of an investigator, a rape crisis advocate, and a nurse examiner can provide victims with information about their medical, legal, and psychological options.

Modus operandi factors important in investigating sex offenses include type of offense, words spoken, use of a weapon, method of attack, time of day, type of location, and the victim's age. Physical evidence commonly found in rape cases includes stained or torn clothing; scratches, bruises, and cuts; evidence of a struggle; and pubic hairs, semen, and bloodstains.

A particular challenge to law enforcement is drug-facilitated sexual assault, with the most common date rape drugs being Rohypnol (also called "roofies" or "ruphees") and gamma hydroxybutyrate or GHB. A timely response is necessary because such drugs may, in only a few hours, be metabolized and rendered undetectable in the victim's bloodstream, or eliminated in the victim's urine.

Other tools in dealing with sexual assault are sex offender registration and community notification programs. After Jacob Wetterling was abducted in October 1989 and never found, Congress passed the Jacob Wetterling Crimes against Children and Sexually Violent Offender Registration Act in 1994. The act required states to create sex offender registries within 3 years or lose 10 percent of their funding. The act also gave states the option of releasing information about registered sex offenders to the public, but did not require it.

Although registries gave police valuable information to identify, monitor, and track sex offenders, they did little to protect the public. Then, in 1994, 7-year-old Megan Kanka was raped and murdered by a paroled sex offender living across the street. In 1996, Congress amended the Wetterling Act to require states to disclose information about registered sex offenders.

Given that each year about 24,000 sex offenders are released to the community after serving an average 6-year prison sentence, a registration and notification system seems logical and necessary. It would also seem to strike a balance between the public's right to be informed and the offender's right to privacy. However, not everyone agrees. A federal court in the District of Columbia struck down that district's "Megan's Law," saying it deprived sex offenders of their Fifth Amendment due process rights without giving them a hearing.

Adding to the challenge of handling sex offenders is that laws vary from state to state, including the level of offense a person is charged with and whether that is a trackable level. Typically, a public notification is only required on the highest level of offenders. This means there are many more mid- and lower-level sex offenders living next door to the general public without the community's knowledge.

Assault

Assault is unlawfully threatening to harm another person, actually harming another person, or attempting unsuccessfully to do so. Simple assault is intentionally causing another to fear immediate bodily harm or death or intentionally inflicting or attempting to inflict bodily harm on another. It is usually a misdemeanor. Aggravated assault is an unlawful attack by one person on another to inflict *severe* bodily injury. It often involves use of a dangerous weapon and is a felony. In specified instances, teachers, people operating public conveyances, and law enforcement officers use physical force legally.

> The elements of the crime of simple assault are (1) intent to do bodily harm to another, (2) present ability to commit the act, and (3) commission of an overt act toward carrying out the intent. An additional element in the crime of aggravated assault is that the intentionally inflicted bodily injury results in (1) a high probability of death; (2) serious, permanent disfigurement; or (3) permanent or protracted loss or impairment of the function of any body member or organ or other severe bodily harm. Attempted assault requires proof of intent and an overt act toward committing the crime.

Special problems in investigating assaults include distinguishing the victim from the suspect, determining if the matter is civil or criminal, and determining if the act was intentional or accidental. Obtaining a complaint against simple assault also is sometimes difficult.

Proving the elements of the offense of assault requires establishing the intent to cause injury, the severity of the injury inflicted, and whether a dangerous weapon was used. Physical evidence in an assault includes photographs of injuries, clothing of the victim or suspect, weapons, broken objects, bloodstains, hairs, fibers, and other signs of an altercation.

Domestic abuse, stalking, and elder abuse all are candidates for categorization as separate crimes, rather than being lumped in the general category of assault for reporting—and thus research—purposes. These offenses were discussed in Chapter 7.

Robbery

Robbery is the felonious taking of another's property from his or her person or in his or her presence through force or intimidation. Robberies are classified as either residential, commercial, street or vehicle-driver robberies, or carjacking, the taking of a motor vehicle by force or threat of force. One type of residential robber is the home invader. Many home invaders are young Asian gang members who travel across the country robbing Asian families, especially business owners.

> The elements of the crime of robbery are (1) the wrongful taking of personal property, (2) from the person or in the person's presence, (3) against the person's will by force or threat of force.

The rapidity of a robbery, its potential for violence and the taking of hostages, and the usual lack of evidence at the scene pose special problems in robbery investigations. Officers responding to a robbery-in-progress call should proceed rapidly but cautiously. They should assume the robber is at the scene unless otherwise advised, and be prepared for gunfire; look for and immobilize any getaway vehicle discovered; avoid a hostage situation if possible; and make an immediate arrest if the situation warrants.

Each element of robbery must be proven separately. To prove that personal property was wrongfully taken, the legal owner of the property must be identified and the property and its value described completely. To prove that property was taken from the person or in the person's presence, the exact words, gestures, motions, or actions the robber used to gain control of the property must be recorded. To prove the property was removed against the victim's will by force or threat of force, a complete description of the robber's words, actions, and any weapon used or threatened to be used must be obtained.

Convenience store robberies pose a special problem because, as the name implies, they are convenient for robbers as well as for customers. Most convenience stores lack security and have poorly trained, inexperienced employees who are encouraged to comply with a robber's demands (Petrocelli 2008b). These stores should maximize natural surveillance, limit the amount of cash in the register and post a notice to this effect, put a height strip near the door to help employees get an accurate height reading with a glance, and set aside a visible area in the store equipped with a table and chair where officers can come to write their reports (Petrocelli 2008b).

Commercial bank robberies are jointly investigated by the FBI, state, and local law enforcement personnel: "The average bank robbery takes less than three minutes, oftentimes occurring so quickly that other customers are not aware of anything happening. About 25 percent of bank robberies occur on Fridays and most occur during the day shift between 9 a.m. and noon" (Petrocelli 2008a, 16). Suggested strategies to reduce bank robberies include enlisting the support of banks, focusing on high-risk branches and specific types of bank robbery, limiting cash access, using dye packs, using tracking devices and bait money, banning hats and sunglasses, employing greeters and hiring security guards, offering rewards, upgrading electronic surveillance, and installing bullet-resistant glass barriers between tellers and customers (Weisel 2007).

Information about the suspect's general appearance, clothing and disguises, weapon(s), and vehicle(s) used should be obtained. Important modus operandi information includes type of robbery, time (day and hour), method of attack (threatened or real), weapon, object sought, number of robbers, voice and words, vehicle used, and any peculiarities. Physical evidence that can connect the suspect with the robbery includes fingerprints, shoe prints, tire prints, restraining devices used, discarded garments, fibers and hairs, a note, and the stolen property.

PROPERTY CRIMES

Many property crimes are difficult to investigate because they typically have little evidence and no eyewitnesses. Physical evidence in property crimes may include fingerprints, footprints, tire impressions, hair, fibers, broken glass, and personal objects left at the crime scene. Other important evidence in property crimes includes tools, tool fragments, tool marks, safe insulation, disturbance of paint, and evidence of forcible entry. The modus operandi of a property crime often takes on added importance because other significant leads are absent. Further, property crimes tend to occur in series, so solving one crime may lead to solving an entire series of similar crimes.

The major property crimes are burglary, larceny/theft, motor vehicle theft, and arson.

Burglary

Burglary is the unlawful entry of a structure to commit a crime. It differs from robbery in that burglars are covert, trying to remain unseen, whereas robbers confront their victims directly. Burglary is a crime against property; robbery is a violent crime against a person. Burglaries are classified as residential or commercial.

The elements of the crime of burglary include (1) entering a structure (2) without the consent of the person in possession (3) with the intent to commit a crime therein. Additional elements of burglary that may be required include (1) breaking into (2) the dwelling of another (3) during the nighttime. A burglary's severity is determined by the presence of dangerous devices in the burglar's possession, by the value of the property stolen, and whether the property or residence was occupied at the time of the offense. Attempted burglary and possession of burglary tools are also felonies. The elements of the crime of possessing burglary tools include (1) possessing any device, explosive, or other instrumentality (2) with intent to use or permit their use to commit burglary.

Officers responding to a burglary call should proceed to the scene tactically, being observant and cautious. They should search the premises inside and outside for the burglar.

Special considerations in investigating burglary include the problem of false alarms, determining the means of entry into a structure, as well as into such objects as safes or vaults, and recovering the stolen property. Jimmying is the most common method used to enter a structure to commit burglary. Attacks on safes and vaults include punching, peeling, pulling or dragging, blowing, burning, chopping, and, for safes, hauling them away.

Physical evidence at a burglary scene often includes fingerprints, DNA, footprints, tire prints, tools, tool marks, broken glass, safe insulation, paint chips, and personal possessions. Important modus operandi factors include the time, the types of premises, the type of victim, point and means of entry, type of property taken, and any peculiarities of the offense.

Mapping can be especially effective in dealing with burglaries, given that burglars often live or work within a 2-mile residential radius. Mapping plus modus operandi information can often effectively zero in on suspects. Burglarized houses are likely to be burglarized again. Therefore, the most important use of data is to facilitate preventive measures such as target hardening after an initial victimization.

Fences, pawnshops, secondhand stores, flea markets, and informants should be checked for leads in recovering stolen property.

Larceny/Theft

Larceny/theft is the unlawful taking, carrying, leading, or riding away of property from another's possession. It is synonymous with theft. Both larceny and burglary are crimes against property, but larceny, unlike burglary, does not involve illegally entering a structure. Larceny differs from robbery in that no force or threat of force is involved. The two major categories of larceny/theft are grand larceny, a felony based on the value of stolen property (usually more than $100), and petty larceny, a misdemeanor based on the value of the property (usually less than $100).

> The elements of the crime of larceny/theft are (1) the felonious stealing, taking, carrying, leading, or driving away of (2) another's personal goods or property (3) valued above or below a specified amount (4) with the intent to permanently deprive the owner of the property or goods. In most states, taking found property with the intent to keep or sell it is also a crime.

Among the common types of larceny are purse-snatching, picking pockets, theft from coin machines, theft from motor vehicles, theft from buildings, jewelry theft, bicycle theft, and shoplifting (including altering the price of an item). (See Figure 10.2.) Closed circuit television (CCTV) is one effective way to detect shoplifters as well as dishonest employees.

One of the most frequent thefts is that of bicycles. More than 1 million U.S. residents have their bicycles stolen each year. Bicycle theft is usually seen as a low police priority, but when viewed in the aggregate, bicycle theft represents a large problem with harmful economic and societal effects (Johnson, Sidebottom, and Thorpe 2008). The FBI Uniform Crime Reports (UCR) puts the annual cost of bicycle theft at between $800 million and $1 billion. Although

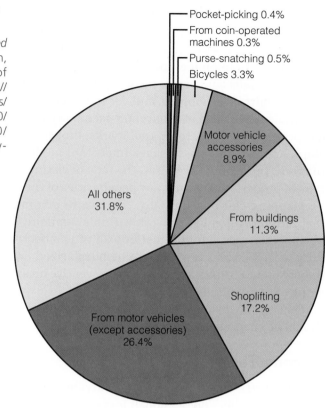

FIGURE 10.2 Larceny/Theft Distribution
Source: *Crime in the United States 2010* (Washington, DC: Federal Bureau of Investigation, 2010). http://www.fbi.gov/about-us/cjis/ucr/crime-in-the-u.s/2010/crime-in-the-u.s.-2010/property-crime/larceny-theft-figure

Pocket-picking 0.4%
From coin-operated machines 0.3%
Purse-snatching 0.5%
Bicycles 3.3%
Motor vehicle accessories 8.9%
From buildings 11.3%
Shoplifting 17.2%
From motor vehicles (except accessories) 26.4%
All others 31.8%

police nationwide recover nearly 50 percent of lost and stolen bikes, less than 5 percent ever make it back to their rightful owners. This could be rectified if bike owners would register with the National Bike Registry. A top priority in reducing bicycle theft is educating the public about using effective bicycle locks and locking practices (Johnson, Sidebottom, and Thorpe 2008).

Of increasing concern is the theft of copper, which, according to the FBI, threatens the U.S. infrastructure ("Precious Metal" 2008). An example of this threat was an incident in which vandals removed 300 feet of copper wire from a Federal Aviation Administration tower in Ohio, threatening to interrupt communications between in-flight aircraft and air traffic controllers. According to the FBI, the demand for copper from developing nations such as China and India has created a "robust" international copper trade; from 2001 to 2008, the price of copper increased more than 500 percent and it remains at unprecedented levels. The thieves, many of whom are drug addicts or gang members, act individually or as part of organized groups. Their targets include electrical substations, railroads, security and emergency services, construction sites and new home developments, and other sensitive sites.

Although jewelry and art theft may be committed by those merely acting on opportunity, professional thieves or organized rings may also be responsible for these crimes. Given the enhanced security usually afforded such items of great monetary value, those who commit jewel or art theft have typically invested more time in planning their heist and may go to greater extremes to protect themselves and their loot, including being heavily armed. The FBI and Interpol are commonly involved in thefts of fine art. Officers investigating jewelry theft should also inform the FBI of the theft, even without immediate evidence of interstate operations.

As with burglary investigations, officers investigating cases of larceny/theft should check with fences, pawnshops, secondhand stores, flea markets, and informants for leads in recovering stolen property.

> The elements of the offense of receiving stolen goods are (1) receiving, buying, or concealing stolen or illegally obtained goods (2) knowing them to be stolen or illegally obtained.

Fraud is intentional deception applied to cause a person to give up property or some lawful right. It differs from theft in that fraud uses deceit rather than stealth to obtain goods illegally. Fraud is committed in many ways, including the use of checks, credit cards, confidence games, and embezzlement. Perpetrators of fraud are rarely prosecuted because the courts often regard fraud cases as civil rather than criminal. An additional challenge lies in establishing the criminal intent required for conviction. Furthermore, most current fraud cases are tied to the Internet, and the perpetrators are difficult to trace, many times being located outside the jurisdiction of the United States. Such inter-jurisdictional cases are difficult to investigate and to prosecute.

Closely related to the preceding types of fraud are debit and credit-card fraud. Retailers and credit card companies incur tens of millions of dollars in losses each year because of credit-card fraud.

> Elements of the crime of larceny by debit or credit card include (1) possessing cards obtained by theft or fraud (2) by which services or goods are obtained (3) through unauthorized signing of the cardholder's name. Bank embezzlements are investigated jointly by the local police and the FBI.

White-collar crime was coined in 1939 by criminologist Edwin Sutherland to describe an offense "committed by a person of respectability and high social status in the course of his occupation" (Sutherland 1983). Later definitions focused more on the offense than the offender and included such elements as illegal acts committed by nonphysical means through deception and concealment during legitimate business activity. Over the years, the term has become synonymous with the full range of frauds committed by business and government professionals, both individuals and corporations.

White-collar or business-related crime includes securities theft and fraud; environmental crime; insurance fraud; credit-card and check fraud; consumer fraud; mortgage fraud; insurance fraud; health care fraud; telemarketing fraud; illegal competition and deceptive practices; bankruptcy fraud; computer-related fraud; embezzlement and pilferage; bribes, kickbacks, and payoffs; and receiving stolen property.

One study has found that in four of six comparisons, white-collar crimes were perceived to be more serious than street crimes (Piquero, Carmichael, and Piquero 2008). Most individuals in the study also perceived that white-collar crimes were as serious—if not more so—than street crimes. Indeed, the economic costs of "suite" crime far exceed the costs of traditional street crime: "We cannot afford to neglect the capacity of corporations, the most powerful actors in the nation, to victimize society. Although corporate crime is usually less spectacular than the usual homicide or robbery, it still does significant harm, and in many respects this harm may far exceed the damage wrought by more traditional modes of criminality" (Cullen et al. 2006, 18).

Detecting fraud and other forms of white-collar crime can be extremely challenging because many of the offenses involve spatial separation between victims and offenders, meaning they never come face-to-face, and many of the crimes are nonself-revealing, such as when a shady auto mechanic claims to have conducted a repair or performed a service and the vehicle owner lacks the expertise to know anything different. "Unlike most so-called traditional street crimes, such as robbery, burglary, auto theft, and assault, white-collar crimes are not obvious. They often do not leave visible traces of their occurrence. Even the victims may not be aware that a crime has taken place, let alone law enforcers" (Benson and Simpson 2009, 207). Without detection, investigation becomes impossible.

White-collar crime has been in the headlines for several decades, with the insider trading scandals of the 1980s, the saving and loan scandals of the 1990s, and the more recent financial and accounting fraud scandals involving Enron, Qwest, Tyco, WorldCom, Adelphia Communications, and others. The FBI has refocused its efforts on white-collar crime, seeking to convict criminals who helped to create or are now exploiting the financial crisis occurring in this country (Kingsbury 2009). For example, in March 2009, the FBI opened more than 200 mortgage-fraud cases and 36 corporate-financial investigations, and the number is expected to grow exponentially: "Congress is already weighing an increase to the FBI's budget to address the spike in frauds related to the economic crisis" (Kingsbury). With mortgage fraud continuing at elevated levels in 2009 and 2010, the Department of Justice implemented a mortgage-fraud takedown in June 2010 called Operation Stolen Dreams, the largest collective enforcement effort to ever address the mortgage fraud problem (*2010 Mortgage Fraud Report* 2011).

Some of the white-collar crimes have gained national attention. One such investigation involves Tom Petters, who, in December 2009, was convicted on all 20 fraud, conspiracy, and money laundering counts in his multibillion-dollar Ponzi scheme trial. In another recent scandal, in March 2009, Bernard Madoff pled guilty to securities fraud, perjury, and other crimes committed during a 30-year span in what some have called the largest fraud in history. The 71-year-old former NASDAQ chairman was accused of bilking investors out of $64.8 billion. There was no plea bargain, and Madoff was sentenced to 150 years in prison in June 2009. Indeed, studies show that Americans seem to support such drastic punishments for those convicted of white-collar crime, generally favoring the same "get-tough" approach on corporate illegality as is commonly held for violent crime (Unnever, Benson, and Cullen 2008).

Ponzi schemes are not the only white-collar crime grabbing headlines. Internet crime increased by 33 percent in 2008, with 275,284 complaints received that involved $265 million in losses compared with 2007 when 206,884 complaints involving $239 million in losses ("FBI/National White Collar Crime Center" 2009).

A problem of increasing concern is *identity theft*, the unlawful use of another's personal identifying information, Historically, higher fraud rates occur when the economy worsens. In 2008, 9.9 million Americans were identity-theft victims, a 22-percent increase over 2007 (Kanable 2009). One reason identity theft has increased so dramatically is that there are more than 200 valid forms of ID or driver's licenses issued in the United States. The increasingly sophisticated computer equipment and photocopying and imaging methods available to the public makes it easy to alter or counterfeit almost any document. The Internet has hundreds of Web sites that sell fake driver's licenses, ID cards, police IDs, and birth certificates on CDs.

Identity theft became a federal crime in 1998 when President Bill Clinton signed the Identity Theft and Assumption Deterrence Act. Although this act looks good on paper, it does not cover thefts less than the $50,000 to $100,000 threshold most attorneys use to determine if federal prosecution should occur.

The rising threat of terrorism makes identity theft an even greater concern. As an example, all 19 of the September 11 hijackers had social security numbers, including several that were stolen. In July 2004, President George W. Bush signed into law a sentence imposing mandatory prison terms for criminals who use identity theft to commit terrorist acts and other offenses.

As with computer-related crime and digital/electronic evidence, many local police departments are ill equipped to deal with white-collar crime and other nontraditional forms of larceny/theft.

Motor Vehicle Theft

Motor vehicle thefts include cars, trucks, buses, motorcycles, motor scooters, mopeds, snowmobiles, vans, self-propelled watercraft, and aircraft. Although motor vehicle theft investigations take much investigative time, they can provide important information on other crimes under investigation. The vehicle identification number (VIN), critical in motor vehicle thefts, identifies the specific vehicle in question and is the primary nonduplicated, serialized number assigned by the manufacturer to each vehicle.

> Categories for motor vehicle theft based on the offender's motive include (1) joyriding, (2) transportation, (3) stripping for parts and accessories, (4) use in committing another crime, and (5) reselling for profit.

Although referred to as "motor vehicle theft," most cases are prosecuted as "unauthorized use of a motor vehicle" because a charge of theft requires proof that the thief intended to deprive the owner of the vehicle permanently, which is often difficult or impossible to establish.

> The elements of the crime of unauthorized use of a motor vehicle are (1) intentionally taking or driving (2) a motor vehicle (3) without the consent of the owner or the owner's authorized agent. Embezzlement of a motor vehicle occurs if the person who took the vehicle had consent initially and then exceeded the terms of that consent.

False motor vehicle theft reports are often filed because a car has been taken by a family member or misplaced in a parking lot, to cover up for an accident or a crime committed with the vehicle, or to provide an alibi for being late. The FBI and the National Auto Theft Bureau provide valuable help in investigating motor vehicle theft.

To apprehend car thieves, many departments are using bait cars, specially outfitted cars placed in areas where they are likely to be stolen, based on trends in the community. A computer monitors the cars' locations and sounds an alarm if anyone gets in. Fairfax County, Washington, uses bait cars equipped with GPS devices, hidden video cameras, and technology that allows the police to remotely shut down the cars' engines or blow their horns loudly.

To improve the ability to recognize stolen vehicles, officers should keep a list of stolen vehicles in their cars, develop a checking system for rapidly determining if a suspicious vehicle is stolen, learn the common characteristics of stolen vehicles and car thieves, take time to check suspicious people and vehicles, and learn how to question suspicious drivers and occupants. Numerous motor vehicle thefts can be prevented by effective educational campaigns and by manufacturer-installed security devices. The Dyer Act made interstate transportation of a stolen motor vehicle a federal crime and allowed for federal help in prosecuting such cases.

Arson

Arson is the malicious, willful burning of a building or property. Fires are classified as natural, accidental, criminal (arson), suspicious, or of unknown origin. They are presumed natural or accidental unless proven otherwise.

> The elements of the crime of arson include (1) the willful, malicious burning of a building or property (2) of another, or of one's own to defraud (3) or causing to be burned, or aiding, counseling, or procuring such burning. Attempted arson is also a crime. Some states categorize arson as either aggravated or simple. Aggravated arson is intentionally destroying or damaging a dwelling or other property by means of fire or explosives, creating an imminent danger to life or great bodily harm, which risk was known or reasonably foreseeable to the suspect. Simple arson is intentional destruction by fire or explosives that does not create imminent danger to life or risk of great bodily harm. Other states use the Model Arson Law, which divides arson into four degrees: first-degree involves the burning of dwellings, second-degree involves the burning of buildings other than dwellings, third-degree involves the burning of other property, and fourth-degree involves attempts to burn buildings or property.

Logic suggests that the fire department should work to *detect* arson and determine the point of origin and probable cause, whereas the police department should *investigate* arson and prepare the case for prosecution. Special problems in investigating arson include coordinating efforts with the fire department and others, determining if a crime has been committed, finding physical evidence and witnesses, and determining if the victim is a suspect.

An administrative warrant is issued when it is necessary for the agent to search the premises to determine the cause and origin of the fire. A criminal warrant is issued on probable cause when evidence of a crime is found on the premises. Entry to fight a fire requires no warrant. Once in the building, fire officials may remain a reasonable time to investigate the cause of the blaze. After this time, an administrative warrant is needed, as established in *Michigan v. Tyler* (1978).

Although the fire department is responsible for establishing when arson has occurred, law enforcement investigators must be able to verify such findings. To do so requires understanding what distinguishes an accidental fire from arson. Basic to this understanding is the concept of the fire triangle, which consists of three elements necessary for a substance to burn: air, fuel, and heat. In arson, at least one of these elements is usually present in abnormal amounts for the structure. Evidence of **accelerants**, substances that promote burning, is a primary form of evidence at an arson scene. The most common accelerant used is gasoline. Also important as evidence are **igniters**, articles used to light a fire. These include matches; candles; cigars and cigarettes; cigarette lighters; electrical, mechanical, and chemical devices; and explosives.

Burn indicators that provide important information include alligatoring (blistering), crazing, depth of char, lines of demarcation, sagged furniture springs, and spalling. The point of origin is established by finding the area with the deepest char, alligatoring, and (usually) the greatest destruction. Fires normally burn upward, are drawn toward ventilation, and follow fuel. Arson is likely in fires that:

▶ Have more than one point of origin.

▶ Deviate from normal burning patterns.

▶ Show evidence of trailers.

▶ Show evidence of having been accelerated.

▶ Produce odors or smoke of a color associated with substances not normally present at the scene.

▶ Indicate that an abnormal amount of air, fuel, or heat was present.

▶ Reveal evidence of incendiary igniters at the point of origin.

Officers investigating vehicle fires should look for evidence of accelerants and determine whether the vehicle was insured. It is seldom arson if there is no insurance. Officers investigating explosions and bombings should pay special attention to any fragments of the explosive device as well as to any powder present at the scene and should attempt to determine a motive. If a computer is found at an arson scene, it is likely that the data on the hard drive is intact, surviving the heat and flames as well as the water and steam from the firefighting efforts.

Arson investigations might also be made more effective and efficient if police officers are cross-trained with firefighters.

OTHER CRIMES

Beyond the eight Index crimes, officers commonly investigate other offenses, such as crimes against children (discussed in detail in Chapter 11), hate or bias crimes, environmental crimes, and computer-related crimes. Many of these offenses involve one or more elements of one or more of the Index crimes. For

---

accelerants

Substances that promote burning; a primary form of evidence at an arson scene; the most common accelerant used is gasoline.

igniters

Articles used to light a fire.

example, crimes against children may include assault, rape, or murder. Bias crimes may be directed at a person (assault, homicide) or property (arson). Environmental crimes may involve theft of a commodity (for example, lumber) or, in some instances, homicide, as was the case when lethal acid was left on the street with the regular garbage and someone exposed to the chemical died. Finally, computer-related crimes may involve various forms of theft, including identity theft, and computers have been increasingly used to perpetrate crimes against children and distribute pornography.

Bias/Hate Crimes

A *hate crime*, according to the FBI, is "a criminal offense committed against a person, property or society which is motivated, in whole or in part, by the offender's bias against a race, religion, disability, sexual orientation or ethnicity/national origin." The FBI's *Hate Crime Statistics* (2010) reports 6,624 single-bias incidents in 2010, with race being the most frequent motivation of hate crime (47.3 percent) followed by religion (20.0 percent), sexual orientation (19.3 percent), ethnicity (12.8 percent), and disability (0.6 percent). Most hate crimes are not reported to the police. The International Association of Chiefs of Police (IACP) has developed a hate crime continuum depicting what can happen if a community ignores racial epithets or hate symbols—relatively nonsevere acts can escalate into assault, arson, and even murder. Consequently, graffiti, epithets, and symbols—precursors to overt hate crime—should be photographed for future evidentiary value and then removed quickly.

Investigators can use several incident characteristics to help them ascertain whether actions are more likely to be hate-based or not (Bodinger-deUriarte 1991). For example, in nonhate-based assaults, the people involved often know each other, whereas hate-based assaults are almost always "stranger" crimes. Regarding the number of perpetrators, most nonhate-based incidents involve one perpetrator and one victim, whereas hate-based incidents involve an average of four assailants for each victim. In nonhate-based incidents, the nature of the conflict tends to be even and the amount of physical damage inflicted is not typically "excessive." In hate-based incidents, however, the conflict tends to be very uneven in number of attackers to victims and the level of violence displayed, with victims of hate-based crimes being three times more likely to require hospitalization than "normal" assault victims. Finally, nonhate-based crimes generally occur in places with no symbolic significance and provide the perpetrator with some personal gain, such as settling a personal score or receiving monetary profit by taking something of value. Hate-based crimes, in contrast, often occur in locations with symbolic significance, such as churches, synagogues, mosques, or cemeteries, and most incidents provide no personal gain or profit to the perpetrator. In fact, it is far more likely that valuable property will be damaged or destroyed in a hate-based crime than taken and sold for profit, as is the typical goal of "traditional" crime (Bodinger-deUriarte 1991).

The Anti-Defamation League has launched a Web site to serve as a database for law enforcement officers investigating hate groups. The site identifies and monitors extremist groups and allows police to search for symbols they might find on literature or tattoos. It also tracks hate group meetings and rallies on a state-by-state calendar.

Environmental Crime

Environmental crimes range from people littering to those illegally disposing of used tires, used oil, biohazardous waste, and other hazardous substances. In some states, property owners can be civilly fined as much as $500 a day if the cleanup is not completed within the required time.

When both civil and criminal proceedings are instituted against a violator, it is known as **parallel proceedings**. The courts have ruled that taking both criminal and civil actions against a violator is not considered double jeopardy. Unfortunately, many law enforcement agencies consider polluting the environment a civil matter and do not devote resources to finding and prosecuting those who break the laws concerning protecting the environment.

parallel proceedings

When both civil and criminal proceedings are instituted against a violator; a frequent occurrence in environmental crimes.

Electronic Crime and Cybercrime

Before the 1990s, computer crime was virtually nonexistent. Where it occurred, it generally involved a single computer, or group of computers networked together, and required the offender to directly access the device, whether to steal data, plant a malicious code within the operating system, or conduct some other type of computer crime. Today, however, one of the hottest crime tools available is a personal computer connected to the Internet, with this *online* element fundamentally changing how law enforcement refers to such offenses—from computer crime to cybercrime: "The Internet's capacity for global interconnectivity has made the scope of the cybercrime problem transnational, the extent of which, confess most experts, is not yet fully understood.... What is known, however, is that cybercrime has touched countless individuals and businesses throughout the United States and has the potential to cause a national disaster" (Orthmann and Hess 2013, 511).

Because computer-related crimes often involve electronic devices other than actual computers, many agencies now refer to such offenses as *electronic crimes*. Electronic crimes and cybercrime are often very technically complex; thus, an in-depth discussion on their investigation is far beyond the scope of this chapter. It is important, however, for patrol officers to be familiar with some of the basic facets and features of these offenses.

> Computer crimes are relatively easy to commit and difficult to detect.

A wide range of criminal offenses are committed with computers, from students changing their grades and school records, to identity thieves wreaking havoc with consumers' lines of credit, to crooks embezzling millions of dollars from large corporations, to pedophiles sharing child pornography and luring innocent children into their illicit activities.

A relatively recent form of computer crime is **phishing**, using fraudulent e-mails and Web sites to fool recipients into divulging personal information. **Spoofing**, which is often associated with phishing, is another newer trend in computer-related crime and involves senders who alter or change the origin or source of an e-mail so that the origin of the e-mail is unknown. Many fraudulent scams use spoofed Internet protocol (IP) addresses. A variety of programs

phishing

Use of fraudulent e-mails and Web sites to fool recipients into divulging personal information.

spoofing

A newer trend in computer-related crime involving senders who alter or change the origin or source of an e-mail so that the origin of the e-mail is unknown; many fraudulent scams use spoofed Internet protocol (IP) addresses.

are available to make spoofing easy to do, and criminals are capitalizing on the anonymity afforded by the Internet along with the difficulty of tracing the source when using this technology. Spoofing has also been used to make prank phone calls, an offense called "telephone spoofing," which is often harmless but can escalate to dangerous levels. Besides the fact that it is very difficult and time consuming to trace spoofed calls, there are also jurisdictional issues because this crime can be committed from far distances, much like Internet fraud. In addition, spoofing itself is currently not illegal in the United States.

Computers and other electronic media that are used to commit crimes will store evidence of those crimes and might provide information on suspects and victims (*Best Practices* 2010). Therefore, investigators must identify and seize all electronic devices that could be connected to the offense. In addition to desktop and laptop computers, electronic evidence may exist on caller identification (ID) boxes, answering machines, cell phones, gaming systems, copy machines, fax machines, scanners and printers, flash drives, and smart cards. Physical evidence may also exist on keyboards and device cases in the form of fingerprints and DNA.

Because digital evidence may be altered, damaged, or destroyed simply by turning a device on or off at the wrong time, it is vital that first responders at computer crime scenes adhere to the ON/OFF rule: If it's on, leave it on. If it's off, leave it off. For more detailed guidelines about how to respond to and investigate computer-related and electronic crimes, the reader is encouraged to consult the U.S. Secret Service's *Best Practices for Seizing Electronic Evidence: A Pocket Guide for First Responders* (2010) and the NIJ's *Digital Evidence in the Courtroom: A Guide for Law Enforcement and Prosecutors* (2007), *Electronic Crime Scene Investigation: A Guide for First Responders* (2008), *Forensic Examination of Digital Evidence: A Guide for Law Enforcement* (2004), and *Investigations Involving the Internet and Computer Networks* (2007).

FALSE REPORTS

Whether officers are investigating violent crimes or property crimes, they should always be aware of the possibility of a false report. People may claim to have been burglarized to collect money for the stolen items from their insurance companies. Or they may set a friend up to "rob" them while they are at work alone and in control of a large amount of cash.

VICTIMLESS CRIMES

victimless crimes

Offenses in which there are no complainants; includes prostitution, pornography, gaming, and drug dealing/using.

A great amount of investigative time is spent on the so-called **victimless crimes**, such as prostitution, gambling, pornography, and dealing/doing drugs. Such crimes are sometimes assigned to a division called *vice investigations*.

> Victimless crimes include prostitution, pornography, gaming, and drug dealing/using.

Opinion polls indicate that most of the public is not all that upset about victimless crimes. However, a crime is a crime, even if the victim does not recognize or acknowledge it. This section addresses the "victimless" crimes of prostitution, gambling, and pornography. Chapter 12 discusses investigating crimes involving drugs.

Prostitution and Pornography

How aggressively police deal with prostitution depends greatly on public expectations. According to Parker (n.d.), "Prostitution, pornography and other forms of commercial sex are a multibillion dollar industry. They enrich a small minority of predators, while the larger community is left to pay for the damages." He further notes, "People used in the sex industry often need medical care as a result of the ever-present violence. They may need treatment for infectious diseases, including AIDS. Survivors frequently need mental health care for posttraumatic stress disorder, psychotic episodes, and suicide attempts. About a third end up chronically disabled and on social security." Further problems are that the sex trade plays an active role in promoting alcohol and drug abuse and that pimps also may use their prostitutes in forgery and credit-card fraud. Perhaps most troubling, however, is the data indicating how young most prostitutes are when they begin their "careers"—the average age for girls is 12 to 14, and for boys and transgender youth it is even earlier, between 11 and 13 (Walker-Rodriguez and Hill 2011).

Although streetwalking prostitutes are the most visible sign of a problem, escort services should not be overlooked. Because escort services advertise in local newspapers, telephone directories, and online Web sites, these sources can be reviewed to reveal their presence. Many prostitutes are homeless, have limited education, and very few social or professional ties with the community. For most, prostitution is not a chosen career but rather a matter of survival, often as the result of a drug habit, combined with the lack of skills or resources.

One common strategy to address prostitution is to focus on the "johns," exposing them to public humiliation. Undercover operations may also be successful in breaking up organized prostitution. In some instances, officers wait outside suspected establishments and talk with exiting customers.

Pornography presents its own unique challenges because of the subjective nature of what is considered "offensive" and the various interpretations allowed of the First Amendment right to freedom of expression. Defining what is *pornographic* is problematic—given the graphic sex scenes on television and in movies, what are the standards today? Most citizens cannot agree. The Internet has also added a new dimension to pornography. Some countries are banning American online services, claiming they are pornographic.

Gaming

The term *gaming* has replaced the older term *gambling* among those who are involved in this activity. In years past, gaming was a focus of law enforcement, with raids on gaming establishments making headlines. Legal gaming includes charitable gaming, paramutual betting, casino gaming, and lotteries. Illegal gaming may attract other vices, such as prostitution, pornography, loan-sharking, and extortion. An NIJ study found that arrestees had significantly more problems gambling than did the general population and had high levels of criminal activity related to their pathological gambling. Nearly one-third of the arrestees identified as pathological gamblers admitted having committed robbery in the previous year, and about 13 percent had assaulted someone for money. In addition, pathological gamblers were much more likely to have sold drugs than were other arrestees (McCorkle 2004).

The most significant forms of illegal gaming are numbers, betting with bookmakers or bookies, and sports pools or sports cards. The Internet is responsible for a large growth in gaming, with hundreds of gaming-related sites, some of which have set up operations offshore.

SURVEILLANCE, UNDERCOVER ASSIGNMENTS, RAIDS, AND STINGS

Many investigations, including those of victimless crimes, use surveillance, undercover assignments, and raids. "Follow that car!" "Don't lose her." "I've been made." "My cover's blown." "It's a raid." "We gotcha." Fictionalized detective work frequently portrays the glamorous side of surveillance, undercover assignments, raids, and stings. In reality, however, such assignments often involve days, weeks, or even months of tedious yet dangerous watchfulness.

> Surveillance, undercover assignments, raids, and stings should be used only when all other investigative alternatives have failed.

Because they are expensive and potentially dangerous, these investigative techniques are not routinely used. When they are used, it is often by specialized units such as drug task forces, gang strike forces, vice squads, and so on.

Surveillance

The purpose of surveillance is to gather information about people, their activities, and associates that may help solve a crime or protect a witness. Surveillance can be designed to serve several functions (Orthmann and Hess 2013, 225):

▶ Gain information required for building a criminal complaint
▶ Determine an informant's loyalty
▶ Verify a witness's statement about a crime
▶ Gain information required for obtaining a search or arrest warrant
▶ Gain information necessary for interrogating a suspect
▶ Identify a suspect's associates
▶ Observe members of terrorist organizations
▶ Find a person wanted for a crime
▶ Observe criminal activities in progress
▶ Make a legal arrest
▶ Apprehend a criminal in the act of committing a crime
▶ Prevent a crime
▶ Recover stolen property
▶ Protect witnesses

A common type of surveillance is the stakeout, a stationary surveillance in which officers set up an observation post and monitor it continuously. Other forms of surveillance include aerial surveillance and audio surveillance, or wiretapping. Before a judge will approve an application for electronic surveillance, those requesting it must show why surveillance is necessary—for example, standard techniques have been tried and failed or standard investigative techniques are too dangerous to try.

Using CCTV cameras to monitor public spaces is increasing, both in the United States and abroad. Despite people's concern about the government watching and recording them as they pass through parks, streets, and other public areas, CCTV use by criminal justice personnel in the United States seems to be increasing: "When implemented with a well-thought plan and used properly, CCTV can potentially be a real force multiplier for law enforcement agencies of any size" (Kanable 2008, 30). Balancing legal electronic surveillance and an individual's right to privacy is a challenge to the criminal justice system.

TECHNOLOGY IN POLICING

SURVEILLANCE

Police surveillance technology has evolved considerably from the binoculars once considered the ultimate surveillance tool to now include devices that see through walls; camera- and transmitter-equipped spheres that hover, watch, and record; facial recognition technology; blur correction software; and throwbots, miniature remote-controlled robots small and tough enough to toss over walls or into otherwise inaccessible areas:

> The Recon Robotics Scout Throwbot…is the shape and size of a two-pound barbell. The "weight" portion of the barbell is actually the device's wheels and motor, and the camera,

batteries, and antennae are on the connecting "bar." A stabilizing tail keeps the camera pointing forward and the antennas pointed up.

The whole device is 7.4 inches wide and 3 inches high, and weighs only 1.2 pounds, and it really is sturdy enough to throw into any environment you can walk into and be able to walk out. Its transmitter/receiver has a range of 100 to 300 feet and it moves at about one foot per second. (Dees 2011, 40)

Source: Dees, Tim. "Surveillance Technology." *Police*, December 2011, pp. 38–41.

Undercover Assignments

An investigation can be overt or covert. **Overt investigations** are conducted openly, usually with officers either in uniform or introducing themselves as officers. **Covert investigations**, in contrast, are done secretively, for example, using surveillance and undercover personnel. Most people are aware of undercover (UC) operations from the television programs and movies in which detectives take on false identities and infiltrate groups engaged in illegal activity. However, undercover operations have been criticized by some as having no place in a free society such as ours.

Undercover operations can offer information not otherwise available. The police cannot be everywhere. They must rely on inside information or tips

overt investigations

Those conducted openly, usually with officers in uniform or introducing themselves as police officers.

covert investigations

Those done secretively, for example, using surveillance and undercover personnel.

where highly skilled criminal activities are involved, particularly lacking identifiable victims or witnesses. Audio recording or video filming a crime is often feasible in undercover operations. This is a surer form of evidence and is more difficult to manipulate than verbal testimony. Undercover practices are costly and susceptible to abuse and unintended consequences. Therefore, they should be used only for serious offenses when alternative means are not available, and then only under careful monitoring.

> Undercover assignments are used to obtain information and evidence about illegal activity when it can be obtained in no other way.

Undercover work can be used (1) to capture fugitives, (2) to establish probable cause to arrest or search, (3) to serve a warrant without use of force, or (4) to interview an uncooperative subject. Undercover operations may even extend into cyberspace. The undercover work itself may be light or deep.

Dangers of Undercover Work   *Light cover* involves deception, but the officer usually goes home at night. While on assignment, the officer may pose as a utility worker or phone company repair person to obtain access to a suspect's home or workplace. Other covers may include that of a writer or member of the news media or a phony photographer.

Deep cover is much more dangerous but can be very effective. The officer lives an assumed identity in an attempt to infiltrate a group or organization. No identification other than the cover identification is carried. Communication with the police department is risky and carefully planned. Plans also are made for what the undercover officer is to do if the criminal operation is "busted" and for how the officer will end the relationship. Officers can risk much working deep under cover, including their own lives. When the operation is completed, they may have to go under witness protection. The officer's family may also be at risk. The deep investigation typically engulfs an individual's entire life, so these officers are usually separated from their families for the duration of a long investigation, which creates tension in their personal lives. Undercover officers may also become close to those they are investigating, which can create severe internal turmoil and identity conflict.

Undercover work requires a "carefully crafted persona and unrelenting self-discipline" (Grossi 2009, 24). The Drug Enforcement Administration (DEA) recommends that undercover officers keep their real first names in case someone on the street who does not know they are working undercover greets them. It is also advisable for UC officers to keep their real birth date so it comes naturally if asked for it.

One danger of using undercover operations is that officers may become what they start out only pretending to be. Another danger of using undercover operations is the potential for a charge of entrapment, discussed in Chapter 14. Also controversial is the use of informants.

Informants   Because of the information informants can provide, many crimes have been solved that would not have been without their assistance.

Sometimes police informers, also referred to as "CIs" for "criminal informants," are paid, but more often their motives for assisting the police are to receive a reduced sentence for a pending criminal matter. Other common motives include concern for the public safety and revenge.

Informants who operate in undercover roles may be involved only in passive observation. They can be used to vouch for and introduce sworn police undercover agents to a suspected person or group and then should be dropped from the investigation. Informants may also play an active role in the criminal activities of those on whom they are informing. Only a small fraction of informers ever testify in court, although the information they provide may be offered to the judge to obtain warrants for arrests, searches, wiretaps, or electronic surveillances.

Some informers go beyond giving information obtained in their natural environment and use disguises and infiltrations. The environment is deceptively shaped to elicit information. For example, an informant is placed in a suspect's cell as a cellmate in the hope that confidences will be transmitted. Other examples are an agent posing as an employee to infiltrate a factory in response to problems such as employee thefts or the police posing as reporters seeking comments from political and social activists.

Known tactics whose legality is questionable include planting informers in a group organized for the legal defense of an activist facing serious criminal charges or having a police officer dressed as a clergyman visit an arrested person in jail. Another common, and often significant, tactic is the "front," such as a cocktail lounge or a neighborhood used-property store set up for a sting operation or specifically created by the police for intelligence purposes.

Once a person has begun to inform, the threat of exposure becomes a factor. Allegiances may shift or become more intense. A criminal who becomes overzealous and tries to play the role of super cop may jeopardize a whole operation. Or, informants may become double agents—that is, clever informants experienced in deception who manipulate and control their police contact, rather than the reverse. Such individuals can also become double informants, having several different police contacts who do not know of each other. This situation may arise more often in cross-jurisdictional investigations. Double informers may share the same information and be reimbursed several times over for the same information.

Because undercover work is complex, it has both positive and negative aspects. Assessing them is difficult. Little research can be done because of the work's covert nature and the courts' and civil rights advocates' suspiciousness.

Raids

The errors involved in the raid in Waco in 1993 underscore the criticality of planning and timing. Although the planners of the raid knew that they had probably lost the element of surprise, rather than rethinking the plan for the raid, they sped up their activities, and the result was a deadly blaze on April 19 and much public criticism. Raids are discussed in greater detail in Chapter 12.

Stings

Sting operations cover a wide variety of crimes, but most have four basic elements (Newman and Socia 2007, 3):

1. An opportunity or enticement to commit a crime created or exploited by police
2. A targeted likely offender or group of offenders for a particular crime type
3. An undercover or hidden police officer or surrogate, or some form of deception
4. A "Gotcha" climax when the operation ends with arrests

Sting operations may involve offering a bribe to a politician suspected of corruption, purchasing illegal drugs in an open-air drug market, buying liquor by a minor, or hiding in an area where drivers are known to exceed the speed limit: "The clearest, defining feature of sting operations nowadays is that there is a point that ends the operations with a 'gotcha,' when police suddenly reveal themselves and catch the offender 'in the act'" (Newman and Socia 2007, 3).

Although surveillance, undercover work, raids, and stings are specialized forms of investigation, a much more common and often relied on source of information is the citizenry of a community, people who can be additional eyes and ears for a department.

INVESTIGATION AND COMMUNITY POLICING

Shifting investigation work from a reactive to a proactive model is in keeping with the community policing philosophy. A new investigative structure might center around developing integrated major crime problem-solving task forces, with detectives developing stronger ties with the community. Citizens become allies in investigations, providing information to the police.

▌AN OFFICER'S PERSPECTIVE
Partnering with Pawnshops

During my time in investigations, there would be an ebb and flow of case workloads. During down times, along with other detectives, I would occasionally go through our Automated Pawn System, a program that required participation from all pawnshops in our state, as well as some located out of state. State law requires anyone who pawns an item to present government-issued identification. This information is then entered into the Automated Pawn System database along with a detailed description of the pawned item.

We would proactively run the names of known thieves and criminal suspects through the system, often discovering stolen items associated with open and inactive cases. These database searches allowed us to close cases with charges and return the items back to their rightful owners. It also allowed us to track suspects and gain video evidence in pawned items related to crimes.

We often had a good working relationship with the pawnshops, which did not want to purchase stolen goods. This cooperation with community businesses was a good example of how investigations and community policing work together toward the same goal.

—*Sgt. Henry Lim Cho*

A shift to community-oriented investigations acknowledges that crime is complex and requires a balanced response, with detectives collaborating among themselves and with community stakeholders.

PROBLEM-ORIENTED POLICING AND INVESTIGATION

The use of problem solving in investigation may seem to be a stretch. Criminal investigation is, by its nature, concerned with solving crimes that have already occurred. Following is the 2003 Goldstein Award Winner for excellence in problem-oriented policing, "The Oakland Airport Motel Program"—The Oakland (California) Police Department Beat Health Unit.[1]

Scanning

In September 2000, the recurring nuisance and criminal activity at a major motel, which is part of an international chain, located near the Oakland International Airport, came to the attention of Officer Brad Gardiner of the Oakland Police Department's Beat Health Unit. Problems included inordinate calls for police service, prostitution, illegal drug activity, abandoned cars, illegal auto repair business in the motel parking lot, and renting of rooms to minors.

Analysis

Data checks, site visits, interviews, undercover surveillance, and comparisons of management practices to other nearby motels led police to conclude that it was the poor management practices at the motel that allowed crime and nuisances to flourish at this motel.

Response

After meetings with on-site motel managers and corporate executives failed to result in improvements at the motel, Beat Health Unit officers and city attorneys filed a drug nuisance abatement lawsuit against the parent corporation. Eventually, through intense negotiations, the parent corporation agreed to improve its management practices and to post a $250,000 performance bond covering a two-year monitoring period to guarantee reductions in crime and nuisance at the motel. It further agreed to pay the City of Oakland about $35,000 to cover the costs of its investigation. Numerous specific improvements were made to the physical environment and management practices at the motel.

Assessment

Two years after the agreement was signed, there have been few calls for police service at the motel, and the property has been returned to productive use. The stipulated two-year monitoring period concluded in March 2003.

---

[1]Source: "The Oakland Airport Motel Program." In *Excellence in Problem-Oriented Policing: The 2003 Herman Goldstein Award Winner and Finalists.* Washington, DC: The Community Oriented Policing Services Office and the Police Executive Research Forum, November 2003.

Judge's Commentary

The Oakland Airport Motel project exemplifies the practice of problem-oriented policing in several significant ways. First, it illustrates the importance of careful documentation of the conditions that give rise to a problem. Particularly when dealing with sophisticated corporate executives, the Oakland police officials and city attorneys took great care to compile irrefutable evidence that a significant amount of crime and nuisance activity was occurring at the motel, that the amount of such activity was greatly disproportionate to that experienced by similarly situated motels, and that the poor management practices at the motel were largely to blame for the problems. Second, the project exemplifies the value of a systematic approach to addressing problems. The Beat Health Unit carefully followed its own step-by-step procedure for building a case against a problem property. This deliberate approach ensured that the investigating officers gathered the necessary information and drew the right conclusions from it before settling on a course of action. Third, and perhaps most significantly, this project exemplifies how police can, with proper documented evidence and careful analysis, shift the ownership of crime and disorder problems away from the police and local government alone, back to those individuals and groups whose actions create the problems and who have the capacity to address them.

SUMMARY

The primary goals of criminal investigation are to determine whether a crime has been committed, legally obtain information and evidence to identify the responsible person, arrest the suspect, recover stolen property, and present the best possible case to the prosecutor. Above all else, the criminal investigation seeks to establish the factual truth surrounding an event. The most critical phase in most criminal investigations is the preliminary investigation.

The successful resolution of a criminal investigation most often hinges on the availability of irrefutable, relevant, and admissible evidence. Advanced Fingerprint Identification Technology (AFIT) is the next generation of IAFIS and provides faster, more accurate identification of prints than previous systems did. Physical fingerprints and DNA fingerprinting are the two forms of positive identification available to investigators.

Detectives must be familiar with techniques to investigate specific crimes. The major violent crimes are homicide, rape, assault, and robbery.

Homicide is classified as criminal (felonious) or noncriminal. The various degrees of murder and manslaughter are criminal homicide, noncriminal homicide (which includes excusable homicide—the unintentional, truly accidental killing of another person), and justifiable homicide (killing another person under authorization of law). A common element in every charge is "causing the death of another human being." Other elements in homicide include premeditation, malicious intent, adequately provoked intent resulting in heat of passion, while committing or attempting to commit a crime that is not a felony, when forced or threatened, culpable negligence or depravity, or simple negligence. Premeditation, the deliberate, precalculated plan to cause death, is the essential element of first-degree murder, distinguishing it from all other murder classifications. After priority matters are completed, the focus of the homicide investigation is to identify the victim, establish the time of death, establish the cause of death and the method used to produce it, and develop a suspect. Special problems in homicide investigations include pressure by the public and the media; difficulty in establishing that it is homicide, rather than suicide or an accidental or natural death; handling serial murders; and, in some cases, reopening cold cases.

Most states have in common the following elements for the crime of rape or sexual assault: (1) an act of sexual intercourse, (2) committed without the victim's consent, (3) against the victim's will and by force.

The elements of the crime of simple assault are (1) intent to do bodily harm to another, (2) present ability to commit the act, and (3) commission of an overt act toward carrying out the intent. An additional element in the crime of aggravated assault is that the intentionally inflicted bodily injury results in (1) a high probability of death; (2) serious, permanent disfigurement; or (3) permanent or protracted loss or impairment of the function of any body member or organ or other severe bodily harm. Attempted assault requires proof of intent and an overt act toward committing the crime.

The elements of the crime of robbery are (1) the wrongful taking of personal property, (2) from the person or in the person's presence, (3) against the person's will by force or threat of force.

The elements of the crime of burglary include (1) entering a structure (2) without the consent of the person in possession (3) with the intent to commit a crime therein. Additional elements of burglary that may be required include (1) breaking into (2) the dwelling of another (3) during the nighttime. A burglary's severity is determined by the presence of dangerous devices in the burglar's possession, by the value of the property stolen, and whether the property or residence was occupied at the time of the crime. Attempted burglary and possession of burglary tools are also felonies. The elements of the crime of possessing burglary tools include (1) possessing any device, explosive, or other instrumentality (2) with intent to use or permit their use to commit burglary.

The elements of the crime of larceny/theft are (1) the felonious stealing, taking, carrying, leading, or driving away of (2) another's personal goods or property (3) valued above or below a specified amount (4) with the intent to permanently deprive the owner of the property or goods. In most states, taking found property with the intent to keep or sell it is also a crime. The elements of the offense of receiving stolen goods are (1) receiving, buying, or concealing stolen or illegally obtained goods (2) knowing them to be stolen or illegally obtained. Elements of the crime of larceny by debit or credit card include (1) possessing cards obtained by theft or fraud (2) by which services or goods are obtained (3) through unauthorized signing of the cardholder's name. Bank embezzlements are investigated jointly by the local police and the FBI.

Categories for motor vehicle theft based on the offender's motive include (1) joyriding, (2) transportation, (3) stripping for parts and accessories, (4) use in committing another crime, and (5) reselling for profit. The elements of the crime of unauthorized use of a motor vehicle are (1) intentionally taking or driving (2) a motor vehicle (3) without the consent of the owner or the owner's authorized agent. Embezzlement of a motor vehicle occurs if the person who took the vehicle had consent initially and then exceeded the terms of that consent.

The elements of the crime of arson include (1) the willful, malicious burning of a building or property (2) of another, or of one's own to defraud (3) or causing to be burned, or aiding, counseling, or procuring such burning. Attempted arson is also a crime. Some states categorize arson as either aggravated or simple. Aggravated arson is intentionally destroying or damaging a dwelling or other property by means of fire or explosives, creating an imminent danger to life or great bodily harm, which risk was known or reasonably foreseeable to the suspect. Simple arson is intentional destruction by fire or explosives that does not create imminent danger to life or risk of great bodily harm. Other states use the Model Arson Law, which divides arson into four degrees: first-degree involves the burning of dwellings, second-degree involves the burning of buildings other than dwellings, third-degree involves the burning of other property, and fourth-degree involves attempts to burn buildings or property.

Other crimes officers must investigate include crimes against children, bias/hate crimes, environmental crimes, and computer-related crimes.

Computer crimes are relatively easy to commit and difficult to detect. Investigations may also involve the so-called victimless crimes, such as prostitution, pornography, gaming, and drug dealing/using.

Many investigations, including those of victimless crimes, make use of surveillance, undercover assignments, raids, and stings. These methods should be used only when all other investigative alternatives have failed. Undercover assignments are used to obtain information and evidence about illegal activity when it can be obtained in no other way.

APPLICATION

To provide better service to the community, the department has decided to add a detective division to its organization. The chief has asked you to develop a policy and procedure for turning cases over to this division, after a patrol officer has conducted the preliminary investigation.

INSTRUCTIONS

Using the form in the Appendix, write a policy on what specific types of cases will be assigned to the detective division. Then write the procedure(s) for assigning cases to this division. Be sure to consider a smooth transition in the investigation from the patrol officer who conducted the preliminary investigation to the detective assigned to handle the case.

EXERCISES IN CRITICAL THINKING

A. Mary Jones, an 18-year-old high school girl, quarreled with her boyfriend, Thomas Smith. At 3 a.m. following the evening of their quarrel, Mary went to Smith's home to return his picture. Smith stated that after receiving the picture, he went to his room, went to bed, and awoke about 8 a.m. When he looked out his window, he saw Mary's car parked out front. Looking into the car, he discovered Mary sitting erect behind the steering wheel, shot through the chest, a .22 revolver lying beside her on the front seat. She was dead—apparently a suicide. The revolver had been a gift to Mary from her father. Smith called the police to report the shooting.

Mary had been shot once. The bullet entered just below the right breast, traveled across the front of her body, and lodged near her heart. The medical examiner theorized that she did not die immediately. When found, she was sitting upright in the car, her head tilted slightly backward, her right hand high on the steering wheel, her left hand hanging limp at her left side.

When questioned, Smith steadfastly denied any knowledge of the shooting. Mary's clothing, the bullet from her body, and the gun were sent to the FBI Laboratory for examination. An examination of her blouse where the bullet entered failed to reveal any powder residues. The bullet removed from her body was identified as having been fired from the gun found beside her body.

1. Is the shooting likely to be a suicide or a homicide? What facts support this?
2. How should the investigation proceed?

B. Ten-year-old Denise was playing in a school parking lot with her 9-year-old stepbrother, Jerry. A car pulled up to the curb next to the lot, and the man driving the car motioned for Denise and Jerry to come over. When the man asked where they lived, Denise described their house. The man then asked Denise to take him to the house, saying he would bring her right back to the lot afterward. Denise got into the car with the man, and they drove away. When they did not return after an hour, Jerry went into the school and told a teacher what had happened. Denise did not return home that evening. The next day the police received a report that a body had been found near a lover's lane. It was Denise, who had been stabbed to death with a pocketknife.

1. What steps should be taken immediately?
2. Where would you expect to find leads?
3. What evidence would you expect to find?
4. Specifically, how would you investigate this murder?

DISCUSSION QUESTIONS

1. What are some motivations for citizens to become informants?
2. How might officers arriving at a crime scene contaminate evidence?
3. What was the purpose of establishing the Violent Crime Apprehension Program (VICAP) at the National Police Academy in Quantico, Virginia?
4. Is the expense involved in testing DNA from crimes such as burglary justified?
5. What are some dangers of undercover operations?
6. What are some purposes of a surveillance? When would a surveillance be useful?
7. How does the general public view the police detective? Where do these images come from?

GALE EMERGENCY SERVICES DATABASE ASSIGNMENTS

▶ Use the Gale Emergency Services database (available for separate purchase) to help answer the Discussion Questions as appropriate.

▶ Use the Gale Emergency Services database to locate and outline one of the following articles to share with the class:

- "Electronic Surveillance: A Matter of Necessity" by Thomas D. Coldbridge
- "Working with Informants: Operational Recommendations" by James E. Hight
- "Best Practices of a Hate/Bias Crime Investigation" by Walter Bouman
- "Computer Forensics: Characteristics and Preservation of Digital Evidence" by Loren D. Mercer
- "Conducting Surveillance Operations: How to Get the Most Out of Them" by John T. Nason
- "The Hate Model" by John R. Schafer and Joe Navarro
- "Major Case Management: Key Components" by Brian P. Carroll

REFERENCES

Benson, Michael L., and Sally S. Simpson. 2009. *White-Collar Crime: An Opportunity Perspective*. New York: Routledge.

Best Practices for Seizing Electronic Evidence: A Pocket Guide for First Responders. Version 3.0. 2010 (March 7). Washington, DC: U.S. Department of Homeland Security, U.S. Secret Service.

Blakely, Amy. 2009. "University of Tennessee's National Forensic Academy." *Law and Order* (May): 75–78.

Bodinger-deUriarte, Cristina. 1991. "Hate Crime: The Rise of Hate Crime on School Campuses." *Phi Delta Kappa Research Bulletin* (10, December): 1–6.

Cameron, Stuart. 2011. "Digital Evidence." *FBI Law Enforcement Bulletin* (August): 14–19.

Commission on Accreditation of Law Enforcement Agencies (CALEA). 2012. *Standards for Law Enforcement Agencies.* 5th ed. Fairfax, VA: Author.

Crime in the United States 2010. 2010. Washington, DC: Federal Bureau of Investigation. Accessed March 20, 2012. http://www.fbi.gov/about-us/cjis/ucr/crime-in-the-u.s/2010/crime-in-the-u.s.-2010.

Cullen, Francis T., Gray Cavender, William J. Maakestad, and Michael L. Benson. 2006. *Corporate Crime under Attack: The Fight to Criminalize Business Violence.* 2nd ed. Albany, NY: Matthew Bender (LexisNexis).

Dees, Tim. 2011. "Surveillance Technology." *Police* (December): 38–41.

Digital Evidence in the Courtroom: A Guide for Law Enforcement and Prosecutors. 2007 (January). Washington, DC: National Institute of Justice. (NCJ 211314). Accessed April 3, 2012. https://www.ncjrs.gov/pdffiles1/nij/211314.pdf.

Electronic Crime Scene Investigation: A Guide for First Responders. 2nd ed. 2008. Washington, DC: National Institute of Justice. (NCJ 219941). Accessed April 3, 2012. http://www.nij.gov/publications/ecrime-guide-219941/chapter6-219941.pdf.

Fantino, Julian. 2007. "Forensic Science: A Fundamental Perspective." *The Police Chief* (November): 26–28.

"FBI/National White Collar Crime Center (NW3C) Release Annual Report on Internet Crime." 2009 (March 30). Washington, DC: Federal Bureau of Investigation, Press Release.

"FBI's Regional Computer Forensics Laboratory Network Increases Number of Accredited Labs." 2009 (April 7). Washington, DC: Federal Bureau of Investigation, Press Release.

Feigin, Matthew. 2009. "Landmark NAS Report Questions Basis of Forensic Sciences in U.S." *Subject to Debate* (April): 3–5.

Forensic Examination of Digital Evidence: A Guide for Law Enforcement. 2004 (April). Washington, DC: National Institute of Justice. (NCJ 199408). Accessed April 3, 2012. https://www.ncjrs.gov/pdffiles1/nij/199408.pdf.

Garrett, Ronnie. 2009a. "The Byte Stuff." *Law Enforcement Technology* (April): 10–16.

Garrett, Ronnie. 2009b. "DNA Saves." *Law Enforcement Technology* (February): 28–37.

Geoghegan, Susan. 2009. "Forensic DNA." *Law and Order* (June): 49–53.

Grossi, Dave. 2009. "Going Under." *Law Officer Magazine* (April): 24–28.

Hate Crime Statistics 2010. 2010. Washington, DC: Federal Bureau of Investigation. Accessed March 22, 2012. http://www.fbi.gov/about-us/cjis/ucr/hate-crime/2010.

Heurich, Charles. 2008. "Cold Cases: Resources for Agencies; Resolution for Families." *NIJ Journal* (July): 20–23.

"Highway Serial Killings: New Initiative on an Emerging Trend." 2009 (April 6). Washington, DC: Federal Bureau of Investigation Headline Archives.

"Increasing Efficiency in Crime Laboratories." 2008 (January). *NIJ in Short: Toward Criminal Justice Solutions.* Washington, DC: National Institute of Justice.

Investigations Involving the Internet and Computer Networks. 2007 (January). Washington, DC: National Institute of Justice. (NCJ 210798). Accessed April 3, 2012. https://www.ncjrs.gov/pdffiles1/nij/210798.pdf.

Jetmore, Larry F. 2007. "The Truth's in the Teeth: Using Forensic Dentistry to Solve Crimes." *Law Officer Magazine* (July): 22–25.

Johns, Susan, and Patricia Rushing. 2009. "Using DNA to Solve Property Crimes." *Community Policing Dispatch* 2 (12, December). Accessed March 20, 2012. http://www.cops.usdoj.gov/html/dispatch/December_2009/dna.htm.

Johnson, Shane D., Aiden Sidebottom, and Adam Thorpe. 2008 (June). *Bicycle Theft.* Washington, DC: Community Oriented Policing Services Office.

Kanable, Rebecca. 2008. "Setting Up Surveillance Downtown." *Law Enforcement Technology* (February): 30–39.

Kanable, Rebecca. 2009. "The Face of Identity Theft." *Law Enforcement Technology* (April): 28–33.

Kingsbury, Alex. 2009 (April 1). "Amid Recession, FBI Makes New Push on Financial Crimes: In the Age of Bernie Madoff, Agents Are Scrambling to Focus on White-Collar Criminals." *U.S. News and World Report.*

Kurash, Aviva. 2009. "New Tools for Sexual Assault Investigations." *Big Ideas* (Spring): 12–13.

Lei, Hsien-Hsien. 2008 (February 20). "Genetic Differences between Identical Twins." Accessed March 20, 2012. http://www.eyeondna.com/2008/02/20/genetic-differences-between-identical-twins/.

McCorkle, Richard C. 2004 (July). *Gambling and Crime among Arrestees: Exploring the Link.* Washington, DC: National Institute of Justice.

McNeil. TiTi. 2009. "Managing Digital Evidence." *Law Enforcement Technology* (January): 30–37.

Newman, Graeme R., and Kelly Socia. 2007 (October). *Sting Operations.* Washington, DC: Community Oriented Policing Services Office.

"The Oakland Airport Motel Program." 2003 (November). In *Excellence in Problem-Oriented Policing: The 2003 Herman Goldstein Award Winner and Finalists.* Washington, DC: The Community Oriented Policing Services Office and the Police Executive Research Forum.

Orthmann, Christine H., and Kären M. Hess. 2013. *Criminal Investigation.* 10th ed. Clifton Park, NY: Delmar Cengage Learning.

Page, Douglas. 2007. "The Bite Stuff?" *Law Enforcement Technology* (February): 112–119.

Page, Douglas. 2008. "Microstamping Calls the Shots." *Law Enforcement Technology* (January): 54–59.

Paige, Lachlan. 2011. "Mapping Human Behavior." *Law Enforcement Technology* (May): 24–29.

Parker, Joe. n.d. "How Prostitution Works." Prostitution Research and Education. http://www.prostitutionresearch.com/how_prostitution_works/000012.html.

Petrocelli, Joseph. 2008a. "Patrol Response to Bank Robberies." *Police* (January): 16–17.

Petrocelli, Joseph. 2008b. "Patrol Response to Convenience Store Robberies." *Police* (August): 20–23.

Piquero, Nicole Leeper, Stephanie Carmichael, and Alex R. Piquero. 2008. "Assessing the Perceived Seriousness of White-Collar and Street Crimes." *Crime & Delinquency* (April): 291–312.

"Precious Metal: Copper Theft Threatens U.S. Infrastructure." 2008 (January 3). Washington, DC: Federal Bureau of Investigation Headline Archives.

Roberts, Darryl W. 2009. "Intimate Partner Homicide: Relationships to Alcohol and Firearms." *Journal of Contemporary Criminal Justice* (February): 67–88.

Serial Murder: Multi-Disciplinary Perspectives for Investigators. 2008. Washington, DC: Federal Bureau of Investigation.

Shelton, Donald E. 2008. "The *CSI* Effect: Does It Really Exist?" *NIJ Journal* (March): 1–8.

Strengthening Forensic Science in the United States: A Path Forward. 2009. Washington, DC: National Academies Press.

Sutherland, Edwin H. 1983. *White-Collar Crime: The Uncut Version.* New Haven, CT: Yale University Press.

Trimpe, Michael. 2011. "The Current Status of GSR Examinations." *FBI Law Enforcement Bulletin* (May): 24–32.

2010 Mortgage Fraud Report: Year in Review. 2011 (August). Washington, DC: Department of Justice, Federal Bureau of Investigation, Financial Crimes Intelligence Unit.

Unnever, James D., Michael L. Benson, and Francis T. Cullen. 2008. "Public Support for Getting Tough on Corporate Crime: Racial and Political Divides." *Journal of Research in Crime and Delinquency* (May): 163–190.

Walker-Rodriguez, Amanda, and Rodney Hill. 2011. "Human Sex Trafficking." *FBI Law Enforcement Bulletin* (March): 1–9.

Weisel, Deborah Lamm. 2007 (March). *Bank Robbery.* Washington, DC: Community Oriented Policing Services Office.

Wilson, David B., David McClure, and David Weisburd. 2010. "Does Forensic DNA Help to Solve Crime? The Benefit of Sophisticated Answers to Naïve Questions." *Journal of Contemporary Criminal Justice* 26 (4, November): 458–469.

CASES CITED

Daubert v. Merrell Dow Pharmaceuticals, Inc., 509 U.S. 579 (1993)

Flippo v. West Virginia, 528 U.S. 11 (1999)

Michigan v. Tyler, 436 U.S. 499 (1978)

People v. Simpson, No. BA097211 (Cal. Super Ct. 1995)

HELPFUL RESOURCES

▶ The National Institute of Justice published *Fire and Arson Scene Evidence: A Guide for Public Safety Personnel*, available online at www.ojp.usdoj.gov/nij/pubs-sum/181584.htm

▶ The Department of Justice published "Searching and Seizing Computers and Obtaining Electronic Evidence in Criminal Investigations," available at http://www.lb9.uscourts.gov/webcites/08documents/CDT_cyber.pdf

▶ The International Association of Chiefs of Police (IACP) also has a guide, *Best Practices for Seizing Electronic Evidence*, available at www.theiacp.org

▶ Another valuable Web site is www.cybercrime.gov, maintained by the Computer Crime and Intellectual Property Section of the U.S. Department of Justice. The site is a collection of documents and links to other sites and agencies that may assist in preventing, detecting, investigating, and prosecuting computer-related crime.

▶ The FBI's *Handbook of Forensic Services*, revised in 2007, provides information on crime scene searches as well as the kinds of evidence that might be found.

▶ Former ATF Special Agent William Queen wrote an excellent book called *Under and*

Alone, detailing his accounts of infiltrating one of the most notorious motorcycle gangs, the Mongols. William Queen, *Under and Alone.* New York: Random House, 2005. ISBN 978-1400060849.

▶ The Anti-Defamation League launched a Web site to serve as a database for law enforcement officers investigating hate groups: http://www.adl.org/learn.

CourseMate

This available CourseMate has an interactive eBook and interactive learning tools, including flash cards, quizzes, and more. To learn more about this resource and access free demo CourseMate resources, go to www.cengagebrain.com, and search for this book. To access CourseMate materials that you have purchased, go to login.cengagebrain.com.

CHAPTER 11

© Hannah Gal/CORBIS

Responding to Children and Juveniles:
Our Nation's Future

DO YOU KNOW . . .

- What greatly influences youths' attitudes toward law and law enforcement?
- Below what age most states consider a person a juvenile?
- What the primary difference between the adult criminal justice and the juvenile justice system is?
- What categories of children are included in the juvenile justice system's jurisdiction?
- What predelinquent indicator often goes unnoticed?
- What special challenge is posed by a missing child report?
- What conduct is included in status offenses?
- What factors enter into the disposition of status offenders?
- How much discretion officers have with status offenders?
- What dispositions are available to officers when dealing with status offenders and what the most common disposition is?
- Who usually enters juveniles into the justice system?
- What rights *In re Gault* guarantees juveniles involved with the juvenile justice system?
- What two programs are widely used throughout the United States to combat the drug and gang problem?

CAN YOU DEFINE?

AMBER Alert
child maltreatment
child welfare model
D.A.R.E.
decriminalization
diversion
8% problem
G.R.E.A.T.
juvenile
juvenile delinquents
juvenile justice model
Munchausen syndrome by proxy (MSBP)
one-pot jurisdictional approach
osteogenesis imperfecta
parens patriae
raves
status offenses
street justice
thrownaways
truancy

INTRODUCTION

"Each professional working with children must understand children, their behavioral patterns and psychological development, and their changing emotional needs as they mature, seek independence, and acquire sexual appetites," says Juvenile Judge Emeritus Lindsay G. Arthur (2010, xv). Police are some of the most important professionals who work with children and juveniles. Law enforcement is commonly the first contact young victims and victimizers have with the juvenile justice system, and serve as the gatekeeper to the rest of the system. The police are charged with protecting youths, both victims and offenders, and dealing fairly with them. A balance is sought between what is in the best interest of the youth and what is best for the community. Also, the crime-fighting philosophy must be balanced with the service ideal.

The importance of the officer on the street cannot be overlooked. Every law enforcement officer, no matter at what level, has an opportunity to be a positive influence on youths. Ultimately, youths' perceptions about the law and law enforcement will be based on one-on-one interactions with law enforcement officers.

> Youths' attitudes toward law and law enforcement are tremendously influenced by personal contacts with law enforcement officers. Positive interactions are critical to delinquency prevention.

This chapter begins with an explanation of who is a juvenile and a brief overview of our juvenile justice system. This is followed by a discussion of law enforcement's response to children in need of help and protection, including victims of child abuse and neglect and those who are runaways, thrownaways, or otherwise missing. Next, police disposition of status offenses, police discretion and the initial contact, and the law enforcement response to serious, chronic, and violent juvenile offenders are presented. This is followed by an explanation of legal procedures when dealing with youths. The chapter concludes with a discussion of programs aimed at youths and a problem-oriented approach to dealing with a juvenile problem.

WHO IS A JUVENILE?

Just who is a juvenile is determined by the legal age set in state statutes. All states have specified an age below which individuals are subject to the juvenile justice system. This age varies from state to state and even within parts of the justice system itself in some states. For example, some state statutes specify that their juvenile courts have jurisdiction over all individuals under age 18, but that the juvenile correctional facilities have jurisdiction over all those under age 21 who were committed to a correctional facility before their 18th birthdays.

The youngest age for juvenile court jurisdiction in delinquency matters ranges from age 6 to age 10. The oldest age for juvenile court jurisdiction in delinquency matters ranges from 15 to 18, with 17 being the most common age.

Previously, the age range was from 16 to 19, with the most common age being 18. This lowering of the oldest age reflects the current tendency to "get tough" on youth in trouble with the law, discussed later in the chapter.

A **juvenile** is a person not yet of legal age. In three-fourths of the states, juveniles are defined as youths under age 18.

juvenile

A person not yet of legal age, usually under the age of 18.

In 2010, there were 74.2 million children under age 18 in the United States, making up 24 percent of the population (Federal Interagency Forum on Child and Family Statistics 2011).

AN OVERVIEW OF OUR JUVENILE JUSTICE SYSTEM

The dual role of protecting both children and the public and investigating behavioral facts is a great challenge facing juvenile officers and any police officer who interacts with youth in any way. The aspect of protection in dealings with juveniles has its roots in the common law of England.

In English common law, the king, through his chancellor, was a substitute parent for abandoned, neglected, and dependent children under a doctrine called *parens patriae*. In the United States, each individual state replaced the king in this responsibility. The doctrine of *parens patriae* allows the state to assume guardianship of abandoned, neglected, and "wayward" children.

parens patriae

A doctrine allowing the state to assume guardianship of abandoned, neglected, and "wayward" children.

Under this doctrine, the state is to act toward the children entrusted to its care as a loving parent would. This is very different from the punitive thrust behind the adult justice system, which removed youths from homes and placed them in lockups and jails. To return to the principle *of parens patriae*, the Illinois Juvenile Court Act of 1899 established the first juvenile court in the United States. This court's primary purpose was to "save" children from becoming criminals.

Historically, the juvenile justice system has been an informal, confidential, nonadversarial system that stresses rehabilitation rather than punishment of youth. This directly contrasts with the punitive nature of the criminal justice system and is reflected in the terminology used in the juvenile justice system, which underscores its emphasis on protecting youth from harmful labels and their stigmatizing effects. For example, youth are not *arrested*; they are *taken into custody*. If the allegations against the youth are true, the youth is called a *delinquent* rather than a *criminal*. Youth sentenced to custodial care upon release receive *aftercare* rather than *parole*.

The juvenile justice system, under *parens patriae*, has historically taken a rehabilitative approach in handling children, rather than the punitive approach taken in the adult criminal justice system.

Although treatment and rehabilitation have been the traditional goals of the juvenile justice system, a trend to "get tough" on young violent offenders has led to increased debate about the mission of this system and a reevaluation regarding the underlying philosophy of the system.

Law enforcement may come in contact with youths who are accused of heinous offenses but who, because of their age, are handled as delinquents instead of criminals. Here, a teenager and two 10-year-old boys walk to a waiting van after their first judicial appearance. The three boys, accused of attacking a homeless day laborer on a street and smashing a concrete block into his face, were each charged by police with aggravated battery.

© AP Images/Jessica Webb Sibley

The Welfare Model versus the Justice Model

child welfare model

Society's attempt to help youths who come in conflict with the law, in which the best interests of the youth are the main considerations.

Since its inception, the juvenile justice system has been guided by a **child welfare model** in which the best interests of the youth are the main considerations. During the 1970s, however, as the rising fear of youth crime coincided with a growing public skepticism about the effectiveness of the juvenile justice system, citizens and lawmakers began calling for more punitive measures against juvenile offenders, especially those who committed serious or violent felonies. The result was a much harsher attitude toward youth crime and a call to "get tough" with youthful lawbreakers, philosophies characteristic of a **juvenile justice model** wherein the courts hold youths responsible and accountable for their behavior. To adopt a justice model does not rule out or diminish the importance of rehabilitative measures employed by juvenile courts. Disapproval of, and punishment for, the wrongful act is probably the single most important rehabilitative measure available to the court.

juvenile justice model

A judicial process in which young people who come in conflict with the law are held responsible and accountable for their behavior.

In many states, the justice model has replaced the welfare model. This is not the only aspect of the juvenile justice system being challenged. Another problematic area is the juvenile justice system's jurisdiction.

The "One-Pot" Jurisdictional Approach

juvenile delinquents

Young people who violate the law.

Our juvenile justice system's evolution, from the beginning, was designed to deal with "wayward" children—that is, **juvenile delinquents**, whose "crimes" could range from talking back to their parents to murder—and with children who were abandoned, abused, or neglected. Early laws, in effect, equated being poor with being criminal.

one-pot jurisdictional approach

Use of the same system to deal with youths who are neglected or abused, those who are status offenders, and those who commit serious crimes.

The juvenile justice system is responsible for children who are neglected or abused, those who are status offenders, and those who commit serious crimes, in what is called the **one-pot jurisdictional approach**.

CHILD MALTREATMENT: ABUSE AND NEGLECT

Not all youths police officers deal with are breaking the law. A great many are victims who need help or protection. Crimes against children were introduced in Chapter 7 and include abuse and neglect (maltreatment), abandonment, exploitation, and kidnapping. Runaways, though technically classified as status offenders, commonly become victims as well.

Child abuse involves causing physical, emotional, or sexual trauma to a child, and *neglect* includes failing to provide proper care and attention to a child's needs. Parents who deny their children the food, clothing, nurturing, or any other basic need children require are guilty of neglect, which can be just as damaging to the child as physical abuse. Frequently, child abuse and neglect occur together, although either one alone constitutes **child maltreatment**, a broader term that encompasses all variations of abuse (physical, emotional, sexual) and neglect (physical, emotional, educational). According to the Centers for Disease Control and Prevention (CDC), "Child maltreatment is any act or series of acts of commission or omission by a parent or other caregiver that results in harm, potential for harm, or threat of harm to a child" ("Child Maltreatment: Definitions" 2009).

In 2010, state and local child protective services (CPS) received an estimated 3.3 million referrals involving the alleged maltreatment of approximately 5.9 children in the United States. Of the nearly 1.8 million referrals that were screened in for and received a CPS investigation, 436,321 were *substantiated*, meaning the investigation found evidence to support the allegation of maltreatment or risk of maltreatment as defined by state law or policy (*Child Maltreatment 2010* 2011). An additional 24,976 were found to be *indicated*, meaning that although the investigation could not substantiate maltreatment under state law or policy, there was reason to suspect that at least one child may have been maltreated or was at risk of maltreatment.

In addition, an estimated 1,560 children died in the United States in 2010 from abuse and neglect. The younger the child, the more likely it was that he or she would be victimized; nearly 80 percent (79.4%) of all child fatalities in 2010 occurred among children younger than age 4. More than 30 percent (32.6%) of child fatalities were attributed exclusively to neglect, and more than 40 percent were by multiple maltreatment types (*Child Maltreatment 2010* 2011). Furthermore, boys had a higher fatality rate (2.51 per 100,000 boys in the population) than did girls (1.73 per 100,000).

Why parents abuse their children is perplexing. Sometimes it is out of frustration. Sometimes it is from unrealistic expectations. Often abusing parents feel their children "have it coming" because of words or actions. And sometimes it is simply, and sadly, the only way parents know to treat their children, having been raised in abusive homes themselves.

Millions of children have been witness to or victims of violence in their homes or communities. Such a history may send these youths down a future course of repeated and increasingly serious run-ins with law enforcement. Even when children are not themselves the direct targets of abuse, they may become "invisible victims" through continued exposure to other abusive relationships.

child maltreatment

A broad term that encompasses all variations of child abuse (physical, emotional, sexual) and neglect (physical, emotional, educational); according to the CDC, "Child maltreatment is any act or series of acts of commission or omission by a parent or other caregiver that results in harm, potential for harm, or threat of harm to a child."

Intergenerational Cycle of Abuse

Violence is learned behavior that often is self-perpetuating. When adults teach children by example that those who are bigger and stronger can use violence to force their wishes on others who are smaller and weaker, children remember the lesson. Children who witness domestic abuse learn that it is okay to hurt the people you care about and that it is acceptable to use violence to get what you want. Children who are abused or neglected may grow up with poor self-images and view the world as hostile and violent, tending to perpetuate dysfunctional behavior in the relationships and families they form as adults.

The connection between children's histories of neglect or abuse and subsequent delinquency, crime, and other problems has been largely ignored by our juvenile justice and social service systems. However, a growing body of empirical evidence shows that those who experience violent, abusive childhoods are more likely to become child or spouse abusers themselves or to display other forms of adult criminal behavior: "Abused and neglected children are 4.8 times more likely to be arrested as [a] juvenile, 2 times more likely to be arrested as an adult and 3.1 times more likely to be arrested for a violent crime than matched controls" (English, Widom, and Ford 2002, iii). These findings replicate earlier studies.

Karmen (2007, 6) describes a cycle of violence in which victims are transformed into victimizers over time: "A group of picked-upon students may band together to ambush their bullying tormentors; a battered wife may launch a vengeful attack against her brutal husband; or a child subjected to periodic beatings might grow up to parent his sons in the same excessively punitive way he was raised. A study that tracked the fortunes of boys and girls known to have been physically and sexually abused over a follow-up period of several decades concluded that being harmed at an early age substantially increased the odds of future delinquency and criminality."

Receiving Reports of Child Maltreatment

Educators are the most common source of reports of abuse and neglect to child protective service agencies. Reports may also come from a variety of other sources such as doctors, neighbors, or even the victims themselves, although that is rare. Professionals in all states, and even citizens in some states, are mandated to report child abuse to responsible authorities. Child welfare investigations substantiate or confirm about one-third of all child maltreatment reports. In some states, child welfare and police conduct investigations jointly; in a few jurisdictions, law enforcement has the sole responsibility for investigation and is increasingly involved in child abuse cases.

The Police Response to Child Maltreatment

Historically, as with spousal abuse, law enforcement agencies were reluctant to pursue reports of child abuse with the same vigor as calls involving other, more traditional offenses. Today, however, the responsibility of the police in regard to abused children is clear. When police are called about child abuse, their first responsibility is to the child. In many states, if it appears the child is in danger, police may take the child into protective custody.

It is good practice for police officers to speak to children as they are responding to the call because, if the incident is in progress or has just occurred, children have not yet had time to be "coached" by the parents or to otherwise have had their statements biased. Young children tend to be blunt and truthful about what they observed. In communities with large immigrant populations, it is not uncommon to speak with the children about the incident anyway because they may be the only ones in the home who speak English. It is important, however, to separate the children from the suspected offender during this interview, to reduce the likelihood of the child being intimidated by the alleged offender, even if the suspect is one of the parents.

In addition, officers responding to a domestic call involving adults must remain aware of the "invisible victimization" suffered by children who witness violence in the home and tend to these young victims as well. Often, when adults are arrested for domestic violence, additional charges of *endangering children* should be made if children were present during the abuse, and those children should also be taken into protective custody. Social services should be contacted immediately to find placements for the children. In some instances, placement can be made with other family members.

The decision to remove a child from the home commonly depends on who the alleged suspect is. If the abuse suspect is a family member, the child may be removed and placed in protective custody by police and social services while the incident is being investigated, and a social worker will be assigned to the family. If the child is assaulted by a neighbor or other "outsider," the child is considered safe with his or her own family and might not be placed.

Officers' next responsibility is to thoroughly investigate the situation. Interviews with family members, medical records, reports from social workers, and interviews with neighbors can all help determine if a charge of child abuse is warranted. Bear in mind that, without consent, medical records are protected and need to be obtained by a search warrant. Police must be especially careful when charges of child sexual abuse are involved because such allegations can do much damage and destroy reputations, even if unfounded. The interviews also can provide information about whether the child can be returned to the home or should be placed in a foster home.

Interviewing child victims and witnesses requires much sensitivity and adherence to certain protocol. In most child abuse cases, children tell the truth to the best of their abilities. Investigators should listen carefully to children and should look at indicators of neglect or abuse. These indicators may be physical or behavioral or both.

Handling child abuse cases is a highly specialized field because children have a different form of communication than do adults and can easily be led in an interview. Although police generally have basic training and can develop interview techniques through field experience, specialized child interviewing training is still not standard among law enforcement. Several types of certifications exist for interviewing children in specific situations, such as alleged maltreatment incidents, sexual abuse cases, and so on.

Two Supreme Court decisions affect children's testimony in abuse and neglect cases. In *Maryland v. Craig* (1990), the Court held that the Sixth Amendment "right to confront witnesses" does not always mandate face-to-face confrontation between a defendant and a child abuse victim-witness at trial, if the child victim-witness will be emotionally traumatized by testifying in the defendant's presence. In *Idaho v. Wright* (1990), the Court ruled that an out-of-court statement by an alleged child sexual abuse victim is not automatically deemed trustworthy nor guaranteed to be admitted at trial, but also ruled that an out-of-court statement may be admitted if it is determined the child making the statement is likely to be telling the truth.

States vary in the standard of proof required to substantiate allegations of child abuse and neglect, ranging from a caseworker's judgment, to some credible evidence, or a preponderance of evidence. However, some cases of abuse are obvious. For example, in a well-publicized 1996 case, a Chicago couple faced multiple charges of child abuse after their four children told authorities their parents had fed them a "regular diet" of boiled rats and cockroaches and had repeatedly raped and drugged them for the previous four years. And in 1999, 2½-year-old Miguel Arias-Baca spent the final moments of his short life getting slammed against the floor. He died slowly and painfully, his brain swelling with blood and his face smeared with his own feces, after his drunken foster father returned home from a Super Bowl party to find the toddler with a dirty diaper.

Sometimes these fatal tragedies result from a single violent episode. Most often, however, they are the culmination of months, even years, of abuse that somehow went unnoticed or fell through the cracks of the child protective and criminal justice services.

Special Challenges Related to Child Abuse Investigations

Problems in investigating crimes against children include the need to protect the child from further harm, the possibility of parental involvement, the difficulty in interviewing children, and the potential need to involve other agencies. Some cases of child abuse present special challenges to responding officers, such as those involving "brittle bone disease" or Munchausen syndrome by proxy and child sexual abuse cases.

Osteogenesis Imperfecta (OI) A challenge related to investigations of child abuse is when a medical condition mimics the signs of physical abuse, as in cases involving **osteogenesis imperfecta**, commonly known as "brittle bone disease," a condition characterized by bones that break easily. Because child abuse is also characterized by broken bones, false accusations of child abuse may occur in families with children who suffer from OI. Similarly, birthmarks or other naturally occurring skin spots may be mistaken for bruising caused by abuse.

osteogenesis imperfecta

A medical condition characterized by bones that break easily; also called *brittle bone disease.*

Unfortunately, when false accusations of child abuse occur, families become victimized. Consequently, it is critical for responding officers to be aware of such conditions and to not automatically discount a parent's denial of child abuse. A thorough investigation will include interviews with social services staff and medical professionals.

Cases in which parents are found to have a history of often changing the hospitals or physicians who treat their children *may* indicate an attempt to hide child abuse. In other instances, children who are frequently admitted to the hospital may be the victims of a form of abuse known as Munchausen syndrome by proxy.

Munchausen Syndrome by Proxy **Munchausen syndrome by proxy (MSBP)** is a psychiatric ailment that causes a person to fabricate a child's illnesses to fulfill the adult's own needs for attention and sympathy. Subjecting a child to unnecessary, even dangerous, medical procedures and treatments certainly constitutes maltreatment.

Child Sexual Abuse Cases As with other forms of neglect or abuse, the sexual victimization of children can have devastating effects on the victims and can lead to an intergenerational cycle of violence and abuse. Although media reports of child sexual abuse tend to sensationalize these crimes, statistics show a decline in child sexual abuse cases.

Investigators should be aware of pedophiles, adults who have either heterosexual or homosexual preferences for young boys or girls of a specific, limited age range. Pedophiles prey on children, who make the perfect victims because they are often naïve and trusting. Teens are particularly at risk because they are likely to engage in communications revolving around sex and relationships. Children also desire attention and affection and are not generally viewed as credible witnesses or victims. Pedophiles' reactions to being discovered usually begin with complete denial and progress through minimizing the acts, justifying the acts, and blaming the victims. If all else fails, pedophiles may claim to be sick.

The Federal Bureau of Investigation (FBI) Behavioral Science Services Unit categorizes child sexual predators as one of two types, based on the victim profile, offender methodology, and threat level (see Table 11.1). Many pedophiles are members of sex rings, and many have moved from prowling the playgrounds to searching for their victims in cyberspace.

Munchausen's syndrome by proxy (MSBP)

A psychiatric ailment that leads a person to fabricate a child's illnesses to fulfill the adult's own needs for attention and sympathy.

Table 11.1 Child Molester Typologies

Child Molester Typologies	Victim Profile	Offender Profile—Methodology	Threat Level
Situational	Often a relative, neighbor, friend, or someone under the authority of the offender. The child is usually under the trusted care of the offender or has some level of trust. The victim might not have definite characteristics that attract the offender and vary for many reasons. The victim in this category may also only be a few years younger than the offender and perhaps becomes a victim in a social setting such as a party.	This offender can range from a one-time act to a long pattern of child sexual abuse. Typically, this offender has a limited number of victims and may abuse out of opportunity. This offender may abuse children for other reasons than genuine sexual attraction.	There are fewer documented cases involving situational molesters because there are fewer victim–offender ratios. This is in addition to the less predictable behavior of this type of offender. The threat of offending and recidivism is lower than with the preferential molester.
Preferential	The victim is more likely unknown to the offender. The offender may meet the child at a random location that typically attracts children or through an online Internet forum. The child may have other issues in his or her life that the offender can exploit to gain trust. The victim is typically a specific gender or age range depending on what the offender is attracted to.	Often older, they look to "groom" a child and build a relationship. They have a definite sexual preference for children and are sexually attracted to them. A common form of building relationships can be through providing attention and tangible gifts. This type of offender is more apt to engage in highly predictable behavior and high-risk activities to locate and seduce victims. The preferential molester is more commonly identified as the pedophile.	Of the two types, the preferential is more dangerous. This is because those that fit in this category have a consistent need to fulfill their sexual desires and they will not stop pursuing them. Although statistically smaller in number than situational offenders, they have the potential to molest a larger number of victims.

Child Pornography on the Internet The Child Protection Act of 1984 prohibits child pornography and greatly increases the penalties for adults who engage in it. The advent of the World Wide Web has greatly facilitated the sharing of child pornography, as well as a range of other Internet crimes against children. One federal initiative to combat child pornography on the Internet is the Innocent Images National Initiative (IINI):

> The Innocent Images National Initiative (IINI), a component of FBI's Cyber Crimes Program, is an intelligence driven, proactive, multi-agency investigative operation to combat the proliferation of child pornography/child sexual exploitation (CP/CSE) facilitated by an online computer. The IINI provides centralized coordination and analysis of case information that by its very nature is national and international in scope, requiring unprecedented coordination with state, local, and international governments and among FBI field offices and legal attachés.

> Today, computer telecommunications have become one of the most prevalent techniques used by pedophiles to share illegal photographic images of minors and to lure children into illicit sexual relationships. The Internet has dramatically increased the access of the preferential sex offenders to the population they seek to victimize and provides them greater access to a community of people who validate their sexual preferences.

> The mission of the IINI is to reduce the vulnerability of children to acts of sexual exploitation and abuse which are facilitated through the use of computers; to identify and rescue child victims; to investigate and prosecute sexual predators who use the Internet and other online services to sexually exploit children for personal or financial gain; and to strengthen the capabilities of federal, state, local, and international law enforcement through training programs and investigative assistance....

> The FBI and the Department of Justice review all files and select the most egregious subjects for prosecution. In addition, the IINI works to identify child victims and obtain appropriate services/assistance for them and to establish a law enforcement presence on the Internet that will act as a deterrent to those who seek to sexually exploit children....

> Online child pornography/child sexual exploitation investigations, which are worked under the FBI's Innocent Images National Initiative, accounted for 39 percent of all investigations worked under the FBI's Cyber Division in fiscal year 2007....

> Between fiscal years 1996 and 2007, the Innocent Images National Initiative has recorded the following statistical accomplishments:

> ▶ Number of cases opened: 20,134
>
> ▶ Number of informations and indictments: 6,844
>
> ▶ Number of arrests, locates, and summonses: 9,469
>
> ▶ Number of convictions and pretrial diversions: 6[1]

---

[1]Source: "Online Child Pornography/Child Sexual Exploitation Investigations." Washington, DC: Federal Bureau of Investigation, 2009.

CHILDREN WHO ARE THROWNAWAYS, RUNAWAYS, OR OTHERWISE MISSING

Sexual abuse and other types of abuse and neglect are common reasons why youth sometimes run away from home. The National Incidence Studies of Missing, Abducted, Runaway, and Thrownaway Children in America (NISMART) has five categories of missing children: (1) thrownaways, (2) runaways, (3) nonfamily abducted children, (4) family abducted children, and (5) lost, injured, or otherwise missing children.

Thrownaways

A **thrownaway** is a child who was told to leave home, who was not allowed back after having left, who ran away and no one tried to recover the child, or who was abandoned or deserted. Runaway/thrownaway children may band together and join other youths who are just "hanging out." Such youths may also pose a problem for law enforcement if they become disorderly.

thrownaways

Youths who were either told to leave, were not allowed back after having left, ran away and no one tried to recover them, or were abandoned or deserted.

Runaways

Running away is leaving home without parental permission. Usually, however, police are more interested in locating and returning the runaway than in entering the youth into the juvenile justice system. Often, no police investigation, social service inquiry, or school inquiry is conducted to determine why these children left home, were truant because of this absence, or continue to run away.

> Running away is a predelinquent indicator, but its importance often is not recognized by the parents, police, school, social agencies, or the courts.

If police dispositions are to be effective, the family must recognize the early signs of maladjustment in children. Running away is the most visible indicator of a possible future victim (assaulted, murdered) or involvement in criminal activity to support individual needs (prostitution, pornography, burglary, theft, robbery).

Missing and Abducted Children

When police are called to deal with a missing-child report, their responsibility is less clear. Many departments lack specific procedures to deal with missing-children calls. In addition, significant variation exists in the initial response to such calls. Officers might obtain a physical description, description of clothing and jewelry, amount of money carried, possible destination and places frequented, and why the person filing the report thinks the child is missing. A picture should also be obtained. Many jurisdictions also have policies about when the information must be entered into the National Crime Information Center (NCIC) system. In California, for example, the law requires that a child's name be entered into the NCIC system within four hours if the child is under age 12.

■ AN OFFICER'S PERSPECTIVE
Handling Runaways

When I take a report of a juvenile runaway and enter it into the statewide system, it remains there until the juvenile is reported found. Often, however, juveniles come back home, and the parents or guardians neglect to notify the police. This becomes a problem when the juveniles have contact with the police later on and, although they may not actually be runaways at that later time, they are in the system as though they are. The officer then has to follow up on this, which is an extremely inefficient use of time.

I have also had calls where the parents are aware of their child's location but, for a variety of reasons, do not want to pick the child up themselves. They believe the police have the responsibility to retrieve the child and can report the child as a runaway as long as the juvenile refuses to come home. In these instances, we inform parents to retrieve their children themselves. If, however, there are people who are preventing the parent from picking up the child, then the situation does become a police issue.

—*Sgt. Henry Lim Cho*

A special challenge in cases where a child is reported missing is determining if the child has run away (a status offense) or has been abducted.

In some cases, one parent believes, correctly or incorrectly, that the other parent is physically or sexually abusing or neglecting the child. The risk of abduction increases if the parent making the accusation was a victim of abuse or neglect as a child. The risk also increases if the suspecting parent has a network of family members or friends who help the abducting parent obtain a new identity and find a new home.

Time is especially crucial in abduction cases: "Most abductions are short term and involve sexual assault; 44 percent of abducted children who are killed are killed in less than one hour of being abducted; 75 percent are killed within 3 hours of being abducted; 91 percent are killed within 24 hours of being abducted; 99 percent of those murdered are killed within 7 days of being abducted" (Swager 2007, 137). Although data shows that sex-related child abduction homicides are statistically rare (100 to 200 cases annually), they are particularly horrific crimes: "Delays in reporting missing children become critical.... Any delay can make a difference in whether the victim is found alive" (Geberth 2004, 33).

Because of the time-sensitive nature of child abductions, many police departments have a child abduction response team (CART) in place. The mission of a CART is to bring expert resources to child abduction cases quickly. Such a team typically consists of seasoned, experienced officers from around the region, each with a preplanned response related to that officer's field of expertise, and may include mounted patrol, all-terrain vehicles (ATVs), helicopters, and K-9s—whatever resources are readily available. A CART

Fingerprints of a child are taken by a police officer in a campaign against child kidnapping. Of all children kidnapped in the United States each year, approximately half of them are murdered. The remainder are generally the object of parental kidnapping (by father or mother), and the act is often a by-product of divorce.

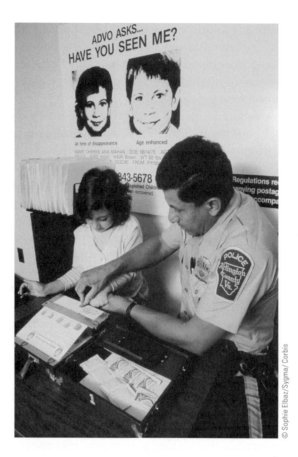

might also include coordinators for the family, the media, the crime scene, the search party, and other agencies involved.

A valuable resource in abduction cases is the America's Missing: Broadcast Emergency Response (AMBER) Alert program. **AMBER Alert** is a voluntary partnership between law enforcement agencies and public broadcasters as an early warning system to notify the public when a child has been abducted. It originated in the Dallas–Fort Worth region after the murder of Amber Hagerman, a 9-year-old girl who was abducted from her home.

AMBER Alert

Voluntary partnerships between law enforcement agencies and public broadcasters to notify the public when a child has been abducted.

All 50 states now have statewide AMBER Alert plans. These alerts may be put on television and radio stations, electronic message systems on highways, and other media. In most departments, the public information officer (PIO) is the communication cornerstone of this network and the primary point of contact for the media, meaning the PIO is responsible for conveying all information from the law enforcement agency to the public via the media and for fielding inquiries from journalists. According to a Department of Justice press release ("Department of Justice Conference" 2008), 426 children have been safely recovered since the AMBER Alert program began, with 96 percent of the recoveries occurring since the program became a nationally coordinated effort in 2002. The program has undertaken a secondary distribution effort in partnership with wireless companies, online service providers, and other private and public entities allowing AMBER Alerts to be sent directly to the public. In addition, tribal nations are working to develop their own plans tailored to their specific needs. According to the press release: "Anecdotal evidence demonstrates that perpetrators are well aware of the power of AMBER Alert, and in many cases have released an abducted child upon hearing the alert."

Before an alert is sent, law enforcement should meet the following criteria: (1) confirm that a child 17 or under has been abducted; (2) believe that the circumstances indicate the child is in danger of serious bodily harm or death; (3) have enough descriptive evidence about the child, abductor, or vehicle to believe an immediate broadcast alert will help; and (4) have entered the child's name and other critical data elements, including the Child Abduction flag, into the NCIC system ("Guidelines for Issuing AMBER Alerts" n.d.).

Yet another resource for law enforcement is a telephone notification system called A Child Is Missing (ACIM). Based in Fort Lauderdale, Florida, ACIM can mobilize an entire community to help search for a missing person. Once an officer at the scene verifies the child is missing, he immediately calls the ACIM toll-free number and gives basic descriptive information to the ACIM technician—name, age, physical and clothing details, and address with zip code where the child was last seen. This is the information that ACIM will give to the public. A technician at ACIM offices in Florida enters the information into a database and discusses with the officer the radius surrounding the child's last known location to determine what size geographic area should be alerted. Using a unique phone system, the ACIM recorded message can be delivered to a thousand phones in 60 seconds. The message ACIM sends out describes the missing person and asks recipients to look out their windows or step outside and check the vicinity in case the missing person is nearby.

Another valuable resource in missing children cases is the National Center for Missing and Exploited Children (NCMEC), which provides two services to law enforcement agencies investigating missing children cases. The first is an age-progression program that creates photographs of a child that approximate what the child would look like now. The greatest age difference they have created is from age 6 to age 31. The second service is called Project KidCare, provided in collaboration with Polaroid Corporation. This service consists of an educational packet and a high-quality photo in a form the NCMEC and law enforcement consider ideal.

If the body of an abducted child is found, the case becomes a homicide investigation. Officers should conduct a neighborhood canvass in the area of the victim's last known location, the victim–killer contact site, the body recovery site, and any other site determined to be important to the investigation. Developing a suspect can be challenging if the offender was transient to the area, rather than someone residing in the community: "The majority of suspects in these cases are White males, averaging 27 years old, single, living with someone else, unemployed or under-employed if working, considered strange by others, with a history of past violent crimes against children" (Geberth 2004, 36).

STATUS OFFENDERS

A special category of offenses has been established for juveniles, designating certain actions as illegal for any person under the age specified by the state.

Status offenses are violations of the law applying only to those under legal age, including curfew violations, drinking alcoholic beverages, incorrigibility, smoking cigarettes, running away from home, and truancy.

status offenses

Violations of the law applying only to those under legal age; include curfew violations, drinking alcoholic beverages, incorrigibility, smoking cigarettes, running away from home, and truancy.

Frequently, status offenses bring young people into contact with police officers, often in a very negative manner. Sometimes the consequences of negative labeling and perhaps confinement with more criminally inclined youths can result in status offenders becoming involved in crime. Several states and the American Bar Association (ABA) have made a case for the **decriminalization** of status offenses, that is, for not treating them as criminal offenses.

Whether states decriminalize status offenses or not, police officers dealing with juveniles should clearly differentiate between simple delinquent behavior (status offenses) and criminal delinquent behavior (crimes regardless of age). One of the most frequent encounters police have with juveniles is dealing with disorderly youths who are just "hanging out," those who violate curfew laws, and those who are truant.

decriminalization

Making status offenses noncriminal matters.

Disorderly Youths Who Are "Hanging Out"

"Hanging out" behavior is well known to most police officers and is a common part of youths' development. To most adolescents, peers become all-important. Parents, teachers, and other authority figures have less influence on adolescents' development and behavior. "Hanging out" is often an indication of lack of direction or purpose and may lead to delinquent behavior, which may be seen as offering excitement. If youths congregate in large numbers inside or outside business establishments, business people and their customers may complain to the police. Some communities have enacted antiloitering laws to discourage groups of youths from "hanging out."

Sometimes the youths have been drinking and are belligerent and unreasonable, making the problem even more difficult. How police officers deal with such situations can make the difference between a peaceful resolution of the problem and a violent confrontation.

Curfew Violators

When youths' behavior is such that the community wants them off the streets at night, a curfew may be established for the public good. The 1990s popularity of curfews as a response to youth crime is simply the most recent revival of a delinquency control measure that has waxed and waned across urban America several times during the last century. Curfew ordinances must demonstrate a compelling state interest and be narrow in interpretation to meet constitutional standards. For example: "The curfew applies to youths under age 17 and between 11 p.m. and 6 a.m., Sunday through Thursday, and midnight to 6 a.m. on Friday and Saturday. Exemptions include juveniles accompanied by an adult, traveling to or from work, responding to an emergency, married, or attending a supervised activity."

Curfews may face resistance from police officers, who see them as babysitting detail and an infringement on crime fighting efforts. Further, many agencies lack adequate personnel to enforce a curfew law. If an officer picks up a child and transports him or her to the station, waits for a parent, and does the necessary paperwork, it could take several hours, taking the officer off the street. Curfew programs should include such strategies as:

▶ Creating a dedicated curfew center or using recreation centers and churches to house curfew violators.

▶ Staffing these centers with social service professionals and community volunteers.

▶ Offering referrals to social service providers and counseling classes for juvenile violators and their families.

▶ Establishing procedures—such as fines, counseling, or community service—for repeat offenders.

▶ Developing recreation, employment, antidrug, and antigang programs.

▶ Providing hotlines for follow-up services and intervention.

In some instances, daytime curfews have been implemented to curb truancy.

Truants

truancy

Loosely defined as habitual unexcused absence from school, considered a status offense because, although compulsory attendance laws vary somewhat from state to state, every state requires children between certain ages to be in school during the academic year absent a valid excuse.

Truancy is a major problem in many school districts. **Truancy**, which is loosely defined as habitual unexcused absence from school, is considered a status offense because, although compulsory attendance laws vary somewhat from state to state, every state requires children between certain ages to be in school during the academic year absent a valid excuse. If a child is not in school, he or she is not learning or gaining the knowledge and problem-solving skills required to move successfully into the adult world of employment and self-sufficiency. Furthermore, youths who are skipping school are very likely to be engaged in proscribed activities such as drug use, property crimes, or even more serious offenses. Research has clearly identified truancy as a precursor to myriad negative outcomes: "A lack of commitment to school has been established by several studies as a risk factor for substance abuse, delinquency, teen pregnancy, and school dropout" (Gonzales, Richards, and Seeley 2002, 3). Other data links high rates of truancy to vandalism and daytime burglary (Baker, Sigmon, and Nugent 2001).

Underage Drinking

Underage drinking is an especially serious status offense because youths who are drinking (or doing drugs) may commit illegal acts while under the influence of drugs or alcohol. A growing body of evidence links alcohol with adolescent violence. Although studies demonstrating a relationship between alcohol use by juveniles and adolescent violence are not new, recent data has confirmed that youth who often engage in underage drinking are significantly more likely to commit violence while sober than are nondrinking youth (Felson, Teasdale, and Burchfield 2008).

Underage drinking causes a wide range of alcohol-related health, social, criminal justice, and academic problems, including drunken driving, disorderly conduct, assaults, acquaintance rape, and vandalism. However, as with curfews, some officers see underage drinking as a low priority because

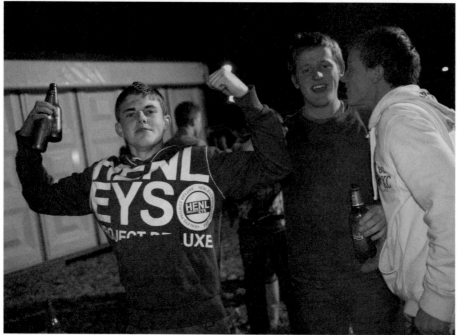

© Keith Morris/age fotostock

Underage drinking can have severe adverse health, social, criminal justice, and academic impacts. Although some officers see underage drinking as "kids just being kids," serious and valid reasons exist for making the enforcement of underage drinking laws a higher priority.

of the perceived legal obstacles in processing juveniles; unpleasant, tedious paperwork; special detention procedures required for minors; lack of juvenile detention facilities or centers that are already above capacity; lack of significant punishment for underage drinking; and personal disagreements regarding underage drinking laws, particularly as they apply to people age 18 to 20. Despite the objections officers may have, serious and valid reasons exist for making the enforcement of underage drinking laws a higher priority.

In conjunction with the Harvard study of binge drinking on college campuses, a survey at Louisiana State University (LSU) was taken regarding alcohol policies at LSU (Campus–Community Coalition for Change 2006). Support or strong support was indicated for making alcohol rules clearer (94 percent), offering alcohol-free dorms (89 percent), and providing more alcohol-free recreational and cultural opportunities such as movies, dances, sports, and lectures (86 percent).

Rave Parties

A problem closely related to underage drinking is that of rave parties. **Raves** are dance parties held in clandestine locations; featuring fast-paced, repetitive electronic music and light shows; and often promising sex, illicit drugs, and alcohol. Drug use is intended to enhance ravers' sensations and boost their energy, so they can dance for extended periods. Ecstasy (also called X) is commonly associated with the rave scene, as is methamphetamine (meth). The principal rave-related concerns for police are drug overdoses, drug trafficking and the associated potential for violence with it, noise (from music, crowds, and traffic), driving under the influence (DUI), traffic control, and parking congestion.

raves

A form of dance and recreation held in a clandestine location; featuring fast-paced, repetitive electronic music and light shows; and often promising sex, illicit drugs, and alcohol.

Approaches law enforcement might use when faced with a rave problem include using nuisance abatement laws, prosecuting rave operators or property owners for drug-related offenses, and educating ravers about the dangers of drug use and overexertion. Currently, raves do not seem to be as prevalent as they were during the 1990s, partially because youth are being better educated about the dangers of meth and X and because that trend in music has passed.

POLICE DISPOSITIONS OF STATUS OFFENSES

Police dispositions range from taking no action to referring the children to social service agencies or to the juvenile court. For status offenses, the police have many alternatives that are guided by the community, the local juvenile justice system, and individual officer discretion.

> In the disposition of matters related to status offenders, how police resolve cases often depends on the officers' discretion, the specific incident, and the backup available.

Whether the police actually arrest a juvenile usually depends on several factors, the most important being the seriousness of the offense. Other factors affecting the decision include age, prior record, family situation, and the youth's attitude. Extralegal factors that should not, but often do, affect police decisions include gender and race.

The decision may also be influenced by public opinion, the media, available referral agencies, and the officer's experience. Officers' actions usually reflect community interests. For example, conflict could occur between the public's demand for order and a group of young people wanting to "hang out." How police respond to such hanging out is influenced by the officer's attitude and the standards of the neighborhood or community, rather than by rules of the state.

Sometimes police may "roust" and "hassle" youths who engage in undesirable social conduct, but officers probably will not report the incident; in this case, street justice is the police disposition. **Street justice** occurs when police decide to deal with a status offense in their own way—usually by ignoring it.

street justice

Decision of police officers to deal with an offense in their own way—usually by ignoring it.

POLICE DISCRETION AND THE INITIAL CONTACT

Between 80 and 90 percent of youths commit some offense for which they could be arrested, yet only about 3 percent of them are. This is largely because they are not caught. Further, those who are caught have usually engaged in some minor status offense that can, in many instances, be better handled by counseling and releasing. This approach allows youths an opportunity to learn from their mistakes without having to officially enter "the system." The result is more desirable for the juveniles and parents involved, and it saves the officer time in dealing with minor status offenses, leaving them available for more serious calls. Although the "counsel and dismiss" alternative may be criticized as being "soft" on juveniles, this approach is often all that is needed to turn a youth around.

> Police officers have considerable discretionary power when dealing with juveniles.

Law enforcement officers have a range of alternatives to take:

▶ Release the child, with or without a warning, but without making an official record or taking further action.

▶ Release the child, but write up a brief contact or field report to juvenile authorities, describing the contact.

▶ Release the child, but file a more formal report referring the matter to a juvenile bureau or an intake unit, for possible action.

▶ Turn the youth over to juvenile authorities immediately.

▶ Refer the case directly to the court, through the district or county attorney.

> Police officers who deal with juveniles may warn them, with or without an official report; turn them over to their parents, with or without an official report; refer them to a social agency; or refer them to juvenile court.

In some instances, youths engaging in delinquent acts are simply counseled. In other instances, they are returned to their families, who are expected to deal with their child's deviant behavior. Sometimes youths are referred to social services agencies for help. And sometimes they are charged and processed by the juvenile justice system.

> The most common procedure is to release the child, with or without a warning, but without making an official record or taking further action.

If police officers refer youths to a community agency, this is known as **diversion**. Whether a youth is diverted will depend on department policy, the availability of appropriate programs, and police awareness of community resources. Typical police referrals are to youth service bureaus, special school programs, boys' clubs, the YMCA, community mental health agencies, and drug programs. Typically, if the juvenile successfully completes the program, the charge is eliminated from his or her record.

diversion

Referring a juvenile out of the justice system and to some other agency or program.

> Most youth referrals to court are from law enforcement.

Remaining referrals to court come from parents, relatives, schools, probation officers, other courts, social services, and other services. The options open to police officers when it comes to serious, violent juvenile offenders are much more limited.

CALEA Standard 44.2.1 states, "In keeping with the doctrine of *parens patriae*, e.g., that the state plays the role of parent to the child rather than adversary, agencies should seek the least forceful alternative when disposing of cases involving juveniles. Agency referral of alleged juveniles for formal legal proceedings should be restricted to those cases involving serious criminal conduct or repeated criminal violations. In general, delinquent acts requiring referral to the juvenile justice system would include all delinquent acts that, if committed by an adult, would be felonies; all delinquent acts involving weapons; all serious gang-related delinquent acts; all delinquent acts involving aggravated assault and battery; all delinquent acts committed by juveniles on probation or parole or by those with a case pending; and all repeated delinquent acts within the preceding 12 months."

Source: Commission on Accreditation of Law Enforcement Agencies (CALEA). 2012. *Standards for Law Enforcement Agencies*, 5th ed. Fairfax, VA: Author.

SERIOUS, CHRONIC, AND VIOLENT OFFENDERS

Of particular concern to law enforcement and society in general are violent juvenile offenders and those who commit serious crimes or display chronic antisocial or delinquent behavior. The classic long-term studies of delinquent youths conducted by Marvin E. Wolfgang and colleagues found that a relatively small group—6 to 8 percent—of male juveniles accounted for the majority—more than 60 percent—of serious offenses committed by juveniles and that by the third arrest, a juvenile delinquent was virtually guaranteed to continue in a life of crime (Wolfgang, Figlio, and Sellin 1972).

Similar conclusions were reported in *The 8% Solution* (2001). The Orange County (California) Probation Department tracked a small group of first-time offenders for 3 years and found that a small percentage (8 percent) of the juveniles were arrested repeatedly (a minimum of four times within a 3-year period) and were responsible for 55 percent of repeat cases. According to the report (1),

8% problem

50–60 percent of juvenile crime is committed by 8 percent of juveniles.

The characteristics of this group of repeat offenders (referred to as "the **8% problem**") were dramatically different from those who were arrested only once. These differences did not develop after exposure to the juvenile justice system, as some might expect; they were evident at first arrest and referral to juvenile court, and they worsened if nothing was done to alleviate the youth's problems. Unfortunately, in wanting to "give a break" to first-time offenders, the juvenile justice system often pays scant attention to those at greatest risk of becoming chronic offenders until they have established a record of repeated serious of ending [bold added].

The good news is that most of the small group of potentially serious, chronic offenders can be identified reliably at first contact with the juvenile justice system. The 8% offenders enter the system with a complex set of problems or risk factors, which the study identified as (1) involvement in crime at an early age and (2) a multiproblem profile including significant family problems (abuse, neglect, criminal family members, and/or a lack of parental supervision and control), problems at school (truancy, failing more than one course or a recent suspension or expulsion), drug and alcohol abuse, and behaviors such as gang involvement, running away and stealing.[2]

LEGAL PROCEDURES WHEN DEALING WITH YOUTHS

In re Gault (1967) established that juveniles have the right to counsel, the right to be notified of the charges against them, the right to confront and examine witnesses, and the privilege against self-incrimination.

These rights must be respected as police officers interact with children and youths.

Custody and Detention

Police can take children into custody by court order if they have reasonable grounds to believe that the child is suffering from illness or injury or is in immediate danger from his or her surroundings or believe the child has run away or because the child has no parent, guardian, custodian, or other person able to supervise and care for the child and return him or her to the court when required.

A landmark Supreme Court case affecting law enforcement is *Schall v. Martin* (1984), which upheld the state's right to place juveniles in preventive detention. Writing for the majority, Justice Rehnquist cited two reasons for upholding the New York statute for preventive detention. The first was that of "protecting a juvenile from the consequences of his criminal activity." The second was protecting the public. In other words, preventive detention fulfills the legitimate state interest of protecting society and juveniles by temporarily detaining those who might be dangerous to society or to themselves.

After police have taken juveniles into custody, they should either release the juveniles to their parents or guardians, take them before a judge, take them to a detention home or shelter, or take them to a medical facility if needed. The parent or guardian and the court are to be notified in writing with all reasonable speed. Delinquents are *not* to be put into a jail or other adult detention facility unless no other option is available. They are put into a room separate from the adults when their detention in an adult facility is necessary for their own safety or that of the public.

An Implementation Guide for Juvenile Holdover Programs (2001, 1) explains, "A juvenile holdover program (JHP) is both an old and a new concept. The old concept—the creativity of law enforcement officers, social workers and probation officers has always been called upon to decide what to do with a juvenile in need of a safe, and perhaps secure, place to wait until a parent can be located or while the system mobilizes to respond to the needs of a child or youth.... The

---

[2]Source: *The 8% Solution* (Washington, DC: OJJDP Fact Sheet #39, November 2001). (FS 200139)

Being taken into custody and locked up can be a turning point for many youths. Is this young girl headed for a lifetime of crime, or can she be rehabilitated?

© Joel Gordon

new concept—communities have developed a variety of different responses to meet the need for a short-term, temporary holding program for juveniles that can be called upon when the need arises." Among the key elements of a JHP are that it is integrated into a network of services for youths, is a short-term alternative, is easily accessible, and has a trained staff. It should also be able to respond to a youth's immediate needs, provide comfortable facilities with minimum services for an overnight stay, and respond to and de-escalate the immediate situation if necessary. The JHP should have screening and assessment capacity and referral expertise and be able to coordinate postrelease services to the youth and family.

Interviewing Juveniles and Custodial Issues

Interviewing in-custody juveniles is different than interviewing in-custody adults. There are occasions when it is appropriate to have parents present when interviewing youths, which can be an added hurdle for law enforcement.

Additional issues are posed when school resource officers (SROs) conduct interviews with juveniles while in school for incidents that have occurred both inside and outside of school. For example, a criminal defense attorney could argue that juveniles may have felt that they were in custody, even if they were in a school setting. Furthermore, juveniles may not be aware that admitting to school administrators or police officers their involvement in incidents that occurred in school may also carry criminal repercussions outside of school. Parents might also take issue with their children being interviewed for possible criminal incidents at a place of learning, where the expectation is for the student to learn and be safe while the parents are not present.

SROs have the additional challenges of working with school administration and school reprimands in these matters. Additionally, there have been cases where school administration has recommended that a juvenile be charged for an incident. It is important to remember that it is not at the discretion of the principal or head administrator of the school in regard to criminal matters; it is ultimately the discretion of the law enforcement officer. In some communities, the relationship between school administration and law enforcement has become such a negative issue that the schools do not have an SRO or liaison officer on the grounds.

Fingerprinting and Photographing Children

In most jurisdictions, law enforcement officers can take fingerprints of children 14 years and older involved in the crimes of murder, nonnegligent manslaughter, forcible rape, robbery, aggravated assault, burglary, housebreaking, purse snatching, and automobile theft. However, children's fingerprint files usually must be kept separate from adult files. The fingerprints are to be removed from the file and destroyed if the youth is adjudicated not delinquent or if the youth reaches age 21 and has not committed a criminal offense after becoming 16.

If police officers find latent fingerprints during a criminal investigation and have probable cause to believe a particular youth committed the crime, they may fingerprint the youth, regardless of the youth's age. If the comparison is negative, the youth's fingerprint card should be destroyed immediately.

Police Records and Files

Law enforcement records and files concerning a child should be kept separate from those of adults. Unless a charge of delinquency is transferred for criminal prosecution, the interest of national security requires, or the court otherwise orders in the interest of the child, the records and files should not be open to public inspection or their contents disclosed to the public. Juvenile records may be sealed in these cases:

▶ Two years have elapsed since the final discharge of the person.
▶ Since the final discharge, the juvenile has not been convicted of a felony, or of a misdemeanor involving moral turpitude, or adjudicated a delinquent or unruly child, and no proceeding is pending seeking conviction or adjudication.
▶ The juvenile has been rehabilitated.

Confidentiality versus Openness

Many states have begun to de-emphasize traditional confidentiality concerns while emphasizing information sharing. During the early 1990s, states made significant changes in how the juvenile justice system treats information about juvenile offenders, particularly violent juvenile offenders. As juvenile crime became more serious, community protection, the public's right to know, and service providers' need to share information displaced the desire to protect minors from the stigma of youthful indiscretions. Legislatures throughout the country have increasingly called for a presumption of open hearings and records, at least for some juvenile offenders.

LAW ENFORCEMENT PROGRAMS AIMED AT YOUTHS

Most children and youths are *not* in trouble with the law. Programs that foster positive relations between youths and the juvenile justice community can provide many benefits to police agencies and the jurisdictions they serve by helping youths continue to stay out of trouble. Law enforcement programs aimed at youths take varied approaches. Some approach delinquency with aggressive enforcement and sometimes referrals. Some are educational school-based programs aimed at preventing drug abuse and gang involvement, two major problems discussed in Chapter 12. And some provide volunteer opportunities and a chance for officers to mentor youths.

Aggressive Enforcement

The North Miami Beach Police Department took aim at the status offense of truancy. Its Police Eliminating Truancy (PET) project is intended to tackle the underlying causes of truancy and, at the same time, reduce the criminal behavior that resulted when juveniles spent their days on the street instead of in school. About 20 percent of the students admitted to committing crimes while truant.

Crime analysis identifies "hot spots" where a high number of Index crimes took place. The PET project assigns two officers to patrol in those hot spots during regular school hours. Officers take truants to the Truancy Evaluation Center (TEC) located in an off-campus classroom. TEC shares space with the department's Alternate to Suspension Program (ASP), whose intensive learning environment and disciplined approach helps many students rededicate themselves to school. A counselor evaluates the truants and then one of three things usually happens. If students have no history of truancy, PET officers take them back to school. Suspended students take part in ASP. Students who seem to be making truancy a habit meet with their parents and the counselor to discuss possible solutions to the problem.

Another positive aspect of aggressive enforcement programs is that youths who are not seriously delinquent can be referred to other programs for help in staying out of trouble in the future.

Referrals/Diversion

Social services agencies, community-based organizations and schools can all play a role in helping a young person develop and keep from entering the juvenile justice system. Although each community will have different resources available, ideally they will have a youth services center knowledgeable of programs available to help children and youths. Prevention programs and early intervention programs can lessen the need for judicial programs, allowing those programs to concentrate on the more serious problem offenders.

Educational Programs

 Two educational programs widely used across the country to combat drugs and gangs are Drug Abuse Resistance Education (D.A.R.E.) and Gang Resistance Education and Training (G.R.E.A.T.).

Probably the best-known school-based educational program is **D.A.R.E.**, the Drug Abuse Resistance Education program. A study by the University of Illinois tracked 1,800 students for 6 years and found that by the end of high school any impact of the program had worn off. In fact, evaluations conducted at the end of the 1990s and beginning of the new millennium were resoundingly critical of this effort: "D.A.R.E. has been the subject of 30 other studies over the past several years and all of them have arrived at the same conclusion—any effect that the program has to deterring drug use disappears by the time students are seniors in high school" (Brown 2001, 76). In response, the curriculum was revised and tested in high schools and middle schools across the nation. One key change in the new version is that police officers are used more as facilitators and less as instructors. Preliminary evaluations of this revised curriculum indicate there has been an improvement in the effectiveness of D.A.R.E. (Perin 2008).

D.A.R.E.

Drug Abuse Resistance Education, a school program aimed at teaching students to say no to peer pressure to use drugs.

Another school-based education program is **G.R.E.A.T.**, the Gang Resistance Education and Training program. This is a proactive approach to deterring violence before it begins. The program builds a foundation focused on teaching children the life skills needed to avoid violence and gang membership. Research on the benefits of this program conducted by Esbensen et al. (2001) found that the program was beneficial: "Beneficial program effects emerged gradually over time so that there was, on average, more pro-social change in the attitudes of G.R.E.AT. students than the non-G.R.E.A.T. students four years following program exposure."

G.R.E.A.T.

The Gang Resistance Education and Training program, a proactive approach to deterring violence before it begins.

A five-year study by the National Institute of Justice also found the program to have modest positive effects on youths (Esbensen 2004). A small percent had lower levels of victimization, had more negative attitudes toward gangs, had more positive attitudes toward police, had less involvement in risk-seeking behaviors, and were involved in more prosocial activities with their peers. The study also found, however, that the G.R.E.AT. program did not reduce gang membership.

Explorer Posts

As the name *Police Explorer Posts* suggests, this program provides an opportunity for youths to explore police work. Explorer Posts are extensions of the Boy Scouts of America and allow young men and women a chance to volunteer their services to their local police departments. The minimum age for most programs is 14. Explorers typically participate in numerous ride-alongs with licensed police officers to get a "front row" view of the day-to-day activities of an officer, and explorers usually undergo three to six months of intensive training covering such areas as first aid, traffic control, firearms safety, fingerprinting, community relations, and the like. After thorough training, they work with sworn officers in numerous capacities. Some agencies allow their explorers to conduct park patrol and may even grant them the authority to cite individuals under city ordinance violations. Every year, there is a National Explorer competition where Explorer Posts throughout the nation come together to compete in various contests, including scenarios such as burglary response, domestics, and traffic stops along with skills competitions in categories such as shooting.

Ride-Along Programs

As the name indicates, ride-along programs allow juveniles, with parental permission, to ride in a police squad with a patrol officer for some time during the officer's shift. As with Explorer programs, ride-alongs are often made available to youths who are interested in the field of law enforcement and provide an opportunity for youths to learn through observation.

Police–Student Internships

Internships also provide students with a more in-depth look at the field of law enforcement. Although program specifics may vary considerably from department to department, internship programs typically include a series of police ride-alongs with patrol officers and time spent with investigators and officers assigned to other divisions within the police department. Internships generally span a period of at least several months, with many lasting a year, and can require a rigorous application and acceptance process. Candidates often must submit a written application, complete a personal interview, and, if selected, pass a background check before they are offered the position. Internship positions are often limited, and competition can be high, because this experience looks very good on a résumé for those with future job aspirations in the law enforcement and criminal justice.

Police as Mentors to Youth

By committing to a mentoring relationship, carefully selected and trained police personnel can have an enormous impact on juveniles who are at risk of becoming chronic offenders and can be the conduit for restoring youthful lives to productive relationships with families, schools, and the community. The Juvenile Mentoring Program (JUMP) of the Office of Juvenile Justice and Delinquency Prevention (OJJDP) supports one-to-one mentoring projects for youths at risk of failing in school, dropping out of school, or becoming involved in delinquent behavior, including gang activity and substance abuse. The OJJDP defines mentoring as a one-to-one supportive relationship between a responsible adult 18 or older (mentor) and an at-risk juvenile (mentee), which takes place on a regular basis, one to two hours per week for an average of at least one year. The three principal program goals for JUMP are (1) to reduce juvenile delinquency and gang participation by at-risk youths, (2) to improve academic performance of at-risk youths, and (3) to reduce the school dropout rate for at-risk youths. The OJJDP awards dozens of JUMP grants to communities throughout the nation each year.

Other Programs

Several other programs whose orientations are less educational also have been instituted by police departments to help deal with problem youths. One of the most common programs is an SRO program, described in Chapter 7. Other well-known programs found throughout the country are the Officer Friendly program and the McGruff police dog ("Take a bite out of crime") program. The McGruff program focuses on crime prevention and safety and helps youths contribute positively to the community.

JUVENILE JUSTICE AND PROBLEM-ORIENTED POLICING

A finalist in the Excellence in Problem-Oriented Policing Awards in 2003 was the "Underage Drinking: More than a Minor Issue" project of the Plano (Texas) Police Department.[3]

Scanning

Officer Richard L. Glenn had noticed that an increasing number of calls for service in his area involved minors in possession of or consuming alcohol. These calls included juvenile problems, noise, party disturbances, and other incidents. The minors involved commonly stated that they could easily walk into a beer store in Plano and purchase alcohol.

Analysis

Officer Glenn noted numerous participants in this problem: the minors that he caught in violation, the store clerks who sold the alcohol, the police department, and the residents of the City of Plano. The harm caused to Plano residents was demonstrated in police calls for service involving juvenile problems, party disturbances, noise complaints, and alcohol-related traffic accidents. Officer Glenn's goal was to reduce the number of stores in Plano selling alcohol to minors.

Response

Officer Glenn implemented a plan to conduct special enforcement details to increase enforcement, gather specific data on which stores were selling alcohol to minors, and educate violators. He used confidential informants under the age of 18 to purchase alcohol under very controlled circumstances. Finding that the problem was pervasive throughout the City of Plano, Officer Glenn identified four main reasons that store clerks sell alcohol to minors and then used this information to educate the community and violators about this problem.

Assessment

Officer Glenn has continued to conduct special enforcement details, and the number of stores selling alcohol to minors in Plano has significantly decreased during the time that he has been working on this project.

Judge's Commentary

Several features of Plano's underage drinking project deserve note. The city is surrounded by dry jurisdictions, making its 159 package stores magnets for an entire region. The problem of underage drinking was particularly significant in

---

[3]Source: "Underage Drinking: More than a Minor Issue." *Excellence in Problem-Oriented Policing: The 2003 Herman Goldstein Aware Winner and Finalists.* Washington, DC: Office of Community Oriented Policing Services and the Police Executive Research Forum, 2003, pp. 37–44.

Plano because the city prides itself on its quality of life, especially for children. After a beat officer sensed an increasing problem of minors in possession of and consuming alcohol, he was stymied in his attempt to gather conclusive data about the problem. This turned out to be one of those problems that fell through the police department's data system's cracks. Specific cases of under-age possession were often handled informally, resulting in no reports and no data. Underage drinking was not a specific code on police reports, so he had no way of determining what proportion of loud parties, noise complaints, juvenile problems, or traffic accidents involved minors in possession. The officer persevered, however, eventually creating his own database to document the scope and seriousness of the problem.

After receiving clearance to address the problem citywide, the officer implemented a systematic enforcement campaign of multiple attempted underage buys at every package store in Plano. This served both as a response to the problem and as a continuation of problem analysis. Offending clerks and their managers were interviewed to determine why underage purchases could be made in their stores. This line of inquiry yielded valuable information that led to additional responses of a nonenforcement nature. The data issues that limited initial problem analysis also made it difficult to demonstrate that this project reduced the impact of underage drinking on noise, disorder, or traffic accidents in Plano. However, the officer's careful and systematic efforts did clearly affect the behavior of store clerks and managers, making it harder for minors to purchase alcoholic beverages in the city.

SUMMARY

Youths' attitudes toward law and law enforcement are tremendously influenced by personal contacts with law enforcement officers. Positive interactions are critical to delinquency prevention. A juvenile is a person not yet of legal age. In three-fourths of the states, juveniles are defined as youths under age 18. The doctrine of *parens patriae* allows the state to assume guardianship of abandoned, neglected, and "wayward" children. The juvenile justice system, under *parens patriae*, has historically taken a rehabilitative approach in handling children, rather than the punitive approach taken in the adult criminal justice system. The juvenile justice system is responsible for children who are neglected or abused, those who are status offenders, and those who commit serious crimes, in what is called the one-pot jurisdictional approach.

Running away is a predelinquent indicator, but its importance often is not recognized by the parents, police, school, social agencies, or the courts. A special challenge in cases where a child is reported missing is determining if the child has run away (a status offense) or has been abducted.

Some youths get into trouble with the law for minor status offenses. Status offenses are violations of the law applying only to those under legal age, including curfew violations, drinking alcoholic beverages, incorrigibility, smoking cigarettes, running away from home, and truancy. In the disposition of matters related to status offenders, how police resolve cases often depends on the officers' discretion, the specific incident, and the backup available.

Police officers have considerable discretionary power when dealing with juveniles. Police officers who deal with juveniles may warn them, with or without an official report; turn them over to their parents, with or without an official report; refer them to a social agency; or refer them to juvenile court. The most common procedure is to release the child, with or without a warning, but without making an official record or taking further action. Most youth referrals to court are from law enforcement.

In re Gault (1967) established that juveniles have the right to counsel, the right to be notified of the charges against them, the right to confront and examine witnesses, and the privilege against self-incrimination.

Two educational programs widely used across the country to combat drugs and gangs are Drug Abuse Resistance Education (D.A.R.E.) and Gang Resistance Education and Training (G.R.E.A.T.).

APPLICATION

As an officer with the Mytown Juvenile Bureau, you have noted some inconsistent handling of juvenile offenders that has caused the juvenile court authorities to worry about youngsters not receiving due process when taken into police custody. You call together a group, including citizens and youths, to rectify the situation by making a statement of need for juveniles and the ultimate purpose in their apprehension. Based on that group discussion, establish a policy to standardize procedures for handling juveniles.

INSTRUCTIONS

Use the form in the Appendix to formulate a policy that provides guidelines to police officers in handling juveniles. Include in the policy those guidelines necessary for processing juveniles taken into custody for various reasons. The policy and procedure should include searching, questioning, and transporting juveniles, as well as public release of information. Necessary reports should be highlighted and dispositions clearly specified. A visit to the local police department or sheriff's office may help determine what to include in the policy and procedure.

AN EXERCISE IN CRITICAL THINKING

D.F.B.'s parents and two younger siblings were killed with an axe on February 18. D.F.B., age 16, was a sophomore in high school and had discussed killing his family with friends. D.F.B. and several friends also had prepared a "hit list" of others to be terminated. Several friends testified, however, that this list was merely a joke.

D.F.B. had no history of delinquent behavior. He had, however, been depressed for several years. D.F.B. expressed fear of his father, but masked the depression with jokes and quick wit at school. Some school reports indicate D.F.B. was depressed when his brother left home (or was ousted) in the fall. Two good friends moved away in the same year. D.F.B. twice attempted suicide, once in June and again in September.

There were 22 wounds on D.F.B.'s father's body, 19 on his mother's body, 8 on his sister's body, and 9 on his brother's body. After his family was killed (sometime around 3:00 a.m. on February 18), D.F.B. obtained cash and purchased groceries. He cut and dyed his hair and then slept in a culvert. He was arrested the following day at the post office while talking on the telephone with a friend. D.F.B. was placed in the custody of the county sheriff.

1. Should D.F.B. be referred for adult prosecution?
    a. Yes, for there is probable cause to believe D.F.B. committed first-degree murder, and there is evidence that D.F.B. is not amenable to treatment.

b. No, because D.F.B. is only 16 years old.

c. No, because D.F.B. has no history of prior delinquent acts.

d. No, because although these acts were criminal, they were actions that came from extreme emotional disturbance during puberty when a body is not matured, and such acts will not be repeated as D.F.B. has now run out of family (which was the singular focus of his anger).

e. No, because police should always use the least restrictive alternative for dealing with any type of juvenile problem.

2. If the county sheriff had known of D.F.B.'s disturbed emotional state of mind before the murders, what action might the police have taken?

a. Initiate a treatment program (patterned along the lines of informal probation).

b. Attempt a deterrence program (athletic, recreational, and club activities).

c. Make a voluntary referral to appropriate community agencies.

d. Establish a counseling service to give one-on-one talks to youths.

e. Only deal with mandatory referral to mental or public health agencies under statutory authorization to make such referrals (e.g., to detoxification programs).

3. Because of the vulnerability of juveniles, greater safeguards are needed, such as these:

a. Greater intrusions than are normally allowed under the Fourth Amendment for adults should be allowed to protect juveniles from damaging home environments.

b. Stronger mandates must be allowed for juvenile treatment programs.

c. Juveniles should not be permitted to waive constitutional rights on their own.

d. More restrictive means should be allowed to protect juveniles from themselves (in the instance of suicide).

e. Juveniles should receive a set of safeguards completely different from those of adults in preliminary investigations (e.g., stop and frisk), questioning, search and seizure, and the arrest process.

DISCUSSION QUESTIONS

1. What are the advantages and disadvantages of a separate system of justice for juveniles?

2. A major principle of English common law is *parens patriae.* Is this philosophy viable in today's society?

3. Should the police be responsible for status offenses, or should some other agency such as the welfare department be given the options of dealing with youths who commit these offenses?

4. Would our society be better off if we treated juveniles like adults in the justice system?

Explain. Should a child's criminal record follow him or her into adulthood?

5. Is the status offender similar to or different from the delinquent? Do status offenders "get worse"? That is, do their offenses escalate into more serious offenses?

6. Should juvenile offenders be subjected to capital punishment?

7. Does your department have a juvenile division? If so, how many officers are involved?

GALE EMERGENCY SERVICES DATABASE ASSIGNMENTS

▶ Use the Gale Emergency Services database (available for separate purchase) to help answer the Discussion Questions as appropriate.

▶ Use the Gale Emergency Services database to read and outline one of the following articles:

- "Violent Crimes among Juveniles: Behavioral Aspects" by William Andrew Corbitt
- "Drug-Endangered Children" by Jerry Harris
- "Idle Hands: What Factors Have Led Adolescence Into a Pharm Frenzy?" by Tabitha Wethal

- "Return to D.A.R.E.: Armed with Scientific Credibility, the New D.A.R.E. Program Makes a Comeback" by Michelle Perin
- "Police Eliminating Truancy: A PET Project" by William B. Berger and Susan Wind
- "Operation Linebacker: Using Status Offenders to Reduce Crime in Communities" by Robert J. Girot
- "Runaway or Abduction? Assessment Tools for the First Responder" by Andre B. Simons and Jeannine Willie

REFERENCES

Arthur, Lindsay G. 2010. "Foreword." In *Juvenile Justice*, 5th ed., by Kären M. Hess, xiv–xv. Belmont, CA: Wadsworth.

Baker, Myriam L., Jane Nady Sigmon, and M. Elaine Nugent. 2001 (September). *Truancy Reduction: Keeping Students in School*. Washington, DC: Office of Juvenile Justice and Delinquency Prevention, Juvenile Justice Bulletin. (NCJ 188947)

Brown, Cynthia. 2001. "D.A.R.E. Officials Responding to Critics, Come Up with New Program." *American Police Beat* (April): 76.

Campus–Community Coalition for Change. 2006 (June). *Alcohol and Other Drug Use by LSU Undergraduates in Three Residential Types*. Baton Rouge: Louisiana State University.

Child Maltreatment 2010. 2011. Washington, DC: U.S. Department of Health and Human Services, Administration for Children and Families, Administration on Children, Youth and Families, Children's Bureau.

"Child Maltreatment: Definitions." 2009 (April 20). Atlanta, GA: Centers for Disease Control and Prevention.

Commission on Accreditation of Law Enforcement Agencies (CALEA). 2012. *Standards for Law Enforcement Agencies*. 5th ed. Fairfax, VA: Author.

"Department of Justice Conference Highlights AMBER Alert System Success, Finds Way to Enhance Program." 2008 (October 14). Washington, DC: Department of Justice press release.

The 8% Solution. 2001 (November). Washington, DC: OJJDP Fact Sheet #39. (FS 200139)

English, Diana J., Cathy Spatz Widom, and Carol Brand Ford. 2002. *Childhood Victimization and Delinquency, Adult Criminality and Violent Criminal Behavior: A Replication and Extension*. Washington, DC: National Institute of Justice. (NIJ 192291)

Esbensen, Finn-Aage. 2004 (June). *Evaluating G.R.E.A.T.: A School-Based Gang Prevention Program*. Washington, DC: National Institute of Justice. (NCJ 198604)

Esbensen, Finn-Aage, D. Wayne Osgood, Terrance J. Taylor, Dana Peterson, and Adrienne Freng. 2001. "How Great Is G.R.E.A.T? Results from a Longitudinal Quasi-Experimental Design." *Criminology and Public Policy* (November): 87–118.

Federal Interagency Forum on Child and Family Statistics. 2011 (July). *America's Children: Key National Indicators of Well-Being, 2011*. Washington, DC: U.S. Government Printing Office.

Felson, Richard B., Brent Teasdale, and Keri B. Burchfield. 2008. "The Influence of Being Under the Influence: Alcohol Effects on Adolescent Violence." *Journal of Research in Crime and Delinquency* (May): 119–141.

Geberth, Vernon. 2004. "Sex-Related Child Abduction Homicides." *Law and Order* (March): 32–38.

Gonzales, Ramona, Kinette Richards, and Ken Seeley. 2002. *Youth Out of School: Linking Absence to Delinquency*. 2nd ed. Denver: Colorado Foundation for Families and Children.

"Guidelines for Issuing AMBER Alerts." n.d. Washington, DC: Office of Justice Programs: AMBER Alert.

An Implementation Guide for Juvenile Holdover Programs. 2001 (June). Washington, DC: National Highway Traffic Safety Administration, Office of Juvenile Justice and Delinquency Prevention, and American Probation and Parole Association. (DOT HS 809260)

Karmen, Andrew. 2007. *Crime Victims: An Introduction to Victimology*. 5th ed. Belmont, CA: Wadsworth.

"Online Child Pornography/Child Sexual Exploitation Investigations." 2009. Washington, DC: Federal Bureau of Investigation.

Perin, Michelle. 2008. "Return to D.A.R.E." *Law Enforcement Technology* (October).

Swager, Brent. 2007. "Tampa's Child Abduction Response Team." *Law and Order* (September): 134–138.

"Underage Drinking: More than a Minor Issue." 2003. In *Excellence in Problem-Oriented Policing: The 2003 Herman Goldstein Aware Winner and Finalists*, 37–44. Washington, DC: Office of Community Oriented Policing Services and the Police Executive Research Forum.

Wolfgang, Marvin E., Robert M. Figlio, and Thorsten Sellin. 1972. *Delinquency in a Birth Cohort*. Chicago: University of Chicago Press.

CASES CITED

Idaho v. Wright, 497 U.S. 805 (1990)

In re Gault, 387 U.S. 1 (1967)

Maryland v. Craig, 497 U.S. 836 (1990)

Schall v. Martin, 467 U.S. 253 (1984)

© AP Images/Detroit News, Ricardo Thomas

CHAPTER 12

Gangs and Drugs:
Two National Threats

DO YOU KNOW . . .

- Whether the gang problem is increasing or decreasing?
- How the National Gang Threat Assessment classifies gangs?
- What activities gang members frequently engage in?
- What the first step in dealing with a gang problem usually is?
- How gang members might be identified?
- How gang problems might be dealt with?
- If drugs and crime have been proven to be related?
- What approaches have been suggested to address the drug problem?
- What three stages are involved in a drug buy?
- What the critical elements in an illegal drug buy are?
- Why the sale and use of illegal drugs is difficult for police to investigate and prosecute?
- How to avoid a charge of entrapment?
- What the predominant approach to the drug problem in the 1980s was? In the 1990s? Currently?
- What drug abatement statutes do?

CAN YOU DEFINE?

entrapment
flashroll
gang
graffiti
horizontal prosecution
moniker
pulling levers
street gang
turf
vertical prosecution

INTRODUCTION

P eople often talk about getting their "gang" together. Belonging to a gang is certainly not a crime. Most people belong to groups or organizations. But when a gang engages in violence or crime, it becomes an issue for law enforcement.

The gang problem is exceedingly complex and is often intertwined with other social and criminal justice problems, including drugs and firearms. However, not all gangs deal with drugs, and not all who use drugs commit other crimes. Law enforcement officers must maintain objectivity and refrain from stereotyping gang members and drug users and pushers, realizing that gang members are also at risk for victimization: "Given the link between gang membership and violent victimization, it is important that gang members be viewed not only as offenders by criminal justice practitioners and researchers. Violent victimization is intertwined with gang membership before, during, and after youths are gang-involved" (Taylor 2008, 133). The same can be said of those involved in using or dealing drugs. Nonetheless, law enforcement agencies must know how to deal with gangs effectively and how to do their part in the war on drugs. Keep in mind, however, that many gangs are not involved in drugs, either using or selling.

The chapter first focuses on the gang problem, beginning with some definitions of gangs and a description of the current gang problem. This is followed by a look at the types of gangs in the United States, their characteristics, and activities. Next is an explanation of why people join gangs and gang culture, organization, and activities, followed by discussions of how to recognize a gang problem, how to identify gang members, and how to investigate illegal activities of gangs. The exploration of gangs concludes with an examination of approaches to the gang problem other than investigation, including community policing, and a brief look at the link among gangs, vice, organized crime, and drugs.

The chapter then turns to the drug problem in the United States, including the seriousness and extent of the drug problem, and some of the specific drugs involved. This is followed by a description of investigative aids and approaches to combating the drug problem, combating street-level narcotics sales, and responding to drug problems in public housing projects. Next, recognizing people on drugs is discussed, followed by a discussion of legislation as a tool in the war on drugs. The chapter concludes with a description of prevention efforts and on how community policing and problem-oriented policing can enhance efforts to deal with both the gang and the drug problems.

[*Note*: Because the topics of gangs and drugs are both very detailed and complex, with entire texts, courses, and, indeed, careers, devoted to addressing these challenges, this chapter cannot possibly cover all of the pertinent information necessary for an effective police response. The companion Web site contains several useful Web resources relating to this chapter.]

GANGS DEFINED

One of the most basic challenges surrounding the issue of gangs is how to define such groups. The National Alliance of Gang Investigators' Associations (NAGIA) defines a gang as "a group or association of three or more persons with a common identifying sign, symbol, or name who individually or collectively engage in criminal activity that creates an atmosphere of fear and intimidation" (*National Gang Threat Assessment* 2009, 3). The current federal law (18 U.S.C. § 521 (a)) defines a criminal street gang as "an ongoing group, club, organization, or association of five or more persons: (A) that has as one of its primary purposes the commission of one or more of the criminal offenses described in subsection (c); (B) the members of which engage, or have engaged within the past five years, in a continuing series of offenses described in subsection (c); and (C) the activities of which affect interstate or foreign commerce."

A definition commonly accepted by law enforcement is that a gang is any group gathering continuously to commit antisocial behavior. For the purposes of this discussion, we will define a **gang** as a group of individuals with a recognized name and symbols who form an allegiance for a common purpose and engage in unlawful activity.

A broadly applicable definition of street gangs has evolved from intense discussions among working groups of American and European gang researchers over six years in an assembly that has come to be known as the *Eurogang program.* The Eurogang consensus nominal definition of a **street gang** is "any durable, street-oriented youth group whose own identity includes involvement in illegal activity" (Klein 2007, 18).

The definition used greatly affects the perceived magnitude of gang problems and may result in over- or underestimation of the nature and extent of the local gang problem. Having a uniform definition would benefit the law enforcement community in several ways. According to the "National Youth Gang Survey Analysis" (2009),

▶ In general, law enforcement agencies report that group criminality is of greatest importance and the presence of leadership is of least importance in defining a gang.

▶ Additionally, law enforcement agencies tend to emphasize the same definitional characteristics in defining a gang irrespective of year of gang onset.

Table 12.1 identifies the defining characteristics of a gang.

In addition to differing definitions for gangs, understanding the threat of gangs is made more complex because of the numerous categories that have been established, to be discussed shortly. First, consider the extent of the gang problem.

THE EXTENT OF THE GANG PROBLEM

The *gang* label has been applied to various groups, from the "Spanky and Our Gang" little rascals of the 1920s to the leather-clad, violent, drug-using outlaw motorcycle gangs of the 1950s and 1960s. The last quarter of the 20th century saw significant growth in gang problems across the country. In the 1970s, less than half the states reported youth gang problems, but by the late 1990s, every state and the District of Columbia reported gang activity. During that same

gang

A group of individuals with a recognized name and symbols who form an allegiance for a common purpose and engage in unlawful activity.

street gang

"Any durable, street-oriented youth group whose own identity includes involvement in illegal activity."

Table 12.1 Definitional Characteristics of Gangs

Definitional Characteristics	Average Rank (1 = Least Important, 6 = Most Important)			
	Larger Cities	Suburban Counties	Smaller Cities	Rural Counties
Commits Crimes Together	4.8	4.9	4.7	4.5
Has a Name	3.9	3.7	3.3	3.5
Displays Colors or Other Symbols	3.3	3.2	3.3	3.2
Hangs Out Together	3.1	3.0	3.6	3.3
Claims Turf or Territory	3.3	3.1	3.0	2.9
Has a Leader(s)	2.6	3.1	3.0	3.5

Source: National Gang Center. *National Youth Gang Survey Analysis.* Retrieved (1/31/2012) from http://www.nationalgangcenter.gov/Survey-Analysis.

period, the number of cities reporting youth gang problems mushroomed nearly tenfold.

The percentage of law enforcement agencies reporting gang problems in 2009 was 17.0 percent in rural counties, 32.9 percent in smaller cities, 51.8 percent in suburban counties, and 86.3 percent in larger cities (Egley and Howell 2011). These percentages have remained fairly stable from those reported in 2006, indicating the gang problems have neither increased nor decreased substantially in the past few years. However, gang prevalence trend data collected by the National Gang Center (NGC), which tracks the distribution and level of the gang problem across the United States, shows that gang prevalence rates in 2009 were "significantly elevated" compared with the rates reported in 2000 and 2001 (Howell et al. 2011).

The gang problem has increased during the past decade.

These findings are supported by the results of the *2011 National Gang Threat Assessment (NGTA)*, which was developed by the National Gang Intelligence Center (NGIC) and the National Drug Intelligence Center (NDIC), both agencies of the Justice Department: "Gangs continue to commit criminal activity, recruit new members in urban, suburban, and rural regions across the United States, and develop criminal associations that expand their influence over criminal enterprises, particularly street-level drug sales. The most notable trends for 2011 have been the overall increase in gang membership, and the expansion of criminal street gangs' control of street-level drug sales and collaboration with rival gangs and other criminal organizations" (9).

It is unclear exactly how many gangs and gang members actively exist in the United States, perhaps because of differing definitions used to identify such activity and membership. For example, Pistole (2008) estimates 30,000 gangs are actively operating within the country, with a total membership of 800,000. According to the *NGTA* (2011), however, there are more than

33,000 gangs throughout the United States and approximately 1.4 million active members in these gangs. The *Assessment* also presents these key findings (9–10):

▶ Gang membership increased most significantly in the Northeast and Southeast regions, although the West and Great Lakes regions boast the highest number of gang members. Neighborhood-based gangs, hybrid gang members, and national-level gangs such as the Sureños are rapidly expanding in many jurisdictions. Many communities are also experiencing an increase in ethnic-based gangs such as African, Asian, Caribbean, and Eurasian gangs.

▶ Gangs are responsible for an average of 48 percent of violent crime in most jurisdictions and as much as 90 percent in several others, according to NGIC analysis. Major cities and suburban areas experience the most gang-related violence.

▶ Gangs are increasingly engaging in nontraditional gang-related crime, such as alien smuggling, human trafficking, and prostitution. Gangs are also engaging in white-collar crime such as counterfeiting, identity theft, and mortgage fraud, primarily because of the high profitability and much lower visibility and risk of detection and punishment than drug and weapons trafficking.

▶ Many gang members continue to engage in gang activity while incarcerated. Family members play pivotal roles in assisting or facilitating gang activities and recruitment during a gang member's incarceration.

▶ Gangs encourage members, associates, and relatives to obtain law enforcement, judiciary, or legal employment to gather information on rival gangs and law enforcement operations. Gang infiltration of the military continues to pose a significant criminal threat, as members of at least 53 gangs have been identified on both domestic and international military installations.

▶ Gang members are acquiring high-powered, military-style weapons and equipment, which poses a significant threat because of the potential to engage in lethal encounters with law enforcement officers and civilians. Typically, firearms are acquired through illegal purchases; straw purchases via surrogates or intermediaries; and thefts from individuals, vehicles, residences, and commercial establishments.

▶ Gangs on Indian Reservations often emulate national-level gangs and adopt names and identifiers from nationally recognized urban gangs. Gang members on some Indian Reservations are associating with gang members in the community to commit crime.

▶ Gangs are becoming increasingly adaptable and sophisticated, employing new and advanced technology to facilitate criminal activity discreetly, enhance their criminal operations, and connect with other gang members, criminal organizations, and potential recruits nationwide and even worldwide.[1]

---

[1]Source: *2011 National Gang Threat Assessment—Emerging Trends* (Washington, DC: U.S. Department of Justice, National Gang Intelligence Center, 2011).

A Los Angeles Crips member flashes his gang's sign.

© Daniel Lainé/CORBIS

TYPES OF GANGS

Just as there are many ways to define gangs, there are many ways to classify or "type" gangs, such as by ethnicity or region of origin (e.g., Asian gangs, African American gangs, Hispanic gangs, etc.), criminal activity (e.g., drug gangs, auto theft gangs), and location of activity (e.g., street, prison). According to Klein (2007, 54–55),

> There is no *one* form of street gang. Gangs can be large or small, long term or short term, more or less territorial, more or less criminally involved, and so on. If one treats all gangs as being the same, then the treatment will often be wrong, perhaps even making things worse.... It is the fact of gang diversity itself that should make us cautious about generalizing too quickly about their nature....
>
> "Compressed" gangs, primarily adolescent groups of 50 to 100 members and less than ten years' duration, are the most common, found in both large and small cities. Least common are "collective" gangs, rather amorphous, but large collections with little internal structure, sometimes held together by loose neighborhood ties and extensive drug dealing. The smallest in size of our five types, but the most tightly structured, is the "specialty" gang, which is not versatile like the other four types, but rather manifests a narrow pattern of criminal behavior. Drug gangs, robbery or burglary gangs, car theft gangs, and skinheads are common examples.[2]

The *2011 NGTA* notes that gangs vary extensively in membership, structure, age, and ethnicity, but three basic types of gangs have been identified and defined by gang investigators: street gangs, prison gangs, and outlaw motorcycle gangs (OMGs) (2011). One Percenter OMGs and neighborhood/local gangs are considered subsets of OMGs and street gangs, respectively (2011).

---

[2]Source: Malcolm W. Klein, *Chasing after Street Gangs: A Forty-Year Journey* (Upper Saddle River, NJ: Pearson/Prentice Hall, 2007).

The *2011 National Gang Threat Assessment* classifies gangs as street gangs, prison gangs, and outlaw motorcycle gangs (OMGs).

The *NGTA* states that *street gangs* are the largest and control the greatest geographical area, with the threat becoming magnified as national- and regional-level street gangs migrate from urban areas to suburban and rural communities. National street gangs typically have several hundred to several thousand members nationwide. Regional-level street gangs typically have several hundred to several thousand members. Local street gangs usually range in membership from three to several hundred. Neighborhood or local street gangs restrict their activity to specific neighborhoods and jurisdictions, often imitating larger, more powerful national gangs (*2011 National Gang Threat Assessment* 2011).

Prison gangs are a serious domestic threat, especially those affiliated with Mexican drug trafficking organizations (DTOs), and maintain substantial influence over street gangs in the communities in which they operate. Prison gangs also operate in local communities through members who have been released from prison and resume their former street gang affiliations.

OMGs are a threat because of their wide-ranging criminal activity, propensity to use violence, and ability to counter law enforcement efforts. The *2011 NGTA* reports that there are approximately 44,000 active OMG members among 3,000 OMGs nationwide, a significant increase in membership from previous years. However, many law enforcement agencies contend that the majority of OMGs and their members are not "active" gang members but rather perform support functions for the One Percenter OMGs, those groups of "motorcyclists who have voluntarily made a commitment to band together to abide by their organization's rules enforced by violence and who engage in activities that bring them and their club into repeated and serious conflict with society and the law. The group must be an ongoing organization, association of three (3) or more persons which have a common interest and/or activity characterized by the commission of or involvement in a pattern of criminal or delinquent conduct" (*2011 National Gang Threat Assessment* 2011, 7). The Bureau of Alcohol, Tobacco, Firearms and Explosives (ATF) estimates there are 300 One Percenter OMGs operating in the United States.

Criminal activity is one of the distinguishing characteristics of a gang and a way to distinguish gangs by "type." Table 12.2 summarizes the major types of criminal organizations, most of which are gangs, listing their names and the types of criminal activity they commonly engage in.

Criminal activities of gangs are discussed in greater depth later in the chapter. A note about street gangs versus drug gangs: Not all street gangs are involved in drug dealing. Although many street gangs do engage in the drug business to a degree, some gangs are formed expressly to deal drugs.

Female Gangs

Although gangs are still male-dominated, female gang membership is on the rise in many communities throughout the United States (*2011 National Gang Threat Assessment* 2011). Scant research exists on the prevalence and activities of female gangs and gang members and, to date, female gangs have

Table 12.2 Criminal Organizations

Type of Group	Subtype of Group	Specific Groups and Distinct Gangs	Criminal Activity
Asian Gangs	Chinese street gangs, Triads, Tongs	Flying Dragons, Fuk Ching, Ghost Shadows, Ping On, Taiwan Brotherhood, United Bamboo, Wah Ching, White Tigers	Extortion of Chinese businesses, gambling, heroin distribution, exploitation of recent immigrants, smuggling of humans
	Japanese gangs (Boryokudan or Yakuza)	Kumlai, Sumiyoshi Rengo, Yamaguchi Gumi	Gambling, prostitution and sex trade, money laundering, trafficking in weapons and drugs
	Korean gangs	American Burger (AB), Flying Dragons, Junior Korean Power, Korean Killers (KK), Korean Power	Prostitution, massage parlors, gambling, loan-sharking, extortion of Korean businesses (particularly produce markets and restaurants)
	Laotian/Cambodian/Vietnamese gangs	Born to Kill (BTK), Laotian Bloods (LBs), Richtown Crips, Tiny Oriental Crips, Tiny Rascal Gang (TRG)[1]	Strong arm and violent crimes related to business extortion; home invasion for theft of gold, jewelry, and money coupled with rape to deter reporting; street crimes; prostitution; drug trafficking; assault; murder
	Hmong gangs	Cobra gang, Menace of Destruction (MOD), Oriental Ruthless Boys, Totally Gangster Crips, Totally Mafia Crips, True Asian Crips, True Crip Gangsters, True Lady Crips (female Hmongs), True Local Crips, Westside Crips, White Tigers	Gang rape, prostitution, burglary, auto theft, vandalism, home invasion, street crimes, strong arm robbery of businesses, drug trafficking, assault, murder
Latin American gangs	Mexican	18th Street gang, Sureños-Mexican Mafia, Norteños-Nuestra Family, Tijuana Cartel–Arellano-Felix organization, Colima Cartel–Amazcua Contreras brothers, Juarez Cartel–Amado Carillo Fuentes group, Sonora Cartel–Miguel Caro Quintero organization, Sinaloa Cartel-Guzman/Leora organization, Guadalajara Cartel–Rafael Caro Quintero/Miguel Angel Felix Gallardo, Gulf Cartel	Drug trafficking (cocaine, crack, heroin, marijuana), counterfeiting, pickpocketing, money laundering, murder
	Cuban	Cuban Mafia	Drug trafficking (cocaine, crack, heroin, marijuana), counterfeiting, pickpocketing, money laundering, murder
	Puerto Rican	Latin Kings, Puerto Rican Stones	Street crimes, drug trafficking, burglary, assault, rape, murder
	Columbian gangs and cartels	Cali Cartel, Medellin Cartel, Norte Del Valle Cartel, North Coast Cartel, Bogota Cartel, Santander DeQuilichao Cartel, Black Eagles, United Self-Defense Forces of Columbia (AUC), National Liberation Army (ELN), Revolutionary Armed Forces of Columbia (FARC)	Drug trafficking (cocaine, crack, heroin, marijuana), counterfeiting, pickpocketing, money laundering, murder
	El Salvadoran gangs	Mara Salvatrucha 13 (MS-13)	Street crimes, strong arming businesses, assault, drug trafficking, rape, murder

Table 12.2 Criminal Organizations (*Continued*)

Type of Group	Subtype of Group	Specific Groups and Distinct Gangs	Criminal Activity
Latin American gangs (continued)	Peruvian gangs	Shining Path—guerilla organization with a mission for Maoist government	Vandalism and other property damage, assault, rape, murder
Jamaican posses		Shower posse, Spangler posse	Drug trafficking (cocaine, crack, marijuana), weapons trafficking, trafficking green cards
Nigerian gangs		Nigerian Criminal Enterprise (NCE)	Heroin smuggling (via mules) and heroin dealing, credit card fraud, infiltration of private security, planned bankruptcy of companies, exploitation of other Africans
Somali gangs		Somali Outlaws, Somalian Hot Boyz, Murda Gang, Somali Mafia, Ma Thug Boys, Ruff Tuff Somali Crips[2]	Street crimes, strong arming businesses, drug trafficking, assault, rape, murder
Russian (or Soviet) gangs		Evangelical Russian Mafia, Malina/Organizatsiya, Odessa Mafia, Gypsy gangs	Theft (diamonds, furs, gold) and fencing stolen goods, export and sale of stolen Russian religious art and gold, extortion, insurance fraud, money laundering, counterfeiting, daisy-chain tax evasion schemes, credit card scams and fraud, smuggling illegal immigrants, drug trafficking
Street gangs	African American, Caucasian, Hispanic, and others	Disciples, Latin Kings, Vice Lords, Dog Pound, and many others, including variants of Bloods/Crips (e.g., Westside Crips or Rolling Crips)	Motor vehicle theft, drug sales (especially crack and marijuana), weapons trafficking, assaults, drive-by shootings, robbery, theft and fencing stolen property, vandalism, graffiti
Drug-trafficking gangs	Traditional street gangs	Bloods, Crips, Gangster Disciples, Latin Kings, and many others	Drug trafficking (heroin, cocaine, crack, and other drugs), violence, arson, indirect prostitution, vandalism, property crime, strong-arm robbery; African American gangs known for crack; Chicano gangs known for heroin and crack
	International drug cartels	Medellin cartel, Cali cartel	Drug trafficking (cocaine, crack, heroin, marijuana)
Graffiti or tagger crews (also tagger posses, mobs, tribes, and piecers)		Known by three-letter monikers such as NBT (Nothing But Trouble) or ETC (Elite Tagger Crew)	Graffiti vandalism, tag-banging in which violence occurs
Prison gangs		Aryan Brotherhood, Black Guerilla Family, Consolidated Crip Organization, Mexican Mafia, Nuestra Familia, Texas Syndicate	Drug trafficking, prostitution, extortion, protection, murder for hire
Outlaw motorcycle gangs (OMGs)		Hell's Angels, Outlaws, Pagans, Bandidos	Drug trafficking (methamphetamine/crank, speed, ice, PCP, LSD, angel dust), weapons trafficking, chop shops, massage parlors, strip bars, prostitution, arson
Hate groups (including militias and terrorist groups, which also share a focus on ideology)		Aryan Nation, Ku Klux Klan (KKK), skinheads (White Aryan Resistance or WAR), American Nazi Party, Christian Defense League	Bombings, counterfeiting, loan fraud, armored car and bank robberies, theft rings

(*Continues*)

Table 12.2 Criminal Organizations (*Continued*)

Type of Group	Subtype of Group	Specific Groups and Distinct Gangs	Criminal Activity
La Cosa Nostra (aka the Mafia)		Families such as Bonnano, Columbo, Gambino, Genovese, and Lucchese	Gambling; loan-sharking; corruption of public officials and institutions; extortion; money laundering; theft of precious metals, food, and clothing; fencing stolen property; labor racketeering; stock manipulation; securities fraud; weapons trafficking; drug trafficking (particularly heroin distribution); systemic use of violence as a tool in business transactions; murder

Note: Although nationality and ethnicity are often unifying characteristics of criminal organizations and used to identify them, this view is overly narrow and promotes ethnic stereotypes. The organization of criminal groups by nationality and ethnicity in this table is not intended to suggest that criminal behavior is characteristic of any group; ethnicity, however, is often a marker to police.
[1]TRGs originated as a Cambodian gang but now allow Laotian members.
[2]Somali gangs often change their name, colors, and signs every few months. For example, the Somali Outlaws, Hot Boys, and Murda Gang are all one gang that has changed its identity. Somali Mafia and Ma Thugs are break-offs of these gangs.

Source: Table data based partly on Deborah Lamm Weisel. "Criminal Investigation." *In Local Government Police Management*, edited by William A. Geller and Darrel W. Stephens. Washington, DC: International City/County Management Association, 2003, p. 270. Modified and updated by Kären M. Hess, Christine H. Orthmann, and Henry L. Cho.

infrequently been the focus of law enforcement. Consequently, police are often less likely to recognize or stop female gang members.

Hybrid Gangs

Although many, if not most, gangs are organized around race or ethnicity and are highly homogeneous with respect to this variable, some street gangs are more racially or ethnically heterogeneous in their membership. Such mixed-race or mixed-ethnicity gangs are known as *hybrid gangs*, a term that originally referred to a gang's ethnic or racial composition. Hybrid gangs in which several small groups, some of them rivals, band together into one larger gang, can be highly violent. Members of hybrid gangs are generally young and particularly profit-driven. These gangs thrive in areas with relatively new gang problems and often include gangbangers who have migrated from larger cities. These gangs represent a "sea of change in gang culture" and bear little resemblance to traditional gangs. Unlike older gangs based on race or neighborhood loyalty, this new generation is singularly focused on making money from drugs, robbery, and prostitution.

WHY PEOPLE JOIN GANGS

Many factors contribute to the development of delinquent gangs, including dropping out of school, unemployment, family disorganization, cultural transition, neighborhood traditions of gang delinquency, and ethnic status. Gangs provide acceptance and protection to inner-city youth, a sense of belonging and being nurtured, and a sort of surrogate family for those who lack a stable, functional traditional family. For some, gangs provide structure—rules to live by and a code of conduct. Often, gangs provide economic opportunity through criminal activity. Others are drawn to a gang simply for the excitement. Table 12.3 lists numerous factors placing an individual at risk for becoming a gang member.

Table 12.3 Risk Factors for Youth Gang Membership

Domain	Risk Factors
Community	Social disorganization, including poverty and residential mobility
	Organized lower-class communities
	Underclass communities
	Presence of gangs in the neighborhood
	Availability of drugs in the neighborhood
	Availability of firearms
	Barriers to and lack of social and economic opportunities
	Lack of social capital
	Cultural norms supporting gang behavior
	Feeling unsafe in the neighborhood: high crime
	Conflict with social control institutions
Family	Family disorganization, including broken homes and parental drug/alcohol abuse
	Troubled families, including incest, family violence, and drug addiction
	Family members in a gang
	Lack of adult male role models
	Lack of parental role models
	Low socioeconomic status
	Extreme economic deprivation, family management problems, parents with violent attitudes, sibling antisocial behavior
School	Academic failure
	Low educational aspirations, especially among females
	Negative labeling by teachers
	Trouble at school
	Few teacher role models
	Educational frustration
	Low commitment to school, low school attachment, high levels of antisocial behavior in school, low achievement test scores, and identification as being learning disabled
Peer group	High commitment to delinquent peers
	Low commitment to positive peers
	Street socialization
	Gang members in class
	Friends who use drugs or who are gang members
	Friends who are drug distributors
	Interaction with delinquent peers
Individual	Prior delinquency
	Deviant attitudes
	Street smartness: toughness
	Defiant and individualistic character
	Fatalistic view of the world
	Aggression
	Proclivity for excitement and trouble
	Locura (acting in a daring, courageous, and especially crazy fashion in the face of adversity)
	Higher levels of normlessness in the context of family, peer group, and school
	Social disabilities

(Continues)

Table 12.3 Risk Factors for Youth Gang Membership (*Continued*)

Domain	Risk Factors
Individual (*continued*)	Illegal gun ownership
	Early or precocious sexual activity, especially among females
	Alcohol and drug use
	Drug trafficking
	Desire for group rewards, such as status, identity, self-esteem, companionship, and protection
	Problem behaviors, hyperactivity, externalizing behaviors, drinking, lack of refusal skills, and early sexual activity
	Victimization

Source: James C. Howell, *Youth Gangs: An Overview* (Washington, DC: Office of Juvenile Justice and Delinquency Prevention, August 1998), 6–7. (NCJ 167249)

Risk factors are not *causes*, per se, and do not preordain a youth to certain gang membership, but they are highly predictive of gang involvement. Evidence indicates that risk factors are cumulative in their effects, meaning the more risk factors a youth possesses, the greater is the likelihood of gang involvement (Hill et al. 1999; Hill, Lui, and Hawkins 2001). Furthermore, having risk factors across numerous domains increases the likelihood of gang membership more than does a simple accumulation of risk factors in one area. It is also important to recognize that, even among high-risk youth, gang membership for most individuals tends to be short-lived, with a gang "career" often lasting for one year or less (Melde and Esbensen 2011).

Research by Bell (2009, 363) found few differences between boys and girls in risk factors associated with gang membership and outcomes associated with gang involvement: "The results indicate that parental social control, attachment and involvement; school safety; peer fighting; age; and race similarly influence boys' and girls' gang involvement."

GANG CULTURE AND ORGANIZATION

Some gang experts talk about the three Rs of the gang culture: reputation, respect, and revenge. Reputation is of prime concern to the gang members, both individually and collectively. They expect, indeed demand, respect. And they are required to show disrespect for rival gang members, called a *dis* in gang slang. Disrespect inevitably leads to the third R—revenge. Every challenge must be answered, often in the form of a drive-by shooting. Noted criminologist David Kennedy is quoted as saying, "The code of the street has reached a point where not responding to a slight can destroy a reputation, while violence is a sure way to enhance it" (Straub 2008, 1).

Gang members have differing levels of commitment and involvement in gang activities. Most gang members are either hard-core, associate, or peripheral members. The hard-core members are those most dedicated to the gang. Knowing how a gang is organized and what level of involvement a member has can be of great assistance to investigators. The hard-core member is least likely to cooperate with the police; the peripheral members are most likely to be cooperative.

A gang's degree of organization influences the behavior observed among its members, with even low levels of organization having important implications regarding criminality: "Indeed, even incremental increases in gang organization are related to increased involvement in offending and victimization" (Decker, Katz, and Webb 2008, 153).

CRIMINAL ACTIVITIES OF GANGS

Street gang members engage in a wide variety of illegal activities, from underage drinking and vandalism to drug use and drug selling, petty theft, auto theft, assault, robbery, and homicide. And although most gang crime consists of relatively minor offenses, such as property damage, theft, and the like, the more serious, albeit infrequent, crimes, such as robbery, assault, and murder, garner more publicity: "It is these more serious offenses that capture media attention, create fear in some communities, and end up receiving the most concentrated attention of the police and the courts" (Klein 2007, 37).

Disagreement exists about "which comes first," so to speak: gang involvement or criminal activity. Some contend that joining a gang leads youths into criminal activity, but others assert criminally minded youth are more likely to become gang-involved. Several studies have shown that although most youths were delinquent before joining a gang, their delinquency increased as a result of joining. Tita and Ridgeway (2007, 208) report, "Research has demonstrated that even after controlling for individual level attributes, individuals who join gangs commit more crimes than do nongang members. Furthermore, the offending level of gang members is higher when they report being active members of the gang. Therefore, gang membership clearly facilitates offending above and beyond individual level characteristics."

> Gang members often engage in vandalism, drug dealings, larceny/theft, burglary/breaking and entering, aggravated assault, motor vehicle theft, and drive-by shootings.

RECOGNIZING A GANG PROBLEM

Many communities are blind to local gang activity. However, gang members usually make their presence known, thriving on attention and recognition. They go unseen only when law enforcement officers, educators, and parents fail to recognize the signs of gang activity. Such failure to recognize or acknowledge the existence of gang activity, whether willingly or through the lack of gang identification training, dramatically increases a gang's ability to thrive and develop a power base.

> The first step in dealing with a gang problem is to recognize it.

Identifying specific gangs can be challenging, but a school or community can be aware of warning signs of a gang problem: graffiti, obvious colors of clothing, tattoos, initiations, hand signals or handshakes, uncommon terms or phrases, and a sudden change in behavior.

Gang graffiti marks the gang's turf.

Stephen Wilkes/The Image Bank/Getty Images

IDENTIFYING GANGS AND GANG MEMBERS

Gang members take pride in belonging to their specific gangs and will make their membership known in various ways.

> Gang members identify themselves by their names, clothing, tattoos, sign language, slang, and graffiti.

moniker

A gang member's street name.

Many gang members have a street name, called a **moniker**. Often, more than one gang member has the same moniker. The color and type of clothing can also indicate gang membership. For example, Bloods are identified by red or green colors. Crips are associated with blue or purple bandanas or scarves. Many have tattoos, and they frequently flash hand signs or use sign language for quick communication. Because each gang has its own distinct hand signing, displaying such signs, also called "throwing down," can be used to identify one another, show respect to peers, or even to disrespect a rival gang.

Gang members speak a distinct language, and knowing street slang can help officers identify persons as gang members and facilitate communication with these individuals during interviews or interrogations. In the field, police officers are likely to hear gang-related street lingo, such as *set, mix, trey-eight, five-oh*, and infinitely more. Because of space limitations, we cannot possibly list all of the slang officers might find useful. However, many online resources are available to familiarize the reader with some of the more common gang slang (see the list of Web links on CourseMate for this chapter). For example, the Gangs OR Us Web site provides an index for gang and hip-hop slang, as well as a link for conducting safe and effective field contacts with gang-involved parolees, relying heavily on the knowledge of gang language.

turf

The territory claimed by a gang, often marked by graffiti.

graffiti

Symbols and slogans written on walls and sides of buildings, often by gang members to mark their turf.

Most gangs establish a specific area, their **turf**, which they mark with **graffiti** (symbols and slogans written on walls and sides of buildings) and will defend to the death. They control their turf through intimidation and violence. Police officers can learn much about gang activity if graffiti appears in their jurisdiction. Graffiti may list gang members' names, often in order of authority. The most graffiti will appear in the center of the turf area. Graffiti crossed out or overwritten is often the challenge of a rival gang. If gang symbols are written upside down, this graffiti is usually written by a rival gang and is a great insult to the gang it depicts. Gang members caught crossing out a rival's graffiti are usually severely beaten or even killed. (See Figure 12.1.)

Weisel (2007, 1) reports, "As with most forms of vandalism, graffiti is not routinely reported to police. Many people think that graffiti is not a police or 'real crime' problem, or that the police can do little about it. Because graffiti is not routinely reported to police or other agencies, its true scope is unknown. But graffiti has become a major concern, and the mass media, including movies and Web sites glamorizing or promoting graffiti as an acceptable form of urban street art, have contributed to its spread."

In the broken windows crime model, graffiti is a foothold crime leading to a neighborhood's decay: "Neighborhoods plagued with graffiti often become breading grounds for loitering, littering, loud music, and public urination.... As 'good' citizens begin to avoid 'that side of town,' the criminal element becomes more comfortable, and these small public disorder crimes snowball into more serious criminal behaviors. When these more serious crimes flourish, it becomes difficult to assess the true cost of the graffiti offense: expenses mount in terms of prevention, arrests, incarceration, and lost revenue" (Petrocelli 2008, 18).

Some agencies and regions have devised checklists to help law enforcement identify gang members, and some states have created databases to track known gang members that have had police contact. The "National Youth Gang Survey Analysis" (2009) reports how respondents identified individuals as gang members:

▶ For larger and smaller cities and suburban counties, a clear majority of agencies emphasize the use of the self-nomination technique compared with other criteria (e.g., arrested or associates with known gang members; tattoos, colors, or other symbols; identified by a reliable source) in identifying and documenting individuals as gang members in their jurisdictions.

▶ The previous pattern is similar for rural counties but with a noticeably greater emphasis on the display of tattoos, colors, or other symbols as a means for designating gang membership.

INVESTIGATING GANGS' ILLEGAL ACTIVITIES

The same procedures used in investigating any other kind of illegal activity apply to investigating gangs' illegal activities. Information and evidence must support the elements of specific offenses and link gang members to those offenses.

It is often difficult to obtain information about a gang's illegal activities because the gang members stick together and will intimidate the people living and working within their turf. Businesspeople and residents alike are usually fearful of telling the police anything, believing the gang will harm them if they do. Furthermore, many immigrant communities, who may be easy targets for gang victimization, have a basic distrust of law enforcement because of the government corruption in their home countries. Many of the same gang

M.O.B. Member of Bloods

CK Crip Killa

Dog paw made up of three dots ⦿⦿⦿

The number **5** and five-point star signify alliance with People Nation

Refer to each other as "dawgs" and "Crip Killers"

Bloods — M.O.B.

BK Blood Killer

The number **6** and six-point star signify alliance with Folk Nation

Refer to each other as "cuz" (cousin) and "Blood Killers"

Crips — crip

Set of People Nation, allied with Bloods

The number **5** and five-point star signify alliance with Bloods

Vice Lords (People Nation)

GD Gangster Disciples, set of Folk Nation, allied with Crips

The number **74** signifying **G**, the 7th letter of the alphabet, **D** the 4th.

Gangster Disciples (Folk Nation)

13 means *Sureño*

Three- or five-point crown signifies Latin Kings

ADR *Amor de rey* (Love of the king)

A.D.R.   **13**   MS - 13

Mi Vida Loca (My crazy life)

Three- or five-point crown signifies Latin Kings

Mi Vida Loca

Latino Gangs: Latin Kings, Sureños 13, MS-13

ABZ Asian Boyz

Tien	Money
Tinh	Love
Tu	Prison
Toi	Crime
Thu	Revenge

Asian Gangs

Aryan Brotherhood

G27 Group 27

Mexican Mafia

Nuestra Familia

Prison

Nickname

Position

Outlaw patch

Top rocker (gang/club)

Logo

Bottom rocker (city/state)

B = Bandidos = **2**

O = Outlaws = **15**

P = Pagans = **16**

HA = Hell's Angels = **81**

Outlaw Motorcycle

FIGURE 12.1 A sampling of gang symbols, including graffiti and hand signs
Source: From Hess/Hess Orthmann, *Criminal Investigation*, 9e. © Cengage Learning.

members who commit crimes against these immigrants may be related in some way or be the children of family friends. Other challenges faced in dealing with victimized immigrant populations, which can seriously thwart effective police investigation of gang activity, are the language and cultural barriers.

If a neighborhood canvass is conducted and information is received, it is important that the canvass not stop at that point. This would implicate the house or business at which the canvass was terminated as the source of information. In addition, more information might be available from a source not yet contacted during the canvass.

Crime scenes that involve gangs are unique. Often, the crime scene is part of a chain of events. When a gang assault occurs, for example, often a chase precedes the assault, considerably widening the crime scene. If vehicles are involved, the assault is probably by a rival gang. If no vehicles appear to have been involved, the suspects are probably local, perhaps even members of the same gang as the victim. This frequently occurs when narcotics, girlfriends, or family disputes are involved. Evidence obtained in gang investigations is processed in the same way as evidence related to any other crime.

Reading Graffiti

Savelli (2004, 9) suggests, "The key to understanding gang graffiti is being able to analyze the symbols, indicators, and terminology used by gangs. Simply, gangs use graffiti to send messages." The purposes of these messages are:

- To mark the gang's turf (territory).
- To disrespect a rival gang or gang member.
- To memorialize a deceased gang member.
- To make a statement.
- To conduct business.
- To serve as artistic expression.

Savelli (2004, 15) notes, "While it is important to read the writing on the walls, it is equally important to cover it over as soon as possible. Don't give the gang a chance to claim your community as their turf by allowing their graffiti to stay intact…. When dealing with graffiti, it is recommended to:

- Photograph it (the whole piece and in sections).
- Analyze it while it is intact.
- Remove it (paint over it, sandblast it, etc.).
- Keep an archive of the photo.
- Document the colors used.
- Document the gang 'Tag' names.
- Document the indicators of 'beef' or violence.
- Get involved in, or create, an antigraffiti program to cover over all graffiti. Get the youths involved!"

Obtaining and Recording Information

The most common way to gather information about gangs is internal contacts with patrol officers and detectives, followed by internal departmental records and computerized files, and then by review of offense reports. An effective records system is critical in dealing with any gang problem. Information is an essential tool for law enforcement and should include the following: type of gang (street, motorcycle, etc.), ethnic composition, number of active and associate members, territory, hideouts, types of crimes usually committed and method of operation, leadership, and members known to be violent.

Departments can use improving technology by combining the efforts of sworn officers and the capabilities of the information technology (IT) staff with its computer-aid dispatch (CAD) and records management system (RMS) to deliver accurate, timely information on gang activity directly to patrol officers who need it, thus maximizing their effectiveness when dealing with known gang members (Posey 2008). Geographic information system (GIS) technology has been used to create computerized maps that analyze the spatial and temporal distribution of gang activity.

TECHNOLOGY IN POLICING

NATIONAL GANG INTELLIGENCE CENTER (NGIC) ONLINE

The challenge to law enforcement in staying current with information regarding today's increasingly adaptable and technically sophisticated gangs has never been greater. A new tool helping gang investigators and frontline officers meet this challenge is NGIC Online, a Web-based information system provided by the National Gang Intelligence Center and accessible through Law Enforcement Online (LEO):

> The system allows law enforcement members to search the system's vast library of intelligence products and images, post announcements, access officer safety reports, request information, and view the status of requests

and submissions to NGIC. The Requests for Information (RFI) portal provides users with the capability to solicit NGIC analytical assistance and communicate with the center's network of national subject matter experts.... Users are encouraged to share their comments, suggestions, and any new intelligence through the site, which allows NGIC to continue to have the most up-to-date and accurate gang information available.

Source: "National Gang Intelligence Center (NGIC) Unveils Online Tool to Share Intelligence and Assist Law Enforcement." *FBI Law Enforcement Bulletin,* Feb. 2012, pp.14–15.

APPROACHES TO THE GANG PROBLEM

The National Gang Center has published a revised edition of *Best Practices to Address Community Gang Problems* (2010), which identifies five core strategies used in the Comprehensive Gang Model.

> Five general strategies are being used to deal with gang problems: (1) community mobilization, (2) opportunities provision, (3) social intervention, (4) suppression, which includes law enforcement efforts, and (5) organizational change and development.

The most effective approach uses a combination of these strategies.

Table 12.4 shows the law enforcement strategies being used, with what frequency and with what perceived effectiveness if used. Although in-state

Table 12.4 Law Enforcement Strategies and Perceived Effectiveness*

Strategy	Used (Percent)	Judged Effective (If Used) (Percent)
Some or a lot of use		
Targeting entry points	14	17
Gang laws	40	19
Selected violations	76	42
Out-of-state information exchange	53	16
In-state information exchange	90	17
In-city information exchange	55	18
Federal agency operational coordination	40	16
State agency operational coordination	50	13
Local agency operational coordination	78	16
Community collaboration	64	54
Any use		
Street sweeps	40	62
Other suppression tactics	44	63
Crime prevention activities	15	56

* Percentage of cities *n* = 211. The number of cities responding to each question varied slightly.

Source: James C. Howell, *Youth Gang Programs and Strategies* (Washington, DC: OJJDP, August 2000), 46. (NCJ 171154)

information exchange was the most used strategy, it was also among those judged least effective. Less than half the departments used street sweeps and other suppression tactics, but their effectiveness was judged high.

Suppression

Suppression tactics include street sweeps, intensified surveillance, hot spot targeting, directed patrol, saturation patrol, aggressive curfew and truancy enforcement, and caravanning (cruising neighborhoods in a caravan of patrol cars). As might be expected, law enforcement agencies view suppression tactics, crime prevention activities, and community collaboration—in that order—as most effective in preventing and controlling gang crime. An effective suppression strategy includes the following critical elements (National Gang Center 2010, 26):

▶ There are formal and informal social control procedures and accountability measures, including close supervision or monitoring of gang youth by agencies of the criminal and juvenile justice systems, and also by community-based agencies, schools, and grassroots groups.

▶ Gang suppression or control is structurally related to community- and problem-oriented policing and to gang enforcement and tactical units.

▶ Police administration and police officers on the intervention team assume key roles in the development and implementation of important aspects of the program through suppression, gang prevention, social intervention, and community mobilization.

▶ Gang crime data collection and analysis (i.e., crime analysis) are established to accurately and reliably assess the gang problem and its changes over time. Definitions of gang-related incidents, gangs, and gang members are maintained. Gang intelligence is routinely collected and analyzed. It is also highly desirable to have gang crime data geo-coded and analyzed, preferably using automated hot spot mapping techniques.

▶ Police contact with targeted youth is regularly and appropriately quantified, shared, and discussed with other members of the intervention team for purposes of team planning and collaboration. Contacts should be generally consistent with the philosophy of community and problem-oriented policing.

▶ Aggregate-level data bearing on the gang problem are regularly shared with all components of the project, particularly the steering committee.

▶ Professional respect and appropriate collaboration between police and outreach workers and other team members are essential.

▶ Tactical, patrol, drug/vice, community policing, and youth division units that have contact with targeted youth and gang members provide support to the intervention team through information sharing and mutual collaboration and support.

▶ Targeted enforcement operations, when and where necessary, are consistent with program goals and are coordinated with the intervention team to have the maximum impact.[3]

Directed patrol has been identified as a useful and effective suppression tactic in dealing with gangs. One example of a successfully implemented directed patrol program is that in Richmond, Virginia, which used crime statistics and crime logs to determine high-crime days and times in the target area. Additional foot, bicycle, motorcycle, and walking officers were added during those times, which resulted in a significant decrease in crime. During the funded periods, Richmond dropped from being the 5th most dangerous city to the 15th. More recently, it has dropped to 29th (National Gang Center 2010).

pulling levers

Cracking down on any type of criminal activity and telling gang members that the crackdown will continue until the violence stops.

Another successful suppression tactic is **pulling levers**, a deterrence response targeting gang members with chronic involvement in serious crime and setting clear expectations for their behavior: If expectations are not met by even one individual, all members of the gang are subjected to intensified supervision and other forms of enhanced enforcement (Dedel 2007). Levers might include arrest for even the slightest infraction such as jaywalking, restricting property (vehicle, housing) ownership, vehicle licensure, enforcing child support payments, asset forfeiture, and warrants. At the same time, prosocial alternatives for compliance such as education and employment opportunities, drug treatment, tattoo removal, and the like are offered, resulting in a carrot-and-stick approach.

---

[3]Source: *National Gang Center. Best Practices to Address Community Gang Problems: OJJDP's Comprehensive Gang Model*, 2nd ed. (Washington, DC: Office of Juvenile Justice and Delinquency Prevention, October 2010). (NCJ 231200)

Very similar to the pulling levers approach is the "focused deterrence" approach, also referred to as the High Point (North Carolina) Intervention. This approach puts offenders on notice that their community wants them to stop dealing drugs, that help is available, and that their particular criminal actions will bring heightened law enforcement attention. Kennedy (2009, 12–13) describes how the High Point Intervention works:

> A particular drug market is identified; violent dealers are arrested; and the nonviolent dealers are brought to a "call-in" where they face a roomful of law enforcement officers, social service providers, community figures, ex-offenders, and "influentials"—parents, relatives, and others with close, important relationships with particular dealers. The drug dealers are told that (1) they are valuable to the community, and (2) the dealing must stop. They are offered social services. They are informed that local law enforcement has worked up cases on them, but that these cases will be "banked" (temporarily suspended). Then they are given an ultimatum: If you continue to deal, the banked cases against you will be activated.[4]

Gang Units and Task Forces

Much like vice and narcotics, gang units are highly specialized in the area of crime enforcement with a focus on gangs. Gang units typically use criminal informants and often are proactive in creating investigations in enforcing laws on gang members. The units also use many of the same methods of enforcement as vice or narcotics, such as surveillance, undercover operations, and so on. This assignment is considered a highly dangerous, as well as respected, aspect of law enforcement.

The National Youth Gang Survey defines a *gang unit* as "a specialized unit with at least two officers primarily assigned to handle matters related to youth gangs." Respondents to the 2006 survey provided the following information regarding the operation of a gang unit in their agencies ("National Youth Gang Survey Analysis" 2009):

▶ Approximately 4 in 10 law enforcement agencies with a gang problem operated a gang unit in 2006, including 54 percent of larger cities.

▶ With the exception of smaller cities, the percentage of agencies operating a gang unit increased yearly and was highest in 2006.

▶ In 2006, 31 percent of law enforcement agencies with a gang problem that did not operate a gang unit reported that one or more officers were assigned to handle gang problems exclusively.

A more recent survey indicates that by year-end 2007, 365 specialized gang units staffed by more than 4,300 sworn officers were operating in 365 of the nation's largest police departments and sheriff's offices (Langton 2010). Virtually all of these units (98 percent) shared criminal intelligence information with neighboring law enforcement agencies.

---

[4]Source: David Kennedy, "Drugs, Race and Common Ground: Reflections on the High Point Intervention," *NIJ Journal* (262, March 2009), 12–17.

Gang units typically engage in one or more of five main functions: intelligence, enforcement/suppression, investigations, intervention, and prevention. The intelligence component gathers information about gangs, analyzes it for trends, and manages other data related to gang activity. The suppression component involves collaboration between police, probation, and prosecution, targeting the most active gang members and leaders. The investigations component focuses on building cases involving gang-related crime. The intervention component includes giving gang members the chance to finish high school or obtain a GED, to have tattoos removed, to obtain gainful employment, and legal assistance. The prevention component includes conflict resolution skills and peer counseling.

In some states with statewide agencies, a gang task force comprises law enforcement officers in multiple jurisdictions. Collaboration among law enforcement agencies can greatly enhance efforts to cope with the gang problem. Multiagency task forces bring together differing perspectives and focus humanpower and resources on a common goal, providing a more effective response to the issue of gangs.

Gang-Related Legislation, Injunctions, and Ordinances

"Highlights of Gang-Related Legislation" (2011) reports the following, and the progress made since 2008, if any, is indicated in parenthesis following each statistic:

- ▶ Of the 50 states and the District of Columbia (DC), all but Vermont have enacted some form of legislation relating to gangs or gang-related activity (up from 46 states plus DC in 2008).
- ▶ 22 states have passed gang prevention laws.
- ▶ 14 states and DC have enacted anti-carjacking statutes.
- ▶ More than half the states have laws that provide for enhanced penalties for gang-related criminal acts (one-half of states had these laws in 2008).
- ▶ The public nuisance laws of 23 states and DC count gang activity among the factors in determining a nuisance. Indiana has defined real estate/ dwellings as "psychologically affected property" if they are the locations of criminal gang activity (22 states in 2008).
- ▶ 41 states and DC have legislation that defines *gang* (36 states in 2008).
- ▶ More than half of the states' legislatures have laws against graffiti.
- ▶ 24 states define *gang crime/activity* (21 states in 2008).
- ▶ 23 states have legislation on gangs and schools (21 states in 2008).
- ▶ 20 percent of the states have enacted laws that deal with gang-related databases.

Some states have also passed laws that automatically increase the severity level of a crime if it is gang-associated in any way.

Civil gang injunctions (CGIs) are neighborhood-level interventions intended to disrupt a gang's routine activities. The injunction targets specific individuals as well as unnamed gang members who intimidate residents by restricting their activities within the boundaries of a defined geographic area.

Another approach to the gang problem in some cities is to pass an antigang ordinance. Such an ordinance was passed in Sunnyside, Washington, to allow police to aggressively pursue individuals who engage in peripheral gang activities. The ordinance makes joining a gang illegal and prohibits hand signals, wearing gang-related clothes, and other typical gang activities. This ordinance, however, is being opposed by the Washington American Civil Liberties Union (ACLU), which claims that it could lead to racial profiling, a finding many gang experts find "baffling," given that race is paramount in gang activity (Moore 2007).

Injunctions and ordinances may be challenged as unconstitutional violations of the freedom of speech, the right of association, and due process rights if they do not clearly delineate how officers may apply such orders. For example, Chicago passed a gang congregation ordinance to combat the problems created by the city's street gangs. During the three years following passage of the ordinance, Chicago police officers issued more than 89,000 dispersal orders and arrested more than 42,000 people. But in *Chicago v. Morales* (1999), the Supreme Court struck down the ordinance as unconstitutional because its vague wording failed to provide adequate standards to guide police discretion.

Vertical Prosecution and Special Prosecution Units

Vertical prosecution and using special prosecution units are methods thought to increase the efficiency and effectiveness of bringing gang-related cases before the court. **Vertical prosecution** involves having one assistant prosecutor or a small group of assistant prosecutors handle a criminal complaint from start to finish through the entire court process. This is in contrast to **horizontal prosecution**, where different assistant prosecutors are responsible for specific phases of the court proceedings. In some jurisdictions, a few assistant prosecutors specialize in gang-related cases.

The other strategies, social intervention, opportunities provision, and community organization, can be seen in the Office of Juvenile Justice and Delinquency Prevention (OJJDP) five-pronged approach to gang reduction.

vertical prosecution

Where one assistant prosecutor or small group of assistant prosecutors handle the criminal complaint from start to finish through the entire court process.

horizontal prosecution

Different assistant prosecutors are responsible for specific phases of the court proceedings.

The OJJDP'S Comprehensive Gang Model and Gang Reduction Program

The OJJDP's Comprehensive Gang Model, which was already introduced, is based on years of experimentation and research on gang prevention. The model's key distinguishing feature is a strategic planning process that empowers communities to assess their own gang problems and fashion a complement of antigang strategies and program activities. Their report, *Best Practices to Address Community Gang Problems* (National Gang Center 2010), presents the best practices for the Comprehensive Gang Model and highlights results of a National Youth Gang Center Survey and a meeting of practitioners regarding their experiences in implementing the model.

The OJJDP's gang reduction program (GRP) uses a five-pronged approach:

1. *Primary prevention* targets the entire population in high-crime, high-risk communities. The key component is a one-stop resource center that makes services accessible and visible to community members. Services include prenatal and infant care, after-school activities, truancy and dropout prevention, and job programs.

2. *Secondary prevention* identifies young children (ages 7 to 14) at high risk and, drawing on the resources of schools, community-based organizations, and faith-based groups, intervenes with appropriate services before early problem behaviors turn into serious delinquency and gang involvement.

3. *Intervention* targets active gang members, close associates, and gang members returning from confinement and involves aggressive outreach and recruitment activity. Support services for gang-involved youths and their families help youths make positive choices.

4. *Suppression* focuses on identifying the most dangerous and influential gang members and removing them from the community.

5. *Reentry* targets serious offenders who are returning to the community after confinement and provides appropriate services and monitoring. Of particular interest are "displaced" gang members who may cause conflict by attempting to reassert their former gang roles.

The first two prongs of this program focus on prevention, which is also the objective of the G.R.E.A.T. Program.

The G.R.E.A.T. Program

The Gang Resistance Education and Training (G.R.E.A.T.) program is a nationally proven approach aimed at stopping gang membership. Its proactive approach seeks to deter violence before it begins. This school-based, law enforcement officer–instructed classroom curriculum was developed in partnership with nationally recognized organizations such as the Boys & Girls Clubs of America and the National Association of Police Athletic Leagues and is intended as an immunization against delinquency, youth violence, and gang membership. The program builds a foundation focused on teaching children the life skills they need to avoid violence and gang membership ("Welcome to the G.R.E.A.T. Web Site" 2012).

A study supported by the National Institute of Justice (NIJ) documented that students who graduated from the G.R.E.A.T. course showed lower levels of delinquency, impulsive behavior, risk-taking behavior, and approval of violence. The study also found that students demonstrated higher levels of self-esteem, parental attachment, commitment to positive peers, antigang attitudes, perceived educational opportunities, and positive school environments.

In 2006, the NIJ awarded a 5-year grant to the University of Missouri at St. Louis to evaluate the revised G.R.E.A.T. program outcomes. The preliminary findings indicate that G.R.E.A.T. students, when compared with non-G.R.E.A.T. students, had more positive attitudes toward police, fewer positive attitudes about gangs, more use of refusal skills, more resistance to peer pressure, lower rates of gang membership, and lower rates of self-reported delinquency ("NYGC Research Update" 2009).

GANGS AND COMMUNITY POLICING

A gang problem is not just a law enforcement problem. A community must provide its young people with meaningful alternatives to draw them away from gangs, such as educational programs, social interaction, recreational activities, and employment opportunities. Providing these services will require cooperation among parents and families, schools, social services, businesses, religious organizations, and other neighborhood resources. As noted gang expert Richard Valdemar points out, "The biggest cause of gangs is we do nothing for the 90 percent who aren't gang members. If all the attention and respect goes to the gang members, then what happens to the kids who aren't getting that attention and are getting beaten up by gang members?" (Basich 2009, 21).

One valuable resource available to all communities is the National Gang Crime Research Center Web site. The community and other law enforcement agencies are also now becoming more involved in dealing with the drug problem, often closely associated with gang problems.

The Police Executive Research Forum (PERF) and the Community Oriented Policing Services (COPS) Office have collaborated on a report, *The Stop Snitching Phenomenon: Breaking the Code of Silence* (2009), aimed at encouraging community members to share vital information and participate in partnership-enhancing activities with their local law enforcement agencies. This stop snitching culture is promoted by drug dealers, gang members, and other criminals who threaten violence against people who provide information to or cooperate in any way with the police. The stop snitching message intimidates witnesses and erodes trust between communities and police, threatening police agencies' ability to prevent and solve crime by impeding investigations, arrests, and convictions, which could severely erode the criminal justice system ("Combating the Stop Snitching Code of Silence" 2009).

THE LINK AMONG GANGS, VICE, ORGANIZED CRIME, AND DRUGS

The Commission on Accreditation of Law Enforcement Agencies (CALEA) Standards include the control of vice, drugs, and organized crime in one standard, acknowledging that some departments may have three separate divisions dealing with these challenges. Because organized crime is often heavily into drugs and some departments consider both groups as gangs, the three areas are combined into one standard. The following standard has been adapted to refer to only drugs and organized crime.

43.1.2

CALEA Standard 43.1.2 states, "The nature of drug and/or organized crime offenses and the considerable amount of undercover work involved in controlling these offenses contribute to the sensitivity of related records. The agency should keep them secure and limit access to authorized persons only... The nature of the operations of these functions often requires frequent and sometimes large expenditures of money. This can include paying informants, purchasing contraband as evidence, and incurring expenses for surveillance activities and equipment."

Source: Commission on Accreditation of Law Enforcement Agencies (CALEA). 2012. *Standards for Law Enforcement Agencies*. 5th ed. Fairfax, VA: Author.

THE DRUG PROBLEM

Gangs are not the only faction involved in dealing drugs. Organized crime is also heavily into this area, as are some "reputable" businesspeople. Drugs and drug-using behavior have been linked to crime in many ways.

> Research supports the link between street-level drug hot spot activity, disorder, and serious crime.

In addition, the use of illicit drugs is a major cause of the soaring rate of incarceration, with an estimated two-thirds of federal and state prisoners and probationers characterized as drug involved.

THE SERIOUSNESS AND EXTENT OF THE DRUG PROBLEM

The *National Drug Threat Assessment 2011* (2011, 4) states, "The trafficking and abuse of illicit drugs in the United States create an enormous drain on the economic, physical, and social health of American society." The following demonstrates the extent of the threat (*National Drug Threat Assessment 2011*, 1–4):

▶ The abuse of several major illicit drugs—including heroin, marijuana, and methamphetamine—appears to be increasing, especially among the young.

▶ Marijuana use among adolescent students has begun to increase after a decade of gradual decline.

▶ An estimated 8.7 percent of Americans aged 12 or older—or 21.8 million individuals—were current illicit drug users in 2009, a statistically significant increase from 8.0 percent in 2008.

▶ The abuse of controlled prescription drugs (CPDs) ranks second only to the abuse of marijuana, according to National Survey on Drug Use and Health (NSDUH) data, with 7.0 million individuals aged 12 or older estimated to have been current nonmedical users of CPDs in 2009. According to the latest available data, the number of prescription overdose deaths exceeds the number of cocaine, heroin, and methamphetamine deaths combined.

▶ Mexican-based transnational criminal organizations (TCOs) dominate the supply, trafficking, and wholesale distribution of most illicit drugs in the United States.

▶ The Southwest border remains the primary gateway for moving illicit drugs into the United States.

▶ The estimated economic cost of illicit drug use to society for 2007 was more than $193 billion.

▶ The NDIC estimates that the annual cost of drug-related crime is more than $61 billion.

▶ The threat posed by the trafficking and abuse of illicit drugs will not abate in the near term and may increase.[5]

---

[5]Source: *National Drug Threat Assessment 2011* (Washington, DC: National Drug Intelligence Center, August 2011).

Laine (2009, 6) reports, "Over the last several years, we have witnessed a remarkable, and horrific, increase in the level of drug-related violence in Mexico. In 2008, more than 6,200 people died as a result of drug-related violence. So far [in April 2009], more than 1,000 people, including police officers, judges, prosecutors, soldiers, journalists, politicians, and innocent bystanders have been killed." Mexican drug cartels are now present in at least 230 U.S. cities, an increase from about 50 cities in 2006 (Laine 2009).

Many of the incidents involve narco-on-narco crime, where one band of criminals rips off a second one and the situation deteriorates into chaos (Marizco 2009). The dealers are mostly loosely knit freelancers, recruiting in bars, swap meets, and even day labor sites. But there are also powerful, highly organized drug cartels fighting one another, threatening to destabilize Mexico. Griffith (2009, 14) notes, "Drug cartels and gangs like Los Zetas have transformed the country into a battlefield. Last year, the drug war officially claimed the lives of 5,000 people and who knows how many people just disappeared, victims of unspeakable horrors after they were kidnapped." He suggests that drug-related kidnapping and brutality, the "signature activities" of the Mexican drug cartels, are on the rise in the United States, noting that in 2008, Phoenix, now the "kidnapping capital of America," had 370 kidnappings. Phoenix Police Chief Anders is quoted as saying, "We're in the eye of the storm. If it doesn't stop here, if we're not able to fix it here and get it turned around, it will go across the nation" (Griffith 2009, 14).

Eventually the drugs transported over the border find their way across the country, posing a huge challenge to local law enforcement.

IDENTIFYING THE DRUGS INVOLVED

Marijuana is the most controversial of the illicit drugs, and a wide spectrum of opinion exists regarding its harmfulness and whether it should be legalized or not. Marijuana, the illicit drug that has previously and pervasively been the most popular drug with teens, has lately taken a backseat to the nonmedical use of pain relievers, with surveys showing more initiates (first-time users) in recent years using these pain relievers than marijuana (Wethal 2008). As far as the link between drugs and crime, data from the National Drug Threat Survey (NDTS) 2010 indicate that crack cocaine and ice methamphetamine are the drugs that most often contribute to crime. Heroin was reported as a significant contributor to property crime (*National Drug Threat Assessment 2011*). A comprehensive collection of drug fact sheets, including photographs, street names, methods of abuse, overdose effects, and the legal status in the United States, is available on the Drug Enforcement Administration's (DEA) Web site: http://www.justice.gov/dea/pubs/all_fact_sheets.pdf.

Street drugs can be identified with a narcotics field test kit. Identification via field-testing, however, can be tricky: "Most of [these drugs] are pills or powders that could be pure, uncut dope or baking soda, marijuana or oregano, and the people that market them aren't widely known for their reverence of truth in labeling" (Dees 2008, 74). Several brands of self-contained, single-use test kits are available that reduce the likelihood of user error and require very small samples: "Between the variations of similar-looking drugs and the quantity of fake or 'bunk' drugs found by street officers, it's unwise to rely solely on appearance or packaging to form probable cause for an arrest. These tests are reliable and inexpensive" (Dees 2008, 79).

Officers must understand that field-testing cannot be used to *establish* probable cause, only *confirm* it. Probable cause, through observation and evaluation of other factors, must already exist before a substance can be field-tested. For example, an undercover officer who buys a small bag of white powder from a suspected cocaine dealer has established probable cause and may run a substance-specific field test for cocaine.

Kanable (2008) recommends that agencies train their own field investigation drug officers (FIDOs). After thorough training and passing an extensive examination, these officers become certified and can conduct chemical color tests for the most common drugs in their jurisdiction. Having the most simple felony possession cases handled in the field allows forensic labs to spend more time on difficult cases. In addition to saving time, these officers can save the agency money; one field test kit costs between $1 and $2, but lab analysis costs $50 or more. As an example, since Utah agencies started doing presumptive screening in the field, they've eliminated about 50 to 60 percent of cases submitted to the lab (Kanable 2008).

INVESTIGATIVE AIDS

One tool to help law enforcement agencies investigate drug trafficking is the DEA's National Drug Pointer Index (NDPIX), a nationwide database that became operational across the United States in 1997. The NDPIX is intended to enhance agent/officer safety, eliminate duplication, increase information sharing and coordination, and minimize costs by using existing technology and 24-hour access to information through an effective, secure law enforcement telecommunications system.

Some investigative aids are not so high-tech. For example, using dogs to detect drugs has been common for decades because their keen sense of smell enables them to detect minute traces of illicit drugs. Canines are effective force multipliers. Law enforcement agencies depend on their K-9s and handlers for many tasks essential to police work, with drug detection topping the list. Ninety percent of surveyed agencies reported they use dogs for this purpose ("Almost 50% of Agencies" 2008).

The Supreme Court has ruled that a canine sniff in a public area or during a lawful traffic stop is not a Fourth Amendment "search." "Assuming the lawfulness of a detention (stop is based on a reasonable suspicion of criminal activity), merely running [a] K-9 around the vehicle or container does not constitute a Fourth Amendment 'search,' and need not be independently justified" (Rutledge 2011, 75). However, use of a narcotics-detection dog to sniff at the door of an apartment or a home has been ruled a search within the meaning of the Fourth Amendment and therefore requires a warrant.

Another assist for investigators is a special high-accuracy laser range finder developed for the U.S. Customs Service. Investigators use the unit to measure the interior dimensions of cargo containers in their search for hidden compartments in which drugs may be smuggled. The small laser beam allows measurements of loaded containers in which physical access to the rear wall is limited. The handheld, battery-operated laser range finder measures distances from 6 to 85 feet with an accuracy of 1 inch.

Flying drones are being used by the U.S. Forest Service to battle pot growers operating in remote California woodlands. The pilotless, camera-equipped aircraft allows law enforcement to pinpoint marijuana fields and size up potential dangers before agents attempt arrests.

APPROACHES TO THE DRUG PROBLEM

A summary of the findings from all rigorous academic studies evaluating a range of street-level drug law enforcement interventions found that strategic crime-control partnerships with a range of third parties are more effective at disrupting drug problems than are law enforcement–only approaches (Mazerolle, Soole, and Rombouts 2007a).

> Approaches that have been suggested to address the drug problem include:
> - Crime control.
> - Punishment.
> - Rehabilitation.
> - Prevention.
> - Legalization.

Figure 12.2 provides an overview of drug-control strategies.

The approaches being suggested should help support the priorities of the *National Drug Control Strategy* (2011), several of which fall squarely within the domain of law enforcement:

▶ Strengthening efforts to prevent drug use in our communities

▶ Seeking early intervention opportunities in health care

▶ Integrating treatment for substance use disorders into health care and supporting recovery

▶ Breaking the cycle of drug use, crime, delinquency, and incarceration

▶ Disrupting domestic drug trafficking and production

▶ Strengthening international partnerships

▶ Improving information systems to better analyze, assess, and locally address drug use and its consequences

Efforts at international source control and national interdiction are beyond the scope of this text. However, local enforcement efforts are of great importance in the efforts to address the drug problem. These efforts often involve drug buys, undercover operations, and raids.

The Drug Buy

Many police departments use criminal informants (CIs) or plainclothes police officers who are part of a drug unit or other specialized team to make drug buys, which are watched by a surveillance team. Often, these buys are taped to provide further evidence of illegal activity. In addition, the surveillance team can step in if trouble develops and the plainclothes officer or informant needs help. Such buys are also useful because they can provide leads to the suspect's other customers and associates, as well as to where the supply is coming from. Often, it is best to simply watch and wait, continuing to make buys and to gather information, rather than to make an immediate arrest.

> Buy operations occur in three well-defined stages: preparations for the buy, the buy itself, and actions needed after the buy to process evidence and information.

AN OFFICER'S PERSPECTIVE
Using Informants

Because a CI is often involved, the operation can be highly dynamic and change at any given moment. Keep in mind that CIs are usually petty criminals themselves trying to work off their own charges. In one investigation where a CI was used to buy drugs from a known gang member, the CI decided to go into the dealer's residence and do drugs with him.

The CI got high, and the transaction lasted an hour. What should have been a quick buy lasted a long time, consuming the resources of the investigating officers who were also on scene. It is important to consider that, when involved in these investigations, you are not dealing with the most reliable people.

—*Sgt. Henry Lim Cho*

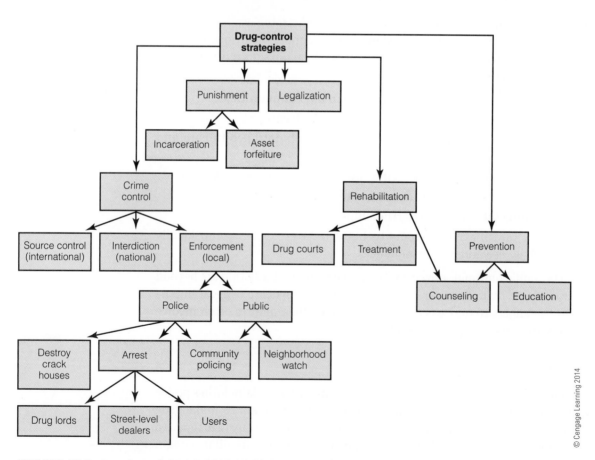

© Cengage Learning 2014

FIGURE 12.2 Overview of drug-control strategies

Preparations for the Buy Officers need to learn all they can about the entire situation. Security is vital. The slightest leak can ruin the operation and endanger the agent. All bills to be used for the buy should be recorded. A backup surveillance team is highly desirable to protect the agent and secure additional evidence. A plan needs to be devised that attempts to cover every contingency. Thorough briefing is essential, but only on a need-to-know basis. When a surveillance team is involved, a set of signals must be arranged. Just before the buy, the officer or informant and vehicle should be searched so an inventory of all items "going into" the buy situation are accounted for and no "tip off" items are present.

The Actual Buy During the buy, any deviation from the plan increases the risk and decreases the chance of obtaining admissible evidence. The agent should control the situation and refuse to accept suggestions made by the seller, although this is not always possible if the buy occurs on a street corner or in a known drug house. Buy location influences the level of control an agent can maintain. Also, the agent should make the buy himself rather than let the informant do it unless, for the purposes of developing intelligence on a certain target, it makes better sense to have a CI do the deal. Sellers should be advised of their rights as soon as they are arrested. They should then be searched to recover the buy money and any other evidence.

After the Buy The drugs should be weighed and tested. Every precaution should be taken to protect their integrity and to maintain the chain of custody as they are checked into the evidence room. All participants should be debriefed. An operational report should be written. Sometimes drug buys are much more sophisticated and complex. Such buys often involve carefully planned undercover operations.

Undercover Operations

One primary approach to dealing with the drug problem is through undercover operations. In such operations, police officers assume a fictitious identity and attempt to infiltrate a drug ring or a drug-dealing gang or to pose as a buyer of drugs.

Undercover investigations are used more routinely in drug cases than perhaps any other type of criminal investigation. The downside to this common tactic is that drug dealers also know it is routinely used, and they have become fairly adept at sniffing out "narcs." Street dealers are also aware of the restrictions imposed on undercover agents, such as the fact that law enforcement officers cannot smoke marijuana legally. As a result, undercover narcotics officers have had to develop more convincing ways to fit into the drug culture.

Critical Elements in an Illegal Drug Buy An undercover agent might dress a certain way, use certain slang, and talk with an accent, or even gargle with beer or hard liquor just before meeting with a dealer. The negotiations conducted by an undercover narcotics officer are similar to those used by a hostage negotiator and require similar communication skills. In the case of the undercover agent, however, the innocent victim whose life may be saved is the agent. To successfully negotiate, undercover agents need as much *information* as possible about the sellers and their needs. Agents often consider that money is the main objective of drug dealers, but security is often even more important. This can be seen in drug dealers' insistence on controlling all aspects of the transaction, especially the location.

Another critical factor in undercover negotiations is *time*. Most drug dealers want to conduct their business as rapidly as possible, keeping the amount of time they have the drugs in their possession to a minimum. Undercover agents also can give the impression of being in a hurry to conduct business, perhaps by having an airline ticket with an impending departure time printed on the envelope jutting from a pocket. Despite the time press to conduct the transaction, it must also be remembered that the passage of time builds trust.

> Information and time are critical elements in an illegal drug buy.

flashroll

Buy money in a drug deal.

Another crucial aspect of the buy is how the **flashroll**, the buy money, is managed. Many undercover narcotics officers who are injured or killed while on assignment usually have mismanaged the flashroll. The most dangerous time is when the drugs and money are in the same place. Grave risks also occur when the flashroll is *not* present. In such instances, undercover agents may not be as guarded as they should be because they feel they are not at that much risk.

If the flashroll is present, agents should allow the dealer to count the money. There is little point in having it on hand if this is not part of the plan. If the agent cannot come up with the full amount requested, it is sometimes a good tactic to simply explain to the dealer that cash is temporarily short. Such an admission can do much to strengthen the agent's cover.

> The sale and use of illegal drugs is difficult to investigate and prosecute because sellers and buyers are willing participants.

entrapment

An action by the police (or a government agent) persuading a person to commit a crime that the person would not otherwise have committed.

Entrapment Whether a sophisticated undercover operation or a simple drug buy is involved, care must be taken to avoid a charge of **entrapment**, which occurs when a police officer (or other government official or person acting on behalf of the police or government) entices someone to commit a crime the person would not normally commit. Repeated requests to buy drugs are sometimes considered entrapment.

In *Hampton v. United States* (1976), Hampton was convicted of selling heroin to DEA agents. The question before the Supreme Court was, If a government informant supplies heroin to a person who then sells it to government agents, is this entrapment? The Court said no; Hampton was "predisposed" to deal in drugs. This view agrees with the majority opinion on entrapment, focusing on the defendant's behavior rather than on that of the officers involved. States vary, however, in whether they support the majority or the minority view. The minority view focuses on how officers or their agents conduct themselves.

To avoid charges of entrapment, those making the buy—be they plain-clothes officers, informants, or undercover agents—should make more than one buy. The more buys made, the weaker the entrapment defense.

Making several drug buys will protect against a claim of entrapment.

Among the other actions to be avoided are pressures such as badgering or coaxing, creating an unusual motive such as sympathy, or making the crime unusually attractive. For example, it might be entrapment if officers said the crime would not be detected or that it was not illegal. Police may create an opportunity for someone to commit crime. It is presumed a law-abiding person would resist the temptation. Agents may also originate the criminal plan. As the California Supreme Court said, "We are not concerned with who first conceived or who willingly, or reluctantly, acquiesced in a criminal project." It is also not entrapment for an officer to take reasonable steps to gain the suspects' confidence.

Proving Guilty Knowledge

Another area police officers involved in drug investigations must consider is the need to prove the person in possession of a package containing illegal substances knew of their presence. This frequently arises in vehicle courier and package delivery cases. Among the facts the courts have found relevant to proving knowledge are (1) inconsistent statements, (2) implausible stories, (3) a large quantity of valuable contraband, (4) nervousness, (5) failure to ask any questions regarding the nature of a trip, (6) more contraband or drug paraphernalia found in the subject's possession, (7) lack of surprise upon discovery of the contraband, (8) scanning for police surveillance, (9) accepting a package without question or surprise, (10) hiding a package once it is delivered, and (11) inquiring about the status of a package in anticipation of its delivery.

Drug Raids

During the 1980s, drug raids made frequent headlines. Tanklike vehicles, special weapons and tactics (SWAT) teams, and sophisticated weaponry all have been involved in drug raids. During such raids, communication is usually critical. It is also advisable to have a narcotic K-9 on standby. Such raids can be highly successful.

In combating the drug problem, law enforcement in the 1980s focused on undercover operations and sophisticated raids. In the 1990s, law enforcement focused on enlisting and educating the public and targeting street-level sales. That emphasis continues into the 21st century.

Combating Prescription Drug Diversion

Two organizations have been formed to help law enforcement tackle the problem of the abuse and diversion of prescription drugs: Prescription Pattern Analysis Tracking Robberies and Other Losses (RxPATROL) and the National Association of Drug Diversion Investigation (NADDI). RxPATROL helps law enforcement solve pharmacy robberies, burglaries, and other major crimes committed in health care facilities through its national computer database.

NADDI is a nonprofit organization that provides prescription drug abuse education to law enforcement, regulatory agents, and health care professionals.

Dealing with Meth Labs

There are two main types of methamphetamine (meth) labs: the super labs, which are highly organized and sophisticated labs using highly trained "cooks" and quality equipment, and "Mom and Pop" labs, generally run by meth users who produce a little extra to sell (Petrocelli 2009). Approximately 90 percent of the labs are considered small-scale, and they exist throughout the country. However, most meth found on the street—more than 80 percent—is produced by super labs, which are concentrated in Southern California and Mexico (Petrocelli 2009). The toxic nature of the smaller labs is a major concern for police and local communities, particularly because of the hazardous waste produced.

> According to National Seizure System (NSS) data, the number of law enforcement officials injured at methamphetamine production sites increased from 32 in 2005 to 62 in 2009. In the first 9 months of 2010, 41 law enforcement officials were injured. Children living in homes where methamphetamine is produced are also at great risk for negative health consequences. According to NSS, the number of children injured at methamphetamine production sites increased from 4 in 2005 to 11 in 2009, while 14 children were injured from January through September 2010. Such children are also at risk from fires and explosions. NSS data show that there were 171 explosions or fires at methamphetamine production sites in 2009, compared with 101 in 2008; in the first 9 months of 2010, there were 160 explosions or fires.[6]

Common signs indicative of a meth lab include chemical odors (especially ammonia ether); coffee grinders and blenders with white residue; large quantities of matches, acetone, lithium batteries, antifreeze, plastic baggies, and glass jars; continuously running exhaust fans; thermoses and plastic liter pop bottles; and constant foot traffic, at all hours, with short stays.

Surveillances and raids are options for law enforcement. However, a more proactive approach to shutting down meth labs is to educate retailers about the ingredients and hardware needed for manufacturing methamphetamine. Several states have approached the meth problem by restricting the sale of cold tablets containing pseudoephedrine, a key ingredient in methamphetamine. Such cold tablets must be locked up, and their sale requires identification and a signature.

Important sources of information include postal carriers, sanitation workers, utility workers, and resident managers and rental property managers. Such individuals should be trained to identify suspicious odors associated with production of meth, including garlic, rotten eggs, cat urine, nail polish remover, and a hospital smell.

If a clandestine drug lab is discovered, extreme caution is warranted as significant danger is posed by interrupting a chemical process at the wrong time and by simply being exposed to chemical fumes:

---

[6]Source: *National Drug Threat Assessment 2011* (Washington, DC: National Drug Intelligence Center, August 2011).

As a patrol officer, your best course of action is to secure any lab and refer entry to trained and equipped specialists. However, circumstances dictate procedures and a tactical situation may require taking action. If so, quickly secure offenders and victims and retreat to safety. Do not interfere with processes, turn on or off any electrical devices, or stop to collect any evidence; leave these things for a trained specialist.

If you enter a clandestine lab, you are exposed, and must be considered contaminated. Expect to be quarantined until hazardous materials specialists arrive. When the hazmat guys do arrive, you will be washed down, stripped of everything you entered with, and possibly be sent for medical evaluation. It is not just for your health—it's for the health of anyone you may encounter until fully decontaminated, including fellow officers, citizens, and family.[7]

COMBATING STREET-LEVEL NARCOTICS SALES

Street drug dealing can be attacked in one of three ways: (1) Attack the demand (scare off buyers), (2) attack the supply (slow the dealer's business), and (3) alter the environment (make the area "too hot" for dealers and buyers): "The greatest deterrent to drug dealing is officer presence. Just being in the area in a marked unit will scare off drug dealers and drug buyers" (Petrocelli 2007, 20).

Citizens know where drug dealing is going on, and if they can be encouraged to report such events, police can concentrate their efforts on those locations receiving the most complaints. Often, police officers want to go higher than the street pusher but should avoid this temptation. If information regarding

Unlike undercover narcotics operations designed to infiltrate drug rings and get to higher-level dealers and distributors, street-level drug raids are a more visible, immediate response and let the community know even low-level pushers will be arrested.

© Henry Cho

---

[7]Source: Laska, Paul R. "Suspicious Packages and Booby Traps." *Police,* May 2011, pp. 68–73. Reprinted by permission of the author.

someone higher up is obtained, it should be given to the narcotics unit for follow-up. The main purpose of the street-level raid is to respond to citizen complaints and to let them see their complaints being acted on—arrests being made. Officers should know where to search a person being detained on suspicion of possession of drugs.

The variety of hiding places for illegal drugs is limited only by the violators' ingenuity. Common hiding places include body orifices, boots, chewing gum packages, cigarettes, coat linings, cuffs, false heels, hair, hatbands, inside ties, lighters, pants, pens and pencils, seams, shoes, shoulder pads, sleeves, and waistbands.

Police-led crackdowns and cleanups such as "Weed and Seed" initiatives have been effective in some communities. These programs target drug hot spots, and during and after the crackdown, the targeted areas receive other services aimed at enhancing the quality of life, including code enforcement, litter removal, and street light repair.

PUBLIC HOUSING AND THE DRUG PROBLEM

To deal with the drug problem in public housing projects, police officers need to understand the workings of the local public housing authorities or agencies (PHAs) managing these complexes. Officers need to work at establishing a relationship with the PHAs and at overcoming the occasional disbelief of management and residents that the police truly want to help. Once this is accomplished, a fact-finding mission should identify key players, provide information about each organization, and determine what programs exist and the participation level. Next the problem should be identified: What is the problem and for whom? Police, residents, housing personnel, the mayor? Does one problem mask another problem? Then a dialogue should be undertaken with key players to enlist support and mobilize the housing project's residents. After that, a strategy should be developed, including goals, objectives, and tactics that might be used. Next, the strategy should be implemented, coordinating all available resources, specifying roles for each key player, and determining a time frame. The final step is to evaluate progress. Was the problem improved or changed?

Various specific strategies have been used to tackle the drug problem in public housing. Some jurisdictions assign liaison officers to high crime public housing areas and may even place a substation in these areas, many of which are grant funded. Other common strategies focus on improving the physical environment: limiting entrances, improving lighting, erecting fences, requiring a pass card to gain entrance to the housing, and keeping trash collected.

Efforts may focus on removing offenders, strengthening enforcement and prosecution efforts, enforcing lease requirements, and seizing assets. The setting and enforcement of strict housing policies in addition to criminal law enforcement often helps—for instance, informing tenants that any drug-related offenses are grounds for automatic eviction.

Efforts may also focus on reducing the demand, focusing on the buyers of the drugs rather than on the sellers either through sting operations or through educational programs, youth diversion programs, or treatment programs.

Another strategy is to work on improving communications by using community surveys and tip lines and by improving communications between narcotics investigators and patrol officers.

RECOGNIZING INDIVIDUALS USING ILLEGAL DRUGS

In addition to being concerned with those who deal in drugs, police officers need to be prepared to manage those who use them. Police officers must be able to recognize when a person is probably under the influence of drugs and must be aware of the dangers the person might present. Table 12.5 summarizes the primary physical symptoms, what to look for, and the dangers involved in the most commonly used drugs, including alcohol.

Police officers must be able to recognize individuals who might be on phencyclidine (PCP), or angel dust. One symptom always present in an individual high on PCP is nystagmus, the involuntary jerking or bouncing of the eye, a possible cause of which is intoxication (recall the discussion in Chapter 5 regarding drunk drivers). Individuals on PCP may display superhuman strength.

Some agencies have drug recognition experts (DREs) who are specially trained to detect and recognize drug-impaired drivers.

LEGISLATION AS A TOOL IN THE WAR ON DRUGS

The government has the power to finance the war on drugs by seizing the drug traffickers' illegally obtained assets. This includes cars and weapons as well as cash. Among items that have been seized are airplanes, vehicles, radio transmitters with scanners, telephone scramblers, paper shredders, electronic currency counters, assault rifles, and electronic stun guns.

Asset Forfeiture

Asset forfeiture is another form of punishment. The U.S. Marshals Service administers the Department of Justice's Asset Forfeiture program, managing and disposing of properties seized and forfeited by federal law enforcement agencies and U.S. attorneys nationwide. The three goals of the program are (1) enforcing the law, (2) improving law enforcement cooperation, and (3) enhancing law enforcement through revenue sharing. Commonly seized assets include real property, vehicles, vessels, aircraft, businesses, financial instruments, and jewelry. Under the Equitable Sharing program, proceeds from the sale of forfeited assets are often shared with the state and local enforcement agencies that participated in the investigation leading to the seizure, enhancing cooperation between state/local agencies and federal agencies ("Asset Forfeiture Program" n.d.).

The COPS office has published a guide, *Asset Forfeiture* (Worrall 2008), that describes applying asset forfeiture to specific crimes, examines legal arrangements for its use, discusses the benefits and consequences of its use, and provides recommendations for launching an asset forfeiture program.

Table 12.5 Drugs of Abuse/Uses and Effects

Drugs	Controlled Substances Act (CSA) Schedules	Trade or Other Names	Medical Uses	Dependence		Tolerance	Duration (Hours)	Usual Method	Possible Effects	Effects of Overdose	Withdrawal Syndrome
				Physical	Psychological						
Narcotics											
Heroin	Schedule I	Diamorphine, Horse, Smack, Black tar, Chiva, Negra (black tar)	None in U.S., analgesic, antitussive	High	High	Yes	3–4	Injected, snorted, smoked	Euphoria, drowsiness, respiratory depression, constricted pupils, nausea	Slow and shallow breathing, clammy skin, convulsions, coma, possible death	Watery eyes, runny nose, yawning, loss of appetite, irritability, tremors, panic, cramps, nausea, chills and sweating
Morphine	Schedule II	MS-Contin, Roxanol, Oramorph SR, MSIR, Dreamer, First Line, God's Drug, Hows, Mister Blue, Morf, Morpho, Unkie	Analgesic	High	High	Yes	3–12	Oral, injected			
Hydrocodone	Schedule II, Product III, V	Hydrocodone w/ Acetaminophen, Vicodin, Vicoprofen, Tussionex, Lortab	Analgesic, antitussive	High	High	Yes	3–6	Oral			
Hydromorphone	Schedule II	Dilaudid	Analgesic	High	High	Yes	3–4	Oral, injected			
Methadone	Schedule II	Amidone, Chocolate Chip Cookies, Fizzies, Maria, Wafer, Pastora, Salvia,	Analgesic	High	High	Yes		Oral, injected			

Drug	CSA Schedules	Trade or Other Names	Medical Uses	Physical Dependence	Psychological Dependence	Tolerance	Duration (hours)	Usual Method	Possible Effects	Effects of Overdose	Withdrawal Syndrome
Oxycodone	Schedule II	Roxicet, Endocet, OxyContin, Percocet, Percodan, Hillbilly Heroin, Kicker, OC, Ox, Roxy, Perc, Oxy	Analgesic	High	High	Yes	3–12	Oral			
Codeine	Schedule II, Products III, V	Acetaminophen, Guaifenesin or Promethazine w/ Codeine, Fiorinal, Fioricet or Tylenol w/ Codeine	Analgesic, antitussive	Moderate	Moderate	Yes	3–4	Oral, injected			
Other Narcotics	Schedule II, III, IV	Fentanyl, Demerol, Methadone, Darvon, Stadol, Talwin, Paregoric, Buprenex	Analgesic, antidiarrheal, antitussive	High–Low	High–Low	Yes	Variable	Oral, injected, snorted, smoked			
Depressants											
Gamma-Hydroxybutyric Acid (GHB)	Schedule I, Product III	Sodium Oxybate, Xyrem®, Easy Lay, G, Georgia Home Boy, Goop, Grievous Bodily Harm, Liquid Ecstasy, Liquid X, Scoop	None in U.S., anesthetic	Moderate	Moderate	Yes	3–6	Oral	Slurred speech, disorientation drunken behavior without odor of alcohol, impaired memory of events, interacts with alcohol	Shallow respiration, clammy skin, dilated pupils, weak and rapid pulse, coma, possible death	Anxiety, insomnia, tremors, delirium, convulsions, possible death

(Continues)

Table 12.5 Drugs of Abuse/Uses and Effects (*Continued*)

| Drugs | Controlled Substances Act (CSA) Schedules | Trade or Other Names | Medical Uses | Dependence | | Tolerance | Duration (Hours) | Usual Method | Possible Effects | Effects of Overdose | Withdrawal Syndrome |
				Physical	Psychological						
Rohypnol	Schedule IV	Circles, Forget Pill, Forget-Me-Pill, La Rocha, Lunch Money Drug, Mexican Valium, Pingus, R2, Reynolds, Roach, Roach 2, Roachies, Rochas Dos, Roofies, Rophies, Ropies, Row-Shay, Ruffies, Wolfies	None in U.S.	Moderate	Moderate	Yes		Oral, snorted	Drowsiness, sleep, amnesia, impaired mental functioning and judgment, confusion, slurred speech, loss of motor coordination, weakness, headache, respiratory depression		
Benzodiazepines	Schedule IV	Valium, Xanax, Halcion, Ativan, Restoril, Klonopin	Antianxiety, sedative, anticonvulsant, hypnotic, muscle relaxant	Moderate	Moderate	Yes	1–8	Oral, injected			
Other Depressants	Schedule I, II, III, IV	Ambien, Sonata, Meprobamate, Chloral Hydrate, Barbiturates, Methaqualone (Quaalude)	Antianxiety, sedative, hypnotic	Moderate	Moderate	Yes	2–6	Oral			

Stimulants

| Cocaine | Schedule II | Coke, Flake, Snow, Crack, *Coca, Blanca, Perico,* Nieve, Soda | Local anesthetic | Possible | High | Yes | 1–2 | Snorted, smoked, injected | Increased alertness, excitation, euphoria, increased pulse rate and blood pressure, insomnia, loss of appetite | Agitation, increased body temperature, hallucinations, convulsions, possible death | Apathy, long periods of sleep, irritability, depression, disorientation |

Drug	Schedule	Trade or Street Names	Medical Uses	Dependence Possible	Physical	Psychological	Duration (hours)	Usual Method	Effects	Effects of Overdose
Amphetamine	Schedule II	Adderall, Dexedrine, Desoxyn, Bennies, Black Beauties, Crank, Ice, Cristal, Krystal Meth, Speed, Uppers	Attention deficit/hyperactivity disorder, narcolepsy, weight control	Possible	High	Yes	2–4	Oral, injected, smoked		
Methamphetamine	Schedule II	Batu, Biker's Coffee, Black Beauties, Chalk, Chicken Feed, Crank, Crystal, Glass, Go-Fast, Hiropon, Ice, Meth, Methlies, Quick, Poor Man's Cocaine, Shabu, Shards, Speed, Stove Top, Tina, Trash, Tweak, Uppers, Ventana, Vidrio, Yaba, Yellow Bam	None		High	Yes		Oral, injected, smoked	Violent behavior, anxiety, confusion, insomnia, paranoia, aggression, visual and auditory hallucinations, mood disturbances, homicidal or suicidal thoughts, increased wakefulness, irregular heartbeat, increased blood pressure, hyperthermia (overheating), convulsions, cardiovascular collapse, extreme anorexia, memory loss, severe dental damage	Death from stroke, heart attack, or multiple organ problems caused by overheating

(Continues)

Table 12.5 Drugs of Abuse/Uses and Effects (Continued)

Drugs	Controlled Substances Act (CSA) Schedules	Trade or Other Names	Medical Uses	Dependence Physical	Dependence Psychological	Tolerance	Duration (Hours)	Usual Method	Possible Effects	Effects of Overdose	Withdrawal Syndrome
Methylphenidate	Schedule II	Ritalin (Illy's), Concerta, Focalin, Metadate	Attention deficit/ hyperactivity disorder	Possible	High	Yes	2–4	Oral, injected, snorted, smoked			
Khat	Schedule I, IV	Abyssinian Tea, African Salad, Catha, Chat, Kat, Oat	None in U.S.					Chewed, smoked, sprinkled on food	Grandiose delusions, paranoia, nightmares, hallucinations, hyperactivity, violence, suicidal depression		
Other Stimulants	Schedule III, IV	Adipex P, Ionamin, Prelu-2, Didrex, Provigil	Vasoconstriction	Possible	Moderate	Yes	2–4	Oral			
Bath Salts and Designed Cathinones (Synthetic stimulants)*	Chemical analog similar to Schedule I	Blue Silk, Cloud Nine, Drone, Energy-1, Ivory Wave, Lunar Wave, Meow Meow, Ocean Burst, Pure Ivory, Purple Wave, Red Dove, Snow Leopard, Stardust, Vanilla Sky, White Dove, White Knight, White Lightening	None					Oral, injected, sniffed, smoked	Agitation, insomnia, irritability, dizziness, depression, paranoia, delusions, suicidal thoughts, seizures, panic attacks, impaired perception of reality, reduced motor control, chest pains, nosebleeds, sweating, nausea	These substances are usually marketed with the warning "not intended for human consumption." Any time that users put uncontrolled or unregulated substances into their bodies, the effects are unknown and can be dangerous.	

* Even though some substances are not currently controlled by the Controlled Substances Act, they pose risks to those who abuse them.

Ecstasy/MDMA and Analogs	Schedule I	Adam, Beans, Clarity, Disco Biscuit, E, Eve, Go, Hug Drug, Love Drug, Lover's Speed, Peace, XTC	None	None	Moderate	Yes	4–6	Oral, snorted, smoked	Heightened senses, teeth grinding, dehydration	Increased body temperature, electrolyte imbalance, cardiac arrest	Muscle aches, drowsiness, depression, acne
K2/Spice	Schedule I	Bliss, Black Mamba, Bombay Blue, Fake Weed, Genie, Spice, Zohai	None					Oral (tea), smoked	Paranoia, panic attacks, giddiness, increased heart rate		
LSD	Schedule I	Acid, Boomers, Mellow Yellow, Microdot, Sunshine, Window Pane	None	None	Unknown	Yes	8–12	Oral	Illusions and hallucinations, altered perception of time and distance	Longer, more intense "trip" episodes	None
Ketamine	Schedule III	Cat Tranquilizer, Cat Valium, Jet K, Kit Kat, Purple, Special K, Special La Coke, Super Acid, Super K, Vitamin K	Anesthetic	Possible	High	Yes	<1 hour	Oral, injected, smoked, snorted	Feelings of disconnection, nausea, flashbacks	Unconsciousness and dangerously slowed breathing	
Phencyclidine and Analogs	Schedule I, II, III	PCP, Angel Dust, Hog, Loveboat, PCE, PCPy, TCP	None	Possible	High	Yes	1–12	Smoked, oral, injected, snorted	Unable to direct movement, feel pain, or remember	Drug-seeking behavior (not regulated)	

(Continues)

Table 12.5 Drugs of Abuse/Uses and Effects (*Continued*)

| Drugs | Controlled Substances Act (CSA) Schedules | Trade or Other Names | Medical Uses | Dependence | | Tolerance | Duration (Hours) | Usual Method | Possible Effects | Effects of Overdose | Withdrawal Syndrome |
				Physical	Psychological						
Other Hallucinogens	Schedule I	Psilocybe mushrooms, Mescaline, Peyote Cactus, Ayahuasca, DMT, Dextro-methorphan (DXM)	None	None	None	Possible	4–8	Oral			
Cannabis											
Marijuana	Schedule I	Pot, grass, Sinsemilla, Blunts, Mota, Yerba, Grifa	None	Unknown	Moderate	Yes	2–4	Smoked, oral	Euphoria, relaxed inhibitions, increased appetite, disorientation	Fatigue, paranoia, possible psychosis	Occasional reports of insomnia, hyperactivity, decreased appetite
Tetrahydro-cannabinol	Schedule I, Product III	THC, Marinol	Antinauseant, appetite stimulant	Yes	Moderate	Yes	2–4	Smoked, oral			
Hashish and Hashish Oil	Schedule I	Hash, Hash oil	None	Unknown	Moderate	Yes	2–4	Smoked, oral			
Anabolic Steroids											
Testosterone	Schedule III	Depo Testosterone, Sustanon, Sten, Cypt	Hypogonadism	Unknown	Unknown	Unknown	14–28 days	Injected	Virilization, edema, testicular atrophy, gynecomastia, acne, aggressive behavior	Unknown	Possible depression

Drugs	CSA Schedules	Trade or Other Names	Medical Uses	Physical Dependence	Psychological Dependence	Tolerance	Duration (hours)	Usual Method	Possible Effects	Effects of Overdose	Withdrawal Syndrome
Other Anabolic Steroids	Schedule III	Parabolan, Winstrol, Equipose, Anadrol, Dianabol, Primabolin-Depo, D-Ball	Anemia, breast cancer	Unknown	Yes	Unknown	Variable	Oral, injected			Agitation
Inhalants											
Amyl and Butyl Nitrite		Pearls, Poppers, Rush, Locker Room	Angina (Amyl)	Unknown	Unknown	No	1	Inhaled	Flushing, hypotension, headache	Methemoglobinemia	
Nitrous Oxide		Laughing gas, balloons, Whippets	Anesthetic	Unknown	Low	No	0.5	Inhaled	Impaired memory, slurred speech, drunken behavior, slow-onset vitamin deficiency, organ damage	Vomiting, respiratory depression, loss of consciousness, possible death	Trembling, anxiety, insomnia, vitamin deficiency, confusion, hallucinations, convulsions
Other Inhalants		Adhesives, spray paint, hair spray, dry cleaning fluid, spot remover, lighter fluid	None	Unknown	High	No	0.5–2	Inhaled			
Alcohol		Beer, wine, liquor	None	High	High	Yes	1–3	Oral			

Source: *Drugs of Abuse, 2011 Edition* (Washington, DC: Drug Enforcement Administration, 2011). Retrieved April 12, 2012 from http://www.justice.gov/dea/pubs/drugs_of_abuse.pdf.

Drug Abatement Statutes

Similar to legislation aimed at the gang problem, recent legislation, such as drug abatement statutes, is also helping in the war on drugs. Such legislation makes it much easier to shut down crack houses and clandestine drug laboratories.

> Drug abatement statutes declare any property where illegal drugs are used or sold to be a public nuisance.

Areas in which new legislation would help include drive-by shootings, witness protection programs, lowering age on juvenile offenses, continuing criminal enterprise, loitering, and pointing a weapon from a vehicle.

PREVENTION

Just as it is always preferable to prevent physical illness rather than treating it when it occurs, so it is always preferable to prevent a drug problem rather than treating it after the fact. One problem associated with drug abuse is the transmission of HIV infections when drug addicts share needles. Needle exchange programs (NEPs) have been found to significantly decrease the spread of HIV infections among intravenous drug users.

One effective way to approach prevention is to focus on known risks. The same factors placing youths at risk for joining gangs can also make them at risk for using drugs or alcohol. *Community risk factors* include extreme economic deprivation; low neighborhood attachment and community disorganization; transitions and mobility; community laws and norms favorable toward drug use, firearms, and crime; availability of firearms; and media portrayals of violence. *School risk factors* include early and persistent antisocial behavior, academic failure beginning in elementary school, and lack of commitment to school. *Family risk factors* include family history of problem behaviors, family management problems, family conflict, and unfavorable parental attitudes and involvement. *Individual and peer risk factors* include alienation and rebelliousness, early initiation of problem behaviors, friends who engage in problem behaviors, and favorable attitudes toward problem behaviors.

It is not enough to simply identify risks, however. Programs must also be put into place to keep youths from abusing drugs.

Educational programs such as D.A.R.E. were discussed in Chapter 11. A booklet, *The Coach's Playbook against Drugs* (n.d.), published by the OJJDP, is aimed at the coaches in youth athletic programs. Most coaches have special relationships with their athletes and can influence their thinking and behavior. The booklet provides a list of "do's and don'ts," as well as how the game will be affected and how team spirit will suffer.

Another approach might be to address what many see as flaws in current drug education programs. One such flaw is to equate drug *use* with drug *abuse*, using the terms interchangeably. But teenagers know the difference. Another flaw is the "gateway" theory, a mainstay of drug education, that use of marijuana leads to use of harder drugs such as cocaine. There is no research evidence to support this. These flaws conflict with what students observe and experience.

WHAT RESEARCH SAYS

Limited research has been done on what works and what doesn't. A review of the evaluation literature on drug law enforcement revealed five categories of intervention: (1) international/national interventions (e.g., interdiction and drug seizure), (2) reactive/directed interventions (e.g., crackdowns, raids, buy-busts, saturation patrol), (3) proactive/partnership interventions (e.g., third-party policing, problem-oriented policing, drug nuisance abatement), (4) individualized interventions (e.g., arrest referral and diversion), and (5) interventions that used a combination of reactive/directed and proactive/partnership strategies (Mazerolle, Soole, and Rombouts 2007b). This review found that "proactive interventions involving partnerships between the police and third parties and/or community entities appear to be more effective at reducing both drug and nondrug problems in drug problem places than are reactive/directed approaches" (Mazerolle, Soole, and Rombouts 2007b, 115).

McCabe (2008, 289) studied the relationship between serious crime, drug arrests, and nuisance abatement using data from New York City between 1995 and 2001, a period in which the city experienced a dramatic decrease in crime. One common explanation for this crime decrease is a version of Wilson and Kelling's broken windows theory. McCabe tested this theory using drug arrest and nuisance abatement closings as an approach to the drug problem. His research showed that the rate of marijuana arrests and the closing of drug locations through nuisance abatement statutes are inversely related to the crime rate and that the rate of controlled substance arrest is directly related to the crime rate.

As has been seen throughout this chapter, gangs and drugs are often a dual problem for communities. Following is an example of how problem-oriented policing has been used to address this dual challenge.

PROBLEM-ORIENTED POLICING AND DRUGS

The following example of problem-oriented policing was a finalist for the 2009 Herman Goldstein Award.

For more than three decades, the Terrace-Bedell neighborhood in the Village of Hempstead in Nassau County (New York) hosted a large open-air drug market plagued by violence. In 2007, 169 major crimes occurred in this six-block area, including 10% of the city's violent crime. The drug market survived three decades of law enforcement efforts. The county district attorney and the Village of Hempstead Police joined with the community to try a different approach designed by David Kennedy. Police gathered enough evidence for arrests of the 50+ principal drug dealers driving the open-air market, but for 18 dealers with no violent histories, a different community intervention was designed. The partnership resulted in the elimination of the drug market, an 87% reduction in narcotics activity, a 10% reduction in Part 1 crime, and a 74% reduction in overall crime in one year. From January to June 2009, there have been no drug arrests. The initiative resulted in building trust between the community and law enforcement allowing the district attorney to redefine her role to include meaningful prevention efforts that serve the community at-large ("Renaming Terror Avenue" 2012).

SUMMARY

The gang problem has increased during the past decade. The *National Gang Threat Assessment* classifies gangs as street gangs, prison gangs, and outlaw motorcycle gangs (OMGs). Gang members often engage in vandalism, drug dealings, larceny/theft, burglary/breaking and entering, aggravated assault, motor vehicle theft, and drive-by shootings. The first step in dealing with a gang problem is to recognize it. Once the problem is recognized, police need to identify gangs and their members. This is not difficult because most gang members identify themselves by their names, clothing, tattoos, sign language, slang, and graffiti.

Five general strategies are being used to deal with gang problems: (1) community mobilization, (2) opportunities provision, (3) social intervention, (4) suppression, which includes law enforcement efforts, and (5) organizational change and development.

Frequently, gangs and drugs are integrally related. Research supports the link between street-level drug hot spot activity, disorder, and serious crime. Approaches that have been suggested to address the drug problem include crime control, punishment, rehabilitation, prevention, and legalization.

Police often use simple drug buys, undercover operations, and raids to combat the drug problem. Buy operations occur in three well-defined stages: preparations for the buy, the buy itself, and actions needed after the buy to process evidence and information. Information and time are critical elements in an illegal drug buy. The sale and use of illegal drugs is difficult to investigate and prosecute because sellers and buyers are willing participants. Making several drug buys will protect against a claim of entrapment.

In combating the drug problem, law enforcement in the 1980s focused on undercover operations and sophisticated raids. In the 1990s, law enforcement focused on enlisting and educating the public and targeting street-level sales. That emphasis continues into the 21st century. Legislation may also help, such as drug abatement statutes, which declare any property where illegal drugs are used or sold to be a public nuisance.

APPLICATION

The chief wants you, the new commander of the narcotics squad, to establish some policies and procedures regarding drug buys. The present guidelines are obsolete. He instructs you to look at the previous general orders and policy and procedure bulletins and to upgrade the operations.

INSTRUCTIONS

Use the form in the Appendix. Identify the problems and needs. Specify what the policy is, why it is needed, and what the police department's responsibility is. In this set of policies and procedures, concentrate on only drug *buy* procedures. Include the preparation, intelligence, surveillance, the buy-money procedures, what to do during and after the buy, what to do when making arrests and processing evidence, and what the report should contain.

AN EXERCISE IN CRITICAL THINKING

On July 8, Mike O'Brien came to an apartment building with five minors to purchase marijuana from a minor who lived in the complex. A group of minors (gang members) was also present in the parking lot for the same purpose. A number of the youths congregated around O'Brien's car, a classic 1966 Chevrolet Impala that O'Brien was in the process of restoring.

Fred Fidel (a member of a rival neighborhood gang) pulled into the parking lot and attempted to pull his vehicle partway into the limited space next to O'Brien's car, almost hitting it. Although none of the building's tenants were assigned designated parking spaces, Fidel habitually parked in the spot directly adjacent to the spot in which O'Brien had parked and in which many of the youths were standing. Although other parking spaces were available, Fidel pulled up to the spot where the youths were standing and repeatedly honked his horn. At that time, O'Brien told Fidel, "If you scratch my car, I'll kick your ass."

Fidel got out of his car, entered into an altercation with O'Brien, and pulled out a knife, brandishing it back and forth in front of O'Brien. O'Brien initially backed away as Fidel walked toward him. Fidel got back into his car and attempted to pull further into the parking space. Fidel then got out of his car, leaving it in such a position that O'Brien would be unable to move his car to leave.

As Fidel walked toward the building, O'Brien went toward him, advising Fidel that he was blocking O'Brien's car and offering to move it for him. During this second confrontation, Fidel again pulled out his knife. O'Brien told him, "Back off; everything is cool." Fidel, however, grabbed O'Brien by the shirt with one hand as O'Brien tried to remove himself from Fidel's grasp and thrust the knife into O'Brien's chest with his other hand.

O'Brien was interviewed by police on the scene, but he bled to death before medical care could be administered. When Fidel was questioned by police, he at first denied possessing a knife or knowing anything about the stabbing. After a few minutes, he changed his account of the event and claimed self-defense.

1. Given the conflicting testimony between the members of the gang and Fidel, is there sufficient evidence to arrest Fidel for second-degree felony murder?

   a. Numerous witnesses give probable cause to believe that Fidel committed felony murder, and therefore, Fidel should be arrested.

   b. Because the only witnesses are juvenile gang members whose testimony is suspect, prosecution will be nearly impossible; therefore, Fidel's testimony should be recorded, but he should not be arrested.

   c. As Fidel clearly was outnumbered and likely felt insecure, he probably wanted only to intimidate O'Brien; so there is insufficient cause to arrest Fidel for second-degree felony murder.

   d. Because of the intended purchase of drugs, Fidel can be arrested for first-degree intentional murder.

   e. Because it is Fidel's word against the gang's, both negate each other, leaving insufficient evidence for arresting and convicting Fidel of second-degree felony murder.

DISCUSSION QUESTIONS

1. How might possible changes in the juvenile justice system be a deterrent to juveniles joining gangs?

2. Does your community have a gang problem? If so, describe it.

3. What role can citizens and community groups usefully play in coping with the drug problem?

4. What must officers consider when establishing a fictitious past for a cover story as an undercover agent?

5. As an undercover agent, if someone asks you if you are a "narc," how do you respond? What attitude will protect your safety?

6. Is drug dealing a problem in your educational institution? Your community?

7. What are some unobtrusive signals surveillance team members can use to cover such situations as when the buy has been completed, when help is needed, and so on?

GALE EMERGENCY SERVICES DATABASE ASSIGNMENTS

▶ Use the Gale Emergency Services database (available for separate purchase) to answer the Discussion Questions as appropriate.

▶ Using the Gale Emergency Services database, find and outline one of the following articles:

- "The Life Development of Gang Members: Interventions at Various Stages" by Mike Meacham and Tony Stokes
- "Street Gangs: Lessons from a Task Force" by Carole Moore
- "Street Gang Mentality: A Mosaic of Remorseless Violence and Relentless Loyalty" by Anthony J. Pinizzotto, Edward F. Davis, and Charles E. Miller III
- "Gangs in Indian Country: The Growing Phenomenon of Native American Gangs" by Liz Martinez
- "Understanding and Tackling Gang Violence" by Karen Bullock and Nick Tilley

- "Return to D.A.R.E.: Armed with Scientific Credibility, the New D.A.R.E. Program Makes a Comeback" by Michelle Perin
- "Jesus Malverde's Significance to Mexican Drug Traffickers" by Robert J. Botsch
- "An Analysis of Clandestine Methamphetamine Laboratory Seizures in Oklahoma" by Rashi K. Shukla and E. Elaine Bartgis
- "Assembling Recidivism: The Promise and Contingencies of Post-Release Life" by Mark Halsey
- "Implementing an Asset Forfeiture Program" by Victor E. Hartman
- "Connecting Drug Paraphernalia to Drug Gangs" by Robert D. Sheehy and Efrain A. Rosario

REFERENCES

"Almost 50% of Agencies Routinely Use K-9s." 2008. *Police* (March): 14.

"Asset Forfeiture Program." n.d. Washington, DC: U.S. Marshals Service.

Basich, Melanie. 2009. "Are Gang Members Hopeless Cases?" *Police Magazine* (May): 21–22.

Bell, Kerryn E. 2009. "Gender and Gangs: A Quantitative Comparison." *Crime & Delinquency* (July): 363–387.

The Coach's Playbook against Drugs. n.d. Washington, DC: Office of Juvenile Justice and Delinquency Prevention. (NCJ 173393)

"Combating the Stop Snitching Code of Silence." 2009. *Community Policing Dispatch* (July).

Commission on Accreditation of Law Enforcement Agencies (CALEA). 2012. *Standards for Law Enforcement Agencies.* 5th ed. Fairfax, VA: Author.

Decker, Scott H., Charles M. Katz, and Vincent J. Webb. 2008. "Understanding the Black Box of Gang Organization." *Crime & Delinquency* (January): 153–172.

Dedel, Kelly. 2007 (March). *Drive-By Shootings.* Washington, DC: Community Oriented Policing Services Office.

Dees, Tim. 2008. "Field Narcotics Testing." *Law Officer Magazine* (June): 74–79.

Egley, Arlen, Jr., and James C. Howell. 2011 (June). *Highlights of the 2009 National Youth Gang Survey.* Washington, DC: Office of Juvenile Justice Delinquency Prevention. (NCJ 233581)

Griffith, David. 2009. "Finding a Cure for a Cancer." *Police* (March): 14.

"Highlights of Gang-Related Legislation." 2011 (December). Tallahassee, FL: National Gang Center, Institute for Intergovernmental Research. Accessed April 11, 2012.

http://www.nationalgangcenter.gov/Legislation/Highlights.

Hill, Karl G., James C. Howell, J. David Hawkins, and Sara R. Battin-Pearson. 1999. "Childhood Risk Factors for Adolescent Gang Membership: Results from the Seattle Social Development Project." *Journal of Research in Crime and Delinquency* 36 (3, August): 300–322.

Hill, Karl G., Christina Lui, and J. David Hawkins. 2001 (December). *Early Precursors of Gang Membership: A Study of Seattle Youth.* Washington, DC: Office of Juvenile Justice and Delinquency Prevention. (NCJ 190106)

Howell, James C., Arlen Egley, Jr., George E. Tita, and Elizabeth Griffiths. 2011 (May). *U.S. Gang Problem Trends and Seriousness, 1996–2009.* Washington, DC: Institute for Intergovernmental Research (IIR) on behalf of the National Gang Center, National Gang Center Bulletin, No. 6.

Kanable, Rebecca. 2008. "Returning Results with FICO Programs." *Law Enforcement Technology* (November): 48–55.

Kennedy, David. 2009. "Drugs, Race and Common Ground: Reflections on the High Point Intervention." *NIJ Journal* (262, March): 12–17.

Klein, Malcolm W. 2007. *Chasing after Street Gangs: A Forty-Year Journey.* Upper Saddle River, NJ: Pearson/Prentice Hall.

Laine, Russell B. 2009. "A Crisis We Must Confront." *The Police Chief* (April): 6.

Langton, Lynn. 2010 (October). *Gang Units in Large Local Law Enforcement Agencies, 2007.* Washington, DC: Bureau of Justice Statistics. (NCJ 230071)

Laska, Paul R. 2011. "Suspicious Packages and Booby Traps." *Police* (May): 68–73.

Marizco, Michel. 2009. "Border Epidemic?" *Law Enforcement Technology* (February): 40–47.

Mazerolle, Lorraine, David W. Soole, and Sacha Rombouts. 2007a (July 22). *Crime Prevention Research Reviews No. 1: Disrupting Street-Level Drug Markets.* Washington, DC: Office of Community Oriented Policing Services.

Mazerolle, Lorraine, David Soole, and Sacha Rombouts. 2007b. "Drug Law Enforcement: A Review of the Evaluation Literature." *Police Quarterly* (June): 115–153.

McCabe, James E. 2008. "What Works in Policing? The Relationship between Drug Enforcement and Serious Crime." *Police Quarterly* (September): 289–313.

Melde, Chris, and Finn-Aage Esbensen. 2011. "Gang Membership as a Turning Point in the Life Course." *Criminology* 49 (2, May): 513–552.

Moore, Carole. 2007. "The ACLU Plays 'Go Fish.'" *Law Enforcement Technology* (November): 98.

National Drug Control Strategy 2011. 2011. Washington, DC: Office of National Drug Control Policy. (NCJ 234320)

National Drug Threat Assessment 2011. 2011 (August). Washington, DC: National Drug Intelligence Center.

National Gang Center. 2010 (October). *Best Practices to Address Community Gang Problems: OJJDP's Comprehensive Gang Model.* 2nd ed. Washington, DC: Office of Juvenile Justice and Delinquency Prevention. (NCJ 231200)

"National Gang Intelligence Center (NGIC) Unveils Online Tool to Share Intelligence and Assist Law Enforcement." 2012. *FBI Law Enforcement Bulletin* (February): 14–15.

National Gang Threat Assessment 2009. 2009. Washington, DC: U.S. Department of Justice.

"NYGC [National Gang Youth Center] Research Update." 2009. Accessed April 11, 2012. http://www.nationalgangcenter.gov/Content/Documents/Evaluation-Updates.pdf.

"National Youth Gang Survey Analysis." 2009. Washington, DC: Institute for Intergovernmental Research.

Petrocelli, Joseph. 2007. "Patrol Response to Street Corner Drug Dealing." *Police* (January): 20–22.

Petrocelli, Joseph. 2008. "Patrol Response to Graffiti." *Police* (March): 18–19.

Petrocelli, Joseph. 2009. "Patrol Response to Clandestine Meth Labs." *Police* (January): 14–17.

Pistole, John S. 2008 (March 3). "Major Executive Speeches." Washington, DC: Federal Bureau of Investigation.

Posey, Ed. 2008. "Using Existing Records to Keep a Closer Eye on Sex Offenders and Gang Members in the Community." *The Police Chief* (June): 38–47.

"Renaming Terror Avenue." Nassau County (New York) District Attorney's Office, Mineola, New York. Accessed April 12, 2012. http://www.popcenter.org/library/awards/goldstein/2009/09-52(F).pdf.

Rutledge, Devallis. 2011. "K-9 Drug Detection Cases." *Police* (January): 74–75.

Savelli, Lou. 2004. *Gangs across America and Their Symbols.* Flushing, NY: Looseleaf Law Publications.

The Stop Snitching Phenomenon: Breaking the Code of Silence. 2009 (June 15). Washington, DC: Community Oriented Policing Services Office.

Straub, Frank G. 2008. "Commissioner Frank Straub Testifies on Reducing Gang and Youth Violence." *Subject to Debate* (June): 1, 4, 5.

Taylor, Terrance J. 2008. "The Boulevard Ain't Safe for Your Kids … Youth Gang Membership and Violent Victimization." *Journal of Contemporary Criminal Justice* 24 (2): 125–136.

Tita, George, and Greg Ridgeway. 2007. "The Impact of Gang Formation on Local Patterns of Crime." *Journal of Research in Crime and Delinquency* (May): 208–237.

2011 National Gang Threat Assessment—Emerging Trends. 2011. Washington, DC: U.S. Department of Justice, National Gang Intelligence Center.

Weisel, Deborah Lamm. 2007 (June 12). *Graffiti.* Washington, DC: Problem-Oriented Policing Services Office.

"Welcome to the G.R.E.A.T. Web Site." 2012. Accessed April 11, 2012. http://www.great-online.org/.

Wethal, Tabatha. 2008. "Idle Hands." *Law Enforcement Technology* (July): 86–94.

Worrall, John L. 2008 (November). *Asset Forfeiture.* Washington, DC: Office of Community Oriented Policing Services.

CASES CITED

Chicago v. Morales, 527 U.S. 41 (1999)
Hampton v. United States, 425 U.S. 484 (1976)

CourseMate This available CourseMate has an interactive eBook and interactive learning tools, including flash cards, quizzes, and more. To learn more about this resource and access free demo CourseMate resources, go to www.cengagebrain.com, and search for this book. To access CourseMate materials that you have purchased, go to login.cengagebrain.com.

The Personal Side of Police Operations

Section I described the basic skills needed to perform the functions of today's law enforcement agencies legally and in the context of a changing society, while using discretion wisely. The need to protect the constitutional rights of all citizens, including those who commit crimes, was emphasized throughout Section I, as was the need to act professionally.

Sections II and III examined the basic police operations as well as specialized functions of police, still emphasizing the importance of respecting individual rights, of acting within the law, and of using discretion professionally.

This section examines the personal side of police operations even as it continues to stress the need for protecting the rights of others and for acting professionally. Today's officers face more stresses than ever before, so it is incumbent on them to be physically and mentally fit. The stresses of the job can be every bit as hazardous as a gun-wielding criminal (Chapter 13). The text concludes with two critical areas in law enforcement, avoiding civil liabilities and doing what is moral and right. Given the great amount of discretion officers have, it is crucial that they select alternatives that are legally and morally acceptable to themselves, their colleagues, and the public they serve (Chapter 14).

CHAPTER 13

The Importance of Physical and Mental Health:
Getting the Job and Keeping Fit for Duty

© Jonathan Newton/The Washington Post via Getty Images

POLICE INSTRUCTOR

DO YOU KNOW . . .

- What the police officer hiring process typically involves?
- What the prime factor in physical fitness is?
- What police-specific physical skills are important?
- What job-related factors detract from police officers' physical fitness?
- What constitutes an effective fitness program?
- What bloodborne pathogens police officers should protect against?
- What the concept of universal precaution recommends?
- What the greatest threat to officers' mental fitness is?
- What the major categories of stressors for police officers are?
- What the effects of stress might include?
- What the awareness spectrum is and where in that spectrum police officers should try to be?
- What the three sides of the border patrol's survival triangle are?
- What the five Cs of basic tactics for survival are?

CAN YOU DEFINE?

acute stress
aerobic training
anaerobic training
awareness spectrum
burnout
burst stress
chronic stress
cross-training
depression
mental fitness
physical fitness
split-second syndrome
survival triangle
universal precaution

INTRODUCTION

Police work has been characterized as long periods of devastating boredom punctuated by sporadic, relatively brief periods of utter terror. Quigley (2008, 62) notes, "Making split-second, life-saving decisions; facing inherent dangers; working shift work and long hours; and constantly interacting with people who are upset, angry, or uncooperative all take a toll on individuals." Much about the job, unfortunately, allows officers to become less physically and mentally fit than they were when they passed the rigorous preemployment screening. Murray (2007, 48) stresses, "Total preparation, in mind and body, prepares officers for physical encounters."

Physical and mental fitness are fundamentally related: mental discipline is needed to maintain or improve physical fitness, and mental alertness requires physical fitness. Physical and mental fitness also affect stress levels and officers' responses to stress. Furthermore, physical fitness, mental fitness, and adaptability to the stresses of police work are all correlated with officers' safety on the job—in effect, their very lives may depend on such physical and mental preparedness.

Although this chapter discusses physical fitness, mental fitness, stress, and officer safety as separate topics, their interrelationship must be kept in mind. The chapter begins with an overview of the police officer hiring process, as adequate mental and physical preparation is essential to getting the job. But the challenge does not end there—to keep the job and keep yourself healthy and sane, ongoing physical and mental health issues must be continually tended to. Thus, the discussion turns to physical fitness, including a look at physical fitness training programs and the health threats posed by bloodborne pathogens and biological and chemical agents. Next, mental fitness is explored, including an explanation of stress and employee wellness programs. The chapter concludes with a discussion of officer safety.

AN OVERVIEW OF THE POLICE OFFICER HIRING PROCESS

The decision to pursue a law enforcement career takes a considerable amount of introspection, self-evaluation, and preparation, both mentally and physically. The path is not one embarked on lightly, and applicants must be prepared for a rigorous test of their mental and physical fitness for duty.

Basic Standards

Each state and police agency has different standards. All states have minimum standards for peace officer licensing certification; however, each agency can have higher or stricter standards then their respective state minimum Peace Officer Standards and Training (POST) requirements. Applicants can find each state's standards by visiting the state POST site online. Individual agency standards may be posted on the department's Web site or may be obtained by contacting a recruiter or human resources officer within the agency or municipality.

Common standards include being 21 years of age or older and having at least a high school diploma or equivalent, as well as no criminal history and being of good moral character. From there, agencies may differ considerably in their hiring standards and employment requirements.

Common Steps in the Hiring Process

The process described here is intended to provide a comprehensive picture of the police officer hiring process. Readers should understand that individual agencies may deviate from this general guideline in the number or order of steps involved.

Application and Résumé Prospective officers very often must complete an application and may be required to submit a résumé and fill out additional supplemental questionnaires. Some agencies will post openings and accept applications for police officer positions only when there is an actual job opening available, and some agencies accept employment applications on an ongoing basis, regardless of immediate need. Typically, larger agencies accept applications on an ongoing basis.

Civil Service Exam and Fitness Test Candidates selected from the application pool will be notified of a time and date for a civil service examination and/or a fitness test. Many agencies consider it more efficient to conduct these two exams at the same time. The civil service examination typically covers police case law, state statutes, and other problem-solving scenarios. The written portion of the test can take several hours. The physical fitness test generally involves a series of physical agility tests to measure standardized fitness levels set by the state POST board or by the agency. Some of the most common physical tests include a timed mile-and-a-half run, push-ups, pull-ups, sit-ups, and an obstacle course that may have a dead-weight carry and wall.

Initial Oral Interview Applicants who successfully complete the previous stages may be invited back for an oral interview in front of a board that typically consists of police officers, human resources personnel, and high-ranking law enforcement administrators, and may include the chief of police. The questions asked often involve scenarios, candidates' personal experiences, and specific criminal justice and law-related knowledge.

Background Investigation and Polygraph Test Candidates who make it to this stage of the hiring process are those at the top level of the applicant pool and are being seriously considered for employment. This step involves an in-depth investigation into a candidate's background, requiring a substantial investment of an agency's time and resources. Candidates will be notified that they have moved on in the process and will be assigned a background investigator, typically a detective, from the interested agency. This phase can take anywhere from a week to several months, depending on the agency's background practice and other variables. An investigator will look into all aspects of a candidate's life to determine if the applicant is of good moral character and has the requisite qualities to be successful as a police officer. During this phase, the assigned investigator may also conduct a polygraph examination.

Psychological Test, Medical Examination, and Drug Screening Candidates who successfully pass the background investigation and polygraph test are then given a psychological examination, which typically takes several hours, and meet with a psychologist to discuss areas of interest or concern revealed during the background investigation. Candidates are also commonly required to submit to a routine physical examination by a medical doctor to ensure the applicant is in good physical health because the job can be physically straining. Often at this time, the applicant is required to provide a urine or blood sample for drug screening.

Secondary Oral Interview/Chief Interview and Conditional Offer Candidates who make it to this stage in the process are typically considered "finalists." Successfully completing the previous stages generally leads to a follow-up or secondary interview, which typically involves only the candidate and the head of the police agency or another high-ranking administrator. During this interview, the police chief may ask more personal questions in an effort to get to know the candidate better. At this time, the chief decides whether to present a conditional offer. If the offer is accepted, the candidate is hired on a probationary basis.

Academy Some agencies require applicants to have successfully completed an academy curriculum as part of their educational standards before the hiring process. Most agencies, however, have candidates go through the academy after the conditional job offer is given and accepted. Police academies can take anywhere from several months to a year. There are various types of academies—some require candidates to reside on site, and some allow candidates to return home daily, but all are based on some level of a paramilitary model. The academy teaches the candidates the relevant state laws and statutes, as well as tactics and skills, such as shooting, and other requirements necessary to work in the capacity of a police officer. At any time while enrolled at the academy, a candidate can be "released" or dismissed for employment for failing to pass certain standards. The environment teaches a wide array of skills but also places constant stress and pressure on candidates. Many candidates who have made it to this stage still fail out of the process.

FTO/Probationary Candidates at this level are at the final phase before tenure in the hiring process. After successfully completing the academy, the officer is assigned a field training officer (FTO), an experienced veteran officer whose job it is to show new recruits how to apply what they learned in the academy to the real world of policing. Some agencies have candidates rotate between several different FTOs during this time, to expose them to different styles of policing.

The FTO process typically involves three phases, beginning with the candidates riding along as observers and ending with the candidates doing the job, having the FTO as their shadows. During this time, the candidates are fully licensed working police officers with the authority and powers to enforce the laws. However, they are not on a permanent status of employment and can be released at anytime during this phase for failing to do the job successfully. The FTO portion can last from two to four months, depending on the agency. If the candidates successfully complete field training, they are released and can begin working as police officers in a full capacity. Again, depending on the agency, the rookie officer may work alone or may be paired with a partner, typically a veteran officer.

The new officer commonly remains on a conditional employment status for the duration of one year. If during this time officers fail to meet the standards of the department, they can be dismissed from employment. Upon completion of the probationary period, officers have full status and, typically, more job security.

Process Summary

The hiring process can be a long and tedious one. However, with high standards come good results. The job is challenging and provides considerable power of authority and great responsibility.

> The hiring process for police officers generally requires candidates to meet basic standards and successfully complete a series of steps, including submitting an application and résumé; taking a civil service exam and physical fitness test; going through an initial oral interview; passing a background investigation and polygraph test; completing a psychological test, medical examination, and drug screening; undergoing a secondary oral interview; receiving a conditional offer of employment; completing the police academy; going through field training; and surviving the probationary period, which typically lasts one year.

The need to hire and retain high-quality police officers to serve and protect the public demands that the standards for employment remain high. But getting the job is only the beginning. Officers must direct continuous attention throughout the duration of their law enforcement career to maintaining their physical and mental health.

PHYSICAL FITNESS

The United States has become fitness conscious. Visit almost any city and you can see joggers and runners, bikers and rollerbladers. Health and fitness clubs are a multimillion-dollar industry. Weight-loss programs have proliferated. Even fast food chains are now offering reduced-fat and fat-free items. People strive to be fit. **Physical fitness** is the body's general capacity to adapt and respond favorably to physical effort.

physical fitness

The general capacity to adapt and respond favorably to physical effort.

The demands of police work require officers to be in top physical condition. Physical fitness may make the difference between success and failure on the job and sometimes may even make the difference between life and death. Furthermore, officers who are not physically fit are not prepared to adequately discharge their duties and may, as a result, be sued. In *Parker v. District of Columbia* (1988), the jury awarded nearly half a million dollars to a man shot twice by a DC police officer during an arrest. The jury reasoned, "Had the officer been physically fit, ... he might have overpowered the suspect instead of reaching for his gun. The officer 'simply was not in adequate physical shape' to do his job." This is not an isolated case.

As one police academy trainer states in his first lesson to cadets: "When you decided to become a cop, you lost the right to be out of shape" (Bartlett 2011, 39). The FBI considers physical fitness so important that its National Academy at Quantico, Virginia, has made CJ340, "Fitness in Law Enforcement," the only required course for all police students attending (Grossi 2007). Fitness is also considered an ethical obligation to one's coworkers: "The uniformed officer simply must be fit enough to offer backup assistance to a fellow officer. If not, it is like showing up at a gunfight without a gun" (Sanow 2009, 95).

Consider the following definition of being *fit for duty*: "If an officer can safely perform his or her duties in an effective manner without jeopardizing his or her life or the lives of others, including other officers, bystanders, even subject and suspect, the officer is fit for duty" (Young 2008, 48). Agencies are encouraged to adopt a fit-for-duty statement supporting officer safety first and foremost: "Being fit for duty is not only an officer safety issue. It is the mark of a professional who is ready to fight to protect him- or herself, fellow officers, and the public" (Young 2008, 49). A study conducted in North Carolina showed impressive results among agencies that implemented fitness programs, including significant improvements in officers' strength and cardiovascular health, a degree of weight loss that allowed participants to stop taking medication for diabetes and hypertension, reduced absenteeism, a decrease in employee turnover, fewer accidents, reduced worker's compensation claims, and a 25-percent overall increase in productivity (Quigley 2008). Additional benefits include a more positive attitude among officers toward their jobs, reduced use of sick time, fewer job-related injuries, and a decrease in use-of-force issues.

Another important benefit of being physically fit is that, often, the mere appearance of fitness might deter an attack: "Offenders, especially desperate ones, size us up. A fit officer's appearance sends an unspoken message that challenging this officer might not be a good life choice" (Johnson 2009, 18).

Many people evaluate fitness on the basis of appearance alone. Although personal appearance can give certain indications of fitness levels, what is going on inside is more important. The prime indicators of physical fitness are endurance, balance, agility, flexibility, strength, power, and body composition.

> Although many factors contribute to a well-conditioned body, the prime factor is the condition of the circulatory (cardiovascular) system, upon which endurance or stamina depends.

Many agencies require active law enforcement officers to pass annual physical fitness tests to continue working in that capacity. Failure to pass may be grounds for dismissal from employment. The requirements of such tests are often similar to those used by the military and set different standards based on age and sex.

Many police departments are also now using body composition rather than height/weight charts in setting their physical standards. Excessive body fat hinders physical motion; it is also a serious risk factor for heart disease, diabetes, and stroke. In addition to the preceding factors involved in physical fitness, several other physical factors are related specifically to how well police officers perform.

Motor skills important to police officers include coordination, speed, and accuracy.

Myths about Physical Fitness

People hold many misconceptions about physical fitness, sometimes as excuses to avoid getting back into shape.

Too Far Gone Many people feel they either are too old or have physically deteriorated to such a degree it is impossible to get back into good physical shape. This is not true. Regardless of age or how "far gone" a person is, if the person is generally healthy and free of serious disease, he or she can become fit through a well-structured physical training program.

Hard Work Will Kill You A rather common misconception is that the harder you work, the quicker you die. This is false—just the opposite is true. People need to exercise regularly or they deteriorate. People "rust out" from inactivity far more than they "wear out" from hard physical work.

Any Kind of Exercise Is Good Again, this is not true. Different exercises and activities have varying degrees of value depending on their intensity, duration, and frequency. Short-duration exercising such as stretching or isometrics offers limited benefits. Likewise, an hour of racquetball, tennis, or softball every few weeks by a usually sedentary person offers only limited benefits and can be extremely dangerous. The most beneficial programs are those done regularly for at least 20 to 30 minutes and directed toward all aspects of total fitness.

Physical fitness may make the difference between success and failure on the job and may even make the difference between life and death.

© Michael Newman/PhotoEdit

No Pain, No Gain When people first begin exercise programs they often experience some stiffness and soreness, but such programs usually should not cause pain. This is not to imply, however, that getting and keeping physically fit is not hard work.

The Quick and Easy Way to Fitness Despite hordes of advertisements to the contrary, getting and keeping physically fit is hard work and requires commitment and discipline. It also takes time—weeks or months—to get into shape. Unfortunately, it takes much less time to get out of shape.

> Police work is often sedentary, is boring, involves irregular hours and rotating shifts, and may promote poor diets, excessive cigarette smoking and consumption of alcohol, and great amounts of stress.

Because of these factors, it is important that police officers engage in some sort of physical fitness training program.

Physical Fitness Training Programs

Because police officers often face situations involving physical restraint, self-defense, or foot pursuit, many police departments have set up both mandatory and voluntary physical fitness programs for officers: "A total fitness program incorporates the development of good lifestyle habits, including regular exercise, good nutrition, weight management, stress management, and substance abuse prevention" (Quigley 2008, 64).

Some agencies provide a "work out on duty" program that allows officers to exercise several times a week while on their regular shifts, if time permits. This is a benefit organizations use to recruit officers and to promote a healthy force. Many of the agencies that have on-site gyms also staff full-time registered dieticians and physical trainers for their officers. Other departments are able to arrange for discounted or fully paid memberships to local health and fitness centers. Law enforcement officers who are required to pass annual physical fitness standards can generally write off most exercise-related expenses for tax purposes. Furthermore, many agencies reward officers for exceeding physical fitness standards.

The kind of program instituted varies from department to department but should include **aerobic training** aimed at the cardiovascular system. This can be biking, cross-country skiing, rowing, swimming, or walking. It also can include treadmills, stationary cycles, and rowing machines. Aerobic training should be done at least three times a week for a minimum of 15 to 20 minutes. It should be preceded by a light warm-up and followed by a brief cooldown. Aerobic training can also incorporate **cross-training**, with an officer biking one day, running one day, and swimming one day.

Speed training should be incorporated into the aerobic portion of the exercise. Police officers are often older than the suspects they chase and are further hindered by the 20 or more pounds of weight added by their gun belts and accessories. Although speed is usually needed in a foot chase, agility is

aerobic training

Physical training aimed at strengthening the cardiovascular system.

cross-training

Alternating between different forms of exercise.

often even more important. Agility can be practiced on an obstacle course or through drills such as those football players use. Jumping rope is another way to improve agility. Eye-hand coordination can be improved through racquetball, tennis, basketball, and softball. Martial arts training can improve an officer's power, flexibility, speed, and balance.

Another important part of an exercise program is *strength training*, or **anaerobic training**. Strength training helps maintain muscle tissue. Strength exercises can also help reduce low-back problems. Aerobic activities do little in this area.

In addition, an officer's physical abilities are frequently tested in such activities as restraining a violent suspect, pushing a disabled vehicle, and lifting an injured person. Among the methods available for building strength are free weights and machines, which usually rely on "progressive resistance," and resistance against one's own body weight, which usually relies on "progressive repetition." Exercises using resistance against one's own body weight include push-ups, pull-ups, dips, and sit-ups.

Flexibility training is also important. This can be done as stretching in the warm-up and cool down portions of aerobic or strength training. Stretching reduces muscle tension, improves coordination, and can prevent injuries. Each stretch should be held for approximately 10 seconds. Breathing should be normal, and no bouncing should be done. It should *not* be painful. If a muscle is stretched to the point of pain, it is being stretched too far.

> An effective physical fitness training program that is varied and of interest to the officer should include aerobic, strength, and flexibility training. It should be engaged in regularly for 20 to 30 minutes a day, at least three days a week.

A 15-year study of physical fitness assessments, which included validation studies performed on more than 5,500 incumbent officers representing 75 federal, state, and local law enforcement agencies, sought to assess the accuracy of a physical fitness test as a predictor of an officer's ability to perform physical job tasks (Collingwood, Hoffman, and Smith 2004). The researchers (33) identified three basic events containing critical and frequent tasks:

1. Roadway clearance, involving lifting, carrying, and dragging debris, and pushing a car
2. Victim extraction, involving sprinting to a disabled vehicle and lifting and dragging a dummy to safety
3. Sustained foot pursuit, involving running up stairs, dodging, jumping, climbing a fence, crawling, vaulting obstacles, striking and moving a dummy, and simulated cutting using resistance bands

The researchers then isolated fitness factors and tests that might measure them. For example, a 1.5-mile run could be used to test the fitness factor of endurance and aerobic power, the vertical jump can test explosive leg strength, and the sit-and-reach test can test extent flexibility (Collingwood, Hoffman, and Smith 2004).

---

anaerobic training

Physical training aimed at strengthening the muscles of the body.

Other Aspects of Physical Fitness

Nutrition plays an important role in a person's overall fitness. Low-cholesterol, low-fat foods can reduce the risks of coronary artery disease (CAD), sometimes called coronary heart disease (CHD) or cardiovascular disease. Cardiovascular disease is the number-one killer of law enforcement officers, but making healthy nutrition choices can add years and quality of life well beyond retirement (Vonk 2009a). Although carbohydrates have been given a bad rap, they are the most important food group for emergency service professionals and athletes alike (Vonk 2009b). They allow officers to fight longer, deliver more powerful strikes, and think and respond more rapidly. Carbohydrates include fruits, vegetables, pasta, bread, rice, and potatoes.

Just as officers get ready for their tour of duty by checking their weapons and other equipment, they should also stock their squad car with appropriate snacks, as they might not get a chance to actually eat a meal. Recommended items include bottles of water, energy bars, trail mix, and bananas (Schreiber 2008). A detailed discussion of what constitutes proper nutrition is beyond the scope of this text. Hundreds, probably thousands, of books are available on the subject for those interested in learning more.

HEALTH HAZARDS

Garrett (2008, 46) reminds us of the obvious: "Police work is a high-risk occupation that often involves physical contact to subdue violent suspects or prisoners. But today's criminals bring more than a potential for violence to the streets, some also carry the silent and less obvious risk of unknown infections. Likewise, once officers restrain a subject, the danger is far from over. The infectious material these individuals transmit may continue to contaminate booking stations, holding cells, or incarceration facilities for some time to come."

> Bloodborne pathogens police officers should protect against include HIV infections and AIDS, hepatitis B, and hepatitis C.

HIV Infection and AIDS

Human immunodeficiency virus (HIV) is typically transmitted from one person to another, usually during unprotected sex or by sharing needles during IV drug abuse. HIV may also be transmitted through blood transfusions. Acquired immune deficiency syndrome (AIDS) is the end stage of HIV infection.

The potential for exposure to HIV/AIDS in police work remains minimal. However, civil liability may result when officers deal with suspects who have AIDS. A police department can be vulnerable both to internal and external civil claims. For example, in *Jane Doe v. Borough of Barrington* (1990), a city was held responsible for failing to adequately train its officers about AIDS, resulting in privacy right violations to the family of an HIV-positive arrestee. Likewise, in *Woods v. White* (1990), the court ruled that individuals have a constitutional right to privacy in information relating to AIDS. Another issue is whether offenders with HIV should be isolated.

The main concerns involve including HIV information in police reports and having officers disclose their own HIV status to coworkers and supervisors. Including a suspect's HIV status in a police report may violate medical information laws, but not including it may raise issues of why an officer acted in a certain way.

Hepatitis B Viral Infection

Hepatitis B viral infection affects the liver and poses a much greater risk than HIV. It can progress to chronic liver disease or liver cancer and death. Symptoms range from fever, aching muscles, and loss of appetite to prolonged nausea, vomiting, and yellowing of the skin (jaundice). Fortunately, a vaccine provides protection for nine years. Since 1992, the Occupational Safety and Health Administration (OSHA) has required law enforcement agencies to offer at no cost the vaccination against hepatitis B to all officers who may have contact with body fluids while on the job.

Hepatitis C Viral Infection

Hepatitis C virus also attacks the liver and is much more treacherous than hepatitis B. Unfortunately, there is no effective treatment or protective vaccine for this disease.

How Bloodborne Pathogens Are Spread

Hepatitis B, hepatitis C, and HIV infection are spread in the same way—through contact with blood, semen, vaginal secretions (sexual contact), and any other body fluid or tissue that contains visible blood. Infection can also occur through contact with the fluid that surrounds an unborn child and the fluid around the heart, lungs, or joints. Body fluids such as sweat, tears, saliva, urine, stools, vomit, nasal secretions, and spit have not been shown to transmit bloodborne diseases, unless they contain visible blood.

These viruses are not spread through the air like cold and flu germs, so contamination will not occur simply from working alongside someone who is infected, from touching them, or by being coughed or sneezed on by them, nor will infection occur from sharing telephones, bathrooms, eating utensils, gym equipment, swimming pools, or water fountains with an infected person.

Other Diseases

Tuberculosis (TB) is transmitted through the air by people who are coughing, hacking, and wheezing. Officers may encounter TB when dealing with people from other cultures, such as immigrants from African regions. *Meningitis* is also spread by airborne transmission. It causes inflammation of the membranes that surround the brain and can result in headaches, fever, vomiting, stiffness in the neck, light sensitivity, and death.

A particularly worrisome and growing health hazard is *methicillin-resistant staphylococcus aureus (MRSA) infection*: "MRSA ... pronounced 'mersa,' is an epidemic plaguing all law enforcement agencies and correctional facilities in the United States. The bacteria causes a drug resistant infection that is as effective as a bullet in wreaking pain, suffering, and even death, killing more than 100,000 people in U.S. hospitals alone every year" (Schneider 2007, 18). Although previously found primarily in hospitals, and still a threat to police officers who may spend their shifts in a hospital setting, guarding a hospitalized suspect or prisoner, the "superbug" is now also found in every area of law enforcement: "MRSA is a type of staph (bacteria) that may cause skin infections that often look like pimples, boils, a spider or other insect bites. These may be red, swollen, painful, and could have pus or other drainage. The infected area may also be warm to the touch and accompanied with a fever. What makes the MRSA type of staph so alarming is its resistance to detection and treatment, earning the moniker 'superbug'" (Haughton 2009, 39–40).

Protecting Oneself

OSHA has developed standards on bloodborne pathogens that require employers to address employee protection in a written exposure control plan describing precautions employees can take to prevent exposures as well as steps to take if exposure does occur. Precautions against bloodborne disease include getting the hepatitis B vaccine, treating all body fluids as infectious (a practice referred to as *universal precaution*), wearing appropriate personal protection equipment (PPE), thoroughly washing your hands and other exposed parts of your body after every personal contact, following department protocol after every exposure (e.g., get tested), and documenting and reporting all exposures.

> The concept of **universal precaution** recommends that all blood and potentially infectious materials other than blood must be treated as if infected.

universal precaution

All blood and potentially infectious materials other than blood must be treated as if infected.

Proper personal hygiene is important, including effective hand washing, showering before leaving work, and having uniforms cleaned at work instead of at home. In addition, the property room and vehicles should be sterilized and disinfected. Numerous sterilizing and disinfecting technologies are now available.

Cuts, scrapes, and puncture wounds can all become infected and should be thoroughly washed and bandaged as soon as possible. Several self-sealing cut closure strips, bandages, and similar products are available for wound care and should be included in an officer's first-aid kit. Avoid sharing personal items, such as towels, washcloths, razors, clothing, or uniforms that may have had contact with an infected wound or bandage (Schneider 2007).

Officers can also become infected from human bites. An officer who is bitten by a human should wash the wound immediately and then see a doctor for the appropriate antibiotics. An officer who is bitten by an animal should impound the animal if possible and have it tested for rabies.

The *tetanus shot* is an important safeguard against infections and should be repeated every 10 years. If, however, a deep or dirty wound is sustained, a tetanus shot should have been given within the last 5 years.

Biological and Chemical Threats

The potential threat of chemical, biological, and other unconventional weapons has increased on the local, state, and federal levels and should be prepared for. Responding to hazardous materials (hazmat) incidents was discussed in Chapter 5.

Keys to Preventing Infections and Other Health Hazards

The FBI's *Handbook of Forensic Services* (Waggoner 2007, 150–152) begins its discussion of protective measures by noting that the concept of following universal precautions is the primary mechanism for infection control. Other protective measures include the following:

▶ Use barrier protection—such as disposable gloves, coveralls, and shoe covers—if contact with potentially infectious materials may occur. Change gloves when torn or punctured or when their ability to function as a barrier is compromised. Wear appropriate eye and face protection to protect against splashes, sprays, and spatters of potentially infectious materials.

▶ Wash hands after removing gloves or other personal protective equipment. Remove gloves and other personal protective equipment in a manner that will not result in contaminating unprotected skin or clothing.

▶ Prohibit eating, drinking, smoking, or applying cosmetics where human blood, body fluids, or other potential infectious materials are present, regardless of personal protection that may be worn.

▶ Place contaminated sharps in appropriate closable, leakproof, puncture-resistant containers when transported or discarded. Label the containers with a BIOHAZARD warning label.

▶ Do not bend, re-cap, remove, or otherwise handle contaminated needles or other sharps.

▶ After use, decontaminate equipment with a daily prepared solution of household bleach diluted 1:10 or with 70-percent isopropyl alcohol or other appropriate disinfectant. Noncorrosive disinfectants are commercially available. It is important to allow sufficient contact time for complete disinfection.

▶ In addition to universal precautions, engineering controls and prudent work practices can reduce or eliminate exposure to potential infectious materials. Examples of engineering controls include long-handled mirrors used to locate and retrieve evidence in confined or hidden spaces and puncture-resistant containers used to store and dispose of sharps and paint stirrers.

Specialized, easily donned protective gear is also available for certain high-risk situations. For example, police-grade Kevlar-lined gloves may be used when searching suspects, especially in drug-related incidents.

MENTAL FITNESS

The ever-present threat of physical injury and infection goes hand-in-hand with the police profession and can cause significant stress and anxiety in officers. A crucial strategy to effectively handle this stress and the physical demands of the job is to pay adequate attention to mental fitness. Mental fitness is not as easily perceived or analyzed, but it is equally as important as physical fitness. In fact, "Research and literature have helped to identify that police work can prove more emotionally dangerous than physically threatening" (Patton 2011, 16). **Mental fitness** refers to a person's emotional well-being—the ability to feel fear, anger, compassion, and other emotions and to express them appropriately. It also refers to a person's alertness and ability to make decisions quickly.

> The greatest threat to officers' mental fitness is negative stress.

mental fitness

A person's emotional well-being—the ability to feel fear, anger, compassion, and other emotions and to express them appropriately; also refers to a person's alertness and ability to make decisions quickly.

STRESS

Most people have a general idea of what stress is. Most people also perceive stress as negative, but this is not necessarily true. A certain amount of stress keeps people alert and functioning. Too much stress, or *distress*, however, can be incapacitating. In ancient China, the symbol for *stress* included two characters—one symbolizing danger, the other opportunity.

Stress may be acute or chronic. **Acute stress** is temporary and may result in peak performance. Adrenaline rushes through the body; heart rate increases; blood pressure, brain activity, breathing rates, and metabolic rates increase—adapting the body for fight or flight. Thousands of years before we became "civilized," our bodies were faced with simple survival, for which either a "fight or flight" response was appropriate.

Chronic stress, in contrast, is ongoing, like being under a state of constant siege. This can lead to severe psychological problems. In his classic work *The Stress of Life* (1956), Dr. Hans Selye suggested that humans subjected to excessive stress undergo a "general adaptation syndrome" consisting of three distinct stages: alarm reaction, resistance, and exhaustion. In the first stage, *alarm reaction*, individuals perceive a threat to their safety or happiness. They recognize their inability to reach their personal or professional goals. The body releases stress hormones. In the second stage, *resistance*, individuals try to cope with the problem. The amount of resistance to the stressors increases, and bodily defense mechanisms are activated. In the third stage, *exhaustion*, individuals feel helpless and hopeless. Bodily resources are also exhausted, and people cannot adequately defend against the stressors.

acute stress

Temporary stress that may result in peak performance; body adapts for fight or flight.

chronic stress

Ongoing, continuous stress; like being under a state of constant siege; can lead to severe psychological problems.

Sources of Stress

Many lists of stressors have been generated, including stressors specific to the police profession. Most of the stressors fall into four main categories, although some overlap exists.

> Sources of stress for police officers include:
> - Internal, individual stressors.
> - Stressors inherent to the police job.
> - Administrative and organizational stressors.
> - External stressors from the criminal justice system and the citizens it serves.

Internal, Individual Stressors Internal stressors vary greatly and can include officers' worries about their competency to handle assignments as well as feelings of helplessness and vulnerability. Mandatory training, court duty, shift work, and overtime can leave police officers feeling trapped in a profession that does not allow room for family and recreational pursuits. Duty-related tasks can occupy so much time that an officer's home life suffers. Shift work may cause officers to routinely miss anniversary or birthday celebrations; their children's concerts, sports activities, and school open houses; and other important family functions. This dearth of time for personal development can translate into divorce, suicide, alcoholism, or burnout.

Vernon (2009, 48) identifies what he calls perhaps the most dangerous condition in law enforcement: the "Knights of the Roundtable Syndrome." Noting that many officers refer to police work as "The Job," Vernon describes how, as part of the syndrome, The Job takes central priority in an officer's life, providing a sense of purpose, significance, and fulfillment, to the detriment of everything else: "We can neglect other very important responsibilities and relationships— *even with our own families.*" He cautions, "It's possible for [officers] to finish their career with no family, no friends—other than a few other cops—and no outside interests. And when The Job ends, as it must, there's nothing."

To avoid this situation, Vernon recommends officers recognize the hazard and actively consider the impact being a police officer has on friends and family. For example, officers might arrange a shift change with a cooperative partner to be able to attend a family function (if department policy allows): "The key is balance. We should do our best in this most significant responsibility, but it should not consume one's life" (Vernon 2009, 48).

Stress Related to Police Work The police role itself is often vague and contradictory. Many people become police officers to fight crime, not to do social work or spend hours writing reports. Officers are surprised to see how much "service" is actually involved in police work and how much time is spent documenting incidents and actions. They are also surprised to learn that their efforts are often not appreciated and that, in fact, their uniform is an object of scorn and derision.

The media often present a distorted view of police work and police officers, resulting in unrealistic expectations by many citizens. Further, the distorted image is displayed repeatedly. Approximately one-third of regular television programming deals with some aspect of the criminal justice system. Citizens come to wonder: If a TV cop can solve three major crimes in an hour, why can't the local police at least keep prostitutes off the street or find the person who vandalized the school?

The police badge may weigh only a few ounces, but it carries a heavy weight for those who wear it. They need to be in constant emotional control. And they experience what is referred to as **burst stress**, that is, having to go from relative calm to high intensity, sometimes life-threatening, activity. This is closely related to what Fyfe (1986) refers to in his classic **split-second syndrome** that affects police decision making in crisis. In such situations, all that can reasonably be asked is that officers respond quickly and that a high percentage of inappropriate decisions should be expected and accepted. The split-second syndrome asserts that if a person has intentionally or unintentionally

burst stress

Having to go from relative calm to high intensity, sometimes life-threatening activity.

split-second syndrome

In some circumstances, officers have very little time to think through decisions; a high percentage of inappropriate decisions should be expected and accepted because the officer must act quickly.

provoked or threatened a police officer, at that instant the provoker rather than the police should be viewed as the cause of any resulting injuries or damages.

Every day officers are ready for the dangers and rigors of the job. When they go off duty, their bodies need downtime, yet day-to-day activities require them to continue pushing their bodies. A common result is fatigue, a dangerous and costly hazard of police work: "Sleep-loss-related fatigue degrades performance, productivity, and safety as well as health and well-being. Fatigue costs the U.S. economy $136 billion per year in health-related lost productivity alone" (Vila 2009, 26). Surveys have found that more than 90 percent of responding officers reported being routinely fatigued, and 85 percent reported driving while drowsy (Vila 2009). Research has attempted to quantitatively assess the dangerousness of sleep deprivation by comparing it with drunk driving. One study found that being awake for 19 hours produces impairments comparable to having a blood alcohol concentration (BAC) of 0.05 percent; being awake for 24 hours is comparable to having a BAC of roughly 0.10 percent (Vila 2009). It is a crime to drive with a BAC of 0.08 percent or above in all 50 states.

Several practices that contribute to the problem of line officer fatigue include secondary employment, overtime, court appearances, and commuting. Although research has documented the reality of a tired workforce, it has also revealed a low-level desire among agency chiefs to have fatigue reduction policies (Senjo and Dhungana 2009).

In addition to fatigue, shift work is associated with other complicating factors. Shift work may contribute to isolation from family and friends as previously noted, as well as contribute to the "blue wall" and "code of silence" perceptions some have. Monthly shift rotations necessitate physical adaptations such as getting used to sleeping different hours, as well as adaptations in officers' social and personal lives. Other stressors inherent in police work include constant threats to safety, such as entering dark buildings in which armed suspects are believed to be hiding and high-speed pursuits; continual exposure to victims in pain as well as unsavory criminals; the immense responsibilities of the job; the authorization to take a life; the ability to save a life; and the need to remain detached yet be empathetic.

Administrative and Organizational Stressors Many management practices and organizational factors can cause stress specific to law enforcement. Stress frequently arises from having to operate from a set of policies and procedures drawn up by individuals who do not have to carry them out. Seldom is the on-the-line officer's opinion on operational policies and procedures sought, even though the individual officer must carry out these policies and procedures.

Researchers have found that the bureaucratic and organizational aspects of police work are actually more stressful than critical incidents are (Best 2009). A PoliceOne poll ("P1Poll" n.d.) revealed that the biggest pet peeve about police work was the bureaucracy (50 percent), followed by lack of funds and outmoded equipment (28 percent). Other sources of administrative and organizational stress include lack of support from administration when a questionable action is taken, the unavailability of needed resources, excessive paperwork, adverse work schedules, unfair discipline, and lack of training and promotional opportunities. The Commission on Accreditation of Law Enforcement Agencies (CALEA) Standard 33 addresses training and career development.

33 CALEA Standard 33 states, "Training has often been cited as one of the most important responsibilities in any law enforcement agency. Training serves three broad purposes. First, well-trained officers are generally better prepared to act decisively and correctly in a broad spectrum of situations. Second, training results in greater productivity and effectiveness. Third, training fosters cooperation and unity of purpose... .

"Career development is a structured process that is utilized by an agency to provide opportunities for individual growth and development at all levels. It is designed to promote productive, efficient, and effective job performance and to improve the overall level of individual job satisfaction."

Source: Commission on Accreditation of Law Enforcement Agencies (CALEA). 2012. *Standards for Law Enforcement Agencies.* 5th ed. Fairfax, VA: Author.

If an agency does not provide effective training and opportunities for growth and development that might lead to promotion, this can certainly cause additional stress for individual officers.

Stressors Related to the Criminal Justice System and Society The criminal justice system and society at large also can induce stress in police officers. Officers are often faced with the court's scheduling of police officers for appearances, prosecutors' decisions not to prosecute a case, defendants "getting off" because of a loophole in the law, the court's perceived leniency, the early release of offenders on bail or parole, corrections' failures to rehabilitate criminals resulting in "revolving door" justice, the exclusion of police officers when plea bargaining is used, and the perceived lack of appreciation for the role of law enforcement.

Effects of Stress

Chronic stress can result in high blood pressure, heart disease, chronic headaches, and gastric ulcers. Other physical effects of stress are chronic back pain, tension headaches, neck pain, gastrointestinal distress, chest pain, skin rashes, and hives. Some disorders such as constipation, heartburn, irritable bowel syndrome, and stomach ulcers can be made worse by stress. Stress can also lead to severe depression, alcohol and drug abuse, aggression, and suicide.

 Police officers tend to have high rates of alcoholism, divorce, posttraumatic stress disorder, burnout, depression, and suicide, often related to the stress of the job.

Whether police divorce and alcoholism rates are higher than such rates for people in other professions is open to question. It is known, however, that the police job seriously interferes with officers' social and home lives, that many officers take their jobs home with them, that spouses worry about the officers' safety, and that rotating shifts make normal social life difficult. Some authorities feel that police suicides are underreported because fellow officers are usually the first on the scene and may cover up the suicide to save the family further pain or embarrassment or for insurance purposes. Police suicide is discussed shortly. It is also clear that stress usually results in other forms of behavior changes.

> Devastating psychological effects of stress include posttraumatic stress disorder, burnout, depression, and suicide.

Posttraumatic Stress Disorder (PTSD) Posttraumatic stress disorder (PTSD) may occur when an individual's life or the life of someone close to him or her has been threatened or from any event that is truly traumatic to the individual. PTSD may cause officers to miss work or lose their jobs entirely. It can ruin marriages and other relationships. This condition was initially discussed in Chapter 8, but one aspect of PTSD that was not covered was how survival stress can affect post-event memory. Officers need to be educated that after a deadly force encounter, their statements may be only a "best guess," as they fill in the blanks in their memory with how they think they must have acted: "In most traumatic and stressful situations, there is usually a sensory overload during which law enforcement officers will experience memory loss; the greater the stress, the greater the potential for memory problems ... Immediately after the incident, there will be post-incident amnesia, with most of the observed information forgotten. The best memory recovery will take place after a healthy night's sleep" (Weiss and Davis 2009, 70).

Burnout When stress continues unremittingly for prolonged periods, it can result in the debilitating condition referred to as *burnout*. **Burnout** has occurred in a person who is "used up," showing a persistent lack of energy or interest in his or her job caused by overwork and stress: "Job burnout is a physical and mental state caused by severe strain placed on the body until all resources are consumed" (Carlton 2009, 66). Strategies to prevent burnout, or to fight it off should it begin to show signs of occurring, include keeping the body healthy, staying fit, watching work hours, talking about it, varying assignments, taking time off, and accentuating the positive aspects of the job (Carlton 2009).

    Unfortunately, burnout generally happens only to those who are initially "on fire"—that is, to enthusiastic, highly productive workers. As one officer said, "I just couldn't go on. It seemed that there was nothing inside of me to keep me going. I couldn't look at one more dead body, one more abused child, or handle one more domestic fight. I'd just had it." Officers who are burned out are at extremely high risk of being injured or killed on duty because they are usually not safety conscious. They are also at risk for depression or suicide.

Depression **Depression** is a serious, life-threatening medical illness. Anyone can be affected, and police officers are no exception. Unfortunately, some in our society stigmatize having depression or seeking help for it.

    Because depression is a medical illness, an imbalance of chemicals in the brain, medication can often be prescribed to treat it. But frequently people do not recognize the symptoms, which can include significant changes in appetite and sleep patterns, irritability, anger, worry, loss of energy, persistent

burnout

Condition experienced by a person who is "used up or consumed by a job," made listless through overwork and stress; the person lacks energy or has little interest in work.

depression

A serious and life-threatening medical illness.

lethargy, feelings of worthlessness or hopelessness, indecisiveness, lack of interest in hobbies, indifference, excessive consumption of alcohol or drugs, and recurring thoughts of death or suicide. The difficulty lies in getting people to recognize the symptoms and to seek treatment. Depression must be treated because it is one of the leading causes of suicide.

Officer Suicide   Alcohol, family problems, the breakup of relationships, and stress all contribute to the high rate of police suicide, about 30 percent higher than what is found in the general population. The stigma attached to suicide can be so great that friends and family members of the person who committed suicide are embarrassed or ashamed to discuss it. Thus, suicide isn't talked about, but every law enforcement officer, supervisor, and administrator needs to know about it.

Help for those at risk of suicide within the department includes counseling units, peer counseling groups, and police chaplains. Outside the department, help might be sought from physicians, priests, ministers, rabbis, attorneys, family, and friends. The Police Suicide Prevention Center's Web site features information about suicide, suicide prevention, and related subjects, as well as links to suicide prevention and mental health sites.

Reducing Stress

Many books and articles deal with stress reduction. Good nutrition and exercise can help. So can taking time for oneself, relaxing, meditating, going for a walk, or finding a hobby. Perhaps the most important step to take for reducing law enforcement-related stress is to have something outside of policing. Leave the stress at work. Have friends outside of the job; regularly spend time with family away from work. Too often law enforcement becomes an individual's identity, and officers live the lifestyle in its entirety. This can be dangerous for those officers because they will not receive certain basic needs from the job alone.

EMPLOYEE WELLNESS PROGRAMS

Many police departments have established an *employee wellness program* (EWP), sometimes referred to as an *employee wellness plan*, geared to helping their officers combat the physical and emotional problems that often come with the stress of the job. Such programs are absolutely essential for officers and agencies alike: "If developed and implemented properly, an EWP improves recruitment and retention, enhances job satisfaction, and reduces employee absenteeism" (McDonough 2011, 1).

Such programs may offer help pertaining to postshooting trauma, alcoholism, drug abuse, marital or other family difficulties, difficult relationships with fellow officers or supervisors, trauma associated with the catastrophic death of a child or spouse, debt management, gambling, staying fit on the job, issues associated with layoffs because of budget cuts, and adjustment to retirement.

Professional counseling, peer counseling, police-spouse support groups, and the like can do much to improve the work climate and productivity of a law enforcement agency. Some advocate that departments take a proactive approach by creating a wellness guide to prepare recruits for the types of violence and other traumatic events ("toxins") they are likely to encounter while performing their police duties: "This material should ... explain, in detail, the long-term, daily exposure to these toxins in police work and how they can lead to burnout and other adverse effects. Additionally, the guide should offer strategies to counter the negative influences pervading police ranks and promote healthy lifestyle choices, such as proper fitness and nutrition" (McDonough 2011, 4).

ADDITIONAL CONSIDERATIONS IN OFFICER SAFETY AND SURVIVAL

A physically and mentally fit officer is a much safer officer. However, officers can do even more to ensure their safety on the job.

Avoiding Complacency

After being in police work for a few years, officers often come to feel invincible, having what is called the "it won't happen to me" syndrome. This is known as the *complacency period*, and it usually happens when officers are four to six years into their policing career. Statistically, most law enforcement officer deaths occur during this time frame. Although they see people all around them being victimized, officers often live in denial that they can become victims themselves. This attitude lulls them into a false sense of security. It is easy for officers to fall into complacency and get lazy with tactics and safety habits. However, such laziness can be fatal: "In most of the situations we encounter on the job, nothing bad happens. As a result, we don't experience a negative consequence from using tactics that we know are unsafe.... The primary reason that we do things we know are tactically unsound is simple: We get lazy. It takes more effort to use good tactics. Tactical laziness gets more officers shot than any other preventable cause" (Webb 2011, 56).

Maintaining Situational Awareness

Most officers injured or killed in the line of duty could have either avoided the confrontation or minimized the injury had they been mentally prepared for the danger, alert, and trained in the proper survival techniques.

> The **awareness spectrum** describes an officer's level of awareness, ranging from environmental unawareness to panicked/blacked out/ perhaps dead. Ideally, officers will be between these two stages—alert but relaxed.

awareness spectrum

Framework for describing an officer's level of awareness, ranging from environmental unawareness to panicked/ blacked out/perhaps dead; ideally, officers will be between these two stages—alert but relaxed.

A frequently taught variation of a situational awareness spectrum is the Cooper Awareness Scale, which instructs that learning to actively observe the environment, constantly evaluate it, and formulate appropriate reaction plans to the observations by shifting up and down a scale of readiness, can enable one to achieve a greater degree of control over one's own fate. At one end of the scale is "Condition White"—a state of obliviousness, when people are "preoccupied" with their thoughts such that they are unaware of the happenings around them and not alert to any changes in their environment. To the question, "When is it acceptable to be in Condition White?," Givens (2004) answers,

"When in your own home, with the doors locked, the alarm system on, and your dog at your feet. Then, you can turn off your mind, if you wish, because you have sufficient layers of protection and warning to enable you to get up, get your gear, and get your head running. If you leave your home, you leave Condition White behind. The instant you leave your home, you escalate one level, to Condition Yellow."

Condition Yellow is "a relaxed state of general alertness, with no specific focal point. You are not looking for anything or anyone in particular; you simply have your head up and your eyes open .... You are difficult to surprise, therefore, you are difficult to harm. You do not expect to be attacked .... You simply recognize the possibility" (Givens 2004). Condition Orange is "a heightened state of alertness, with a specific focal point. The entire difference between Yellow and Orange is this specific target for your attention" (Givens 2004). Finally, Condition Red is being mentally prepared for conflict and ready to fight, regardless of any actual action taken.

Givens (2004) stresses, "Your main enemy is reaction time. If you are not aware of your surroundings, and fail to see the suspicious character, he may overwhelm you before you can marshal an effective defense.... If you're caught in Condition White, you will need five to six seconds to realize what is happening, get your wits together, and respond. You simply don't have that much time." Officers who fail to prepare adequately for a deadly encounter, either mentally or physically, will likely find themselves in Condition Black, a catastrophic breakdown in performance in which the mind is overwhelmed and the body fails to deliver a successful defensive reaction.

Officers can improve their mental preparedness by running possible scenarios in their minds during downtime: "You can mentally respond to an active shooter at the local high school, a barricaded subject in the courthouse, an assault in progress at a residence, or a silent alarm at a bank. You mentally can process your response to a driver with a gun getting out of a vehicle during a traffic stop or your safe approach to respond to a report of shots fired" (Lohner 2011, 20–21).

TECHNOLOGY IN POLICING

THE DANGERS OF TECHNOLOGY

Many law enforcement agencies spend a great deal of resources on the high-liability aspects of policing, such as shooting proficiency, handling combative subjects, and emergency driving skills, yet they neglect to address the more routine threats faced every day. Ironically, "In today's world, one of the biggest unrecognized threats to officer safety and survival is technology. There is no denying that the use of technology has made an officer's life more efficient. But that efficiency has come at an overlooked price: compromising aspects of the officer's safety. The downside to technology is that it creates an inherent loss in environmental awareness" (Murgado 2011, 16).

Examples of digital distractions include typing on an in-car mobile data computer (MDC) while driving; calling and texting on cell phones; and using an in-car ticket printer: "It's already bad enough that officers pay more attention to their MDC instead of to the passengers in the car they stopped. There have been instances where suspects have escaped unnoticed" (Murgado 2011, 18). The obvious danger is that officers have limited to no peripheral vision when they focus all of their attention on a computer or printer monitor, leaving them vulnerable to attack in their vehicles.

Recognizing Indicators of Aggression

Among officers' survival skills is the ability to recognize the indicators of aggression—to be prepared for an attack before it happens. Among the common indicators of aggression are the folded-arm stance, hands on hips, an invasion of personal space, finger pointing, wandering attention, ignoring verbal commands, pacing, standing with fists clenched, and talking through clenched teeth: "Pre-fight tensions will cause jaw muscles to bulge, fists to close, and facial muscles to contract" (Glennon 2008). Other "telegraphed" indicators of hostile intent include:

▶ *Scanning*, where the subject is paying attention to the surrounding area rather than the interviewer, looking for the officer's backup, witnesses, escape routes, or even his own buddies.

▶ The *target glance*, which refers to the obvious preoccupation an offender has with a particular area of an officer's body or with any of the officer's weapons. One of the most common target glances involves the suspect eyeing an officer's gun, perhaps considering a "gun-grab."

▶ *Eye blinks,* because under stress, people will either blink very rapidly or very slowly.

▶ The *pugilistic stance*, or fighting stance, where one leg and side of the body (usually the strong side) is dropped behind the other. Any shifting of the weight or stance may be a significant indicator of an impending attack.

Paying attention to such indicators is critical to officer safety, indeed, sometimes to officer survival (Glennon 2008).

Part of being alert is being aware of objects that can pose a danger to police officers. A crucial axiom among officers is "hands kill." Be sure you can always see subjects' hands and anything they may be holding. Many everyday items can be used as dangerous weapons, for example, a ball point pen or a plastic straw can serve as a knife, a tightly rolled newspaper or magazine can serve as a baton, and a set of keys firmly locked between the fingers and raked across exposed skin can serve as brass knuckles.

Safe Driving

Driving is the most dangerous activity police officers perform (LaTourrette 2011). Official data indicate that automobile and motorcycle accidents accounted for approximately 46 percent of law enforcement fatalities in 2010; 7 deaths were classified "felonious," and 52 were "accidental" (*Law Enforcement Officers Killed and Assaulted 2010*). One common-sense approach to reducing these statistics is to insist that officers wear their seat belts, but many agencies do not have such a policy. Examination of pursuit policies might be another approach to reducing vehicle-related fatalities.

The Border Patrol's Survival Triangle

Another approach to officer safety and survival is suggested by the Border Patrol's "survival triangle," illustrated in Figure 13.1.

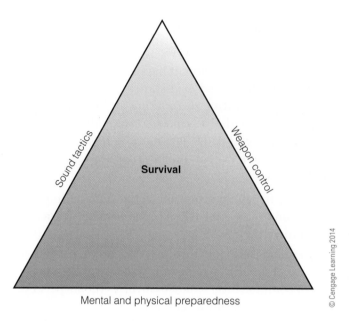

FIGURE 13.1 Survival Triangle

survival triangle

Model for police survival; consists of mental and physical preparedness, sound tactics, and weapon control.

 The Border Patrol's **survival triangle** consists of these components:
- Mental and physical preparedness
- Sound tactics
- Weapon control

The focus of this chapter has been on the base of the survival triangle, physical and mental preparedness. The second side of the survival triangle is sound tactics, which consist of the five "Cs": cover, concealment, control, containment, and communications. Effective, constant communications is the single thread that stitches all the pieces together.

The five Cs for survival tactics are cover, concealment, control, containment, and communications.

The third side of the survival triangle is weapons control. This is addressed in the following checklist:

1. Do you know the capabilities and limitations of yourself and each of your weapons?
2. Are your weapons clean and functional?
3. Are they loaded? How are they loaded? What type of ammunition are they loaded with? Does your partner know the answers to these questions?
4. Are your weapons immediately accessible to you? Or are they on the seat next to you where they might slide out of reach under your leg, or in the trunk, or the back seat? Close to you is not the same as accessible in a dynamic confrontation!

5. Do you practice constant forearm contact with your sidearm? (This is an excellent habit to acquire.)

6. Have you mastered a good technique for weapon retention?

7. Can you practice fire discipline?

8. Have you mentally prepared yourself to use your weapons? Lag time is a killer.

Witness reports of officers who were shot indicated some made no attempt to draw or use their weapons once they were down. Other reports stated that officers were shot by assailants while lying on the ground pleading, with arms raised to deflect gunshots. Even though they had full use of their arms and hands, they made no attempt to use their weapon for protection. Officers should also take safety precautions for keeping their service revolvers at home as well as carrying them when off duty.

Avoiding 10 Fatal Errors

According to the FBI (*Law Enforcement Officers* 2010), 56 law enforcement officers were feloniously killed in the line of duty in 2010. Of these felonious deaths, 15 were caused by ambush situations, 14 occurred during arrest situations, 8 while investigating suspicious persons/circumstances, 7 during traffic pursuits/stops, 6 answering disturbance calls, 3 during tactical situations (barricaded offender, hostage situation, high-risk entry, etc.), 2 while conducting investigative activity (surveillance, search, interview, etc.), and 1 while transporting or maintaining custody of a prisoner.

Based on the investigation of hundreds of line-of-duty deaths of experienced law enforcement officers, a list of "10 deadly sins" has been compiled identifying the major causes of useless, unnecessary deaths, a list that all "boots on the ground" officers should review periodically ("Ten Fatal Errors" n.d.):

1. *Attitude:* If you fail to keep your mind on the job or you carry personal problems into the field, you will make errors. It can cost you or fellow officers their lives.

2. *Tombstone courage:* No one doubts that you have courage. But in any situation where time allows—*wait* for the backup. There are few instances where alone and unaided you should try to make a dangerous apprehension.

3. *Not enough rest:* To do your job, you must be alert. Being sleepy or asleep on the job is not only against regulations, but you endanger yourself, the community, and all your fellow officers.

4. *Taking a bad position:* Never let anyone you are questioning or detaining manipulate you into a position of disadvantage. Always be aware of position. Maintain the advantage. There is no such thing as a routine arrest or stop.

5. *Danger signs:* As an officer, you should recognize "danger signs." Fast movement and strange cars are warnings that should alert you to watch and approach with caution. Know your community and watch for what looks to be "out of place."

6. *Failure to watch the hands of a suspect:* Is he reaching for a weapon or getting ready to strike you? How else can a potential killer strike but with his hands?

In our society today, it is mandatory that officers maintain their weapons skills through continuous training. Here, a police sergeant fires a beanbag round at a paper target during Special Response Team training. Officers on the team all qualify with submachine gun shooting as well as with handguns. They then practice with the less-lethal beanbag rounds, fired by a shotgun, which are designed to incapacitate an individual while reducing the chance of killing the subject.

7. *Relaxing too soon:* Observe carefully. Are you certain the crisis is over? Don't be quick to relax simply because the immediate and apparent threat has been neutralized.

8. *Improper use or no handcuffs:* See that the hand that can kill is safely cuffed. Once you have made an arrest, handcuff the prisoner immediately and properly.

9. *No search or poor search:* There are so many places to hide weapons that your failure to search is a crime against fellow officers. Many criminals carry several weapons and are prepared to use them against you.

10. *Dirty or inoperative weapon:* Are your weapons clean? Will they fire? How about the ammunition? When did you last fire so that you can hit a target in combat conditions? What's the sense of carrying any firearm that may not work when you need it the most?[1]

The Warrior Attitude

Survival is a constant theme in American law enforcement, but survival isn't enough. To survive simply means to remain in existence: "I want law enforcement personnel to go home the same way they left—unharmed, unscathed, and ready for duty; no wheelchairs, medical aids, crutches, or coffins. I want officers to *prevail*" (Spaulding 2009, 46). To prevail, officers need a *combative mindset*, which Spaulding defines as "a previous decision based on reason and intellect to be ready and willing to fight back."

[1]Source: "The Ten Fatal Errors that Have Killed Experienced Lawmen." Reprinted by permission of the National Association of Chiefs of Police.

SUMMARY

The hiring process for police officers generally requires candidates to meet basic standards and successfully complete a series of steps, including submitting an application and résumé; taking a civil service exam and physical fitness test; going through an initial oral interview; passing a background investigation and polygraph test; completing a psychological test, medical examination, and drug screening; undergoing a secondary oral interview; receiving a conditional offer of employment; completing the police academy; going through field training; and surviving the probationary period, which typically lasts one year.

Physical fitness is the body's general capacity to adapt and respond favorably to physical effort. Although many factors contribute to a well-conditioned body, the prime factor is the condition of the circulatory (cardiovascular) system, upon which endurance or stamina depends. Motor skills important to police officers include coordination, speed, and accuracy.

Police work is often sedentary, is boring, involves irregular hours and rotating shifts, and may promote poor diets, excessive cigarette smoking and consumption of alcohol, and great amounts of stress. These factors can be offset by physical fitness training programs. An effective physical fitness training program that is varied and of interest to the officer should include aerobic, strength, and flexibility training. It should be engaged in regularly for 20 to 30 minutes a day, at least three days a week.

Bloodborne pathogens police officers should protect against include HIV infections and AIDS, hepatitis B, and hepatitis C. The concept of universal precaution recommends that all blood and potentially infectious materials other than blood must be treated as if infected.

Mental fitness is as important as physical fitness. The greatest threat to officers' mental fitness is negative stress. Sources of stress for police officers include internal, individual stressors; stressors inherent to the police job; administrative and organizational stressors; and external stressors from the criminal justice system and the citizens it serves. Police officers tend to have high rates of alcoholism, divorce, posttraumatic stress disorder, burnout, depression, and suicide, often related to the stress of the job. Devastating psychological effects of stress include posttraumatic stress disorder, burnout, depression, and suicide.

Officer safety is another important aspect of keeping prepared for duty. The awareness spectrum describes an officer's level of awareness, ranging from environmental unawareness to panicked/blacked out/perhaps dead. Ideally, officers will be somewhere in between these two extremes—alert but relaxed. The Border Patrol's survival triangle, useful for all police officers, consists of mental and physical preparedness, sound tactics, and weapon control. The five Cs for survival tactics are cover, concealment, control, containment, and communications.

APPLICATION

You have noticed that many of your fellow officers are stressed out, and the department has no program to assist them. You approach your supervisor and offer to discuss this with your colleagues and then develop a policy dealing with stress management.

INSTRUCTIONS

Use the form in the Appendix to develop a department policy regarding stress management. The policy should point out various types of stressors officers must cope with and various services available to help officers. It also should bring employee assistance programs to the attention of the officers. It should include how to contact an individual or a group for help. Consider such programs as Alcoholics Anonymous, marriage counseling, financial advisors, psychological counseling, and any other services locally available. The policy should stress that officers may keep their contacts confidential and that no department interference will be generated that might impair or threaten an officer's job because that officer seeks assistance.

AN EXERCISE IN CRITICAL THINKING

You are a five-year veteran of the State Police Department and take pride in remaining physically fit for duty. Your agency requires that you pass an annual physical fitness test to continue to work out on patrol. You work hard every year to meet these standards and to exceed them. When you first started on the force, you were partnered with Officer Bailey. Officer Bailey and you graduated from the academy together and have worked the streets together ever since. Initially, Officer Bailey was in good physical shape and passed all of the standards that are required by your agency. However, in the last few years, you have noticed that Officer Bailey has continued to gain a significant amount of weight and developed poor eating habits while you have worked together. You have made a point to bring this up on several occasions, only to be told to mind your own business. You are concerned with Officer Bailey's welfare, but also with your own safety as well as the public's safety when performing your duties. You rely heavily on Officer Bailey as your partner in day-to-day operations. The gradual weight gain has caused you to pick up Officer Bailey's slack in your normal duties. In the most recent annual fitness test, you observe Officer Bailey intentionally miss a few of the obstacles when not observed by the proctor and claim that he passed them. You know for a fact that he did not.

Recently, you responded to a domestic violence incident where a husband was actively assaulting his wife upon your arrival. When the husband saw both of you, he ran from the scene. As you began to chase after him along with Officer Bailey, Officer Bailey stopped after a few feet, bent over, could not catch his breath and yelled for you to help him. You stopped to make sure your partner was okay, which resulted in the assailant getting away. After a few minutes, Officer Bailey was fine and stated that he is just out of shape. The following day you are both called to your sergeant's office to explain what happened and why the suspect was not arrested. You are aware that the victim has also generated a complaint.

1. What would your response be to your supervisor?
   a. Protect your partner; he has been with you since day one and there is the "Code of Silence." You will just have to continue picking up his slack until you can convince him to change his ways.
   b. Tell your supervisor that the suspect was just too fast and that neither of you could catch him, even though you both tried.
   c. Tell your supervisor that you believe Officer Bailey has some health issues that may have contributed to the escape and that are affecting his work performance as well. However, do not go into further detail; leave it for Officer Bailey to explain.
   d. Tell your supervisor of the ongoing health issues you have observed with Officer Bailey, express your concerns for safety, and also advise him that you know Officer Bailey did not successfully pass the recent annual physical fitness test and made his way through anyway by cheating.

2. How would you address the issue with Officer Bailey after the incident?
   a. Express your concerns over his safety, your own safety, and the safety of others given his recent inability to perform some of his duties.
   b. Tell him that you will notify your supervisors of him cheating on the annual fitness test.

c. Since he has been with you since day one, get together with Officer Bailey to come up with plan on what to say to supervisors. Then work out a deal about how you will be responding to calls together in the future because he is no longer physically able to do some things.

d. Do not address it with him. Leave it alone, pick up his slack, and hope that he realizes it and eventually does something about it on his own.

DISCUSSION QUESTIONS

1. Is peer counseling—"cops working with cops"—better for helping troubled officers than outside professional counseling? Is it better for short-term or long-term impact?

2. Is there one best way to handle officers who have drinking problems? Explain.

3. One reason police officers are reluctant to seek therapeutic services is that they fear their careers will be jeopardized. How can this obstacle be overcome?

4. Is it a good idea for every police department to have its own police psychologist? What are the advantages of in-house versus outside psychological assistance?

5. Are police officers confronted with the same stressful problems faced by everyone in society, such as firefighters, construction workers, business people, and military personnel?

6. Do the media create unnecessary stress for police officers in your community? If so, how?

7. How do police administrations contribute to the stresses of police officers? What role does the department play in dealing with the stress faced by an officer's spouse or family? Why should it become (or not become) involved?

GALE EMERGENCY SERVICES DATABASE ASSIGNMENTS

▶ Use the Gale Emergency Services database to help answer the Discussion Questions as appropriate.

▶ Use the Gale Emergency Services database to find and outline one of the following articles:

- "The Effects of Sleep Deprivation" by Glory Cochrane
- "HIV/AIDS in Law Enforcement: 'What-If' Scenarios" by John Cooley
- "Surviving Assaults: After the Physical Battle Ends, the Psychological Battle Begins" by Arthur W. Kureczka

- "Police Trauma and Addiction: Coping with the Dangers of the Job" by Chad L. Cross and Larry Ashley
- "The 'Modern Warrior': A Study in Survival" by Richard H. Norcross
- "Physical Fitness in Law Enforcement: Follow the Yellow Brick Road" by Patti Ebling
- "Fit for Duty: How to Train for the Real Deal" by Carole Moore

REFERENCES

Bartlett, Derrick D. 2011. "Why We Work Out." *Police* (March): 36–41.

Best, Suzanne. 2009. "Proactive Stress Management for Police Executives." *Big Ideas* (Spring): 9–10.

Carlton, Jerry. 2009. "Preventing the Long and Lonely Ride to Officer Burnout." *Law Enforcement Technology* (March): 64–70.

Collingwood, Thomas R., Robert Hoffman, and Jay Smith. 2004. "Underlying Physical Fitness Factors for Performing Police Officer Physical Tasks." *The Police Chief* (March): 32–37.

Commission on Accreditation of Law Enforcement Agencies (CALEA). 2012. *Standards for Law Enforcement Agencies.* 5th ed. Fairfax, VA: Author.

Fyfe, James J. 1986. "The Split-Second Syndrome and Other Determinants of Police Violence." In *Violent Transactions*, edited by Anne Campbell and John Gibbs, 207–223. New York: Basil Blackwell.

Garrett, Ronnie. 2008. "Super Bugs: Coming to a Department Near You." *Law Enforcement Technology* (March): 46–51.

Givens, Tom. 2004 (May). "States of Awareness, the Cooper Color Codes." *Sharpen the Blade*. Accessed April 16, 2012. http://www.teddytactical.com/SharpenBladeArticle/4_States%20of%20Awareness.htm.

Glennon, Jim. 2008. "Pre-Attack Indicators: Conscious Recognition of Telegraphed Cues." *PoliceOne.com News* (February 12). Accessed April 16, 2012. http://www.policeone.com/police-products/training/articles/1660205-Pre-attack-indicators-Conscious-recognition-of-telegraphed-cues/.

Grossi, Dave. 2007. "Tactical Wellness." *Law Officer Magazine* (October): 26–27.

Haughton, Brian P. 2009. "The MRSA Menace." *Tactical Response* (March–April): 38–44.

Johnson, Robert Roy. 2009. "Officer Fitness." *Law and Order* (January): 18.

LaTourrette, Tom. 2011. "Safety and Health Protection Efforts in the Police Service." *The Police Chief* (June): 74–78.

Law Enforcement Officers Killed and Assaulted 2010. 2010. Washington, DC: Federal Bureau of Investigation. Accessed April 16, 2012. http://www.fbi.gov/about-us/cjis/ucr/leoka/leoka-2010/officers-feloniously-killed/feloniouslykilled.

Lohner, Wyn. 2011. "What Does It Take to Excel?" *FBI Law Enforcement Bulletin* (August): 20–23.

McDonough, Mark E. 2011. "The Employee Wellness Plan: A Strategy for Fighting the 'Evil from Within.'" *FBI Law Enforcement Bulletin* (December): 1–6

Murgado, Amaury. 2011. "The Threat of Technology." *Police* (July): 16–18.

Murray, Ken. 2007. "The Seven Survivals." *Law Officer Magazine* (December): 48–49.

Patton, Gary L. 2011. "Coping with the Career: A Review of Acquired Life Patterns of Veteran Officers." *FBI Law Enforcement Bulletin* (June): 16–23.

"P1Poll: What Is Your Biggest Pet Peeve about Police Work?" n.d. *PoliceOne Member News*. Accessed April 12, 2012. http://www.policeone.com/polls/1354587-What-is-your-biggest-pet-peeve-about-police-work/.

Quigley, Adrienne. 2008. "Fit for Duty." *The Police Chief* (June): 62–64.

Sanow, Ed. 2009. "Fitness Is an Ethical Obligation." *Tactical Response* (January–February): 95–96.

Schneider, Jason. 2007. "MRSA Infections: Tougher than Kelvar." *Law Enforcement Technology* (September): 18–23.

Schreiber, Sara. 2008. "Healthy Choices: Training for Firearms, Fugitives and … Trans-Fat?" *Law Enforcement Technology* (September): 10–16.

Selye, Hans. 1956. *The Stress of Life*. New York: McGraw-Hill.

Senjo, Scott R., and Karla Dhungana. 2009. "Field Data Examination of Policy Constructs Related to Fatigue Conditions in Law Enforcement Personnel." *Police Quarterly* (June): 123–136.

Spaulding, Dave. 2009. "Mindset Matters." *Law Officer Magazine* (April): 46–47.

"Ten Fatal Errors That Have Killed Experienced Lawmen." n.d. National Association of Chiefs of Police. http://www.aphf.org/errors.html.

Vernon, Bob. 2009. "Knights of the Roundtable." *Law Officer Magazine* (June): 48.

Vila, Bryan. 2009. "Sleep Deprivation: What Does It Mean for Public Safety Officers?" *National Institute of Justice Journal* (262, March 27): 26–31.

Vonk, Kathleen. 2009a. "Law Enforcement and Nutrition." *Tactical Response* (January–February): 30–33.

Vonk, Kathleen. 2009b. "The Nitty-Gritty of Proper Nutrition." *Law and Order* (February): 14–17.

Waggoner, Kim, ed. 2007. *Handbook of Forensic Services*. Quantico, VA: FBI Laboratory Publication.

Webb, Howard. 2011. "Force of Habits." *Police* (September): 56–59.

Weiss, Jim, and Mickey Davis. 2009. "Survival Stress Research and Post-Event Memory." *Tactical Response* (March–June): 66–70.

Young, Dave. 2008. "Redefining Fit for Duty." *Police* (August): 42–49.

CASES CITED

Jane Doe v. Borough of Barrington, 729 F. Supp. 376 (D.N.J. 1990)

Parker v. District of Columbia, 850 F.2d 708 (D.C. Cir. 1988)

Woods v. White, 899 F.2d 17 (7 Cir. 1990)

© AP Images/John Fitzhugh

CHAPTER 14

Liability and Ethics:
Is It Legal? Is It Moral?

DO YOU KNOW . . .

- Under what three types of state liability (tort) law officers may be sued?
- On what basis most civil lawsuits against police are brought?
- What the most common civil actions brought against the police involve?
- What can protect against civil liability?
- Whether incident reports are important in defending against civil suits?
- How to minimize lawsuits?
- What the most common defenses used by police officers against civil liability lawsuits are?
- Whether officers can countersue?
- Whether ethical issues are usually absolute or relative?
- According to conventional wisdom, what the defining characteristics of the police culture are, and what the result is?
- What three areas in discussions of law enforcement ethics are controversial?
- What the key elements in corrupt behavior are?
- What the most important factor in police officers becoming corrupt is?
- What other factors may cause officers to become corrupt?

CAN YOU DEFINE?

absolute issue
blue lie
civil action
Civil Rights Act
collective deep pocket
discretionary acts
exculpatory evidence
intentional tort
libel
litigious
malfeasance
malicious prosecution
ministerial acts
negligence
nonfeasance
perjury
police placebo
relative issue

- If scandals are caused by "bad apples" or "bad barrels"?
- What basic ethics tests can be used to assess behavior?
- What maxim should guide ethical decisions?
- Who is most responsible for the ethics of a law enforcement agency?

Section 1983
slander
slippery slope
strict liability
tort
vicarious liability

INTRODUCTION

Law enforcement officers must act within the law. If they do not, they may be found criminally liable for misconduct under Title 18, U.S.C., Section 242, as well as under state criminal law. Most lawsuits against law enforcement officers, however, deal with civil matters and are filed under Title 42, U.S.C., Section 1983.

In carrying out their official duties, law enforcement officers must protect the constitutional rights of their public. The consequences of violating such rights in a criminal investigation were discussed in Chapter 3. Actions in violation of a suspect's constitutional rights can cost a favorable decision. In addition, the suspect can sue the police.

Police operations also involve considerable discretion, and discretion is central in the debate regarding the "letter of the law" versus the "spirit of the law." Very simply, a letter of the law approach tends to be quite rigid and take a black-and-white, right-or-wrong stance in assessing situations, whereas a "spirit of the law" philosophy generally considers contextual factors, recognizing the various shades of gray that often accompany specific incidents. This variable application of discretion, too, can result in actions viewed as conduct "not becoming a police officer" and thereby subject officers to civil lawsuits.

Law enforcement officers must act legally, and they must act ethically. *Ethics* refers to standards of fair and honest conduct. It involves *integrity*, doing what is considered just, honest, and proper. Ethics looks at human conduct in the light of *moral principles*—that is, set ideas of right and wrong. Moral principles can be established by individuals, set forth by a particular society or culture, laid down by a religious body or doctrine, or established by a given subculture. In most instances, an individual's moral principles derive from a combination of all of these. Further, in our pluralistic country, many differences exist in what is considered right and wrong.

This chapter begins with an overview of civil liability and Section 1983, the Civil Rights Act. This is followed by common charges brought against police officers. Next is a discussion of defenses in civil lawsuits—of ways to reduce their occurrence and of the possibility of countersuits. The discussion of legal liability ends with a look at legal liability and community policing.

The chapter then changes its focus from what is legal to what is moral or ethical. This discussion begins with an overview of ethics and of ethics in law enforcement. This is followed by a discussion of some gray areas in police ethics and outright unethical behavior. Next, basic ethics tests are presented, along with information about internal affairs investigations. The chapter concludes with discussions of ethics and community policing and integrating ethics into the SARA model.

CIVIL LIABILITY: AN OVERVIEW

The United States has been called a **litigious** society—that is, its citizens are very likely to sue over any perceived wrong. When someone who feels wronged by another person sues that other person, even though the action involved may not be a crime, such a lawsuit is called a **civil action**. In civil law, the wrongdoing itself is called a **tort**. Sometimes an action is considered both a tort and a crime. For example, a person who strikes someone could be charged with assault (a crime) and sued for the assault (a tort). An individual found guilty of a crime is *punished* by paying a fine, serving a jail or prison sentence, or both. An individual found guilty of a tort is made to make *restitution,* usually in the form of a monetary payment.

An estimated 30,000 civil actions are filed against the police every year, with between 4 and 8 percent resulting in verdicts against the police. The threat of a lawsuit may influence officer decisions such as to arrest or to use force and how much. There have been instances when an officer did not fire on a suspect who was pointing a gun at him. Uncertain as to whether the gun was real, the officer hesitated and was shot to death, more fearful of a lawsuit than of being killed. Officers may find themselves in a "Catch 22"—sued if they take action or sued if they don't.

litigious

Highly likely to sue.

civil action

A lawsuit for perceived wrongs against individuals for which restitution is sought in civil court.

tort

A civil wrong, the equivalent to a crime in criminal law.

▌ AN OFFICER'S PERSPECTIVE ▌
Which Is Worse: Death or a Lawsuit?

In officer survival training, trainers commonly reference the quote, "It is better to be judged by 12 than carried by 6." Translation: You may have to deal with the most negative of repercussions in a courtroom, but you will still be alive, which matters most. This is as opposed to being wrong, and dead.

Because of America's litigious culture, officers are forced to continue their education and training to properly do their jobs. The increasing standards foster more educated officers, which is not a bad thing, but education cannot teach reactionary instinct. You either have it or you don't.

—Sgt. Henry Lim Cho

Law enforcement officers can be sued in just about every phase of police operations. Each time officers are sued, it exposes them to possible personal embarrassment in the community and on the job. It may result in job loss. It may mean financial ruin. Equally damaging is the undermining of respect for the rule of law when officers are found guilty. Although the increase in lawsuits is alarming, it is still true that few lawsuits against police officers can be traced to extremely poor judgment or malicious acts by one or more officers. The responsible behavior of officers is a definite deterrent to any action against them.

strict liability

Refers to an act where the injury or damage is so severe and the harm should have been foreseen so that intent or mental state need not be proven.

> Officers may be sued under three types of state liability (tort) laws: strict liability, intentional tort, and negligence.

Strict liability refers to an act where the injury or damage is so severe and the harm should have been foreseen so that intent or mental state need not be proven—for example, reckless operation of a vehicle. **Intentional tort** refers to an act where the officer's intent to engage in the behavior must be

intentional tort

An act where the officer's intent to engage in the behavior must be proven, for example, wrongful death or false arrest.

negligence

An act where intent or mental state does not matter; what must be proven is if some inadvertent act or failure to act created an unreasonable risk to another person, for example, speeding resulting in a traffic crash or not responding to a 911 call.

proven—for example, wrongful death or false arrest. **Negligence** refers to an act where intent or mental state does not matter. What must be proven is whether some inadvertent act or failure to act created an unreasonable risk to another person—for example, speeding resulting in a traffic accident or not responding to a 911 call.

SECTION 1983, THE CIVIL RIGHTS ACT

Section 1983

The Civil Rights Act; it states that anyone acting under the authority of the law who violates another person's constitutional rights can be sued; the legal authority for most lawsuits against law enforcement officers and agencies.

Most civil lawsuits brought against law enforcement officers are based on Statute 42 of the U.S. Code, **Section 1983**, also called the **Civil Rights Act**. This act says that anyone acting under the authority of the law who violates another person's constitutional rights can be sued.

Civil Rights Act

States that anyone acting under the authority of the law who violates another person's constitutional rights can be sued; see also *Section 1983*.

This act, passed in 1871 after the Civil War, was originally part of the Ku Klux Klan Act of 1871, one part of which is now called the Civil Rights Act of 1871. The act was designed to prevent the abuse of constitutional rights by officers who "under color of state law" deny defendants those rights. The act states, "Every person who, under color of any statute, ordinance, regulation, custom, or usage, of any State or Territory, subjects, or causes to be subjected any citizen of the United States or other person within the jurisdiction thereof to the deprivation of any rights, privileges, or immunities secured by the Constitution and laws, shall be liable to the party injured in an action at law, suit in equity, or other proper proceeding for redress."

vicarious liability

Makes others specifically associated with a person also responsible for that person's actions.

In other words, Section 1983 says that anyone acting under the authority of the law who violates another person's constitutional rights can be sued. This includes law enforcement officers. It now may also include their supervisors, their departments, and even their municipalities. **Vicarious liability** makes others specifically associated with a person also responsible for that person's actions. Most lawsuits naming supervisory officers are attempts to get to more, wealthier, and better-insured defendants through vicarious liability. Suing every possible individual and agency involved creates a **collective deep pocket** from which astronomical judgments can be collected.

collective deep pocket

A pool of defendants from which astronomical financial judgments can be collected; created by suing every possible individual and agency involved in an incident.

Section 1983 lawsuits may involve First Amendment issues such as freedom of speech, religion, and association; Fourth Amendment matters such as arrest and detention, search and seizure, and use of force; Fifth Amendment issues in interrogation and confessions; Sixth Amendment concerns regarding the right to counsel; and Fourteenth Amendment claims of due process violations. It is important for law enforcement officers to understand Section 1983 because it is often the basis for a civil action against police.

COMMON CHARGES BROUGHT AGAINST POLICE OFFICERS

As noted, most cases being tried are based on Section 1983, alleging police violation of constitutional rights. More recently, several lawsuits have been brought for failure to protect or investigate. Two important distinctions determine personal liability of city officers and employees for acts committed while on duty: discretionary versus ministerial acts and malfeasance versus nonfeasance.

Discretionary acts are those actions officers perform using their own judgment. Policies and procedures for the acts leave decisions up to the officers. If police officers are carrying out a duty requiring judgment, they cannot be liable for damages unless they are willfully or grossly negligent. Making an arrest is an example of a discretionary act. **Ministerial acts** have to do with the way the duty is to be performed. If officers fail to perform the duty as prescribed, they can be sued. If, for example, a department has a policy against shooting a gun from a moving squad car and an officer does so and injures someone, the officer can be sued.

Malfeasance refers to acts of misconduct or wrongdoing, while **nonfeasance** refers to failure to take action. In the infamous Rodney King incident, officers participating in the beating might be charged with malfeasance in civil proceedings. Those who stood by and did nothing to interfere might be charged with nonfeasance.

> The most frequent civil lawsuits against police involve false arrest or imprisonment, malicious prosecution, use of unnecessary or excessive force and police brutality, wrongful death, negligent operation of a vehicle, failure to protect, failure to identify, and negligent service.

discretionary acts

Those actions officers perform using their own judgment; policies and procedures for the acts leave decisions up to the officers.

ministerial acts

Duties prescribed by law as some of the tasks of an administrative office.

malfeasance

Acts of misconduct or wrongdoing.

nonfeasance

Failure to take action, with the result being injury or damage to another person.

False Arrest or Imprisonment

The largest number of lawsuits, accounting for about 50 percent of all lawsuits filed, is for false arrest and imprisonment. False arrest and false imprisonment are exceptionally vulnerable to lawsuits because such suits are filed with ease and can be filed as group actions. False arrest and false imprisonment are almost synonymous under the law. Both are usually alleged against the officer.

Arrest is broadly defined as taking an individual into custody by physical or constructive restraint with the intention of charging the individual in a court of law. Physical force need not be used to accomplish arrest or imprisonment. The assertion that would be brought to the court's attention in such a lawsuit is that the officer lacked probable cause to arrest. An absolute defense in such a case is that probable cause *did* exist. The courts look at two important factors when examining liability for false arrest: (1) the information known to the police officer at the time the arrest was made and (2) the reasonableness of the officer's action given all the circumstances at the time of the arrest.

A common problem occurs when police officers respond to retail stores' calls for assistance in arresting people suspected of shoplifting. Most agencies have standardized procedures requiring the apprehending store employee to make a formal citizen's arrest. In this case, a claim of false imprisonment may be filed against both the store and the police officer.

Many other false-arrest suits result from drunk and disorderly arrests and from warrantless arrests under pro-arrest domestic violence statutes.

Malicious Prosecution

An area of liability closely associated with false arrest and imprisonment is malicious prosecution. **Malicious prosecution** is a proceeding instituted in bad faith without any probable cause in the belief that the charges against the defendant can be sustained. The cause of action in the civil suit is usually for damages suffered. This type of civil action arises most frequently when one citizen formally charges another citizen and the defendant is not successfully prosecuted.

Excessive Force or Brutality

The second largest numbers of civil actions against police officers are filed in the areas of excessive force or brutality. Such a suit can be the result of lawful or allegedly unlawful arrest and will usually name a supervisor as a defendant along with the officer(s) actually involved.

The specific allegations may be civil assault and battery. *Assault* refers to conduct that may result from a well-founded fear of imminent peril. *Battery* is the unlawful, hostile touching or shoving of another, no matter how slight. Some states have combined the two into a single charge of assault. In some instances, criminal charges may be brought as well. For example, if a police officer were to strike a handcuffed prisoner with a nightstick hard enough to shatter the bones in the prisoner's face, the prisoner could bring a civil action *and* press criminal charges against the officer.

Courts have held an officer liable for assault and battery if that officer strikes a suspect or uses an aerosol irritant on the suspect for talking back, or if an officer continues to beat a defendant who has stopped resisting. Almost every state now has statutes that define the extent to which police officers can use physical force in specific situations. All officers should become thoroughly familiar with their states' statutes in this area.

Most states allow officers to use some physical force short of deadly force to make an arrest or prevent an escape. Officers may also use physical force, short of deadly force, to defend themselves. Recall that *Graham v. Connor* (1989) established that police officers could be held liable for using excessive force, with the test for liability being "objective reasonableness."

Lawsuits are also likely when use of deadly force is involved. As stated in Chapter 3, the use of *deadly force* to make an arrest or prevent an escape is generally permitted only when:

▶ The crime committed was a felony involving the use or threatened use of imminent physical force against a person.

▶ The crime committed was an inherently dangerous felony such as kidnapping, arson, or burglary in a dwelling, and the officer felt that the escape of the felon would contribute to the possible death or harm of others if not stopped (having known the felon has already committed one of those severe felonies).

▶ The officer's life or personal safety, or the safety of others, was endangered in the particular circumstances involved.

▶ The person was an escapee from a correctional facility.

The Commission on Accreditation of Law Enforcement Agencies (CALEA) Standards address use of force in the first standard dealing with law and authority.

> **CALEA Standard 1** states, "Policies, procedures, and training on topics such as use of force and officer discretion have typically touched upon the legal aspects of these issues; in some jurisdictions this may even be mandated. Accredited agencies look beyond simply what might be legal, providing sound written guidance consistent with agency values that often conveys a sense of responsibility and compassion that transcends all laws."
>
> Source: Commission on Accreditation of Law Enforcement Agencies (CALEA). 2012. *Standards for Law Enforcement Agencies.* 5th ed. Fairfax, VA: Author.

It is doubtful the court would uphold the use of deadly physical force in cases involving property crimes unless there was imminent danger to the officer or other individuals.

The use of physical force by police officers to prevent destruction of evidence is controversial. Generally, the force used must be reasonable under all circumstances. Deadly physical force is *never* permitted in preventing the destruction of evidence. The swallowing of drugs in an arrest is an issue for which courts have not given police any guidelines. Cases have included everything from officers sticking their fingers down suspects' throats to officers taking suspects to hospitals to have emergency personnel give them enemas. Handcuffing an arrested person who is resisting arrest also has been deemed excessive force in some instances, as discussed in Chapter 3.

Wrongful Death

Closely related to excessive force and brutality complaints is the area of wrongful death actions. Wrongful deaths can be caused either by intentional or negligent acts or by omissions of police officers. Intentionally inflicting fatal injuries causes the greatest number of wrongful death actions. Circumstances that lead to wrongful death suits include shooting an unarmed, fleeing misdemeanant; a fleeing felon when the felon could have been subdued without deadly force; any misdemeanant to effect an arrest; excited delirium deaths; cases where TASERs or oleoresin capsicum (OC) pepper spray were used; and shooting in self-defense of an actual or threatened attack when the attacker did not use great bodily force.

Negligent killings account for a much smaller number of deaths and usually arise in the following situations:

▶ Shooting to halt a motor vehicle and striking a passenger. (Most police departments have regulated this practice by forbidding firing at a moving vehicle.)

▶ Accidentally shooting a bystander.

▶ Reckless firing of warning shots. (Many police departments forbid the firing of warning shots.)

▶ Poor aim when shooting to wound a suspect. (This includes accidentally striking a hostage or accidentally discharging a firearm, wounding, or killing an innocent person.)

Officers participating in raiding parties, such as those making drug arrests, must act reasonably. Any lawsuits that may emanate from their actions will encompass all officers participating in the raid. The lawsuit can extend to the supervisors, the department, and the city itself. Some wrongful death suits arise from police pursuits or negligent operation of squad cars.

Negligent Operation of a Vehicle

Another area of specific liability is the operation of a police vehicle. Liability in this particular area has increased dramatically in recent years. Police officers are charged with the same standard of care as the general public and are found liable under a straight negligence theory for the negligent operation of vehicles. Statutes allowing police officers to disregard stop signs and other traffic laws and cautions are now being interpreted by the courts to require officers to use reasonable care under existing circumstances. The requirement of reasonable care is particularly critical when "hot pursuit" is involved and the police vehicle is unmarked and lacks a siren and red lights. Liability concerns have led many departments to adopt "no pursuit" policies.

Failure to Protect

Another broad area of officer liability involves lawsuits alleging "failure to protect." This can take several forms, including failure to answer calls for help, failure to respond in a reasonable amount of time, failure to arrest, failure to investigate, and so on. Some "special relationships" have been found to exist in certain circumstances, and failure to protect can involve several types of situations.

General Failure to Protect One of the most common situations occurs when a victim assumes the police will provide protection and then relies on that assumption. Publishing a 911 number, according to some courts, implies that the police will protect those who call that number.

Failure to protect also occurs when the police tell a victim they will let the victim know when someone is released from custody or from prison and fail to do so. Failure to protect witnesses who have cooperated with police and whose cooperation brings them into contact with the suspects also has resulted in lawsuits.

Failure to Arrest or Restrain People Committing or About to Commit Violent Crimes This is usually classed as an act of negligence. For example, an officer failed to get a drunken motorist off the road before the motorist caused a serious accident. Failure to arrest a person known to be dangerous when probable cause exists can also lead to suits for damages subsequently done by that person.

Failure to Respond to Calls for Assistance If police officers have reason to believe someone is in imminent danger, they must take action or face the possibility of a lawsuit. In *Thurman v. City of Torrington* (1984), the victim, an estranged wife who was stabbed by her husband, received a $2.3 million award because the police had refused to act on her complaints.

Failure to Identify

At times, failure to identify oneself as a police officer before making an arrest can lead to liability on negligence theory. The liability would be for incurred damages or injuries that might have been avoided if the officer had given proper identification.

Negligent Service

The past decades have seen an increase in civil lawsuits claiming negligence by police officers, departments, and municipalities in providing traffic services. Police officers or agencies may be liable if they know of a potentially dangerous condition and fail to take reasonable action to correct the existing hazard. They may also be liable if they fail to warn oncoming traffic of an existing hazard.

Some courts do hold police officers responsible for providing assistance at a crash scene. Other courts, however, contend that although the police have a duty to help at a crash scene, officers become liable only after establishing a special relationship with the victim.

Traffic-related incidents are not the only area in which charges of negligent service can be made. Some cases suggest that the negligent administration of first aid by police officers can be the basis for an action in negligence in which an officer's act or omission becomes the cause for complaint. In addition, some lawsuits have been filed in attempts to make officers liable for not recognizing existing medical impairments. Though these cases are rare, officers should be aware of them. Most have not been successful, and many have centered around individuals who appeared to be drunk and were treated as being drunk, but who in actuality were suffering heart attacks or having epileptic seizures.

One of the main responsibilities of a police officer is to administer first aid to victims.

© David Butow/CORBIS SABA

Other Areas of Civil Liability: Libel and Slander

libel

Written defamation of another's character; false statements that tend to humiliate a person and degrade that person in the esteem of others.

slander

Spoken defamation of another's character; false oral statements that tend to humiliate a person and degrade that person in the esteem of others.

Another type of civil liability officers face, albeit infrequently, involves allegations of libel or slander. Usually known as *defamation of character* suits, these cases involve false written (**libel**) or spoken (**slander**) statements that can humiliate or degrade a person in the esteem of others. These suits often pivot around statements made during arrests because much of the court process and testimony are privileged communications and should not be repeated by the police officers. Proving the statement's truth is a defense to such actions. Although this area has produced limited litigation against the police to date, officers should be aware of the possibility for such lawsuits.

REDUCING THE OCCURRENCE OF CIVIL LAWSUITS

According to Means (2007, 33), "Nothing whatsoever reduces legal problems and liability risks in law enforcement like good interpersonal communication skills. We all know officers who can go in a biker bar, make an arrest, and leave with a friend. Other officers could start a fight in a Quaker Friends meeting." The critical need for effective communication spills into every aspect of police work and will not be discussed further here except to note that it is one vital way to avoid lawsuits.

Police officers and agencies can expect more rather than fewer lawsuits unless specific steps are taken. Ultimately, the risk of civil liability rests on the individual actions of each police officer. Police departments can develop extensive policies and procedures to help ensure that their officers act in a way that will deter civil lawsuits.

> Protection against lawsuits includes:
> - Effective policies and procedures clearly communicated to all.
> - Thorough and continuous training.
> - Proper supervision and discipline.
> - Accurate, thorough police reports.

At the heart of protecting against lawsuits are the department's *policies and procedures.* A department's procedures manual should clearly state that a fundamental mission of the department is to protect everyone's civil rights and that officers and supervisory personnel have an affirmative duty to intervene if they witness the violation of civil rights by anyone, including fellow officers: "By definition, policy is a course of action, a guiding principle or procedure considered expedient, prudent, or advantageous. By practice, the policies of a law enforcement agency dictate the protocol by which officers are expected to conduct their duties, often carrying with it the added responsibility of mitigating potential liability resulting from those duties. By all accounts, it is often more restrictive than what the law requires, than what cops desire, and more than what their employers would want in an ideal world" (Scoville 2008, 56).

In many areas requiring police discretion, policies seek to prevent abuses of authority, minimize threats to the community, mitigate the need for civil redress, and generally keep the employing agency out of the headlines, rather than guiding officers in what is expected under general circumstances: "Policies are formal declarations of what an agency is expected and willing to do. They have import. They have purpose. Perhaps one day, they will allow greater leeway for officers to exercise their authority and greater latitude for the men and women who evaluate their discretions so that if they can't temper justice with mercy, then perhaps with a little common sense.... For some the writing is on the wall: 'To err is human. To forgive is against department policy'" (Scoville 2008, 63).

Adopting performance standards such as the CALEA internationally accepted accreditation program can go far in reducing the risk of being sued. Data from a 2011 PhD thesis indicate that CALEA-accredited law enforcement agencies have 45 percent fewer civil lawsuits, 44 percent less financial resources spent on litigation costs, and 168 percent less monetary amounts paid out in adverse judgments (Gaut 2011). In addition, many insurance companies provide lower insurance rates for those who meet these standards or local or state standards that have been validated.

Burch (2008, 69) asks, "How do you train officers to balance doing what they are told with using some common sense? How do you train them to sort out following the letter of the policy or they will be in trouble versus following the spirit of the law or they will be in trouble?" This is a true training challenge.

Training should include the basic rookie training as well as ongoing in-service training and specialized training. Training must include the policies and procedures of the department. It also must include continual updating on changes in laws that affect police operations, as discussed earlier in the text.

Proper supervision and discipline are also vital to avoiding lawsuits. Discipline can be viewed both positively and negatively. On the positive side, police departments should foster professional discipline within their officers—that is, they should encourage an atmosphere in which officers act according to established policies and procedures. Departments should be able to say of their personnel that they are well-disciplined officers. On the negative side, officers who do not act according to established policies and procedures should be reprimanded (disciplined).

Another key area in preventing lawsuits is *thorough, accurate police reports* establishing the reasonableness of officers' actions, especially important in use-of-force reports. Grossi (2008) prefers to call these documents *subject management reports*, focusing on something the subjects did (or failed to do) that caused the officer to have to use some level of force to control them and take them into custody. Indeed, increasing numbers of agencies are changing the names of these reports to such titles as "Response to Resistance" reports, to reflect the shift in focus from the force used by an officer to the resistance used by a subject.

Effective subject management reports serve numerous purposes. They can be used by the training unit to document what is and is not working on the street and highlight where more training is needed. They can be used by the crime analysis team to identify crime hot spots. They can also give a judge, jury, or hearing officer a clear understanding of who and what an officer was up against (Grossi 2008).

As many as one in every 60 officers in the United States is currently being sued for a use of force incident: "To successfully combat a use of force lawsuit, an officer must do two things. First, and most importantly, the officer needs to be right (i.e., reasonable) in the use of force. Second, the officer must carefully and clearly document why he or she was right and reasonable. Any inaccuracy or omission in the report will be used to attack the officer's integrity and professionalism" (Joyner 2009).

Officers tend not to see their own writing errors because they are familiar with what they have just written. In a hurry to submit a report and move on to a new activity, too many officers turn in error-filled documents before effectively reviewing them. A brief separation from the report, in both time and space, is often enough to overcome this problem. Set the report aside for 10 minutes and then go back to review it, using these three steps (Bowden 2009):

▶ First, check for completeness in the information blocks and in the narrative. Is all necessary information included?

▶ Second, check the content. Read the narrative to make sure it flows well, makes sense, and speaks clearly.

▶ Third, check for spelling and capitalization. Reading it backward forces you to look at every word separately.

> The importance of documentation cannot be emphasized enough. Comprehensive, well-written incident reports are vital to defenses against civil suits.

Videotaping traffic stops also provides officers with documentation of their actions, especially in cases involving driving while intoxicated (DWI) arrests. Griffith (2009a, 8) suggests that all officers remember this dictum: "There is always a camera watching you, and it would be better if you had one too." Data from the International Association of Chiefs of Police (IACP) shows that the vast majority (93 percent) of officers charged with misconduct are exonerated when video evidence is available (Griffith 2009b). This statistic provides strong incentive to heed the advice. Body cameras are becoming increasingly popular among law enforcement agencies, with some administrators predicting they will become standard equipment in the foreseeable future ("Cameras" 2012).

> To minimize lawsuits at a more personal level, law enforcement officers should:
> - Know and follow their department's policies and procedures.
> - Stay in the scope of their duties.
> - Always act professionally.
> - Know and respect their constituents' rights.
> - Seek advice if in doubt.
> - Carefully document their activities in their reports.
> - Maintain good community relations.
> - Keep current on civil and criminal liability cases and know the laws.

CIVIL SUIT DEFENSES AND COUNTERSUITS

Despite all efforts to reduce the likelihood of being sued and minimize department and officer exposure to civil liability, lawsuits will happen. In fact, in the law enforcement culture, there is a saying, "If you haven't been sued, you aren't doing your job." This speaks to the reality that at some point during your career, *you will be sued*, regardless of whether it is a frivolous accusation. It is not uncommon for a veteran officer to have been sued several times throughout his or her career. This affects all demographics of law enforcement.

When the inevitable lawsuit occurs, officers, agencies, and municipalities have several common defenses available to them.

> The normal defenses used by police officers, departments, and municipalities being sued are that:
> - They did not intend to deprive the plaintiff of constitutional rights.
> - They acted in good faith.
> - They acted with what was considered reasonable judgment at the time and with valid authority.

In many instances, civil suits brought against law enforcement officers either have no basis or are frivolous. Some people consider the best defense to be a good offense and, therefore, sue the officer who arrested them, thinking it might put them in a better bargaining position.

> Law enforcement officers and agencies can countersue if they are falsely accused of a civil offense.

In one case, a deputy sheriff responded to a public drunkenness complaint at a convenience store. When he arrived, the deputy approached the suspect and asked that he come outside with him to discuss the problem. The suspect filed a brutality complaint against the deputy, claiming the deputy grabbed him by the throat and physically dragged him out of the store. The evidence obtained from the convenience store security camera showed that the deputy did not grab the suspect by the throat, and even held the door open for him when they left the store. The trial judge awarded the deputy sheriff $25,000 in damages as a result of the false accusations.

Law enforcement officers also can sue even if they have not been sued. Prosecutors, police, and sheriff's deputies are entitled to the same right to recover for wrongful injury as any other citizen.

LEGAL LIABILITY AND COMMUNITY POLICING

If community policing becomes a reality in a jurisdiction, citizens will better understand why the police do what they do. Citizens should also be less likely to bring suit against officers if they view them as partners. Likewise, police officers operating under a community policing philosophy will have a service orientation and will be less likely to infringe on the constitutional rights of those with whom they work. This may also lead to officers policing in a more ethical manner.

ETHICS: AN OVERVIEW

Ethics usually involves what is often referred to as the *conscience*, the ability to recognize right from wrong and to follow one's own sense of what is right. Some believe conscience is an innate moral sense; people are either born with it or not. Others believe it is a power acquired by experience—that is, it can be taught or consciously ignored.

A complexity in ethical behavior is whether the issues addressed by ethics are absolute or relative. For example, is killing a human being always "bad" (absolute) or is it even "good" at times (relative)?

absolute issue

An issue with only two sides, viewed as either/or, black or white.

relative issue

An issue with a range of morally acceptable options, which are of several shades of gray rather than either black or white.

> An **absolute issue** is one with only two sides—the decision is between "black" and "white." A **relative issue** is one with a multitude of sides, that is, varying shades of "gray" between the two absolute positions. Ethical issues are usually relative and are affected by the police culture.

Ethics involves looking at moral rules recognized by individuals with a conscience and held to be either absolute or relative. What one individual considers ethical behavior may be considered highly unethical behavior by another individual. An example of this is the Hmong practice in which adult males marry very young girls. To Hmong people, this is moral and right. To many Americans, this is immoral and wrong.

Ethics *is* complex and presents serious challenges to those who seek to behave ethically. Consider, for example, which of the following ethical principles are behind your behavior:

▶ Do unto others as you would have them do unto you.

▶ Do what will accomplish your goal or vision in the most efficient manner.

▶ Do whatever you please so long as it does not cause harm to anyone else.

▶ Might makes right.

Ethics includes integrity, that is, doing right when no one is watching. Ethical integrity is paramount in a profession endowed with power, authority, and discretion, and thus, it is the most important value a law enforcement officer can have: "Everything in law enforcement works outward and upward from the foundation of integrity" (Lohner 2011, 20). Figure 14.1 illustrates the dynamics of integrity in a police career, including the personal, departmental, and external forces affecting an officer's behavior.

Jetmore (2008a, 104) points out, "Deciding what's right or wrong is a large part of what police officers do, and state statute books are full of laws, so why is it tough to figure out the right thing? It's because our society entrusts the police to decide under what circumstances to enforce the law. Simply because an officer has the legal power to do something doesn't make it the right thing to do." He (106) explains that improper conduct can be rationalized because of the disparity that exists between official policy and the reality of what occurs on the street and because of the nature of police discretion in making decisions. Jetmore (2008b, 68) also notes the sharp difference between the philosophical definition of *ethics* used in the academic world and that of the real-life definition facing officers confronting the "claw and the fang" world of "drive-by shootings,

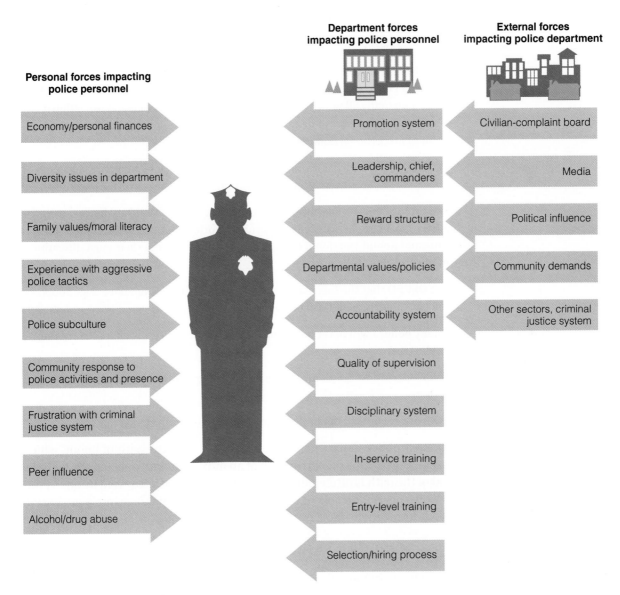

FIGURE 14.1 Dynamics of Police Integrity
Source: *Police Integrity: Public Service with Honor* (Washington, DC: National Institute of Justice, January 1997), 92.

murders, the effects of drugs, suicide, widespread homeless, AIDS, domestic violence, poverty, child abuse, etc."

The Law Enforcement Oath of Honor

1.12

CALEA Standard 1.12 states, "A written directive requires all personnel, prior to assuming sworn status, to take and subsequently abide by an oath of office to enforce the law and uphold the nation's Constitution or basic law of the land, and, where applicable, those of governmental subdivisions."

Source: Commission on Accreditation of Law Enforcement Agencies (CALEA). 2012. *Standards for Law Enforcement Agencies.* 5th ed. Fairfax, VA: Author.

On October 21, 1988, the IACP passed the following resolution (Bennett et al. 1999, 24–29):

> WHEREAS, integrity is acknowledged by the International Association of Chiefs of Police to be one of the most significant needs throughout the world and for virtually all professions, and because the International Association of Chiefs of Police seeks to demonstrate worldwide leadership in the advancement of professional honor, integrity, and ethics, and
>
> WHEREAS, an oath is universally recognized to be a solemn pledge someone makes when they sincerely intend to commit to what they advocate and affirm,
>
> WHEREAS, sincere commitment to an oath can provide vital guidance during a life's most crucial decisions, a moral anchoring that can endure the test of time and a solid emotional foundation for officer's facing their most difficult moments; now, therefore be it
>
> RESOLVED that the International Association of Chiefs of Police does adopt the Law Enforcement Oath of Honor.
>
> On my honor I will never betray my badge, my integrity, my character, or the public trust.
>
> I will always have the courage to hold myself and others accountable for our actions.
>
> I will always uphold the Constitution and the community I serve.[1]

In most police departments, new officers recite the oath of honor, which stresses integrity. The indoctrination of an individual into policing through the recital of the oath is often marked with ceremony and witnessed by one's family, friends, peers, and colleagues. It is a proud rite of passage into a profession steeped in tradition. The newcomers soon become part of the police culture.

Codes of Ethics

Another focus in most departments is a code of ethics, which further define what is expected of officers. One departmental force influencing police officers is often a *code of ethics* that sets forth accepted standards of behavior for a profession. The code of ethics is often framed and hanging on the wall. Such codes usually have at least three important themes:

▶ Justice or fairness is the single most dominant theme. Officers are not to take advantage of people or accept gratuities.

▶ The importance of the law and the police as tools of the Constitution is a second theme. Police behavior must be totally within the bounds set by the law.

▶ The third theme is that police must at all times uphold a standard of behavior consistent with their public position.

---

[1]Source: Bennett, Charles; Bushey, Keith; Cummings, Patrick; Doherty, Ann Marie; Hesser, Larry; Jahn, Mike; and Melton, Richard. "The Law Enforcement Oath of Honor." *The Police Chief*, October 1999, pp. 24–29.

Often, however, the police department's formal code of ethics and its informal code of ethics are entirely different. The informal code of ethics results from what is commonly referred to as the police culture.

The Police Culture

This culture has been studied for more than 40 years and may include some of the following beliefs unique to the profession and that may promote unethical behavior: The police are the only real crime fighters. Loyalty counts more than anything. It is impossible to win the war on crime without bending the rules. The public is demanding and nonsupportive.

> Conventional wisdom holds that the defining characteristics of the police culture are social isolation and group loyalty, resulting in a code of silence. This phenomenon is also called the *thin blue line*.

Officers have to decide where their *first loyalty* lies—to fellow officers or to enforcing the law. The answer is in the oath of honor every officer takes upon accepting the call to the badge. The officer promises to support, protect, and defend the Constitution of the United States, the constitution and laws of his state, and possibly the laws and ordinances of his county or city. Fellow officers, the chief, or the sheriff are not mentioned. Nonetheless, many officers will put loyalty to their colleagues above loyalty to the public or even to the department, often by abiding by the code of silence.

The Code of Silence

The National Institute of Ethics (NIE) conducted, between February 1999 and June 2000, what some consider the most extensive study ever performed on the police code of silence (Trautman 2000). Of the 3,714 officers and recruits who participated in the study,

▶ 79 percent said that a law enforcement code of silence exists and is fairly common throughout the nation.

▶ 52 percent said that the fact a code of silence exists does not really bother them.

▶ 24 percent said the code of silence is more justified when excessive force involves a citizen who is abusive.

▶ 46 percent said they would not tell on another cop for regularly smoking marijuana off duty.

Another survey by the NIE, with 1,116 officers participating, found that 46 percent of the officers stated they had witnessed misconduct by another employee but had not taken action (Trautman 2001). Of those officers, 47 percent said they had felt pressure to take part in the code of silence from the officers who committed the misconduct. According to Trautman (2001, 69), "Anger was the most frequent incident for which the code of silence was used; 41 percent were excessive use of force circumstances." A code of silence breeds, supports, and nourishes other forms of unethical actions. Furthermore, "The 'Us vs. Them' mentality is usually present within the minds of those who participate in the Code of Silence" (Trautman 2001, 71).

> The code of silence and the Us versus Them mentality often bond. Loyalty becomes more important than integrity.

Developing loyalty and the code of silence is an understandable phenomenon among people who spend significant time together. This intimate bond is unique to professions such as law enforcement where officers may have to sacrifice their lives for their partners, and the partners are willing to do the same for them. However, the bottom line is that an officer cannot subscribe to both the code of ethics and the code of silence. Quinn (2004) cautions,

> As terrible as it is, there is no escaping the Code. It is as inevitable as your childhood diseases and just as necessary. Each stinging battle with the Code will be either an inoculation of the spirit and an opportunity to grow stronger or a crippling injury to your integrity. Regardless of the outcome there will be vivid images you can't erase from your memory. There will always be the mental and physical scars to remind you of your battles. (24–25)

> But, each encounter can leave you better prepared both physically and mentally for the tough challenges ahead, if you are willing to admit you're not superman, and you recognize your "dark side" for what it is. Because only when we know the Code of Silence for what it is can we gain some control over it. Either way, you won't escape unscathed because at some point in time you are going to "Walk with the Devil" in order to get the job done. (25)

> Every day is a new challenge and ethical police conduct is often an uphill battle. Even the best of cops have days when they want to give up and do whatever it takes to put a child molester, baby murderer, or other lowlife in prison. When you sit inches away from these scum and they brag about the truly horrific things they have done to an innocent it's easy to abide by the Code—if that's what it takes. When the evidence isn't perfect, you just use a little creative report writing and this guy will never harm another person again. Illegal searches, physical abuse, or even perjury, you know you will be in the company of many good cops who have done the same. But are they really good cops? (13–14)

> The choice of being a "Peace Officer" means there will be many battles in solitary combat with other cops and with yourself. You will not win them all—you cannot—the cards are stacked against you. There will be no medals, awards ceremonies, or cheering crowds for the battles you do win. But there will be honor and integrity—in your life and in your work. (18)[2]

Using the code of silence to "cover" for a colleague is usually clearly unethical. But many areas of policing are not so clear.

---

[2]Source: Michael W. Quinn, *Walking with the Devil: The Police Code of Silence (What Bad Cops Don't Want You to Know and Good Cops Won't Tell You)* (Minneapolis, MN: Quinn and Associates, 2004).

GRAY AREAS IN POLICE ETHICS

> Three areas in discussions of law enforcement ethics are controversial: police use of deception, police acceptance of gratuities, and professional courtesy.

Police Use of Deception

As Klockars (1995, 552) comments, "At the core of the ethical life of the officer is a profound moral dilemma. On the one hand, the officer's obligations to the values of civilized society oblige him or her to coerce people effectively. On the other hand, the officer's obligation to coerce people effectively requires that he or she suspend the very values that civilized society treasures."

Klockars (1995, 552) describes two types of lies commonly used by police officers in doing their duties. The first is the **police placebo** (sometimes referred to as the "little white lie"): "Police officers find it ethically defensible to lie when the lie is told to benefit the person lied to and no more effective means of dealing with the problem is available." Klockars gives as an example two mentally ill brothers well known to police who believed they were being pursued by invisible agents from outer space. The brothers were told by officers that they had reported the so-called invasion to Washington and were sending out a squad of equally invisible investigators to protect the brothers.

The second type of lie is the **blue lie** (Klockars 1995, 553): "'Blue lies' are different from police placebos in that they are not told to help or comfort the person lied to but, rather, to exert control." Klockars gives as an example a police officer attempting to remove an abortion protestor from an abortion clinic waiting room. She insisted they'd have to carry her out. The officer told her he had just had a hernia repaired and was afraid if he lifted her, he would tear out his stitches. He even offered to show her, but his lie was sufficient to get her to leave peacefully.

In some circumstances, lies may be justified by investigative necessity. While performing their duties, officers may engage in a significant amount of deceptive conduct essential to public safety. Consider lying to suspects, conducting undercover operations, and even deploying unmarked cars. Presenting a suspect with false evidence, a false confession of a crime partner, or a false claim that the suspect was identified in a lineup are but a few of the deceptive practices police officers have used for years during interrogations. These investigatory deceptive practices are necessary when no other means would be effective, when they are lawful, and when they are aimed at obtaining the truth.

Alpert and Noble (2009, 237) agree that police often use the preceding practices in interrogation, but note, "Although they are allowed to be dishonest in certain circumstances, they are also required to be trustworthy, honest, and maintain the highest level of integrity." Some deceptive practices may lead to unintended consequences such as false confessions. One such contested practice is entrapment, introduced in Chapter 12 and discussed again shortly as a form of unethical behavior.

police placebo

A lie told by the police when the lie benefits the person lied to and when no more effective means of dealing with the problem is available; also known as a *white lie*.

blue lie

A lie told not to help or comfort the person lied to but, rather, to exert control.

Moore (2007, 146) contends, "It's a fact of life in law enforcement: criminals don't often go quietly into the night. Many times police are forced to use deceptive means to corral suspects who continue to elude arrest. And as long as the means are legal, then as far as I'm concerned whatever it takes to get the job done is fine." She gives as an example an officer who posed as a reporter to lure a suspect with outstanding warrants into a position to be arrested. The media cried foul, claiming entrapment. It simply was not. As the Supreme Court has repeatedly acknowledged, "Criminal activity is such that stealth and strategy are necessary weapons in the arsenal of the police officer" (*Sorrells v. United States* 1932). "Nor will the mere fact of deceit defeat a prosecution, for there are circumstances when the use of deceit is the only practicable law enforcement technique available" (*United States v. Russell* 1973).

When deception does cross the line to become entrapment, it is not an issue of the conduct becoming unethical—it is a matter of the conduct becoming illegal. *Sorrells* was the first time the Supreme Court recognized the entrapment defense and drew a line between capturing the unwary innocent and netting the unwary criminal. In this case, a federal prohibition agent, undercover as a tourist, engaged Sorrells in conversation. After gaining the defendant's confidence by sharing common war experiences, the agent asked for some liquor and was twice refused. The third time he asked, however, Sorrells gave in and was then arrested and subsequently prosecuted for violating the National Prohibition Act. Speaking for the Court, Chief Justice Hughes said the defendant should have had the defense of entrapment available. This defense prohibits law enforcement officers from instigating a criminal act by those "otherwise innocent in order to lure them to its commission and to punish them."

Gratuities

Another gray area of ethics includes the acceptance of gratuities. The formal law enforcement code of ethics disapproves of *gratuities*, material favors, or gifts given in return for a service. However, many citizens feel there is nothing wrong with a business giving freebies, such as gifts or free admission, to a police officer. Many officers believe these are small rewards for the difficulties they endure in police work.

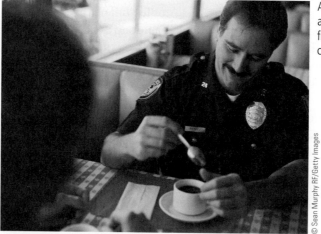

Accepting gratuities such as free coffee can be the first step toward becoming corrupt.

© Sean Murphy RF/Getty Images

Allowing Gratuities

- They help create a friendly bond between officers and the public, thus fostering community-policing goals.

- They represent a nonwritten form of appreciation and usually are given with no expectation of anything in return.

- Most gratuities are too small to be a significant motivator of actions.

- The practice is so deeply entrenched that efforts to root it out will be ineffective and cause unnecessary violations of the rules.

- A complete ban makes officers appear as though they cannot distinguish between a friendly gesture and a bribe.

- Some businesses and restaurants insist on the practice.

Banning Gratuities

- The acceptance violates most departments' policies and the law enforcement code of ethics.

- Even the smallest gifts create a sense of obligation.

- Even if nothing is expected in return, the gratuity may create an appearance of impropriety.

- Although most officers can discern between friendly gestures and bribes, some may not.

- They create an unfair distribution of services to those who can afford gratuities, voluntary taxing, or private funding of a public service.

- It is unprofessional.

FIGURE 14.2 Arguments For and Against Gratuities
Source: Mike White. "The Problem with Gratuities." *FBI Law Enforcement Bulletin,* July 2002. p. 21. Reprinted by permission of the author.

The question becomes, What gratuities are acceptable and under what circumstances, if any? Certainly gratuities are acceptable in many other professions. But in a profession involving great discretion, gratuities can be extremely problematic. They can give the appearance of preferential treatment, even if such preferential treatment does not exist. As O. W. Wilson was fond of saying, "Nobody ever gave a cop something for nothing." Figure 14.2 summarizes the arguments for and against accepting gratuities.

▌ AN OFFICER'S PERSPECTIVE ▌
Gratuities: To Accept or Not to Accept?

Many people who support the police and want to show gratitude may do something like bake them cookies. In one community, some citizens wanted to thank their public safety professionals, so they baked cookies for the local firefighters and police officers. The firefighters accepted them with thankfulness. The police, however, had to turn them away saying they could not accept gratuities, which offended the citizens.

The argument behind the difference between the firefighters being able to accept the cookies and the police being unable to do so is that the police have the influence of authority over individuals.

In jurisdictions with such absolute policies regarding gratuities, it is still hard to turn away the small child who made cookies for the police simply because she wants to someday become a police officer. She clearly has no expectation of anything in return—it is a pure gesture of gratitude.

—*Sgt. Henry Lim Cho*

An example of a questionable ethical situation would be a gas station that offers complimentary coffee to the police. Although this not an expensive item, there are certain possible expectations that may occur from accepting the coffee. Perhaps the owner expects to get out of a speeding ticket if stopped by the local police he gives free coffee to. Even if there are no expectations such as this, perhaps the fact that officers know that this establishment offers them free coffee results in them frequenting the business more often than other local business. Another business that does not offer this complimentary service might argue that it is not being protected or frequented as equally as the business that does.

Accepting gratuities may be the first small step on the road to more unethical behaviors and eventually to corruption.

Professional Courtesy

Professional courtesy has existed in the medical profession for centuries, physicians taking care of each other and their families, lawyers representing each other and their families, usually for no fee. However, the situation in law enforcement is different. Wolfe (2009) describes how, in his one-squad-car town, with him the only officer under the chief, the chief explained how cops need to help other cops when they were in trouble. This is certainly true in the case where one officer's home is devastated by a hurricane or tornado, but this is not what the chief was talking about. He used the example of an off-duty cop who crashed his car while driving drunk. If there were no witnesses, he would have no problem "looking the other way," giving the officer a ride home, and cleaning up the accident scene. He stressed that cops had to watch out for one another, to take care of each other, to extend them *professional courtesy*.

Sometimes off-duty officers who are pulled over for speeding will be sure to make their badge visible to the officer who stopped them, in what may be an attempt to get out of a ticket. In many cases, this tactic works. However, many—citizens and officers alike—consider this to be an abuse of the badge.

Wolfe suggests that how each officer handles the matter is up to the individual officer. Consider the offender's attitude. Might a verbal warning solve the problem? And remember, anyone can order a badge. A call to the supervisor to verify the ID might be in order. Nonetheless, the safest and most ethical practice is to treat off-duty officers as you would treat any citizen.

Professional courtesy should not mean that one officer lets another officer go simply because he or she carries a badge. To Wolfe, it means that when another officer is in his jurisdiction, that officer will behave so as to not require contact with him. In other words, officers who come into his jurisdiction must act professionally and he, in turn, will do likewise. He, like many, does not condone using the badge as a "get out of jail free" card.

UNETHICAL BEHAVIOR

Police routinely deal with the seamier side of society, not only drug addicts and muggers, but middle-class people involved in dishonesty and corruption. The constant displays of lying, hiding, cheating, and theft create cynicism and threaten even the strongest code of ethics, especially when these behaviors are carried out by judges, prosecutors, superiors, and politicians. The following are some rationales police might easily use to justify unethical behavior:

▶ The money is there—if I don't take it, someone else will.

▶ I'm only taking what's rightfully mine; if I got a decent wage, I wouldn't have to get it on my own.

▶ I need it—it's a good cause—my wife needs an operation.

▶ I put my life on the line every day—I deserve it.

Trautman (2009) offers four primary reasons good cops do unethical things:

1. They lie to themselves with excuses.

2. They experience momentary selfishness.

3. They just make a bad decision.

4. They are afraid of "being ostracized" for doing the right thing.

Training plays a critical role in setting the stage for new recruits and the unwavering expectation that officers maintain and abide by the highest ethical standards possible throughout their career, including how to avoid the pitfalls of unethical deception and corruption.

Unethical Deception

Deceptive behavior might be viewed on a continuum, with lies justified by necessity and based on circumstances on one end and intentional, unethical, deceptive conduct at the other end. As discussed, police are sometimes justified in walking through a gray zone of deception as a means to an end, and lies of the former variety might be excused, even if not accepted. Lies of the latter type, however, can cause great harm and often leave no option other than the termination of officer's employment. Unethical deception might include falsely testifying in court ("testilying"), failing to reveal exculpatory evidence, or creating false evidence implicating someone in a criminal act.

False Testimony The deceptive practice of giving false testimony to imprison a criminal is clearly unethical. Although the officer's intent—removing a criminal from society—may be laudable, and the officer may truly believe he is engaging in a greater good, this lie under oath (**perjury**) violates a standard of reasonableness and appropriateness under the circumstances, considering the status obligations of the person engaging in the lie. Although the intent may be legitimate, the actions are unethical. This malice is the motive by which any sense of limits or constraint or fidelity to law and policy is destroyed. Motive or intentions can be mixed, so a person may deceive to pursue some worthwhile, utilitarian goal (such as public safety) and at the same time have a total disregard for the rights of the suspect and for the laws, policies, and limits that apply to policing.

perjury

Lying under oath.

Withholding Exculpatory Evidence Another type of unethical deception occurs when police withhold evidence that might benefit the criminal defense. A *duty to disclose* was established in the landmark case of *Brady v. Maryland* (1963), in which the U.S. Supreme Court ruled that the government has a duty

exculpatory evidence

Evidence favorable to a defendant in a criminal case that could tend to prove that the accused party is innocent or cast doubt as to their guilt, often referred to as "*Brady* Material."

to divulge material evidence to the defense that could tend to change the outcome of a trial. This decision placed an affirmative constitutional duty on prosecutors to disclose any and all **exculpatory evidence**, often referred to as "*Brady* Material," or evidence favorable to a defendant in a criminal case that could tend to prove that the accused parties are innocent or cast doubt as to their guilt. This duty has been extended to law enforcement agencies through case law, requiring police to notify the prosecutor of any potential exculpatory information (Rothlein 2007).

Giglio v. United States (1972) expanded the *Brady* decision by requiring prosecutors to provide information to the defense that could tend to impeach a witness, including information about the credibility of police officers and the veracity of their testimony (Rothlein 2007). Under the *Giglio* doctrine, a prosecutor is required to notify the defense if the potential witness is an officer with a past record of falsifying reports or other conduct that could affect their truthfulness.

These rulings affect police in that officers with a documented history of lying while in an official capacity, falsifying official reports, or expressing bias will likely be unable to testify in court because their credibility is compromised and could be challenged. This situation creates liability for agencies and for officers, directly affecting their ability to perform a critical aspect of their job (testifying). Being forever labeled an impeachable witness presents an operational deficit that can essentially destroy a police officer's career. The best way for agencies to protect against any civil litigation based on the *Brady* or *Giglio* rulings is to ensure that (Rothlein 2007):

▶ All officers receive proper training on the obligation and duty to disclose exculpatory material.

▶ The agency has a policy requiring officers to document exculpatory information and provide it to the prosecutors.

▶ The agency has trained investigators concerning their obligations under the *Giglio* doctrine, including informing prosecutors of information that could impeach the testimony of their officers.

Corruption

Unethical behavior in its extreme form results in corruption. Corruption is not just a 21st-century police problem. Much police corruption is drug related, for example, stealing money or drugs from drug dealers, selling stolen drugs, planting drugs on suspects, and protecting drug operations. A police officer making a modest salary may be greatly tempted by easily gaining the equivalent of two years' salary by making one "favorable" decision for the drug trafficker. Other corrupt behaviors may or may not be drug related, such as conducting unconstitutional searches and seizures, providing false testimony, and submitting false crime reports. Although examples of police corruption vary, they all have key elements in common.

The key elements in corrupt behavior are (1) conduct prohibited by law (2) involving misuse of position (3) resulting in a reward or personal gain for the officer.

Several factors contribute to becoming corrupt, such as ego, greed, sex, or the exercise of power; tolerance of the behavior by the community; socialization from peers or the organization; inadequate supervision and monitoring of behavior; lack of clear accountability of employees' behavior; and no real threat of discipline or sanctions.

> Perhaps the most important factor in police officers becoming corrupt is the extraordinary amount of discretion they have.

In a 1981 FBI Academy graduation address, Chief Justice Burger stated, "The policeman on the beat, or in the patrol car, makes more decisions and exercises broader discretion affecting the daily lives of people every day and to a greater extent, in many respects, than a judge will ordinarily exercise in a week." Where officers run into trouble is when they apply inappropriate values to their discretionary decisions, such as what can occur with the ends-versus-means dilemma.

The Ends-versus-Means Dilemma The "ends" of policing are noble: keep the peace, bring criminals to justice, serve and protect the public. Some officers come to believe that the ends justify the means by which they are accomplished, and they resort to unlawful behavior in the name of justice. This type of unethical behavior is also called *noble cause corruption*: "The only values officers must employ in the delivery of their police services are the values of the profession. They are not to use their own personal values in their decision-making processes while enforcing the law.… Noble cause corruption in policing occurs when good officers substitute in their personal values for the values of the profession and the law. It is an ends-justifies-the-means rationalization associated with public service wherein officers break the law to enforce the law" (Martinelli 2011, 61).

The Slippery Slope Another theory on why good cops turn bad is that something seemingly insignificant, such as accepting free coffee or meals, can put an officer on a **slippery slope**, leading to major crimes. According to Trautman (2001, 68), "Research repeatedly confirms that most scandals start with one employee doing relatively small unethical acts and grow to whatever level the leadership allows." He calls this the *corruption continuum*.

slippery slope

One small indiscretion can lead to more serious misbehavior and finally to actual corruption.

Being above the Law Another explanation for police officers becoming corrupt is that they are taught in the academy that in many areas they may break the law; for example, they can exceed speed limits, go through red lights, and carry concealed weapons.

Violating the law may impair crime control by alienating the public, lessening their willingness to assist the police. In addition, when police violate the law, they forfeit the cooperation they need and increase the likelihood that encounters with the public will generate hostility and violence, placing police officers at risk.

> In addition to the existence of discretion, officers may become corrupt because they believe the ends justify the means, they begin with accepting gratuities and progress to larger indiscretions, they believe they are above the law, or they engage in the code of silence.

Rotten Apples versus Rotten Barrels

Although corruption begins with individual officers, controversy exists about whether a rotten apple spoils the barrel or the other way around. It is commonly thought that a few "bad apples" can cause a whole department's reputation to suffer when a scandal is uncovered. Some scandals, such as the Rodney King incident, can cause the whole profession's reputation to suffer.

 The culture of the police department (the barrel) can allow or eliminate corrupt behavior (bad apples).

Fortunately, only a small percentage of officers are corrupt. As noted, most corrupt behaviors begin with unethical behavior rather than outright corruption.

BASIC ETHICS TESTS

Some questions, such as the question of gratuities, might appear to be black-and-white (absolute) issues to most, but many other ethical decisions police officers must make are not black and white at all, but are instead varying shades of gray (relative issues). To arrest or not? To inform on someone or not? To lie to suspects to build a case or not? In such instances, the answer is seldom obvious. How do police officers decide what is and is not ethical behavior?

 Some basic ethics tests include asking oneself, Am I doing the right thing? At the right time? In the right way? For the right reason? How would I feel if it were to be made public?

Trautman (2009) suggests three steps to take when thinking about an ethical decision: (1) clearly understand the issues, (2) evaluate the facts, and (3) make the decision by applying objective standards to the dilemma. He says officers should ask themselves,

▶ What would I do if my family was behind me?
▶ Is it worth my job and career?
▶ How will I feel about myself 20 years from now?
▶ Would those who love me be proud or ashamed?

Many people believe all behavior should be guided by the Golden Rule: Do unto others as you would have them do unto you. Other, less positive people have coined the Silver Rule: Do unto others before they do unto you. A simple maxim might guide police officers when they wrestle with ethical decisions:

There is no right way to do a wrong thing.

Police officers have awesome powers over other people's lives. They must act legally and ethically to be true professionals and to be true to themselves as individuals. It has been said that there is no pillow so soft as a clear conscience.

Ethical behavior within a law enforcement agency is ultimately the responsibility of each individual officer within that agency.

A BRIEF WORD ABOUT INTERNAL AFFAIRS INVESTIGATIONS

When police corruption or unethical behavior is suspected or alleged, a department is obligated to respond and investigate, often by initiating an internal affairs (IA) investigation. Policing the police is a difficult job, and many such investigators are referred to as "the rat squad" by officers outside the IA division.

Internal affairs sections traditionally are reactive, responding to citizen complaints and reports of misconduct and policy violations from other department members (Dees 2003). Although IA investigators protect the public from abusive or unethical police, they also work to protect individual officers from unfounded allegations. Five functions of the IA process are (1) protecting the public, (2) protecting the department, (3) protecting the employee, (4) removing unfit personnel, and (5) correcting procedural problems (Kelly 2003).

Figure 14.3 illustrates how an issue can flow through the system to become an IA investigation. As shown, issues come to the attention of the department

FIGURE 14.3 Sorting Chart: How a Case Gets to Internal Affairs
Source: Deputy Chief Todd Sandell, Richfield (Minnesota) Police Department, 2009. Reprinted by permission.

at the *intake* stage from internal (other officers) and external (the public) sources. At intake, a first-line supervisor, usually a sergeant, determines if the issue is a concern or a complaint. Complaints are further sorted as minor, serious, or criminal, with the cases involving serious administrative policy concerns being those processed into the IA division.

Colaprete (2005, 112) emphasizes, "Police administrators are constantly faced with political pressure, media attention, the requirements of legal and collective bargaining agreements, and the protection of the community in the conduct of all internal investigations." If there is even a hint of criminal behavior by the officer, the matter should be separated into both a criminal and an administrative investigation. The criminal investigation should be conducted first, including the *Miranda* warning if applicable. This is followed by the administrative investigation, including a *Garrity* warning if applicable.[3]

The first step is to review all evidence. Next, obtain copies of all associated elements of the case. These can include a copy of the crime or arrest report, a computer printout of the call-for-service, a copy of radio transmissions, and any other retrievable items. A fundamental component of most investigations is interviewing all involved parties.

ETHICS AND COMMUNITY POLICING

The roots of community policing can be found in Sir Robert Peel's instructions to the Metropolitan Police in 1829: "The primary objective of an efficient police department is prevention of crime: the next that of detection and punishment of offenders if crime is committed.... In attaining these objectives, much depends on the approval and cooperation of the public, and these have always been determined by the degree of the esteem and respect in which the police are held." As police officers get involved with the community and work together to solve problems, they may change the way they think and, more importantly, the way they behave.

INTEGRATING ETHICS INTO THE SARA MODEL

Trautman (2009) asserts, "Law enforcement does a shameful job of preparing cops to make difficult ethical decisions. This is particularly tragic considering the fact that virtually every time an officer is justifiably fired or arrested it

---

[3]The Supreme Court ruled in *Garrity v. New Jersey* (1967) that a violation of the Fourteenth Amendment occurs when the government uses a police officer's statement in a criminal trial against that officer. Officers accused of misconduct can be threatened with loss of their jobs if they do not cooperate with an internal investigation. *In other words, anything used in a criminal trial may be used in an administrative trial, but the reverse is not true.*

Under the *Garrity* rule, "An employer has the right to require employees to answer questions regarding their conduct as long as those questions are narrowly drawn and directly related to the duties they were hired to perform. The employer may use these statements in disciplinary actions involving the employee which could result in termination of employment." However, if the employer uses *Garrity* to compel an officer to answer questions, employers are prohibited from giving this information to police or having it used during a criminal trial. The officer must request *Garrity* protection. Officers can protect themselves by getting in writing a *Garrity* protection, a written notification that they are making their statement or report involuntarily.

resulted from a bad ethical decision." Agencies are duty-bound to train about the moments most likely to destroy an officer's career.

The Boston Police Department has done just this by establishing a task force to integrate ethics analysis into the SARA problem-solving model by using the dilemmas-options-consequences (DOC) method as well: "The DOC method puts moral decision making in the day-to-day realm of an officer's professional and personal life. The DOC method challenges officers to carefully consider their decisions, as well as the short- and long-term consequences of those decisions" (Romano et al. 2000, 98).

Romano et al. (2000, 99) say if a decision maker is facing a dilemma that "feels" wrong, he or she should ask questions such as:

▶ What feels unsatisfactory? What feels wrong?

▶ Who or what is presenting a choice to me?

▶ Is there a moral or ethical threat to me or someone else?

▶ Will I, or someone in the community, be affected or hurt physically or emotionally?

▶ Will I, or someone in the community, be treated disrespectfully or without dignity?

▶ Is my quality of life, or the quality of life of someone in the community, threatened?

Once the dilemma is defined, the action or response phase involves the following questions:

▶ What are my options?

▶ What are the extreme options?

▶ Am I considering all options?

▶ Am I being open-minded and creative about my options?

▶ Do my options rely only on me, or could I use a resource or someone's help? What are those resources? Whose help could I use?

For each option, the consequences must be assessed by asking questions such as the following:

▶ What happens because of my choice? What happens if I do nothing?

▶ Who is affected by what I do? How will they be affected? How will I be affected?

▶ Will I be preserving and protecting the quality of life and the dignity of others?

▶ Will I be preserving my moral and ethical integrity? Will I be preserving the moral and ethical integrity of my organization?

▶ What are the short-term effects? What are the long-term effects?

As Romano et al. (2000, 102) suggest, "Ethical problem solving incorporates values, human dignity, and respect into the problem-solving process. It encourages officers to include stakeholders, rather than exclude stakeholders. This method raises the standards in the community and will ultimately positively affect the qualify of life in that community."

SUMMARY

Officers may be sued under three types of state liability (tort) laws: strict liability, intentional tort, and negligence. Most civil lawsuits brought against law enforcement officers are based on Statute 42 of the U.S. Code, Section 1983, also called the Civil Rights Act. This act says that anyone acting under the authority of the law who violates another person's constitutional rights can be sued. The most frequent civil lawsuits against police involve false arrest or imprisonment, malicious prosecution, use of unnecessary or excessive force and police brutality, wrongful death, negligent operation of a vehicle, failure to protect, failure to identify, and negligent service.

Protection against lawsuits includes effective policies and procedures clearly communicated to all, thorough and continuous training, proper supervision and discipline, and accurate, thorough police reports. The importance of documentation cannot be emphasized enough. Comprehensive, well-written incident reports are vital to defenses against civil suits.

To minimize lawsuits at a more personal level, law enforcement officers should know and follow their department's policies and procedures; stay in the scope of their duties; always act professionally; know and respect their constituents' rights; seek advice if in doubt; carefully document their activities in their reports; maintain good community relations; keep current on civil and criminal liability cases; and know the laws. The normal defenses used by police officers, departments, and municipalities being sued are that they did not intend to deprive the plaintiff of constitutional rights, that they acted in good faith, and that they acted with what was considered reasonable judgment at the time and with valid authority. Law enforcement officers and agencies can countersue if they are falsely accused of a civil offense.

Police officers should be concerned with acting legally to avoid civil lawsuits, as well as with acting ethically. Ethics deals with standards of honesty, fairness, and integrity in behavior. An absolute issue is one with only two sides—the decision is between black and white. A relative issue is one with many sides, that is, varying shades of gray between the two absolute positions. Ethical issues are usually relative and are affected by the police culture. Conventional wisdom holds that the defining characteristics of the police culture are social isolation and group loyalty, resulting in a code of silence. This phenomenon is also called the *thin blue line*. The code of silence and the attitude of Us versus Them often bond. Loyalty becomes more important than integrity.

Three areas in discussions of law enforcement ethics are controversial: police use of deception, police acceptance of gratuities, and professional courtesy. Accepting gratuities may be the first step on the way to corrupt behavior. The key elements in corrupt behavior are (1) conduct prohibited by law (2) involving misuse of position (3) resulting in a reward or personal gain for the officer. Perhaps the most important factor in police officers becoming corrupt is the extraordinary amount of discretion they have. In addition to the existence of discretion, officers may become corrupt because they believe the ends justify the means, they begin with accepting gratuities and progress to larger indiscretions, they believe they are above the law, or they engage in the code of silence. The culture of the police department (the barrel) can allow or eliminate corrupt behavior (bad apples).

Basic ethics tests include asking oneself, Am I doing the right thing? At the right time? In the right way? For the right reason? How would I feel if it were made public? There is no right way to do a wrong thing. Ethical behavior within a law enforcement agency is ultimately the responsibility of each officer within that agency.

APPLICATION

The chief of police has been concerned about officers coming to him wanting advice about what to do when business people give them gratuities such as boxes of candy, children's toys, bottles of liquor, and other items useful to an officer and the officer's family. The officers are concerned as to how much they can take, when they can take it, and whether they should report to the administration upon receipt. The chief asks a committee, of which you are chair, to develop a policy and procedure to clarify how officers are to respond to such offers.

INSTRUCTIONS

Write a policy and procedure specifying the need for uniformity in accepting gratuities and gifts and if they are to be accepted at all. Include what can be accepted and under what circumstances.

EXERCISES IN CRITICAL THINKING

A. In the early morning hours, Jacqueline McKone stepped outside her apartment and witnessed what she said was the uncalled-for arrest and beating of a young Black man, 21-year-old Dennis Cherry. McKone was a legal assistant in an attorney's office, completing coursework to become a court reporter. She reported that four police officers held Cherry, and one, whom she identified as Ed Nelson, hit him. Cherry, she reported, had done nothing to attract the police or to resist their efforts to arrest him. The incident occurred more than a block away from the Convention Center, to which police had come to close down a dance.

Several officers, including Nelson, tried to intimidate McKone as she stood watching the scene. She said this to herself, however: I can't stop it, but I will watch this whole thing and report it. When Lieutenant Bruce Jones arrived on the scene, she approached him to report what she had witnessed.

1. When Lieutenant Jones arrived at the scene, what should have been his treatment of McKone?

   a. To tell McKone that the police were simply following arrest procedure and that because she was not present at the beginning of the incident or close enough to hear all that Cherry said to police, she could not be expected to understand what actually happened.

   b. First, to ask if she had been harmed; second, to apologize for what she had witnessed; and then, to provide her with the information needed to contact civilian review.

   c. First, to interview the police officers who conducted the arrest, then to interview McKone, and then to explain to McKone that although Cherry denied it, the police said he tried to hit them, which justified their treatment of Cherry.

   d. To ignore McKone other than to tell her that she could bring her views and testimony to the Police Civilian Review Authority.

   e. To gently remind McKone that it was not wise to offend local police, especially well-liked officers such as Nelson, and to point out that if she called the news media and filed a complaint, she would get a series of hateful, racist responses accusing her of having a Black boyfriend or of being a "nigger lover."

B. In June, a police officer received information from a confidential, reliable informant. He had observed a film depicting a 16-year-old girl engaging in sex with a Rottweiler dog while at the home of Robert Bonynge. The officer applied for a search warrant for Bonynge's residence. The affidavit accompanying the application reiterated the information received from the informant and stated that the officer sought the search warrant "to seize any film involving child pornography and bestiality." The warrant permitted seizure of the following:

> Pornography films involving female juveniles and a Rottweiler dog and any contraband that would violate the state statute governing the pornography laws. Any filming equipment and duplicating equipment.

The affidavit was attached to the warrant. The police executed the search warrant at Bonynge's residence. A police lieutenant observed the Rottweiler dog on the premises and numerous videocassettes, 8-millimeter movies, photographs, and magazines depicting sexual scenes involving young females, possibly juveniles. The officers seized hundreds of films and photographs including several commercial videotapes of popular motion pictures. The officer stated that it was his experience that "obscene material is planted in the middle of what appears to be a commercial tape to make it difficult to locate."

1. Were the videotapes seized in violation of Bonynge's Fourth Amendment rights?

   a. Yes, because the Fourth Amendment gives individuals the right to be free from unreasonable search and seizure and declares that warrants shall particularly describe the place to be searched and the person or things to be seized, and not all the videotapes were of pornographic subjects.

   b. Yes, because a warrant limits the discretion of the executing officers as well as gives notice to the party searched, and the materials seized were not described with sufficient particularity.

   c. No, because a warrant to search a residence gives rights to search all parts of that residence and seize any evidence found.

   d. Yes, because pornography is an ethical issue that must be left to individual discretion—no law or police action is appropriate.

   e. No, because the officers who swore out the affidavit also executed the search; they had the benefit of the more specific language of the affidavit.

2. Which of the following would be unethical?

   a. The temporary seizure of constitutionally protected material (in this case, of every film and videotape regardless of content).

   b. Providing a prior adversary hearing before authorizing the seizure of allegedly obscene material for the purpose of destroying it.

   c. Accepting gratuities from bookstores or commercial theaters involved in the distribution or exhibition of pornographic materials and being loyal to fellow officers who accept gratuities.

   d. Varying the times when you take breaks, eating meals at different times and places, filling out reports at irregular times and places to protect yourself from temptation, and blowing the whistle on colleagues who routinely bend rules.

   e. Exercising discretion while extending due process to criminal suspects and victims alike (such as withholding the identity of the 16-year-old girl).

DISCUSSION QUESTIONS

1. Have any misconduct lawsuits been filed against local police officers? Check with your police department to see what their history of civil lawsuits has been.

2. How much training is enough to avoid lawsuits under Section 1983? Explain your reasoning in the areas of firearms, search and seizure, and laws of arrest.

3. How could a Section 1983 action be brought where an officer in the locker room preparing for duty accidentally discharged his revolver, striking a custodian? What would be the justification for a lawsuit in this case?

4. In what areas of law enforcement should police officers be exempt from lawsuits, if any?

5. What are some temptations that lead to police misconduct or corruption?

6. Can ethical standards that apply to police officers be circumvented when it comes to apprehending drug dealers? If so, to what extent?

7. Do you feel there is value in civilian review boards?

GALE EMERGENCY SERVICES DATABASE ASSIGNMENTS

▶ Use the Gale Emergency Services database (available for separate purchase) to answer the Discussion Questions as appropriate.

▶ Use the Gale Emergency Services database to find and outline one of the following assignments:

- "Getting Along with Citizen Oversight" by Peter Finn
- "Managing for Ethics: A Mandate for Administrators" by Timothy J. O'Malley
- "Organizational Ethics through Effective Leadership" by Brandon V. Zuidema and H. Wayne Duff

- "Above Reproach" by Brian Parsi Boetig
- "Law Enforcement Ethics Do Not Begin When You Pin On the Badge" by Norman Stephens
- "To Arrest or Not Arrest" by Carole Moore
- "Crime Scene Ethics: Take It or Leave It" by Douglas Page
- "Ethics and Law Enforcement" by J. Kevin Grant
- "Institutional Integrity: The Four Elements of Self-Policing" by John H. Conditt, Jr. List and briefly explain what the four elements of self-policing are according to Conditt.

REFERENCES

Alpert, Geoffrey P., and Jeffrey J. Noble. 2009. "Lies, True Lies, and Conscious Deception: Police Officers and the Truth." *Police Quarterly* (June): 237–254.

Bennett, Charles, Keith Bushey, Patrick Cummings, Ann Marie Doherty, Larry Hesser, Mike Jahn, and Richard Melton. 1999. "The Law Enforcement Oath of Honor." *The Police Chief* (October): 24–29.

Bowden, John. 2009. "Proof Is in the Review." *PoliceOne.com* (January 30). Accessed April 20, 2012. http://www.policeone. com/police-technology/ruggedized-laptops/articles/ 1769178-Proof-is-in-the-review/.

Burch, Jay. 2008. "Letter of the Policy versus Spirit of the Policy: The Loss of Common Sense in Policing?" *Law and Order* (November): 69–74.

"Cameras." 2012 (January). In *How Are Innovations in Technology Transforming Policing?*, 13–24. Washington, DC: Police Executive Research Forum, Critical Issues in Policing Series.

Colaprete, Frank. 2005. "Internal Affairs Interviews." *Law and Order* (June): 112–115.

Commission on Accreditation of Law Enforcement Agencies (CALEA). 2012. *Standards for Law Enforcement Agencies.* 5th ed. Fairfax, VA: Author.

Dees, Tim. 2003. "Internal Affairs: Management Software." *Law and Order* (May): 88–95.

Gaut, William T. 2011 (August). *Examining the Relationship between Law Enforcement Accreditation, Citizen Complaints, Civil Lawsuits, and Adverse Monetary Judgments.* Prescott Valley, AZ: Northcentral University, PhD dissertation. Partial findings accessed April 19, 2012, on CALEA Web site. http://www.calea.org/content/did-you-know.

Griffith, David. 2009a. "The All Seeing Eye." *Police* (June): 8.

Griffith, David. 2009b. "Turning Cops into Cameras." *Police* (June): 38–41.

Grossi, Dave. 2008. "Tactics for Survival Writing." *Law Officer Magazine* (October): 30–33.

Jetmore, Larry R. 2008a. "Investigative Ethics." *Law Officer Magazine* (August): 104–108.

Jetmore, Larry R. 2008b. "Investigative Ethics: Part 2." *Law Officer Magazine* (September): 68–69.

Joyner, Chuck. 2009. "A Proper Use of Force Report— Protection against Liability." *PoliceOne.com News* (May 20). Accessed April 20, 2012. http://www.policeone.com/ police-products/less-lethal/TASER/articles/1834524-A- proper-use-of-force-report-protection-against-liability/.

Kelly, Sean F. 2003. "Internal Affairs Issues for Small Police Departments." *FBI Law Enforcement Bulletin* (July): 1–6.

Klockars, Carl B. 1995. "Police Ethics." In *The Encyclopedia of Police Science*, 2nd ed., edited by William G. Bailey, 549–553. New York: Garland.

Lohner, Wyn. 2011. "What Does It Take to Excel?" *FBI Law Enforcement Bulletin* (August): 20–23.

Martinelli, Thomas J. 2011. "Noble Cause Corruption and Police Discretion." *The Police Chief* (March): 60–62.

Means, Randy. 2007. "The Greatest Liability Reduction Tool." *Law and Order* (December): 32–33.

Moore, Carole. 2007. "Deceptive Techniques." *Law Enforcement Technology* (August): 146.

Quinn, Michael W. 2004. *Walking with the Devil: The Police Code of Silence (What Bad Cops Don't Want You to Know and Good Cops Won't Tell You).* Minneapolis, MN: Quinn and Associates.

Romano, Linda J., Jack McDevitt, Jimmie Jones, and William Johnson. 2000. "Combined Problem-Solving Models Incorporate Ethics Analysis." *The Police Chief* (August): 98–102.

Rothlein, Steve. 2007. *Brady v. Maryland: Do You Understand Your Obligations?* Indianapolis, IN: Public Agency Training Council, Legal & Liability Risk Management Institute.

Accessed April 20, 2012. http://www.patc.com/special/Brady-vs-Maryland.pdf.

Scoville, Dean. 2008. "Rules of Engagement." *Police* (October): 56–63.

Trautman, Neal. 2000. *Police Code of Silence*. Arlington, VA: International Association of Chiefs of Police.

Trautman, Neal. 2001. "Truth about Police Code of Silence Revealed." *Law and Order* (January): 68–76.

Trautman, Neal. 2009. "Overcoming the Moments Most Likely to End Your Career." *LawOfficer.com* (June 15). Accessed April 20, 2012. http://www.lawofficer.com/article/needs-tags-columns/surviving-ethical-dilemmas.

Wolfe, Duane. 2009. "Defining 'Professional Courtesy.'" *PoliceOne.com News* (June 5). Accessed April 20, 2012. http://www.policeone.com/off-duty/articles/1839305-Defining-professional-courtesy/.

CASES CITED

Brady v. Maryland, 373 U.S. 83 (1963)

Garrity v. New Jersey, 385 U.S. 493 (1967)

Giglio v. United States, 450 U.S. 150 (1972)

Graham v. Connor, 490 U.S. 386 (1989)

Sorrells v. United States, 287 U.S. 435 (1932)

Thurman v. City of Torrington, 595 F. Supp. 1521 (D. Conn. 1984)

United States v. Russell, 411 U.S. 423 (1973)

 CourseMate

This available CourseMate has an interactive eBook and interactive learning tools, including flash cards, quizzes, and more. To learn more about this resource and access free demo CourseMate resources, go to www.cengagebrain.com, and search for this book. To access CourseMate materials that you have purchased, go to login.cengagebrain.com.

Policies and Procedures Sample Form

Policies and Procedures Sample Form

Name of agency:	Date issued:
Procedure directive #:	Page _____ of _____
Effective date:	
Subject:	
Goal:	
Policy:	

Policy #:	Page _____ of _____
Procedures:	
	_____
	Chief of Police

GLOSSARY

Numbers in (parentheses) indicate the chapter in which the term can be found.

A

absolute issue—An issue with only two sides, viewed as either/or, black or white. (14)

absolute privilege—Information or testimony that cannot be received; there are no exceptions (see *privileged information*). (2)

accelerants—Substances that promote burning; a primary form of evidence at an arson scene; the most common accelerant used is gasoline. (10)

acute stress—Temporary stress that may result in peak performance; body adapts for fight or flight. (13)

admission—Statement containing some information concerning the elements of a crime, but falling short of a full confession. (2)

Advanced Fingerprint Identification Technology (AFIT)—The next generation of IAFIS; provides faster, more accurate identification of prints than previous systems did. (10)

aerobic training—Physical training aimed at strengthening the cardiovascular system. (13)

agroterrorism—A subset of bioterrorism, it is the intentional release of animal or plant toxins to generate widespread public fear and economic loss and undermine social stability. (9)

AMBER Alert—Voluntary partnerships between law enforcement agencies and public broadcasters to notify the public when a child has been abducted. (11)

anaerobic training—Physical training aimed at strengthening the muscles of the body. (13)

arrest—The official taking of a person into custody to answer criminal charges; involves at least temporarily depriving the person of liberty and may involve the use of force. (3)

asymmetric war—One in which a much weaker opponent takes on a stronger opponent by refusing to confront the stronger opponent head on or to adhere to proscribed "rules of engagement." (9)

awareness spectrum—Framework for describing an officer's level of awareness, ranging from environmental unawareness to panicked/blacked out/perhaps dead; ideally, officers will be between these two stages—alert but relaxed. (13)

B

battered woman syndrome—Defense used by women who have been beaten by their husbands and who then kill those husbands, apparently while completely sane and in control. (7)

battering—The use of physical, emotional, economic, or sexual force to control another person. (7)

beachheading—Deliberate questioning first and then Mirandizing and requestioning—an unconstitutional interrogation strategy. (2)

Beheler Admonition—A statement given to a suspect who comes to the police station to be interviewed, voluntarily, without arrest, that conveys the message, "You are not under arrest. You are free to leave anytime you want." (2)

bioterrorism—Involves using viruses, toxins, or fungi—classes of organism that include anthrax, botulism, and smallpox—as weapons of mass destruction. (9)

blood-alcohol concentration (BAC)—The weight of alcohol in grams per milliliter of blood. (5)

blue lie—A lie told not to help or comfort the person lied to but, rather, to exert control. (14)

broken windows metaphor—Broken windows in a neighborhood make a statement that no one cares enough about the quality of life in the neighborhood to bother fixing things that need repair. (1)

bullying—Repeated pattern of aggressive behavior that involves an imbalance of power and that purposefully inflicts harm on the bullying victim. (7)

burnout—Condition experienced by a person who is "used up or consumed by a job," made listless through overwork and stress; the person lacks energy or has little interest in work. (13)

burst stress—Having to go from relative calm to high intensity, sometimes life-threatening, activity. (13)

C

Carroll doctrine—Because automobiles are mobile, officers may search them without a warrant if they have probable cause to believe the car contains evidence of a crime; established in *Carroll v. United States* (1925). (3)

chain of custody—Documented account of who has had control of evidence from the time it is discovered until it is presented in court; also called *chain of possession.* (6)

chain of possession—See *chain of custody.* (6)

child maltreatment—A broad term that encompasses all variations of child abuse (physical, emotional, sexual) and neglect (physical, emotional, educational); according to the CDC, "Child maltreatment is any act or series of acts of commission or omission by a parent or other caregiver that results in harm, potential for harm, or threat of harm to a child." (11)

child welfare model—Society's attempt to help youths who come in conflict with the law, in which the best interests of the youth are the main considerations. (11)

chronic stress—Ongoing, continuous stress; like being under a state of constant siege; can lead to severe psychological problems. (13)

civil action—A lawsuit for perceived wrongs against individuals for which restitution is sought in civil court. (14)

civil disobedience—Intentional breaking of a law to prove a point or to protest something. (6)

Civil Rights Act—States that anyone acting under the authority of the law who violates another person's constitutional rights can be sued; see also *Section 1983.* (14)

closed question—Limits the amount or scope of information that a person can provide—for example, "What color was the car?" (the opposite of an open-ended question). (2)

cognitive interview—Interviewing method that puts witnesses mentally back at the scene of an incident and encourages them to tell the whole story without interruption. (2)

collective deep pocket—A pool of defendants from which astronomical financial judgments can be collected; created by suing every possible individual and agency involved in an incident. (14)

collective efficacy—Cohesion among neighborhood residents combined with shared expectations for informal social control of public space that inhibits both crime and disorder. (6)

community policing—"Philosophy that promotes organizational strategies, which support the systematic use of partnerships and problem-solving techniques to proactively address the immediate conditions that give rise to public safety issues such as crime, social disorder, and fear of crime." (1)

compliance—A complete lack of physical resistance. (3)

conditional privilege—The official information privilege—that is, the information can be received but the source of the information can be protected. (2)

confession—Information supporting the elements of a crime that is provided and attested to by any person involved in committing the crime; can be oral or written. (2)

contagion effect—Media coverage of terrorism inspires more terrorism—it is, in effect, contagious. (9)

contamination—An undesired transfer of information between items of evidence. (10)

continuum of contacts—Almost limitless variations of contacts between the public and the police, ranging from no contact to incarceration or even the death penalty. (3)

covert investigations—Those done secretively, for example, using surveillance and undercover personnel. (10)

critical-incident stress debriefing (CISD)—Officers who experience a critical incident, such as a mass disaster or large accident with multiple deaths, are brought together as a group for psychological debriefing soon after the event. (8)

cross-training—Alternating between different forms of exercise. (13)

cruising—Driving around and around a predetermined, popular route, usually through the heart of a town or city; a social activity of teenagers. (5)

***CSI* effect**—"Where unrealistic portrayals of the science have translated to equally unrealistic expectations from not only the public but also other professions that operate within the justice system" who have unrealistic expectations about what crime scene investigators can do. (10)

curtilage—A house and the area immediately surrounding it. (3)

cyberterrorism—The use of high technology to disable or delete critical infrastructure data or information as a means of promoting a religious or political ideology and that targets innocent civilians, elements of the business sector, or government agencies. (9)

D

D.A.R.E.—Drug Abuse Resistance Education, a school program aimed at teaching students to say no to peer pressure to use drugs. (11)

de facto arrest—A detention without probable cause that is factually indistinguishable from an arrest. (3)

deconfliction—Avoiding conflict. (9)

decriminalization—Making status offenses noncriminal matters. (11)

depression—A serious and life-threatening medical illness. (13)

differential police response strategies—Practice of varying the rapidity of response as well as the responder based on the type of incident and the time of occurrence. (4)

directed patrol—Use of officers' discretionary patrol time to focus on specific department goals. (4)

discovery crimes—Offenses that have been completed and whose scenes have been abandoned before the crimes are noticed; in contrast to *involvement crimes.* (4)

discretionary acts—Those actions officers perform using their own judgment; policies and procedures for the acts leave decisions up to the officers. (14)

discretion—The ability or power to act or decide a matter on one's own. (1)

diversion—Referring a juvenile out of the justice system and to some other agency or program. (11)

DNA profiling—Use of the unique genetic structure of an individual for identification; blood, hair, and other body tissues and fluids may be used in this process. (10)

dog shift—Typically the shift from 11 p.m. to 7 a.m. (1)

drug recognition expert (DRE)—Specially trained individual who can determine if someone is under the influence of drugs; also called *drug recognition technician*. (5)

drug recognition technician (DRT)—See *drug recognition expert*. (5)

dual motive stop—A stop in which the officer stops a vehicle to investigate a traffic violation but also because the driver looks suspicious; also called a *pretext stop*. (5)

due process of law—The fundamental principle of American justice that requires notice of a hearing or trial that is timely and that adequately informs the accused persons of the charges; it also gives the defendant an opportunity to present evidence in self-defense before an impartial judge or jury and to be presumed innocent until proven guilty by legally obtained evidence. (3)

E

ecoterrorism—Seeks to inflict economic damage on those who profit from the destruction of the natural environment. (9)

8% problem—50–60 percent of juvenile crime is committed by 8 percent of juveniles. (11)

elder abuse—The physical, sexual, or emotional abuse; financial exploitation; neglect; or abandonment of a person aged 65 or older. (7)

emergency management—The coordination and integration of all activities necessary to build, sustain, and improve the capability to prepare for, protect against, respond to, recover from, or mitigate against threatened or actual natural disasters, acts of terrorism, or other human-made disasters. (8)

emergency operations center (EOC)—The location from which personnel operate during a natural disaster or other type of emergency. (8)

enforcement index—A figure based on the ratio of tickets issued for hazardous driving violations to the number of fatal and personal injury crashes; standard suggests that for each fatal and personal injury crash, between 20 and 25 convictions for hazardous moving violations indicates effective traffic enforcement. (5)

entrapment—An action by the police (or a government agent) persuading a person to commit a crime that the person would not otherwise have committed. (12)

equivocal death investigation—May have two or more meanings and may be presented as either a homicide or a suicide, depending on the circumstances. (10)

estimative language—Language based on analytical assessments and judgments rather than on facts or hard evidence. (9)

exclusionary rule—Courts cannot accept evidence obtained in illegal searches and seizures, regardless of how relevant the evidence is to the case (*Weeks v. United States* 1914). (3)

exculpatory evidence—Evidence favorable to a defendant in a criminal case that could tend to prove that the accused party is innocent or cast doubt as to their guilt, often referred to as "*Brady* Material." (14)

exigent circumstances—Conditions surrounding an emergency situation in which no time is available to secure an arrest or search warrant. (3)

expressive violence —That resulting from hurt feelings, anger, or rage. (7)

F

felony syndrome—Obtaining complete information only on felony cases, deeming them to be the only "real" police work. (2)

FEMA—The Federal Emergency Management Agency, a federal agency charged with building and supporting the nation's emergency management system. Its mission is to reduce loss of life and property and protect our nation's critical infrastructure from all types of hazards through a comprehensive, risk-based, emergency management program of mitigation, preparedness, response, and recovery. (8)

field inquiry—The unplanned questioning of a person who has aroused a police officer's suspicions. (2)

flashbangs—Devices that explode with a loud bang and emit brilliant light; used by police as a diversion. (6)

flashroll—Buy money in a drug deal. (12)

forensics—The application of scientific processes to solve legal problems, most notably within the context of the criminal justice system. (10)

frisk—A brief patdown following a stop to determine if a person is armed. (3)

fruit of the poisonous tree doctrine—Evidence obtained as the result of an earlier illegality (e.g., an unconstitutional search or seizure) is inadmissible as evidence and must be excluded from trial. (3)

functional equivalent—Refers to places other than actual borders where travelers frequently enter or exit the country, such as international airports. (3)

fusion center—Manages and facilitates the flow of information and intelligence across all levels and sectors of government and private industry, turning information and intelligence into actionable knowledge. (9)

G

G.R.E.A.T.—The Gang Resistance Education and Training program, a proactive approach to deterring violence before it begins. (11)

gang—A group of individuals with a recognized name and symbols who form an allegiance for a common purpose and engage in unlawful activity. (12)

geographic information systems (GIS)—Enhance traditional mapping by adding information from various other databases. (6)

goals—Broad, general intentions. (1)

good faith—Belief that one's actions are just and legal. (3)

graffiti—Symbols and slogans written on walls and sides of buildings, often by gang members to mark their turf. (12)

H

hazmat incident—An incident involving hazardous materials. (8)

heterogeneity—Diversity. (1)

horizontal prosecution—Different assistant prosecutors are responsible for specific phases of the court proceedings. (12)

hotspots—Geographic locations where crime incidents tend to cluster. (4)

I

igniters—Articles used to light a fire. (10)

impact evaluation—Assessment that determines if a problem declined. (4)

implied consent law—A law stating that those who request and receive driver's licenses agree to take tests to determine their ability to drive; refusal will result in license revocation. (5)

incident management—Refers to how incidents are managed across all homeland security activities, including prevention, protection, response, mitigation, and recovery. (8)

incivilities—Subtle signs of a community not caring about disorder, including rowdiness, drunkenness, fighting, prostitution, and abandoned buildings. (6)

inevitable discovery doctrine—Created as an exception to the exclusionary rule to allow evidence to be admissible even if seized in violation of the Fourth Amendment when it can be shown that the evidence would have inevitably been found through lawful means. (3)

informant—A person who provides information in a criminal action and whose identity must be protected. (2)

information—Raw data. (1)

instrumental violence—That used to exert control. (7)

intelligence—The product of evaluation, manipulation, and analysis of information through which context, value, and validity have been added. (1)

intentional tort—An act where the officer's intent to engage in the behavior must be proven, for example, wrongful death or false arrest. (14)

interoperability—The ability of public safety officials to communicate with each other seamlessly in real time over their wireless communications network either by voice or through data transmissions. (2)

interrogation—The questioning of hostile witnesses or suspects from whom officers try to obtain facts related to a crime as well as admissions or confessions related to the crime. (2)

interview—The planned questioning of a witness, victim, informant, or other person with information related to an incident or a case. (2)

"in the presence"—Perceived by an officer through his or her senses (does not refer to proximity). (3)

involvement crimes—Offenses in which the victim and the suspect confront each other; in contrast to *discovery crimes*. (4)

J

jihad—A holy war. (9)

juvenile delinquents—Young people who violate the law. (11)

juvenile justice model—A judicial process in which young people who come in conflict with the law are held responsible and accountable for their behavior. (11)

juvenile—A person not yet of legal age, usually under the age of 18. (11)

L

leading question—One that suggests an answer—for example, "You wanted your boss dead, isn't that correct?" (2)

libel—Written defamation of another's character; false statements that tend to humiliate a person and degrade that person in the esteem of others. (14)

litigious—Highly likely to sue. (14)

Locard's principle of exchange—When two objects come into contact, information or material, however minute, is exchanged. (10)

lockdowns—Periods when students are detained in classrooms while police and dogs scour the building searching for contraband or any danger to a safe educational environment. (7)

M

malfeasance—Acts of misconduct or wrongdoing. (14)

malicious prosecution—A proceeding instituted in bad faith without any probable cause in the belief that the charges against the defendant can be sustained. (14)

mental fitness—A person's emotional well-being—the ability to feel fear, anger, compassion, and other emotions and to express them appropriately; also refers to a person's alertness and ability to make decisions quickly. (13)

mere handcuff rule—A policy stating that in the interest of officer safety, all persons arrested and transported shall be handcuffed; it disregards the fact that handcuffing is a form of force and should be used only if the situation warrants. (3)

ministerial acts—Duties prescribed by law as some of the tasks of an administrative office. (14)

Miranda **warning**—A statement of a suspect's rights when that suspect is being questioned: the rights to remain silent, to talk to an attorney, and to have an attorney present during questioning, the attorney to be provided free if a suspect cannot afford one. (2)

mission—An organization's reason for existence, its purpose. (1)

mission statement—Written statement of an organization's reasons for existence or purpose. (1)

moniker—A gang member's street name. (12)

Munchausen's syndrome by proxy (MSBP)—A psychiatric ailment that leads a person to fabricate a child's illnesses to fulfill the adult's own needs for attention and sympathy. (11)

N

negligence—An act where intent or mental state does not matter; what must be proven is if some inadvertent act or failure to act created an unreasonable risk to another person, for example, speeding resulting in a traffic crash or not responding to a 911 call. (14)

nonfeasance—Failure to take action, with the result being injury or damage to another person. (14)

nystagmus—The involuntary bouncing or jerking of the eye, a possible cause of which is intoxication. (5)

O

objectives—Specific activities to accomplish a goal. (1)

one-pot jurisdictional approach—Use of the same system to deal with youths who are neglected or abused, those who are status offenders, and those who commit serious crimes. (11)

open question—One that allows for an unlimited response from the witness in his or her own words—for example, "What can you tell me about the car?" (the opposite of a closed-ended question). (2)

osteogenesis imperfecta—A medical condition characterized by bones that break easily; also called *brittle bone disease*. (11)

overt investigations—Those conducted openly, usually with officers in uniform or introducing themselves as police officers. (10)

P

pandemic—An infectious disease that occurs over a large geographic area and affects a significantly high percentage of the population. (8)

parallel proceedings—When both civil and criminal proceedings are instituted against a violator; a frequent occurrence in environmental crimes. (10)

parens patriae—A doctrine allowing the state to assume guardianship of abandoned, neglected, and "wayward" children. (11)

participatory leadership—Allows officers to influence decisions affecting them and seeks to form a cohesive team. (1)

patdown—A brief feeling of a person's outer clothing to determine if a weapon is present; also called a *frisk*. (3)

perjury—Lying under oath. (14)

phishing—Use of fraudulent e-mails and Web sites to fool recipients into divulging personal information. (10)

physical fitness—The general capacity to adapt and respond favorably to physical effort. (13)

plain language—"Communication that can be understood by the intended audience and meets the purpose of the communicator"; it is "designed to eliminate or limit the use of codes and acronyms, as appropriate, during incident response involving more than a single agency." (2)

plain view—Term describing evidence that is not concealed, that is easily seen by officers while performing their legal duties. (3)

police operations—Activities conducted in the field by law enforcement officers as they "serve and protect"; usually include patrol, traffic, investigation, and general calls for service. (1)

police placebo—A lie told by the police when the lie benefits the person lied to and when no more effective means of dealing with the problem is available; also known as a *white lie*. (14)

policy—A statement of principles that guide decisions. (1)

positional asphyxia—A type of strangulation that results if a person's body position interferes with breathing. (3)

posttraumatic stress disorder (PTSD)—A debilitating stressful reaction to a trauma that may last for months or years; can be experienced by victims and by those who help the victims. (8)

preliminary investigation—The on-the-scene interviews of victims and witnesses, interrogations of suspects, and search of the crime scene itself. (6)

premeditation—The deliberate, precalculated plan to cause death; the essential element of first-degree murder, distinguishing it from all other murder classifications. (10)

pretext stop—A stop in which the officer stops a vehicle to investigate a traffic violation but also because that the driver looks suspicious; also called a *dual motive stop*. (5)

preventive patrol—Efforts to thwart or deter crime and civil disorder through an ongoing police presence or potential presence. (4)

primary victim—One who actually is harmed. (2)

privileged information—Information that does not need to be divulged to the police or the courts because of the existence of a special relationship, such as that between spouses or between lawyers and their clients. (2)

probable cause—That it is more likely than not that a crime has been committed by the person whom a law enforcement officer seeks to arrest: depends on what the officer knew *before* taking action. (3)

problem-oriented policing (POP)—A proactive approach to patrol and policing that focuses on problems to be solved rather than incidents to be responded to. (4)

procedural law—Deals with process, or how the law is applied. (3)

procedures—Step-by-step instructions for carrying out departmental policies. (1)

process evaluation—Assessment that determines if a response was implemented as planned. (4)

property crimes—Offenses in which no physical contact with the victim occurs, including arson, auto theft, burglary, and larceny/theft. (6)

proportionate assignment—Determination of area assignments by requests for service based on available data; no area is larger than the time it takes a car to respond in three minutes or less. (4)

proximate—Closely related in space, time, or order; very near. (4)

proxy data—Pieces of evidence not seen as they are created but which are only the remnants of an event left behind. (10)

pulling levers—Cracking down on any type of criminal activity and telling gang members that the crackdown will continue until the violence stops. (12)

R

racial profiling—The act of selecting an individual for further scrutiny or assessing the likelihood of criminal conduct or wrongdoing based solely on that person's race or ethnic background; discriminatory enforcement of the law. (5)

random patrol—A strategy based on the theory of probability in which an ongoing patrol presence is presumed to (1) increase the chances that an officer will detect and disrupt crime occurring in public places and (2) deter potential offenders because the unpredictable nature of patrol means there is a chance a squad car or foot patrol will come along at any minute. (4)

rapport—A relationship of mutual trust, conformity, accord, and respect; a sense between two people that they can communicate comfortably and openly. (2)

raves—A form of dance and recreation held in a clandestine location; featuring fast-paced, repetitive electronic music and light shows; and often promising sex, illicit drugs, and alcohol. (11)

reader-friendly writing—Communicates in plain, straightforward language; avoids police jargon and abbreviations; and considers its audience. (2)

reasonable suspicion—An objective and particularized basis, supported by specific and articulable facts, for suspecting an individual of criminal activity. (2)

reasonable suspicion—More than a general hunch or "gut feeling" based on intuition; an objective and particularized basis for suspecting an individual of criminal activity that must be based on specific and articulable facts. (3)

regulations—Rules put out by a lower level of government governing the actions of employees of the city, including police department personnel. (1)

relative issue—An issue with a range of morally acceptable options, which are of several shades of gray rather than either black or white. (14)

response time—The time elapsed from when the police are called to when they arrive on the scene. (4)

road rage—"An assault with a motor vehicle or other dangerous weapon by the operator or passenger(s) of one motor vehicle on the operator or passenger(s) of another motor vehicle and is caused by an incident that occurred on the roadway." (5)

routine activity theory—Principle of environmental criminology that states crime occurs at the intersection of a motivated offender, a suitable target, and an absent or ineffective guardian. (6)

routine patrol—Unstructured patrol throughout a beat in an effort to deter crime by creating a sense of police omnipresence; often considered synonymous with random patrol. (4)

S

saturation patrol—A technique that uses a large number of patrol officers for specific enforcement in a concentrated area, such as a "hot spot" or high-crime corridor, or for enhanced enforcement during specific events, such as a "safe and sober" campaign. (4)

scofflaws—Persistent lawbreakers. (5)

secondary victim—One who is not actually harmed but who suffers along with the victim—a spouse or parent, for example. (2)

Section 1983—The Civil Rights Act; it states that anyone acting under the authority of the law who violates another person's constitutional rights can be sued; the legal authority for most lawsuits against law enforcement officers and agencies. (14)

selective enforcement—The ability to decide when to impose legal sanctions on those who violate the law, whether issuing traffic tickets or arresting someone. (1)

slander—Spoken defamation of another's character; false oral statements that tend to humiliate a person and degrade that person in the esteem of others. (14)

slippery slope—One small indiscretion can lead to more serious misbehavior and finally to actual corruption. (14)

sovereign citizens—A loose network of individuals scattered across the United States who believe that the original citizens of the United States were free from all government control and that the federal, state, and local governments today operate illegally. (9)

split-force patrol—Assigns multiple units to a single geographical area or beat; while one unit responds to calls, the other unit continues to proactively patrol that beat. (4)

split-second syndrome—In some circumstances, officers have very little time to think through decisions; a high percentage of inappropriate decisions should be expected and accepted because the officer must act quickly. (13)

spoofing—A newer trend in computer-related crime involving senders who alter or change the origin or source of an e-mail so that the origin of the e-mail is unknown; many fraudulent scams use spoofed Internet protocol (IP) addresses. (10)

stake-in-conformity variables—Include marital status, employment, residential stability, and age—all variables offenders might lose if convicted for a repeat offense. (7)

statement—A legal, detailed account of events related to a crime. (2)

status offenses—Violations of the law applying only to those under legal age; includes curfew violations, drinking alcoholic beverages, incorrigibility, smoking cigarettes, running away from home, and truancy. (11)

Stockholm syndrome—In a hostage situation, the process of transference, with the hostages feeling positively toward their captors (and negatively toward the police) and the captors returning these positive feelings. (6)

stop-and-frisk situation—One in which law enforcement officers briefly detain a suspicious person for questioning and pat the person's outer clothing to ensure that the person is not armed. (3)

stop—Brief detention of a suspicious person by law enforcement officers for questioning. (3)

street gang—"Any durable, street-oriented youth group whose own identity includes involvement in illegal activity." (12)

street justice—Decision of police officers to deal with an offense in their own way—usually by ignoring it. (11)

strict liability—Refers to an act where the injury or damage is so severe and the harm should have been foreseen so that intent or mental state need not be proven. (14)

substantive law—Deals with content, or what behaviors are considered crimes. (3)

survival triangle—Model for police survival; consists of mental and physical preparedness, sound tactics, and weapon control. (13)

swatting—An emerging trend by pranksters involving communication centers in which a false report is filed, via the Internet, to the emergency dispatch center to deploy SWAT teams to a residence where the occupants are oblivious to the situation. (8)

T

terrorism—"The unlawful use of force and violence against persons or property to intimidate or coerce a government, the civilian population, or any segment thereof, in furtherance of political or social objectives." (9)

Terry **stop**—An officer with articulable reasonable suspicion that a crime is occurring, has occurred, or is about to occur may conduct a brief investigatory stop, including a patdown for weapons if the officer has reason to suspect the person is armed and dangerous. (2)

thrownaways—Youths who were either told to leave, were not allowed back after having left, ran away and no one tried to recover them, or were abandoned or deserted. (11)

tort—A civil wrong, the equivalent to a crime in criminal law. (14)

totality of circumstances—All relevant variables in an arrest, including an individual's age, mentality, education, nationality, and criminal experience, as well as the reason for the arrest and how it was explained to the individual being arrested. During an interrogation, it also includes whether basic necessities were provided and the methods used during the interrogation. (2)

traffic calming—Describes a wide range of road and environment design changes that either make it more difficult for a vehicle to speed or make drivers believe they should slow down for safety. (5)

triage—Prioritizing, sorting out by degree of seriousness, as in medical emergencies. (8)

truancy—Loosely defined as habitual unexcused absence from school, considered a status offense because, although compulsory attendance laws vary somewhat from state to state, every state requires children between certain ages to be in school during the academic year absent a valid excuse. (11)

turf—The territory claimed by a gang, often marked by graffiti. (12)

U

Uniform Crime Reports (UCRs) —The FBI's national crime reporting system, published annually as *Crime in the United States*. (6)

universal precaution—All blood and potentially infectious materials other than blood must be treated as if infected. (13)

V

vehicle pursuit—"An active attempt by a law enforcement officer on duty in a patrol car to apprehend one or more occupants of a moving motor vehicle, providing the driver of such vehicle is aware of the attempt and is resisting apprehension by maintaining or increasing his speed or by ignoring the law enforcement officer's attempt to stop him." (5)

vertical prosecution—Where one assistant prosecutor or small group of assistant prosecutors handle the criminal complaint from start to finish through the entire court process. (12)

vicarious liability—Makes others specifically associated with a person also responsible for that person's actions. (14)

victimless crimes—Offenses in which there are no complainants; includes prostitution, pornography, gaming, and drug dealing/using. (10)

violent crimes —Offenses in which physical contact with the victim occurs, including assault, murder, rape, and robbery; sometimes called crimes against persons. (6)

W

waiver—A purposeful, voluntary giving up of a known right. (2)

Z

zero-tolerance policies—School policies that mandate predetermined consequences or punishments for specific offenses—for example, suspension or expulsion for possession of drugs or a weapon. (7)

INDEX